INTERNATIONAL
ORGANIZATIONS

INTERNATIONAL ORGANIZATIONS

principles
and
issues

second edition

A. LeRoy Bennett
University of Delaware

PRENTICE-HALL, INC., *Englewood Cliffs, N.J. 07632*

Library of Congress Cataloging in Publication Data

Bennett, Alvin Le Roy
    International organizations.

    Bibliography: p.
    Includes index.
    1. International agencies.   2. International
organization.   3. Regionalism (International
organization)   I. Title.
JX1995.B43   1979   341.2   79-13139
ISBN 0-13-473447-5

© 1980, 1977 by PRENTICE-HALL, Inc., Englewood Cliffs, New Jersey 07632

PRINTED IN THE UNITED STATES OF AMERICA

10 9 8 7 6 5 4 3

editorial/production supervision and interior design: CATHIE MICK MAHAR
cover design: JERRY PFIEFFER
manufacturing buyer: HARRY P. BAISLEY
cover photograph: STAN WAKEFIELD

PRENTICE-HALL INTERNATIONAL, INC., *London*
PRENTICE-HALL OF AUSTRALIA PTY. LIMITED, *Sydney*
PRENTICE-HALL OF CANADA, LTD., *Toronto*
PRENTICE-HALL OF INDIA PRIVATE LIMITED, *New Delhi*
PRENTICE-HALL OF JAPAN, INC., *Tokyo*
PRENTICE-HALL OF SOUTHEAST ASIA PTE. LTD., *Singapore*
WHITEHALL BOOKS LIMITED, *Wellington, New Zealand*

To

Clarence A. Berdahl
Scholar, Mentor, and Friend

Contents

4

BASIC PRINCIPLES AND ORGANIZATION OF THE UNITED NATIONS 54

5

SOME BASIC ISSUES OF THE UNITED NATIONS 76

6

PEACEFUL SETTLEMENT OF DISPUTES 104

7

COLLECTIVE SECURITY AND ITS ALTERNATIVES — THEORY AND PRACTICE 143

8

THE SEARCH FOR JUSTICE UNDER LAW 182

9

CONTROLLING THE INSTRUMENTS OF WAR 214

10

PROMOTING ECONOMIC WELFARE 239

11

PROMOTING SOCIAL PROGRESS 270

12

THE 1970s:
A DECADE OF WORLD CONFERENCES 310

13

THE STRUGGLE FOR SELF-GOVERNMENT 337

14

VARIETIES OF REGIONALISM 366

15

INTERNATIONAL ADMINISTRATION
AND THE SEARCH FOR LEADERSHIP 405

Preface

This book is the culmination of thirty years as an observer and student of international organizations and as a teacher of the subject. During that period of time, the United Nations, as the primary general-purpose intergovernmental organization, has fluctuated between success and failure and has met with both public support and skepticism. The author is normatively committed to the indispensability of international organizations, such as the United Nations, in an age when people and nation-states must adapt to a shrinking and increasingly interdependent globe.

In this study the author follows no single model and is eclectic in his interests. The focus is on the philosophy and principles of international organizations and on a broad range of issues with which these organizations try to deal. A balance is struck between comprehensive coverage of the problems, inquiries and decisions that face these organizations daily, and the limitations that must be observed in tailoring a textbook for a one-semester course. The use of several tables, charts, and case studies provides devices for summarization and illustration of detailed activities. Yet comprehensiveness has not been sacrificed by omitting discussion on any major activity of international organizations. Neither has it been assumed that the student possesses prior detailed knowledge of the subject.

In the second edition the main outlines of the original text have been maintained with the addition of a new chapter on the series of world conferences of the 1970s. Besides comprehensive updating the author has made numerous changes based on suggestions from users of the first edition. He would like to thank all those who contributed so constructively to the improvement of the text. He also acknowledges the excellent support of the Prentice-Hall staff and the very special efforts of his wife, who assisted in every stage of preparing the manuscript.

A.L.B.

1

By Way of Introduction

The foundation of international organizations was built in ancient times, but the organizations themselves did not appear until the last few decades, when they were formed among political structures known as nation-states. Before being linked by these organizations, the nation-states already had diplomatic, economic, legal, and even war relationships.

The international system as a whole consists of these nation-states, their interactions, international organizations, and the interactions of private actors. As only one part of the whole, international organizations are necessarily affected by the other parts. Because these international organizations are new, they have a minor rather than a major influence on world relationships, and again, are shaped by these relationships more than shaping them.

Nevertheless, the idea of international organization is gradually becoming more complex and influential, as shown by both the words and actions of government spokespeople. Although they may not go so far as to surrender sovereign powers to international organizations, they do find them indispensable for other purposes. New nations demonstrate this in their eagerness to be admitted to the United Nations. Despite great differences, the big powers in the UN do not seem anxious to withdraw, and all countries find the organization useful for sounding out ideas and for contact with other nations.

The United Nations has a more elaborate structure than the League of Nations did, which in turn, was more complex than pre-World War I organizations. At the same time, regional and private international organizations since 1945 also have increased in both numbers and influence. We may assume then that this process will continue, and that international organizations will become an increasingly important part of international relationships.

Since 1945 regional and private international organizations have also rapidly expanded in numbers and influence.

THE ROLE OF INTERNATIONAL ORGANIZATION IN TODAY'S WORLD

International organization has been viewed, at one extreme, as the vanguard of an emerging world government, and, at the other, as an exercise in futility in fostering cooperation among sovereign states. Neither of these extreme views does justice to the role of international organizations in the present age. Today the state, possessing ultimate power and authority, remains the primary political unit. Yet change, accommodation, and a proliferation of interstate and transnational contacts are the hallmarks of an increasingly interdependent world.

The state system shows no sign of rapid deterioration or transformation into new forms. States are reluctant to sacrifice any sovereignty to supranational entities. Yet humans are rational and capable of effecting adjustment or modification of the system. Change is not only a major phenomenon of the modern world but is occurring at an accelerating rate. Many changes have already taken place which must be considered in analyzing the relations of nations. The post-World War II world is vastly different than the world of the 1930s. The range of changing conditions is indicated by the rise of super-powers armed with superweapons, the collapse of the old colonial empires, and focus of attention upon new problems of economic development, overpopulation, the environment, the use of outer space, and control of ocean resources. Another change is the rapid development within the present century of an elaborate structure of international organizations, private and public, universal and regional, multipurpose and specialized.

Modern international organizations may be classified as inter-

governmental organizations (IGOs) and nongovernmental organizations (NGOs, or INGOs, to distinguish international private agencies
from those limited to a single country). The major emphasis in this
study is on IGOs because of the impact on world affairs of governmental actors. However, the increasing influence of nongovernmental
actors, of both profit-seeking and non-profit-seeking varieties, is
noted at several points throughout the text. The common characteristics of both IGOs and non-profit-seeking INGOs include (1) a
permanent organization to carry on a continuing set of functions;
(2) voluntary membership of eligible parties; (3) a basic instrument
stating goals, structure, and methods of operation; (4) a broadly
representative consultative conference organ; and (5) a permanent
secretariat to carry on continuous administrative, research, and
information functions. IGOs are, additionally, established by treaty
and usually, in order to safeguard state sovereignty, operate at the
level of consent, recommendation, and cooperation rather than
through compulsion or enforcement.

States continue as the dominant political units, but international
organizations can perform useful functions within the state system.
For the present these organizations are more the adjuncts (and
perhaps only minor ones) of the state system rather than the incipient units of a new political system.

As adjuncts of the state system, international organizations can
and do play a number of significant roles. Their chief function is to
provide the means of cooperation among states in areas in which
cooperation provides advantages for all or a large number of nations.
In many cases they furnish not only a place where decisions to
cooperate can be reached but also the administrative machinery for
translating the decisions into action. Another function is to provide
multiple channels of communication among governments so that
areas of accommodation may be explored and easy access will be
available when problems arise. In conflict situations not only may
grievances by the parties directly involved be aired, but also the
influence of other nations may be exerted to prevent precipitous
action that may threaten the interests of many states.

States will continue to exercise power, and many conflicts will
result. In a nuclear age states are not free to exercise ultimate force
in most conflict situations. They must exercise self-restraint and
accept stalemate, a change in conditions, or compromise. If states
are willing to explore the possibilities of accommodation and compromise, modern international organization has made available a new
dimension beyond the previously existing channels of diplomacy and

peaceful settlement. The United Nations, the Specialized Agencies, and regional organizations provide multiple and continuous contact points through which accommodation can be exercised.

States are still the parties in conflict. They are free to bring their disputes to an international agency or refuse to participate. They are free to bargain or to make no concessions. They may accept decisions and comply with the spirit of resolutions agreed to by a majority of the members of the agency or refuse to cooperate in carrying out these recommendations. If a state must be coerced, it will be by action of other states. International organizations generally have no independent means of carrying out coercion. Even if world public opinion is a sometimes mildly effective pressure influencing the behavior of states, the expression of that opinion is as likely to be through government spokesmen in international agencies as through other channels.

But states, needing to minimize the effects of conflict, find the many and diverse agencies of international organization useful for that end. The United Nations, for example, provides several major organs whose functions include the resolution of conflict. In addition, the principles of the Charter provide a yardstick for guiding deliberations toward peaceful solutions. The influence of other members can be readily brought to bear in meetings and in private consultations.

In other situations not involving sharp clashes of interests, as in some of the technical work of international organizations, cooperation is facilitated by the existence of these organizations for reaching agreements that have mutual advantages for all states concerned. An agreement to control the spread of disease across international boundaries or to facilitate the interchange of mail can have few possible disadvantages to any nation involved.

Since the states of the modern world must, in so many areas, cooperate, adjust, accommodate, and compromise to promote their common welfare, to solve problems not limited to national boundaries, and to lessen conflict, it is entirely logical for them to create elaborate agencies of international organization for these ends. These agencies are more diverse and numerous than at any previous time in the rather short history of international organization. It is also logical to assume that they will continue to be used by states as indispensable though limited tools for a wide variety of purposes. The range of their purposes is a reflection of the complex set of relationships among nations at this stage in history. Since the trend of world events is toward increased contacts and a growing diversity of problems, we may reasonably expect international organizations to become also increasingly diverse in number and purposes rather than to diminish in significance.

INTERNATIONAL ORGANIZATION
IN A WORLD OF PARADOXES

The major political forces and the economic and social factors influencing those political forces produce a most confused and bewildering pattern of international relationships today. The confusion of the pattern is the result of countervailing forces working at cross purposes. The result is a series of dilemmas and paradoxes which confound those who would seek easy or quick solutions to international problems.

One of the most basic of these paradoxes is the insistence upon state sovereignty, supremacy, and independence in a shrinking, interdependent world. Each state declares its right to determine its own course of action regardless of the effects upon other states, and, at the same time, is increasingly dependent upon the actions of other states in vital areas of mutual concern such as trade, communications, economic development, and world peace. Rigid adherence to the absolute right of each state to be bound in international affairs only by its own positive assent to the specific course to be followed, places formidable obstacles in the path of resolving conflicts of interests. Only when a high coincidence of interests occurs can agreements be reached, since majority rule is incompatible with the necessity of unanimity based on the sovereignty of each and every state. Many world problems resulting from mutual interests and interdependence cannot be dealt with effectively as long as no other agency than the sovereign state has the power or means to make or enforce decisions affecting large numbers of states.

Closely related to the paradox of the sovereign power of states in an interdependent world is the conflict between convergent and divergent national interests. Each state may try to enhance its own power, prestige, and economic prosperity partially by seeking advantages at the expense of other states, or it may find mutual advantages with other states through agreements to cooperate for the supposed or real benefit of all parties. An ideology may act as a unifying force within a group of states yet act as a divisive factor in relation to states with competing ideologies. A defense pact may represent a mutuality of interests among the members of the pact but serve as a threat to nonmembers. Weak nations may feel threatened by powerful nations yet, on occasion, find protection in their power. Poor nations may envy rich nations, but both may find advantages in measures which enlist the resources of the rich in an effort to develop the economic prosperity of the poor. Even the chief adversaries of the Cold War for the past quarter-century find an increasing number of areas of mutual advantage including the avoidance of nuclear holocaust.

Interdependence and convergent national interests lead to co-operative actions. These cooperative actions may take place inside or outside of international organizations such as the United Nations, but the existence of such organizations facilitates cooperation and thus serves the interests of the member states.

On the other hand, divergent national interests and the emphasis upon state supremacy and sovereignty lead to conflict among states. Since the means of waging economic and political conflict reside in the individual states, and since engaging in conflict may seem to be advantageous to the parties to a dispute or situation, international peace and tranquility are frequently threatened by clashes of interests. In these situations agencies such as the United Nations are limited in their utility because their power and means are limited. They have never been endowed with the powers of a government or of a superstate. They may serve as a place where disputes may be discussed and pressures may be exerted by other states wishing to avoid extreme forms of conflict between the disputants, but they lack effective or independent means for intervention to preserve peace or dictate a solution. The custodians of the means for protecting the interests of the world as a whole are still more than 150 sovereign states, especially the rich and powerful states, which can wield the strongest pressures. The need for more effective international controls to resolve conflicts may seem apparent to many people, but the world continues to rely upon and perhaps even strengthen the role of the individual state. International organizations may serve as occasionally useful tools of the state, but they constitute no threat to the state's sovereignty.

Another paradox of the modern world lies in separation of international and domestic concerns. As the world shrinks through the effects of technology and communications, the line between domestic and international problems becomes increasingly blurred. Internal events have their international implications. Both the theory and practice of the United Nations recognize this dilemma. The United Nations Charter in Article 2 declares that the United Nations may not "intervene in matters which are essentially within the domestic jurisdiction of any state," but in the same sentence says, "but this principle shall not prejudice the application of enforcement measures under Chapter VII." Chapter VII deals not only with breaches of the peace and acts of aggression, but also with threats to the peace. The authors of the Charter foresaw the difficulty of delineating domestic and international issues. It is sufficient to note at this point that their foresight has been borne out in practice and that the impossibility of drawing a satisfactory division between domestic and international matters is one of the recurrent dilemmas of the United Nations and of the world.

The lag in the rate of development of political and social institutions in a rapidly changing world is a frequently noted theme among social scientists. This lag is apparent in the development of international organizations. We are willing to create such organizations as long as they are based primarily on the principle of voluntary cooperation, preserving all the major prerogatives of the state that have been developed over a period of 500 years. The result is the creation of a great deal of machinery with very little power or ability to resolve the rising tide of issues resulting from the international contacts, which seem to increase by geometric proportions. A rising tide of revolutionary international problems is met with the slow, evolutionary development of international institutions. This increasing imbalance between the scope of our problems and our means to solve them can lead to disillusionment, frustration, disaster, a breakdown of the international system, or controlled or uncontrolled revolutionary political changes. Tradition and an excessively conservative set of attitudes toward international political change could easily be humankind's own worst enemy.

Another anomaly becomes apparent by comparing the elements which produce order within national societies with the inadequacy of these elements at the international level. A relative degree of order is a value clearly sought in most national states. The means to achieve such order include government machinery backed up by a monopoly of force, and attempts to build support and unity through education, language, religion and/or ideology, economic ties, tradition, symbolism, culture, and appeals to loyalty. Of course, national states vary widely in the degrees to which they have achieved internal order and unity.

In general, however, the international system is marked by less development of integrative factors than is found at the national level. In most cases member states are unwilling to accord to international organizations independent decision-making powers of a legislative, executive, judicial, or enforcement nature. Exceptions in the European Economic Community or in the supposedly binding effect of certain United Nations Security Council decisions only prove the general rule. The means available for building a sense of world community are weak in contrast to those available within national states for strengthening the elements of national unity.

However, these contrasts between national and international factors may be overdrawn by ascribing to states an anthropomorphic quality which ignores the fact that individuals and groups, not abstractions called states, are the actors in both national and international affairs. Also, recognition must be given to Dag Hammarskjöld's two concepts of the United Nations: (1) as static conference machinery for resolving conflicts of national interests, or, more realistically (2) as a dynamic instrument of governments for developing cooperative executive- and legislative-type actions. These more complex approaches to analysis of national and international political processes, when considered along with the variety of stages of political development within states, will prevent the oversimplification of too sharply contrasting national with international conditions.

Behind many of the paradoxes discussed above is the paradox of human rationality and humanitarianism versus the individual's egoistic, selfish, and emotional qualities. If enough attention and intellectual talent is directed to the problem, rational persons may decide that present international relationships are unsatisfactory and that humankind has common values, including survival, which should take precedence over lesser values. Some few intellectuals have come to these conclusions, but thus far these ideas have not permeated the power centers of national governments to any great degree. Not only would such ideas have to become more widely held, and greater amounts of research be directed to the problems of international order, peace, and conflict management, but also means would have to be devised for bringing about the revolutionary changes required in the international system. Such developments would encounter tremendous counterpressures from vested interests whose immediate economic interest, political power, or emotional attachments to existing political and social institutions would be seemingly or really threatened. The greatest obstacle of all, however, would be, in a compartmentalized world, to bring about a focusing of major intellectual talents upon the common interests of humankind. The allocation of national resources and talents will more probably continue to be directed toward the enhancement of national military power, political advantage, and economic prosperity in short-run perspective, without sufficient regard for their effects on other major segments of the globe. Rational, intelligent individuals may also differ in their assessment of the necessity for greater emphasis upon the common interests of humankind.

A restatement of some of the dilemmas and their attendant conditions discussed above would bring into focus the paradox of maximum international problems and limited means of resolving these problems. World problems become more severe both as a result of increasing contacts of states and people and as a consequence of more sophisticated means of influence and destruction. Science and technology applied to many areas, including the military, create multiple tensions and conflict. We are frequently reminded that these same developments may be used for the benefit of humanity to help eliminate the greatest threats to human security and well-being. The truth seems to be, however, that the means are largely lacking for mustering the benefits of science for the solution of people's major problems. We are constantly reminded that the gap between rich and poor nations continues to widen. Examples are few of under-developed countries becoming successfully developed and prosperous in the past four or five decades, nor are there indicators that many will succeed in this process by the year 2000. Trade and balance-of-payments problems sometimes have overtones of a relationship between an exploited area and its exploiter, and, even among relative equals, trade barriers continue to exist. Foreign capital needs of underdeveloped countries are frequently unmet because potential investors feel the risks involved are too great, or because of a lack of guarantees against expropriation, or because the indigenous economy and government are unable to use effectively the resources that might otherwise be furnished for economic development.

Minor wars continue to break out and threaten to spread to greater proportions. Confrontations between nuclear powers are dangerous but frequent. The means of dealing with economic, military, and political problems remain inadequate. The methods of dealing with twentieth-century problems are essentially outmoded. New initiatives and a spirit of cooperation are sorely needed, but a shift of focus to regional and global levels will be difficult to achieve.

IDEOLOGICAL ROOTS OF INTERNATIONAL ORGANIZATION

One feature of today's world scene is the existence of nearly 300 public and approximately 2500 private international organizations. Nearly all of these have been established within the past century, with the greatest development since World War II. Although this movement to establish international organizations is mostly confined to the past 100 years, the ideas and practices upon which modern international organization is built can be traced through many

centuries. This heritage of ideas and practices is related to the
purposes and procedures of today's international organizations,
whose goals, generally speaking, stress accommodation and cooperation across national boundaries.

The basic concepts and practices underlying modern intergovernmental organizations involve diplomacy, treaties, conferences, rules
of warfare, the regulation of the use of force, peaceful settlement of
disputes, the development of international law, international trade,
international economic cooperation, international social cooperation,
cultural relationships, world travel, world communications, cosmopolitanism, universalism, peace movements, the formation of leagues
and federations, international administration, collective security,
and movements for world government. All these ideas and practices
originated prior to the last 100 years, but they constitute the basic
building blocks for existing international organizations and for any
emerging organizations of the future.

Many political philosophers, in every period of recorded history
and in eastern as well as in western civilizations, have advocated
theories and practices compatible with and supportive of international accommodation and the easing of intergovernmental tensions. At the opposite extreme were such writers as Hegel, Hobbes,
and Machiavelli, who upheld the power and aggrandizement of
individual states or rulers. It is to the group of philosophers who
formulated ideas for resolving state differences and for promoting
intergovernmental cooperation that today's organizations owe their
major ideological debt.

War prevention and regulation has been a primary purpose of
both the League of Nations and the United Nations. A broad legacy
of ideas for controlling warfare can be found in the literature of
political philosophy. Attitudes toward war, from ancient to modern
times, ranged from those who advocated war as state policy to those
who considered it a paramount evil to be eliminated. Between these
extremes fell a substantial number of scholars who deplored war but
accepted it as inevitable or necessary under some circumstances. In
this last category were such ancient Greek philosophers as Plato
(427–347 B.C.) and Aristotle (384–322 B.C.). In his *Laws* Plato
esteemed wisdom and justice above courage. He believed that a state
should not neglect its military defense, but the ideal state would be
an isolated, self-sufficient unit with as little dependence on the rest
of the world as possible. Aristotle was also ambivalent in his attitude
toward war. He generally opposed war except in self-defense, but in
his *Politics* he justified the conquest of inferior people because he
believed that some people were suited only to serve as slaves.

In this same pattern, major spokesmen for the Church during the Middle Ages generally accepted war under certain conditions, although deploring it in general. Wars should be just. Wars against the infidel (i.e., the Crusades) were approved but wars among Christians were undesirable. St. Augustine (354-430) set the pattern for much of the later Church doctrine. He disapproved of wars of conquest but accepted wars of defense and wars that were intrinsically justified as means of redressing grievances. Thomas Aquinas (1225-1274) deplored war as inhuman and wasteful but accepted St. Augustine's doctrine of just wars and approved the Crusades.

Many philosophers have taken an unequivocal position against war and have viewed it as an evil to be eliminated. Ancient Chinese philosophers, such as Confucius (551-479 B.C.), deplored the use of coercion and advocated good faith and moderation as the key doctrines of interstate relations. Another Chinese, Mo Ti (fifth century B.C.), showed even greater aversion to war. Based on his view that killing and conquest in war are crimes similar in kind to murder and theft, though greater in degree, Mo Ti totally rejected war, not only as a criminal act, but also as an economic waste.

The Dutch scholar Desiderius Erasmus (1466-1536), as a humanist, pacifist, and internationalist, expressed clearly his rejection of war. His aversion to military action was based on his respect for human life. Erasmus deplored war as brutal, wicked, wasteful, and stupid. Furthermore, he believed that wars result from the ambitions of princes and are generally unprofitable to both victors and vanquished.

Among other philosophers totally opposed to war was William Ellery Channing (1780-1842), who was one of the pioneers of the American peace movement. Channing attacked war as the greatest of all moral evils because it dehumanizes man and makes him a destroyer of his fellow men. It was his contention that war always brings more evils than it removes. The resultant human suffering and destruction are inexcusable. Channing was not sanguine about the rapid elimination of military conflict, for he believed that education was the only effective means to eliminate war.

Just prior to World War I, Norman Angell, an English publicist, drafted an indictment of war which attracted wide attention and was translated into several languages. His book *The Great Illusion* had as its main theme the idea that modern wars were unprofitable for both the victors and the vanquished. Furthermore, military preparedness was socially and economically wasteful and futile. Like Channing, he believed that people's ideas would have to change before effective peace machinery could be erected.

Condemning war does not provide an alternative for settling disputes or for channeling peaceful change. Substitutes that have been proposed have taken a variety of forms, which may now be examined.

One alternative to state conflict is world unity in the form of universal empire. Historically, the most extensive and durable approximation of world empire was the consolidation of territory under the Roman emperors for a period of several hundred years. Dante Alighieri (1265–1321) looked back to this "golden age" with admiration and nostalgia, for to him the restoration of the conditions of the Roman Empire represented the most hopeful approach to universal peace. His ultimate goal was an opportunity for man to develop his intellect, but this could only be accomplished under conditions of universal peace, and peace was most easily attained through universal empire. Dante believed that the success of Roman rule served as proof that it represented a natural order.

A world unity based on political authority may be compared and contrasted with the world view of cosmopolitanism based on such concepts as the brotherhood of man. The schools of philosophy represented by the Cynics and the Stoics were basically cosmopolitan in their outlook. These philosophies were influential in the late centuries of the pre-Christian era and the early centuries of the Christian era in both Greece and Rome. Because they involved a world outlook, these patterns of thought could serve as a bridge from the era of Greek city-states to the era of the Macedonian and Roman Empires. Both the Cynics and the Stoics believed that one person or one place was as good as any other. The Cynics' view was essentially negative and rejected patriotism and the need for separate states. The Stoics held a positive philosophy based on the idea of men joined by universal reason in a universal society. Reason was the essential ingredient in man's universal equality. Both Cicero and Seneca were influential Roman Stoics. Cicero believed in a universal and superior law of justice derived through reason, whereas Seneca emphasized virtue through service to a world society. Erasmus, whose views on war were previously noted, was also cosmopolitan in his beliefs and experience. He was an international scholar who traveled widely throughout Europe, exchanging ideas with leading scholars from England to Italy and maintaining an extensive correspondence with them.

During the past four centuries philosophers have advocated such diverse approaches to world order as the development of international law, decolonization, disarmament, and free trade. As will be noted in the later discussion of more elaborate plans for peace, some of these approaches appear in combination with other suggested methods for attaining international order, but a few scholars have stressed a single factor approach as the key to peace. One of the latter was Hugo Grotius (1583-1645), often referred to as the father of modern international law. Grotius believed that law is necessary in the relations among nations and that it serves as a limitation upon sovereignty. In his 1625 *De Jure Belli et Pacis* ("On the Law of War and Peace") he expanded the principles developed by earlier scholars for a comprehensive system of international law. Jeremy Bentham in his *Principles of International Law* (1786-1789) focused on the emancipation of all colonies and general disarmament as twin fundamental principles for attaining an orderly world. One of the ablest critics of colonialism was J. A. Hobson, a British economist. In *Imperialism* (1902) he attacked colonialism on both economic and political grounds. Hobson anticipated the mandate and trusteeship systems of the League of Nations and the United Nations by advocating international responsibility for colonial states to ensure against exploitation of non-self-governing peoples. A principal advocate of free trade as the main key to world peace was Richard Cobden, an influential member of the British Parliament in the mid-nineteenth century. Cobden linked colonialism to war and believed that free trade would eliminate both.

Several elaborate plans for international peace machinery are worthy of special attention. Each of these proposals involves the setting up of confederacies or loose political unions of one type or another, but none goes so far as to advocate the creation of a superstate or world federation with direct representation of citizens.

The earliest of the more intricate proposals for lessening conflict was that of Pierre Dubois (1250-1322). He suggested an alliance of Christian rulers under French leadership. Wars against the infidel would be encouraged, but peace among Christian nations would be enforced by cooperative action against violators. Penalties would be severe, including confiscation of goods, cutting off food supplies, and military sanctions. Dubois proposed that all disputes be settled by arbitration, with final appeals to the Pope. As a counselor to Philip the Fair of France, Dubois also called his plan to the attention of Edward II of England and of the Pope, but his suggestions received no official support.

In 1623 another Frenchman, Émeric Crucé addressed a detailed proposal for peace to monarchs and princes in Europe. Basing his ideas on the principle of the interdependence of states, he proposed a universal organization, not limited to Christian rulers, primarily for the promotion of trade. Crucé emphasized, as adjuncts to in-

creased trade, the practical arts, travel, and agreements for the stabilization and exchange of currencies and for the standardization of
weights and measures. Disputes would be heard by an assembly of
permanently accredited ambassadors with decisions by majority vote.
Enforcement, if necessary, would be by mutual military sanctions.

In 1694 William Penn published his *Essay toward the Present and
Future Peace of Europe,* and early in the following century the
Abbé de Saint-Pierre circulated his *Plan of Perpetual Peace* among
rulers and philosophers in Europe. Both of these plans proposed the
establishment of a general parliament or assembly to settle all disputes by a three-fourths vote with collective sanctions including
armed force. The Abbé thought that peace would promote the
greater prosperity of all, and he proposed a series of bureaus to
develop cooperation in commercial law, weights and measures, and
monetary systems.

In his thinking about plans for peace, Immanuel Kant begins with
an analysis of the nature of man. Man has two sides: on the one
hand, he is selfish, egoistic, and acquisitive; on the other hand, he is
reasonable. Man's reason provides discipline to balance the selfish
side of his nature. Man escapes from political anarchy to the acceptance of law and government through the discipline provided by
reason. Nations, too, will gradually move from international anarchy
to order when reason dictates that wars are too costly and unprofitable. Since despotic rulers are not likely to promote peace, Kant foresaw in *Perpetual Peace* (1795) a world society made up of republican
states as the ideal basis for peace. The main elements in Kant's plan
included a federation open to voluntary membership of any state; a
congress to settle disputes; no standing armies; no territorial changes
by conquest, inheritance, or purchase; no loans for external purposes; no interference by one state in the internal affairs of another;
the right of self-determination; and world citizenship and freedom of movement between countries based on a universal law of
hospitality.

Prior to the League of Nations, the most elaborate and revolutionary set of proposals for international peace machinery was detailed by William Ladd, an American Quaker, in his *Essay on a Congress of Nations* (1840). He used the institutions of both the Swiss
and American governments as his models. He advocated the establishment of a Congress of Nations and a Court of Nations with legislative
and judicial powers to develop and apply international law. The congress, composed of ambassadors, would develop law by unanimous
decision in the form of treaties. The court would hear cases sub-

mitted with the mutual consent of contending states, and would apply principles of international law, if established, or, in their absence, principles of equity and justice. Ladd provided no executive authority, for he thought that public opinion would serve as an adequate means of enforcement. Believing that an enlightened public opinion is more effective than physical power, Ladd advocated the abolition of standing armies, and he stated that men generally obey law more because of opinion than because of compulsion.

In spite of the access of many of the philosophers discussed above to rulers or to government circles, the impact of their ideas upon governmental practices seems to be minimal. The growth of international institutions has come only in the nineteenth and twentieth centuries. The development of internationalism was retarded for a number of reasons. In the first place, the ideas presented in the preceding pages, while often familiar to rulers, were not necessarily dominant or exclusive in their impact upon the rulers' thoughts and behavior. Second, no age until the present one was marked by a set of conditions conducive to an increased emphasis on international cooperation. Some of these conditions are of very recent origin. Among them are new weapons of war and the potential for wars to become global, and the emergence of dozens of newly independent states whose aspirations for development cannot be achieved without external policies of support. Other more gradually developing factors are encompassed within the term "interdependence" with all its complex components.

Throughout most of human history, the forces of political fragmentation have been dominant. In the modern era national states had to emerge and engage in competition before the climate for increased cooperation could develop. The seventeenth and eighteenth centuries were marked by a consolidation of state power, rivalries in war and for colonial empires, and the intensification of nationalism. These tendencies were bolstered by philosophies that stressed individualism. As applied to states, an emphasis on individualism tends more toward rivalry than cooperation.

Even today the forces of nationalism outweigh those of internationalism. In newly emergent states nation-building is a primary concern. Older states emphasize national security, economic interests, and prestige. Cleavages between nations are more potent factors than the forces of unity. The world is segmented by elements of language, customs, religion, ideology, political structure, economic rivalry, human acquisitiveness, fear, and suspicion. The impact of the implications of interdependence has not yet penetrated human consciousness to a significant level of influence. Entrenched interests, backed by powerful instruments of influence and enforcement, will resist changes in the international system which are perceived as a potential threat to those interests. The forces of social and political conservatism will, in all probability, prevent radical change in the direction of world unity. Furthermore, parochialism may better represent the capacity and inclination of human thought than the complexities of a global philosophy. If some exponents of theories of human aggression and territorial drives are correct, this tendency toward philosophical parochialism is powerfully reinforced by basic human emotions and drives.[1] Altogether, the movement toward political internationalism has but limited momentum, and the forces of fragmentation remain dominant.

CONCLUSION

Although nation-states or their spokesmen are the primary actors and nationalism is the chief motive force in world politics, a few developments have occurred in recent decades to enhance the possibilities of international cooperation and unity. The industrial revolution and scientific developments have shrunk global distances and resulted in increased international and transnational contacts. Within the past century there has been an accelerating trend in the formation of international private and public organizations. New problems have arisen which are of global proportions and which may respond only to global treatment. Among these are population, food supply, energy supplies, mass poverty, environmental controls, outer space, the oceans and seabed, and insurance against human annihilation. To a degree never existing before, all humans are interdependent for their lives and welfare. Yet the number of states and the intensity of nationalistic feelings are at an all-time high. This persistent paradox requires either resolution or the application of intelligence to controls, restraint, and cooperation among independent political units. The very impact of the bourgeoning contacts and transactions across national borders may gradually force the lowering of barriers that interfere with human freedom of interaction. Any shift toward internationalism must be accompanied by confidence that the new arrangments offer as much individual security as is now

---

[1] See, for example, the writings of Robert Ardrey, Konrad Lorenz, Sir Arthur Keith, and Raymond A. Dart.

afforded by sovereign states. World community will not evolve quickly or without the serious growing pains that accompany philosophical, emotional, social, and political change. But even before fundamental changes occur, international organizations may serve a useful function in channeling a portion of state interactions and in providing vehicles for increased cooperation. In spite of their limited role, international organizations have become indispensable instruments within the international system.

2

A Great Experiment— the League of Nations

World Wars I and II engendered two rather contradictory forces. One was a unity and a determination in each country to make every effort and sacrifice necessary to win the war. Thus, nationalism and patriotism were intensified. But at the same time, the hatred of all wars and the resolution to prevent them also were increased. Although not everyone thought that international cooperation was the best way to avoid future conflict (e.g., those Americans opposed to the League of Nations), most citizens and world leaders became convinced during these wars that international organizations could help to prevent future military conflict.

But the problem of reconciling these contradictory forces, heightened feelings of nationalism and a greater hatred of war, was carried over into the newly created organizations for peace. Because existing nationalism had been reinforced by the wars, no leaders would surrender any important area of national sovereignty. The result was a really toothless international organization, dependent on the collective power of individual member-states and on their desire to cooperate to avoid crises.

Another problem preventing these organizations from having any potency was the establishment of a peace policy enforced by the victorious powers. The enemy states at first were refused membership in these postwar international organizations and then were admitted only by permission of the major Allied powers. Too, the dominance of these powers was secured by assigning them permanent positions on the main enforcing organ of the international agency and by protecting them against enforcement penalties by the privilege of a veto. Thus the great powers had a double guarantee that no effective action could be directed against them, and yet were the ones directing enforcement action. The major Allies dictated territorial settlements and executed them through self-help assisted by the new international machinery of a League of Nations or a United Nations. Potentially explosive tensions were almost assured, because there still were no satisfactory means of peaceful change, and because the ultimate sanction continued to be military interference, despite the hope that the new organizations would assist in preventing armed conflict.

FOUNDING OF THE LEAGUE OF NATIONS

The war in Europe had scarcely begun when groups were organized in several European countries and in the United States for the specific purpose of planning how to maintain peace in the postwar period and prevent future wars. The first efforts were private, although leading political figures in some instances expressed an interest in the same kind of ideas at an early stage. Organized official support came somewhat later than the initial private activities, and, in several cases, the official documents borrowed heavily from the ideas of the private groups. Opinion leaders in the citizenry thus influenced and shaped governmental policy with regard to the postwar peace maintenance system.

In the United States the most important private group in postwar planning was the League to Enforce Peace, founded in Philadelphia in June, 1915. Former President William Howard Taft was a major leader of this movement.

At first President Woodrow Wilson was reluctant to identify himself with the ideas of the League to Enforce Peace, but in May, 1916, he addressed a meeting of the organization, and gradually he came to endorse many of their principles. By January, 1917, Wilson, in an address to the United States Senate, advocated a "League for Peace" backed by superior collective force. One year later, in an address to Congress, he presented his famous Fourteen Points as the war aims of the United States government. The last of the points called for a League of Nations in the following terms: "A general association of nations must be formed under specific covenants for the purpose of affording mutual guarantees of political independence and territorial integrity to great and small States alike." The Fourteen Points were subsequently adopted, with minor exceptions, as the war aims of all the Allied powers. Thus the Allied heads of governments were committed to the establishment of a security organization as a part of their plans for peace.

In Great Britain the first government-sponsored plans for a League of Nations were initiated by a committee of historians, diplomats, and lawyers under the chairmanship of Lord Phillimore, a judge and professor of international law. The official French version, produced by a ministerial commission under the chairmanship of Léon Bourgeois, laid considerable stress on an elaborate system of sanctions.

The Phillimore plan had the greatest influence on the first American draft prepared by Colonel E. M. House, a close personal adviser of the President. Having prepared his own first draft for a League of Nations, Wilson left for Paris in December, 1918, a month after the armistice and a month before the peace conference was to open and, on a tour of European capitals, was received with great enthusiasm by huge crowds.

After President Wilson's arrival in Paris, a plan for the proposed League authored by General Jan Christiaan Smuts of South Africa attracted wide attention because it was released to the general public and because it was clearly and persuasively presented with each proposal accompanied by supporting explanation. This *Practical Suggestion*, as it was entitled, among its innovations suggested a mandate system for the colonies of the defeated powers, a council of permanent and rotating members, and a series of technical committees to carry on the economic and social work of the organization.

This brief outline of some of the main threads of planning during 1914–18 for a League of Nations demonstrates the variety of contributions and sources that preceded the work of writing the Covenant. Although President Wilson was credited with being the main champion of this development, private and public groups and individuals in many countries deserve recognition for playing highly significant roles.

On January 18, 1919, the peace conference convened in Paris. Just one week later, at the instigation of the United States and British delegations, a resolution was adopted which provided that the plans for a League of Nations would become an integral part of the peace treaties, and that a commission should be created to work out the details of the League's constitution. President Wilson was then designated as chairman of a nineteen-member commission composed of two members from each of the great powers and one each from nine smaller states. The membership was notable for its inclusion of all the major contributors to preliminary planning for a league who were present in the Paris delegations. These were Wilson and House from the United States, Cecil and Smuts representing the British Empire, and Bourgeois of France. The commission was aided by David Hunter Miller of the United States and Cecil Hurst of Great Britain, who produced a combined draft proposal of the Covenant which became the working document for all further commission deliberations.

The commission met in the evenings beginning February 3 and eleven days later had hammered out a draft Covenant, which it presented to the plenary conference and to neutral and other smaller states for their comments and suggestions. Wilson immediately sailed back to the United States to assess the reaction at home, which might necessitate further modifications in the proposals.

The most significant changes that resulted from this period of general discussion and criticism were in response to American reactions, especially those originating among United States Senators, including the opponents of the League idea. Several revisions to meet these objections were made when Wilson returned to Paris. The most important were (1) specific mention of the Monroe Doctrine's consistency with Covenant obligations, (2) recognition of the right of withdrawal from League membership, (3) a statement that unanimity in voting was required except in cases exempted by the terms of the Covenant or peace treaty, and (4) a safeguard against interference in domestic questions.

The commission held only five more meetings after Wilson's return to Paris on March 14 and was able to agree on the incorporation of the major additions outlined above and other minor modifications from a variety of sources. Decisions also had to be made concerning the location of the seat of the League at Geneva, the appointment of Sir Eric Drummond as the first Secretary-General, the provision for an organizing committee to plan for the permanent establishment of the League, the selection of the four states which would serve as initial nonpermanent members of the Council, and the agreement upon a list of neutral states that would be invited to become original members of the organization by acceding to the Covenant.

The final draft of the Covenant was laid before a plenary session of the peace conference on April 28, 1919, and the Covenant and all the supporting agreements were approved unanimously. A week later

Acting Secretary-General Drummond received authority from the organizing committee to begin the recruitment of the Secretariat staff and the preparatory work for the first sessions of the League organs. He established temporary headquarters in London. Since the League Covenant was a part of the Treaty of Versailles, the official birthday of the organization was delayed for eight additional months until the treaty was ratified and took effect on January 10, 1920.

ESSENTIAL FEATURES OF THE LEAGUE

All except three of the forty-five states named in the annex to the Covenant deposited the necessary notices of ratification by early 1920 and became original members of the League of Nations. Some question had been raised at the peace conference concerning the eligibility of the British Dominions, especially India, for inclusion in the list. The most severe critics claimed that Great Britain was given six votes in the Assembly.[1] In addition to the original members, other "fully self-governing States, Dominions, or Colonies" could be admitted to membership by a two-thirds vote of the Assembly, provided that they gave "effective guarantees" of their willingness to accept the necessary international obligations.[2] The right of withdrawal with two years' notice was specifically provided, and a member could be expelled by unanimous vote of all other members of the Council for violation of Covenant obligations.

The United States was the only major state that never joined the League. With this exception, the League approximated universal membership with sixty-three states as sometime members, although, with withdrawals in the 1930s, the maximum at any given date was sixty.

Because of President Wilson's preeminent role in promoting the League idea, it is ironic that the United States defected from League membership. Although a majority of the members of the United States Senate favored membership, the opponents, led by Senator Lodge, used the device of burdening the treaty with reservations to prevent the required two-thirds approval. Throughout the history of the League, the official attitude of the United States toward the League gradually changed from one of hositility and aloofness to increasing cooperation in a variety of League activities, primarily

---

[1] This argument is an interesting prelude to the dispute over separate memberships for the Union Republics of the Soviet Union in the United Nations.

[2] Covenant of the League of Nations, Art. 1, sec. 2.

through the agency of a most able consul in Geneva, Prentiss Gilbert, and his staff.

Germany was admitted to the League in 1926, and the Soviet Union was admitted in 1934. Both, immediately on admission, were given permanent seats on the Council, in recognition of their importance. The first withdrawals became effective in 1927 and 1928 when Costa Rica withdrew because of the financial burden of membership followed by Brazil whose national pride suffered from a refusal to grant it permanent membership on the Council. Germany and Japan announced their intention to withdraw in 1933, and in the late 1930s there was a rash of defections.

The only case of expulsion was against the Soviet Union in late 1939 for its invasion of Finland. This was ironic since, in most respects, the Soviet Union, during its five-year membership, insisted more strongly than any other state on scrupulous observance by all members of Covenant obligations, and since there were several acts of aggression by other League members against whom there was no demand for expulsion.

The most important set of goals of the League of Nations related to promoting peace and preventing wars. Ten of the twenty-six articles of the Covenant dealt with the means for achieving this set of goals. Although war was not totally outlawed by the Covenant, the intention was clear that through peaceful settlement of disputes wars should be prevented, and that any aggressor who resorted to war in violation of the Covenant should be dealt with promptly and effectively by the collective action of all other members.

Two basic principles underlay the League system for peace maintenance (1) members agreed to respect and preserve the territorial integrity and political independence of other states, and (2) any war or threat of war was a matter of concern to the whole League. If states were unable to settle their disputes by negotiation, they agreed to submit them to arbitration, judicial settlement, or consideration by the League Council. The disputants agreed not to go to war in any circumstances until at least three months following a decisions of the body hearing the dispute. In order to facilitate judicial settlement, Article 14 of the Covenant charged the League Council with responsibility for establishing a court, and this duty was promptly carried out. If in hearing a dispute the Council made a unanimous set of recommendations, excepting any disputing parties, all League members agreed not to go to war with any state which complied with the recommendations. If unanimity could not be achieved, the members were free to take individual action.

Article 16 of the Covenant provided the teeth for enforcement action against a state which broke its agreements to keep the peace. The sanctions provided under collective action were potentially severe and effective if the obligations had been vigorously and scrupulously fulfilled. A violation of Covenant obligations was to be interpreted as an act of war against all other members. The offending state was to be subjected to immediate total economic and political isolation with the direct and indirect costs shared equitably by all members. Supposedly, such measures were automatic and obligatory. The council was empowered to recommend military sanctions including the allocation of national contributions to a joint military force composed of land, sea, or air contingents. No offending state could withstand such pressures if all other members cooperated in applying maximum available measures against it.

The League's program of war prevention also included provisions for disarmament "to the lowest point consistent with national safety." The success of these provisions depended upon Council initiative and member acceptance of general disarmament plans. The Covenant also criticized the manufacture of arms by private industry and sought its elimination. Finally, the members agreed to publicize information on armaments and industries readily convertible to arms production and this agreement resulted in the publication by the League of an annual *Armaments Yearbook.*

Although the major emphasis in the Covenent was upon peace maintenance, some recognition was given to the desirability of international economic and social cooperation. The Covenant provided no special machinery for carrying on, supervising, or coordinating these efforts, although a commitment was included for the establishment of one or more organizations to secure "fair and humane conditions of labor for men, women and children,"[3] and an autonomous International Labour Organization was established as a part of the Treaty of Versailles. The Secretariat was designated as a clearing-house for relevant information not collected by any other international bureau or commission. The Covenant also indicated the desirability of bringing all existing and future public international bureaus under the direction of the League. This goal was never achieved, although in very limited areas the League became the central coordinating agency.

In addition to a concern for labor conditions, the Covenant included references to several specific economic and social problems. These were (1) just treatment of non-self-governing peoples, (2) supervision of traffic in women and children, (3) supervision of traffic in dangerous drugs, (4) supervision of the arms trade, (5)

---

[3] Covenant, Art. 23.

freedom of communications and transit, (6) equitable treatment of international trade for all states, and (7) the prevention and control of disease. Whether appropriate or not for special emphasis in such a document, another provision of the Covenant singled out voluntary national Red Cross organizations as suitable for encouragement and promotion.

As a substitute for outright annexation of the colonies taken from the Central Powers at the end of the war, a mandate system was instituted declaring that the well-being of the peoples of these territories formed "a sacred trust of civilization" and that the "tutelage of such peoples should be entrusted to advanced nations." The "advanced nations" who took over this supervision were Britain, France, Japan, Belgium, South Africa, Australia, and New Zealand, with Britain and France assuming a lion's share of responsibility for multiple territories. The Mandatories were declared to be acting on behalf of the League and were to submit an annual report on each territory to the Council through the Mandates Commission. The Mandates Commission, as created, was composed of experts serving in their individual capacities rather than as government representatives.

Three categories of mandates were described in the Covenant, distinguished from one another by their political development or proximity to self-government and independence. These became known as A, B, and C mandates with the A category recognized as nearing statehood, and the C category as least able to achieve statehood within the foreseeable future. The Mandatories of the C group were authorized to administer them as integral parts of their own territory.

Another objective of the League of Nations was the abolition of secret treaties. The Covenant provided that all treaties should be submitted to the Secretariat for publication and that no treaty should be valid unless so registered. The *Treaty Series* of the League was the resulting record of compliance. The Assembly was also charged with a general responsibility for the review and revision of outmoded treaties, but this function remained virtually dormant.

The League machinery was centered around three major organs : the Assembly, the Council, and the Secretariat. The first two were delegate bodies in which each member state had one vote; the Secretariat was composed of international civil servants whose role included impartial service to the organization as a whole.

All members of the League were automatically members of the Assembly. Although casting a single vote, each member state's delegation to the Assembly could consist of three representatives and three alternates with supporting advisory and secretarial staff. No schedule of meetings was provided by the Covenant, but the practice of annual meetings of approximately one month's duration became the established pattern.

The Assembly accomplished most of its work through six main committees. These dealt with (1) legal questions, (2) technical organizations, (3) reduction of armaments, (4) budget and finance, (5) social and humanitarian questions, and (6) political questions. Each member was entitled to be represented on all committees. Although this arrangement was unwieldy, it had the advantage of providing the spectrum of national viewpoints in the committee stage of consideration of each issue. Small delegations from less affluent countries were hard pressed to participate fully and effectively in every phase of Assembly action.

Committee decisions could be taken by majority vote, but final approval on most issues had to face the requirement of unanimity in a plenary session of the Assembly. This presumably difficult barrier was by-passed by a number of special provisions, practices, and devices. Matters of procedure required only a majority vote. Other important matters, such as admission of members and election of members of the Council, were specifically exempted from the unanimity rule. Members exercised restraint in the use of their liberum veto and, unless a matter was of vital concern to one or more states, they generally abstained rather than choosing to block a resolution supported by a substantial majority of states. Abstentions rather than vetoes could sometimes be assured through bargaining and cooperation concerning the wording of resolutions for the purpose of removing or softening elements irritable to particular national sensibilities. If unanimous agreement was impossible, the resolution could be changed to one expressing a wish or the sense of the Assembly, and it then could be treated as a procedural matter. Since most League sanctions relied more on moral than on physical or tangible force, the differences among the effects of various types of decisions were largely matters of degree.

Although the original size of the League Council was intended to be five permanent and four elected members, the defection of the United States produced an equal balance between the two categories. This was the minimum size of the Council throughout its history. The Covenant permitted the Council and Assembly to prescribe changes in both categories of membership. The total membership varied from eight to fifteen, with permanent membership of three to six members and a variation in elected membership between four and eleven. The permanent members were originally designated as the United States, Great Britain, France, Italy, and Japan. Germany was given permanent Council status upon its admission to the League in

1926, and the Soviet Union was identically treated in 1934. The withdrawals of Germany, Japan, and Italy from League membership in the 1930's decreased the proportion of permanent to nonpermanent Council members. Nonmembers of the Council were invited to sit as temporary Council members whenever a dispute or other matter of special concern to that state was considered by the Council.

The Covenant's allocation of powers and duties between the Assembly and the Council indicates the greater importance attached to the Council by the framers of the document. Another evidence of the lesser role predicted for the Assembly was the intent of some of the participants in the Paris conference that the Assembly meet only at three- or four-year intervals but that Council sessions be much more frequent. The list of powers and duties assigned to the Assembly was brief, although some of the Assembly's roles were basic and significant. They included (1) the admission of members to the League, (2) the control of the budget, (3) the selection of nonpermanent members of the Council, (4) the formulation of rules concerning the selection and terms of Council members, (5) the consideration of matters referred to it by the Council, and (6) the instigation of plans for the revision of treaties.

The list of Council responsibilities was more formidable than that of the Assembly. The Council was assigned (1) the conciliation of disputes, (2) the expulsion of members of the League that violated the Covenant, (3) the supervision of the mandates, (4) the approval of staff appointments to the Secretariat, (5) the authority to move the League headquarters, (6) the formulation of plans for disarmament, (7) the recommendation of methods for carrying out the provisions of the Covenant for the peaceful settlement of disputes and the application of sanctions, and (8) the obligation to meet at the request of any League member to consider any threat to international peace.

A few powers were shared by the Council and Assembly. Instead of sharply delineating the spheres of responsibility for the most basic functions of the League, a broad mandate in identical terms was given to each. Both the Council and Assembly were authorized to "deal at . . . [their] meetings with any matter within the sphere of action of the League or affecting the peace of the world."[4] Both were also authorized to seek advisory opinions from the Permanent Court of International Justice. Three other responsibilities required joint action of the Council and Assembly. These were (1) the ap-

[4] Covenant, Art, 3, sec. 3; and Art. 4, sec. 4.

pointment of the Secretary-General, (2) the election of members of the Permanent Court of International Justice, and (3) the approval of changes in the allocation of permanent and nonpermanent seats on the Council.

A reading of the Covenant makes it evident that the framers of that document laid greater stress on the Council than on the Assembly. It was natural that the great powers should expect to continue their dominance of the processes for maintaining peace as they dominated the decisions at the peace conference. In practice, however, the Assembly became the main focus of attention within the League. The Assembly, at its first session in 1920, seized the initiative and established precedents that enhanced its prestige vis-à-vis the Council. The practice of general debate involving speeches by the heads of delegations of small as well as large states provided the closest approximation that had yet been achieved to the establishment of a world forum. The report of the Council was treated as a basis for broad debate, analysis, and criticism so that the Council was assumed to be responsible to the Assembly through an annual review of its activities. The Assembly also called for an annual report by the Secretary-General, the review of which brought the entire range of League activities within its purview. The Assembly was not hesitant to invade spheres of influence assigned in the Covenant to the Council and regularly and extensively dealt with such areas as disarmament and mandates. The Assembly set up committees to consider important matters in the interim between its own annual sessions and expected these committees to report back to the parent body. The members of the League regularly sent their most able and responsible spokesmen to represent them in Assembly as well as in Council sessions. Finally, the first Assembly adopted the policy of annual rather than less-frequent meetings as its permanent pattern. "Thus in a single session the Assembly had definitely constituted itself as the central organ of the League."[5]

Like the Assembly, the Secretariat had to establish most of its own precedents. There was an almost total absence of guidelines in the Covenant. Most of the responsibility and credit for the success of the work of the Secretariat was due to the initiative of the first Secretary-General, Sir Eric Drummond, who served in that capacity from 1919 to 1933. He was succeeded by his deputy, Joseph Avenol, who resigned in 1940. From 1940 until 1946 Sean Lester presided over a skeleton staff in what was essentially a caretaker operation.

[5] F. P. Walters, *History of the League of Nations* (London, Oxford University Press, 1952), I, p. 127.

From the beginning, the Secretary-General assembled a widely representative staff of able assistants. An important precedent was set in establishing the principle that members of the Secretariat were responsibile to the Secretary-General and to the organization as a whole and were not answerable to their own governments. This is the basic requirement for a truly international civil service.

Sir Eric Drummond interpreted his role as being mainly limited to efficient administration rather than assuming a position of political leadership in the policies of the League of Nations. His function was that of impartial civil servant, and, as such, he gained the confidence of the representatives of all members of the organization. The Covenant granted him no broad discretionary powers except in the selection of staff and the direction of the work, and he chose to interpret his mandate modestly. As head of the continuous branch of the League, he efficiently coordinated all of the League's diverse activities, organized and directed the Secretariat, furnished supporting services to the Council and Assembly, and impartially and proficiently carried out their directives. He was available to the delegates for consultation but was never accused of a breach of confidence. By playing a limited role he avoided the political pressures to which the Secretaries-General of the United Nations have been subjected.

Around the main organs of the League a satellite group of more than twenty auxiliary organizations developed which varied in the intensity of their affinity to the central organs. These included three major technical organizations: (1) the Economic and Financial Organization, (2) the Organization for Communications and Transit, and (3) the Health Organization. In addition, there were several permanent advisory commissions, such as the Mandates Commission and the Advisory Commission on Opium and Other Dangerous Drugs; a number of temporary commissions such as the Preparatory Commission for the Disarmament Conference and the Special Committee on Contributions in Arrears; a few administrative bodies such as the office of the High Commissioner for the Free City of Danzig and the Advisory Commission for Refugees; two autonomous organizations, the Permanent Court of International Justice, and the International Labour Organization; and several special institutions such as the International Institute of Intellectual Cooperation in Paris and the Institute for the Unification of Private Law in Rome. While it might reasonably be assumed that such a diverse and decentralized set of organizations would result in a chaotic and unmanageable pattern of activities, the Assembly acted as a general reviewing body, and the Secretariat provided continuous and fairly effective coordination of the wide range of agency programs.

Although the Permanent Court of International Justice was theoretically a separate organization from the League of Nations, it was in several respects closely affiliated with the League. A previous reference was made to the Covenant's provision that the Council was responsible for formulating plans to establish the Court. The Court was an integral part of the League's formulas for peaceful settlement of disputes, and both the Council and Assembly could seek advisory opinions from the Court. Although membership in the two organizations was separate and independent, the relationship was in most respects as close as is the present one in which the International Court of Justice is designated as a major organ of the United Nations.

The total budget for the League during the years of principal activity varied between 2.5 and 7 million U.S. dollars annually. This included the budgets for the Court and the International Labour Organization as well as the expenses of most of the auxiliary commissions. The attitude of the members always seemed to be one of extreme economy, and the budget was scrutinized thoroughly with an eye to cutting expenses.

The amendment process explained in Article 26 of the Covenant was ambiguous in that it provided a requirement for ratification of amendments but was silent on the process and standards for their proposal. Amendments would take effect when ratified by a majority of League members including all members of the Council.

In spite of the difficulty of the amending process (a difficulty that increased with the expansion in the size of the Council), three necessary sets of amendments were adopted in the first few years of League history. These provided the Assembly with the authority to allocate expenses of the League and to set up rules for elections to the Council, and clarified the role of judicial settlement through the Permanent Court of International Justice in the League processes for peaceful settlement of disputes.

SUCCESSES AND FAILURES OF THE LEAGUE OF NATIONS

In spite of any accomplishments in other areas of cooperation, the success of modern international organizations such as the League of Nations or United Nations is most often judged on the basis of their handling of disputes and their utility in avoiding war. This is the case because of the destructiveness of modern warfare and because of the central role assigned to peace-keeping in establishing these organizations. The negotiatiors who frame the treaties that serve as constitutional documents for a League or United Nations may be unable or unwilling to create the conditions that can realistically control aggression and the resort to war, but the organization's success or failure is ultimately assessed primarily in terms of its utility in the control of political and military conflict.

During the early years of League experience, there were high hopes that the organization could ameliorate tense situtations that exhibited the potentiality for erupting into major conflict. The League machinery was utilized for the hearing of at least thirty disputes during the first decade of its existence, and a majority of these were resolved satisfactorily. This successful record was in part due to the involvement of small or middle powers in most of the situations and to the resulting ability and willingness of the large powers to bring sufficient pressure to assure a settlement without recourse to war.

One of the potentially most serious incidents of the early years was expeditiously handled and successfully resolved in 1925. This was a Greek-Bulgarian border dispute in which an invasion of Bulgarian territory by Greek troops was brought to the Council's attention by the Bulgarian government. The Council President, Briand of France, requested a cease-fire and a withdrawal of troops, and the Council met within three days. The Council dispatched military observers to the scene to determine whether normal conditions had been restored, and a commission of inquiry was set up to recommend terms of settlement and indemnity. The prompt and positive action of Briand and the Council restored peace with a minimum of hostilities and damage.

The great tests of the League's ability to settle disputes involving the major powers began in 1931. In September of that year the Japanese launched a series of attacks in Manchuria on the initial pretext that they were protecting their rights involved in their lease of railway property. With the capture of Mukden, their purpose to take over Manchuria became apparent. The League Council hesitated to take effective action since Great Britain and France were unwilling to apply economic or military sanctions and the United States indicated that it would not support any drastic measures. An attempt, under Article 11 of the Covenant, to send a commission of inquiry was vetoed by Japan, but China later appealed to Article 15 under which the votes of the disputing parties could not block a decision. China also asked for a transfer of the question to the Assembly to indicate its disappointment with the Council's performance. The United States somewhat stiffened its attitude with the publication of the Stimson Doctrine of nonrecognition of territorial changes in violation of the Kellogg-Briand Pact for the renunciation of war, and the Assembly gave approval to this doctrine as the official attitude of the League.

The Lytton Commission, a five-member group from the big powers, was eventually dispatched to Manchuria but arrived there nearly seven months after the original incident. In the meantime the Japanese had completed their conquest of Manchuria and had established a puppet government with the name of the new state changed to Manchukuo. The Lytton report castigated the Japanese for their military aggression, but no further action was taken by the League or its members to force the government of Japan to comply with its recommendations. The ineffectiveness of the League in the face of aggression by a major power was a blow to the prestige of the organization and served as an indication to other states bent on conquest that the will to apply sanctions was lacking on the part of the most powerful League members.

Perhaps the greatest challenge to the League's political effectiveness was Italy's conquest of Ethiopia. By early 1934 Mussolini was building up military forces and supplies in Eritrea and Italian Somaliland. In December of that year an armed clash of serious proportions occurred at Wal-Wal in what was generally conceded to be Ethiopian territory. Emperor Haile Selassie requested that the matter be submitted to arbitration under the terms of an earlier treaty with Italy, but Italy responded with demands for an apology and reparations. The Ethiopian government then requested that the matter be placed before the League Council whereupon Italy, in order to postpone Council action, agreed to the proposed arbitral procedure.

The British and the French, fearful of Hitler and courting the support of Mussolini in Europe, gave to the Italian dictator tacit assurances that they would not unduly interfere with his African ambitions and aided in delaying Council consideration of the Ethiopian complaints. In August representatives of the British and French governments met with Italian representatives to try to negotiate an African territorial settlement, but the suggested concessions to Italy were rejected by Mussolini as unacceptable.

Finally, on October 3, 1935, a full-scale invasion of Ethiopia was launched by the Italian forces in Eritrea. The small, poorly trained, and inadequately equipped Ethiopian army was no match for the modern, mechanized Italian divisions and bomber squadrons, and the final result could never be in doubt unless Italian supply lines were cut. The Italians also resorted to the extensive use of mustard gas, in spite of other advantages that made this violation of treaty obligations seem unnecessary as well as inhumane.

The response of the League to the news of the attack was prompt and unprecedented. Within four days of the initial invasion, the Council voted unanimously, except for Italy, that the Italian government was an aggressor in violation of the Covenant and that Article 16, providing for economic and possibly military sanctions, should be applied against Italy. This was the first time that the collective security provisions of the Covenant had been invoked, and, surprisingly, they were to be employed against a major power.

In order to bring Article 16 into effect, action by the Assembly was required. Although that article seems to demand the automatic application of economic sanctions, the members, in 1921, had adopted an interpretation that each state reserved the right to determine if it would engage in sanctions. On October 11, fifty of the fifty-four League members endorsed cooperative action against Italian aggression.

To provide for uniformity in the application of sanctions, a coordinating committee of the fifty states endorsing the League action was formed. The members agreed to stop the sale of arms to Italy but not to Ethiopia, to cut off credit to the Italian government and to Italian businesses, to prohibit imports from Italy, and to embargo the sale to Italy of strategic war materials (including rubber, tin, aluminum, and manganese), which were substantially controlled by the boycotting states.

These measures struck a severe blow to the Italian economy but were insufficient to prevent the conquest of Ethiopia. Within a few months the Italian gold reserves were dwindling to a critical point, and the lira had to be devalued. Italy's foreign trade was reduced to a small fraction of its previous level. Additional effective sanctions, which undoubtedly could have stopped the military action, were rejected. Embargoes were excluded on food, coal, steel, and oil. The sanctions committee refused to cut off Italian access to the Suez Canal or to blockade the Italian mainland. Diplomatic relations were continued with Italy. The British and French governments had agreed not to push sanctions to the point of risking war with Italy, and, in December, 1935, the Hoare-Laval proposal for giving Italy control of most of Ethiopia shocked public opinion in most of the world. The proposal was, however, unacceptable to Mussolini as well as to Haile Selassie.

In July, 1936, sanctions against Italy were abandoned, just two months after Mussolini's announcement of victory and his assumption of the title Emperor of Ethiopia. The initiative for the conciliation of Italy came from the British who feared the resurgence of a German threat and were reacting to Hitler's remilitarization of the Rhineland in March of that year. Although the hope proved vain,

Italy's support was courted in the resistance to German belligerence. Other European states, including the Scandinavian countries, opposed the lifting of sanctions but could do little but accede to the British proposal. The effectiveness of continued limited sanctions was never tested, and the first such application had to be branded a failure. The League members, in their anxiety over European threats to the peace, were unwilling even to refuse to recognize the legitimacy of the Italian hegemony over Ethiopia.

The first experiment in applying sanctions against a major power ended in disillusionment concerning their effectiveness, although there had been limitations placed upon their application. The Russian spokesman in the League pointed out that the failure was due to halfheated measures, rather than to any deficiency in the formula of Article 16. The proof that collective security measures cannot work was not convincing in this situation, since the will to apply sanctions was the real subject under test. The disappointment in the results was best expressed in a warning by the Haitian delegate to the Assembly, who pleaded, "Let us never forget that one day we may be somebody's Ethiopia."

Following the failure to take effective action against Japanese and Italian aggression, the League processes for the collective control of political conflict degenerated. The faltering will for dynamic response to crises was now dead. Each member concentrated on its own desire to avoid involvement in acts of aggression against other states. Following Hitler's abrogation of the Treaty of Versailles and the Locarno Pact through the remilitarization of the Rhineland, Germany met no League opposition in taking over Austria and Czechoslovakia. The League failed to intervene in the Spanish civil war in spite of the internationalization of the war through Italian, German, and Soviet involvement. China was virtually rejected in its pleas for League action against Japan when Japan invaded China in 1937 as the opening stage of World War II in the Far East. In September, 1938, the Council approved the application of sanctions against Japan, by individual League members, but this was a hollow gesture, and no appreciable change of policy by any state resulted.

From the earliest days of the League, the members realized that the procedures of the Covenant lacked guarantees that all disputes would be settled peacefully. Several attempts were made, both inside and outside the League, to close the gaps and build an airtight security system. Most of these proposals were linked to plans for general disarmament. After years of preliminary planning, a League-sponsored general disarmament conference convened in 1932 but failed to reach any compromise among competing formulas for disarmament.

As a part of its search for security guarantees, France, in 1925, succeeded in obtaining the agreement of other European states to the Locarno Pact. France feared the resurgence of German power on the continent, and the Locarno Pact guaranteed the boundaries between Germany, France, and Belgium with British and Italian adherence to the agreement. The League Council was to act as the agent for determining boundary violations. Other pacts were concluded between France, Germany, Poland, and Czechoslovakia, which attempted to assure the freezing of the territorial status quo in East Europe.

The Kellogg-Briand Pact, or General Treaty for the Renunciation of War, in 1928, was widely acclaimed as a landmark in the search for peace but proved ineffective as a bulwark against aggression. Because it was promoted by the United States, it was hailed as an important link between the League ideas and United States policy. The two major principles were simple: (1) war was renounced as an instrument of national policy, and (2) the parties agreed to settle all disputes by peaceful means. The treaty was received so enthusiastically that sixty-four states quickly ratified it. In subsequent years its weaknesses became apparent. It provided no means of enforcement and was therefore only a moral declaration. Wars of self-defense were declared by Secretary Kellogg to be outside the treaty's purview, yet every state is the judge of its own reasons for taking up arms, and all conflicts tend to be self-judged as defensive.

In spite of scant attention paid to economic and social matters in the Covenant, a vast amount of valuable work was carried on in these areas, and, in the 1930s, these activities became the most successful contributions of the League to the attempted solution of world problems. Starved by a lack of adequate funds, the economic and social work of the League nevertheless ran the gamut of activities that were continued on a grander scale by the United Nations, and furnished valuable experience on which the United Nations Economic and Social Council and more than a dozen specialized agencies could build. A network of committees, organizations, and conferences was developed to foster this wide range of activities, and a major portion of the Secretariat was devoted to supporting this work. One of the valuable services in the economic and social sphere was the gathering and dissemination of knowledge, and the Secretariat furnished much of the necessary effort in research, in acting as a central clearing-house for information, and in publication of reports.

The growing importance of the economic and social work of the League culminated in a demand during the late 1930s for reorganization of that aspect of the basic League structure with a view both to greater recognition of the role of economic and social activities and to a more detached and independent status for the agencies in those fields. Greater independence would relieve the economic and social organs from dominance by the political arms of the League and would encourage greater cooperation by nonmembers such as the United States. In May, 1939, a committee under the chairmanship of Stanley Bruce of Australia was formed to study the problem of reorganization. The report, published in August, proposed a new Central Committee for Economic and Social Questions to supervise and coordinate all League social and economic affairs. It would be open to nonmember states who would make financial contributions to its work. It would not be subject to close supervision by the Council or Assembly, and its composition could include experts as well as government delegates.

In addition to its recognition of the expansion of the economic and social work of the League at a time when its political efficacy was suffering eclipse, the Bruce Report represented the experience of the League in providing an adequate structure for a wide range of activities that the architects of the Covenant had not foreseen. The demands for more and more activities in the economic and social spheres culminated in this landmark report, which, though never implemented in the League because of the advent of war, laid all the essential groundwork for the elaborate economic and social structure of the United Nations. The report is a prime example of the ways in which League experience made valuable contributions to the establishment of an improved international organization at the close of World War II.

GENERAL ASSESSMENT OF THE LEAGUE OF NATIONS

The League of Nations represented both a radical and a conservative trend in the development of international relations. It was radical because, for the first time, the ideas and ideals of several philosophers who had advocated a universal organization for promoting peace and cooperation among nations were incorporated into state policy. It was radical because it dared to encompass within a single organization the means for dealing with a wide range of problems on which international action was desirable if not imperative. It was radical because it was innovative in creating the political, judicial, economic, social, and administrative agencies that would serve basically as a model for the United Nations. The lessons of the League's twenty years of experience also served well to modify and strengthen the pattern of the United Nations.

The trend in establishing the League was conservative because it was based on an existing international order and no attempt was made to redirect the sources of authority and power. The sovereignty of national states remained undisturbed in an organization based primarily on the principle of voluntary cooperation among those states. The innovations of the League did not include any radically new practices. The methods for settling disputes, the use of conferences, the techniques of international administration, and the principles of equality of states and of the right of a state to be bound only by its own consent were long-established features of the international scene. The new element was the superimposition upon the existing order of a comprehensive and permanent system of periodic conferences and continuous administration. The fact that the new direction received substantial approval in spite of the League's inability to prevent World War II is evidenced by the demand for a similar but expanded organization after that war and the survival without significant change of such auxiliary agencies as the World Court and the International Labour Organization.

The early optimism concerning the League may be attributed in part to the general desire for peace and cooperation among nations in the aftermath of World War I. Because of its lack of independent power and authority the League was destined to reflect the general state of international relations rather than to represent a positive force for redirecting the course of international affairs. As long as all members realized mutual advantages through cooperation, the League provided them with a useful avenue for achieving their common goals. When Germany, Italy, and Japan began to challenge the status quo and when each nation was prompted by economic distress to resort to measures that increased economic rivalry, the League mirrored the lack of cooperative will among its members.

 Many reasons have been advanced for the League's failure to survive. The absence from membership of major states such as the United States and, during shorter periods, the Soviet Union and Germany was a handicap to concerted action. The Covenant suffered from some gaps and technical weaknesses, but, in the critical tests, it was the lack of will of the members rather than of available devices that accounted for ineffective measures. Even the halfhearted sanctions against Italy came within inches of stopping aggression or reversing its results. The attempts to use the League as an instrument for maintaining an unsatisfactory and unstable status quo established in Europe by the victors in World War I doomed the attempts to failure, since no safety valves were provided to allow adjustment through the channels of peaceful change. The problem of providing means for peaceful adjustment as a substitute for military conflict remains a dilemma of international organization today.

Basically, the League of Nations failed (and the United Nations may fail) because it was ill equipped to accomplish its goals. It was based on principles that were inadequate to assure peace and co-operation. All national confederations have collapsed or been transformed due to lack of centralized power and due to rivalries among the component units. An international organization with real enforcement powers is incompatible with the principle of absolute national sovereignty. The world was not ready in 1919 or in 1945 to transfer effective control over military forces and compulsory jurisdiction over disputes to the international level.

The fading distinction between domestic and international problems may hasten the creation of more effective international agencies in the future, but the basic cleavages that divide one nation from another are not much different today from those in the period of the League. Economic rivalries, differences in languages, culture, levels of prosperity and political systems, prejudice, and a lack of trust stand as barriers to the creation of the kind of international system that may be required to make a League of Nations or United Nations a more effective instrument for dealing with world problems.

If the League of Nations is measured against a yardstick of hopes and possibilities for achieving world peace and cooperation, it fell short of its goal. If, on the other hand, it is measured by the standard of previous advances toward world order, it represented a breakthrough in the development of international organization. If the process of development does not reverse itself, the League will continue to stand as a landmark in the evolutionary process of achieving a more orderly world.

3

❧

The Genesis
of
the United Nations

Just as World War I led to the formation of the League of Nations, World War II led to the establishment of the United Nations. In each case, both statespeople and scholars tried to develop ways of maintaining peace and stability when the war ended.

Despite the desire for peace, after each war there were many conservative elements working to prevent the creation of an international organization radically different from that existing before the war. Included in these conservative elements were nationalism, existing international relationships, the desire to continue and to promote national and individual economic, social, political, and ideological interests, and also suspicion and fear of alien political and cultural systems in a hostile world climate.

The United Nations, established in 1945, is a balance of conservatism and change. Because the League of Nations had failed to prevent war, the United Nations Charter sought to correct the League Covenant's deficiencies. The architects of the UN also attempted to divorce the new organization from any lingering stigma of the League and to convince others that the UN was a completely new creation, not just a revised League. But at the same time, the negotiators were unwilling, and perhaps unable, to think in terms other than those of nationalism, national sovereignty, national interests, and established patterns of international relationships. The result was no more radical than a new automobile model might be, in which the lines and trim are different, but basic engineering is the same.

PRELIMINARY STAGES OF POSTWAR PLANNING

With much of Europe overrun by Axis military forces or under threat of annihilation by bombing, a greater proportion of postwar planning during World War II than during World War I was concentrated in the United States. Dozens of private organizations in the United States generated ideas and plans for a peace-keeping organization and reacted to proposals from other sources. The Department of State created some modest planning machinery by January, 1940, and gradually intensified postwar planning efforts as the deadline approached for translating ideas into a finished Charter.

The Department of State was able to draw ideas for a postwar organization from a wide range of private organizations. One of the most active and influential was the Commission to Study the Organization of Peace, established in 1939 under the chairmanship of James T. Shotwell and composed of leading scholars concerned with international organization. This commission has continued in existence to the present time, but its first four reports, issued during the period 1941–44, outlined a basic philosophy and detailed proposals for a world organization. Another active agency was the Commission for a Just and Durable Peace, established by the Federal Council of Churches of Christ in America. John Foster Dulles, subsequently Secretary of State, served as the commission's chairman. Another group of Catholic, Jewish, and Protestant religious leaders in October, 1943, published the *Declaration on World Peace.* A Universities Committee on Postwar International Problems with headquarters at the World Peace Foundation in Boston coordinated the deliberations and ideas of approximately 100 local cooperating faculty groups. Both labor and management demonstrated their interest in postwar peace plans through committees of the American Federation of Labor and the United States Chamber of Commerce. A select committee of fifteen United States citizens experienced in the work of international organizations, under the chairmanship of Judge Manley O. Hudson, published in 1944 a comprehensive *Design for a Charter of the General International Organization.* Other active groups included the Council on Foreign Relations, the League of Nations Association, the Americans United for World Organization, and the Foreign Policy Association.

All of the above efforts, and others among private groups in the United States, antedated the first official plans made public in the form of the Dumbarton Oaks Proposals in the fall of 1944. The State Department recognized the widespread public interest in the Dumbarton Oaks Proposals and responded to a request from the Americans United for World Organization and the Commission to Study the Organization of Peace for a briefing session for representatives of interested national organizations. Arrangements were made for delegates from nearly 100 organizations to participate in a briefing and discussion of the proposals on October 16, 1944. This high degree of interest of concerned citizens, acting through private organizations, was sustained throughout the period of the drafting of the United Nations Charter at San Francisco and continued into the initial years of the new organization.

The impetus for a postwar international organization was not confined to the United States. In Great Britain the League of Nations Union under the leadership of Lord Robert Cecil published proposals for an international authority closely paralleling the League of Nations provisions. Some efforts in private planning were international in scope. In 1940 the International Chamber of Commerce and the Carnegie Endowment for International Peace jointly initiated a planning project through the cooperation of national committees. The major concentration of these committees was upon postwar economic reconstruction and trade relations. Two cooperative enterprises between citizens of the United States and Canada concentrated on the field of international law. One involved a series of discussions in 1942–43, participated in by 200 judges, lawyers, professors, government officials, and others with special competence and interest in international law. The final report of this group was entitled *The International Law of the Future: Postulates, Principles, Proposals.*[1] The second United States-Canadian cooperative effort was sponsored by the Canadian and American bar associations. As a result of a series of regional conferences attended by more than 600 lawyers, judges, teachers, and legal practitioners, a joint statement was issued entitled *The International Court of the United Nations Organization.*[2]

From this review of private planning activities it is evident that government agencies could draw upon a wide cross section of concerned and informed opinion in formulating postwar organization plans. The United States Department of State gathered, organized,

[1] *International Conciliation*, no. 399, April 1944, pp. 251–374.
[2] *International Conciliation*, no. 411, May 1945, pp. 343–62.

and analyzed the proposals from dozens of sources and incorporated some of the ideas into the official planning process.

The willingness of American leaders to help create and to play a leading role in a general international organization represented a significant departure from the refusal of the United States to join the League of Nations. President Roosevelt and Secretary of State Cordell Hull were committed to the establishment of a general international organization and were determined to avoid the disillusioning experience of President Wilson with the League of Nations. Congressional leaders of both major political parties declared their support for cooperation in a postwar organization. Senator Arthur Vandenberg of Michigan was instrumental in securing the endorsement of a conference of Republican leaders at Mackinac Island in September, 1943, for United States participation in an international organization. Later that month the House of Representatives passed the Fulbright Resolution, favoring the creation of postwar international peacekeeping machinery and participation therein by the United States. A corresponding resolution sponsored by Senator Connally was adopted by the Senate in early November.

Although the Department of State initiated postwar planning activities in January, 1940, the most intensive and important work in this area was begun after United States involvement in the war against the Axis. Early in 1942 a new Advisory Committee on Postwar Foreign Policy with an elaborate system of subcommittees was established within the department. Most of the personnel for these committees were co-opted from outside the State Department from both public and private sectors. Supporting all of the planning activities of the State Department from 1940 through the completion of the United Nations Charter was the Division of Special Research of the department. Under the capable direction of Leo Pasvolsky, the research division acted as secretariat for the series of planning committees and subcommittees throughout the war years. In addition to serving as head of the research division, Pasvolsky also held the portfolio of Special Assistant to the Secretary of State for International Organization and Security Affairs and the title of Executive Director of the Advisory Committee and of its successor agencies that drafted the Charter. During 1942, as the tempo of postwar planning activities within the department rapidly increased, the personnel of the research division was expanded from ten to more than seventy.

During the period 1940–43 the pressures for a postwar organization of a regional or a decentralized nature seemed dominant. President Roosevelt during these years favored a decentralized system of agencies for nonsecurity matters and advocated "great power" responsibility for curbing aggression. Winston Churchill leaned toward a regional approach to peace-keeping, and early British plans reflected this bias. Functional decentralization was bolstered by the United Nations Conference on Food and Agriculture at Hot Springs, Virginia, in May, 1943, which agreed upon the establishment of the Food and Agriculture Organization, and by the Bretton Woods Conference of July, 1944, which established the International Bank for Reconstruction and Development and the International Monetary Fund. The State Department Advisory Committee in 1942–43 tended to move so much in the direction of a regional emphasis under the chairmanship of Under Secretary Welles that in June, 1943, Secretary Hull took over the active role of chairman and re-directed the plans along the lines of his own global preferences. By late 1943 a global approach seemed assured with accommodation within the comprehensive organization for separate and cooperating regional and functional organizations.

World attention was focused upon postwar planning through a series of meetings of heads of the major Allied states or of their foreign ministers. Each of these meetings resulted in the signing and proclamation of a document declarative of postwar goals. The first in this chain of pronouncements was the Inter-Allied Declaration signed in London in June, 1941, by representatives of British Commonwealth governments and European governments-in-exile. Without referring specifically to the establishment of an international organization, the signatories pledged their cooperation in working for the elimination of the threat of aggression and in striving for economic and social security for all free peoples.

Two months later President Roosevelt and Prime Minister Churchill met aboard ship off Argentia, Newfoundland, and agreed upon the terms of a document referred to as the Atlantic Charter. In arriving at a compromise concerning some of the points to be included and the phraseology, Churchill was persistent in pushing for a reference to the establishment of an "effective international organization." Roosevelt considered the phrase too strong but finally accepted the principle that aggressor nations should be disarmed "pending the establishment of a wider and permanent system of general security." The Atlantic Charter was promulgated before the United States entered the war, but in January, 1942, the representatives of twenty-six nations allied against the Axis powers signed the Declaration by United Nations in Washington, D.C. This document included the first use of the term "United Nations," and in it the signatories subscribed to the principles of the Atlantic Charter as their war and peace aims in addition to a pledge of full cooperation and effort in defeating the Axis states. As they later became involved in the war, a score of additional states adhered to the declaration.

On October 30, 1943, the foreign ministers of the USSR and the United Kingdom, Secretary of State Hull, and the Chinese ambassador to the Soviet Union issued a declaration in Moscow that, for the first time, clearly pledged their efforts for the establishment of a general international organization. The paragraph which contained this pledge stated that the four governments

> . . . recognize the necessity of establishing at the earliest practicable date a general international organization, based on the principle of the sovereign equality of all peace-loving states, and open to membership by all such states, large and small, for the maintenance of international peace and security.

One month after the Moscow Declaration, President Roosevelt, Premier Stalin, and Prime Minister Churchill, meeting in Tehran, announced in their final communiqué

> We recognize fully the supreme responsibility resting upon us and all the United Nations to make a peace which will command the goodwill of the overwhelming masses of the peoples of the world and banish the scourge and terror of war for many generations. . . . We shall seek the cooperation and active participation of all nations large and small . . . [for] the elimination of tyranny and slavery, oppression and intolerance. We will welcome them, as they may choose to come, into a world family of Democratic Nations.

From this series of declarations it is apparent that by the end of 1943 the leaders of the major powers were committed to the establishment of a postwar general international organization. The task that remained was the formulation of detailed plans to which a large number of governments could subscribe. This process involved not only compromise among the divergent views and interests of the big powers, but the eventual resolution of some of the differences between the goals of the small and the large states.

THE DUMBARTON OAKS CONVERSATIONS

By mid-1944 the pace of detailed planning within individual major Allied governments had acquired sufficient momentum to provide working plans for a conference of those big powers. The purpose of this conference was to produce a tentative or preliminary draft of a constitution for a postwar international organization, subject to further elaboration and modification by an expanded conference of Allied and neutral states. This two-step conference process allowed the big powers first to agree among themselves on the essential elements of the organization and then to present a united front in resisting fundamental changes proposed by the smaller states while accepting their suggestions for filling in details and modifying provisions which the major powers considered as nonvital.

The United States government suggested an exchange of preliminary plans and invited the other major Allies to meet in Washington, D.C., in August, 1944. Because the Soviet Union was not at this time involved as an ally of China in the Pacific war, the parties agreed that the conversations would take place in two phases. During the first phase the representatives of the United States and the United Kingdom would confer with the Soviet representatives, and immediately afterward the Chinese delegates would replace the Soviet delegates for a second round of consultations. The meetings were held at Dumbarton Oaks, an extensive estate in the Georgetown section of Washington, D.C. The informal conversations at Dumbarton Oaks may be characterized as a working conference of a technical nature at a fairly high diplomatic level.

The Dumbarton Oaks conversations brought about substantial agreement on the major elements of a plan for an international organization. The final document, published on October, 9, 1944, was neither complete nor in satisfactory form for a finished Charter, but it served, together with subsequent additions by the Big Four, as the fundamental framework of the emerging United Nations. While it was presented to the world merely as a working document to be used as a basis for further discussion, comment, and amendment, it represented much more in reality. It embodied the areas of agreement on essential principles among the major powers, and from these principles those powers could not readily be detached. Throughout the subsequent San Francisco Conference the Dumbarton Oaks participants demonstrated their tenacity in adhering to their previous mutual agreements and commitments, in spite of attacks, suggestions, and criticisms from other states.

The participants at Dumbarton Oaks concentrated their efforts on the security provisions of the emerging Charter. The dominance of the great powers in the war effort was to be carried over into the peacekeeping measures for the postwar period. The central organ for this purpose was to be a Security Council in which the Big Five would have permanent membership. The agreements provided for three other major organs — a General Assembly, a Secretariat, and a Court. Except for the incorporation of the Court into the general organization, the basic structure was similar to that of the League of Nations. At Dumbarton Oaks no provision was made for a trusteeship system, and the Economic and Social Council was to be a subsidiary to the General Assembly rather than being declared a major organ.

The Dumbarton Oaks Proposals left a number of gaps to be subsequently filled. The most important was the voting formula in the Security Council. At Dumbarton Oaks an impasse had been reached on this issue. The Soviet Union insisted on an unlimited veto privilege for the permanent members of the Council, whereas the other parties thought that such a provision would result in excessive rigidity and stalemate. The Soviet Union also requested individual membership in the organization for all sixteen of her Union Republics on the basis of their constitutional autonomy, a claim somewhat analogous to, but more exaggerated than, membership by India and the Philippines prior to their complete independence. Other unsettled questions included the nature of the Court (whether it should be new or a continuation of the Permanent Court of International Justice) and arrangements for transition from the League of Nations to the new organization. Some sections of the proposals needed elaboration also. Notable among these were the provisions for the Secretariat and for the economic and social activities of the organization.

FROM YALTA TO SAN FRANCISCO

In early February, 1945, Roosevelt, Churchill, and Stalin, accompanied by their foreign ministers, met at Yalta in the Crimea to discuss a wide range of subjects relating to the war and postwar plans. Many of the discussions were unrelated to proposals for a United Nations organization; among these subjects were the Polish and Balkan questions, the establishment of occupation zones in Germany, and the entry of the Soviet Union into the Pacific war.

The most important decision reached at Yalta concerning the unfinished business of Dumbarton Oaks was the acceptance of the United States proposals for the voting formula in the Security Council. Under this formula unanimity of the big powers would be required on substantive matters including any enforcement action in response to a breach or threat to the peace or act of aggression, but none of the permanent members could use the power of veto to block a procedural vote, and a party to a dispute was required to abstain on a decision by the Security Council to discuss the dispute. Since the proposal provided the means for the big powers to prevent enforcement action against themselves, Stalin finally became convinced that their position was adequately safeguarded by this arrangement.

Stalin accepted the western position on the voting formula partially in exchange for a concession on multiple membership for the Soviet Union. The original demand for membership for sixteen Union Republics was first reduced to three and then to only two — the Ukraine and Byelorussia. Roosevelt reluctantly accepted this offer, although he anticipated some difficulty concerning Congressional and public acceptance at home, and he stated that he would have to keep open the possibility of asking for a similar multiple vote for the United States. The question of whether the Ukraine and Byelorussia would be invited as full and equal participants in the forthcoming conference to write the Charter was not fully settled at Yalta.

The conferees further agreed that the general conference on international organization would be held at San Francisco beginning on April 25 and that the United States would issue the invitations. China and France would be asked to cosponsor the conference if they so desired. France subsequently attended but did not act as sponsor. It was agreed that the invitations would declare that the Dumbarton Oaks Proposals and the Yalta voting formula would serve as a basis for conference discussion.

The Big Three at Yalta also reached an understanding concerning the essential principles of trusteeship in the Charter. No territories were to be specifically designated as trust territories until after the San Francisco conference, but the three categories to which trusteeship could be applied were (1) existing mandates under the League of Nations, (2) territories detached from the enemy as a result of the present war, and (3) any other territory voluntarily placed under trusteeship. Further details concerning the trusteeship system were to be elaborated on the basis of additional consultation among the sponsoring states prior to the San Francisco conference.

Rumblings of discontent with the Dumbarton Oaks Proposals became apparent at a special Inter-American Conference on Problems of Peace and War held in Mexico City from February 21 to March 8, 1945. Secretary of State Stettinius traveled directly from Yalta to Mexico City to chair the United States delegation. In spite of attempts by that delegation to head off attacks on the big-power agreements, the Latin American representatives expressed their dissatisfaction with the Dumbarton Oaks Proposals. In a broad resolution on the subject of the establishment of a general international organization, the conference listed several suggestions for change, including (1) stress on universality of membership, (2) amplification of the powers and role of the General Assembly, (3) expansion of the jurisdiction and competence of the International Court, (4) an expanded role for regional organizations within the general framework, and (5) adequate representation of Latin America on the Security Council. The voting formula agreed upon at Yalta was published too late to be a target for attack at Mexico City. The attitudes expressed, however, gave due notice of the battles to come at San Francisco between the large and the small states.

THE SAN FRANCISCO CONFERENCE

The United Nations Conference on International Organization (UNCIO), which opened in San Francisco on April 25, 1945, faced not only the problems of reconciling conflicting positions among states, but also problems of size, effective organization, communications, and national pride and prestige. All forty-six states that had adhered to the United Nations Declaration and that had declared war on one or more Axis powers accepted invitations to participate and, by agreement of the participants, Argentina, Byelorussia, the Ukraine, and Denmark were added to the roster. The Soviet Union urged the inclusion of the provisional government of Poland, but that recommendation was rejected, although Poland was subsequently allowed to sign the Charter as an original member. The fifty participating states were represented by 282 official delegates and by more than 1,400 delegation advisers and staff members. A Secretariat of more than 1,000, furnished by the United States as host country, served the conference in official roles, and more than 4,000 auxiliary personnel provided less professional services. News coverage was provided by more than 2,600 accredited press and radio personnel.[3] After some debate over the languages to be used, English and French were adopted as the working languages of the conference, and these two plus Russian, Chinese, and Spanish were accepted as official languages. The resulting requirement of reproducing debates in two languages and many documents in five languages placed a heavy burden on the Secretariat.

In San Francisco the smaller states made their most concerted attack on the voting formula in the Security Council. The attack was led by H. V. Evatt, Australian Minister for External Affairs, and was joined by spokesmen from most of the other medium and small states. The objections were both to the principle of a privileged position for the five permanent members of the Security Council

---

[3] These conference statistics are adapted from Clyde Eagleton, "The Charter Adopted at San Francisco," *American Political Science Review*, Vol. 39 (October, 1945), p. 935.

and to the lack of clarity concerning the application of the veto in specific situations. All attempts at modificiation of the formula or the removal of its applicability from such areas as pacific settlement of disputes were rebuffed by the major powers. On one occasion Senator Connally of the United States dramatized the intransigence of the Big Five by tearing to pieces a copy of the proposed Charter and announcing that without the veto there would be no Charter. In the end the smaller states had to accept the formula without change. The applicability of the veto even outside the strict areas of peace and security, such as Charter amendment, admission of members, and selection of a Secretary-General, withstood all attacks and remained a bastion of great-power privilege.

The small powers achieved slight gains in San Francisco in the matter of clarification of the voting formula. They collectively submitted to the sponsoring powers a twenty-three part questionnaire requesting answers to questions concerning the applicability of the veto in specific situations. After some disagreement among the Big Four over the issue of the right to use the veto to block preliminary discussion of a dispute (settled only through an appeal to Stalin in Moscow to relax the Soviet hard line), the sponsoring powers issued a general reply to the questionnaire. The reply carried the label "Statement by the Delegations of the Four Sponsoring Governments on Voting Procedures in the Security Council." The statement clarified the interpretation of the Big Four without answering the questionnaire item by item. The smaller states were dissatisfied with the general rigidity of the applications of the veto but had to accept the interpretations as representing the limits of big-power concessions. On one point the small states were particularly disappointed. If an issue arose over whether a question was substantive or procedural, the sponsoring powers stated that that preliminary question would be settled by a substantive vote. Thus the way was opened for the so-called double veto. The statement did include a list of matters that could be decided by a procedural vote of any seven of the eleven Security Council members. This list became a future guarantee against further invasions of the procedural areas through interpretation by the permanent members of the Security Council, and also limited the range of future possibilities for using the double veto. In general the big powers have treated their published statement in San Francisco to be as binding as the Charter.

Although the smaller states were unsuccessful in removing the veto power from the process for amending the Charter, they received some concessions toward calling a review conference to revise the

Charter. Provision was made that such a conference could be called at any time by a two-thirds vote in the General Assembly and by a vote of any seven members of the Security Council. Furthermore, the proposal to call such a conference would be placed on the agenda of the tenth annual session of the General Assembly at which time the required vote in the General Assembly would be reduced to a majority together with any seven affirmative votes in the Security Council. However, any amendments proposed by a conference would still require ratification by all the permanent members of the Security Council as well as by two-thirds of all members of the United Nations.

Many other states shared the concern expressed by the Latin American states at the Mexico City conference with regard to the continued importance of regional arrangements and the relationship of regional organizations to the United Nations. The chapter on regional arrangements was redrafted at San Francisco to enhance the emphasis on the importance of regional organizations in the peaceful settlement of disputes and in enforcement actions. The most significant change resulting from small-state pressure was the recognition in Article 51 of the Charter of the right of collective self-defense in cases in which the Security Council was immobilized. This provision left a wide lattitude for action by such a group as the Organization of American States.

Since the Dumbarton Oaks Proposals contained no provisions on trusteeship or colonial matters, nearly all details of this section of the Charter had to be developed at San Francisco. The sponsoring powers intended to confer prior to the San Francisco conference on the details of a trusteeship plan, but other pressures prevented this consultation, and the door was thus open to diversified influences in developing these chapters of the Charter. The final result was two lengthy chapters on the trusteeship system, including the creation of the Trusteeship Council which was accorded major organ status. The creation of the Trusteeship Council as a major organ and the raising of the status of the Economic and Social Council to similar rank increased the number of major organs from four, as suggested at Dumbarton Oaks, to six.

One of the greatest accomplishments of the small states in San Francisco was the drafting of Chapter XI of the Charter, entitled "Declaration Regarding Non-Self-Governing Territories." This unprecedented statement has been hailed as a bill of rights for all politically dependent peoples. It contained the key principle that in the administration of such territories the interests of the inhabitants are paramount, and it obligated the colonial powers to advance the inhabitants' political, economic, social, and educational welfare. It further obligated the administering states to transmit regular reports to the Secretary-General on the economic, social, and educational conditions in these territories. This concern for politically subjugated peoples carried over into the experience and practice of the United Nations and culminated in the adoption by the General Assembly in 1960 of a declaration stating that all peoples have a right to independence and self-determination.

In enhancing the emphasis upon economic and social activities of the United Nations, the smaller states received support from the United States delegation. In San Francisco the Economic and Social Council was declared to be a major organ, although, constitutionally as well as in practice, its activities have been reviewed and closely scrutinized by the General Assembly. A comparison of the Dumbarton Oaks Proposals with the adopted Charter demonstrates the expansion of the role of the Economic and Social Council. Areas of competence were spelled out in greater detail. Specific references were added for promoting respect for and observance of human rights and fundamental freedoms. The powers and functions of the Economic and Social Council were expanded to include the drafting of conventions and the calling of international conferences on subjects within its areas of competence. The greater detail of this section of the Charter provided a firm base for the widely diversified program of economic and social work that has been developed by the United Nations during more than a third of a century.

In trying to diminish the influence of the big powers through the Security Council, the small powers in San Francisco sought to enhance the importance of the General Assembly, the Secretariat, and the International Court of Justice. The most significant addition to the powers of the General Assembly was incorporated into Article 10 of the Charter which gave to the General Assembly the broad authority to "discuss any questions or any matters within the scope of the present Charter or relating to the powers and functions of any organs provided for in the present Charter." This sweeping grant of power has served to justify a broad range of General Assembly activities both of a supervisory and of an initiatory nature. The meager provisions of the Dumbarton Oaks Proposals concerning the Secretariat and the Secretary-General were enlarged, and the staff received additional guarantees in the Charter of their independence from undue interference by the member states. A decision to establish a new Court was made before the Conference convened, and, prior to the San Francisco sessions, a committee of jurists had been assembled in Washington, D.C., to draft a statute for the Court. This statute was adopted in San Francisco as a part of the Charter. The new statute was nearly identical to that of the Permanent Court of International Justice. Nevertheless, the International Court of Justice was incorporated into the United Nations as a major organ rather than having an independent status as in League days. Attempts by several states to confer compulsory jurisdiction on the Court were unsuccessful. Such a step would have constituted a major surrender of sovereignty, a step that a majority of nations were not yet ready to take.

LAUNCHING THE NEW ORGANIZATION

The Charter provided that it would become effective upon ratification by the five permanent members of the Security Council and by a majority of the other signatories. The Charter was signed by representatives of all the participating states on June 26, 1945. The first state to deposit its instrument of ratification was the United States. In late July the Senate approved the Charter by a vote of 89-2, a far cry from the debates on and defeat of the Convenant in 1919-20. By October 24, 1945, the required number of ratifications had been deposited with the United States government, and the Charter came into force.

A preparatory commission had been working in London prior to the effective date of the Charter to make the necessary arrangements for launching the new organization. This work was continued through the ensuing weeks until a permanent organization could be created. With the first meeting of the General Assembly in London, on January 10, 1946, the United Nations as a functioning entity was under way.

During late 1945 the decision had been made to locate the headquarters of the United Nations in the United States. Temporary quarters were used at Hunter College in the Bronx and at Lake Success on Long Island with additional facilities in the New York City building on the grounds of the New York World's Fair. After months of search for a suitable site for a permanent headquarters, an offer was made by John D. Rockefeller, Jr., to give for this purpose a tract of land between Forty-second and Forty-eighth Streets and adjacent to the East River in Manhattan. Although this site was much more restricted in size than the space previously sought, the offer was accepted. With an interest-free loan of 65 million dollars from the United States government, the principal buildings were planned, built, and occupied by the early 1950s.

The period from conception to launching for the United Nations, like that for the League of Nations, was of several years' duration. Both organizations were the products of major wars. Both were based on ideas and experience from a variety of sources, but both were promoted primarily by the United States Presidents and their advisers. Both primarily represented the principles and ideas acceptable to the major powers, but the United Nations Charter was debated by a broad cross section of states, and the small powers managed to make some significant changes and additions to the proposals of the powerful states. With rapid acceptance by all the signatory states, the United Nations held out somewhat greater promise at its inauguration than had the League with its truncated membership. However, the proof of its efficacy remained to be tested through experience and trial.

4

❧

Basic Principles
and Organization of
the United Nations

The United Nations Charter outlines all the United Nations' subsequent relationships and programs. The Charter also is a multilateral treaty establishing the pattern of agreements among and obligations of its members and as such, is an important addition to international law. As a written constitution, the Charter provides the UN's organizational structure, principles, powers, and functions.

Because the United nations is, at most, a weak confederation, its members' obligations are limited and only their cooperation can bring about the implementation of UN functions. The organization has no means of enforcing its measures, unlike individual governments, and even the final interpretation of Charter obligations is made by its members.

As with most constitutions, not all principles and practices can be determined by merely reading the Charter. Interpretation and actual usage of the document have been far more important than the few amendments added to it. Only by examining United Nations practices can its Charter's functions, nonfunctions, and malfunctions be really understood. Sometimes its constitutional principles have acted either as catalysts or as barriers to action; at other times, the attitude and will of the members have been more influential.

OBJECTIVES OF THE UNITED NATIONS

Obviously, a statement of objectives or goals for an organization guarantees nothing toward their fulfillment, and, if the goals have real importance or significance for the welfare of humankind, the process of fulfillment is of greater value than the verbalization of aims. However, the coming together of fifty nations to form an international organization indicates a desire to accomplish certain common purposes, and the agreement on a statement of these purposes, usually incorporated into the opening passages of the basic final document of such a conference, specifies the range and limits of the areas of mutual concern. Whether achievable or not, this statement of objectives points the direction for action and gives shape to the program for the organization.

The statement of purposes in the United Nations Charter is both general and redundant. The aims are broad enough to express the desire of war-weary nations for an organization and program capable of helping them to avoid future military contests and to improve economic and social relationships among states. At the same time general and vague goals provide a basis for ready agreement because they can suggest to the representatives of nations with divergent interests a variety of subgoals, interpretations, and means of implementation. The redundancy results from the repetitious character of the Preamble and Article 1 of the Charter.

The primary goal of both the League of Nations and the United Nations is to maintain international peace and security. The means for goal achievement include peaceful settlement of disputes and collective measures for the prevention and removal of threats to the peace or acts of aggression. Major sections of the Charter detail the instruments and methods for implementing this objective. The Security Council is assigned primary responsibility for peace maintenance but shares this function with the General Assembly and the International Court of Justice. Chapter VI of the Charter is devoted to methods of peaceful settlement of disputes, and Chapter VII outlines measures to be taken in the more serious situations involving threats to the peace, breaches of the peace, and acts of aggression. In an additional chapter, the role to be played by regional organizations in maintaining peace is suggested.

Second only to peace maintenance, the Charter emphasizes the aim of promoting international economic and social cooperation. The Economic and Social Council is to serve as the major organ for implementing this goal with substantial support from the General

Assembly and from such autonomous international specialized agencies in the economic and social sphere as governments may create and bring into formal relationship with the United Nations. Additional support in promoting economic and social cooperation may come from subsidiary bodies of the Economic and Social Council and through consultations with nongovernmental organizations. Some of the obligations under the trusteeship provisions of the Charter and some of the guarantees made to all non-self-governing peoples also fit into the economic and social category.

A third professed purpose of the United Nations is to promote respect for human rights for all peoples. The reference in Article 1 to human rights and fundamental freedoms lacks any specific or detailed meaning and provides no guidelines for implementation. No further definition appears elsewhere in the Charter. Major responsibilities for promoting human rights are assigned to the General Assembly and to the Economic and Social Council. The Economic and Social Council is directed to set up one or more commissions in the area of human rights and is empowered to make recommendations and prepare draft conventions on human rights. The encouragement of respect for human rights and fundamental freedoms is declared to be a basic objective of the trusteeship system. The safeguarding of human rights may be inferred from the obligation of colonial powers to recognize "that the interests of the inhabitants of [non-self-governing] territories are paramount . . . to promote to the utmost . . . the well-being of the inhabitants of these territories, and . . . to ensure . . . their political, economic, social, and educational advancement."[1]

All other statements of purposes in either the Preamble or Article 1 of the Charter are more notable for their vagueness than for their specific meaning and for their lack of citing means of implementation than for their specifying means for affecting change. These vague goals include (1) developing friendly relations among nations, (2) acting as a center for harmonizing the actions of nations in the attainment of the more specific goals, (3) taking appropriate measures to strengthen universal peace, (4) practicing tolerance and living together in peace as good neighbors, and (5) establishing justice and respect for international law.

BASIC PRINCIPLES OF THE CHARTER

Immediately following the primary statement of purposes, the Charter, in Article 2, establishes the basic rules of conduct or prin-

[1] Charter of the United Nations, Art. 73.

ciples upon which the United Nations is founded and, it is hoped, upon which it will operate. In addition to the list in Article 2, several other general rules are scattered throughout the Charter. Although all provisions of the Charter are, in theory, legally binding, these principles are statements of basic standards or norms undergirding the structure and operation of the United Nations system. These principles, therefore, represent the most fundamental obligations of members of the United Nations and are the basic legal standards to which they promise adherence.

The first, and probably the most fundamental, principle is the sovereign equality of the members. Of course, equality refers to legal status rather than to size, power, or wealth. Some inequality is recognized in according permanent Security Council membership to the great powers and in the unequal assignment of responsibilities and financial assessments. Nevertheless, the Charter substantially perpetuates and reinforces the well-established principle of international law of the legal equality of states and generally accords voting rights on the basis of one state–one vote.

The fact that the United Nations is an organization of sovereign states places drastic restrictions on the independent power of the organization. Sovereignty indicates that the members reserve the power of ultimate decision-making for themselves and confer no real authority upon the international agency. This reservation of authority requires the United Nations to depend for its effective performance on the willingness of the members to cooperate in collective action and to accept stalemate or frustration when cooperation is withheld in favor of national interests. A few restrictions upon sovereignty are incorporated into the Charter, as, for example, in the mandatory obligation to carry out certain decisions of the Security Council, but, in practice, this obligation has proven to be nearly meaningless. The admission to membership of non-self-governing political units such as the Ukraine serves as an exception to the strict application of the principles of sovereignty. However, the principle of sovereignty is one of the cornerstones upon which the United Nations is constructed.

Closely related to the primary goal of the United Nations to maintain international peace and security are the twin principles that all member states (1) shall refrain from the threat or use of force in any manner inconsistent with United Nations purposes, and (2) shall settle their international disputes by peaceful means. The substitution of peaceful settlement for the reliance on force has been disappointing in the United Nations record. Portions of the Charter that envision the establishment of international military forces have not been implemented. The United Nations has lacked the means to ensure either, in the first instance, that disputes will be submitted to international agencies for settlement, or, in the second place, that settlement procedures or enforcement will be effective. Although international peace will always be a relative rather than an absolute condition, the number of unsettled disputes, the numerous instances of recourse to force, and the frequent refusals to submit disputes to United Nations agencies attest to the lack of success since 1945 in substituting peaceful settlement for reliance upon force.

Two other Charter principles closely related to those of peaceful settlement and international enforcement are (1) the obligations of members to support enforcement actions of the United Nations, and to refrain from giving assistance to states that are the objects of United Nations preventive or enforcement action, and (2) collective responsibility to require nonmember states to conform sufficiently to Charter principles to ensure the maintenance of international peace and security. The obligation to support United Nations enforcement actions is essential to the integrity and reasonable degree of effectiveness of the organization. Without the cooperation of nonmember states any assurance of efficacious action by the United Nations is diminished. The experiences of the League of Nations with the lack of will by members to apply and enforce League principles, and the uncertainties concerning support for League measures by a nonmember such as the United States serve as cogent reminders of the importance of both principles.

An essential but self-evident principle of the Charter is the obligation of all members to fulfill in good faith all the obligations assumed by them in the Charter. This promise is nothing more or less than a statement of the basic norm underlying all international treaties and international law. Without this obligation the United Nations Charter has no real meaning beyond its literary value, since enforcement is dependent upon the actions of the individual members. Because the right to interpret such obligations also rests ultimately with individual states, the possibilities for state commitment to Charter obligations vary from vigorous action to a nullity.

The list of principles in Article 2 of the Charter concludes with a severe limitation upon United Nations authority. This limitation is the "domestic jurisdiction" clause, which forbids the United Nations "to intervene in matters which are essentially within the domestic jurisdiction of any state." The impossibility of always drawing a clear distinction between domestic and international affairs makes reconciliation of this clause with the positive obligations of the Charter difficult. Practice demonstrates that varying interpretations of specific dispute or conflict situations often produce disagreement over the domestic or international nature of these situations. Such disagreements are inevitable, but the United Nations is so generally ineffective that individual nations have little to fear concerning interference from the United Nations in their internal affairs. An exception to the application of the domestic jurisdiction principle is granted in the last clause of Article 2 in which the Security Council is authorized to take enforcement action under Chapter VII of the Charter without restriction by the domestic jursidiction rule. Chapter VII deals with the most drastic measures that the Security Council may apply with respect to threats to peace, breaches of peace, or acts of aggression.

Although the whole of Article 2 of the Charter is devoted to basic principles, at least a half dozen other Charter provisions can reasonably be put in the same category of fundamental standards. The Preamble and Article 1 contain references to human rights not only as goals but also as recognized principles. The phrase in the Preamble "to reaffirm faith in fundamental human rights, in the dignity and worth of the human person, [and] in the equal rights of men and women" should be interpreted more as a matter of principle than as guidelines for a program. Article 1, which deals primarily with the purposes of the United Nations, also includes an obligation for "respect for the principle of equal rights and self-determination of peoples."

Another principle of the Charter is the statement found in Article 51 of the "right of individual or collective self-defense" against armed attack. The primary responsibility for dealing with acts of aggression resides in the Security Council, and member states are obligated to report their responses to attack to the Security Council but are not required to wait for effective United Nations action before taking self-defense measures. The possiblities for using regional self-defense arrangements in lieu of United Nations channels have in practice proven to be another major obstacle to the maximum utilization of the Security Council or the General Assembly for restoring peace in situations in which armed force is involved. By ignoring the obligation to report individual or collective self-defense measures to the Security Council or by the use of the veto in the Security Council, a major power may nullify the role of the United Nations and proceed to handle the situation either independently or through regional channels. Whether Article 51 provides mainly a supplement to or a substitution for the effective role of the Security Council in disputes involving armed force depends upon the cooperative attitude of the member states, but the implications for the United Nations as a dynamic instrument for peace are far-reaching.

Greater detail concerning regional arrangements and their relationships to the United Nations is provided in Articles 52–54 of the Charter. The major principle stated in this portion of the text is that regional arrangements shall not, in general, be considered as precluded by the Charter as long as their provisions and activities "are consistent with the Purposes and Principles of the United Nations."

Several additional principles are incorporated into the chapter of the Charter on miscellaneous provisions, which includes Articles 102–05. The first of these provides that every treaty and international agreement shall be registered by the members with the Secretariat and that no treaty not so registered shall be invoked before any United Nations organ. A second principle in this chapter declares that, in case of conflict, obligations under the Charter shall take precedence over obligations in other international agreements. Both of these principles are duplicates in all but the precise phraseology of provisions of the League of Nations Covenant.

Articles 104 and 105 provide the standards for establishing the juridical capacity of the United Nations and its privileges and immunities and those of its agents and representatives. The details of these provisions remained to be supplied in subsequent conventions. The two principal instruments for supplying these details are the Convention on the Privileges and Immunities of the United Nations, to which most members except the United States subscribe, and the Headquarters Agreement between the United States and the United Nations.

The principles discussed in this section constitute a substantial body of basic norms on which the United Nations structure and functions are superimposed. Although this group of norms is not always clear as to meaning and is not internally consistent, it represents, in combination with the purposes of the organization, the essential statement of the philosophy of the United Nations. Since a philosophy is not very useful without implementation, the international behavior of states will determine whether these norms or others are predominant in world politics.

MAJOR ORGANS OF THE UNITED NATIONS

The Charter designates six agencies as major organs of the United Nations, These are (1) the General Assembly, (2) the Security Council, (3) the Economic and Social Council, (4) the Trusteeship

Council, (5) the Secretariat, and (6) the International Court of Justice.

The General Assembly

If any of the six major organs of the United Nations is paramount and central to the organization, it is the General Assembly. This centrality was not necessarily established by design in the Charter but was soon achieved through vigorous exercise by the General Assembly of its clearly designated functions and through its assertion of additional authority in areas, such as the maintenance of peace and security, in which its Charter mandate is ambiguous. The growth in the relative importance of the United Nations General Assembly is comparable to the transition by which the League of Nations Assembly asserted its precedence over the other League organs. The details which illustrate the enhancement of the General Assembly's relative importance will emerge in the further study of the functions and proceedings of the United Nations.

The General Assembly serves as an arena for general debate for the United Nations and as the only existing approximation of a world forum. Of the six major organs the General Assembly is the only one in which all member states are represented. Each year the delegates from almost all the recognized states in the world meet and discuss an agenda encompassing an extremely broad range of general and specific international issues. The General Assembly exercises coordinating and supervisory functions for all other agencies within the United Nations orbit and thus brings to a focus in its debates the most complete scope of United Nations activities. With so many viewpoints to be expressed and with so many functions and issues centered in one body, it should not be surprising that the General Assembly has difficulty working its way through its complicated agenda within a three-month period each year.

The Charter provides for regular annual sessions of the General Assembly and such special sessions as may be required. Regular sessions begin on the third Tuesday in September, and delegates usually anticipate adjournment before Christmas, but the pressure of normal business or a crisis situation, such as the Congo crisis, will prompt a reconvened session after a Christmas holiday.

The Charter provides for the calling of special sessions of the General Assembly, and ten such sessions have met. The subjects and years are Palestine (1947), Palestine (1948), Tunisia (1961), Financial and Budgetary Problems (1963), Review of Peacekeeping Operations and Southwest Africa (1967), Raw Materials and Development (1974), Development and International Economic Cooperation

(1975), Financing of United Nations Interim Force in Lebanon (1978), Namibia (1978), and Disarmament (1978).

In the summer of 1950 the Security Council was able to avoid a stalemate over the Korean situation because the Soviet Union boycotted the Council meetings during the first seven months of that year. Several resolutions on Korea were adopted by the Council during the Soviet absence. When the General Assembly met in the fall of 1950, the United States and six other states introduced a Uniting for Peace Resolution providing, among other related matters, for the convening, on as little as twenty-four-hour notice, of emergency special sessions of the General Assembly. Under the threat of future Security Council impotence in the face of Korea-type situations, the Assembly members overwhelmingly adopted the resolution in spite of Soviet-bloc opposition and claims of illegality. However, in June, 1967, the Soviet delegation called for an emergency special session of the General Assembly under the provisions of the Uniting for Peace Resolution. This emergency session dealt with the crisis in the Middle East. Four previous emergency sessions had been held on the Suez crisis (1956), the Hungarian crisis (1956), Lebanon and Jordan (1958), and the Congo crisis (1960).

The bulk of the work of the General Assembly is carried on in the seven main committees to which the agenda items are allocated according to subject matter. These committees are the First or Political and Security Committee; Special Political Committee, created to relieve the overworked First Committee; Second or Economic and Financial Committee; Third or Social, Humanitarian and Cultural Committee; Fourth or Trusteeship Committee, to which questions relating to non-self-governing territories are also assigned; Fifth or Administrative and Budgetary Committee; and Sixth or Legal Committee. Each member of the United Nations is entitled to be represented on each of the main committees, a formidable assignment for small understaffed delegations who find full participation impossible and who must allocate their limited resources according to their best assessment of national priorities. Subcommittees are also appointed to expedite the work of the main committees.

The General Assembly has used generously its authority under Article 22 of the Charter to "establish such sudsidiary organs as it deems necessary for the performance of its functions." In addition to its main committees, there are in existence, at any given time, approximately fifty other subsidiary bodies created by the General Assembly.

The most comprehensive and important function of the General Assembly is its power to discuss and recommend. Article 10 of the Charter grants an almost unlimited mandate to the General Assembly in regard to the range of subjects that the body may consider. The mandate extends to "any questions or any matters within the scope of the present Charter or relating to the powers and functions of any organs provided for in the present Charter." Two significant limitations restrict an otherwise indeterminate list of matters that may be of concern to the General Assembly. The first limitation is the provision in Article 12 of the Charter that specifies that the General Assembly may discuss but may make no recommendation on "any dispute or situation" that is concurrently under consideration by the Security Council. This limitation may be avoided by action in the Security Council to remove the item from its agenda, an action that requires a procedural vote not subject to veto. The second limitation involves the fundamental nature of international organization at this stage of development. Since states are reluctant to surrender sovereign powers to international agencies, the General Assembly's authortiy is limited to recommendations that are not binding on member states. Whether recommendations will be enforced or even observed as guidelines depends upon the cooperation and action of individual states.

The General Assembly's powers of discussion and recommendation are supplemented by powers of inquiry, study, and investigation. If the grants of power to study and investigate were not specifically included in the phraseology of Articles 10–14 of the Charter, they could be implied as a necessary adjunct to the powers of discussion and recommendation. In practice the General Assembly has liberally interpreted its scope of functions and powers.

A second function assigned to the General Assembly is the supervision and review of all activities of the United Nations. The General Assembly acts as a central coordinating body for the other United Nations organs and agencies. In this capacity it receives and reviews annual reports from the Secretary-General, the Security Council, the Economic and Social Council, and the Trusteeship Council. The General Assembly also considers periodic reports from the subsidiary agencies that it has created under its broad grant of authority in Article 22 of the Charter.

Although the Charter designates the Economic and Social Council and the Trusteeship Council as major organs of the United Nations, Articles 60 and 85 seem to place them in a subordinate role to the General Assembly. This dichotomy results both in an unclear relationship between the General Assembly and the respective councils, and in some duplication of effort when the work of the councils is annually reviewed in the Second, Third, and Fourth main committees of the General Assembly.

Deciding financial matters constitutes a third major function of the General Assembly. The General Assembly has the authority to consider and approve the budget, to apportion expenses among the members, and to examine and make recommendations on the budgets of the separate specialized agencies. Budgetary powers may be used as instruments of control in substantive areas, and, in fact, clashes over policy control through financial means caused a major crisis in the 1960s.

The General Assembly exercises the most important elective functions within the United Nations, and these responsibilities constitute a fourth major area of powers and functions of the Assembly. Within the General Assembly resides the exclusive power to elect the nonpermanent members of the Security Council, all members of the Economic and Social Council, and the nonadministering members of the Trusteeship Council that are not permanent members of the Security Council. The selection of judges of the International Court of Justice is the joint responsibility of the General Assembly and the Security Council. The General Assembly also appoints the Secretary-General upon the recommendation of the Security Council. Thus, the Assembly has a voice in the composition of all the other major organs of the United Nations, with the single exception that, since 1969, due to the reduction in the number of trust territories, all elective posts on the Trusteeship Council have been eliminated.

Another power that may be interpreted as a part of the elective function is the General Assembly's control over admission of states to membership in the United Nations. Except for the original members, the General Assembly shares with the Security Council control over admission of states. A two-thirds vote is required in the General Assembly to admit an applicant. By a similar vote the Assembly may suspend the rights and privileges or may expel a member state, but all of these actions are dependent upon a prior recommendation of the Security Council. In summary of its elective functions, the General Assembly's influence extends not only to the composition of all other organs of the United Nations but to its own composition as well.

The final area of major responsibility of the General Assembly is its role in Charter amendment and revision. This constituent function includes the General Assembly's power to propose amendments by a two-thirds vote. However, any such proposal must be ratified by two-thirds of the member governments including all the permanent members of the Security Council. The constituent function also extends to the General Assembly's authority to call a general conference for Charter revision. Although two-thirds of the General

Assembly and any nine members of the Security Council may, at any time, call a revision conference, such a move would be futile unless all the permanent members of the Security Council were favorable toward ratification of any resulting proposed amendments.

Because the General Assembly has such a broad variety of functions and responsibilities, and because its large membership, which has approximately tripled since 1946, makes it an unwieldy body, there have been several proposals for increasing the efficiency of the Assembly. Studies and suggestions have been produced at frequent intervals, but few changes have been effected. Criticisms have been aimed at the number and length of speeches in general debate, at the lack of promptness in convening meetings, at the delays in starting and completing committee work, at the ineffective use of subcommittees, and at the time consumed in roll-call votes. An electric voting device has been installed, but other reforms to limit debate or speed up committee work depend more on human factors of speakers and chairmen than on devices or rules. The right of all members to be heard in a world forum probably dooms any hopes for radical streamlining of Assembly procedures and shortening of sessions.

The Security Council

The big powers, which dominated both the war effort against the Axis and postwar planning for an international organization, visualized the Security Council as the paramount organ of the United Nations. Providing a mechanism to aid in maintaining international peace and security was to be the primary purpose of the new organization, and enforcement would depend upon the power of the large states. With a continuation of the cooperation that had existed in wartime among the Allies, threats to international peace and security could be effectively met and solutions to disputes could be found. Without cooperation among the most powerful states, solutions were virtually impossible. Therefore, the big powers, it was felt, should have positions of authority on the Security Council commensurate with their responsibilities for maintaining world peace and security.

The four powers that particpated in the Dumbarton Oaks conversations — the United States, the Soviet Union, the United Kingdom, and the Republic of China — invited France to join them as permanent members of the Security Council. At first, six other nonpermanent members of the Security Council were to be elected for two-year terms, but, according to an amendment adopted in 1965, the number of nonpermanent members was expanded to ten. Primary responsibility for maintaining peace and security was concentrated in the Security Council, and unanimity among the permanent members was required on all votes on substantive matters.

During the early months of United Nations history, the pre-eminence of the Security Council seemed likely to develop. During the first three years the Security Council held an average of more than 130 meetings per year and debated a substantial number of critical political issues. The development of the Cold War, however, doomed the continued collaboration among the great powers that was necessary for effective Security Council action. Growing dis-agreement manifested itself in the increasing use of the veto by the Soviet Union, in stalemate in trying to agree on effective measures for Security Council action, and in the use of special sessions and other devices by which peace and security questions could be trans-ferred to the General Assembly. The nadir of Security Council activity was reached in 1959 when that body met only five times. In recent years the Security Council's role and activity have somewhat revived due in part to East-West détente and to the common interests of the United States and the Soviet Union in resisting mounting pres-sures of small, underdeveloped nations that can, and often do, dominate voting in the General Assembly. In spite of this recent trend, the Security Council has not measured up to its anticipated preeminent role in the United Nations.

The nonpermanent seats on the Security Council are distributed according to both Charter principles and non-Charter agreements and rules. The term is for two years with half of the number elected by the General Assembly each year. The Charter specifies that a member may not be immediately reelected. In 1946 a "gentlemen's agreement" was made to allot two seats to Latin America, and one each to Western Europe, Eastern Europe, the British Commonwealth, and the Middle East. The Soviet Union assumed that the East Euro-pean choice would be subject to Soviet control. These expectations were dashed when, beginning in 1950, that seat was filled, in succes-sion, by Yugoslavia, Greece, and Turkey, and later, under growing pressure for Asian and African representation, by the Philippines, Japan, and Liberia, among others. The growing demands for Asian and African representation finally resulted, in 1965, in the adoption of the first amendments to the Charter, providing for an enlargement of the Security Council from eleven to fifteen members. The General Assembly adopted a resolution allotting the ten elective seats as follows: five for Africa and Asia; two for Latin America; one for Eastern Europe; and two for Western Europe and other states.

Because the Security Council is compact in size and because its types of responsibilities are not diverse, its organizational structure has remained relatively simple. The most important subsidiary agencies have been ad hoc bodies established to deal with aspects of disputes and situations on the Security Council agenda. The length of service of such bodies is dependent upon the nature of the assignment and the duration of the dispute. Fact-finding commissions can finish their assignments within a few weeks, but agencies such as the United Nations Representative for India and Pakistan or the United Nations Force in Cyprus assume a tenure of several years' duration.

In order to deal with crisis situations, the Security Council is a continuous organization capable of meeting on any given day. Each member state must keep a representative available in the headquarters area at all times. The rules of the Security Council require meetings of the Council at intervals of no more than fourteen days, but this rule is frequently breached by common consent. The frequency of meetings is pragmatically determined by such considerations as the existence of disputes or threatening situations, the willingness of states to bring these situations before the Security Council, and the nature of the dispute and parties involved in relation to any prospects for the Security Council to contribute to the resolution of the controversy or to provide a propaganda advantage for any state or group of states.

In contrast to the full-year term of the General Assembly's President, the presidency of the Security Council rotates monthly by English alphabetical order of states. The President has some control over the agenda, the calling of meetings, and Council debate, but his rulings are subject to challenge by the Security Council.

The primary function of the Security Council is to maintain international peace and security. In carrying out this function the Security Council may place on its agenda for consideration any dispute, threat to the peace, breach of the peace, or act of aggression, with due consideration to the principle of domestic jurisdiction. In accepting the Charter, all members agree that the Security Council acts on their behalf and that they will carry out any Council decisions. This means, in theory, that Security Council decisions are binding, but compliance is difficult to enforce. A preliminary difficulty is the infrequency of agreement among Security Council members on a firm and effective course of action in any given dispute or situation. Details and examples of Security Council action with regard to peaceful settlement of disputes will be dealt with in chapter 6.

As a subsidiary aspect of its responsibility for maintaining international peace and security, the Security Council is also charged with the obligation to formulate plans for the international regulation of armaments. The term "regulation" seems to have been deliberately adopted rather than "reduction" or "disarmament." Relatively little progress has been made in carrying out this Charter provision as the threat of nuclear catastrophe and the acquisition of arms by large and small states continue unabated.

A secondary but important function of the Security Council is its participation in the elective process that it shares with the General Assembly. Before the General Assembly can admit a state as a new member of the United Nations, the Security Council must recommend admission. Since admission of states is a substantive matter, any permanent member of the Council may block admission by a negative vote. The process of selecting a Secretary-General is identical to the requirements for admission of members and is, therefore, also subject to the veto. The only instance in which a majority vote of the Security Council is sufficient for a decision is in the selection of judges of the International Court of Justice. The judges are elected by an absolute majority vote of the General Assembly and of the Security Council, proceeding independently of each other.

The Security Council has the responsibility to supervise, through the agency of the Trusteeship Council, any strategic trust territories. All others are subject to General Assembly supervision. Only one trust territory, the Territory of the Pacific Islands, with the United States as trustee, was ever designated in this category.

Throughout the history of the United Nations the prestige of the Security Council has fluctuated greatly. From an optimistic beginning, through a period of growing frustration manifested by frequent exercise of the veto and the use of the Council as an East-West propaganda arena, the Security Council sank in world esteem to a low point in the 1950s. As disillusionment with the effectiveness of the Security Council grew, attempts were made to strengthen the General Assembly or to utilize the initiative of the Secretary-General to fill the gap. In the 1960s some signs of revitalization of the role of the Security Council began to appear. Meetings were more frequent, and stalemate was avoided by the increased use of abstentions, the adoption of resolutions by consensus, restraint in the exercise of the veto, and efforts to accommodate conflicting views in the formulation of resolutions before they were brought to a vote. The effectiveness of the Security Council is inextricably tied to the utility of the whole United Nations, and that utility ultimately depends on the attitudes and cooperation of the member governments.

The Economic and Social Council (ECOSOC)

At the insistence of the smaller powers, and based on the League of Nations experience, appropriate emphasis and structure in the economic and social areas were incorporated into the Charter in San

Francisco. The Economic and Social Council of eighteen members (enlarged by amendment in 1965 to twenty-seven and in 1973 to fifty-four members) was created as one of the six major organs of the United Nations. All members are elected by the General Assembly for three-year terms with one-third of the terms expiring each year. No state is entitled to continuous membership, but, as a practical matter, to assure adequate support of programs, all of the permanent members of the Security Council except Nationalist China have been regularly reelected. Other seats are rotated on a regional basis. Small and underdeveloped states are in the majority in ECOSOC and can pass resolutions favorable to their own interests, since all measures are adopted by simple majority vote. Implementation is another matter because financial support from prosperous states is necessary to give effect to most economic and social programs.

In broad terms, the mission of the Economic and Social Council is to promote the welfare of all peoples everywhere. To consider the diversified agenda necessary for such a sweeping mandate, ECOSOC meets twice annually with a spring session in New York and a summer session in Geneva.

Because the economic and social activities of the United Nations are less spectacular and less controversial than the area of political disputes and confrontation, the work of ECOSOC and its associated agencies is little heralded in world headlines. Yet, more than three-fourths of the United Nations budget is spent in support of economic and social programs.

The functions of the Economic and Social Council may be divided into three general categories (1) deliberation and recommendations, (2) research and reports, and (3) coordination. Since each category is significant in the work of ECOSOC, the order of listing is not indicative of any rank order of importance.

The field of Economic and Social Council deliberation includes matters related to human rights, refugees, economic and social development, culture, education, health, food supply, trade and transportation, population, narcotic drugs, housing, labor conditions, and communications. All of these topics appear on the Council agenda from time to time, but some topics receive major emphasis. Various aspects of human rights have been of persistent concern since the 1940s. Since 1960, with the adoption of General Assembly declarations proclaiming the 1960s as the First Development Decade and the 1970s as the Second Development Decade, ECOSOC has been heavily engrossed in the problems and aspirations of the developing nations.

The Economic and Social Council performs an indispensable function in calling for a wide variety of research studies and reports on subjects within the range of its competence. Adequate statistical data as a basis for rational programing is often nonexistent. Methods of statistical measurement lack standardization, and the results, therefore, lack reliability. ECOSOC has attempted to fill the gaps, standardize procedures, and act as a clearing-house for information. United Nations studies and reports constitute a primary source of data for governments and private researchers. A portion of the research function is carried out through the subsidiary regional and functional commissions of ECOSOC. Substantial numbers of the United Nations Secretariat personnel are engaged in research and in the preparation of studies and reports in support of ECOSOC activities. Some of the major results of the economic and social research activities of the United Nations include the *World Economic Survey*, the *Report on the World Social Situation*, the *United Nations Statistical Yearbook*, the *United Nations Demographic Yearbook*, and the *United Nations Yearbook on Human Rights*. The specialized agencies affiliated with the United Nations carry on extensive research projects with ECOSOC acting as a coordinating agency.

Because of the diversity of programs and the numerous agencies involved in international economic and social work, the task of coordination is of signal importance and difficulty among the functions of the Economic and Social Council. Ideally, ECOSOC should operate as a focal point for all efforts in this area, should set up priorities, should allocate projects, and should eliminate duplication of effort and conflict of interest among agencies. Such perfection in coodination is never attained in complex organizations, and the types of relationships among the agencies involved contribute to the difficulties of the Economic and Social Council in achieving an orderly and efficient program. So many activities lie outside the effective jurisdiction of ECOSOC that, even with ideal conditions of budget, will, personnel, unity of purpose, and organizational efficiency, a well-coordinated program would, nevertheless, be difficult to establish. Furthermore, a fifty-four-member body with limited powers is not an ideal agency of coordination.

In recognition of these problems, the General Assembly in 1974 called for the appointment of a committee of experts to propose structural changes for enhancing the effectiveness of the economic and social programs of the United Nations. One of the results of the committee's recommendations was the creation in 1978 of a Secretariat post of Director-General for Development and International Economic Cooperation, second only in rank to the Secretary-General of the United Nations. This and other measures for streamlining the diverse machinery and programs under the aegis of ECOSOC may help to lessen the most severe problems of coordination.

Further information concerning the range and types of economic and social agencies in the United Nations system and their relationships to ECOSOC are detailed in chapter 10.

The Trusteeship Council

The Trusteeship Council, like the Economic and Social Council, is in the anomalous position of being designated as a major organ of the United Nations and yet being subject to General Assembly authority and review of its activities. In supervising the administration of strategic territories, the Security Council theoretically replaces the General Assembly as the final review agency, but this function is never exercised. At the San Francisco meeting the purpose of conferring major-organ status on the Trusteeship Council was to emphasize the importance attached by some representatives to the task of safeguarding the rights of non-self-governing peoples.

The role of the Trusteeship Council is to provide, on behalf of the international community, supervision of those non-self-governing territories that are designated as trust territories. The administration of each territory is carried out by a specified state, but certain supervisory responsibilities are performed by the General Assembly through the agency of the Trusteeship Council. Articles 87 and 88 of the Charter indicate the main methods for exercising this supervisory role. These methods are (1) the preparation of a detailed questionnaire on the political, economic, social, and educational advancement of the inhabitants of the territory, to be used as a basis for an annual report by the administering authority; (2) a comprehensive oral examination of the spokesmen for the administering authority based on the reply to the questionnaire, and a written report from the Trusteeship Council to the General Assembly; (3) the receipt and examination of petitions from individuals or groups within the trust territory; and (4) periodic visits to each trust territory by delegates of the Trusteeship Council. More effective supervision of conditions within trust territories is provided by these devices than existed under the mandates system of the League, although publicity and persuasion are today, as they were in the League period, the only sanctions available to pressure an administering authority into compliance with recommendations. However, the use of inspection by visiting missions is a new device that was not available to the League agencies, and petitions need no longer be submitted through the administering government, as was the case under the mandates system.

By 1950, eleven territories had been put under trusteeship with seven states acting as trustees. All except Somalia under Italian trusteeship had been former mandates within the League system. South Africa refused to place its former mandate, South West Africa, under a trust agreement, insisting instead on the unilateral right to annexation. Only one territory, the Trust Territory of the Pacific Islands under United States trusteeship, was declared a strategic area, making it theoretically subject to Security Council rather than General Assembly supervision.

Three categories of territories were designated in Article 77 of the Charter as proper subjects for trusteeship agreements:

1. Territories previously under mandate. All except those given independence after World War II and South West Africa were made trust territories.
2. Territories detached from enemy states as a result of the war. Only Somalia, detached from Italy, was assigned to Italy as trustee for a ten-year period and was granted independence in 1960.
3. Territories voluntarily placed under the system by the governing states. No such territories were placed under trusteeship.

The language of Article 77 was permissive not mandatory; no state was reqired to place any of its territories under trusteeship, but the force of opinion favored the transfer of the former mandates to the status of trust territories.

The Trusteeship Council's composition is determined by a complex formula. All members of the United Nations that administer trust territories are ex officio members of the Trusteeship Council. Any permanent members of the Security Council that are not administering powers also have automatic membership. In order to attain parity in numbers between administering and nonadministering states, the General Assembly elects sufficient additional members to achieve this equality. At the maximum, during the 1950s, the Trusteeship Council had fourteen members with the United States, the United Kingdom, and France among the seven administering states, the Soviet Union and China as nonadministering permanent members of the Security Council, and five other members elected by the General Assembly. As trust territories gained their independence, the number of elective members diminished to one and then to none, leaving only the five permanent members of the Security Council on the Trusteeship Council in the unequal ratio of four nonadministering to one administering member. By 1981, if the independence of the Trust Territory of the Pacific Islands is granted as scheduled, the Trusteeship Council will cease to function for lack of any business to perform. Details concerning several facets of the goals and work of the Trusteeship Council during its active years will be elaborated in chapter 12.

The Secretariat

The United Nations Secretariat is a body of international civil servants headed by the Secretary-General. Unlike the General Assembly and the three councils, the Secretariat is not composed of delegate spokesmen for their respective governments. Rather, it is constituted of full-time employees of the organization, who must preserve their neutrality in the interests of serving the entire membership and of promoting the international goals of the United Nations. This neutrality is safeguarded by the provisions of Article 100 of the Charter, which provides for the following:

1. In the performance of their duties the Secretary-General and the staff shall not seek or receive instructions from any government or from any other authority external to the Organization. They shall refrain from any action which might reflect on their position as international officials responsible only to the Organization.
2. Each Member of the United Nations undertakes to respect the exclusively international character of the responsibilities of the Secretary-General and the staff and not to seek to influence them in the discharge of their responsibilities.

These paragraphs indicate clearly the double responsibility incumbent upon both staff and governments to preserve the international character of the Secretariat. The independence of the Secretariat members from national pressures was a principle not clearly stated in the Covenant but established at the inception of the League of Nations by its first Secretary-General.

The Secretary-General is appointed by the General Assembly, acting by a two-thirds vote, upon recommendation of the Security Council. In the absence of any Charter specification, the first General Assembly established the length of term for the Secretary-General as five years. The greatest hurdle to selection is agreement on a candidate by the major powers, since any permanent member of the Security Council may exercise a veto. Stalemates are a general threat in the selection process, and the term of the first Secretary-General had to be extended by the General Assembly without concurrence by the Security Council.

Four Secretaries-General have served the organization. Trygve Lie of Norway held the office from 1946 to 1953. He was succeeded by Dag Hammarskjöld of Sweden who served until his death in an airplane crash in central Africa on September 17, 1961. After an interval of nearly seven weeks, U Thant was appointed first as Acting Secretary-General and later for two successive terms as Secretary-General. Kurt Waldheim of Austria assumed the office in January, 1972.

The major functions of the Secretary-General are outlined clearly in the Charter and include the following (1) to be the chief administrative officer of the organization, (2) to act as secretary to all the major delegate bodies of the United Nations, (3) to perform functions assigned to him by the General Assembly and the three Councils, (4) to make an annual report to the General Assembly on the work of the organization, and (5) to appoint the Secretariat staff under regulations established by the General Assembly. The Secretary-General also has the authority to act on his own initiative to bring to the attention of the Security Council any matter that in his opinion threatens international peace and security.

In practice, the role of the Secretary-General has expanded far beyond the anticipations of the architects of the Charter. This expansion has resulted both from circumstances and from the initiative of each of the incumbents in the office. The role of the Secretary-General and other facets of the theory and practice of an international civil service will be detailed in chapter 15.

The International Court of Justice (ICJ)

The sixth major organ of the United Nations is the International Court of Justice with headquarters in The Hague. The Statute of the ICJ is an integral part of the Charter and is almost identical to the Statute of the previous Permanent Court of International Justice (PCIJ). However, unlike the League arrangement in which the PCIJ and its membership were independent of the League, all members of the United Nations are automatically members of the ICJ. Additional states may become parties to the Court Statute under arrangements approved by the General Assembly and the Security Council. Switzerland, Liechtenstein, and San Marino have adhered to the Statute under these conditions.

The Court is composed of fifteen judges elected by concurrent vote of the General Assembly and the Security Council. No two judges may be of the same nationality, and the Court as a whole should represent the principal legal systems of the world. Judges serve nine-year terms with the terms of five judges expiring every third year. No limit it set on the number of terms for which a judge may be reelected.

In hearing a specific case, if there is no judge on the Court of the nationality of one or more of the states that are parties to the case, such state or states may appoint a national judge to sit for that case. These additional judges participate with full voting rights.

Cases are decided by majority vote of the participating judges. Nine judges constitute a quorum. In case of a tie, the President of the Court has a casting vote.

The Court hears those cases that are referred to it by the contending parties. The Court may, however, determine that the case, because of its nature, is not subject to judicial determination, or that the parties have no legal right to submit the case to the Court. Only states may bring cases before the Court, but no state is required to submit any case for hearing and decision. This lack of compulsory jurisdiction is a major deficiency of international as contrasted with national legal systems.

In addition to hearing cases, the ICJ is authorized to give advisory opinions on legal questions. The Charter provides that the General Assembly and the Security Council may request such opinions and that the General Assembly may authorize other organs and the specialized agencies to request opinions on legal questions within the scope of their activities. The Economic and Social Council, the Trusteeship Council, and all the specialized agencies except the Universal Postal Union have been granted general authority of this kind, but more than three-fourths of all requests to the Court for advisory opinions have been made by the General Assembly.

Although suffering from numerous deficiencies, the Court plays an important role in the development of an international legal system. This role will be explored further in chapter 8.

5

❧

Some Basic Issues
of
the United Nations

Besides the principles and the major organs discussed in the previous chapter, certain issues should be understood as a background for a later examination of the programs and activities of the United Nations and its agencies. These issues are questions of membership, representation, voting, amendment, and finance. Among these are constitutional issues as fundamental as the matters of principle and structure covered in chapter 4. Other parts of these questions reach beyond legal relationships into United Nations practices.

THE MEMBERSHIP ISSUE

Membership in an international public (intergovernmental) organization may be either exclusive or inclusive, limited or universal. Regional organizations or certain special-purpose organizations may naturally be limited in membership, since the vital interests of all states will not be sufficiently affected by the activities of the organization to warrant universality. However, a strong argument can be made for universality in organizations that are concerned with worldwide problems whether the programs of those organizations are general and complex, as in the case of the League of Nations or

United Nations, or whether they are more limited in scope, as exemplified by the specialized agencies of the United Nations. Inherently weak organizations, dependent on the cooperation of members for effective action, are further handicapped if one or more major power centers lie outside the organization's consultation agencies. The absence of the United States from League membership and the limited duration of Soviet and German participation are generally cited as major deficiences of League efficacy. The absence until 1973 of representatives of East and West Germany and the refusal from 1950 to 1971 to seat delegates from the People's Republic of China in United Nations bodies similarly weakened the implementation of adopted resolutions and introduced an element of uncertainty into the negotiating process itself. For example, arms-control measures or territorial and political settlements, when arranged through United Nations channels, will be more secure if backed by Chinese and German guarantees in addition to the support of the other major powers.

Universal membership was a vague goal but was rejected as a basic principle in both the League of Nations and United Nations. Enemy states in the preceding world war were excluded as original members. A list of original members was drawn up, and these were able to activate their membership by ratifying the Covenant or the Charter. All other states had to submit to an admission process involving a vague set of admission criteria. At the San Francisco conference several states, primarily from Latin America, advocated automatic and universal membership in the United Nations for all independent states. Lip service was given to the desirability of universality, but the hurdles of an admission procedure were retained. In spite of the rejection of the principle of automatic membership by both the League and United Nations, the goal of universality may be achieved if three conditions are present: (1) if the terms and procedures for admission are not too difficult or rigid, (2) if the existing members are cooperative and committed to achieving universality, and (3) if nonmembers are willing to seek membership. Prevalent theories of sovereignty preclude the possibility of compulsory membership.

In general practice autonomous states are considered to be the units eligible for membership in international organizations. The League of Nations expanded the list of eligibles by stating that "any fully self-governing state, dominion or colony" might be admitted by a two-thirds vote of the Assembly. India was included as an original League member, although its full sovereignty was not established until 1947. The United Nations also granted exceptions to the requirement of statehood in its list of original members. The Soviet Union claimed a right of separate membership for each of its sixteen union republics; the concession to include the Ukraine and Byelorussia as original members did not meet generally accepted standards of statehood. India and the Philippines were also accorded the status of original members prior to the transfer of sovereignty.

The membership provisions of the League Covenant proved no obstacle in moving toward near-universal membership. The mini-states of Liechtenstein, San Marino, and Monaco were rejected on grounds that their small size precluded their ability to effectively carry out the obligations of membership. The United States was the only major state that never joined the organization.

The provisions of the Covenant that permitted termination of membership thwarted any hopes for sustaining the near universality of the League. The methods for terminating membership included (1) withdrawal with two years' notice of intent, (2) expulsion by the affirmative vote of all other members of the Council, and (3) refusal to accept the terms of an amendment to the Covenant. The third method (a manifestation of one of the principles of sovereignty) was never invoked. The Soviet Union was expelled in 1939 after its military attack on Finland, and was the only case of expulsion. With-drawals, on the other hand, were frequent, beginning with notifica-tion of intent by Costa Rica in 1924 and Brazil in 1926, continuing with similar action by Japan and Germany in 1933, and concluding with a flurry of twelve such announcements in 1936–40.

The United Nations closely followed the League pattern in setting up categories of original membership and admitted member-ship. The original members included the states that participated in the San Francisco conference or previously signed the Declaration of the United Nations issued in January, 1942. All fifty-one states that were eligible for original membership ratified the Charter before the end of 1945. The process of admission involves a recommenda-tion by the Security Council (a substantive matter subject to veto by any permanent member) followed by a two-thirds vote of the General Assembly. Membership is open to all "peace-loving states which accept the obligations contained in the present Charter and, in the judgment of the Organization, are able and willing to carry out these obligations."[1]

From 1945 to 1955 the admission of members to the United Nations became a Cold War issue between the Soviet Union and the West. The battleground was the Security Council. Between 1946

[1] Charter of the United Nations, Art. 4.

and 1950 nine states that were not clearly candidates of one or the other bloc were admitted to the United Nations. From 1950 to 1955 the membership remained frozen at sixty, although by 1952 twenty-one additional states had applied for admission with a majority of these applications dating from the first two years of United Nations existence. A stalemate developed in which the Soviet Union was unwilling to vote for prowestern candidates and vice versa. The western strategy, led by the United States, was to force as many Soviet vetoes as possible in order to dramatize the "obstructionist" stance of that power. The Soviet Union was compelled to veto Italy's admission on five different occasions, and more than half of all Soviet vetoes in these early years were on membership applications. Since Soviet-sponsored candidates were unable to obtain the required seven affirmative votes in the Security Council, the United States was saved from the use of the veto. The Soviet Union on occasion accused the West of a "collective veto."

States on both sides of the Iron Curtain that, by any objective standards, met all the Charter criteria for membership were hapless victims of Cold War politics. Justifications were given by both sides for their opposition to candidate states. The West opposed Bulgaria, Hungary, and Rumania for alleged violations of human rights; Bulgaria and Albania for their role in the Greek border incidents; and Albania for its lack of cooperation with the United Nations in the Corfu Channel dispute. The Soviet Union objected to candidates because they had no diplomatic relations with the Soviet Union (Portugal, Jordan, Ireland); because peace treaties with them had not been concluded (Italy, Austria); because of Axis sympathies (Ireland, Portugal); because of membership in the "aggressive Atlantic bloc" (Italy); because of doubts concerning their status of full sovereignty and independence (Jordan, Ceylon, Japan); and because of serving as a base for United States aggression (Japan). These excuses for prolonged exclusion of states from United Nations membership provided a thinly veiled legality that was intended to disguise the unexpressed motives of the Cold War adversaries. However, the underlying motives became clear when it is noted that all pro-Communist candidates were opposed by the West and all non-Communist applications were vetoed by the Soviet Union. Charter criteria for admission were robbed of significant meaning in a contest for political power in the United Nations.

During the ten-year impasse over the admission of more than a score of potential members, several attempts were made through the General Assembly to break the deadlock. In 1946 Australia proposed changes in the admissions procedure to grant the General Assembly the sole power over admissions. Similar plans had been previously rejected at the San Francisco conference. In 1947 Argentina proposed that the General Assembly interpret the Charter as permitting General Assembly action on either *positive* or *negative* membership recommendations of the Security Council. Peru in 1952 suggested that the General Assembly proceed on the assumption that all votes on candidates in the Security Council were procedural and not subject to veto. The Argentine and Peruvian suggestions were clearly in conflict with an advisory opinion issued in 1950 by the International Court of Justice at the request of the General Assembly in which the Court declared that the Charter required a Security Council recommendation for admission prior to General Assembly action and that no recommendation could be made in the event of a negative vote by any permanent Council member. The General Assembly also passed a series of resolutions and set up special committees to study the question and consult with Council members; these measures were intended to pressure the Security Council into finding a solution to the impasse.

Since the admissions problem was basically political rather than procedural, compromise of competing interests had to be the final solution in the form of a "package deal" or admissions en bloc. The United States had proposed such a trade-off in 1946, and the Soviet Union had objected, but during most of the ten-year stalemate, the positions of the two major powers were reversed. In December, 1955, the deadlock was finally broken under increased pressure from many sources, and a package deal was agreed upon to admit sixteen states simultaneously. In the period since 1955 admissions procedures have proved no impediment to a burgeoning membership approaching universality.

During the period since 1955 so many additional members were admitted to the United Nations that the membership more than doubled, and new anxieties arose concerning the impact of a large membership on the organization. As soon as a territory achieved statehood it generally sought and was accorded United Nations membership. Most of the newly admitted members were located in Africa or Asia. Some new members were so small in population, area, and resources that increasingly they were referred to as ministates. Small states with voting power equal to that of large states could carry resolutions in the General Assembly by the sheer volume of votes, although they might represent a small proportion of the world's population, resources, or other indices of power. Emphasis shifted in the General Assembly to the issues of development and anti-colonialism. Neither the United States nor the Soviet Union seemed to be any longer capable of delivering automatic majorities for their own measures, and the initiative in many areas passed to the underdeveloped nations. The new vocabulary of international affairs deemphasized the East-West split in favor of heavy emphasis on North-South rivalry and the demands of the Third World. The wisdom of according equal status to political units as small as the Seychelles, Dominica, Sao Tome and Principe with populations of less than 100,000 each and to more than twenty other members with populations under a million each may reasonably be questioned. The resources of some of these mini-states are so limited that payment of the minimum scale of the United Nations budget and the expense of maintaining representation at United Nations meetings are a serious financial burden. The size of the General Assembly and its main committees has become more and more unwieldy. The pressure for increased representation of the Afro-Asian bloc resulted in Charter amendments to expand the membership of the Security Council and the Economic and Social Council. Scholars and representatives from the developed countries have recently increased their inquiries into limited membership and weighted voting in international organizations. However, it is unlikely that the United Nations will, in the near future, take any measures to limit ministate membership.[2]

Few states remain outside the United Nations. Switzerland, although it provided the headquarters and was an active member of the League of Nations, has interpreted some of the obligations of the Charter as inconsistent with its traditional policy of neutrality. It has, however, joined most of the specialized agencies and is a party to the International Court of Justice. North and South Korea have not been admitted to membership but reunified Vietnam was admitted in 1977. From its inception in 1949 until November, 1971, the People's Republic of China was unrepresented at the United Nations, but this problem was primarily one of credentials, recognition, and representation rather than of membership.

No provision is made in the Charter for withdrawal from membership, and this omission seems to have had a salutary influence on the trend toward universality. Only one state, Indonesia, has ever announced its withdrawal, but, after an absence of twenty months, it returned to full participation. Indonesia's complaint was the election of Malaysia to a Security Council seat. No readmission process was deemed necessary, since only a notice of Indonesia's

[2] Michael M. Gunter, "What Happened to the United Nations Ministate Problem?" *American Journal of International Law,* 71 (January 1977), 110-24.

statement of intent but no official acceptance of its withdrawal had been issued by the United Nations. Other representatives have absented themselves from meetings of United Nations organs for periods of days or months, but these boycotts were not intended as more than gestures toward the potential threat of withdrawal.

Articles 5 and 6 of the Charter provide for suspension and expulsion of members from the United Nations. The procedural requirements are the same in both cases. The General Assembly may suspend or expel a member by a two-thirds vote upon the recommendation of the Security Council. The suspension or expulsion of a permanent member of the Security Council is impossible, since that member can, through its veto power, block action against itself. No action has ever been taken under Article 5 or 6, although African states have exerted pressures to try to bring about the expulsion of South Africa.

Membership in the specialized agencies affiliated with the United Nations is independent of United Nations membership. Most states belong both to the United Nations and to most of the specialized agencies. Several of the specialized agencies have a membership larger than that of the United Nations. Several specialized agencies admit non-self-governing territories as full or associate members. The Soviet Union initially was reluctant to join any of the agencies except the Universal Postal Union, the International Telecommunication Union, and the World Meteorological Organization, but gradually has extended its interests to include membership in most agencies except those in the financial area.

PROBLEMS OF REPRESENTATION

The practices regarding representation of members in the United Nations are based to a greater degree upon custom and necessity than upon specific Charter provisions. However, Charter specifications do provide, both concretely and by implication, a skeletal framework for the representation pattern. Member states may have not more than five representatives in the General Assembly and one each in the Security Council, Economic and Social Council, and Trusteeship Council, if a member of those bodies. Nothing in the Charter itself anticipates the practice of appointment of alternates or the extensive use of advisers attached to the larger delegations. The elaborate committee structure developed by the General Assembly and the numerous commissions established by the Economic and Social Council contribute to the practicability of involving a wide range of experts as spokesmen for governments in these subsidiary bodies.

Consistent with the basic principle of the sovereignty of members, the Charter does not specify any qualifications for representatives. Representatives are the spokesmen for their governments and, as such, are subject to those governments with regard to qualifications, appointment, tenure, and compensation. With modern communications, representatives can receive detailed instructions from the home government concerning the content of speeches, bargaining positions, and voting patterns.

Nearly all member states maintain a permanent mission to the United Nations. The mission is similar to an embassy, except that its personnel are accredited to the United Nations rather than to a host government. The head of the mission normally carries ambassadorial rank as well as the title "permanent representative to the United Nations." The total working force in a mission varies from less than a half-dozen to approximately 200 depending on the resources of the country and the depth of its involvement in United Nations affairs.

The Charter does not clearly indicate the necessity for each member to maintain a permanent mission in New York. Only the members of the Security Council are required "to be represented at all times at the seat of the Organization" so that the Council may function continuously. However, all United Nations members are involved in the annual General Assembly sessions, which last at least three months and which occasionally may be prolonged for most of the year. Most members also serve on one or more councils or commissions, which meet at intervals throughout the year. Additionally, New York provides a center for continuous negotiation and consultation among the governments of the world on a one-to-one basis or in larger groups. Finally, the adoption of the Uniting for Peace Resolution in 1950 obligated all members to keep representatives available for emergency sessions of the General Assembly, which can be called on twenty-four-hour notice. The representatives on the permanent staff of their missions find their assignments in New York as demanding of time and energy as an assignment to most other diplomatic posts.

During General Assembly sessions the mission staff in New York may be augmented at all levels of responsibility often to the point of doubling the number of personnel. The minister for foreign affairs frequently heads the delegation, although he may remain in New York for only a few days at the opening of the session. Other delegates and alternates from the home government may be designated to serve with the permanent representative to the United Nations and other diplomats on his regular staff. Advisers and supporting personnel from the foreign office or other areas of needed expertise may be assigned to temporary duty at mission headquarters for the duration of the Assembly session. In the larger missions specialists are useful in such fields as political affairs, finance, economic development, social problems, human rights, arms control, legal questions, military affairs, administration, press relations, public relations, protocol, liaison activities, and various geographic areas of the world. Secretaries, clerks, guards, maintenance personnel, chauffeurs, and other supporting personnel perform necessary auxiliary services for the professional staff of the mission.

In a number of ways the national missions to the United Nations are more important than embassies to individual countries. The United Nations headquarters is the closest approximation to a world capital and serves as a neutral territory where negotiations can take place without loss of prestige by any party to the negotiations. Informal discussions can be arranged outside of the meetings of official bodies. Constant contact among representatives facilitates negotiation and communication. No ambassador has greater prestige than that of the head of a mission. The mission staff not only carry out policy determined in their national capital, but, to a greater degree than in most embassies, they help formulate foreign policy. They serve as a sounding board, a channel for multiple contacts, and a source of information and advice on the widest possible range of matters that come before the United Nations. In the foreign policy process they not only communicate the outputs of the system, but they furnish valuable inputs for the formulation of the policy.

Governments generally appoint experts in the appropriate areas to represent them in the delegate bodies of the various specialized agencies. A health expert serving in a delegation to the World Health Organization (WHO), an educator as a representative to UNESCO, or a nutritionist appointed to attend the conference of the Food and Agriculture Organization (FAO) will each be convinced that his special field is so important that it deserves increased emphasis and greater financial support. The problem for governments is to balance all competing interests, instruct delegates concerning overall policy and limitations on commitments, and coordinate the dozens of strands of policy carried out through the diverse agencies related to the United Nations. Each ministry of foreign affairs (or its counterpart by any other title) must be so organized and staffed as to provide reasonable coordination and control.

For more than twenty years the most persistent and dramatic problem concerning United Nations representation was the China issue. Beginning in 1950 the issue appeared annually, in one form or another, among the General Assembly's items of business. From 1951 through 1960 a debate was avoided by the adoption of a proposal to postpone action, thus eliminating the item from the formal agenda. From 1961 through 1970 the question appeared as a proposal to accept the credentials of the representatives of the Peking rather than of the Taiwan regime. At the same time a resolution, sponsored by the United States, was adopted to treat the problem as an "important question" requiring a two-thirds vote. However, such items may be removed at any time from the "important question" category by a majority decision in the General Assembly. The same thorny problem of Chinese representation was raised from time to time in the Security Council, and the Soviet representatives absented themselves from the Council for nearly seven months in early 1950 in protest against the continued seating of the Taiwan representatives.

Since the question was presented in the General Assembly as a matter of credentials, the issue, in a strict legal sense, was one of representation rather than one of membership. China was an original member of the United Nations and had a permanent seat on the Security Council (Article 23 of the Charter, in naming the permanent members of the Council, uses the title the Republic of China, the official title retained by the Nationalist Government). Furthermore, agreements made at the close of World War II recognized Taiwan to be a part of China, and both rival governments claimed sovereignty and legitimacy over all the area of China. Therefore, the acceptance of the representatives of the Nationalist regime was a recognition of the right of those representatives to speak for all of China—the mainland and Taiwan.

It is clear that the China issue was as much a political contest as it was a legal question. Prior to 1971 the world was more or less evenly divided in the number of states that recognized each rival claimant to legitimacy. Neither Chinese government would exchange diplomats with another country unless that country broke diplomatic relations with its rival. The United States maintained its commitment to the perpetuation of the Taiwan regime and to the defense of the island against attack from the mainland. During the 1960s many of the United States' closest allies grew restless with the anti-Peking pressure from Washington and refused to follow United States policies of nonrecognition and economic boycott of the People's Republic of China. To those states, recognizing a regime that controlled more than 98 percent of the total population and more than 99.5 percent of the land area of China seemed more logical than maintaining the fiction that a government on Taiwan, after twenty years of exile from the mainland, could speak for 850 million Chinese.

Because of the concern of some United Nations members for the fate of the Nationalists on Taiwan, and because of the desire to encourage self-determination for the island population who have never lived under Communist control, several proposals were made either for a "two Chinas" or a "one China, one Taiwan" solution to the problem. These proposals generally took one of two stances: either that Peking was entitled to the China seat and Taiwan should be admitted as a new member, or that two regimes had succeeded to the original entity of China and that both should be accommodated within the United Nations framework.

For twenty years the United States government led the fight to deny representation in the United Nations to the Peking regime. The principal devices used were the procedural tactics of annually rejecting the question as an agenda item (1951–60) or of requiring a two-thirds vote to seat the Peking representatives (1961–70), plus behind-the-scenes pressures on other delegations and their governments. The graph on page 87 demonstrates the gradual loss of efficacy of these tactics, culminating in the acceptance of the Communist representatives in 1971 when the United States switched its position to one of favoring a Security Council seat for the Peking regime while maintaining places for both delegations in the General Assembly. By this time the pro-Peking tide was running so strongly that the United States proposal was defeated and the representatives of the People's Republic were accorded sole representation for China accompanied by the expulsion of the Nationalist representatives.

The decisions made in the twenty-sixth session of the General Assembly leave the future of Taiwan unsettled. Just prior to the vote to expel them, the Nationalist representatives announced their withdrawal from participation in the United Nations. The People's Republic claims to represent the people on Taiwan but cannot establish de facto control unless the United States withdraws its protection from the island. As a separate entity Taiwan with a population of 16 million is larger than three-quarters of the members of the United Nations. For more than thirty years the mainlander minority of 15 percent of the population has exercised government domination over the 85 percent who are native Taiwanese. No hard evidence exists to prove whether in a free exercise of self-determination the Taiwanese would opt for permanent separation from the mainland. If a new state of Taiwan were created and if it applied for United Nations membership, it would face the grim reality of a Chinese

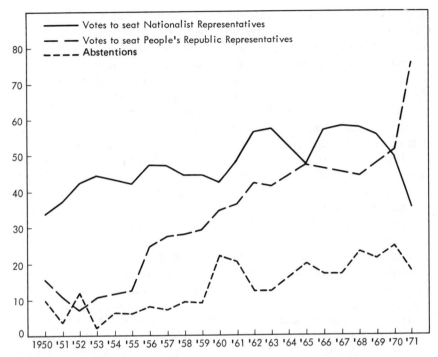

Voting in the General Assembly on the Representation of China (no vote in 1964)

veto on its application. Thus one impasse would be replaced by another.

VOTING RULES AND PRACTICES

Modern international organization, as it has developed over the past century, has been faced with the enigma of reconciling democratic decision-making processes with the theory of the absolute sovereignty of states. The tradition of sovereignty as practiced prior to the twentieth century in international conferences and treaty making required unanimity among all parties according to the principle that no state could be bound without its own consent. States, regardless of population or resources, were also considered equal, and each state was entitled to exercise the right of one vote for each state. Some exceptions to both the principle of unanimity and the principle of state equality developed in the nineteenth century in such agencies as the river commissions of Europe, but the tenacity of these ideas is demonstrated by the first-stated principle of the United Nations Charter that "the Organization is based on the principle of the sovereign equality of all its Members." Although the Charter requires unanimity only among the permanent members of the Security Council on nonprocedural matters (which, it should be noted, constitutes a breach of the equality principle), the formation of the United Nations was intended to fit into long-established patterns of international conduct rather than to revolutionize them.

The League of Nations preserved the principles of unanimity and state equality, although significant exceptions were made to each. Each member of the Council or Assembly could defeat a general recommendation in either body by a negative vote, but abstentions were common and were used as a means of avoiding obstruction of the will of a substantial majority of states when vital national interests were not at issue. The committees of the Assembly operated by majority vote, and procedural matters in either the Council or Assembly required only majority support. When the Council was considering a case under Article 15 of the Covenant, the vote of any party to the dispute was not counted, and, under Article 16, a state could not veto its own expulsion from the League. The Covenant specified that the very basic decision of admitting new members to the League could be made by a two-thirds majority. However, the traditional right not to be bound without the state's own consent was preserved in the prerogative of every member to dissent from any amendment to the Covenant with such dissent constituting termination of membership in the League. Although each state had one vote in the Council or Assembly, the inequality of states was recognized by assigning permanent membership on the Council to the most powerful nations. Membership on the Council carried more than honorific significance because of the powers and functions assigned to that organ.

The gradual abandonment of the unanimity rule in international organizations has been facilitated by the nature of those organizations. As long as international agencies are more administrative than prescriptive, more cooperative than coercive, as long as they are lacking in true legislative and enforcement powers and are limited to discussion and to recommendations that are unenforceable on individual states, the members of such organizations see no great threat to their sovereignty if they agree to modify the requirement of unanimity. Majority or qualified majority votes allow the passage of recommendations that authorize administrative action in the less controversial areas of international relationships; at the same time, each state's retention of ultimate enforcement powers guarantees that its vital interests are not surrendered.

The United Nations preserves this balance of sovereign rights and the necessity to abandon unanimity in order to facilitate the adoption of administrative directives and expressions of the will of a majority of members. The League of Nations rule of unanimity is abandoned in the General Assembly in favor of either majority or two-thirds votes for decisions. Security Council decisions can be taken by a qualified majority, but the permanent members are protected by the rule that any one of them can block action by a negative vote on nonprocedural matters. Since the Security Council was originally intended to deal with the most vital issues of national interest and since the big powers possess the preponderance of means for enforcement, such an arrangment may be considered a necessary departure from the complete abandonment of unanimity. Further flexibility is provided by the interpretation that an abstention does not constitute a veto. Thus, the representative of any one of the permanent members of the Security Council is free to express three choices ranging from approval, through mild disapproval but unwillingness to be obstructionist, to effective blocking of a decision by negative vote. The net result of the voting arrangements in the General Assembly and the Security Council is to facilitate activities in the common interest without threatening the sovereign prerogatives of the big powers.

Voting in the lesser agencies of the United Nations is by simple majority. This rule applies to the Economic and Social Council, the Trusteeship Council, and the committees and commissions subordinate to the major organs. Since all actions of these bodies are subject to review by the General Assembly and are not self-executing or automatically enforceable, the less strict criterion for agreement among members may be tolerated without serious challenge to traditional theories of national sovereignty.

In the World Bank group of specialized agencies the traditional rule of an equal vote for each state has given way to weighted voting roughly proportionate to the financial contributions of the members. In these agencies — the International Bank for Reconstruction and Development, the International Monetary Fund, the International Finance Corporation, and the International Development Association — the United States casts approximately 25 percent of the vote. Except in these financial agencies, proposals to modify the one state–one vote principle in favor of weighted voting based on one or more factors such as contributions, population, or measures of financial or other resources have never been seriously debated by United Nations agencies. The influx of numerous mini-states into the organization may raise questions concerning the imbalance between the voting power of states and their ability to contribute to the resolution of world problems or their inequality in the numbers of persons affected by decisions. But although these theoretical considerations may develop, the smaller states will not be inclined to surrender lightly an advantage based on the centuries-old principle of state equality.

The voting formula in the Security Council was discussed in Dumbarton Oaks, hammered out in Yalta, and retained intact in spite of the onslaught of the small and medium states in San Francisco. All votes in the Security Council require the approval of nine of the fifteen members (seven of the eleven members before the amendments of 1965). On substantive (nonprocedural) matters the nine votes must include the affirmative votes of the five permanent members of the Council. Thus a single negative vote by a permanent member on a substantive question constitutes a veto, although the word "veto" does not appear in the Charter. According to the explanatory Statement of the Sponsoring Powers issued in San Francisco, certain matters were to be considered clearly procedural, but if a question rose as to whether a matter was procedural or substantive, the preliminary question was subject to the substantive voting requirement. This interpretation opens the door to a "double veto" procedure. According to established practice, an abstention or an absence is not equivalent to a veto in spite of the language of Article 27, which specifies "an affirmative vote of nine members including the concurring votes of the permanent members."

The hopes of the smaller states that the permanent members of the Security Council would use their power of veto sparingly have not been borne out in practice. In reluctantly accepting the voting formula established in San Francisco, the spokesmen for the smaller states appealed for restraint in the exercise of the veto. By the 1970s all of the big five had used the veto more than once and the Soviet Union had cast more than 100 vetoes, or nearly 80 percent of the total.

An examination of the pattern of vetoes reveals, however, something less than the flagrant abuse of power. Approximately two-thirds of all vetoes were cast in the first ten years of the United Nations, and during that period fifty vetoes were used to block admission of states to United Nations membership. The excessive number of Soviet vetoes on the question of admission is accounted for by the strategy of the western states under United States leadership in forcing separate votes on each candidate and repeatedly asking for admission of the same candidates. The western states, in turn, could block the admission of any pro-Soviet state by any combination of five abstentions or negative votes.

The veto was intended to protect the vital interests of the big powers, and it has operated to accomplish that purpose. During the earlier years of the United Nations, the Soviet Union's vital interests were frequently threatened because of western control of the issues before the Security Council and because of the minority position of the Soviet Union. During the 1970s the United States began to resort to the veto more than any other power for an average use of twice per year, while the Soviet Union seldom needed recourse to this device. However, the veto is a weapon always available to any of the Big Five.

During the early years of the United Nations, the General Assembly made a number of efforts to influence the Security Council to eliminate certain categories of questions from the exercise of the veto power. The suggested categories included the admission of members and actions for the pacific settlement of disputes. These efforts were fruitless in instigating any change of rules or attitudes.

In recent years a spirit of restraint has manifested itself in the decreased use of the veto and in the increased use of abstentions. There is evidence also of more frequent consultations to phrase resolutions in terms not seriously objectionable to any major power. This spirit of accommodation may be partially due to a spirit of détente between the United States and the Soviet Union. It is also probably due to a realization of a common interest among the big powers in restoring the Security Council, in which they can exercise maximum influence, to a position of greater importance vis-à-vis the General Assembly. With the influx of large numbers of members since 1955, manipulating the General Assembly has become increasingly more difficult for any of the great powers. Under these conditions the arena of the Security Council looks relatively more attractive to both superpowers for the debates over major issues. Restraint in the use of the veto, as well as other forms of accommodation, will avoid transfer of these issues to the General Assembly.

Voting in the General Assembly has presented fewer problems than in the Security Council. Each member, regardless of population or resources, casts one vote. It is theoretically possible for states representing less than 15 percent of the world's population to muster a two-thirds vote in the General Assembly. But since the General Assembly, in most actions, is limited to recommendations that depend for implementation on moral suasion and national cooperation, action by small states is generally not considered a major threat to the larger states. Nevertheless, the passage of resolutions that are meaningless in terms of effecting change may destroy confidence in the United Nations and undermine its future efficacy. In 1974 Ambassador Scali of the United States blasted the Third World members for using "the tyranny of the majority" not only for passing resolutions that are unenforceable but also for making procedural decisions in handling Middle Eastern and South African issues.

In the General Assembly important matters require a two-thirds majority of the members present and voting. Other decisions can be taken by a simple majority of those present and voting. Article 18 of the Charter lists certain categories of "important questions" requiring the two-thirds rule. These are (1) recommendations with respect to the maintenance of peace and security, (2) the election of nonpermanent members of the Security Council, (3) the election of members of the Economic and Social Council and of the Trusteeship Council, (4) the admission of new members to the United Nations, (5) the suspension of the rights and privileges of membership, (6) the expulsion of members, (7) questions pertaining to the operation of the trusteeship system, and (8) budgetary questions. Additional categories of questions requiring a two-thirds vote may be added (and likewise removed) by simple majority. Abstentions are not counted in determining the "present and voting" requirement. With large numbers of abstentions on some questions, a two-thirds affirmative vote on an important matter may represent only a minority of the total membership.

Under some sections of the Charter, either an absolute or a two-thirds majority of all members — not just those "present and voting" — in the General Assembly is required for decisions. Elections to the International Court of Justice require a majority of all states. Amendments to the Charter may be proposed by a vote of two-thirds of the members of the General Assembly. The votes required for calling a general review conference under the provisions of Article 109 of the Charter are based on the full membership. In all of these cases abstentions or absences would have the same effect as negative votes in determining the results of the ballots, since the affirmative votes must constitute more than half (or two-thirds when specified) of the membership.

According to Article 19 of the Charter, a member state may have its voting rights in the General Assembly suspended if it is more than two years in arrears in its budget contributions. The crisis of 1964 over the possible application of this provision is detailed below in the section of this chapter dealing with financial problems of the United Nations.

Both the General Assembly and the Security Council in recent years have frequently used the technique of announcing the adoption of resolutions by consensus without a formal vote. In fact, in several sessions of the General Assembly, a majority of all decisions were made in this manner. The consensus procedure is a method of adopting measures without formal objection and one which avoids confrontation through voting. Decision making by consensus allows for behind-the-scenes compromise and avoids embarrassment to some states. However, it is no panacea. Consensus resolutions may be watered down to a low level of relevance. Also nations frequently nullify the appearance of harmony and prolong debate by adding a series of stated reservations to the resolutions after passage by consensus.

Bloc voting and caucusing by groups of states with allied interests have been notable aspects of General Assembly practice. The early dominance of United States influence gradually eroded to be replaced finally by the unity of the have-not states on issues of economic development and anticolonialism, which now constitute the bulk of the agenda. Caucusing and informal consultation serve several useful purposes including the tempering and reconciliation of extreme positions, a saving of time in the sessions of an otherwise unwieldy Assembly, and the planning of advance strategy for the promotion of common interests. However, one should note that votes in the United Nations are an imperfect measure of influence in world affairs, since votes cannot alter world power relationships to any significant degree.

FORMAL AND INFORMAL CHARTER AMENDMENT

Writing and adopting a constitution is regarded as the most fundamental act of government. Although existing international organizations lack many of the attributes of national governments, each has a constitution in the form of a multilateral treaty that prescribes the purposes, structure, and modes of procedure of the organization. Since amendments may generally amplify, modify, or delete any of the provisions of a constitution, the amending process is as basic as the original constituent act. The requirements for adopting amendments to a constitution or charter almost invariably demand a higher order of agreement than is required for ordinary legislation or resolutions. The amending process should be neither so difficult as to make basic change impossible nor so easy as to contribute to frequent tampering with fundamental structures and powers. In an international organization of sovereign states, ease of amendment would run counter to the reluctantly surrendered tradition that no state may be bound without its own consent. Therefore, the difficulty of the amending process of the United Nations Charter should surprise no one.

The Charter provides two methods of proposing amendments but a single formula for ratification. Amendments may be proposed by a vote of two-thirds of the total membership of the General Assembly and will then come into force if ratified by the governments of two-thirds of the members, including all the permanent members of the Security Council. Amendments may also be proposed by a two-thirds vote of a general review conference. Such a review conference can be convened at any time by the General Assembly and the Security Council. Until 1968 the requirement for calling a conference was a two-thirds vote of all members of the General Assembly and a vote of any seven members of the Security Council. In that year an amendment became effective to raise the Security Council requirement to nine votes as a supplement to the earlier enlargement of Security Council membership. Amendments proposed by a review conference do not become effective until ratified according to the same formula as required for amendments initiated by the General Assembly. Nevertheless, the states most dissatisified with various provisions of the Charter as adopted in San Francisco insisted on the possibility of calling a review conference in the hope of reexamining a broader range of fundamental changes than might result from piecemeal proposals from the General Assembly.

Article 109 also provides that if a review conference has not been held before the tenth annual session of the General Assembly, the proposal to call such a conference shall be placed on the agenda of that session and the required vote is reduced to a majority of all members of the General Assembly and any seven members of the Security Council. In 1955 it was clear to most members that a review conference would be an exercise in futility since there was no basis for agreement upon previously suggested reforms. Instead of calling a conference, the General Assembly created a committee of the whole to study the situation and to revive the question at an "appropriate time" under "auspicious circumstances." This combination of time and circumstances did not occur, and after 1967 the committee became inactive. In 1974 the General Assembly created a new Special Committee on the Charter which has encountered stiff opposition by the major powers to proposals by the nonaligned states for substantial reforms affecting the relative roles of the General Assembly and Security Council.

During the first fifteen years under the Charter, Cold War issues in combination with the difficulty of the amending process blunted all attempts at change through formal amendment. With the influx of large numbers of new members from Africa and Asia, the pressures upon the great powers for structural adjustments in the size of the Councils mounted. In 1963 the General Assembly adopted proposed amendments to increase the size of ECOSOC from eighteen to twenty-seven members and to increase the membership of the Security Council from eleven to fifteen. These amendments entered into force August 31, 1965, upon the deposit of sufficient government ratifications, and the enlarged Councils sat for the first time in 1966. In 1973 ECOSOC was enlarged to fifty-four members.

The dynamics of fundamental change in the United Nations have been exercised more through informal than through formal amendment. Most constitutions grow by means of custom, interpretation, and elaboration, and the United Nations Charter is no exception. Examples of such developments are numerous. Although contrary to the terms of the Charter, the custom of disregarding abstentions and absences in Security Council voting is firmly established. The adoption in 1950 of the Uniting for Peace Resolution substantially altered the relative roles of the General Assembly and Security Council without a formal amendment. The phenomenon of bloc voting on certain issues in the General Assembly is a development as fundamental in nature as any provision of the Charter. The General Assembly's liberal interpretation of its authority to demand information from colonial powers, to exercise pressure toward ending colonial rule, and to declare the independence of Namibia from South Africa are examples of expansions of authority in the colonial sphere unforeseen in a strict interpretation of Charter provisions.

Charter provisions may be expanded by custom and usage or may be allowed to atrophy by disuse. One of the most evident examples of the lack of implementation applies to Article 43, according to which armed forces were to be made available to the Security Council by all members of the United Nations for the purpose of maintaining international peace and security. The agreements anticipated by this article were never drawn up because of fundamental disagreements among the major powers over the terms of the agreements and underlying security questions.

The United Nations experience with formal and informal amendment of the Charter suggests several basic questions. Is the formal amendment procedure too rigid to allow necessary adjustment to changing world conditions? Will the members discover enough flexibility through custom, interpretation, and elaboration to overcome the obstacles of a difficult amendment process? Is the disuse and misuse of the United Nations due more to inherent defects in its Charter or to attitudes, practices, and prerogatives of sovereign states in a loosely structured international system? If the members become convinced that a more integrated international system is necessary, is the United Nations Charter a viable instrument on which to build, or must it be replaced with a radically different instrument? If states view the United Nations as tangential to the mainstream of international affairs, those questions remain highly academic and inconsequential. If a more orderly world is ever to be achieved, the answers to such questions become vital.

FINANCIAL PROBLEMS

Since the total annual costs of all United Nations–related activities amount to a fraction of 1 percent of the members' military budgets, one might reasonably assume that budgetary questions should not represent a major difficulty for the organization. Yet, in the early 1960s a financial crisis threatened the continued existence of the United Nations, and the repercussions of that crisis carried over into the 1970s.

Control of the budget is one of the powers lodged in the General Assembly. The Secretary-General annually presents budget estimates to the Assembly, and these estimates are reviewed by the Advisory Committee on Administrative and Budgetary Questions. The two sets of recommendations are examined by member governments both individually and in the Fifth Committee of the General Assembly before adoption in a General Assembly plenary session. In determining the assessment of costs to individual states, the Assembly is assisted by the Committee on Contributions.

In reality several budgets exist in the United Nations. The basic budget for running the administrative machinery and meeting the costs of the major organs and their auxiliary agencies is the regular budget. This budget has grown from an initial figure in 1946 of less than 20 million dollars to more than twenty times that figure in the 1970s and currently tends to increase by 5 to 10 percent each year. The basic causes of increasing costs are (1) inflationary trends, (2) increased membership, (3) expanding programs and agencies, and (4) devaluation of the U.S. dollar. In recent years the big powers have complained of the rates of annual increase, but the more numerous developing nations have defended the expanding costs because the increased activities have been considered vital to their interests.

Contributions to the regular budget are assessed among the members according to a formula that is based ostensibly on ability to pay. In 1946 in the initial determination of the percentage of the total budget to be allotted to each member, the Committee on Contributions was instructed to consider (1) national income, (2) per capita income, (3) economic dislocations resulting from the war, and (4) the ability of members to obtain foreign currencies. On the basis of these factors, the United States should have been asked to pay nearly 50 percent of the original budget, but this figure was arbitrarily reduced by 10 percent to 39.89 percent in order to lessen the financial dependence of the United Nations on a single member. A further agreement was reached to reduce gradually the maximum assessment to one-third and subsequently to a target of 25 percent. A minimum assessment of .04 percent was also set for the states with the lowest assets. In 1973 this minimum was reduced to .02 percent and in 1978 to .01 percent. Since sixty-seven members pay the minimum of .01 percent each and another seventeen pay .02 percent each, it is theoretically possible for a majority of the General Assembly to represent a total contribution of less than 1 percent of the budget. At the other extreme the ten largest contributors pay more than three-fourths of the budget but cast fewer than 7 percent of the votes.

Not all costs of maintaining the regular operations of the United Nations must be assessed against the members, but neither does the budget represent the full costs of United Nations membership. The United Nations raises approximately 9 million dollars annually from miscellaneous income from sales and services, and about five times that amount is derived from staff assessments made against Secretariat salaries to offset income-tax payments of employees who are United States nationals. To the assessments levied against each member state must be added the expense of maintaining a mission headquarters and staff in New York, and, for most members, maintaining smaller staffs in Geneva and at the headquarters of the specialized agencies. For the least affluent states these costs generally exceed the amount of the regular budget assessment.

Ever since the establishment of the United Nations Children's Fund (UNICEF) in 1946, the United Nations has supplemented its regular budget with special budgets for economic and social programs. These budgets are supported by voluntary contributions rather than by assessment. Some of the major funds in this category in addition to UNICEF are the United Nations Development Program (UNDP), with an annual budget larger than that of the regular United Nations budget; the United Nations Relief and Works Agency for

Palestine Refugees; the World Food Program; and voluntary funds administered by the United Nations High Commissioner for Refugees. Since all members are free to determine whether and how much they will contribute to these funds, the patterns of contribution vary widely from the assessment figures of the regular budget. For many years the United States pledged 30–80 percent of these special funds with a fixed dollar limit, but this previous generosity has given way to an attitude in the United States Congress of cutting most voluntary contributions to 25 percent or less.

A third category of budgets is that of the specialized agencies affiliated with the United Nations through the Economic and Social Council. As a part of the autonomous character of these agencies, each enjoys a high degree of independence in determining its budget, with probably the most effective coordinating control operating through member governments. The United Nations General Assembly is limited to reviewing and making recommendations on these budgets. Since the United Nations and the specialized agencies share a great deal of responsibility for economic development and technical assistance programs, including a division of the funds pledged to the United Nations Development Program, controls also operate through administrative coordinating agencies within this sphere of activities.

Within each of the specialized agencies, budgetary assessments are allocated on a scale roughly equivalent to that for the United Nations regular budget. Modifications must be introduced to account for variations in membership. The total of all the budgets of the specialized agencies generally exceeds that of the regular United Nations budget. For the three types of budgets discussed thus far, the total amount in 1978 is more than 1.5 billion dollars per year.

The fourth category of budgets, peacekeeping expenses, has been the most controversial and has caused the financial crisis that became acute in the 1960s and that has continued to threaten the stability and viability of the organization. The principal problem has resulted from attempts to assess peacekeeping costs on the same basis as regular budget assessments, although separate accounts were set up for each major peacekeeping operation. The high costs, especially of the Congo operation, also exacerbated the problem.

The earliest manifestations of the crisis surfaced with the refusal of the Soviet bloc and several Arab states to contribute to the support of the United Nations Emergency Force (UNEF) established in 1956. In spite of opposition and bitter debate, the proposal of the Secretary-General to assess the costs on the same basis as the regular assessments received the necessary support for adoption by the

General Assembly. When the United Nations Forces in the Congo (ONUC) was created in 1960, the application of the same formula created greater problems because the annual costs of the Congo operation were greater than the entire regular United Nations budget and because additional members, including France, refused to pay the peacekeeping assessments. The total United Nations cost of the UNEF from 1956 to 1967 was approximately 200 million dollars, and the cost of the ONUC from 1960 until its withdrawal in 1964 was in excess of 400 million dollars. These costs are exclusive of the ordinary costs of salaries and equipment of the forces, which are borne by the states that furnish the forces.

As Ruth Russell suggested in 1970, the United Nations financial crisis is not primarily a result of *incapacity* of the members to pay but a result of their *unwillingness* to do so.[3] The issue is more political and legal than financial. In addition to the legal question of what constitutes "expenses of the Organization" under Article 17 of the Charter, the political disputes involve the legitimate roles of the General Assembly and the Security Council, and the issue of who should pay for peacekeeping operations.

The Secretary-General, backed by the United States and sufficient votes to pass the supporting resolutions, maintains that the expenses of peacekeeping operations initiated by either the Security Council or the General Assembly are expenses that the General Assembly has a right to assess under the authority of Article 17 and that all members are obligated to pay. The Soviet Union, France, and other states that refused to pay the costs of either the UNEF or the ONUC or both declare that only the Security Council can authorize a peacekeeping action and that the General Assembly has usurped powers not granted in the Charter. The Soviet Union would assess all peacekeeping costs against the aggressors—France, the United Kingdom, and Israel in the Middle East crisis of 1956 and Belgium in the Congo. Egypt, claiming to be the victim of aggression, also objected to paying the subsequent peacekeeping costs. A third position on the issue of peacekeeping costs is that taken by several Latin American states, who contend that the General Assembly is authorized to assess these expenses but should assess them according to a special formula that would place the primary burden on the permanent members of the Security Council with token assessments for states with less ability to pay. They would ask the major powers to pay the bulk of such expenses as the price of their special power,

[3] Ruth B. Russell, *The General Assembly: Patterns/Problems/Prospects* (New York: Carnegie Endowment for International Peace, 1970), p. 35.

privilege, and responsibility in the United Nations.

⟨In order to clarify the legal aspects of the financial dispute, the General Assembly in 1961 sought an advisory opinion from the International Court of Justice. In July, 1962, the Court delivered its opinion sustained by a 9–5 vote. The majority of the Court rejected the contention that the question was purely political and not subject to juridical opinion. On the substantive question, the Court declared that the peacekeeping expenses constitute "expenses of the Organization" within the meaning of Article 17 of the Charter. The position of the Secretary-General supported by General Assembly resolutions was thus vindicated by the Court's opinion.⟩

General Assembly resolutions and Court opinions were insufficient, however, to raise the necessary funds for the peacekeeping operations. The Secretary-General drew on the Working Capital Fund, and some member states made voluntary contributions, but the expense of simultaneously maintaining two peacekeeping forces exceeded the available financial resources of the United Nations. As an emergency measure the 1961 General Assembly authorized the issuance of 200 million dollars worth of United Nations bonds to be repaid in installments over a twenty-five-year period. Approximately 85 percent of the authorized limit was subscribed to with the United States purchasing 50 percent of the total. This temporary stopgap failed to solve the permanent problem.

The financial crisis came to a head in the 1964 General Assembly session. A provision of Article 19 of the Charter states that a member that is at least two years in arrears in its budget contributions shall be deprived of its vote in the General Assembly. The Soviet Union, because of its refusal to pay peacekeeping costs, was more than two years delinquent, and France would reach that point before the General Assembly was scheduled to adjourn. The United States threatened to apply Article 19, and the Soviet Union indicated that if the sanction were applied, it would leave the organization. The contest of wills resulted in a stalemate, and a strange phenomenon ensued. A voteless session of the General Assembly was conducted during which all necessary decisions were taken by consensus through informal consultation of the President of the Assembly with the delegates. Votes were actually registered in the anterooms instead of on the Assembly floor. Thus, a gentlemen's agreement to postpone the showdown permitted the organization to survive what threatened to be its deathblow, at least as a nearly universal organization.

By the opening of the twentieth session of the General Assembly in 1965, the United States abandoned its attempt to enforce Article 19 since it lacked support from most members for such extreme sanctions. In 1965 a Committee of Thirty-Three was established to review the financial dilemma resulting from the peacekeeping issue. Since that time a series of committees has not been able to resolve the problems in a manner acceptable to all parties. A suggestion was adopted in 1965 to call for voluntary contributions to alleviate the bankrupt position of the United Nations, and the understanding seemed to be that the Soviet Union and France would contribute if they were free to choose their own terms of contribution. Although more than a score of members made pledges, the Soviet Union and France refused voluntary contributions unless their action was matched simultaneously by the United States. In the game of power politics, the United Nations was the destitute stepchild. The Soviet Union not only refused to pay for peacekeeping operations but withheld from its regular assessments amounts equal to its share of the service debt for United Nations bonds.

As a practical matter the United Nations has sought alternative means of financing other peacekeeping operations. The Security Council established the United Nations Force in Cyprus (UNFICYP) in March, 1964, and provided that its financing should come from three sources: (1) the governments providing the contingents, (2) the government of Cyprus, and (3) voluntary contributions. The mandate for the force has been continued from year to year, and financial support has been precarious, but the solution has proven less troublesome than the financing of the UNEF or the ONUC. The costs of a United Nations Observation Mission in Yemen and of an executive authority and a supporting security force in West Irian were split equally by the contending governments.

Somewhat surprisingly, in the light of past financial difficulties, the Security Council, in authorizing in October, 1973, a new 7,000-member peacekeeping force in the Middle East, provided for its costs to be assessed on a modified scale based on the regular budget. The major powers could support this decision since it was made in the Security Council, which is considered by the Soviet Union and France to be the proper arena for such action. Under these circumstances defaults on the payment of assessments are unlikely as long as no disagreement arises among the major powers concerning the neutral role played by the force in its efforts at pacification. The 1978 peacekeeping force in Lebanon was similarly authorized by the Security Council, but both the Soviet Union and China announced their refusal to contribute to its financial support.

The United Nations has not recovered from the financial crisis of the 1960s. Repeatedly, the Secretary-General has appealed to the members to resolve the impasse and to rescue the organization from bankruptcy. If the United Nations is suffering a crisis of confidence, the heart of the situation is the unwillingenss of the members to seek, through a spirit of mutual cooperation, solutions to the financial and other problems of the organization. Although past decisions for peacekeeping financing may have been unwise, the vitality of the organization should now be restored in the interests of world order. Only the member governments have the power and will to restore that vitality.

From time to time suggestions have been made for future United Nations financing that would give the organization independence from reliance on government assessments. About 2 percent of current revenue comes from such sources as charges for services and sales of publications and stamps, but most proposals for independent financing seek much more substantial sums. Some of the suggestions for future sources of revenue for the United Nations include.

1. A surcharge on international mail or on international communications to be earmarked for the United Nations
2. A fee for the use of international waterways
3. Substantial fees for services performed by the United Nations or the specialized agencies
4. A "finder's fee" for aid in discovering and developing new resources

5. Exploitation of the resources of the oceans and seabeds through a United Nations operating agency or, more likely, through leasing rights to private or national agencies
6. Exploitation of the resources of Antarctica
7. Licensing fees or other charges for the use of outer space
8. Taxes earmarked for United Nations use but collected by member states
9. Taxes on international travel or international passport fees
10. Private or foundation contributions with suitable exemptions from national taxation

Several of these sources seem logical since, for example, no nation can claim jurisdiction under existing international law to the oceans beyond their territorial limits or to unlimited rights in outer space.

Unfortunately, any of these proposals that would raise considerable amounts of independent revenue for the United Nations would face strong opposition from the members. To make the United Nations less dependent on the financial support of its member governments, especially of the larger states, would be a major blow to national sovereignty and control and would radically alter the nature of the organization. The smaller and developing states might welcome the additional leverage and resources available for promoting their economic and social interests. The big powers would view the financial independence of the United Nations as a threat to their influence in the organization. The same attitudes that produced the financial crisis of the 1960s will probably not permit radical innovations in patterns of financing in the foreseeable future.

6

❧

Peaceful Settlement
of
Disputes

In earlier chapters we discussed the history of the ideology and practice of international organization, the precedents set by the League of Nations, and the legal and organizational framework and the underlying issues of the United Nations. With this background, we now will examine the more specific efforts of the UN to transform theories, goals, and principles into programs for solving world problems.

IMPORTANCE OF PEACEFUL SETTLEMENT

Although the United Nations is a multifunctional organization, foremost among its functions is the maintenance of world peace. Both the League of Nations and the United Nations were created near the end of the greatest wars of the century primarily to act as instrumentalities for eliminating armed conflict and for strengthening means for conflict control and resolution. In the long run, arms reduction and control and the development of world law might serve as means for promoting peace, and, on occasion, collective action against threats to or breaches of the peace might be required, but the keystone of the formula for avoiding international violence is to strengthen the commitment to and the machinery for peaceful settlement of disputes.

The primacy of peaceful settlement processes in both the League of Nations and the United Nations is evidenced by the emphasis upon these processes in the Covenant and in the Charter — an emphasis based on both placement and detail within the documents. The goals of promoting peace and security are mentioned first in these texts, and peaceful settlement of disputes is also first and fundamental among the means for goal attainment. Other goals such as (1) developing friendly relations among nations, (2) harmonizing the actions of nations, (3) taking appropriate measures to strengthen universal peace, and (4) practicing tolerance and living together in peace, included in the United Nations Charter, reinforce the desire for avoiding war. The principles of the organizations emphasize the obligations of member states to refrain from the threat or use of force and to settle international disputes by peaceful means. The means available for the processes of peaceful settlement both outside and inside the new organizations are elaborated in these constitutional documents. In the Covenant the material on pacific settlement of disputes is more detailed than on any other subject. In the Charter the chapter on pacific settlement immediately follows the general provisions on purposes, membership, and organization. These data attest to the concern of the authors of the League Covenant and the United Nations Charter for the processes of peaceful settlement of disputes.

In an age of nuclear, biological, and chemical weapons, the attention to peaceful settlement procedures is a prudent approach to world order. The risks of mass annihilation, the insecurity of massive deterrence, the increase of interdependence among nations, the proliferation of cheap and increasingly destructive weapons, the psychological uncertainty of the behavior of leaders under stress, and the threats of escalation, human error, and accident place the future of much of the human race in constant jeopardy. If survival is a foremost human value, then peaceful settlement of disputes is enhanced as an alternative to the risks of conflict and nuclear war. The other goals of the United Nations may be worth striving to attain for the enrichment of human welfare, but if rivalries and tensions are unrestrained and if peaceful settlement fails to prevent nuclear holocaust, all other human gains may be wiped out in a few moments. Such tragic prospects should provide sufficient incentive to use all means available to avoid international confrontations and to seek new and imaginative methods for reducing tensions. Any risks involved in taking such initiatives are probably less than those involved in a blind contest of wills among competing sovereign states. Peaceful settlement requires a spirit of cooperation and compromise among national states, but any other course holds little promise for survival in an interdependent world of states with nuclear capability.

CHARTER PROCEDURES AND METHODS

In the area of pacific settlement of disputes the architects of the Charter were not notably innovative. The world's statesmen were not ready to commit their governments to any radical departure from established practices. The sovereignty of states and the protection of the prerogatives of the major powers were the basic conditions around which all other features of the Charter had to fit. Therefore, the familiar methods of pacific settlement, firmly established in international law and practice, were the ones mentioned in the Charter as the devices to be used by states or by United Nations organs in handling disputes; also, the processes to be followed for the consideration of disputes brought before United Nations bodies were singularly similar to the formulas established twenty-six years earlier in the League of Nations Covenant. Except for greater detail and a supposedly clearer delineation of functions between the Security Council and the General Assembly (a distinction that in practice became blurred), the processes for pacific settlement provided for in the two constitutional documents were fundamentally identical.

The Charter provides a logical progression of steps to be followed by states involved in disputes. Each member promises in adhering to the Charter to settle all disputes by peaceful means and to refrain from the threat or use of force. If a dispute does arise, the parties should, before submission to a United Nations organ, "seek a solution by negotiation, inquiry, mediation, conciliation, arbitration, judicial settlement, resort to regional agencies or arrangements, or other peaceful means of their own choice."[1] If the dispute is not so resolved, then a party to the dispute or any member of the United Nations or the Secretary-General may bring the matter to the attention of the Security Council or of the General Assembly. The assumption was originally made that the Security Council would, in most cases, be the referee since primary responsibility for the maintenance of international peace and security was lodged in the Council. When a dispute does come before the Security Council, that body's

---

[1] Charter of the United Nations, Art. 33.

first and simplest option is to suggest to the disputants that they settle their dispute by one of the means of peaceful settlement listed above.

Since the traditional means of peaceful settlement of disputes listed in Article 33 of the Charter are the basic methods applied to the resolution process both inside and outside the United Nations, a clear understanding of each method is in order. Some variations and refinements of traditional methods have been developed by United Nations organs, but the essential means correspond to procedures and practices developed over hundreds of years.

Negotiation is the most common method for settling international differences. It involves direct discussion between or among the parties to the dispute with the objective of reaching an agreement. No outside party is involved in the process. Negotiation is the essence of the practice of diplomacy.

Good offices is the only traditional method of dispute settlement not listed in Article 33 of the Charter but one frequently used by United Nations organs. Good offices involves the assistance of a third party, or state not a party to the dispute. The third party, in adhering strictly to the limits of good offices, may offer only a channel of communications or facilities for the use of the parties but may not offer any suggestions for terms of settlement. By providing a neutral ground for negotiation or by offering to carry messages between the disputants, the third party displays a friendly desire to promote a settlement without getting involved in the issues at stake.

Inquiry is a process of fact-finding by a neutral team of investigators. Often the facts underlying a controversy are in dispute, and clarification by an impartial commission may facilitate settlement. The report of the investigating commission does not suggest terms of settlement but may help to establish conditions conducive to settlement.

Mediation is a procedure involving the suggestion of terms of settlement by a third party. The mediator enters into the negotiations between the disputing parties seeking terms of compromise acceptable to the disputants. An effective mediator may not impose his will upon the parties without losing the confidence of one or more of them in his neutrality.

Conciliation is similar to mediation except for the legal distinction that the third party is a commission or international body whose aid has been sought in finding a solution satisfactory to the disputants. Special commissions have often been created by the United Nations to attempt conciliation. As in mediation, the object is peace through compromise on terms acceptable to the parties, not the imposition of terms by the commission of conciliation or the application of abstract principles of law or justice. In practice the United Nations organs have tended to use the terms "conciliation," "mediation," and "good offices" without adherence to their strict legal distinctions.

Arbitration is a means of applying legal principles to a controversy within limits previously agreed upon by the disputing parties. A panel of judges or arbitrators is created either by special agreement of the parties or by an existing arbitral treaty. In agreeing to submit the dispute to arbitration, the disputants also agree in advance to be bound by the decision. An arbitral agreement known as a *compromis* specifies the method of selecting the arbitral panel, the time and place of the hearing, and any limitations upon the facts to be considered or the principles of law or equity to be applied in arriving at a decision. Historically, arbitration has enjoyed several periods of popularity beginning with its use by the ancient Greeks and gaining in use during the nineteenth and early twentieth centuries, but it has almost disappeared from general use in the period since 1945, except for the specific area of trade disputes.

Adjudication or *judicial settlement* is a process of submitting a dispute to an international court for decision. Unlike arbitration, the court is subject to no preliminary limitations upon its procedures, evidence to be considered, or legal principles to be applied, except those stated in the statute by which it was created. However, nations, jealous of their sovereignty, have been reluctant to grant to international courts any form of compulsory jurisdiction or to submit appropriate cases to existing courts. As a result, the International Court of Justice has languished for lack of business to an even greater extent than its predecessor, the Permanent Court of International Justice. As with arbitration, once the parties have agreed to submit a case to adjudication, the decision rendered is considered binding, although adequate means of enforcement in instances of noncompliance are lacking.

When a dispute is called to the attention of the Security Council, the first step is to adopt the question as an agenda item. Prolonged disputes previously adopted as agenda items and never officially removed from the list of items of which the Council is "seized" (the official United Nations terminology referring to the current agenda) may be taken up again at any future time without this preliminary step. Because the General Assembly may not make recommendations on a dispute or situation under Security Council consideration, the Secretary-General is required to maintain and publish a "list of matters of which the Security Council is seized." If the dispute is new, the preliminary debate on the adoption of the agenda may require from a few minutes to several days. Questions of domestic jurisdiction or other sources of doubt concerning the legality, wisdom, or practicality of Security Council involvement may delay approval of the agenda. By discussing for many hours the pros and cons of the appropriateness of Security Council consideration, some of the substantive issues of the dispute may be thoroughly aired and may serve to focus public attention upon these issues even if the agenda item is subsequently rejected. One example of such prolonged preliminary debate occurred in April, 1952, when the Security Council was requested to consider the situation in Tunisia over French objections that the matter was one of domestic jurisdiction. After several days of debate, the item failed to gain the seven votes required to adopt it as an agenda item.

After the Security Council agrees to consider a dispute or situation, the case for each disputant may be presented by sympathetic members of the Council or by the representatives of the disputing states. Any party to a dispute has a right to participate, without vote, in the discussion of that dispute. Other nonmembers of the Council may also be invited, at the discretion of the Council, if their interests are affected. On some occasions these provisions have led to a crowded Council chamber and to lengthy debate because of requests to participate by large numbers of "interested" parties. Of course, every complex question for discussion is also supported by elaborate documentation including communications from the contending governments. This allows each member of the Security Council to consider evidence other than that presented orally.

If, during the course of debate, some of the Security Council members become convinced that a decision or suggestion by the Council is possible or desirable, one or more resolutions will be introduced with the hope of adoption by Council vote. Resolutions may be sponsored by one or by several members of the Council. In most cases, extensive consultation will occur outside the Council chamber both before and after resolutions are introduced. Amendments to resolutions may be submitted, and not all proposals will necessarily be voted on. In spite of consultation among the members, all proposed resolutions on a given issue may fail for lack of nine supporting votes or because of an occasional veto by a permanent member, although abstentions are more frequent than vetoes in recent years. Another common phenomenon is that resolutions, in order to receive adequate support from the members, may be so watered down that they fail to be effective in alleviating the conditions of which the aggrieved party or parties have complained. Resolutions of this least-common-denominator variety may contribute to deterioration of public respect for the efficacy of the Security Council.

In dealing with a dispute, the Security Council may decide to refer the matter to another body or may itself suggest terms of settlement. If Security Council action is blocked by a veto, any nine members may remove the item from the agenda and request an emergency session of the General Assembly under the Uniting for Peace Resolution discussed in chapter 7. By Council resolution the dispute may be referred to a regional organization or to a specially created commission of inquiry or conciliation. The Council may also appoint a mediator or recommend that the Secretary-General arrange for a mediator or for one or more agents to offer good offices. The Council also has the option of suggesting to the parties that they continue or resume negotiation or that they arrange to submit the dispute to arbitration or judicial settlement, although the latter two means have largely fallen into disuse.

One device not mentioned in the Charter, which has been used to good effect while other means for final settlement are being sought, is calling on parties already engaged in armed hostilities to abide by a cease-fire. The drawing of a cease-fire line and the temporary cessation of hostilities may make possible the working out of a permanent settlement, as in the Indonesian-Dutch dispute, or it may contribute only to the checking of large-scale fighting and loss of lives for prolonged periods, as in the Kashmir and Palestine disputes. In either case, whether "settlement" is achieved or not, Security Council members generally prefer an armistice in which the adversaries face each other from their respective sides of a cease-fire line to warfare with its human and economic costs.

Until a dispute is finally resolved, the Security Council may retain the item on its agenda for a period of months or years. This allows for reconsideration on short notice (1) to follow up the results of previous Council recommendations, (2) to seek new, more effective means for settlement, or (3) to consider new developments in the situation. As long as means for international decision making and enforcement are unsatisfactory, the persistence of unresolved issues over long time spans will remain a feature of international relations.

Although it is less well equipped to deal with disputes than the Security Council, the General Assembly may be called upon to consider controversies referred to it by a party to the dispute, by members of the Security Council, or by any other member or group of members of the United Nations. Unwieldy size and lack of binding power for its recommendations are just two of the Assembly's obvious disadvantages as an agent for handling acute international differences. But in spite of these handicaps the Assembly has played a much larger role in disputes than foreseen by the planners in San Francisco. This enhanced role is discussed at many other points in this book.

If the parties to a dispute can agree that a satisfactory result may be obtained by judicial settlement, they may submit their case, by mutual agreement, to the International Court of Justice. More details of the role of the Court will be developed in chapter 8, but it may now be noted that the number and the importance of cases submitted to the Court has not been impressive. States are reluctant to use the Court for judicial settlement, and the recent trend has been toward less rather than greater use of this agency for conflict resolution.

The Secretary-General and his staff play a wide variety of roles in dealing with disputes. These range from merely receiving and transmitting information between governments and United Nations organs to calling the attention of those organs to threatening situations or to acting as the principal agent of the Security Council or the General Assembly in mediating a dispute or carrying out the steps called for in United Nations resolutions. The influence and activities of the Secretary-General have been, in practice, much more pervasive than would have been generally predicted in 1945.

The keynote of United Nations responses to disputes and threats to peace has been flexibility. From the variety of procedures outlined above, the organs of the United Nations have been able to select appropriate responses for widely varying circumstances depending upon the limitations imposed by both the situation and the willingness of member governments to support one or another course of action. To the extent that disputes have on occasion been dealt with effectively, the factor of flexibility has made a major contribution.

UNITED NATIONS EXPERIENCE — SURVEY AND CASE STUDIES

A complete account of United Nations activities in the area of pacific settlement of disputes could not be given in a single chapter or even in a single volume. Although member states do not choose to submit all appropriate controversies or situations "which might lead to international friction or give rise to a dispute" to consideration by United

DISPUTES CONSIDERED BY THE SECURITY COUNCIL AND THE GENERAL ASSEMBLY JANUARY 1946–JUNE 1977

Dispute	Considered by — Security Council	Considered by — General Assembly	Year First Introduced	Duration of Consideration — 1 Year or less	Duration of Consideration — 1–5 Yrs.	Duration of Consideration — More than 5 Yrs.
Middle East						
Iranian Question	X		1946	X		
Syrian-Lebanese Complaint	X		1946	X		
Palestine Question	X	X	1947			X
Egyptian Question	X		1947	X		
Status of Jerusalem	X	X	1947		X	
Palestine Refugee Question		X	1948			X
Anglo-Iranian Oil Dispute	X		1951	X		
Israeli Complaint against Egypt on Suez Canal	X		1954	X		
Gaza Area Incidents	X		1955	X		
Suez Canal Question	X	X	1956			X
Syrian Complaint against Turkey	X	X	1957	X		
Lebanese Complaint against UAR	X	X	1958	X		
Jordanian Complaint against UAR	X	X	1958	X		
Case of Adolf Eichmann	X		1960	X		
Question of Oman		X	1960			X
Question of Kuwait	X		1961	X		
Question of Yemen	X		1963		X	
Complaint by UK against Yemen	X		1966	X		
Situation in the Middle East	X	X	1967			X
Situation in and around Jerusalem	X	X	1968			X
Question of Bahrain	X		1970	X		

				Year	
Dispute over Certain Islands in Persian Gulf			X	1971	X
Iraqi Complaint against Iran			X	1974	X
Israeli Practices Affecting Human Rights in Occupied Territories	X	X		1968	X
Middle East Problem Including Palestinian Question		X		1976	X
Situation in Occupied Arab Territories		X		1976	X
Exercise by Palestinian People of Inalienable Rights		X		1976	X

Asia and Far East

				Year	
Indonesian Question		X		1946	X
Korean Question	X	X		1947	X
India-Pakistani Question	X			1948	X
Hyderabad Question				1948	X
Soviet Threats to Political Independence of China		X		1949	X
Armed Invasion of Taiwan		X		1950	X
Alleged Bombing by U.S. of Chinese Territory		X		1950	X
Intervention of China in Korea		X		1950	X
Relief and Rehabilitation of Korea	X			1950	X
Alleged Bacterial Warfare in Korea		X		1952	X
Complaint of Mass Murder of Korean and Chinese POWs by U.S.		X		1952	X
Burmese Complaint against Rep. of China		X		1952	X
North Korean and Chinese Atrocities		X		1953	X

113

TABLE CONTINUED

Dispute	Considered by		Year First Introduced	Duration of Consideration		
	Security Council	General Assembly		1 Year or less	1–5 Yrs.	More than 5 Yrs.
Thai Request for Aid of Peace Observation Commission	X		1954	X		
Detention of UN Military Personnel in Violation of Korean Armistice Agreement		X	1954		X	
Acts of Aggression by U.S. Navy against People's Rep. of China		X	1954	X		
Violations of Freedom of Seas in China Area		X	1954	X		
West Irian Question		X	1954			X
Question of Chinese Coastal Islands	X		1955	X		
Laotian Situation	X		1959	X		
Question of Tibet		X	1959			X
Question of Goa	X		1961	X		
Human Rights in South Vietnam		X	1963	X		
Cambodian Complaints of Aggression by U.S. and South Vietnam	X		1964	X		
Question of Malaysia	X		1964	X		
Gulf of Tonkin Incidents	X		1964	X		
Situation in Vietnam	X		1966	X		
Complaint by U.S. against North Korea	X		1968	X		

115

TABLE CONTINUED

Dispute	Considered by Security Council	Considered by General Assembly	Year First Introduced	Duration of Consideration 1 Year or less	Duration of Consideration 1–5 Yrs.	Duration of Consideration More than 5 Yrs.
Complaint of Dem. Republic of Congo Concerning Act of Aggression	X		1967	X		
Complaints by Zambia against Portugal	X		1969	X		
Complaints by Senegal against Portugal	X		1969	X		
Complaints by Guinea against Portugal	X		1969	X		
Complaint by Guinea against Portugal	X		1970	X		
Complaint by Guinea against Portugal	X		1971	X		
Complaint by Senegal against Portugal	X		1971	X		
Complaint by Zambia against South Africa	X		1971	X		
Complaint by Senegal against Portugal	X		1972	X		
Complaint by Zambia against South Africa	X		1973	X		
Occupation by Portuguese Forces of Sectors of Guinea-Bissau		X	1973	X		
Situation Concerning Western Sahara		X	1974		X	
Situation in the Comoros	X		1976	X		

Dispute			Year		
French-Somalia Incident in Afars and Issas	X		1976	X	X
Complaint of South African Aggression against Angola	X		1976	X	
Complaint by Zambia against South Africa	X		1976	X	
Complaint by Mauritius of Act of Aggression by Israel against Uganda	X		1976	X	
Complaint by Lesotho against South Africa	X		1976	X	
Complaint by Botswana against Rhodesia	X		1977	X	
Complaint of Aggression against Benin	X		1977	X	X
Question of South Africa	X		1977	X	X
Complaint by Mozambique against Rhodesia	X		1977	X	X
Europe					
Greek Question	X	X	1946		X
Spanish Question	X	X	1946		X
Free Territory of Trieste	X		1947		
Corfu Channel Question	X		1947		
Czechoslovakian Situation	X		1948	X	
Berlin Situation	X		1948	X	
Human Rights in Balkans		X	1948	X	X
Soviet Wives of Foreign Nationals		X	1948	X	
Conditions for Free Elections in Germany		X	1951	X	
Complaint by Yugoslavia of Hostile Activities of Neighbors		X	1951	X	

TABLE CONTINUED

Dispute	Considered by — Security Council	Considered by — General Assembly	Year First Introduced	Duration of Consideration — 1 Year or less	Duration of Consideration — 1–5 Yrs.	Duration of Consideration — More than 5 Yrs.
Complaints of U.S. Intervention in Domestic Affairs of other Countries (3 separate complaints)		X	1951	X		
		X	1952	X		
		X	1956	X		
Austrian Peace Treaty		X	1952	X		
U.S. Complaint of Attack on its Aircraft	X		1954	X		
Cyprian Question	X	X	1954			X
Hungarian Question	X	X	1956			X
Flights of U.S. Armed Aircraft toward Soviet Frontiers	X		1958	X		
Complaints of U.S. Violations of Soviet Airspace	X		1960	X		
Status of Bozen Residents		X	1960		X	
Relations between Greece and Turkey	X		1964	X		
Situation in Czechoslovakia	X		1968	X		
Complaint by Iceland against United Kingdom	X		1975	X		
Complaint by Greece against Turkey	X		1976	X		
Western Hemisphere						
Aggression against Guatemala	X		1954	X		
Cuban Complaints against U.S.	X	X	1960		X	

	Year				
Venezuelan Complaint against Dominican Republic	1960	X		X	
Boundary Dispute between Venezuela and British Guiana	1962		X	X	
Haitian Complaint against Dominican Republic	1963	X		X	
Panamanian Complaint against U.S.	1964	X		X	
Situation in Dominican Republic	1965	X			X
Complaint by Haiti of Act of Aggression	1968	X		X	
Question of Panama Canal	1973	X		X	
Complaint by Cuba against Chile	1973	X		X	

Nations organs, the documentation of the more than 130 disputes debated by the Security Council and General Assembly during a thirty-one-year period is voluminous. Even a summary of each dispute would require much space and would be tedious to follow. The data in this section is, therefore, condensed by the use of a table supplemented by sufficient detail concerning selected controversies to sample and illustrate a variety of approaches used by United Nations agencies in dealing with disputes.

No sharp distinctions can be drawn, in United Nations practice, among pacific settlement, collective security, and the newly developed techniques of peacekeeping or preventive diplomacy. All situations that involve the use of collective security or peacekeeping techniques also contain elements of pacific settlement. The accompanying table includes all disputes submitted to the United Nations without classifying certain of them as having been partially dealt with by methods that may be labeled collective security or peacekeeping. However, the theory and practice of collective security and peacekeeping will be treated more fully in the following chapter and will include case studies of several additional disputes to which the techniques of collective security or peacekeeping have been applied.

Through the selection of a few case studies, a wide range of conditions may be illustrated concerning the ability of United Nations organs to contribute to the peaceful settlement of disputes. The case studies that follow have been selected because they demonstrate a variety of circumstances in which the United Nations has been involved in attempts at conflict resolution. The selection is based on these specific criteria: (1) to show examples of a wide variety of techniques utilized, ranging from simple to complex, in attempting to resolve the several disputes; (2) to illustrate varying degrees of great-power involvement or direct interest in the dispute; (3) to include disputes of varying duration; (4) to give examples of consideration by the Security Council only, by the General Assembly only, and by both; and (5) to demonstrate degrees of success or failure in resolving the issues involved or in terminating the dispute.

The Iranian Question

The earliest dispute to come before the Security Council was a complaint by Iran in January, 1946, that Soviet troops, still occupying the Azerbaijan region, were interfering with the internal affairs of Iran by encouraging a separatist movement there. The Soviet representative denied the charges, and the Council, after brief discussion, requested that the adversary governments resume negotiations and that the Security Council be kept informed of results. In March the matter was discussed again. The issue was dropped in May when Iran reported the withdrawal of Soviet troops.

The Iranian case illustrates several points regarding the handling of disputes by the Security Council. The Council is unable to use strong measures or coercion against a major power. The only weapon available is an appeal to Charter principles and to the good faith of the disputants, supported by publicity and world opinion. There is no way to measure the degree to which international exposure of the situation served as an impetus for the Soviet response. In any event, the matter was shortly settled. There have been several other situations in which no more drastic action by the Security Council or the General Assembly than general debate and an appeal to the parties to negotiate has brought about settlement of disputes. In the absence of contrary evidence, it may be reasonably assumed that in such cases settlement through negotiations was hastened by United Nations exposure and pressure.

The Indonesian Question

During World War II nationalist sentiment spread rapidly in Indonesia, making a return to Dutch hegemony in the islands highly unlikely. Two days after the Japanese surrender, nationalist leaders declared the independence of Indonesia. No force could effectively challenge their claim until, six weeks later, British troops were ordered into the islands to disarm the Japanese military forces there. The British command recognized the de facto control of the nationalists, but Dutch troops and government officials were able to re-enter the islands so that two opposing governments and military forces claimed sovereignty in Indonesia.

In January, 1946, the Ukraine brought charges in the Security Council that the British were using Japanese troops against the nationalist movement. In early February pro-nationalist proposals by the Ukraine and Egypt failed to gain sufficient votes for adoption, and the Council dropped further consideration of the matter for more than a year.

In Indonesia military clashes were continuing between Dutch and nationalist forces. Representatives of both sides carried on prolonged negotiations during 1946, resulting in a truce arrangement in October and the signing of the Linggadjati Agreement in March, 1947. The principal feature of this agreement was the recognition of a dual authority in Indonesia with a commitment to form a federal democratic state and a Netherlands-Indonesian Union within two years.

Continued truce violations and disagreements culminated in large-scale military action initiated by the Dutch in July, 1947.

On July 30, at the urging of both Australia and India, the Security Council adopted the Indonesian situation as an agenda item. The Council called on both parties to cease hostilities and to settle their differences by peaceful means. Both sides promptly issued cease-fire orders, but violations were reported within a few days. On August 25 the Council reminded the disputing parties of their cease-fire obligations, requested the consuls of Council members who were represented in Batavia (the Dutch name for Djakarta, the capital of Indonesia) to report to the Council on the degree of cease-fire observance, and authorized the creation of a Committee of Good Offices to aid in reaching a settlement. This committee was composed of Belgium chosen by the Netherlands, Australia chosen by Indonesia, and the United States chosen by the first two members.

The Committee of Good Offices arrived in Indonesia in late October and, after nearly three months of negotiation, succeeded in bringing the two disputants into substantial agreement on most points at issue. A so-called Renville Agreement was signed on January 17, 1948, aboard the U.S.S. *Renville*, which served as neutral territory for the negotiations. The agreement included a truce and eighteen principles as a basis for a final settlement.

By June, 1948, the tensions between the parties had again developed to the danger point. Each accused the other of undermining the spirit of some of the Renville Agreement terms. Military clashes became frequent, and further negotiations ceased. In December the Netherlands began full-scale military operations, captured the president of the republic and other officials, and overran much of the territory previously under the control of the republic. The Committee of Good Offices placed responsibility on the Netherlands for this violation of the Renville Agreement. During the last week in December, the Security Council adopted resolutions calling for an immediate cessation of hostilities and the release by the Netherlands of political prisoners.

When no change occurred in the Indonesian situation, the Security Council, on January 28, 1949, adopted a sweeping resolution. It repeated the demands of the December resolutions; it recommended the establishment of an interim federal government by March 15, 1949, the election of a Constitutional Assembly by October 1, and the transfer of sovereignty to the United States of Indonesia by July 1, 1950; and it converted the Committee of Good Offices to the United Nations Commission for Indonesia and gave it enlarged duties and authority.

In March the Netherlands released the republican leaders and proposed the calling of a round-table conference in The Hague for the purpose of arranging a final settlement of the Indonesian question. In April, with the aid of the United Nations Commission, negotiations were resumed, and by August all the basic elements of the Security Council resolutions had been complied with. The round-table conference was scheduled to begin on August 23 in The Hague. The participants were representatives of the Netherlands, the Republic of Indonesia, spokesmen for areas of Indonesia other than the republic, and the United Nations Commission for Indonesia.

The Hague Conference reached agreement on (1) the transfer of sovereignty not later than December 30, 1949, (2) a Netherlands-Indonesian Union for defense and economic cooperation, and (3) transitional measures including the withdrawal of armed forces. Formal transfer of sovereignty actually took place on December 27, and Indonesia became an independent state. In September, 1950, it was admitted to United Nations membership.

The Security Council made all of the important United Nations decisions in the Indonesian case. Some discussion occurred in the General Assembly, but that body's role was ancillary to that of the Security Council. A strong course of action was possible because of fundamental agreement among the major powers. The cause of Indonesian independence was supported by all the permanent members of the Council, and the behavior of the Dutch in violating truce agreements bolstered the resolve of the Security Council members to push for an early transfer of sovereignty.

In spite of strong measures to resolve the Indonesian question, the Security Council never declared that it was acting under Chapter VII of the Charter, which deals with actions involving threats to the peace or breaches of the peace. Australia had proposed a specific reference to Chapter VII, but the Security Council avoided any legal questions that might result from such a reference. Action was taken without specific reference to any article of either Chapter VI, which deals with the pacific settlement of disputes, or Chapter VII, which specifies measures to be taken in the more severe situations calling for various forms of sanctions or collective action. Through this vagueness a flexibility of response could be achieved, and a precedent was set for future United Nations flexibility and avoidance of legal straitjackets.

The flexibility of the Security Council response was also demonstrated by the variety of devices used in the Indonesian situation. Several cease-fires were called for and observed for varying periods of time. Observer functions and fact-finding were performed by the

consular offices in Batavia. The Commission of Good Offices furnished channels of communication between the disputants and offered a neutral meeting ground. The United Nations Commission for
Indonesia engaged in conciliation efforts by suggesting terms of settlement and participated in the final conference in The Hague. The
Security Council itself suggested the general terms of settlement
in its resolutions. By a combination of firmness and flexibility the
Security Council no doubt reduced the scope of hostilities in Indonesia and hastened the final settlement.

Former Italian Colonies

According to the peace treaty with Italy at the end of World
War II, the disposition of Libya, Italian Somaliland, and Eritrea was
to be determined by France, the United Kingdom, the Soviet Union,
and the United States. If, within one year they could not agree (and
this proved to be the case), they were to turn the matter over to the
General Assembly for solution. After much study and debate, the
Assembly, in November, 1949, adopted a resolution that provided
for additional investigation with regard to Eritrea and for a decision
on the final status of the other two territories.

Libya was to become an independent state not later than January
1, 1952. A United Nations commissioner was appointed and was to
be assisted by a ten-member council in drawing up a constitution and
preparing for self-government. Since Libya was a poor country with
a population of approximately 1 million, all appropriate agencies of
the United Nations, including the specialized agencies, were urged to
aid it with technical and financial assistance. A National Assembly
was chosen, a federal form of government was adopted, and on
December 24, 1951, Libya was proclaimed an independent state.
Libya immediately applied for United Nations membership, but its
application was vetoed by the Soviet Union, and it was admitted
only as a part of the "package deal" in December, 1955. Libya continued to receive special attention in the aid programs of the United
Nations until the discovery of large petroleum resources moved it
from very low to very high per capita income in the space of a
decade.

According to the Assembly's 1949 resolution, Somaliland was to
be placed under trusteeship for a period of ten years and was then to
become independent. Italy was to serve as the administering authority with the aid of an advisory council set up by the United Nations.
In 1959 a constituent assembly was elected, and a new constitution
was approved in May, 1960. Independence was declared on July 1,

1960, and in September, Somalia (which also includes the former British Somaliland) became a United Nations member.

A brief delay was necessary before a final decision on the future of Eritrea could be reached. An investigating commission was instructed to determine the wishes of the various groups in Eritrea and to suggest a plan for their political future. On-the-spot surveys were taken as a basis for the commission's report. In December, 1950, the General Assembly approved a plan according to which Eritrea would be federated with Ethiopia as an autonomous unit under the Ethiopian Crown. A United Nations commissioner was to assist with the transitional steps. A new constitution came into effect in September, 1952.

The disposition of the former Italian colonies was handled entirely by the General Assembly as prearranged by the major powers. Although the major powers were unable to agree, the General Assembly rather promptly settled upon distinct plans for each of the three territories. Some criticisms of the proposals were voiced, but the results seemed as satisfactory as could have been expected from any alternative courses of action. The political and economic viability of Libya was questioned, and some special aid was required for several years, but the discovery of oil alleviated major economic problems. Doubts could be raised concerning Italy's role as trustee for Somaliland both because Italy was the former imperial state and because Italy was not yet a United Nations member. However, the administration of Somaliland for a ten-year period under close United Nations scrutiny was conducted as well as the administration of most trust territories, and the transition to full independence was prompt and efficient. Not all elements within Eritrea could agree upon their desired status, and a residual separatist movement remains, but the arrangement was reasonably satisfactory to most groups. In general, the Assembly performed a difficult and complicated assignment quite effectively.

Indian-Pakistani Question

One of the most prolonged, and still unsettled, disputes before the United Nations is the Indian-Pakistani question, alternately referred to as the Kashmir dispute. Military confrontations between the parties have twice flared into major wars that involved fighting outside as well as inside Kashmir. In fact, the 1971 war was fought over the separate issue of the struggle for Bangladesh independence to which fighting on the Kashmiri front was but incidental.

In 1947, when India and Pakistan were partitioned and became independent, one of the princely states free to accede to either India or Pakistan or to remain independent was the state known by the collective title of Jammu and Kashmir. The majority of the population was Muslim, but the maharajah was Hindu. The maharajah opted for accession to India, and India accepted, subject to later verification by plebiscite.

In January, 1948, both India and Pakistan called to the attention of the Security Council the potentially serious situation in Kashmir. The Indians claimed that tribesmen aided by Pakistan had invaded Jammu and Kashmir. Pakistan charged that the accession to India was illegal and that India was violating other agreements with Pakistan.

On January 20 the Security Council established the United Nations Commission for India and Pakistan (UNCIP) to which it assigned responsibilities of investigation, good offices, and mediation. The UNCIP members, representing five states, arrived in the area in July, 1948, and the next month proposed a cease-fire and detailed arrangements for a truce and the holding of a plebiscite. Because of disagreements between India and Pakistan over details, the cease-fire did not come into effect until January 1, 1949, and the final delineation of the cease-fire line was not established until nearly seven months later. During this interval a United Nations Military Observer Group in India and Pakistan (UNMOGIP) was set up to observe and report on the cease-fire, and U.S. Admiral Chester Nimitz was nominated as plebiscite administrator.

In December, 1949, the UNCIP submitted its final report to the Security Council voicing its frustration in trying to reach agreement on military withdrawals and the conditions for a plebiscite. The Council then requested the President of the Security Council, General McNaughton of Canada, to negotiate with India and Pakistan, but in February he reported no significant progress. In April, 1950, the responsibilities of the UNCIP were turned over to Sir Owen Dixon of Australia, who was given the title United Nations Representative for India and Pakistan. In September he reported failure to reach agreement on outstanding issues and asked to be relieved of his responsibilities. In April, 1951, Dr. Frank Graham of the United States was appointed to succeed Sir Owen. The Council vainly suggested that, after three months, any remaining points of difference that could not be resolved with the aid of the United Nations representative should be submitted to arbitration. Graham made limited progress on some points of negotiation, but the unresolved issues after several additional years of effort were crucial to a final settlement, and the general stalemate continued.

In January, 1957, the Security Council took up the Pakistani complaint that India had held a constituent assembly in Kashmir and drawn up a constitution that provided for the integration of Kashmir into India in violation of earlier agreements for a plebiscite. The Council President, Gunnar Jarring of Sweden, was requested to visit India and Pakistan to explore the possibilities of reaching a settlement on the Kashmir issue. On April 29 he reported no progress. Jarring's suggestion to submit certain basic issues to arbitration had been accepted by Pakistan but rejected by India on the grounds that no other measures were appropriate until Pakistan took steps toward military withdrawal since it was still engaging in aggression.

In 1962 and again in 1964, Pakistan requested that the Security Council take up the question of Kashmir. In spite of days of debate, no constructive course of action could be agreed upon by the Council.

On September 3, 1965, the Secretary-General reported to the Security Council that between January and mid-June the UNMOGIP had verified 218 cease-fire-line violations by Pakistan and 159 by India. Since August 5 illegal activities on both sides had further increased. These activities included artillery fire, crossing the line by armed Pakistanis not in uniform, and occupation by Indian troops of positions on the Pakistani side of the cease-fire line. The Security Council by unanimous resolution called upon both sides to stop aggression immediately and to return to their respective positions behind the cease-fire line. Instead, military activity intensified, and India invaded Pakistan in areas around Lahore and Sialkot. The Security Council, on September 6, called on the parties to stop all hostilities and return their forces to positions held before August 5. The Council requested the Secretary-General to assist in implementing this resolution; U Thant spent the next week in India and Pakistan arranging for a cease-fire, which became effective on Septemper 22. The number of military observers in UNMOGIP was more than doubled, and a new temporary United Nations India-Pakistan Observation Mission (UNIPOM) was dispatched to the areas along the India-Pakistan border where Indian forces had crossed into Pakistan.

Frequent cease-fire violations occurred during the remainder of 1965, and the Security Council pressed India and Pakistan to implement the withdrawal of forces to the positions held before August 5. The prime minister of India and the president of Pakistan met in Tashkent under Soviet auspices and on January 10, 1966, issued a joint declaration stating that all troop withdrawals would be accomplished by February 25. The Secretary-General verified that the schedule had been met, the UNIPOM group was disbanded, and the UNMOGIP force was gradually reduced to its normal contingent.

The 1971 civil war in East Pakistan culminated in Indian military invasion of that area in December and resulted in the declaration of Bangladesh as an independent state. Fighting occurred in Kashmir as well, but the war did not bring about any change in the situation in that region. The cease-fire line continues to divide Jammu and Kashmir, the UNMOGIP patrols the line and reports violations, India claims the legitimacy of the incorporation of Kashmir territory into India, and Pakistan insists that its claim to the entire territory is equally valid. The basic issues have been unresolved for more than a quarter century.

United Nations efforts to resolve the Kashmir issue represent an exercise in repeated frustration, since the parties are unwilling to reach a compromise solution. The prospects for a plebiscite have now receded, and India considers the accession of Kashmir to India to be a *fait accompli*. A cease-fire line has divided the area since 1949 with a group of forty to fifty military observers responsible for reporting violations along a line nearly 500 miles long. With the exception of the General Assembly's consideration of the Bangladesh phase in 1971, the Security Council has maintained jurisdiction over the dispute in spite of occasional stalemates due to the use of the veto. On other occasions, when crises occurred, resolutions were passed by unanimous vote or with one or more abstentions. Except for a big-power stalemate over Bangladesh, the ability of the Security Council to take positive action has forestalled demands for General Assembly involvement.

The Security Council has used a very wide range of devices in seeking a solution to the Kashmir issue. It has called repeatedly for cease-fires, and a cease-fire line was established in 1949. Fact-finding or inquiry functions were assigned to the original five-member commission sent to the area and to the two observer groups created subsequently. The instructions to the United Nations Commission for India and Pakistan also included charges to use good offices and mediation. The two United Nations representatives for India and Pakistan acted primarily as mediators. The Security Council twice dispatched its current President to the subcontinent as mediator and authorized the Secretary-General to use his personal influence in bringing the 1965 war to a halt. The Council, on one occasion, and its President, on another, suggested the submission of certain issues to arbitration, but the parties to the dispute would not agree to the use of this procedure. The Soviet Union also exercised good offices and mediation in bringing about the 1966 Tashkent agreement. In spite of flexibility and persistence, the Kashmir issue has remained impervious to resolution. However, for long periods since 1949 fighting has been limited to minor incidents along the cease-fire line rather than breaking out into major military actions.

Race Conflict in South Africa

One of the bitterest, most persistent, and least soluble problems confronting the United Nations has been the question of the racial policies of the South African government. In one form or another the problem has been debated since 1946. The first complaint was made by India concerning South African policies toward the Indian minority in South Africa. In 1952 a second issue — that of apartheid, or separation of the races — was added to the agenda of the General Assembly. After 1962 these separate items were combined into a single question of apartheid in all its aspects. All complaints during the 1940s and 1950s were made to the General Assembly, but beginning in 1960, with prodding from new members (especially those in the African group), the Security Council periodically joined the General Assembly in debating the issue and passing resolutions. If strong measures are ever to be applied against South Africa, Council action is preferable to Assembly decision because the Charter is more explicit in granting the power to impose sanctions to the Council than to the Assembly. Furthermore, sanctions imposed by the Council are theoretically binding on all members, and the cooperation of the permanent members is necessary to make sanctions effective.

The race issue in South Africa raises some fundamental questions. Are its racial policies, as South Africa claims, purely a domestic question and, therefore, immune under Article 2 of the Charter from United Nations jurisdiction? Or can the United Nations bring action either on the grounds that South Africa has flagrantly violated its human-rights obligations under the Charter, or on the grounds that South African race policies so affect and offend other states as to constitute a threat to international peace and security? In an interdependent world, where can the line be drawn between sovereign rights and collective prerogative; between domestic matters and international concerns? The position of the parties is irreconcilable, yet each is based on fundamental Charter principles.

Political power in South Africa is concentrated in the one-fifth of the population who are white. Those who are black, Asian, or of mixed blood are denied access to the economic and social resources by which they may escape from poverty and lack of opportunity. The policies of apartheid require the complete separation of nonwhites from whites in the society except for strictly regulated conditions under which nonwhite labor may be used in the nation's economic enterprises. Recent policies have set aside 13 percent of the land as African Reserves, or Bantustans, where the blacks may live, but economic necessity and the dearth of resources in the reserves result in more than half the blacks living outside the reserves.

The whites enjoy a high standard of living, but the apartheid policies perpetuate the poverty of the nonwhites. In 1976 South Africa granted independence to Transkei, one of the former Reserves, but most nations, at the urging of the Organization of African Unity and the United Nations General Assembly, have refused to recognize the transfer of sovereignty, labeling it a device for denying South African citizenship to nearly two million blacks.

The Asians in South Africa, as well as the blacks, have been the objects of government discrimination. In a total population of more than 20 million, Asians number about 600,000. India made the first complaint to the General Assembly in 1946 and was joined by Pakistan in 1947 in claiming discrimination against the Asian minority in violation of treaties between the countries and of Charter obligations. A series of General Assembly resolutions requesting South African negotiations with India and with Pakistan were ignored by South Africa, and various individuals and commissions authorized by the Assembly to assist in arranging negotiations were rebuffed by South African refusal to cooperate.

On the broad aspects of apartheid, the General Assembly has annually adopted sweeping resolutions requesting (1) South Africa to modify its policies, (2) member states to take retaliatory action against South Africa, (3) special committees to study the situation and recommend action, (4) the Security Council to use economic sanctions or to consider the expulsion of South Africa from the United Nations, and (5) the specialized agencies to take action by all appropriate means to apply pressure on the South African government to modify its policies. An additional resolution has called for the dissemination of information concerning the apartheid policies. These resolutions have made little apparent impact on South African leaders; new legislative measures have been enacted from time to time to enforce apartheid policies even more strictly. In protest over the General Assembly's invasion of what South Africa claims to be a matter of domestic jurisdiction, that government for three years, beginning in 1955, refused to participate in General Assembly sessions and has subsequently refused to attend any committee meetings dealing with the apartheid issue. In a reverse move, the Assembly in 1970, for the first time, questioned the legitimacy of the credentials of the South African delegation to the General Assembly, but on technical grounds the delegates were allowed to participate in spite of this manifestation of disapproval. However, on November 12, 1974, the General Assembly upheld a ruling by its President excluding South Africa from participation in the remainder of its twenty-ninth session.

The Security Council first became involved in the apartheid issue in 1960 after the Sharpeville incident in which nearly 250 black demonstrators against South Africa's "pass laws" were killed or wounded. The passbooks serve as identification and as work and travel permits for blacks. The Security Council, on April 1, 1960, adopted a resolution stating that a continuation of South Africa's racial policies might endanger international peace and security. In 1962 the General Assembly requested member states to (1) break off diplomatic relations with South Africa, (2) close their ports to South African vessels, (3) forbid their ships to enter South African ports, (4) prohibit all imports from or exports to South Africa, especially sales of arms or ammunition to that country, and (5) refuse landing rights to all South African aircraft. Some members of the Security Council have not been willing to impose such sweeping sanctions, but in 1963 the Council called on all states to embargo the sale of arms, ammunition, and military vehicles to South Africa, including equipment or materials for arms manufacture in South Africa.

According to a report of the Special Committee on Apartheid submitted to the Security Council in 1970, the arms embargo was not effective. Interpretations, loopholes, and violations resulted in a constant strengthening of South Africa's military capabilities. The extension of apartheid to Namibia (South West Africa) and threats to strengthen South Africa's entente with Portugal and Rhodesia justified strong Security Council sanctions and the closing of all embargo loopholes. France was accused of being the main supplier of military goods; France defended its position on the grounds that it sold to South Africa arms only for external defense and not for internal repression. The African nations' response to this argument was that no external threat to South Africa exists.

The Security Council in July, 1970, adopted another resolution which carefully avoided action against South Africa under Chapter VII of the Charter, but which condemned arms-embargo violations and called for the embargo's full implementation. Significantly, France, the United Kingdom, and the United States abstained on the resolution. The United Kingdom and the United States claimed prior treaty commitments for certain types of sales of defense materials to South Africa. All three states declared that some of the provisions of the resolution were too sweeping. On December 8, 1970, the same three states, joined by South Africa, Portugal, and Australia, voted against a General Assembly resolution, favored by ninety-one states that included provisions for (1) deploring the continued cooperation of certain states and economic interests with South Africa in military, economic, and political fields; (2) urging the Security Council to take effective measures against South Africa including measures under Chapter VII of the Charter; and (3) urging all states to terminate diplomatic, military, economic, and technical relations with South Africa. Finally, in 1977 the Security Council approved a mandatory arms embargo against South Africa.

Pressure on South Africa has been exerted through several of the United Nations specialized agencies, through the Organization of African Unity (OAU), and through the Conference of Non-Aligned Nations. South Africa has withdrawn from some of the specialized agencies including UNESCO, the Food and Agriculture Organization, and the International Labor Organization. It is no longer a member of the Economic Commission for Africa, a regional commission under the United Nations Economic and Social Council. The OAU has acted as a principal generating force behind United Nations actions against South Africa. However, South African overtures for dialogue with other African leaders have broken the united front of OAU opposition, as several black African heads of state have favored such dialogue.

Most analysts agree that total economic and political sanctions against South Africa would be the most effective pressure that could be applied toward forcing a major policy change. The principal trading partners of South Africa — the United Kingdom, the United States, France, and West Germany — are unwilling to support universal economic sanctions, and their cooperation is essential for effective Security Council action. South Africa's arms strength continues to increase, not only through imports but also by licenses for internal production of military equipment and supplies. The Special Committee on Apartheid reports that the volume of trade has recently increased between South Africa and its major trading partners and that the flow of investment from the United Kingdom and the United States continues at a substantial level.

In addition to all of the previously mentioned efforts to exert pressure on South Africa, two other United Nations activities should be noted. In 1961 the Secretary-General visited South Africa for conversations concerning the apartheid policies. Although the conversations were cordial, no changes in policy occurred and the declared intention by both parties to continue the consultations was never implemented. The other activity involves the creation of two trust funds, a United Nations Trust Fund for South Africa and a United Nations Educational and Training Program for South Africans. These funds are intended to provide legal assistance, relief for dependents and refugees, and education for prisoners, dependents, and refugees or persons arrested or displaced because of the apartheid measures of

South Africa. The funds are modest in relation to need, but the Scandanavian countries have been especially generous in their financial support.

The impasse over the apartheid policies of the South African government continues. A solution by military sanctions seems remote. Total economic sanctions could be effective, but support is lacking. Even the arms embargo has been partial and inadequate. Gradual changes of policies could eventually result from internal pressures. The white population is far from unanimous in its support of apartheid, and the economy, though prosperous, suffers from inefficient use of blacks. In the meantime, world pressures will continue through many channels, particularly the United Nations, to try eventually to restore human rights to the South African majority.

Situation in the Dominican Republic

From 1961 to 1966 the political situation in the Dominican Republic was very unstable. General Trujillo Molina ruled the republic as a dictator from 1930 until his assassination in 1961. After a transition period Juan Bosch was elected president but served only nine months before being overthrown by a military coup. In April, 1965, a rebel group under Colonel Caamano Deno temporarily seized power only to be ousted four days later by a junta under General Wessin y Wessin, which in turn was replaced after nine days by a regime headed by General Imbert Barreras. The city of Santo Domingo was the main battleground in a civil war between the right-wing forces of General Imbert and the left-wing forces of Colonel Caamano.

On the same day that General Wessin y Wessin attained temporary power, President Johnson ordered United States marines into Santo Domingo. The first reason given for intervention was to protect endangered American lives, but official statements soon added the motive of preventing a Communist government from gaining control in the Dominican Republic. The United States response to the situation was massive; within a few days a force of 24,000 men was sent to the island. This contingent was reduced when, under United States pressure, the Organization of American States (OAS) with several members dissenting, authorized the dispatching to Santo Domingo of an Inter-American Peace Force. However, troops from five other countries made up only approximately one-sixth of this peace force, the balance being United States troops already in the republic.

On April 29, 1965, the United States government informed the

United Nations Security Council through the Secretary-General that on the previous day United States forces had been sent to the Dominican Republic to protect American citizens and that the OAS had been asked to consider the situation. On May 1 the Soviet Union requested an urgent meeting of the Security Council to consider the question of United States armed interference in the internal affairs of the Dominican Republic. The first series of Security Council meetings was held between May 3 and May 25.

The OAS became involved in the Dominican situation earlier than the United Nations, engaged in a wider range of activities, and provided the main channels by which a political settlement was finally achieved. In addition to the authorization of the Inter-American Peace Force mentioned above, the foreign ministers of the OAS, two days before the first Security Council debates, established and sent to Santo Domingo a commission composed of representatives of Argentina, Brazil, Colombia, Guatemala, and Panama. This commission was charged with responsibilities for facilitating the restoration of peace, seeking a cease-fire, and evacuating endangered persons. Less than three weeks later, after the arrival in Santo Domingo of a United Nations representative and a small United Nations military observer corps, the OAS commission issued a report in which the majority of the commission stated that United Nations intervention in the Dominican situation had obstructed their efforts, and they asked to be relieved of their responsibilities. The OAS foreign ministers on May 20 transferred the responsibilities of the commission to the Secretary-General of the OAS, who was already in the Dominican Republic, and requested that he coordinate his efforts with those of the United Nations representative.

On June 2 the OAS notified the Security Council of the appointment of an ad hoc committee, composed of representatives of Brazil, El Salvador, and the United States, to offer good offices for restoring normal conditions in the Dominican Republic. The Inter-American Commission on Human Rights, at the request of both Dominican contending groups, began activities in the republic in early June and continued its investigations and reports for several months. Its work was supported by the Commission of Criminologists, which investigated certain atrocity charges. The ad hoc committee was finally successful in bringing about negotiations between the parties, leading to the establishment of a provisional government on September 3 under Hector Garcia-Godow and to the election on June 1, 1966, of Joaquin Balaguer as president. The last contingents of the Inter-American Peace Force left the Republic on September 20, 1966.

The Dominican question was considered by the Security Council in twenty-eight meetings in May, June, and July, 1965. The clash of national interests and opinions was apparent throughout the debates and precluded agreement on strong measures for an effective United Nations role in restoring peace in the Dominican Republic. The representatives of the Soviet Union, France, Jordan, and Uruguay were highly critical of both United States intervention in the republic and the primary role of the OAS as the peacekeeping agency. Uruguay, which had been one of five OAS members to oppose the creation of the Inter-American Peace Force, accused the United States of violating the principles of the United Nations Charter and Articles 15 and 17 of the Charter of the OAS, which specifically prohibit intervention "directly or indirectly, for any reason whatever, in the internal or external affairs of any other State" or military occupation of the territory of any state. The United States was charged with utilizing the OAS for its own ends and with deploying its military forces in such a way as to bring advantage to the right-wing army under General Imbert.

Although several other members of the Security Council supported the United States contentions that the OAS was the most proficient instrument for restoring peace in the Dominican Republic and that the provisions of the United Nations Charter with regard to the role of regional organizations were being adhered to, no agreement was possible for authorizing the OAS to act as the agent of the United Nations in the situation. Because of the split among the members a series of proposed resolutions failed to gain sufficient support for adoption. The only significant resolution was adopted on May 14 when, by unanimous vote, the Security Council approved a call for a strict cease-fire and authorized the Secretary-General to send a representative to the Dominican Republic to report on the situation. A small group of military observers under General Rikhye was dispatched to the republic on May 15, and two days later Jose Antonio Mayobre, executive secretary of the Economic Commission for Latin America, who had been designated as the Secretary-General's representative, arrived in Santo Domingo.

From May, 1965, until the installation of the new government in the Dominican Republic in the summer of 1966, the work of Mayobre and his staff represented the main contribution of the United Nations to restoring stable conditions there. He consulted with the leaders of the contending factions and with agents of the OAS and others in the Dominican Republic and, through the Secretary-General, kept the Security Council fully informed of the day-to-day situation and new developments in the republic. After June 18, 1965, in spite of sporadic incidents, the cease-fire remained generally effective. Although Mayobre and the Secretary-General continued to report to the Security Council, the Council held no meetings on the Dominican question after July 26, 1965.

The Dominican situation demonstrates the impotency of the United Nations in coercing a major power. Although, by any reasonable interpretation, the United States was guilty of violating Articles 15 and 17 of the OAS Charter and the principles of territorial integrity and political independence guaranteed in the United Nations Charter, it was able to gain the acquiescence of a majority of OAS members for a set of policies substantially supporting its position and actions. Although the United States scrupulously complied with the provisions of Article 54 of the United Nations Charter to keep the Security Council informed of its own and OAS actions, the equally clear mandate of Article 53 that "no enforcement action shall be taken under regional arrangements or by regional agencies without the authorization of the Security Council" was violated. Proposals by the United States for Security Council approval of OAS actions were unacceptable to other Council members. The United States overreacted both to the threat to American lives and to the possibility of a Communist takeover in the Dominican Republic, and lost credibility and prestige in pressuring OAS members for support.

The United Nations and the OAS found themselves as uncomfortable partners in the Dominican situation. The United Nations representative acted mainly as observer and reporter to furnish objective assessments of the situation and the sources of fault in each major incident. The OAS ad hoc committee was an important force in bringing the opposing factions together to work out a permanent settlement. The United States military forces were not used impartially but, at times, acted as a buffer between opposing factions.

No one can accurately predict what internal political developments would have transpired if the Dominican crisis had been treated strictly as a domestic question. It may, however, be asserted that the United Nations, the OAS, and the United States all lost prestige as a result of the episode.

CHANGING ROLES
OF UNITED NATIONS ORGANS

There is little question that the General Assembly has played a larger role in the processes of peaceful settlement of disputes than would have been predicted in 1945. The big powers, who dominated the determination of the basic formulas for the new organization in

Dumbarton Oaks and San Francisco, tried to establish the preeminent position of the Security Council in handling disputes. They looked upon the Security Council as an organ designed to perform this one, paramount function. They attempted to secure the superior position of the Council over the Assembly by conferring upon the Council "primary responsibility for the maintenance of international peace and security," by making Council decisions legally binding on all members, and by prohibiting the General Assembly from making recommendations on any dispute or situation while the matter is under Security Council consideration. By a number of devices the General Assembly has extended its involvement into this Security Council domain. These devices include generous interpretations of Assembly powers and functions as stated in the Charter and the adoption of special expedients such as an Interim Committee and the Uniting for Peace Resolution. The Uniting for Peace Resolution has served as a basis for calling five *emergency* special sessions of the General Assembly, each of which dealt with a dispute that the Security Council was unable to resolve. In addition, five of the ten General Assembly special sessions called under the regular Charter provisions for such sessions were also concerned with disputes or situations that could possibly threaten international peace and security.

An examination of the table of disputes and a review of the case studies in the preceding section of this chapter can serve as evidence of the degree of General Assembly involvement in the processes of pacific settlement of disputes. Nearly 25 percent of all disputes submitted to the United Nations have been dealt with solely by the General Assembly. Another 21 percent have been considered by both the Security Council and the General Assembly. Thus, the General Assembly has been involved in nearly half of the disputes investigated by the United Nations. Among the six case studies presented in this chapter, the General Assembly exclusively handled the disposition of the Italian colonies and shared with the Security Council the responsibilities for dealing with two other problems — the Indonesian question and race conflict in South Africa.

At the same time, the General Assembly has not superseded the Security Council as the primary agency for considering disputes. More than half of all disputes on the agendas of the United Nations organs have been handled exclusively by the Security Council. When to this list is added the group of cases in which both the Security Council and General Assembly have been involved, the result is that the Security Council has exercised total or shared responsibility for more than 75 percent of all disputes considered.

Predictions in the 1950s that the General Assembly might become the predominant agency for dispute settlement have been proven wrong. In the period when the Cold War was most intense, when the Security Council was most plagued by vetoes and stalemates, and when the General Assembly had lost any inhibitions about encroaching upon Security Council prerogatives and had equipped itself to hold emergency sessions on twenty-four-hour notice, there was some basis for predicting the atrophy of the Security Council. When, in 1959, the Council held but five meetings in twelve months, the trend seemed clear to some persons. Since 1960 the activity of the Security Council in disputes has again accelerated as states have submitted a majority of their complaints first or exclusively to the Council. In the 1970s, 90 percent of all disputes were referred to the Security Council.

The reasons for the revival of Security Council activity are many. The Council has always been better equipped than the Assembly to handle disputes, by virtue of size, organization, availability, locus of world power, and authority granted by the Charter. The big powers share a common interest in focusing activity in an organ that is more subject than the Assembly to their control and in which the veto can serve as the ultimate protection of national interests. The resulting pattern since 1960 has been a decrease in the number of vetoes, an increase in the use of abstentions, and an increase in consultation among Council members in order to arrive at compromises in the terms of resolutions so that a favorable vote may be achieved. The announcement of a consensus without formal vote, as practiced in 1967 in the Middle East crisis and on several occasions since, is one more device for avoiding embarrassment to the members through positions taken in public debate.

A tacit division of labor exists between the Security Council and the General Assembly with regard to consideration of disputes. New disputes, especially of a crisis nature, are generally referred to the Security Council. If a dispute is unresolved and becomes a perennial problem, the General Assembly frequently becomes involved. Exceptions occur, but, since 1960, examples of cases submitted solely to the General Assembly are scarce. In the period covered by the 1970–71 Annual Report of the Secretary-General, only one new dispute was reported, a complaint by Guinea, and this was submitted to the Security Council. The General Assembly during that year dealt with aspects of nine disputes, all of which were persistent or long-term and six of which had previously been considered by both the Council and the Assembly. During the same twelve-month period the Security Council, in addition to hearing the new Guinea complaint, considered aspects of five other recurrent disputes all of which had received previous attention by both the Assembly and the Council. Even regarding the persistent questions that claim the prolonged attention of both organs, some specialization occurs. Within the broad dimensions of a complex situation, new outbreaks or crises demanding immediate attention will generally be referred to the Security Council, whereas the General Assembly will consider those aspects that allow prolonged study and deliberation.

Since 1955 the broadest category of disputes with which the General Assembly has been concerned is that of decolonization. An examination of the list of disputes on the Assembly agenda shows that in recent years over half of all disputes are related to the struggle of newly emerging states for independence and self-determination.

The General Assembly stands ready to deal both with emergencies and the less-urgent aspects of disputes when the Security Council is deadlocked. In the series of Middle East crises since 1947, the responsibility has been frequently shifted back and forth between the two bodies. The availability of the Assembly may stimulate the permanent members of the Security Council to seek accommodation rather than stalemate in order to preserve the prerogatives of that organ in which they enjoy a privileged position.

The enhanced role of the Secretary-General in dispute settlement has been noted at some points in this chapter and will be reinforced in subsequent chapters, but this growing importance should be emphasized in discussing the changing roles of United Nations organs. The case studies in this chapter demonstrate some of the multiple and invaluable functions performed by the Secretary-General in direct negotiation, appointment of representatives or mediators, and furnishing of full, prompt, and accurate information to the Council and the Assembly. In the following chapter his role in the recruitment, deployment, and direction of peacekeeping forces will be explained and illustrated. The Secretary-General and his staff must be not only efficient, but also patient, tactful, and impartial in dealing with disputing parties and with members of the Council or the Assembly. The Council or the Assembly may determine broad policy, but the responsibility for implementation falls on the Secretariat. In many cases the critical details of implementation demand a wide range of additional decisions and leave room for initiative by the Secretary-General and his assistants. The history of dispute settlement in the United Nations amply demonstrates that the Secretariat has played a much more important role in this area than did its predecessor in the League of Nations as well as a more crucial role than was indicated by the specific provisions of the United Nations Charter.

The Secretary-General has also prevented some disputes from

being submitted to the Council or the Assembly by arranging for settlement through his good offices when the disputing parties cooperated in such action. On two occasions in 1958-59 and in 1962-64 the Secretary-General, at the invitation of Cambodia and Thailand, sent his personal representative and a small staff to those countries to assist in settling mutual charges of acts of aggression and border disputes. The second mission was invited to stay for two years with all costs met equally by the two governments. The Secretary-General reported his actions to the Security Council, but no request was ever made for Security Council consideration of the issue. In 1969 the Secretary-General was requested to send a representative to Equatorial Guinea to assure the orderly withdrawal of Spanish military forces and to prevent hostile acts on both sides. Both parties were cooperative, and the representative reported satisfactory conditions in effecting the withdrawal. However, in this instance and again in regard to the appointment in 1970 of a representative to settle the future status of Bahrain, the Soviet representative protested that the Secretary-General was invading the prerogatives of the Security Council. The Secretary-General pointed out that the parties to the disputes sought his assistance for peaceful settlement prior to the necessity for submitting the dispute to the Security Council and that this procedure is in full compliance with the admonition of Article 33 of the charter: "The parties to any dispute . . . shall, first of all, seek a solution by . . . peaceful means of their own choice." Since the disputes between Cambodia and Thailand and between Equatorial Guinea and Spain were never submitted to the Security Council or the General Assembly, they are omitted from the table of cases in this chapter.

GENERAL APPRAISAL
AND FUTURE REQUIREMENTS

The record of the United Nations in the area of pacific settlement of disputes leaves much to be desired. Many controversies develop that are not submitted to the United Nations but are handled through other means. This reluctance to use United Nations channels may result as much from a desire by the parties to maintain their freedom of action as it does from a lack of confidence in United Nations processes. Patterns of national behavior stemming from deeply ingrained feelings of nationalism and sovereign rights stand as bulwarks against the use of international channels for conflict resolution. The forces of nationalism and sovereignty also prevented the establishment, in the first place, of an organization with independent sources of power sufficient to impose solutions upon reluctant minorities. The ability to resist international coercion is abundantly demonstrated by the substantial number of unresolved issues that remain on the agendas of United Nations organs for prolonged periods of time. Weak proposals for responding to threats of peace are also a negative element in the United Nations record and result from the absence of adequate means of enforcement and the necessity to compromise among competing national interests.

In the light of its inherent weaknesses, the record of the United Nations in conflict resolution is surprisingly encouraging. Of more than 130 disputes considered by the Council and the Assembly, not more than a dozen remain as persistent long-range problems defying final solution. Some have been resolved by action of the parties after United Nations debate, but in others the Security Council, the General Assembly, and the Secretariat have made positive contributions to the final settlement. This success has been due, in part, to the pragmatism and flexibility of the organs in not being unduly hampered by narrow interpretations of grants of authority and in seeking a variety of means for conflict resolution peculiarly adapted to the circumstances of each dispute. Every established device, plus a few innovations and variations on these devices, has been applied to the controversies considered by United Nations organs. Cease-fires and observer missions have been effective in many circumstances in lessening hostilities. The use of peacekeeping forces will be examined more fully in chapter 7. In prolonged disputes the influence of the United Nations has generally been exerted to prevent escalation or to stabilize the situation at a minimum level of conflict. The substantial number of disputes submitted to the United Nations reflects a need that is fulfilled by the existence of such an organization and a willingness on the part of some of the parties to rely on United Nations contributions to seeking solutions to the problems. Small states have been especially willing to request United Nations aid in conflict resolution.

Regional organizations have played a relatively modest role in dispute settlement. Since 1945 the OAS has assisted in settling several disputes not submitted to the United Nations but has not been utilized by the Security Council in the manner envisioned in Chapter VIII of the United Nations Charter. Other regional organizations have not achieved notable success in dispute settlement. In the Dominican affair cooperation between the United Nations representatives and those of the OAS was sometimes grudging and uncomfortable and at other times nonexistent. The dominant influence of a big power may either neutralize a regional organization's capacity for impartial conciliation in a dispute or serve as a lever for settlement if the major power's chief interest is in peace and stability between disputants. Regional organizations perform many useful functions, but their greatest contribution has not been in conflict resolution.

While the availability and the flexibility of United Nations agencies have made major contributions to the positive accomplishments of the organization in dispute settlement or control, the attitudes and the policies of the members is the most critical factor. In a world of sovereign states, which are the final repositories of power, the behavior of those states will determine the spread or containment of conflict. States may defy international pressures, as in the case of South Africa, or they may be willing to seek accommodation through negotiation or the United Nations, or they may work for the strengthening of international means for assuring world order. As contacts multiply among nations, the number of conflicts will also increase. The avoidance of nuclear war should serve as a powerful incentive toward peace.

As increasing numbers of thoughtful leaders weigh the odds between eventual catastrophe and survival under the present international system, they may devote some of their energies toward the strengthening of present means or the creation of new means for the orderly and just settlement of disputes. The provision of efficient channels of dispute settlement lies at the heart of any adequate system of organizing a society. The stakes in developing such a system at the international level are increasing rapidly. In tomorrow's world the necessity for humankind to provide satisfactory means for conflict resolution on a global scale is greater than was the imperative for similar national institutions at the time of gestation and birth of each state. The necessity is greater because it is *vital* — the continuation of life is basic to all other human values.

7

꧁

Collective Security
and
Its Alternatives-
Theory and Practice

There are at least six methods of attempting to settle international disputes. They are (1) no action taken by the disputing parties, allowing the dispute to remain unsettled over a period of time; (2) settlement through the parties' own initiative, using negotiation or other peaceful means of their choice; (3) intervention by an international agency to facilitate peaceful settlement; (4) collective action by an international agency to restore order after international peace has been breached or threatened; (5) coercive self-help, including recourse to war between the parties; and (6) intervention by other states to promote or secure their own interests. A principal reason for founding the League of Nations and the United Nations was to eliminate, as far as possible, the recourse to war. Members of both these organizations also were encouraged to seek by themselves peaceful settlement of disputes through other channels. Chapter 6 investigated the role of international organizations in peaceful settlement. This chapter will explore their role in more serious situations, in which disputes have progressed to actual or imminent hostilities. Implicit here is the question of what can or should an international organization do when peaceful settlement has failed or is avoided?

THE NATURE OF COLLECTIVE SECURITY

The theory of collective security is not unique to the twentieth century. Some scholars credit certain aspects of the Amphictyonic Council of ancient Greece and of the Truce of God of the Middle Ages as limited collective-security systems. Several philosophers discussed in chapter 1 advocated means of controlling conflict that might reasonably be labeled collective-security measures. Nevertheless, the first attempt to adapt the vague concepts of collective security to a worldwide system for preventing war was the establishment of the League of Nations in 1919.

The proponents of collective security viewed it as a method of controlling war in a world of sovereign states. Experience had brought disillusionment with the capability of a balance-of-power system to maintain peace. The world was not ready to surrender enough national sovereignty to make possible the establishment of a world government, even one with limited powers. The idea of collective security seemed to provide the bridge between the crumbling world of past centuries and the kind of ideal world yet to be created.

The theory of collective security rests on the assumption that all nations share a primary interest in maintaining peace. In order for collective security to operate, peace must be viewed as indivisible, and threats to peace anywhere must be treated as the concern of all members of the international system. Furthermore, all members must agree in advance to react promptly and effectively against threats to peace and must be organized in such a way as to provide the procedures for collective response to such threats. The aggressor nation will be faced with such overwhelming opposition from all other members of the system that peace will be promptly restored. In fact, the promise of preponderant opposition will usually dissuade incipient aggressors from their inclinations toward breaches of international peace.

Although collective-security theory, in the abstract, sounds plausible, several basic conditions are required for its effective application. The first is a commitment on the part of all members of the international system to peace as a paramount goal requiring the subordination of other goals of foreign policy. If, in practice, collective security is to succeed, each state must commit itself to act in concert with other states as a party interested more in peace restoration than in other national interests or in relationships with the state accused of threatening international peace. A second condition is the ability of the members of a system not only to reach initial consensus for establishing the system, but also to find a consensus in each situation that a threat to peace or a breach of peace does or does not exist. Furthermore, their consensus must extend to the identification of the aggressor state or states against whom collective action is required. Once an aggressor is identified, a collective determination must be made of an appropriate response to apply prompt and effective sanctions against the aggressor for the purpose of stopping the aggressive acts. Although a military response may be decided upon, the theory calls for police action to restore peace, not war against an enemy.

A collective-security system will work best if power is widely dispersed. Since the theory requires the possible application of preponderant force against an aggressor, the presence of a very powerful state capable of defying the collectivity reduces the odds for effective action against any and all aggressors.

The ideal collective-security system requires a membership approaching universality. Several reasons for this requirement are obvious. The consensus on peace as a primary goal is reduced to the degree that states exist outside the system. Challenges to the system are less likely from parties committed to all the conditions underlying the system. Impartial decisions can be better guaranteed if all parties can be heard and all relevant evidence examined. Limited membership also limits the amount of resources available for sanctions against an aggressor and increases the liability of each member for contributions to an effective response. In addition, in an organization of limited membership, the capability of one state to defy the collectivity is enhanced. A powerful state may be immune from the threat of sanctions in a relatively small organization but may respond to pressure when faced with the possibility of preponderant force against it.

Many scholars accept certain regional organizations as collective-security organizations in some of their functions. In order to qualify as collective-security organizations, they must incorporate the conditions of consensus and commitment to peace and collective response that are fundamental to collective-security theory. They must include in their membership most of the states in their region. The collective-security aspects of their terms of agreement are directed against threats from within the region rather than from outside the region. However, the arguments presented above for universality in a collective-security arrangement indicate the possible advantages of a worldwide system.

The term "collective security" has been so distorted from its classical meaning as to jeopardize its precision as a theory of international relations. On occasion it is loosely applied to any arrangement for collective defense against potential enemies outside as well as inside the membership of the collectivity. Such a perversion of meaning disregards some of the essential conditions of collective-security theory and fails to distinguish collective security from the alliance system, which it was designed to replace.

Collective security should be clearly differentiated from collective defense. Collective-defense arrangements, such as NATO, involve alliances for mutual protection against outside attack. The appropriate response to such an attack is war against an enemy, not the restoration of peace through appropriate measured responses. Several collective-defense arrangements will be examined in chapter 14.

Collective security may be internally consistent as a theory for world order but impractical and faulty in its acceptance and application by sovereign states bent on protecting national interests and suspicious of the motives of other states. In practice, the consensus on peace as a primary goal, which is the basis for collective security, may conflict with other national interests demanding equal or greater priority. Complex forces influence each state in a given situation to diminish that state's commitment to the impartial application of sanctions against an aggressor nation.

The theory of collective security assumes that a situation can be agreed upon demanding collective action and that an aggressor can be identified against whom that action should be directed. In a large number of cases, these basic assumptions prove to be incorrect. Evidence is seldom clear either that a threat to peace or a breach of peace has occurred or that a particular state has committed the aggressive act. Each state can usually produce evidence that it is the victim of aggression rather than the aggressor. A clear-cut and comprehensive definition of aggression has proven to be difficult to develop. This difficulty leaves the determination of aggression in each situation to the subjective and perhaps biased collective judgment of the members of the organization. The determination that a threat to peace or a breach of peace has occurred and demands international action is equally complex and difficult. At what point does a threat assume proportions or characteristics that justify international intervention? Where can a line be drawn or a set of rules established to distinguish between domestic matters and matters of international concern? In answering such questions the subjective judgment of the members of the collective-security organization must again be substituted for objective standards. Such judgments are influenced not only by national interpretation of conflicting evidence and by economic and political ties to the disputing parties, but also by the reluctance of a state to participate in a collective action if there is little promise of advantage to that state from such participation.

Collective security demands a singleness of purpose and devotion to the principle of peace maintenance that states show little evidence of accepting today. Even if the other difficulties of applying collective-security principles could be overcome, the selfish and competitive aspect of international relations would present a major obstacle to success. States are not equally willing and able to participate in collective action against aggression anywhere in the world. National goals, values and interests, and international commitments compete with the demands of collective security for action against aggression. National security takes precedence over collective security. Cultural and traditional ties, trade and investment, military alliances and ideology are balanced against a general commitment to world peace. Costs and convenience of collective action also enter the calculus of national decisions.

If a common commitment to maintaining peace by prompt, effective, collective action could be guaranteed, there is little doubt that aggressive action by a single state could be checked and, in most cases, deterred. If power is sufficiently dispersed, the threat of massive sanctions would be effective against both large and small states. No state could hope to defy the united will and effort of all other states acting in concert. Faced with such odds, the would-be aggressor, under rational leadership, would avoid the penalties resulting from being subjected to sanctions.

Although certain parts of the theory of collective security are valid, the faults inherent both in some of its basic assumptions and in the reluctance of states to adopt and apply all its principles impair its effectiveness as a keystone for present-day international organization. As some scholars have pointed out, if the world situation were conducive to the success of a system of collective security, we would also be ready for world government.[1] National leaders are not yet prepared to put a common human interest ahead of a host of national interests.

THE LEAGUE OF NATIONS AND COLLECTIVE SECURITY

Woodrow Wilson was firmly committed to the proposition that collective security would stop or forestall wars, and he guided the ef-

---

[1] See, e.g., Inis L. Claude, Jr., *Swords into Plowshares: The Problems and Progress of International Organization*, 4th ed. (New York: Random House, 1971), p. 256.

forts to incorporate a collective-security formula into the League of Nations Covenant. Article 10 of the Covenant stated that:

> The members of the League undertake to respect and preserve as against external aggression the territorial integrity and existing political independence of all Members of the League.

The principle of common concern was added to the formula in Article 11 through the declaration that:

> Any war or threat of war, whether immediately affecting any of the Members of the League or not, is hereby declared a matter of concern to the whole League, and the League shall take any action that may be deemed wise and effectual to safeguard the peace of nations.

In order to provide "teeth" to enforce the general principles of collective security, Article 16 provided for sanctions.

> Should any Member of the League resort to war in disregard of its covenants under Articles 12, 13, or 15 [which outlined procedures for peaceful settlement of disputes], it shall *ipso facto* be deemed to have committed an act of war against all other Members of the League, which hereby undertake immediately to subject it to the severance of all trade or financial relations, the prohibition of all intercourse between their nationals and the nationals of the covenant-breaking State, and the prevention of all financial, commercial or personal intercourse between the nationals of the covenant-breaking State and the nationals of any other state, whether a Member of the League or not.

Note that the economic sanctions of the Covenant were intended to be *total* and *automatic*. If military sanctions were required, a further provision of Article 16 obligated the Council to make recommendations to the members concerning their contributions to such forces. Article 17 provided that collective actions could also be taken against nonmembers of the League.

The experience of the League reveals a reluctance by the members to adhere to the collective-security obligations of the Covenant. Instead of total and automatic application of economic sanctions, the obligations were treated as selective and voluntary for each member in each situation. In 1921 the Assembly adopted resolutions that declared that for each state the application of economic sanctions under Article 16 was optional, not mandatory. Loopholes were discovered in the Covenant formula for collective security and taken advantage of to avoid inconvenient enforcement obligations.

League members failed every test in the 1930s to apply effective sanctions against aggressor nations. In 1931 the Japanese invaded Manchuria, and the League response was a belated investigation after Japanese occupation was completed. The resulting report suggested no more effective measures than nonrecognition of the territorial changes that had occurred.

In 1935-36 economic sanctions were actually imposed against Italy after its attack on Ethiopia. Fifty League members agreed to an embargo on arms and on financial aid to Italy and a ban on imports from Italy. Although these measures seriously affected the Italian economy, they did not encompass the most critical sanctions of an embargo on oil, or a blockade of Italian ports, or a denial of access to the sea routes, especially the Suez Canal through which Italy was able to move and supply its invasion forces. The United States continued to trade with Italy except for arms. The League discontinued its economic sanctions in the summer of 1936 at a time when Italy's economic health was at a critical stage. The opportunity to prove the effectiveness of economic sanctions was missed because of inadequate measures applied for too short a time span. Behind the failure of methods was a failure of national will on the part of League members and nonmembers.

No sanctions were imposed on Germany in Hitler's series of aggressive acts. In 1936 German forces reoccupied the Rhineland in violation of both the Treaty of Versailles and the Locarno Pact. In 1938 Germany further expanded its territory at the expense of Austria and Czechoslovakia. Germany had withdrawn from League membership, and the League seemed paralyzed in the face of spreading aggression.

In 1937 Japan began its further conquest of Chinese territory. Both the League Council and the Assembly reacted to condemn the Japanese action, and the Council invoked Article 16 of the Covenant, but no widespread sanctions were imposed.

In December, 1939, the League Council made one last futile gesture in the direction of sanctions by expelling the Soviet Union from the League. The expulsion was prompted by the Soviet invasion of Finland and was ironic for several reasons. This was the only expulsion of a member in the history of the League in spite of similar patterns of aggression by other states. The League action to expel the Soviet Union came after the beginning of World War II and after the League had been abandoned by numerous states, leaving only a hollow shell in which all confidence had been lost. The condemnation of the Soviet Union had no effect on the course of events, whereas if strong measures had been adopted and enforced in earlier cases of aggression, the chances for success would have been somewhat greater. All opportunities to test the validity of League sanctions as a means to stop aggression had been lost.

CHARTER PROVISIONS AND REALITIES

The architects of the United Nations Charter attempted to distinguish clearly between the functions of peaceful settlement of disputes and of collective security by placing each in a separate chapter of the Charter. Chapter VI of the Charter is entitled "Pacific Settlement of Disputes"; Chapter VII is labeled "Action with Respect to Threats to the Peace, Breaches of the Peace, and Acts of Aggression." All specific references to sanctions are contained in Chapter VII, but the Security Council has maintained flexibility and has avoided legal restraints by dealing with most situations without reference to any particular Charter provision. In this way the distinction between peaceful settlement and collective action has become blurred and a new process not specifically described in the Charter has evolved in United Nations practice. This process is referred to as peacekeeping and will be further explored in subsequent sections of this chapter.

The Charter provisions for sanctions may be viewed in some respects as improvements over and in other respects as retrogressions from the corresponding Covenant terms. No automatic sanctions are provided for in the Charter, but it has been noted in the previous section that declarations by League members nullified the compulsory nature of League economic sanctions. United Nations members are legally obligated under Article 25 of the Charter to accept and carry out Security Council decisions under any section of the Charter. If the Security Council invokes Article 39, it then shall determine that a threat to the peace, breach of the peace, or act of aggression exists and shall decide on a course of action to maintain or restore peace. Article 40 allows the Security Council to take interim or provisional measures. Article 41 outlines the provisions for applying economic, communicatory, and diplomatic sanctions. Article 42 authorizes the Security Council to call for military sanctions. Other articles in Chapter VII forsee supplementary treaty agreements to provide, for immediate use at the call of the Security Council, national military contingents for United Nations enforcement action; specify the functions of a Military Staff Committee to assist the Security Council; and guarantee the right of individual or collective self-defense until the Security Council has acted. In Chapter VII of the Charter the possible role of the General Assembly is not mentioned, showing the original intention to make the invoking of sanctions the exclusive prerogative of the Security Council.

All of the major shortcomings of collective-security theory apply as much to the United Nations provisions for invoking sanctions as they did to the League provisions. Before sanctions can be applied there must be (1) an agreement that an aggression or threat to peace exists, (2) the identification of the guilty party, and (3) unanimity or acquiescence among all permanent members of the Security Council that action is warranted. States maintain all of the means to impose sanctions and are reluctant to take coercive action against allies, trading partners, or states with whom they share cultural or ideological affinities or friendly relations. Every state is not equally interested in maintaining peace or resisting violent change. Because of cleavages among the permanent members of the Security Council, a coincidence of interests, necessary for prompt and effective application of sanctions, infrequently occurs. National interests of the powerful states take precedence over international obligations to support the principle of the indivisibility of peace.

The "teeth" that were lacking in League enforcement were supposed to be furnished under the terms of Article 43 of the Charter. That article provides for prompt negotiation of agreements by which United Nations members will make available on the call of the Security Council "armed forces, assistance, and facilities" for use in applying military sanctions. Depending upon the terms of the subsequent agreements, either a standing international force or standby contingents of national forces subject to immediate Security Council call will be created. The Military Staff Committee, representing the chiefs of staff of the permanent members of the Security Council, is to advise the Council on the implementation of Article 43 and to direct any armed forces called into United Nations service. However, the members were able to agree on only two major principles: (1) that most forces should be furnished by the big powers, and (2) that any forces should remain under national jurisdiction until summoned for specific duty by the Security Council. On all other principles and details there was total stalemate. No agreements could be reached on the size of standby forces, the allocation of quotas to individual members, or the types of forces to be furnished by each state. Because of the suspicions and intransigence of the major powers, Article 43 has become dormant, and the anticipated international forces available for military action against aggressors have never materialized.

One of the major problems in applying collective-security theory is the identification of aggressors and acts of aggression. One possible approach is to develop a comprehensive definition of aggression that can act as a standard and be applied to each situation as it arises. The alternative approach is to determine for each situation, by vote of an authorized agency and on the basis of the total body of available evidence, whether a state is guilty of aggression. In the absence of objective standards such an approach is necessary, and, according to some authorities, is the preferred method of dealing with the problem of aggression. Those who oppose the adoption of a definition of aggression argue that a formula can never be comprehensive or will be too inflexible, and that the application of a formula cannot give proper weight to provocation and various forms of subversion and propaganda in a variety of complex situations.

United Nations efforts to define aggression were initiated in San Francisco in 1945. Subsequently, the question received study by the International Law Commission and then was assigned by the General Assembly to a series of special committees. Finally, in 1974, the last of these special committees agreed on a rather general definition limited to the use of armed force. This definition was approved by the General Assembly as a guide to the Security Council in determining the existence of acts of aggression. Whether the adoption of such legal criteria will actually influence political decisions of this nature is problematical.

Although the Security Council was intended as the exclusive agent to apply sanctions under Chapter VII of the Charter, the General Assembly has invaded this field and the closely related areas of dispute settlement and peacekeeping. The Security Council is frequently immobilized, by disagreement among its permanent members, in taking action in response to threats to or breaches of international peace. Only the accident of Soviet absence, in pique over the Chinese-representation issue, allowed the Security Council, in 1950, to authorize collective action in Korea. The return of the Soviet representative to the Council table on August 1, 1950, precluded any further agreement on the basic issues in Korea. At the initiative of the United States, the General Assembly proceeded at its next session to add specific means of dealing with breaches of the peace to its general grants of authority in the Charter, such as its power in Article 10 to "discuss any questions or any matters within the scope of the present Charter."

The specific instrument for enlarging the General Assembly's realm of concern and action is the Uniting for Peace Resolution adopted on November 3, 1950. The most important provision of the resolution is the agreement for calling an emergency special session of the General Assembly within twenty-four hours whenever the Security Council is deadlocked and "fails to exercise its primary responsibility for the maintenance of international peace and security in any case where there appears to be a threat to the peace, breach of the peace, or act of aggression." Emergency sessions of the

Assembly can be called by an nine (previously seven) members of the Security Council or by a majority of United Nations members. The resolution also requests member states to designate and train armed-forces units for United Nations service on the call of either the Security Council or the General Assembly. This provision is an attempt to plug the gap left by the nonimplementation of Article 43. To further assist the General Assembly in carrying out its expanded functions, the resolution established a Peace Observation Commission and a Collective Measures Committee, both of which lapsed into inactivity after performing brief useful functions in support of the general purposes of the Uniting for Peace Resolution.

The General Assembly has never called for collective military sanctions of the type envisaged in the Uniting for Peace Resolution, but it has been involved in many other actions in the field of peace and security. It has authorized peacekeeping forces in the Middle East and has branded the People's Republic of China as an aggressor in Korea. Five emergency special sessions of the Assembly have dealt with important aspects of disputes when the Security Council was deadlocked. The adoption of the Uniting for Peace Resolution clearly expanded the General Assembly's potential role to cover all the areas of competency in the area of collective security established for the Security Council in Article 39. The Assembly can now substantially accomplish by a two-thirds vote what the Council can achieve by unanimity of the permanent members and a total of nine affirmative votes. The one remaining difference is that the Assembly can only recommend action while Council decisions are supposedly binding on all members. However, in a world in which states are jealous of their freedom of action, this difference is more apparent than real.

The use of sanctions in the practice of the United Nations has been very limited and has been singularly ineffective in those few instances in which sanctions have been invoked. Most applications of sanctions have been made without specific reference to Chapter VII of the Charter, thus permitting each state legal freedom of action in deciding whether or not to comply. Article 42, which provides for military sanctions, has never been invoked, and in only two cases have economic sanctions under Article 41 been applied. In 1966 the Security Council applied partial economic sanctions against Southern Rhodesia, and in 1968 these were extended to comprehensive sanctions. Under the terms of Article 41, these sanctions were supposedly compulsory and were intended to bring the white-dominated regime of Ian Smith to its knees. However, the noncooperation of South Africa and Portugal greatly reduced the impact of the economic boycott, and the Smith regime survived. In 1977 the Security Council adopted a mandatory arms embargo against South Africa.

In a few cases the Security Council or the General Assembly has adopted a resolution calling for sanctions without designating the action as falling under Chapter VII of the Charter. Under these conditions states have treated compliance with the resolution as voluntary. In 1946 the General Assembly requested United Nations members to break diplomatic ties with the Franco government in Spain and recommended that Spain be barred from membership in the specialized agencies affiliated with the United Nations. The charge against the Franco regime was that it was illegally instituted with aid from the Axis powers. In 1950 these recommendations were rescinded by the General Assembly. In May, 1948, the Security Council, in a resolution calling for a cease-fire in Palestine, requested all governments "to refrain from importing or exporting war material into Palestine, Egypt, Iraq, Lebanon, Saudi Arabia, Syria, Transjordan, and Yemen during the cease-fire." In 1951 the General Assembly, after branding the People's Republic of China as an aggressor in Korea, asked for an embargo on strategic goods to China.

Sanctions have been requested by both the General Assembly and the Security Council against South Africa. The General Assembly recommendations, adopted in 1962, are more sweeping than those adopted the following year by the Security Council. The Assembly requested the breaking of diplomatic relations, an embargo on all trade with South Africa, and the closing of ports and airports to South African ships and aircraft. The Security Council asked all states to embargo arms, ammunition, military vehicles, and materials or equipment for arms manufacture. In 1977 these measures were made mandatory. As noted in the previous chapter, compliance with these resolutions has been incomplete and generally ineffective in drastically slowing South Africa's rate of economic growth or its military preparedness.

The total experience of the United Nations with regard to handling threats to peace, breaches of peace, and acts of aggression has been filled with disappointment and frustration. No permanent international military force has been formed, and the Military Staff Committee has become a body without substance. Compulsory economic sanctions have been applied only twice and have been breached without effective retaliation by the international community. Military sanctions, invoking Article 42 of the Charter, have never been utilized. The Korean action fell short, in significant ways, of fulfilling the requirements of a true application of collective-security principles. These shortcomings are explained in detail in the Korean case study included in a subsequent section of this chapter. The search for a definition of aggression has been full of pitfalls. Cleavages among the permanent members of the Security Council have frustrated effective collective action. The attempts by the General Assembly to fill the breach in the collective-security system have encountered noncooperation by enough states to frequently blunt the impact of the proposed measures.

The failure of collective-security measures calls for substitute innovations that can contribute to international peace and security in situations that do not respond to peaceful settlement procedures. United Nations agencies and personnel have shown some ingenuity in developing peacekeeping techniques not anticipated in the charter. These innovations are considered in the following sections of this chapter.

PEACEKEEPING INNOVATIONS

If the United Nations' experience in handling disputes were based solely on the peaceful settlement and collective-security procedures of the Charter, the degree of success would be considerably lower than history has proven it to be. The Charter has grown, not only through formal arrangements such as the Uniting for Peace Resolution, but also through innovative practices of United Nations agencies. One such development is the technique of peacekeeping, which has been applied to more than a dozen critical problems brought before the United Nations.

Peacekeeping is unique in that it fits neither the classical pattern of peaceful settlement nor the model of collective security. Peacekeeping techniques have been applied both to disputes between states and to internal situations threatening civil war. By the time the term "peacekeeping" came into the United Nations lexicon, the techniques involved had already been applied in several cases, which have retroactively been considered a part of the peacekeeping experience of the United Nations. Other terms, including "preventive diplomacy" and a "United Nations presence" have become closely identified with the process of peacekeeping. It was during the tenure of Dag Hammarskjöld as Secretary-General that these techniques were clearly recognized as a unique contribution to conflict resolution, and Hammarskjöld's name became associated with the successful development and refinement of peacekeeping practices.

Peacekeeping may be compared with collective security only in the respect that each *may* involve the deployment of military forces. In all other attributes the two processes are different. In peace-keeping operations the objective is not to defeat an aggressor, but to prevent fighting, act as a buffer, keep order, or maintain a cease-fire. Peacekeeping forces are generally instructed to use their weapons only in self-defense. Their mission is to keep the peace using measures short of armed force, a role more closely resembling that of police than of military. In order to be effective, they must maintain an attitude of neutrality and impartiality regarding the adversaries. Furthermore, the peacekeepers must be present with the consent of the disputing parties, or at least the consent of one of them and the toleration of the other. One or all disputants must have invited the peacekeeping force since there is no international territory on which they can be stationed, and sovereignty requires consent for their presence on national soil. This consent indicates a desire by the disputants to avoid conflict. A group carrying UN insignia interposed between contending forces will dampen hostilities because neither side wishes to incur international opprobrium by attacking a symbol of a global desire for peace.

In contrast to the intention to draw collective-security forces mainly from the great powers, the practice in peacekeeping has been to insulate each situation from major-power involvement, influence, or confrontation. Peacekeeping forces have been mainly supplied by medium and sometimes by a few smaller powers whose neutrality is unquestioned by the disputants. The major powers have contributed transport and other forms of logistical services and substantial financial support for peacekeeping activities, but, by relying upon direct involvement of military or patrol units from smaller states, they have avoided the otherwise inevitable charges of intervention. Special circumstances occasionally permit an exception to the rule of major power nonparticipation, as was the case with British contributions of personnel to the United Nations Force in Cyprus where British troops were already stationed, but the general rule is not nullified by such an exception.

Peacekeeping operations, because of diverse circumstances leading to their creation, vary widely in function and size. They may perform duties of observing, patrolling, acting as a buffer force, keeping or restoring order, or negotiating. Peacekeeping contingents may range in size from less than a score of observers, to a military force of 5,000–7,000 in the Middle East or in Cyprus, to a maximum of 20,000 in the Congo.

According to a report issued by the President of the General Assembly and the Secretary-General in 1965, United Nations peacekeeping operations may be divided into two categories — observer operations and operations involving the use of armed-forces units. Of the fifteen peacekeeping missions, only five have involved multinational armed forces of more than 3,000 personnel: the United Nations Emergency Force (UNEF) in Egypt from 1956 to 1967; the United Nations Congo Operation (ONUC), established in 1960 and terminated in 1964; the United Nations Force in Cyprus (UNFICYP), in existence since 1964; UNEF-II dispatched to the Middle East in 1973; and the United Nations Interim Force in Lebanon (UNIFIL) created in 1978. A United Nations Security Force (UNSF), composed primarily of 1,500 Pakistani troops also served as the military arm of the United Nations Temporary Executive Authority (UNTEA) in West Irian in 1962-63. In spite of its title, the United Nations Disengagement Observer Force (UNDOF) of 1,250 personnel, placed in 1974 on the Golan Heights as a buffer between Israel and Syria, should be classified in the armed-forces category of peacekeeping units. All other operations were of such size and nature that they may be classified as observer-type missions.

Both official United Nations sources and outside scholars identify twelve pre-1970 United Nations actions as peacekeeping operations.[2] Since 1970, the UNEF-II, the UNDOF, and the UNIFIL, referred to above, should be added to the list. In addition to the larger operations identified above, the other peacekeeping missions include the United Nations Special Committee on the Balkans (UNSCOB), established in 1947 to investigate the Greek border situation; the United Nations Truce Supervision Organization (UNTSO), operating since 1949 to report on cease-fire and armistice violations by Israel and its neighbors; the United Nations Commission for Indonesia (UNCI), charged with observing cease-fires and with aiding negotiations for Indonesian independence in 1949; the United Nations Military Observer Group in India and Pakistan (UNMOGIP), responsible since 1949 for patrolling the cease-fire line in Kashmir; the United Nations Observer Group in Lebanon (UNOGIL), dispatched to Lebanon briefly in 1958 to check allegations of infiltration across Lebanese borders; the United Nations Yemen Observation Mission (UNYOM), charged with supervising the disengagement of military forces during 1962-64 in the civil war in Yemen; the United Nations India-Pakistan Observation Mission (UNIPOM), established to patrol the border between India and Pakistan during and im-

---

[2] See, e.g., the General Assembly records of the work of the Special Committee on Peacekeeping Operations (the Committee of Thirty-Three) and Larry L. Fabian, *Soldiers Without Enemies: Preparing the United Nations for Peacekeeping* (Washington, D.C.: The Brookings Institution, 1971).

mediately after the 1965 war between those countries; and the UNTSO-Suez Canal observer group under the UNTSO direction but stationed in the Suez Canal area after the June, 1967, war.

Although four of the United Nations peacekeeping missions were established before Dag Hammarskjöld became Secretary-General, he is generally identified with the development of peacekeeping practice and the refinement of its techniques. Two of the largest operations, the UNEF and the ONUC, were initiated during his tenure in office. These large-scale undertakings placed heavy demands upon the Office of Secretary-General for the recruitment, organization, deployment, and administration of multinational forces. Hammarskjöld also developed much of the philosophy, terminology, and rationale in support of peacekeeping as a distinctive feature of United Nations practice, and defended peacekeeping against those who questioned its legitimacy, its sources of authority, its methods of financing, and the role of the Secretary-General in its operation.

Peacekeeping was a part of a broader approach of Dag Hammarskjöld to maintaining and promoting peace. The term "quiet diplomacy" has been used to describe his style in skillful negotiations, conducted with tact, persistence, and impartiality, but without fanfare. The term "United Nations presence" refers to all of the fifteen peacekeeping operations, but, in addition, refers to the use of personal representatives of the Secretary-General in the settling of controversies such as the border disputes between Cambodia and Thailand in 1958–59 and in 1962–64. The term "United Nations presence" has also been applied to United Nations mediators and their staffs, commissions of good offices or conciliation, smaller groups of military observers such as the one sent to the Dominican Republic in 1965, and other similar groups dispatched to the scene of a conflict by the authority of either the Security Council or the General Assembly. "Preventive diplomacy" is a term associated with Hammarskjöld's approach to problems of peace, encompassing all aspects of peacekeeping and the related activities mentioned above. The theory of preventive diplomacy rests on the assumption that it is better to forestall conflict than to allow it to spread. All peacekeeping and related techniques contribute to that end.

Peacekeeping represents, on the one hand, one of the most innovative developments in United Nations practice, but, on the other, a source of major problems to the world organization. The larger operations have been relatively expensive and have put a strain on the United Nations budget from which it has never recovered. The combined costs of the ONUC and the UNEF were approximately 600 million dollars, and the attempt to assess these costs on the members on the same basis as the regular expenses of the organization led to refusals to pay and a mounting indebtedness and series of deficits in United Nations financing. Most peacekeeping projects since 1960 have sought alternative means of financing to avoid exacerbation of an already acute situation. More details of these financial problems were discussed in chapter 5.

The United Nations financial crisis is a manifestation of a more deeply seated political and philosophical conflict over peacekeeping. Although thirteen of the fifteen peacekeeping operations were initially approved by the Security Council, the Soviet Union sees the exceptions, particularly the first UNEF operation, as part of the attempt to alter the control of the big powers over all aspects of peace and security matters. The Congo undertaking was also transferred in certain stages to the General Assembly, so that the two most expensive peacekeeping enterprises were removed from the possibility of Soviet veto. Thus, the General Assembly asserted its authority to create, direct, and assess the costs of peacekeeping forces. The Soviet Union not only has affirmed the exclusive jurisdiction of the Security Council over peacekeeping activities, but also has argued that costs should be mainly borne by states engaging in aggressive action. Other states have joined the Soviet Union in refusing to pay for undertakings of which they do not approve, and many small states have suggested that the big powers should pay the lion's share of peacekeeping expenses.

The majority of United Nations members support the position that the General Assembly should possess some means to take effective action in cases in which a Security Council stalemate occurs, but no consensus exists on the precise nature and scope of General Assembly authority or on the means to distribute the financial burden. The Special Committee on Peacekeeping Operations (the Committee of Thirty-three) has struggled since 1965 to resolve the fundamental questions of the respective roles of the Security Council, the General Assembly, and the Secretariat in all aspects of peacekeeping, from the approval of new missions to the means for financial support. The issues are so complex and the attitudes so divergent that any progress is more likely to be piecemeal than comprehensive.

One of the problems of peacekeeping is the source of manpower for participation in peacekeeping missions. A group of middle powers, including the Nordic states, Canada, and India, have been enthusiastic supporters of the peacekeeping philosophy, have furnished men and material for peacekeeping missions, and have provided leadership in short- and long-range planning for more effective United Nations peacekeeping activities.

Why have the middle-sized powers been such a strong source of support for peacekeeping activities? They are in a unique position to contribute personnel because of their reputation for neutrality. They have not been tainted with imperialism nor, with the exception of the North Atlantic Treaty Organization, with association with movements that jeopardize their reputation for impartiality. They have sufficient economic resources to meet the costs involved without undue citizen sacrifice. Their position in world affairs is such that they have a heavy stake in the avoidance of military conflict. Leaders such as Lester Pearson of Canada have emerged as enlightened advocates for the strengthening of techniques, including peacekeeping, that may ensure world peace. The humanitarian concerns of a discerning citizenry furnish a base for generous support for causes that promote world peace as well as for a wide range of United Nations economic and social activities. These countries perceive a close affinity between their national interests and United Nations goals and principles.

Some indication of participation by middle-sized powers in United Nations peacekeeping activities is readily discernible from the table on page 161. All of the Nordic states and Canada have furnished forces for more than half of all peacekeeping missions undertaken by the United Nations, and have contributed to at least three of the five largest operations — the ONUC, the UNEF, the UNFICYP, UNIFIL and the UNEF-II. The Nordic countries have cooperated in limited ways in joint planning and training for future peacekeeping requirements, and Canada invited other states to participate in a conference in Ottawa in 1964 to discuss United Nations peacekeeping.

Although the number of missions in which a state has participated is an indicator both of its willingness to contribute and of its acceptability as an impartial party, other factors are significant in assessing the contribution of any given country to United Nations peacekeeping efforts. India, because of relatively large military contingents in the ONUC and the UNEF, outranks all other states in the size of total forces that have served in peacekeeping missions.[3] However, in relation to the number of men in its armed services, less than 2 percent of India's forces were in United Nations missions at any given time, whereas for Ireland's small army the corresponding figure exceeded 15 percent. The Netherlands has been involved in more United Nations missions than India, but only in observer missions or in furnishing small contingents of specialists. Therefore,

---

[3] Fabian, *Soldiers Without Enemies,* p. 161.

ELEVEN MOST FREQUENT PARTICIPANTS IN PEACEKEEPING MISSIONS

Country	No. of Missions	UNS-COB	UNT-SO	UNCI	UNM-OGIP	UNEF	UNO-GIL	ONUC	UN-TEA-UNSF	UNY-OM	UN-FI-CYP	UNI-POM	UNTSO, Suez Canal	UN EF-II	UN-DOF	UNI-FIL
Canada	12	—	X	—	X	X	X	X	X	X	X	X	—	X	X	X
Sweden	12	—	X	—	X	X	X	X	X	X	X	X	X	X	—	X
Denmark	9	—	X	—	X	X	X	X	—	X	X	X	—	—	—	X
Finland	9	—	X	—	X	X	X	—	—	—	X	X	X	X	—	X
Ireland	9	—	X	—	—	—	X	X	X	—	—	X	X	X	—	X
Norway	8	—	X	—	X	X	X	X	—	X	—	X	—	—	—	X
Netherlands	7	X	X	—	—	—	—	X	—	—	X	—	—	—	—	—
Austria	6	—	—	—	—	X	X	X	X	X	X	—	X	X	X	—
India	6	—	X	—	X	—	X	X	—	X	X	X	—	—	—	—
Italy	6	—	X	—	X	X	X	X	—	X	—	X	—	—	—	—
New Zealand	6	—	X	—	X	—	X	X	—	—	X	X	—	—	—	—

Source: Adapted in major part from data included in Larry L. Fabian, *Soldiers Without Enemies: Preparing the United Nations for Peacekeeping* (Washington, D.C., The Brookings Institution, 1971), Appendix B, and updated from United Nations official publications.

the total number of Dutch personnel involved is less than 1 percent of the number from India or Sweden.[4]

Factors to be considered in assessing the contributions of states to United Nations peacekeeping must include the following: (1) number of missions, (2) number of personnel, (3) population, (4) size of armed forces, (5) gross national product and per capita income, (6) size of defense budget, (7) financial and logistical support, and (8) basis for deployment (i.e., whether military contingents have volunteered for United Nations duty or whether they are regular units of the armed services). No single index can adequately measure the cooperation and commitment of a nation to United Nations peacekeeping efforts. However, an assessment based on all available factors would indicate that the Nordic states, Canada, Ireland, and India deserve special credit for their leadership and support.

A major problem in United Nations peacekeeping is the availability and training of personnel for emergency situations. The necessity to dispatch quickly a force of several thousand to the Middle East in 1956 resulted in the use of military contingents that had no previous training in the special techniques of peacekeeping. In 1958 and 1959 Secretary-General Hammarskjöld took the initial steps toward correcting this deficiency. He recognized that both national states and the Secretariat must plan for effective peacekeeping participation. The Secretariat first issued a study based on the UNEF experience, and the Secretary-General then directed a letter to the states that had previously furnished personnel for peacekeeping missions in the Middle East. At approximately the same time the Nordic states began preliminary consultations aimed at providing standby forces specially trained for United Nations peacekeeping duy. Several other states indicated a willingness to earmark forces for possible use in emergencies. During the 1960s a dozen states authorized or promised standby forces. Some planned to earmark units of their regular armed forces, and others visualized the use of volunteers, often from military reserve personnel. The training of medical, communications, and other specialized units was recognized as part of future needs.

Several commitments for standby forces remained unfulfilled in the 1970s, and plans were delayed in other cases because the number of personnel required for existing missions in Cyprus, the Middle East, and Kashmir exceeded the quota of standby forces promised by individual states for future missions. States have responded

[4] *Ibid.*, p. 144.

generously to past emergencies, but the need for planning and special training continues.

CASE STUDIES IN COLLECTIVE SECURITY AND PEACEKEEPING

Examples of United Nations peacekeeping activities are fairly numerous, but collective-security theory has been rarely applied in United Nations practice. The one approximation of collective security by military means is the case of the Korean conflict. Several attempts to apply economic or diplomatic sanctions were described in a previous section of this chapter. None of these attempts was notably successful in bringing to terms the state against which sanctions were imposed. In the one instance in 1968 of supposedly compulsory and comprehensive economic sanctions taken under Chapter VII of the Charter against Rhodesia, the desired impact was blunted by the noncooperation of South Africa and Portugal.

United Nations peacekeeping missions are so integrated with other problems of dispute settlement as to be inseparable for purposes of general discussion. The case studies of peaceful settlement presented in the previous chapter incorporated substantial information concerning three of the fifteen United Nations peacekeeping missions. Two of these groups — the United Nations Military Observer Group in India and Pakistan (UNMOGIP) and the United Nations India-Pakistan Observation Mission (UNIPOM) — were associated with the prolonged Indian-Pakistani dispute. The United Nations Commission for Indonesia (UNCI) contributed to United Nations efforts to facilitate the granting of independence to Indonesia in 1949. Additional information concerning the theory, practice, and problems of peacekeeping as applied to all fifteen peacekeeping missions has been previously presented in this chapter. Some gaps in our data can, perhaps, be best filled by a further examination of the Korean dispute (as an attempt to apply the principles of collective security) and of several of the peacekeeping missions not previously discussed in great detail.

The Korean Question

Korea became divided at the thirty-eighth parallel of latitude as a result of the agreement in 1945 between the Soviet Union and the United States that each power would temporarily occupy one of the two sectors, accept the surrender of the Japanese forces there, and work out provisions for establishing a permanent government for an independent and unified country. When negotiations for a unified Korea reached an impasse, the United States in 1947 first submitted the question to the General Assembly. The Assembly adopted a resolution providing for elections for a National Assembly to be conducted under the surveillance of a United Nations Temporary Commission on Korea and subsequently for the prompt withdrawal of occupying forces. The commission was refused access to the territory north of the thirty-eighth parallel but observed the conduct of elections for a government in the southern half of the territory, which was recognized by the General Assembly as the only legitimate government in Korea. Immediately thereafter, a government was established in the zone of Soviet occupation also claiming legitimacy for all of Korea.

In 1948 the General Assembly created a second commission charged with facilitating the political, economic, and social unification of Korea and observing and verifying the withdrawal of occupying forces. The commission reported in 1949 that United States forces had been withdrawn from South Korea but could not verify the claims of Soviet withdrawals from the North. No progress was made toward unification.

On June 25, 1950, the United Nations Commission on Korea reported a large-scale invasion across the thirty-eighth parallel by North Korean forces. At the request of the United States government, the Security Council met that Sunday afternoon. The Soviet boycott of the Security Council permitted the adoption of three crucial Council resolutions during the next two weeks. The first declared the armed attack by North Korean forces a breach of the peace (but not necessarily an act of aggression) and called for the cessation of hostilities and the withdrawal of North Korean forces. The second, adopted two days later, recommended that member states assist the Republic of Korea in repelling the attack and in restoring international peace and security in the area. The third resolution authorized a unified command using the United Nations flag and requested the United States to designate a commander and organize the combined forces.

The Security Council resolutions gave legitimacy to United States massive involvement in assisting the South Korean government and furnished the basis for the incorporation of contingents from other members into a United Nations army under United States command. Before the Security Council resolution on June 27, President Truman had already ordered United States forces to give air and sea support to South Korea. General Douglas MacArthur, who was directing

United States operations in Korea, was designated on July 8 as the Commanding General of the unified forces in Korea, including the forces of the Republic of Korea.

The unified force which fought in Korea under the United Nations banner was far from a model of an ideal collective-security force. The United States supplied 50 percent of the ground forces, 85 percent of the naval forces, and more than 90 percent of the air forces. When the South Korean contingents are added to these figures, more than 90 percent of ground and naval forces and almost all of the air forces came from these two countries. Fifteen other states furnished military units of at least battalion size, and an additional five states sent medical units to serve under the unified command. Token offers of smaller size were not accepted. Almost forty states and several specialized agencies and nongovernmental organizations contributed to the relief and rehabilitation work in Korea, but in this area also the United States furnished the bulk of the contributions. Security Council and General Assembly resolutions and a multilateral force under a unified command using the United Nations flag were symbols of great moral and psychological significance, but they mainly supplied international legitimacy for United States efforts to aid South Korea in repelling aggression. The United States possessed the combination of resources, national interests, and military forces stationed nearby to play the primary role in resisting the invasion. Other countries had obligations elsewhere that restricted their degree of involvement. Examples include French military commitments in Indochina and British commitments in Malaya. Soviet absence from Security Council sessions permitted United States policies to receive endorsement as United Nations policies. Further support at the international level came in the form of General Assembly resolutions passed by overwhelming majorities.

Virtually all of Korea became a battleground in 1950 and 1951. Several weeks elapsed after the attack on June 25 before United States forces could launch a successful counterattack against the North Korean invaders, who had overrun nearly the entire peninsula. As the battle front moved northward, a major question of purpose had to be faced. If the goal was to repel an invasion, a crossing of the thirty-eighth parallel by United Nations forces was unjustified. If the primary objective was to establish a unified Korea, the pursuit and defeat of the North Korean forces could be warranted. A resolution on October 7, 1950, by the General Assembly recalled the original goal of unification, and General MacArthur's army continued to advance toward the Yalu River, which separates Korea from China.

Early in November contact was first reported with military units of the People's Republic of China, and a few weeks later substantial numbers of Chinese attacked the United Nations forces. The war had suddenly assumed a new dimension. The Chinese forces assisted the North Koreans in driving the United Nations armies southward beyond the thirty-eighth parallel. Seoul, the South Korean capital, was captured by the northern invaders for the second time within six months. In January, 1951, the retreat southward was halted, the North Korean and Chinese forces were gradually pushed back across the thirty-eighth parallel, and the front became relatively stabilized near that location.

In January, 1951, the General Assembly established a cease-fire commission to recommend appropriate measures for ending the conflict. The commission's proposals were rejected by the government of the People's Republic of China. On February 1 the General Assembly adopted a resolution branding the People's Republic as an aggressor in Korea and on May 18 recommended that all states embargo the shipment of arms, ammunition, implements of war, items useful for producing war material, petroleum, and transportation items to the People's Republic and to North Korea.

Armistice negotiations began in July, 1951. For two years these negotiations were stalled over questions relating to the exchange and repatriation of prisoners of war. An armistice agreement was signed in July, 1953, and a demilitarized zone was established. Negotiations for a final settlement were carried on in Panmunjom in the demilitarized zone, but no agreement could be reached, and in December these sessions were terminated.

In February, 1954, the foreign ministers of France, the Soviet Union, the United Kingdom, and the United States announced that a conference would be called in Geneva in April to discuss a settlement of both the Korean and the Indochinese questions. Participants for the Korean issue would be the four convening powers, the People's Republic of China, North Korea, South Korea, and other countries that had contributed armed forces for the United Nations action in Korea.

The Geneva Conference debated the Korean question for several weeks but the participants were unable to agree on a settlement. Both sides favored unification, but on unreconcilable terms. The status quo of 1953 remains in the 1970s. A divided Korea with hostile forces on each side of a demilitarized zone and frequent charges of armistice violations seem to be permanent features of the Korean scene.

Although the Korean problem is the nearest approximation by

the United Nations to collective security through military sanctions, it falls short of the conditions for applying the classical theory of collective security. Unanimity among the great powers did not exist. One great power carried out a policy that it would have executed with or without United Nations support. That great power and the invaded political unit furnished most of the forces for repelling the invasion. Small contingents from fifteen other states lent credibility to the action as a United Nations mission but served more as a symbolic than as a decisive factor in the fighting.

Security Council and General Assembly resolutions were couched in broad general terms rather than advocating specific actions. States were left free to comply voluntarily with these directives to whatever degree suited their purposes. The General Assembly branded the People's Republic of China as an aggressor, but the Security Council declared only that there had been a breach of the peace. The Council invoked Article 39 of the Charter but never utilized the stronger measures of Articles 40-42. The only specific sanctions, which were voluntary, not binding, were those requested by the General Assembly.

The Korean action ended in a stalemate. However, the invasion was repulsed. A United Nations commission was present to observe the invasion and to give impartial reports to United Nations headquarters. The Security Council was able to act in the absence of the Soviet representative. More than fifty states in a total membership of sixty declared their moral support in the General Assembly for the action taken in the name of the United Nations. As a result of the situation in the Security Council, the General Assembly proceeded at its earliest opportunity to strengthen its ability to deal with disputes when the Security Council is deadlocked. In spite of the failure to apply collective-security techniques fully, the Korean episode was a landmark in United Nations history and furnished some limited positive contributions to United Nations practice.

United Nations Emergency Force (UNEF)

Hostility, incidents involving violence, and a series of wars have marked the history of Israel's relations with its Arab neighbors since 1947, the year before Israel was proclaimed as an independent state. The original UNEF force was created in 1956 during the second major war in that area and remained as a buffer between Israel and Egypt until Egypt requested its removal in 1967 at the outbreak of the six-day war.

The first war between Israel and its neighbors had been brought to a close by the signing of armistice agreements in 1949. The United Nations Truce Supervision Organization (UNTSO) was created at that time to supervise the armistice. From 1949 until 1956 an uneasy truce existed with many complaints to the Security Council concerning incidents and clashes. The refugee situation was also acute and defied solution.

In 1956 the Palestine dispute assumed a new dimension in a war involving invasions of the Suez Canal area by Israel, the United Kingdom, and France. In July, Egypt announced the nationalization of the canal. Some temporary progress was made toward negotiating differences among Egypt, the United Kingdom, and France over issues of canal ownership, management, and use, but these negotiations were abruptly halted by news that Israeli forces had invaded Egyptian territory and were advancing toward the canal. The Security Council met promptly on October 30, but on the same day the United Kingdom and France, fearing the interruption of canal traffic, issued an ultimatum to Egypt and Israel to pull back from the canal or face British and French military intervention. Proposed Council resolutions requesting immediate withdrawal of Israeli forces were vetoed by France and the United Kingdom, whereupon a Yugoslavia-sponsored resolution was adopted to call for an emergency special session of the General Assembly under the 1950 Uniting for Peace Resolution. Next, on October 31, British and French air attacks against Egypt in the canal area were begun, followed two days later by invasion by land forces. The Egyptians sank ships in the canal, blocking navigation for several months.

On November 1, 1956, the General Assembly began its first emergency special session with the subject matter limited to the Suez crisis. On the following day a resolution was adopted calling for a cease-fire, a withdrawal of forces, and prompt action toward reopening the canal. The British and the French indicated that they would comply only if a United Nations force moved into the area to insure the carrying out of details concerning the armistice and the reopening of the canal. On November 4 Lester Pearson of Canada introduced a resolution calling for the creation of the United Nations Emergency Force (UNEF). Plans for the force were formulated by the Secretary-General and approved by the Assembly on November 5 and 7. By November 15 the first contingents arrived in Egypt, which had agreed to accept the force on its soil. Twenty-four states offered to contribute military personnel, but a force of 6,000 from ten countries was assembled in Egyptian territory by February, 1957, none of whom were drawn from the permanent members of the

Security Council, UNEF personnel continued to patrol the borders between Israel and Egypt in the Gaza and Sinai areas for more than ten years.

The arrival of UNEF units did not immediately assure the withdrawal of all forces to their prewar positions. The last British and French troops left Egypt on December 22, 1956. Israel had occupied most of the Sinai Peninsula including controlling positions over navigation in the Gulf of Aqaba and the Straits of Tiran. Not until arrangements were made for the UNEF to assure freedom of navigation in these waterways was Israel willing to withdraw its forces. The process was completed on March 8, 1957.

Tensions, incidents, and complaints to United Nations organs concerning the Middle East situation did not disappear during the period that the UNEF patrolled the buffer zone. The UNEF's presence kept incidents along the Israeli-Egyptian borders to a minimum, but, during these years, the Security Council heard frequent charges of armistice violations from Israel and its neighbors.

Ominous signals of impending war became apparent in May, 1967. In a report to the Security Council on May 19, the Secretary-General highlighted the deterioration of the situation in the Middle East. The number of incidents between Syria and Israel had been steadily increasing for several months, and a major armed clash had occurred on April 7. The activities of El-Fatah had also become especially inflammatory and unsettling. In mid-May Egyptian troops advanced to the Gulf of Aqaba and demanded that UNEF units turn over key strategic positions to them. On May 18, the Egyptian representative to the United Nations, Mohamed Awad El-Kony, delivered to U Thant an official request from his government for the withdrawal of UNEF forces from Egyptian territory, where they had been for more than ten years. U Thant inquired of Israeli authorities whether they would accept the forces on the Israeli side of the border, but, consistent with the original refusal by Israel in 1956 to allow UNEF personnel on its territory, the reply was negative. The Secretary-General consulted his advisory committee on UNEF and the states furnishing contingents, and they agreed that the buffer force was in an untenable position and that there was no choice but to remove it. U Thant flew to Cairo to try to get a reversal of the Egyptian decision but was unsuccessful.

The Security Council, which, in spite of the chain of threatening conditions, had not been called into session previously in 1967, held twenty-one meetings between May 24 and June 14. Before June 5 the Council engaged in general debate on the Middle East situation but no resolutions were adopted. The Council seemed impotent to find a course of action to stem the tide of events leading to another Middle East war.

In the early hours of June 5, the Security Council representatives were summoned to an urgent session by the news of the outbreak of full-scale warfare between Israel and its neighbors. One of the first results of the fighting was the killing of nine UNEF soldiers from India by Israeli gunfire. Although the evacuation of UNEF forces had begun in May, the last units could not be removed from the area until June 17, and these units were unhappily caught between the lines of the belligerent armies. Other reports to the Council on June 5 dramatized the gravity of the general situation.

During the brief period of fighting, the Israeli forces were successful on all fronts. They occupied the Sinai Peninsula and advanced to the Suez Canal. They occupied the west bank of the Jordan River and pushed the Syrians back from the Golan Heights area. These occupied territories then became a major issue in subsequent negotiations for a settlement of the Middle East question.

On June 6, 1967, the Security Council unanimously adopted a simple cease-fire resolution, attaching no blame for the war nor specifying any conditions for a return to relative peace. Within the next three days the cease-fire was accepted by all belligerents. During succeeding months the situation remained impervious to solution, in spite of the convening of another emergency session of the General Assembly, the passage in November of a Security Council resolution establishing principles on which a settlement should be based, and the prolonged efforts of a United Nations special representative, Gunnar Jarring. The UNTSO observers were present in small numbers on the various fronts, but the larger UNEF force was not re-created until after another major war in October, 1973.

The creation of the UNEF is especially significant because it furnished a model for the peacekeeping movement. Although previous small observer forces came to be retrospectively labeled as peacekeeping actions, the scale of the UNEF and the principles clearly enunciated for its operation provided a pattern of organization and a philosophy for all subsequent peacekeeping units. The development was innovative since it did not follow Charter prescriptions. The foresight and imagination of men like Lester Pearson and Dag Hammarskjöld generated a new concept, which has proven useful in numerous situations.

The UNEF was an instrument for relative peace in the Middle East for more than ten years. However, its ultimate success or failure was dependent not only on the skills and initiative of the Secretaries-

General but also on the cooperation and support of the disputing states and the major powers. In spite of the lack of financial support by the Soviet Union and France and the demand by Egypt in 1967 to withdraw the force, the acceptability and durability of the basic concepts established in 1956 are attested to by the creation in 1973 and 1974 of two new similar forces in the area with the endorsement of all parties that had previously withheld support and cooperation.

The United Nations Congo Operations (ONUC)

Of all United Nations peacekeeping operations the ONUC (the acronym follows the French word order) was the largest, most controversial, and most expensive. Military units were present in the Congo for four years, and for three of those years numbered 15,000 to 20,000 men. Thirty-four countries participated in the ONUC, and other countries, including the major powers, contributed transport and logistical support. Costs assigned to the United Nations budget amounted to 400 million dollars in addition to expenses borne by states contributing forces. These amounts do not include the costs of extensive civil and technical aid to the Congo through both the regular and special-aid channels of the United Nations.

The Congo operation was controversial because there was no clear mandate for the ONUC and because several sets of internal and external interests sought to exploit the ONUC or the chaotic internal conditions in the Congo for their own ends. Two Secretaries-General attempted to follow a noninterventionist course in restoring order and in assisting a Congo government to acquire the capability for handling its own political, economic, and social problems. But in the process they were attacked by self-seeking internal and external spokesmen and were denied the necessary financial support to keep the United Nations solvent. The Soviet attacks on Dag Hammarskjöld were especially virulent and took the form of demands for his resignation and the replacement of a single Secretary-General with a troika, which would have extended the veto to the top echelon of the Secretariat.

The former Belgian Congo (presently named Zaire) is a large, almost landlocked state in central Africa, ranking third among African states in area and fifth in population. At the time independence was granted only thirty Congolese in a population of 14 million were university graduates, and all middle- and upper-echelon government posts and military officer positions were filled by Belgians or other Europeans. The decision to grant independence to the Congo was made suddenly, with no preparation of the Congolese for the responsibilities of self-rule.

On July 5, 1960, five days after independence, Congolese soldiers mutinied against their Belgian officers, and civil disorder occurred in many parts of the Congo. Belgian authorities requested permission to use Belgian troops, stationed at two bases retained by treaty, to restore order in the Congo but were refused by Prime Minister Patrice Lumumba. On July 10 after riots spread and many Belgians fled the Congo, the Belgian troops intervened to restore order in several cities. On the following day President Moise Tshombe of Katanga declared the independence of his province as a separate state.

Unable to cope with the growing chaos, President Kasavubu and Premier Lumumba first requested aid from the United States and were advised to appeal to the United Nations. On July 14 the Security Council adopted a resolution calling upon Belgium to withdraw its troops from the Congo and authorizing the Secretary-General to provide military and technical assistance to the Congolese government until the national security forces were capable of maintaining internal order.

In response to the resolution of July 14, the Secretary-General, with the cooperation of member states, created the United Nations Operation in the Congo (ONUC). On July 15 more than 1,350 troops from Ghana and Tunisia arrived in the Congo, and within a month the United Nations force exceeded 14,000. According to the guidelines established by Hammarskjöld, no units were accepted from permanent members of the Security Council or from any state that, in the judgment of the Secretary-General, had a special interest in the situation. Priority was also given to participation by African states, twelve of which contributed units. The guidelines also provided that the troops were responsible only to the Secretary-General, that they must not intervene in the internal affairs of the Congo, and that they should use force only in self-defense. All of these conditions were consistent with the general principles that had been gradually evolved for peacekeeping operations.

The goals for the ONUC were established by a series of Security Council resolutions in 1960–61 and by a resolution adopted on September 20, 1960, by the General Assembly's emergency session on the Congo. These goals are summarized by Ernest W. Lefever in his study of the Congo operation as follows:

Restore and maintain law and order.

Protect life and property throughout the country.

Transform the Congolese army into a reliable instrument of internal security.

Restore and maintain the territorial integrity of the Congo.

Prevent civil war and pacify tribal conflict.

Protect the Congo from external interference in its affairs, particularly through the elimination of foreign mercenaries hired by secessionist Katanga.[5]

All of these purposes and the guidelines for the conduct of the operations were generally adhered to, although continued crises in the Congo after the withdrawal of the ONUC demonstrated the absence of stability. This lack of stability should surprise no one since the transformation of the Congo from a chaotic to an orderly society in four years under the most adverse conditions would have been an achievement beyond reasonable expectation.

The chaotic conditions in the Congo are epitomized by the situation there between September, 1960, and August, 1961, when no single government existed with which the United Nations could deal. On Septermber 5, 1960, President Kasavubu dismissed Prime Minister Lumumba, and Lumumba retaliated by dismissing Kasavubu. On September 12 the army chief of staff, Joseph Mobutu, arrested Lumumba and subsequently took over the government in Leopoldville (now Kinshasa) and suspended Parliament. Lumumba later escaped, was rearrested, transferred to Katanga province, and executed by one of Tshombe's mercenaries in January, 1961. By early 1961 at least four separate governments claimed legitimacy in the Congo. Kasavubu and Mobutu in Leopoldville were recognized by a majority of United Nations members and claimed national jurisdiction. Gizenga, a Lumumba supporter with headquarters in Stanleyville in Orientale province, also claimed national jurisdiction and was recognized by the Soviet bloc and by several African states, which withdrew their forces from the ONUC in protest over the failure of the United Nations to support the legitimacy of Lumumba and Gizenga. In Katanga, Tshombe claimed the right of that province to separate statehood and continued to engage Belgian mercenaries to enforce his autonomy. Albert Kalonji in Kasai province sought autonomy through agreements at various stages with Tshombe and with Kasavubu. In August, 1961, the eleven-month constitutional crisis was ended with the selection of Cyrille Adoula as premier of a government that all factions endorsed as the only legitimate government of the Congo.

Tshombe soon proved that he was unreliable in his support of the Kasavubu-Adoula government. Tshombe was motivated by personal ambition, but other factors encouraged his secessionist plans.

[5] Ernest W. Lefever, *Crisis in the Congo: A United Nations Force in Action* (Washington, D.C.: The Brookings Institution, 1965), p. 177.

Katanga was by far the richest province of the Congo. Belgian interests, including financial ones, favored the secessionist movement. Mercenaries from Belgium, France, South Africa, and the Rhodesias willingly supported the political intrigues. Sympathy for Tshombe's plans could also be found in Rhodesia, Britain, France, and some segments of the United States population. Fighting occurred between Tshombe's forces and the ONUC in August and September, 1961. After the second incident Secretary-General Hammarskjöld arranged a personal conference with Tshombe and was on his way to keep that engagement when he was killed in the crash of his plane. A cease-fire was agreed to on September 21 but was soon violated by Katangese mercenaries and native armed forces. On November 24 the Security Council gave Acting Secretary-General U Thant an unprecedented mandate "to take vigorous action, including the use of a requisite measure of force, if necessary, for the immediate apprehension, detention pending legal action and/or deportation of all foreign military and para-military personnel and political advisers not under the United Nations Command, and mercenaries . . ."[6] In order to defend themselves and carry out their mandate, ONUC forces were required to engage in limited military activities rather than adhere to the ideal role of policemen. Tshombe made a series of agreements for the unification of the country and promptly broke each one. It was not until January, 1963, that all military and political opposition ceased in Katanga.

Partially because of financial problems and partially because its principal mandate had been achieved, the ONUC was withdrawn from the Congo by June 30, 1964. The country was still deficient in many elements required for unity, order, and political and economic progress, and internal disorders and political upheavals were frequent during the next four years. After the withdrawal of the ONUC, technical assistance and development aid programs of the United Nations and the specialized agencies continued to serve some of the basic economic, social, and political needs of the Congo.

In concluding his study of the Congo operation, Ernest W. Lefever summarizes his overall assessment of its shortcomings and successes as follows:

> The Congo peacekeeping effort was a novel, controversial, and a less-than-efficient enterprise. It sometimes fumbled. It made many small mistakes. It was assailed on all sides. It precipitated a financial crisis for the United Nations. But in the final analysis, the U.N. Force must be judged by its contribution to international stability, regardless of what other interests

[6] Security Council Resolution S/5002, November 24, 1961.

it might have served. So judged, the mission succeeded. It contributed to peace and security in Central Africa and in the wider world.

As the largest and most complex internationally authorized and administered operation in history, the Congo peacekeeping effort is rich in lessons and warnings for the future.[7]

West Irian Question

When Indonesia achieved independence from the Netherlands in 1949, the status of West New Guinea (West Irian) remained unresolved. Both Indonesia and the Netherlands continued to claim jurisdiction over the territory. Because of the inability of the parties to agree on the future status of the territory, the General Assembly debated the issue in 1955 and in 1961 without notable success. In late 1961 and early 1962 military clashes between Dutch and Indonesian forces occurred in West New Guinea.

Secretary-General U Thant appealed to the Netherlands and Indonesian governments to avoid warfare and requested that representatives of the two governments consult with him in order to keep the peace and facilitate a permanent settlement. Consultations were carried on, and U Thant appointed Ambassador Ellsworth Bunker of the United States to assist as a mediator in the dispute. An agreement for the transfer of authority over West New Guinea was signed at United Nations headquarters on August 15, 1962.

The agreement on the future status of West Irian provided that, on October 1, 1962, the United Nations would take over from the Dutch the administration of the territory for a period of seven months after which the administrative authority would be transferred to Indonesia. Indonesia agreed to conduct a future plebiscite under United Nations supervision to determine the wishes of the native Papuans concerning their permanent status.

In order to carry out the United Nations interim administrative role, a United Nations Temporary Executive Authority (UNTEA) was created with a United Nations Security Force (UNSF) as its military or police arm. The cost of the United Nations peacekeeping and administrative functions was shared by Indonesia and the Netherlands.

The West Irian case is notable in a number of ways. The transfer of sovereignty and the temporary United Nations administration proceeded smoothly and effectively. The leadership of the Secretary-General resulted in a cessation of hostilities and prompt agreement on the terms of a settlement. The UNTEA set a precedent by pro-

---

[7] Lefever, *Crisis in the Congo*, p. 181.

viding for direct administration of a territory by the United Nations. No financial burden created additional United Nations budgetary problems. The Security Council played no role in the dispute. The General Assembly and the Secretary-General assumed responsibility for all United Nations contributions to the calming of a potential threat to international peace and security. The entire operation in 1962 and 1963 is a positive accomplishment of the United Nations as against numerous other examples of frustration or failure. The only blight upon this record came in 1969 when Indonesia used eight consultative assemblies in West Irian to approve a questionable "act of free choice" endorsing permanent status of the territory as a part of Indonesia. Several recommendations of the United Nations Representative for safeguarding the self-determination procedures were rejected by the Indonesian authorities.

The United Nations Force
In Cyprus (UNFICYP)

The need for a United Nations Force in Cyprus is prompted by a complex political and social situation in that island state. Nearly 80 percent of the population is of Greek origin; most of the remainder are Turkish. Turkey ruled Cyprus from the sixteenth to the nineteenth century, but ancient cultural ties link Cyprus to Greece. Because of proximity to Turkish territory, the island is strategically important to Turkey, but the importance of naval bases in the eastern Mediterranean also enhances its strategic importance to the United Kingdom, which controlled Cyprus from 1878 to 1960. The president of Cyprus, Makarios, is also archbishop of the Orthodox Church, and his predecessors in the Church for more than a century have led a campaign for *enosis* (union with Greece). Some of the Turkish segments of the population favor partition of the island into Greek and Turkish political units. A further complicating factor is that the threats of hostilities between Greece and Turkey over the Cyprus issue constitute also a threat to the unity of interests in NATO. Since the Soviet Union has strong interests in the eastern Mediterranean area, the major powers as well as Greece and Turkey are vitally concerned with the situation in Cyprus.

In 1954, 1956, and 1957 Greece requested the General Assembly to consider the question of self-determination for Cyprus. No action resulted except for resolutions suggesting that the parties concerned seek a solution through negotiation. Terrorist activities spread in Cyprus after 1955, and the internal situation became increasingly tense. Consultations in Zurich and in London in February, 1959, resulted in an agreement for the future status of Cyprus negotiated among the prime ministers of Greece, Turkey, and the United Kingdom, and Archbishop Makarios for the Greek Cypriots, and Fazil Kuchuk representing the Turkish Cypriots.

Out of the Zurich and London consultations came a set of principles that were later embodied in several legal instruments, the most important of which were the constitution for the government of Cyprus and a Treaty of Guarantee. The governmental provisions resulted from compromise among competing interests and have proved unworkable in practice. Some of the most important provisions include the following:

1. The republic would have a president from the Greek Cypriot population and a vice-president from the Turkish Cypriot population each possessing veto power over key issues.
2. The Turkish Cypriots were assigned 30 percent of the seats in the House of Representatives and 30 percent of the positions in the civil-service and security forces (although constituting about 18 percent of the population). In the army the ratio was 60 percent Greek Cypriots to 40 percent Turkish Cypriots.
3. Certain taxing powers and authority over cultural, educational, and religious affairs were reserved to two communal legislatures, one for each ethnic community.
4. Each of the five largest towns would have two city councils, one for each ethnic community.
5. The basic governmental structure could not be amended or altered.
6. The Treaty of Guarantee allowed Great Britain, Greece, and Turkey to take individual or joint action to maintain or restore the status quo in Cyprus.[8]

It was inevitable that a government designed for stalemate would shortly find itself unable to operate effectively. The government failed to implement the quotas for Turkish Cypriots in the civil service, and the minority retaliated by obstructing financial legislation. Governmental functions were paralyzed, and threats of violence increased. In November, 1963, Makarios proposed thirteen drastic constitutional changes. The following month fighting began between local regular and irregular forces, and Greece and Turkey made threatening gestures of intervention. Violence in Cyprus resulted in hundreds of casualties and thousands of refugees who fled from their villages and homes. The British tried to restore order in the island but without notable success.

[8] James A. Stegenga, *The United Nations Force in Cyprus* (Columbus, Ohio: Ohio State University Press, 1968), pp. 24-25.

The Security Council considered the Cyprus issue in late December, 1963, and again in February and March, 1964. No agreement was reached in the December meetings. In January, at meetings in London, the NATO powers tried to hammer out an arrangement for a NATO peacekeeping force in Cyprus, but Makarios insisted that the Security Council must be involved. Also in January the governments of Cyprus, the United Kingdom, Greece, and Turkey requested the Secretary-General to appoint a personal representative to observe the situation in Cyprus, and U Thant complied by appointing General Gyani of India.

On March 4, 1964, the Security Council unanimously approved the creation of the United Nations Force in Cyprus (UNFICYP) for a period of three months. Three- and six-month extensions prolonged the authorization for the operation over the next several years. The Secretary-General was given authority over the force and its financing. The peculiar circumstances in Cyprus made possible the acceptance of a British component of the UNFICYP, which has varied from more than 40 percent to less than 20 percent of the total manpower. An original target of a force of 6,000 to 7,000 men was achieved within the first two months after the adoption of the March resolution. Nine countries have furnished contingents of military or police personnel for the UNFICYP. Lessening of tensions, fewer shooting incidents, and the need for decreasing costs led to the reduction of the force by 1969 to 3,650 men, including 175 civilian police from four countries.

In 1974 the situation in Cyprus took an ominous turn. A new Greek military government sent 650 Greek officers to the island to lead the national guard. On July 15 a military coup overthrew the Makarios government. Turkey, in turn, on July 20 invaded Cyprus with 6,000 troops and gradually gained effective control of much of the northern and eastern sections of the island. Makarios was later able to return to Cyprus and reestablish a government, which claimed legitimacy for all of the territory, but, in February, 1975, a Turkish Cypriot Federated State claimed hegemony over the areas occupied by Turkish forces. In spite of the mediation attempts of Secretary-General Kurt Waldheim and of United States government officials, the impasse over political unity or partition of the island continued.

The costs of maintaining the UNFICYP have been borne by countries furnishing contingents, by the government of Cyprus, and by voluntary contributions. NATO countries have furnished more than 90 percent of the voluntary contributions, with the United States and the United Kingdom giving nearly two-thirds of the amount. In recent years the budget for the UNFICYP has incurred a constant deficit to add to the United Nations financial problems. The Soviet Union and France have not contributed to the costs, although they have approved successive extensions of the life of the UNFICYP.

The mandate for the UNFICYP was to prevent a recurrence of fighting and to contribute to the maintenance of law and order and a return to normal conditions. Relative peace was restored in Cyprus except for a series of incidents in 1967 and the major crisis of 1974. However, the basic causes of conflict between the majority and minority segments of the population have not been altered. A return to the full operation of the 1960 constitution is now impossible.

The search for a solution to the problem of Cyprus, which would allow the removal of the UNFICYP, is more in the realm of pressures from NATO members and of the United Nations mediator and the special representative of the Secretary-General than of the UNFICYP command. The original mandate for the UNFICYP in 1964 included the authority for the Secretary-General to appoint a mediator to seek a permanent solution in Cyprus and both the mediator and special representative have sought reconciliation of conflicting interests since that time. The issues are so impervious to rational solution that success remains a remote possibility.

The maintenance of a United Nations peacekeeping force in a divided and tension-ridden country is a costly, inconvenient, but necessary enterprise. Andrew Boyd reminds us of the possible consequences of withdrawing the UNFICYP.

> Can it be seriously contended that it would be better to leave the Cypriots to kill each other until the neighbor countries are dragged into a wider war? The UN operation in Cyprus is easy to criticize — until you give a little thought to the alternatives.[9]

GENERAL ASSESSMENT
OF UNITED NATIONS PRACTICE

Given the world situation from 1945 into the 1970s, the principle of collective security is probably unworkable and unrealistic. The strength of nationalism and the safeguarding of sovereignty preclude automatic collective responses by states whose interests are not directly enhanced by stopping aggression wherever it may occur. National rivalries and competing alliance systems prevent

[9] Andrew Boyd, *Fifteen Men on a Powder Keg: A History of the United Nations Security Council* (New York: Stein and Day, 1971), p. 298.

universal responses to threats to international peace. Basic disagreement over the terms for implementing Article 43 of the Charter to provide an international police force was the prelude to other clashes that have frequently immobilized the United Nations as an instrument for peace. The general lack of recourse to Chapter VII of the Charter reflects the lack of unanimity of the United Nations members in seeking solutions to the most serious situations threatening world peace and stability. Until international peace becomes the *primary* goal of the foreign policies of the world's nations, collective security or any adequate substitute at the global level will remain an unattainable illusion.

In the face of collective-security stalemate, the United Nations has devised new methods for dealing with a limited range of threatening situations. Military forces from the lesser powers have been utilized, not to defeat aggressors, but to keep or restore peace, generally without recourse to arms, at the invitation of a host country on whose soil they are stationed. The ingenuity of statesmen such as Lester Pearson has been linked with the resourcefulness and administrative capability of successive Secretaries-General and the cooperation of governments furnishing troops to make possible innovations in peacekeeping procedures. Going beyond peaceful settlement, but stopping short of enforcement by collective might, these procedures have been dubbed "Chapter Six and One-half," since they fill the interstices between peaceful settlement and collective-security actions. In more than a dozen situations the presence of observer or military corps, supplemented by preventive diplomacy efforts of the Secretary-General or his representatives or assistants, have acted to stabilize or defuse crisis conditions. The financial costs have threatened the United Nations with bankruptcy, but the positive benefits may be immeasurable in monetary terms.

A systematic study of conflict management by international organizations from 1945 through 1970 reveals the relative strengths and weaknesses, successes and failures, in handling disputes of the United Nations, the Organization of American States, the Arab League, the Organization of African Unity, and the Council of Europe.[10] The detailed conclusions of this study cannot be elaborated here but a few highlights follow:

> 1. More than two-thirds of all conflicts were referred to the United Nations; of the regional organizations the OAS was most active in conflict management.

[10] Ernst B. Haas, Robert L. Butterworth, and Joseph S. Nye, *Conflict Management by International Organizations* (Morristown, N.J.: General Learning Press, 1972).

2. The UN excels in dealing with high-intensity conflict, decolonization disputes, interstate issues not related to major world problems, and conflicts among smaller (but not smallest) and middle powers.
3. Only the OAS deals effectively with insignificant disputes or low-violence disputes and internal conflict.
4. International organizations are largely ineffective in Cold War disputes.
5. Joint leadership between the UN Secretary-General and either a superpower or a middle-sized power produces an excellent success record.
6. The UN excels in using elaborate field operations in the most threatening disputes; regional organizations excel in using fact-finding, mediation, and conciliation in less dangerous disputes.
7. Both the OAS and the UN are high in versatility in terms of good performance on many dimensions, but the UN has performed the more complex tasks of conflict management.

In order to make the United Nations a more effective instrument for dealing with aggression and threats to international peace, much remains to be done. The prospects for reenergizing Article 43 of the Charter and obtaining the cooperation of the great powers in applying collective-security measures as a matter of principle are not great. Limited progress has been made in earmarking and training standby forces in several countries for future United Nations peacekeeping missions. The Secretariat has accumulated valuable experience and has initiated projects for the efficient recruitment, deployment, supply, and direction of forces that may be called into United Nations service on missions not yet foreseen. Several private organizations and individuals have directed their efforts toward such activities as the creation of peace academies to prepare persons with a wide range of necessary skills for a constructive role in restoring peace in future crises. That these meager efforts can ever balance the expenditures and training for wars and preparations for warfare is a dim prospect in the current international climate. In the meantime, the United Nations has shown its ability to adapt to limited crisis situations on an ad hoc basis, and the utility of past operations provides encouragement for further efforts in this direction.

8

The Search
for
Justice Under Law

Humans are political beings who develop orderly processes and institutions to establish relationships among themselves. All human societies have rules substituting order for chaos in intersocietal relations. Laws establish norms governing a society. As a society becomes more complex, its laws also become broader and more detailed. Some laws may be written; others are not, but rather are established customs and usages followed by the society, which are as binding as written laws.

Societies exist on many levels. But there is not yet an effective world society, with laws broad enough to establish norms for the most basic relationships between persons or political units operating on an international or global level.

Today's international organization is an undeveloped, imperfect, yet potentially useful step toward world order. Evolving and implementing more effective international laws are two goals of such organizations as the League of Nations and the United Nations. Other goals necessary for world order are settling disputes peacefully and maintaining peace, which pertain more to the very basis and activities of these organizations, and which were examined in chapters 6 and 7. Applying international legal principles to such disputes or threats to international peace is one way of resolving conflict.

International law also is used in other aspects of international organizations and relationships. In this chapter we will show further how law is established at the international level.

LAW IN NATIONAL AND INTERNATIONAL SYSTEMS

Today's world is characterized by the existence of more than 150 national states that claim attributes of independence and sovereignty and that are organized for governmental purposes on the basis of law. We have previously defined law as a body of established norms for the governance of a society. The essential condition for law is the recognition of rules that are binding as a result of a group conviction to that effect by the members of the community.

States vary widely in the characteristics of their legal systems. Newly established states may possess little written law and in some cases a minimum of customary law. A state may have within it a high degree of consensus on the basic norms for governance, or it may be divided by factions among which struggle and compromise will produce a stormy and uncertain further development of legal rules. Lawmaking powers may be concentrated in few hands, or they may be widely shared. A central body of law may regulate most of the relations of the members, or legal authority may be decentralized through several levels of government. Government regulation may impinge on every aspect of individual existence, or minimal controls or support may exist.

In spite of wide variations, certain common characteristics of national legal systems are notable. Except for occasional rebellions the members of the society agree that state authority should exist and that the laws should be generally respected and obeyed. Some of the rules should be written in the form of political creeds, constitutions, legislation, court decrees, executive orders, and administrative rulings. There should be both duly constituted authority to enact new law and the means to enforce the law on reluctant or dissident members or groups within the society. Courts or similar agencies should interpret and apply the law to controversies. Consensus should generally provide compliance with the law so that violations of law are the exception, not the rule. Legal norms should be sufficiently stable to maintain the understanding necessary as a basis for consensus. Both individuals and groups are the subjects and beneficiaries of the law.

International law is deficient in several of the attributes that contribute to the effectiveness of national legal systems. Traditionally, only states have been considered the subjects of international law, although, in recent years, in such areas as human rights and war crimes, a trend toward the applicability of international law to individuals has been emerging. These same states have retained a monopoly of the means of coercion and have only slowly and reluctantly created supranational agencies vested with the authority to enforce the will of the collectivity upon the individual state. War, means of peaceful settlement, collective security, and world public opinion seem inadequate substitutes at the international level for the kind of action that may be taken against recalcitrant individuals or dissident groups to force compliance with established legal norms within national states.

Other deficiencies of international law include the lack of satisfactory means for developing, applying, and enforcing legal norms. Although national as well as international law is developed, in part, through custom, no true legislative bodies with responsibility for developing new law exist at the international level. Legislation is a swifter and more flexible means of adding to or changing a body of law than the slower and uncertain process of development through custom. The counterpart of national legislation at the international level is the multilateral lawmaking treaty, but these treaties are produced by ad hoc conferences or by international agencies performing other major functions, not by permanent bodies established to exercise primarily legislative functions. Although occasional claims are made that international agreements may be enforced against non-subscribers to the agreements, the general interpretation of international law is that treaties are binding only on states that specifically assent to their terms. Legislation by majority rule, binding on all members of the society, has few counterparts in international practice.

With limited exceptions the few international courts that exist exercise no general compulsory jurisdiction. In broad terms each state decides when to submit disputes to court jurisdiction subject to its own convenience and interests. States may agree in advance to submit certain types of controversies to court decision, but reservations and interpretations applying to such obligations allow international courts to languish from inactivity. However, national courts also apply international law in their decisions.

Perhaps the inadequacy of enforcement machinery is the most unsatisfactory aspect of the international legal system. No international agencies are authorized to enforce international law. The means of enforcement are monopolized by national states, which are reluctant to curtail their own power and to entrust their security to international agencies.

In summary, each state claims sovereign authority to be its own interpreter of its rights, its own source of authority, and its own strength to maintain its rights. In these respects the international legal system is a primitive arrangement under which threats to order and impediments to justice are as much to be anticipated as their antithetical conditions within well-developed national legal systems.

An assessment of the deficiencies of international law may lead erroneously to the conclusion that no legal principles operate across national boundaries, but an inadequate system does not signify the absence of any system. The impression that international law is of little significance may be reinforced by the resort of states to self-help in those dramatic situations that elicit emotional responses and make world headlines. Emphasis upon deficiencies and crises tends to obscure the broad utility of international law in the daily and orderly relations of states.

The two most important sources of international law are the customs of states and lawmaking treaties. The development of customary law is dependent on the length of time required for state practice to become established as law and on the acceptability of majority practice. Nevertheless, custom accounts for a substantial body of international law in the same way that it establishes many norms for accepted behavior in national societies. As international contacts multiplied in recent decades, lawmaking treaties became increasingly common. International treaties or conventions, like national legislation, tend to convert customary law into statutory law and to clarify and extend its principles. That is, the absence of international legislative bodies has not prevented the acceptance by states of hundreds of conventions specifying mutual obligations and prerogatives. When these conventions are negotiated among and ratified by a large proportion of the world's national governments or when a pattern of bilateral or limited-party treaties forms a network binding most of the world's states to common terms, a body of international legislation is established by treaty.

Article 38 of the Statute of the International Court of Justice specifies three other sources of international law that the Court may apply. These secondary sources are (1) general principles of law recognized by civilized nations, (2) judicial decisions, and (3) the teachings of the most highly qualified publicists of various nations.

One of the imperfections of international law is that it does not totally or specifically cover all subjects and circumstances. However, even with gaps, courts should be able, by applying analogies from the primary and secondary sources cited above, to "find the law" necessary for deciding cases not specifically covered in previously established principles of international law. Although the gaps may be wider in international than in municipal law, national courts also are required, on occasion, to fill the lacunae in the law and, thus, to establish new law.

For all its imperfections, international law plays an important role in the twentieth century. A substantial body of such law has accumulated because nations have been dealing with each other for hundreds of years and the contacts and legal agreements multiply with each decade. The significance of international law is dramatized by Professor Louis Henkin in a negative approach to the subject.

> If one doubts the significance of this law, one need only imagine a world from which it were absent. . . . There would be no security of nations or stability of governments; territory and airspace would not be respected; vessels could navigate only at their constant peril; property — within or without any given territory — would be subject to arbitrary seizure; persons would have no protection of law or of diplomacy; agreements would not be made or observed; diplomatic relations would end; international trade would cease; international organizations and arrangements would disappear.[1]

If the absence of organized sanctions is the greatest deficiency of international law, this inadequacy may cause one to overlook the most important sanction of both national and international systems. The main reason national systems work is the broad acceptance of legal norms by the bulk of the community — not the provision of punishment for violators. The convenience of the society is buttressed by this broad consensus. The regularity of relations among states is also guaranteed by consensus and reciprocity. The means for handling violations are inadequate, but the mutual interests of the members of the international community require compliance with international law as the normal pattern of behavior.

LEGAL DEVELOPMENTS BEFORE 1945

The modern state system was of European origin, and a body of international law developed as an adjunct of the state system. In the seventeenth century the law established by the practices of states was clarified in the writings of such scholars as Suarez and Grotius. During this early period of development of international legal princi-

---

[1] Louis Henkin, *How Nations Behave: Law and Foreign Policy* (New York: Praeger, 1970), pp. 22-23.

ples, the emphasis upon the law of war was much greater than upon the peaceful relations of states.

In the nineteenth century arbitration of disputes came into practice under the leadership of the United States and Great Britain. A settlement of the *Alabama* claims was made in 1872 through arbitral procedure. In the early twentieth century a number of standing arbitration treaties were agreed to, and several disputes were submitted to the jurisdiction of the Permanent Court of Arbitration, created as a result of the Hague Peace Conference of 1899. The Court continues in existence but has been little used since 1914.

The Permanent Court of International Justice (PCIJ) was not a part of the official organization of the League of Nations, and membership in the Court was separate from League membership, but other linkages were very close. Article 14 of the Covenant specified that the League Council was responsible for formulating plans for the PCIJ, which was to be competent to hear and determine international disputes and to give advisory legal opinions at the request of the Council or Assembly. The Statute of the Court, in the form of a treaty, was promptly developed, opened to state ratification, and came into force in September, 1921. Judges were chosen by concurrent majorities of the Council and the Assembly, and the budget of the PCIJ was provided as a part of the League budget. Although more than fifty states became members, the United States never joined the Court.

The Court was never permitted to decide the most vital issues affecting the interests of the major powers, but its work has generally been assessed as significant and highly professional and impartial. By 1940 the PCIJ had handed down thirty-two decisions and twenty-seven advisory opinions. The Court was authorized to exercise jurisdiction over disputes arising under hundreds of treaties drawn up during this period. The reputation of the Court was such that, when the United Nations was formed, the Statute of the new Court was nearly identical with that of the PCIJ.

Whereas the early emphasis of international law had been upon the law of warfare, the main thrust of efforts after 1918 turned to the promotion of peace. The establishment of the League of Nations and the PCIJ reflects this emphasis. The League was recognized as inadequate for guaranteeing peace, so supplementary actions were taken to reinforce the means for preventing war. The movement for disarmament took shape in the Washington and London naval conferences of 1921 and 1930. A general disarmament conference under League sponsorship, after years of preparatory work, foundered under basic national disagreements over the means and methods to be followed in achieving world disarmament. The Locarno Pacts of 1925 set up obligations to enforce the territorial integrity of European states. In 1928 the Kellogg-Briand Pact, or Pact of Paris, attempted to outlaw war by renouncing it as an instrument of national policy. This pact was ratified by most of the world's governments but proved ineffective in the face of the aggressive actions of the expansionist states in the 1930s. The General Act for Pacific Settlement formulated the same year was not widely accepted.

Other noteworthy attempts to expand the influence of international law include the adoption, in 1925, of a protocol against gas warfare, and the convening of a Hague conference, in 1930, for the purpose of codifying laws of nationality, the territorial seas, and state obligations toward aliens. Although the specific results of the Hague conference were disappointing, it represented a part of a widespread continuing effort to develop and clarify various aspects of international law. The International Labor Organization was more successful than most agencies in securing wide acceptance of international conventions; in this instance the subject matter pertained to the social welfare of workers.[2]

THE CHARTER AS AN INSTRUMENT OF INTERNATIONAL LAW

As a multilateral treaty that prescribes principles and rules for the behavior of states and that is subscribed to by most national governments, the United Nations Charter is a part of the developing body of international law. Such a statement, however, does not do justice to the relative contribution of the Charter to the dynamics of the process of legal development. The significance of the Charter as compared with other treaties lies in its principles, its scope, and its capacity for generating a chain of activities that, in turn, produce further additions to international law.

The Charter lays down principles that are of sweeping significance to the relations of states. The most fundamental is the promise of all members to settle their disputes by peaceful means and to refrain from the threat or use of force against other states or in any manner inconsistent with the purposes of the Charter. This obligation is a departure from previous reliance on force, and the Charter

---

[2] See chapter 11 for further details on ILO contributions to international social legislation.

seeks to make the obligation universal. The means of enforcement and the degrees of compliance have been imperfect, but the principle has been regularly applied in United Nations consideration of disputes and in the behavior of states, with the result that wars of one state against another have been kept down in spite of increased contacts, sources of tension, and numbers of states. Louis Henkin strongly asserts that:

> . . . I say confidently, the law of the Charter, the wide acceptance of that law by governments and peoples, the authority of the United Nations and world opinion behind the law, and other political reactions (stronger because war has been outlawed) can claim substantial credit for the fact that the world has avoided major war since 1945. The sense that war is not acceptable conduct has taken some hold; nations more readily find that their security and other national interests do not require the use of force after all; even where force is used, the fact that it is now illegal must be taken into account and limits the scope, the weapons, the duration, the purposes, the justifications.[3]

The Charter is more significant in expanding international law than most treaties because of the range of activities provided for in its various articles. The Charter establishes a general, multipurpose organization. It goes beyond a statement of agreed principles and obligations by authorizing the creation of an elaborate set of major and subsidiary agencies. It envisions six major organs, numerous committees or commissions, and the establishment of a pattern of relationships between the central organization and a network of specialized agencies, regional organizations, and nongovernmental organizations throughout the world. Tens of thousands of persons are thus involved in a wide range of political, legal, economic, social, and humanitarian activities with the United Nations as the focal point of the efforts. The Charter is significant because it is the fundamental law or constitution for the only general-purpose, nearly universal organization that exists in today's world. Even if it does not establish a true government, it creates an elaborate structure through which states have obligated themselves to cooperate for many mutually advantageous ends.

The United Nations is a dynamic organization in which many agencies engage in active programs and in which a wide range of decisions are made. One by-product of these activities and decisions is the gradual expansion of international law. Not only do agencies such as the International Court of Justice and the International Law Commission (to be discussed in more detail in the following sections

---

[3] Henkin, *How Nations Behave*, p. 137.

of this chapter) play a major role in developing law, but some of the decisions of other organs gradually acquire the status of law. An extensive analysis of this process has been made by Rosalyn Higgins, who states in the introduction to her study:

> Collective acts of states, repeated by and acquiesced in by sufficient numbers with sufficient frequency, eventually attain the status of law. The existence of the United Nations — and especially its accelerated trend toward universality of membership since 1955 — now provides a very clear, very concentrated, focal point for state practice. Here, then, is the reason for looking to United Nations practice in a search for the direction of the development of international law.[4]

At exactly what point the collective action of states taken in United Nations organs becomes accepted as customary international law is not easily ascertainable, but that the process occurs is beyond reasonable doubt.

The United Nations Charter is not a static legal instrument but has grown through interpretation and usage. International law has been altered as the Charter has been modified and amplified by such interpretation. The Charter was written in general and often deliberately ambiguous terms. It is subject to interpretation by the member states and by each organ, and as with any flexible constitution, the Charter expands and takes on new meaning with widely accepted interpretation and the resulting practice. Examples are myriad, and include the practice of abstentions in the Security Council, the assumption of unforeseen powers by the General Assembly, the degree of initiative exercised by the Secretary-General, and the substitution of peacekeeping procedures for an unworkable system of collective security.

The United Nations General Assembly, the International Law Commission, the specialized agencies, and United Nations commissions under the aegis of the Economic and Social Council have all taken initiatives and carried on preparatory work resulting in treaties that are significant landmarks in the growing body of international law. A few of the most important examples include the Treaty Governing the Exploration and Use of Outer Space (1967), four conventions on the law of the seas (1958), the Vienna Conventions on Diplomatic and Consular Relations (1961 and 1963), the Convention on the Settlement of Investment Disputes (1965), the Genocide Convention (1948), the Covenants on Human Rights (1966), and the Convention on the Law of Treaties (1969).

[4] Rosalyn Higgins, *The Development of International Law through the Political Organs of the United Nations* (London: Oxford University Press, 1963), p. 2.

Although international law may emerge from many sources within the United Nations, the General Assembly is assigned special responsibility for its development. Article 13 of the Charter specifies that the "General Assembly shall initiate studies and make recommendations for the purpose of . . . encouraging the progressive development of international law and its codification." These responsibilities are exercised in part through (1) the Assembly's Sixth (Legal) Committee, (2) the International Law Commission, (3) the Assembly's own interpretations and practice, and (4) international conferences that are called for formulating treaties on specific subjects.

Another way in which the General Assembly reinforces and verifies international law is by declarations of the existence of legal principles. When such declarations, referring to specific principles, are sustained by the supporting votes of nearly all members, the legal norms involved are given added weight as clearly established elements in international law. Examples of such declarations include the Declaration on the Granting of Independence to Colonial Countries and Peoples (1960), which was adopted by a vote of 89–0 with nine abstentions, and the 1961 General Assembly resolution on apartheid in South Africa as a flagrant violation of the Charter, which was adopted by a vote of 97–2 with one abstention.

THE ROLE OF THE INTERNATIONAL COURT OF JUSTICE

The International Court of Justice (ICJ) is the principal judicial arm of the United Nations. It is designated as one of the six major organs of the United Nations and is the successor to the Permanent Court of International Justice (PCIJ) established by the League of Nations. The Statute of the Court is an integral part of the United Nations Charter, and a government's act of ratification involves acceptance of both documents. Under special provisions Switzerland, Liechtenstein, and San Marino, which are not United Nations members, have adhered to the Court Statute. The general facts concerning the composition, procedures, headquarters, and functions of the Court were outlined in chapter 4 of this text and will not be repeated here.

One of the deficiencies of the international legal system as compared with national systems is the lack of compulsory jurisdiction of the ICJ. One attribute of sovereignty that states refuse to surrender to international authority is their freedom to choose whether or not they will submit any particular case for judicial determination. Once they have agreed to submit a case to the Court, they are bound by the principles of international law to accept and carry out the decision, although there is no satisfactory means for enforcement of decisions, and refusal to comply has, on one occasion, occurred.

An attempt to partially overcome the lack of compulsory jurisdiction was written into the Statute of the ICJ in Article 36. This article provides in Section 2 that any party to the Statute may declare that it recognizes as compulsory in relation to any other state accepting the same obligation, the jurisdiction of the Court in all legal disputes concerning:

a. the interpretation of a treaty;
b. any question of international law;
c. the existence of any fact which, if established, would constitute a breach of an international obligation;
d. the nature or extent of the reparation to be made for the breach of an international obligation.

Article 36, Section 2, was an attempt to build a bridge between the principle of sovereignty and that of compulsory jurisdiction. The aim was to open an area in which a degree of international order could be established through the judicial process.

This "optional clause" has not resulted in the submission of a wide range of disputes over legal questions to the Court for settlement. By July, 1977, only forty-five states had filed declarations of acceptance of the "optional clause." Several states have attached reservations to their acceptance of the compulsory jurisdiction of the Court. The most sweeping of these reservations was made by the United States in the so-called Connally amendment, which specified that the jurisdiction of the Court would not apply to "disputes with regard to matters which are essentially within the domestic jurisdiction of the United States *as determined by the United States of America.*" Not only does this reservation practically nullify the compulsory-jurisdiction clause by allowing the United States to decide unilaterally that any case it wishes not to submit is "essentially" one of domestic jurisdiction, but it also allows, under the legal principle of reciprocity, any other party to a case involving the United States to invoke the same privilege. All attempts at repeal of the self-judging Connally reservation have been futile.

The proportion of economically underdeveloped countries that have accepted the compulsory jurisdiction of the Court, with or without reservations, is smaller than that of the developed countries. Only two South American governments have filed acceptances, and most of the Arab countries of the Middle East have not accepted compulsory jurisdiction. The high response from Europe and from such countries as Canada, Australia, and New Zealand is often attributed to the reflection of the Court and of the body of international law of European norms and standards of justice, since that area is the source from which modern international law developed.

Court Judgments

With more than 140 states as parties to the Statute of the ICJ and with 45 of them as adherents to the compulsory jurisdiction provisions (albeit with some significant reservations), it might reasonably be assumed that the Court would have a full docket of cases. Since only one such court exists and since international conflicts of interest are legion, the expectation is reinforced that the Court would be swamped with pending litigation. These assumptions concerning the amount of business before the Court have not been borne out in practice. The reasons include (1) distrust of the Court, (2) distrust of the judicial process, (3) unwillingness of states to submit their interests to outside determination, or (4) bad faith by states in carrying out their obligations assumed under the United Nations Charter and the Court Statute. The reasons for the neglect of the Court will be further examined in the subsequent sections of this chapter.

The table on page 194-96 lists all the cases placed before the ICJ from the election of the first panel of judges in 1946 through 1973. The first case, the Corfu Channel Case, was referred to the Court a year after the Court's initial organization. The peak periods for the submission of new cases came in 1949-51, 1953-55, and 1957-59.

The 1960s are in sharp contrast with the 1950s in the amount of business before the Court. In the 1950s twenty-nine cases were submitted to the ICJ; in the 1960s the number was only six cases on four subjects as both the South West Africa question and the North Sea Continental Shelf controversy involved pairs of related cases on single subjects. In fact, in spite of six years of litigation in the South West Africa case and eight years in the Barcelona Traction Light and Power Company case, the ICJ was twice for brief periods in 1970 and 1971 completely without any pending business of any kind including requests for advisory opinions. If states will not submit cases to the Court, the ICJ will be unable to fulfill its potential contribution toward developing and applying the rule of law at the international level.

INTERNATIONAL COURT OF JUSTICE CASES AND ADVISORY OPINIONS (1947-77)

I. Cases in Which Judgments Were Rendered

Title	Parties	Dates
1. Corfu Channel	United Kingdom v. Albania	1947–49
2. Fisheries	United Kingdom v. Norway	1949–51
3. (a) Asylum	Colombia/Peru*	1949–50
(b) Request for Interpretation of Judgment in Asylum Case	Colombia v. Peru	1950
(c) Haya de la Torre	Colombia v. Peru	1950–51
4. Rights of Nationals of the United States in Morocco	France v. United States	1950–52
5. Ambatielos	Greece v. United Kingdom	1951–53
6. Anglo-Iranian Oil Co.	United Kingdom v. Iran	1951–52
7. Minquiers and Ecrehos	France/United Kingdom*	1951–53
8. Nottebohm	Liechtenstein v. Guatemala	1951–55
9. Monetary Gold Removed from Rome in 1943	Italy v. France, United Kingdom, and United States	1953–54
10. Certain Norwegian Loans	France v. Norway	1955–57
11. Right of Passage over Indian Territory	Portugal v. India	1955–60
12. Application of Convention of 1902 Governing the Guardianship of Infants	Netherlands v. Sweden	1957–58
13. Interhandel	Switzerland v. United States	1957–59
14. Aerial Incident of 27 July 1955	Israel v. Bulgaria	1957–59
15. Sovereignty over Certain Frontier Land	Belgium/Netherlands*	1957–59
16. Arbitral Award Made by the King of Spain on 23 December 1906	Honduras v. Nicaragua	1958–60
17. (a) Barcelona Traction, Light and Power Co., Ltd.	Belgium v. Spain	1958–61
(b) Barcelona Traction, Light and Power Co., Ltd. (New Application)	Belgium v. Spain	1962–70
18. Temple of Preah Vihear	Cambodia v. Thailand	1959–62
19. South West Africa	Ethiopia v. South Africa; Liberia v. South Africa	1960–66
20. North Cameroons	Cameroon v. United Kingdom	1961–63
21. North Sea Continental Shelf	Federal Republic of Germany/Denmark; Federal Republic of Germany/Netherlands*	1967–69
22. Appeal Relating to the Jurisdiction of the ICAO Council	India v. Pakistan	1971–72
23. Fisheries Jurisdiction	United Kingdom v. Iceland	1972–74
24. Fisheries Jurisdiction	Federal Republic of Germany v. Iceland	1972–74
25. Nuclear Tests	Australia v. France	1973–74
26. Nuclear Tests	New Zealand v. France	1973–74

II. Case Pending in 1977

Title	Parties	Dates
1. Aegean Sea Continental Shelf	Greece v. Turkey	1976–

III. Cases Removed without Judgment

Title	Parties	Dates
1. Protection of French Nationals and Protected Persons in Egypt	France v. Egypt	1949–50
2. Electricite de Beyrouth Co.	France v. Lebanon	1953–54
3. (a) Treatment in Hungary of Aircraft and Crew of United States	United States v. Hungary	1954
(b) Treatment in Hungary of Aircraft and Crew of United States	United States v. USSR	1954
4. Aerial Incident of 10 March 1953	United States v. Czechoslovakia	1955–56
5. (a) Antarctica	United Kingdom v. Argentina	1955–56
(b) Antarctica	United Kingdom v. Chile	1955–56
6. Aerial Incident of 7 October 1952	United States v. USSR	1955–56
7. Aerial Incident of 27 July 1955	United States v. Bulgaria	1957–60
8. Aerial Incident of 27 July 1955	United Kingdom v. Bulgaria	1957–59
9. Aerial Incident of 4 September 1954	United States v. USSR	1958
10. Compagnie duPort, des Quais et des Entrepots de Beyrouth and Société Radio-Orient	France v. Lebanon	1959–60
11. Aerial Incident of 7 November 1954	United States v. USSR	1959
12. Trial of Pakistani Prisoners of War	Pakistan v. India	1973

IV. Advisory Opinions

Title	Requested by	Dates
1. Conditions of Admission of a State to Membership in the UN	UN General Assembly	1947–48
2. Reparation for Injuries Suffered in the Service of the UN	UN General Assembly	1948–49
3. Interpretation of Peace Treaties with Bulgaria, Hungary, and Rumania	UN General Assembly	1949–50
4. Competence of the General Assembly for the Admission of a State to the UN	UN General Assembly	1949–50
5. International Status of South West Africa	UN General Assembly	1949–50

Title	IV. Advisory Opinions Requested by	Dates
6. Reservations to the Convention on the Prevention and Punishment of the Crime of Genocide	UN General Assembly	1950-51
7. Effect of Awards of Compensation Made by the UN Administrative Tribunal	UN General Assembly	1953-54
8. Voting Procedure on Questions Relating to Reports and Petitions Concerning the Territory of South West Africa	UN General Assembly	1954-55
9. Judgments of the Administrative Tribunal of the ILO upon Complaints Made Against UNESCO	UNESCO Executive Board	1955-56
10. Admissibility of Hearings of Petitioners by the Committee on South West Africa	UN General Assembly	1955-56
11. Constitution of the Maritime Safety Committee of the Inter-Governmental Maritime Consultative Organization	IMCO Assembly	1959-60
12. Certain Expenses of the UN [Art. 17(2) of the Charter]	UN General Assembly	1961-62
13. Legal Consequences for States of the Continued Presence of South Africa in Namibia (South West Africa) Notwithstanding Security Council Resolution 276 (1970)	UN Security Council	1970-71
14. Application for Review of Judgement No. 158 of the United Nations Administrative Tribunal	Committee on Applications for Review of Administrative Tribunal Judgements	1972-73
15. Western Sahara	UN General Assembly	1974-75

*Proceedings instituted by special agreement

The table of ICJ cases also demonstrates that a substantial number of controversies are removed from the Court's jurisdiction in the preliminary stages with the result that the Court never reaches the point of formulating a judgment. These removals before judgment fall into two categories. The larger group are those in which a plaintiff state presents a case to the Court with a request that the defendant state agree to accept the Court's jurisdiction for the settlement of the dispute. When the state against which the charge is made refuses to submit to the Court's jurisdiction, the Court has no choice but to remove the case from its list. Most of the cases involving aerial incidents and the two cases relating to Antarctica claims are in this category. The remaining cases that fail to reach the judgment stage are removed at the request of the plaintiff, usually on the grounds that a satisfactory settlement or method of settlement has been agreed to by the parties. This procedure is similar to a settlement out of court in civil cases in municipal law. Since these cases require relatively little of the judges' time and consideration, the Court's work load has been lighter than the list of cases and opinions might suggest.

Another point, obvious to any well-informed person who examines the list of ICJ cases, is that the major international conflicts since 1945 have been dealt with by bodies other than the Court. Judgments by the ICJ have been requested in none of the more serious clashes that have come before the political organs of the United Nations — clashes such as Korea, the Congo, Palestine, Suez, Cyprus, or Rhodesia. The level of conflict involved in Court cases is also low as compared with the situations dealt with mainly outside the United Nations, such as Vietnam, Biafra, the Cuba missile crisis, Northern Ireland, or the Chinese border clashes. This is not to say that no questions of legal principles are involved in all these examples or that the issues involved are unsuitable for judicial determination. Rather, it is an indication that the nations of the world, and particularly the most powerful states, do not entrust questions of national interest to impartial determination based on the established rules of international law.

If the cases decided by the Court are not notable for their involvement with world headlines, they may, nevertheless, help to establish an ever-growing set of principles, which, by slow accretion, add to the body of international law. Another major significance of Court judgments is the avoidance by the parties of settlement through resort to violence or other means not based on the rule of law. Willingness to submit a case to legal determination not only establishes patterns of compliance with legal norms for the states involved, but, it is hoped, serves as an example to other states of the desirability of this method of peaceful settlement of disputes.

A brief summary of a few of the Court's most important cases will illustrate the ICJ's adjudicatory role. The selection is based on the significance of legal principles involved and on the degree of general interest in the cases.

Corfu Channel Case   On October 22, 1946, two British destroyers passing through the Corfu Channel adjacent to Albania struck mines, and forty-four naval personnel lost their lives. The channel had been swept in 1945, so the assumption was made that the mines had been recently laid by Albania or another party. The British on November 12 and 13, without Albania's consent, used minesweepers to clear the channel. In January, 1947, the United Kingdom submitted the dispute to the Security Council, which, after some investigation and debate, adopted a resolution recommending that the parties refer the dispute to the ICJ for settlement.

Albania had voluntarily been represented before the Security Council during the Corfu Channel debate and had accepted the resolution to refer the question to the Court but raised preliminary questions challenging technical aspects concerning the Court's jurisdiction. The Court rejected Albania's preliminary objection by a vote of 15–1. The only judge dissenting was the ad hoc judge from Czechoslovakia appointed by Albania under the right of a party to a case not represented on the Court to choose a person to sit for that case.

After disposing of the preliminary objection, the Court turned to the main issues of the case and handed down a judgment on April 9, 1949. The Court ruled that the minefield could not have been laid without the knowledge of Albania, that Albania was responsible for the loss of life and damages, and that compensation should be paid. The Court also decided that the British ships enjoyed the right of innocent passage through an international waterway, although part of the channel lies within the territorial waters of Albania. In sweeping the mines on November 12 and 13, 1946, the British were held by a unanimous Court to have violated Albanian sovereignty. In a third judgment on December 15, 1949, the ICJ fixed the amount of compensation due the United Kingdom from Albania at 843,947 pounds sterling.

The Corfu Channel case is significant because it is the only situation in which the Security Council ever recommended referral of a dispute to the Court. The case is also notable as the only judgment of the ICJ that one of the parties refused to honor; Albania has never paid the assessed compensation to the United Kingdom. Important questions concerning the law of the seas were basic to the judgments, and the Court performed impartially on the basis of legal principles.

Fisheries Case In 1935 the Norwegian government issued a decree reserving exclusive fishing rights for its nationals within a four-mile zone along its northern coast. In 1949 the United Kingdom instituted proceedings before the ICJ objecting, not to the four-mile zone, but to the manner in which Norway had determined the limits of the zone. Norway's coastline is very irregular and it had used straight baselines drawn between fixed points on the mainland and islands rather than following the configuration of the coast. The Court was asked to determine whether the method used and the specific baselines were contrary to international law.

The Court decided both basic questions in favor of Norway. The majority opinion found that the method used by Norway was well established in international law and that Norway had been using a similar method for several decades without objection by other states. Baselines must follow the general direction of the coast and Norway's specific methods did so.

The case was followed with particular interest by many maritime states since it involved significant questions concerning territorial waters. Other aspects of such questions persist to the present, and the International Law Commission and a series of conferences have attempted to resolve some of the related issues.

South West Africa Cases South West Africa was assigned as a Class C Mandate under Article 22 of the League of Nations Covenant to the jurisdiction of South Africa. Class C status permitted South Africa, subject to safeguards for the interests of the indigenous population, to administer the area as an integral part of its own territory. When the United Nations was formed, all former mandates not granted independence, except South West Africa, were placed under trusteeship. South Africa claimed that, with the demise of the League, it was under no obligation to place South West Africa under trusteeship, and stated its intention to annex the territory under its sovereign control. In 1949 South Africa discontinued its annual reports on South West Africa and refused to forward petitions from inhabitants of the territory to the United Nations.

In December, 1949, the General Assembly requested an advisory opinion of the ICJ concerning the international status of South West Africa and the resulting obligations of South Africa. In July, 1950, the Court rendered an opinion covering several aspects of the issue. The Court advised that (1) South Africa's obligations under the original mandate continued and it was required to submit reports to the General Assembly as the successor organ to the League machinery; (2) although Chapter XII of the Charter provides a means by which South West Africa could be placed under trusteeship, it was not mandatory that South Africa do so; (3) the degree of supervision by the General Assembly was to be, as far as possible, neither greater nor less than that exercised by the League; and (4) South Africa could not unilaterally alter the status of South West Africa and would have to obtain the consent of the General Assembly for any such modification.

South Africa refused to recognize the validity of the Court's advisory opinion and continued to ignore all United Nations attempts to work out means for compliance with its terms. The General Assembly established a series of committees to seek means for implementing the terms of the opinion and to investigate conditions in South West Africa. Beginning in 1957 the Assembly pointed out to member states the possibility of taking legal action through the ICJ under the terms of the original mandate. Such a case would necessarily have to be instituted by a state that was a member of the League of Nations.

In 1960 Ethiopia and Liberia instituted proceedings against South Africa before the ICJ. They charged that South Africa (1) had failed to carry out its duties as a mandatory power, (2) had extended the policy of apartheid to South West Africa, (3) had violated the human rights of the population of South West Africa and prevented progress toward self-government, and (4) had failed to render annual reports or to forward petitions to the General Assembly. South Africa responded by raising preliminary objections to the jurisdiction of the Court and to the right of Ethiopia and Liberia to act as plaintiffs. In 1962 the Court replied to the preliminary objections by ruling that, as had been indicated in the 1950 advisory opinion, South Africa's obligations under the mandate continued, that the ICJ was the appropriate forum in which to air the complaint, and that Ethiopia and Liberia, as former members of the League, were entitled to bring the charges of violation of the obligations under the Mandate. The fact that the Court was sharply divided 8-7 on the preliminary questions was an omen of the possibility of a final opinion unfavorable to the Ethiopian and Liberian position. Changes in Court personnel between 1962 and 1966 contributed to converting this possibility into reality.

After four more years of written and oral proceedings and after consideration of two additional procedural motions by South Africa, the ICJ in July, 1966, handed down its final judgment in the South West Africa cases. The judgment did not deal with the substantive issues raised by Ethiopia and Liberia but rested upon the legal status of the plaintiffs and their right to institute proceedings to enforce the mandate, a question which, according to widely held opinion, had been disposed of in the 1962 Court rulings. The Court found that the plaintiffs had failed to establish their right or interest to enforce the mandate since the Covenant did not provide for the right of each League member individually to require from the mandatories the performance of their obligations. Such a right was vested only in the League organs, and, since the League was now defunct, no means of legal enforcement was possible. The Court noted that the absence of a means of legal enforcement in the international field occurred frequently.

The ICJ's ruling was greeted with dismay by most African states as well as by a majority of United Nations members, which had been carrying on a campaign against the remnants of colonialism and against all forms of racial or ethnic discrimination. The dismay was compounded by the expectation that the Court would rule on the substantive, not the procedural, aspects of the case since the 1962 preliminary judgment had been based, in part, on Article 7 of the Mandate, which established the right of League members to invoke the compulsory jurisdiction of the Court in any dispute involving the Mandate. The ruling was made more unpalatable by the fact that the vote of the justices was 7–7 with Sir Percy Spender of Australia using his prerogative in such cases, as President of the Court, to cast an additional "casting vote" to break the tie.

The members of the United Nations were frustrated in their hopes for using the ICJ as one more avenue for putting pressure on South Africa to grant early independence to South West Africa. After the adverse decision they turned from legal means to an intensification of their efforts through political channels. Disillusionment with the court increased as a result of the 1966 decision, and the movement away from the adjudicatory process was intensified.

Advisory Opinions

The ICJ may be requested to give advisory opinions on any legal questions by the Security Council, the General Assembly, or any other organ or specialized agency of the United Nations that has been authorized by the General Assembly to make such requests. The General Assembly has extended such authorization to the Economic and Social Council, the Trusteeship Council, the Interim Committee of the General Assembly, the Committee on Applications for Review of Administrative Tribunal Judgments, the International Atomic Energy Agency, and all of the specialized agencies except the Universal Postal Union. Prior to 1978 the ICJ had rendered eleven advisory opinions at the request of the General Assembly, one at the request of the Security Council, one at the request of the Executive Board of UNESCO, one at the request of the Assembly of the Inter-Governmental Maritime Consultative Organization, and one at the request of the Committee on Applications for Review of Administrative Tribunal Judgments.

Advisory opinions are not binding but are authoritative statements of the principles of international law applying to the specific situations on which the advice of the Court is sought. Advisory opinions often delineate the rights and duties of states or international agencies, or provide an interpretation of an international treaty or other instrument. Advisory opinions are useful to establish a basis for further action and could be sought much more frequently by international bodies. The Security Council has been particularly delinquent in seeking the Court's advice on legal issues, a delinquency that reflects the emphasis upon political not legal approaches by that body and an indication of the reluctance of the major powers to subject their policies to international legal norms.

A majority of Court opinions have been accorded due respect through compliance with the terms of the rulings, but the record is far from perfect. In an advisory opinion of March, 1950, the Court ruled that Bulgaria, Hungary, and Rumania were obligated to cooperate in setting up commissions to safeguard human rights as provided in the peace treaties with those countries. When all three refused to comply, the Court further advised that a substitute method of appointment of commissioners was not justified, and a stalemate resulted. It has been noted above with regard to the South West Africa situation that South Africa refused to respect the advisory opinion of the Court concerning its several continuing obligations under the terms of the Mandate. A number of states, led by the Soviet Union and France, refused to honor a 1962 Court opinion on the right of the General Assembly to assess the costs of certain peacekeeping operations of the United Nations on the same basis as the regular budget of the organization. Lack of respect for Court opinions contributes to the weakening of the international legal order and is one more evidence of the need for means of enforcing international legal rules and standards.

Only five requests for advisory opinions have been registered with the ICJ since 1955 as compared with ten between 1947 and 1955. In part this decline is due to the greater need in early years for legal opinions to clarify points of confusion in a newly created set of international organizations. In substantial measure, however, the trend is one aspect of the direction of international relations in which states use political rather than legal means for conducting their foreign policies.

Some of the ICJ's advisory opinions have dealt with fundamental and significant legal matters. A few examples will illustrate this aspect of the work of this Court.

Conditions of Admission of a State to Membership in the United Nations (Article 4 of Charter) In 1946 and 1947 fifteen states applied for admission to membership in the United Nations, and, during that period, only four were admitted. The unsuccessful candidates were the victims of an East-West political contest in which the United States and the Soviet Union each managed to block the candidates favored by the other through the voting requirements in the Security Council. There was little doubt that most of the applicants could meet the standards for admission, if impartially applied, but the reasons given for the rejections served as legal rationalizations for political expediency in which neither major power was willing to see the influence of the other in the United Nations extended.

In order to clarify some of the issues behind the deadlock, the General Assembly asked the ICJ for an advisory opinion. The request raised two major questions. One question was in regard to whether a member state is juridically entitled to make its consent to the admission of a new member dependent on conditions not expressly provided by Article 4 of the Charter. The second question concerned whether a member can make its consent subject to the condition that other states be admitted at the same time.

In rendering its advisory opinion in May, 1948, the Court disposed of two preliminary questions. It found that the issues involved in the request were properly legal, not political, questions, and it upheld its own competence under the Charter and the Statute of the Court to interpret the Charter.

In dealing with the substantive issues raised by the General Assembly, the Court advised that the conditions for admission of members specified in Article 4 of the Charter were exhaustive and that members were not justified in adding other conditions. From this conclusion it then follows that the admission of one member cannot be made contingent upon the admission of another. Each member's admission should be based on its own qualifications unconnected to any other conditions.

The handing down of this opinion did not immediately resolve the membership impasse but it clarified some of the issues involved in the admission process. The major powers continued to block membership applications on grounds that in their self-judgment would fall within the qualifications for membership specified in Article 4 of the Charter. Another attempt to escape the stalemate was made by the General Assembly in 1949 by requesting the Court to advise on whether the General Assembly could admit a state to membership in the absence of a positive recommendation by the Security Council. The Court replied that such a procedure would violate the clear intent of the Charter. The membership dilemma was finally resolved in 1955 with a "gentleman's agreement" for a "package deal" in spite of the Court's previous advice that one state's admission should not depend upon the simultaneous admission of another state.

Reparation for Injuries Suffered in the Service of the United Nations By 1948 several agents of the United Nations had been killed or injured while carrying out their official duties. The assassination of the United Nations mediator in Palestine, Count Folke Bernadotte, was the most publicized of these incidents. The United Nations had provided compensation in these cases and wished to establish its legal right to attempt to recover these amounts by claims against the states responsible for the deaths or injuries.

In December, 1948, the General Assembly sought an advisory opinion from the ICJ in which the principal issue was whether the United Nations had the capacity to bring an international claim against the responsible government with the purpose of obtaining reparation for damage caused to the United Nations and to the victim. In the event of an affirmative reply to the main issue the General Assembly also wished to know how the action by the United Nations could be reconciled with such rights as might be possessed by the state of which the victim was a national.

The advisory opinion of the Court was a landmark in establishing the international personality of the United Nations with attendant rights in international law. The Court ruled that the member states in setting up the United Nations intended to confer upon it the capacity to operate on the international plane and to exercise rights and duties necessary to carry out its functions. Its privileges are not necessarily identical with those of a state, but the organization must be deemed to have such powers as, even if not expressly stated in the Charter, are essential to the performance of its duties. This is a principle of implied powers that opens the door to a generous interpretation of the prerogatives of international organizations. With regard to the secondary question of reconciling the United Nation's right to claim damages with those of an interested state, the Court advised that neither party has priority and that any conflict of interest might be resolved by accommodation.

Effect of Awards of Compensation Made by the United Nations Administrative Tribunal In December, 1952, Secretary-General Trygve Lie dismissed or suspended a number of Secretariat employees who were United States nationals. The grounds for dismissal were the refusal of the staff members to testify before a United States federal grand jury or before Congressional committees on questions of subversion. Twenty-one of these former employees appealed their cases to the Administrative Tribunal established by the General Assembly in 1949 to review charges of violation of staff members' contracts. The Administrative Tribunal awarded compensation to eleven of those dismissed in the amount of 179,420 dollars. The United States led the opposition in the General Assembly to appropriating the funds for compensation and, as a compromise measure, the Assembly decided to request an advisory opinion of the ICJ.

The question answered by the Court was whether the General Assembly had the right on any grounds to refuse to give effect to an award of compensation made by the Administrative Tribunal in favor of a United Nations staff member whose contract had been terminated without his assent. In determining the answer the ICJ examined the nature of the Administrative Tribunal and found that, although the Tribunal was created by the General Assembly, it was intended to be a judicial, not an advisory, body with authority to make decisions from which there was no appeal. The judgments were, therefore, binding on the General Assembly, which was obligated to appropriate funds for the awards. Challenges to the power of the Assembly to create the Tribunal or to confer upon it its assigned powers were rejected. Thus a broad interpretation of implied powers not explicitly stated in the Charter was relied upon by the Court to arrive at its ruling, an approach consistent with the earlier Reparation for Injuries opinion.

The Awards of Compensation ruling was made against the dramatic background of hysteria in the United States concerning alleged subversion among government and United Nations employees. Although the United States government lost the battle for refusing to pay compensation to its dismissed nationals, it managed to get major concessions from the Secretariat concerning the future screening of United States personnel employed by the United Nations. The costs of such concessions were high in terms of the independent international position of the Secretariat and in terms of general morale among its personnel. These factors are examined in more detail in chapter 15.

Several additional advisory opinions are referred to at other points in this and other chapters of the text. The opinion on the International Status of South West Africa was discussed above as background for the South West African Cases decision in 1966. Altogether three separate opinions on questions pertaining to South West Africa were handed down between 1950 and 1956 and these opinions form a part of the picture of the struggle for independence treated in chapter 13. A fourth opinion on South West Africa delivered in 1971 is the latest important development in this sequence.

The opinion by the Court in 1962 on the right of the General Assembly to assess peacekeeping costs as a part of the regular expenses of the United Nations was discussed in relation to the section on financial problems in chapter 5 and in regard to peacekeeping practices in chapter 7. Together with the preceding treatment of selected advisory opinions, these references form a basis for judging the significant role played by the Court in delivering advisory opinions on basic legal problems that have faced the United Nations.

THE ROLE OF THE INTERNATIONAL LAW COMMISSION

The Charter makes the General Assembly responsible for initiating studies and making recommendations "for the purpose of . . . encouraging the progressive development of international law and its codification."[5] In order to carry out this function the Assembly established the International Law Commission as its principal instrument for making the necessary studies and recommendations. After some delays in the General Assembly over details for its establishment, the International Law Commission began its work in 1949. Its twenty-five members are chosen as experts in law representing the major legal systems of the world, and no two may be of the same nationality. The pattern of composition was thus copied from that of the ICJ.

The procedures of the International Law Commission have been slow, but this slowness is inherent in the processes of developing international law. The commission has also followed a pragmatic and flexible course in drawing no sharp distinction between its two functions of progressive development and codification of law. In many instances its efforts on a single subject involve clarification and standardization as well as the filling of gaps in existing law. The steps usually followed in developing and codifying law are (1) selection of an appropriate topic by the commission, (2) approval of the topic by the General Assembly, (3) appointment of a member of the commission as rapporteur on the subject, (4) report and preliminary suggested draft by the rapporteur, (5) discussion and revision by the commission, (6) submission to governments for comment, (7) revision by the commission on the basis of governments' suggestions, (8) submission of the revised draft to the General Assembly, (9) consideration in the Assembly's Sixth Committee, (10) decision by the

---

[5] Charter of the United Nations, Art. 13, sec. 1.

General Assembly to convene an international conference to consider the draft, (11) consideration and revision by the international conference, (12) signature of any adopted convention by state representatives, (13) ratification by governments, (14) deposit of sufficient ratifications to bring the new convention into force. With so many hurdles to overcome many efforts at codification become stalled or are aborted.

However, the International Law Commission has been successful in initiating studies that have led to the adoption of important conventions. At its initial session the commission drew up an agenda of fourteen topics for its investigation. The General Assembly has from time to time requested additional studies. One general area in which a series of multilateral treaties has been adopted as a result of groundwork by the commission is the law of the sea. A conference in Geneva in 1958 adopted four separate conventions on the territorial sea, the high seas, fisheries, and the continental shelf. Further complex unresolved problems concerning the oceans were considered by a conference in 1960 and by the Third United Nations Law of the Seas Conference which began in 1973 and was prolonged by the difficulties of achieving compromise among diverse interests. Additional details on these issues are given in chapter 12. Initial work by the International Law Commission also resulted in the adoption of the Vienna Convention on Diplomatic Relations (1961) and the Vienna Convention on Consular Relations (1963). These conventions modified and clarified diplomatic and consular practices, some of which had been established at Aix-la-Chapelle in 1818. A third area in which the work of the International Law Commission led to the formulation of a multilateral treaty is with regard to the problem of statelessness. International conferences at Geneva (1959) and New York (1961) finally adopted and opened for ratification a Convention on the Reduction of Statelessness.

According to many legal experts, the most fundamental accomplishment of the International Law Commission has been its preparatory work concerning the law of treaties. Treaties are especially important because they constitute a major source of international law. Careful work by the commission resulted in the adoption by a two-year conference of the Vienna Convention on the Law of Treaties (1969). By this convention many uncertainties in the customary law of treaties are removed.

In addition to its contributions to the formulation of international conventions, the International Law Commission has submitted other significant reports to the General Assembly. These studies include, *inter alia*, (1) model rules of arbitral procedure, (2) the principles of the Nuremberg trials, (3) a declaration of the rights and duties of states, (4) a code of offenses against the peace and security of humankind, (5) the question of defining aggression, and (6) the effect of reservations to multilateral conventions.

Evaluations of the contributions of the International Law Commission vary. There is little doubt of the eminence of some of its members. The original membership of the commission included such distinguished legal experts as Sir Benegal Rau of India, James L. Brierly of the United Kingdom, Manley O. Hudson of the United States, V. M. Koretsky of the USSR, and George Scelle of France. Its meticulous preparatory work for the law of treaties might alone justify the existence of the commission for its more than thirty years.

Professor Percy E. Corbett points to one of the difficulties that the International Law Commission has faced from the beginning.

> The division of the world into competing power blocs, aggravated, if not caused, by the conflict of ideologies, made the International Law Commission a forum for political polemics, a distortion undeterred by the fact that its members were supposed to be independent experts rather than representatives of governments.[6]

Yet, in general, Professor Corbett praises the commission, calling its total output "a remarkable achievement"[7] and highlighting

> its merits not only as a standing drafting committee, but as a body where, in spite of the nonofficial character of its members, even the political and cultural differences of their countries undergo a first round of reconciliation. . . . The enlargement of the Commission from the original fifteen experts in 1948 to twenty-five in 1961 gives new assurance that all main currents of legal thought will find representation, and at the same time gives the newly established nations of Asia and Africa a necessary sense of participation in the adaptation to present needs of a legal order which they had little or no part in elaborating.[8]

OTHER AGENCIES PROMOTING WORLD LAW

The Sixth (Legal) Committee of the General Assembly deals with a wide range of legal problems assigned to it by the Assembly. It regularly reviews the recommendations and reports from the International Law Commission. The Sixth Committee could be used more

[6] Percy E. Corbett, *The Growth of World Law* (Princeton, N.J.: Princeton University Press, 1971), pp. 51–52.
[7] *Ibid.*, p. 60.
[8] *Ibid.*, p. 68.

extensively, but many legal questions are often assigned to one of the committees handling political issues in situations in which political and legal questions are intertwined. The Sixth Committee was utilized to draft one important treaty, the Convention on Genocide.

One of the earliest acts of the General Assembly was its approval and opening for ratification of the General Convention on Privileges and Immunities of the United Nations. Because of its fundamental importance to the operation of the United Nations, this convention was drafted by a subcommittee of the legal committee of the United Nations Preparatory Commission and was ready for consideration at the first session of the General Assembly. After review by its Sixth Committee the Assembly approved the Convention in February, 1946.

The General Assembly occasionally declares and even creates law by resolution. In 1961 and 1963 it adopted unanimous resolutions declaring principles for space that were later incorporated into the 1967 Treaty on Outer Space. On other occasions actions by the Assembly have led to important subsequent treaties. As a result of the cooperation stemming from the proclamation of an International Geophysical Year in 1957 and 1958, the Antarctic Treaty was made possible among the states having claims in that area. The treaty provides for continued cooperation among the parties and prohibits all military activity in Antarctica.

In order to support the legal work of the United Nations and to advise on legal matters, the Secretariat incorporates within its structure an Office of Legal Affairs. Because of the initiatives taken by the Secretary-General, the advice of the legal counsel, who heads the office, and of his staff are vital to the Secretary-General. The Secretariat also registers and publishes international treaties and agreements in the United Nations Treaty Series.

From time to time the General Assembly establishes bodies to study or promote a discrete aspect of international law. In 1963 the Assembly created a Special Committee on Principles of International Law Concerning Friendly Relations and Cooperation Among States. The committee was asked to assist the Assembly with the study of seven principles for improving state relations and cooperation. In 1965 the Assembly established a ten-member Advisory Committee on a Program of Technical Assistance to Promote the Teaching, Study, Dissemination and Wider Appreciation of International Law. The advisory committee was assigned the task of advising the Secretary-General in a program carried out by the Secretariat, UNESCO, the United Nations Development Program, and the United Nations Institute for Training and Research. In 1966 the Assembly created a twenty-nine-member (later expanded to thirty-six members) United Nations Commission on International Trade Law with a broad program to promote the improvement of the law of international trade and with a close relationship to the United Nations Conference on Trade and Development.

Since its inception the Commission on Human Rights, under the aegis of the Economic and Social Council, has devoted its main energies to the development and encouragement of multilateral treaties within its field of competence. After first producing the Declaration of Human Rights, the commission turned its attention to converting the nonbinding declaration into two covenants, one on economic, social, and cultural rights and the other on civil and political rights. States were slow to ratify these covenants, but in 1976 they received sufficient ratifications to come into force. Under United Nations auspices other treaties have been produced dealing with such subjects as equal rights for women, forced labor and slavery, the elimination of all forms of discrimination, the status of refugees and the reduction of statelessness.

The International Labor Organization (ILO) has since 1919 opened for ratification more than 130 conventions dealing with every aspect of labor welfare. By setting standards and incorporating these standards through ratification into the domestic law of states, these conventions can serve as a model for similar efforts in other fields. Fuller treatment of the contributions of the ILO to labor law is presented in chapter 11.

In 1966 a Convention on the Settlement of Investment Disputes between States and Nationals of Other States entered into force. The treaty had been worked out through several years of preliminary effort by the International Bank for Reconstruction and Development. The unique feature of this convention is its provision for binding arbitration of disputes in which private investors as well as states are involved.

Regional organizations have made significant contributions to the development of international law and judicial practice. The European Court of Justice, which is the judicial arm of the European Community, has handed down hundreds of decisions and rulings on disputes among the western European members. Parties to the cases may be member states, community organs, or private individuals or agencies. The European court also rules on preliminary questions referred from municipal courts. Court decisions are binding upon the parties and upon municipal organs of government, but the problem of enforcement is not satisfactorily resolved.

The Council of Europe sponsored a European Convention on Human Rights, which came into force in 1953. The convention provides for a European Commission on Human Rights, which screens most complaints, and a court of last resort, the European Court of Human Rights, which is composed of one judge from each of the eighteen members of the Council of Europe. Although few cases are brought to the court, the degree of satisfaction with the system seems high. Individuals may bring complaints to the commission, and the emphasis is upon quiet adjustment of differences. Unique breakthroughs in the practice of international law are represented by the compulsory jurisdiction and the access of private parties to the European Court of Justice, the European Commission on Human Rights, and the European Court of Human Rights.

Since the creation of a Commission of Jurists by the Inter-American Conference of 1906, a substantial number of conventions have been produced by that body and its successors in the Organization of American States. The conventions cover a broad range of subjects but none of them has been ratified by every member of the organization. The work of the commission was divided in 1948 between an Inter-American Council of Jurists and an Inter-American Juridical Committee, and less progress has been made since that date.

Dozens of private agencies focus all or a portion of their energies on the promotion of international law as an instrument of world order. For a fairly complete summary of the work of both private and public agencies in this field, the student should examine the May–June, 1967, issue of *Intercom*, published by the Foreign Policy Association in New York. Only a partial listing will be included here.

The International Chamber of Commerce has carried on a variety of activities to promote international law with regard to trade and investments. In 1953 it took the initiative through the Economic and Social Council to call attention to the need for enforcement of commercial arbitral awards. An international conference was called in New York in 1958 and the following year the Convention on the Recognition and Enforcement of Foreign Arbitral Awards came into force. The chamber established a Court of Arbitration in Paris in 1924, which has heard more than 2,000 cases involving individuals, corporations, and governments in disputes providing for arbitration in the enforcement of contracts. The chamber has also established standards for fair treatment of international investment and for the terms of international contracts.

The World Peace Through Law Center in Geneva was established in 1963. Among its activities are the sponsorship of biennial world conferences and World Law Day; the establishment of sixty subject-matter committees and national committees; the publication of reports, bulletins, and pamphlets; and the maintenance of a world legal information and reference service.

The Institute for World Order, Inc., in New York carries on a broad educational program through schools and colleges. It makes available publications and films and conducts seminars for students and teachers. It also is conducting a World Order Models Project to promote alternative futures for the world of the 1990s with an emphasis upon the elimination of war.

The United World Federalists have been very active in the United States since World War II in promoting the concept of peace through law. The Federalists spread their influence through publications and meetings, but they also serve as a well-organized pressure group to influence the United States Congress on issues within their range of interests.

Other organizations are too numerous to describe. A partial list would include the American Society of International Law, the American Bar Association's committees on World Peace Through Law and on Peace and Law Through the United Nations and its section of International and Comparative Law; the International Commission of Jurists; the Duke University Rule of Law Research Center; the Commission to Study the Organization of Peace; the Carnegie Endowment for International Peace; and the Fund for Education in World Order.

ASSESSING OUR PROGRESS

Because of certain defects and gaps in the system, the development of international law appears to many critics to be one of the weakest elements in the evolution of international organization and in the struggle for world order. These defects are not difficult to identify and a comparison with national legal systems dramatizes the deficiencies of the international system.

A single court lacking compulsory jurisdiction is inadequate to meet the minimal standards of a world system of justice. If most international legal disputes were assured of a hearing in a judicial forum, the International Court of Justice would be unable to conduct all of the hearings. Instead the Court languishes from a lack of business. The decision in the South West Africa cases contributed to a loss of confidence in the Court but is not the principal factor in its being neglected. The political organs of the United Nations have failed to utilize the ICJ for advisory opinions on many subjects. More importantly, national governments have refused to submit their differences to impartial judicial judgment thus subordinating their national interest in the evolution of world order to the supposed advantages of protecting immediate interests. The lack of adherence to the optional clause of the Court Statute and the attachment of crippling reservations to acceptance of that clause are other factors contributing to the inactivity of the ICJ.

Even if a system of courts with compulsory jurisdiction existed, other defects in the international legal system would be apparent. Individuals as well as states and international organizations should have rights and duties under the law. Custom and multilateral treaties produced by occasional conferences are slow and inefficient methods of developing a comprehensive body of law. Means of enforcement will remain unsatisfactory as long as no independent enforcement agencies exist at the international level.

In spite of deficiencies a substantial system of and a body of international law exist. Except in a few critical areas international law is observed and respected. New states look to legal norms to protect them against insecurity, and mature states find the conduct of international affairs impossible except within the framework of law. An increasing body of commercial law is evolving and disputes are being settled by recourse to legal agencies and principles. New treaties have been adopted and widely respected not only in the realm of commerce but also with regard to labor, human rights, Antarctica, space, and the seas. A few bright spots appear in the area of arms limitation and regulation. The desire of every state to belong to the United Nations and to a network of regional and world organizations and to use the processes of these organizations for common ends is a beginning toward further development of world law.

In spite of slowness and politicization, the International Law Commission has been successful in developing standards and the texts for conventions in crucial areas of law. It has been willing to pioneer in the codification and development of law on the most fundamental subjects regarding interstate relations.

Perhaps it is the private agencies that most clearly indicate the future hope for a more orderly world. The acceptance of the peace-through-law concept has permeated a wide range of nongovernmental organizations. This concept is fundamental to the philosophy on which the United Nations is built; the renunciation of the use of force and the settlement of disputes by peaceful means is the keystone principle of the organization. National political leaders cling stubbornly to national sovereignty and independence in a world in which traditional approaches are inadequate to the needs of humankind. The realization of the need for orderly legal processes in critical areas of international relations may eventually reach the level of national political leadership in a majority of the world's states. Pressures from private groups will speed this process.

9

❧

Controlling
the
Instruments of War

War is as old as the existence of competing political units and as ubiquitous as the common cold. Like the cold, people for some time have tried to eliminate it, with about equal success. Theories about the causes of war range from those of the human's supposedly inherent violence to those of war as exploitation in a class struggle. Reactions to war stretch from its acceptance as a continuation of political intercourse by other means to its deprecation as wasteful, inhumane, and irrational.

Although wars always have been devastating, those of the twentieth century have introduced new methods of actual and potentially total destruction. The Thirty Years War during the seventeenth century was perhaps, for the area involved, as bloody and ravaging as any so far. Yet in the twentieth century, the two world wars involved more countries, more men, more widespread combat arenas, more expense, and more lethal weapons that any before. The new nuclear weapon was the first with a capacity to destroy all human life on this planet.

The resulting arms races affect both rich and poor nations alike. Few have been able to resist maintaining expensive military forces and weapons systems. The most powerful countries have been caught up in both an escalating arms race and in the development of more sophisticated weapons — conventional, nuclear, chemical, radiological, and bacteriological. Poor states accept military aid from the rich and spend great sums of their own on military preparedness. In Ruth Leger Sivard's study, using the most reliable available statistics, of the twelve countries that in 1974 spent more than ten percent of their gross national product (GNP) on military preparedness, eight had per capita GNPs of less than 600 dollars.[1] Obviously, this is an oppressive burden for poverty-stricken countries. Throughout the world, military and space research receive more public research and development funds than all social needs combined. The affluent donor nations spend over fifteen times as much on military budgets as they contribute to the poor nations in official economic assistance. From 1961 to 1975, the cost of arms imports of the developing nations increased twice as fast as either their increase in receipts of development aid or their rise in per capita GNP.[2] Neither rich nor poor can support such high levels of military preparedness without neglecting other areas of human needs that, if fulfilled, can contribute more positively to human well-being.

Proposals for disarmament and arms controls have been numerous; steps toward their success have been few or often have been retrogressive. Since the advent of the nuclear age, the demand for control has been increased by the knowledge of the power of the new weapons and of their better delivery systems. Yet a common interest in survival has not produced an agreement to eliminate or control weapons and military forces. Fear, suspicion, envy, pride, and all those negative qualities dividing the human race have continued to dominate those international relations closest to restraining or eliminating the ability of nations to destroy each other.

A DISCOURAGING HISTORY

Throughout history philosophers have advocated disarmament as one means of controlling international conflict or of lowering the level of suffering and destruction caused by war, but their ideas have made little appreciable impact upon those who wielded political power. This discrepancy between philosophical thought and state practice was noted above in chapter 1. Jeremy Bentham, Immanuel Kant, William Ladd, and Richard Cobden were especially strong in their advocacy of disarmament as a means to peace.

[1] Ruth Leger Sivard, *World Military and Social Expenditures 1977* (Leesburg, Virginia: WMSE Publications, 1977).
[2] *Ibid.*

Occasional state actions or pressures for disarmament appeared in the ninteenth century. As early as 1816 the Russian tsar suggested general disarmament, but this and similar suggestions by several heads of state during the century evoked no favorable response from other governments. In 1817, under the terms of the Rush-Bagot Treaty, Great Britain and the United States agreed to the demilitarization of the Great Lakes, an important step in the attitude of friendly confidence that has pervaded most U.S.-Canadian-British relations for 150 years.

The Hague conferences of 1899 and 1907 were called by the Russian tsar in the hope of reaching agreements on disarmament and means of peaceful settlement of disputes. The 1899 conference succeeded only in adopting an innocuous and meaningless resolution urging states to reduce their military budgets, but no firm agreements could be reached. The 1907 conference noted the ongoing increase in armaments and decided that nothing could be done at the time to stop the arms race. An agreement to meet again in 1915 was aborted by war.

At the close of the war a series of treaties, including the Treaty of Versailles, provided for disarmament and demilitarization in certain areas. Germany was forced to accept severe limitations on its armaments, and the Rhineland, Danzig, and other areas were demilitarized.

Article 8 of the Covenant of the League of Nations dealt with disarmament and related questions. A firm pledge of "reduction of national armaments to the lowest point consistent with national safety" left open the underlying conditions of security that would make agreement possible on levels and formulas for reduction. The League Council was charged with the responsibility for initiating plans for disarmament, and League members pledged the exchange of "full and frank information" on levels of military preparedness including information on industries convertible to war-support production. The information contained in these reports was published in the League's *Armaments Yearbook.* Finally the members agreed "that the manufacture by private enterprise of munitions and instruments of war is open to grave objections," and again the Council was directed to "advise how the evil effects attendant upon such manufacture can be prevented."

During the period 1920-24 two commissions appointed by the League Council were unable to agree on plans for disarmament. However, confidence still existed that a universal disarmament agreement could be formulated and adopted, and in 1925 the Council appointed a Preparatory Commission to do the preliminary work necessary before convening a World Disarmament Conference. Commission membership included three nonmembers of the League — the United States, the USSR, and Germany. At this point the intention was clear to call the conference within three years.

During its five years of intermittent effort, the Preparatory Commission came up against fundamental national cleavages concerning approaches to disarmament and the relation of disarmament to security guarantees and to enforcement measures. France wanted security before disarmament. The United States refused to be linked to any system of international sanctions. Germany chaffed under the special restraints imposed by the Treaty of Versailles and demanded equality. The USSR insisted on total disarmament. Basically, the United States and Great Britain maintained that disarmament in itself would lead to security, while France argued that disarmament could come only after security measures were instigated and that international enforcement must be incorporated into disarmament plans. Agreement seemed impossible. The final instrument of the Preparatory Commission was a draft convention, which failed to resolve the fundamental national differences and which left numerous gaps to be filled, contrary to all reasonable expectation, by the World Disarmament Conference.

In spite of dim prospects for success, the World Disarmament Conference was finally convened in February, 1932. Additional indicators in the international climate foretold the possibility of failure. The Nazis were rising in power in Germany, and Japan had invaded Manchuria. Economic unrest was fed by the Depression. The spirit of political cooperation was fragile.

Instead of following the normal pattern for international conferences of adjournment after a few weeks of intensive effort, the World Disarmament Conference dragged on intermittently for more than two years. Several new and revised plans were considered, but each was unacceptable to one or more major powers. The United States, Great Britain, Germany, France, and Italy consulted during periods of conference recess. Any hope for agreement was shattered, when, in 1933, first Japan and then Germany announced their withdrawal from the League and from the conference. Final adjournment came in June, 1934, with no tangible achievement to show for nearly a decade of planning and negotiation.

The one area of partial success in disarmament efforts during this period was in naval disarmament. At the Washington Naval Conference in 1921-22, the United States, Great Britain, Japan, France and Italy agreed to limit the size of battleships and aircraft carriers, scrap certain ships, and build no new capital ships for ten years. In the London Naval Treaty of 1930 the United States, Great Britain, and Japan agreed to extend the building moratorium on capital ships, limited the size of destroyers and submarines, and set ceilings for their total tonnages of cruisers, destroyers, and submarines. The resurgence of Japanese militarism and territorial ambitions in the Pacific marked the abandonment of the naval treaties.

The experiences of the interwar years seemed to indicate the fallacy of the direct approach to disarmament, which held that armaments in themselves were the main source of insecurity among nations and that disarmament would automatically bring an easing of international tensions. Negotiators from many countries were unwilling to enter into disarmament agreements unless linked with security and enforcement measures. Such arrangements as were negotiated were readily evaded or discarded when they were incompatible with the political goals of the state. Simplistic approaches to disarmament failed to come to grips with the basic elements of state relations, which included the prerogative of waging war to gain or protect supposed national interests. Armaments, both then and today, are considered as primary instruments of national security—the most fundamental goal of the foreign policy of most states. Therefore, armaments will not be lightly surrendered without substitute means of assuring that security.

ARMS CONTROL ISSUES

Since 1945 three major developments have affected and complicated the desire for arms control or disarmament as factors in maintaining a peaceful world. The first of these is the development of nuclear and other means of destruction thousands of times more lethal than previous weapons. The second factor, recently showing signs of diminishing in significance, is the bipolar rivalry of two superpowers, reinforced by a clash of ideologies. The third development is the emergence of dozens of new states whose demands produce a degree of instabilitiy in international relations.

The terms "arms control" and "disarmament" are often linked but are neither synonymous nor mutually exclusive alternative approaches to the problem of dealing with armaments. Disarmament means a reduction in the means to engage in war and may be qualitative, quantitative, or both. Arms control may involve a reduction in armaments levels but need not do so. Arms control involves mutual restraint and a seeking of stability in arms competition through regulation. More emphasis has been placed on arms control than on disarmament since 1945 at the same time that an escalating arms race has been in progress.

Arms control and disarmament cannot be divorced from the world setting in which agreements must be negotiated. Stability in arms control can be achieved more easily in a stable international climate. If levels of fear, suspicion, and incompatability of goals are high, negotiation becomes more difficult. Feelings of insecurity and mistrust may lead to an arms race, which may result in greater insecurity.

For a major portion of the postwar years, the Soviet Union and the United States were the leaders of competing power blocs, each attempting to attain superiority in individual and collective strength. Military alliances were the order of the day. Competing ideologies served as the philosophical basis for rivalry of political, economic, and social systems. These ideologies depicted the world competition in terms of good versus evil — evoking a messianic zeal on each side of the curtain that separated East from West.

As each power block began to crumble, new forces unconducive to arms agreements developed. The nuclear monopoly of the United States and the Soviet Union was broken, and many states developed the potentiality for a nuclear arsenal. The cleavage within the Communist bloc produced an intense rivalry for bloc leadership with China as the challenger. Many aspects of Chinese policy were enigmatic, and China's stance was more militant and revolutionary than that of the Soviet Union, which had begun to moderate. China possessed limited nuclear capability but remained outside the channels of negotiation for arms control. The French no longer trusted United States assurances of nuclear protection and developed their own capabilities, also refusing to be bound by international limitations.

The emergence of dozens of new states in the Third World, while only indirectly related to arms control, nevertheless complicated the problem of seeking agreements. New lines of cleavage were drawn between North and South, rich and poor. Military assistance was often thrust upon countries that could ill afford to build a military establishment. Established ruling cliques might use such aid to assure their continuation in power, or the aid might appeal to national pride and prestige, but it often delayed the solution of problems related to most basic needs of an impoverished nation. Poor countries are adversely affected if they become the battlegrounds for limited wars involving the affluent states. The developing countries, in general, do not accept the international status quo and seek revolutionary change. The resulting lack of stability is an unsettling factor in seeking international agreements on many subjects including arms control.

The development of nuclear weapons has had a revolutionary effect upon problems of arms control. For the first time in history, the new weapons posed the threat of annihilation of whole populations or perhaps all of humanity. Their full-scale use became unthinkable or likened to an act of madness. Even with limited use, millions would die and no effective defense against attack could be devised. Self-restraint or international control were the only rational alternatives.

Emphasis upon self-restraint developed into an extensive body of deterrence theory. The mutual possession by potential adversaries of an arsenal of nuclear weapons of unprecedented destructive capability and the threat of massive retaliation against any nuclear aggressor forced a nuclear stalemate or tacit agreement not to use these weapons. Rather than seek disarmament the adversaries developed larger, more accurate, more diversified, and better-protected arsenals, and communicated to the potential enemy their willingness to use these weapons if attacked or if certain vital national interests were threatened. The effectiveness of deterrence depended upon making the threat to use nuclear weapons credible to the adversary. The situation became a test of wills in a balance of terror in which each side exercised restraint in pushing the other beyond the level of acceptable threat to their interests. While an arms race continued, confidence grew on both sides that the other would not launch an unprovoked attack or threaten vital national interests. A mutual desire for survival encouraged mutual restraint. Nevertheless, the knowledge that almost unimaginable destructive capability could be called into action created an unsettling international psychological situation.

Deterrence theory and practice demand that the potential enemy not be allowed to gain an overwhelming advantage and make effective retaliation impossible. At no time must the adversary be capable of delivering a paralyzing first strike. Each side must at all times maintain a second strike or retaliatory capability to deliver unacceptable losses or damage on the nation that strikes the first blow. These conditions impose the necessity to continue research for new and more effective weapons, to harden or protect missile sites to make them virtually impossible to destroy, and to provide mobile launching facilities, such as submarines, to ensure a retaliatory capability.

The existence of huge nuclear arsenals poses the threat of nuclear war by accident, by miscalculation, or by escalation from nonnuclear to nuclear levels. Multiple safety devices are incorporated into the design of nuclear weapons and their delivery systems, and combinations of human, mechanical, and computer controls are used to insure against accidental arming and release of nuclear devices. Misinterpretation of signals from the adversary or the confusing of other objects on detection screens for the approach of enemy missiles could possibly trigger the launching of a "retaliatory" strike, when no real threat exists. Studies of human reaction under stress and the possible action of fanatics or unstable individuals are not reassuring factors in the politics of survival. No system can probably be devised that assures 100 percent safety against human and mechanical error and that at the same time provides the ability to launch quickly a retaliatory strike in response to a deliberate attack by another state. Missile technology has created a dichotomy between the necessity for quick decisions based on flawless information in the event of a real threat of destruction and the requirement of due deliberation and the elimination of every possibility of error before touching off a holocaust because of insufficient or inaccurate data.

Numerous military conflicts have occurred in the period since 1945, and all have been restricted to the use of nonnuclear weapons, but these circumstances are no infallible guarantee against future escalation of nonnuclear into nuclear war. If the aims of nuclear powers with interests in a given conflict are limited and if tacit mutual understandings of these limits exist, then the means used are likely to remain limited. However, if crucial interests are severely threatened, the temptation to raise the level of conflict could escalate into major conflagration. The existence of nuclear potential presents the possibility of maximum use by a desperate state whose survival or basic values are perceived to be threatened.

Another problem that tends to goad nuclear powers to seek limited arms control is proliferation of nuclear capability. Originally there was but one nuclear power, then two, then five, then six, and tomorrow perhaps dozens. The problem is frequently referred to as the Nth power problem. The spread of nuclear weapons is made possible by the diffusion of scientific and technical knowledge, by the decreasing cost of producing a basic weapon, and by national pride and a loss of confidence in the willingness and ability of nuclear powers to protect nonnuclear states against aggression. Fear of the intentions of neighbors may also lead states to seek nuclear capability for protection. This factor was undoubtedly present in the Chinese development of nuclear weapons and may lead to proliferation in the Middle East.

One of the concerns concomitant to disarmament proposals is whether the economy of individual countries will be adversely affected by reductions in military spending. Most analysts agree that sufficient economic knowledge exists to meet the challenge and, to a greater degree than the lack of knowledge, the problem would involve psychological factors, will, and the adequacy of government processes in applying the necessary measures. The talents now absorbed in military research and development could be redirected toward the enrichment of life in developed economies or toward the solution of the most basic problems of the developing nations.

Several national and international, public and private studies have been made of the economic and social consequences of disarmament. One of the most notable was carried out by a team of ten experts representing a cross section of economic systems at various levels of development. The report of this consultative group transmitted to the Economic and Social Council by the Secretary-General in March, 1962, concluded with the following summary of their findings:

> The Consultative Group is unanimously of the opinion that all the problems and difficulties of transition connected with disarmament could be met by appropriate national and international measures. There should thus be no doubt that the diversion to peaceful purposes of the resources now in military use could be accomplished to the benefit of all countries and lead to the improvement of world economic and social conditions. The achievement of general and complete disarmament would be an unqualified blessing to all mankind.[3]

Another United Nations study, issued in 1971, affirmed the conclusions of the earlier report.

The continued testing of nuclear devices raises the conflict between the necessity to test in order to develop a nuclear deterrent capability and the adverse human and ecological effects of testing. States newly committed to acquiring nuclear weapons are unwilling to renounce any aspects of experimentation concomitant to that acquisition. Major nuclear powers assert that they need to test in order to maintain parity in nuclear capability and to prevent their adversary in the arms race from acquiring a paralyzing first strike advantage.

Unlimited testing threatens humanity to a degree only exceeded by nuclear war itself. Even with precautions to clear the blast area of human life, risks to present and future generations accompany every test, especially those in the atmosphere. In atmospheric tests water, soil, and air currents are saturated with radioactive fallout known to be lethal within an area of almost 10,000 square miles for a

---

[3] UN Document E/3593/Rev. 1, p. 52.

twenty-megaton bomb, but periling human well-being over a much wider range. Carried by air currents, the threat of health or genetic damage may spread over several continents.

The period from 1954 to 1963 was one of increasing concern for the harmful effects of atmospheric testing. Skin burns incurred by Japanese fishermen on the fishing boat *Lucky Dragon* nearly 100 miles from ground zero, and thyroid abnormalties discovered among inhabitants of the Marshall islands following the United States Bikini test, in 1954, dramatized the dangers of continuing to saturate the atmosphere with radioactive substances. Scientific reports on the possible contamination of food supplies and the long-term effects of certain atomic substances such as strontium-90 distributed over remote areas by air currents heightened the demand for cessation of indiscriminate or unnecessary testing.

With the adoption of the test-ban treaty in 1963, which eliminated all except underground tests, these fears were diminished but not entirely eliminated. Some radioactivity is a problem in underground tests and possible damage to plant and animal life and the danger of setting off earthquakes persist. Furthermore, France and China have refused to adhere to the limited test-ban treaty, and China continues to contaminate the atmosphere through aboveground nuclear explosions. France voluntarily discontinued atmospheric testing in the South Pacific in 1975 after protests and the filing of actions in the International Court of Justice by Australia and New Zealand. Only future generations can fully ascertain the genetic effects of radioactive substances already released into the human environment.

The basic objectives of arms reduction are international security and stability. Phased disarmament must meet the demands for a balanced impact upon the principal negotiators. Because of differences in types of weapons and forces maintained by various parties the formulas for each stage of arms reduction, in order to maintain security for all concerned, are complicated and difficult to negotiate. Reciprocal reductions cannot be based purely on percentage or numerical cuts by all or major states. Security involves psychological factors that must be weighed before a new balance at a lower level of preparedness can be subscribed to and achieved. Since security is not based on military preparedness alone but upon a total world situation involving political, social, and economic relationships among and within national states, the ability to maintain a sense of relative security free of excessive risks for all nations calls for a delicate balance not easily achieved. In fact, these difficulties explain, in major portion, the painstaking and frustrating nature of disarmament and arms-control negotiations.

Each state engaging in arms control or disarmament negotiations must seek as many safeguards as possible before it agrees to change its defensive or offensive posture and capabilities. It must weigh the extent to which the good faith of all parties can be depended upon to secure the new arrangements. The degree of mistrust will shape the nature of the terms of agreement. Means of dealing with violations and the risks attendant to violations must be considered. Controls and means of verification of compliance with treaty arrangements must be explicitly or implicitly involved in the bargaining process. In the absence of international controls, reliance on self-help will require national means of ascertaining compliance with agreements, the maintenance of means to defend national-security interests, and, perhaps, a degree of trust in the motives of the other negotiating parties. With sophisticated surveillance means and techniques, the requirement of on-the-spot inspections has diminished as a bargaining factor.

The lack of international agencies with means to police disarmament or arms-control agreements creates roadblocks for arriving at such agreements. States are unwilling to substitute international authority for self-help in enforcing disarmament arrangements. If the international climate were conductive to the creation of an international agency with means to assure complicance with arms control or reduction measures, then other diminutions of national sovereignty might also be possible. Or, to state the case conversely, disarmament and arms control would be more easily attainable in a world ready to accept limited world government. In fact, a world authority could not tolerate means of massive destruction concentrated in the hands of its component members. Until the forces that drive humankind together outweigh the divisive elements of world politics, the difficulties and problems outlined in the preceding pages dealing with arms control issues will persist. The risks involved in weapons competition are not in themselves a sufficient compulsion to cause the human race to convert the international system of today into a single world authority capable of controlling the instruments of mass annihilation.

CONTINUED FRUSTRATIONS WITHIN
AND OUTSIDE THE UNITED NATIONS

The United Nations Charter contains no firm commitment to arms reduction but charges the Security Council with the responsibility for formulating plans for a system for the "regulation of armaments." The General Assembly is also permitted to consider the principles governing disarmament and arms regulation and is empowered to submit recommendations on these principles to the Security Council or to the member governments. In spite of the Charter's lack of emphasis upon disarmament, as contrasted with the details of Article 8 of the League Covenant, proposals and machinery for both disarmament and arms control have been profuse and varied since 1946, although they have yielded small returns. The immediate pressure for control was heightened by the first use of atomic weapons at Hiroshima just six weeks after the signing of the Charter. The lack of progress is due to the same factors of mistrust, search for security, national intransigence, and lack of effective international authority that prevented the adoption of earlier proposals for disarmament or arms regulation. The issues of arms control remain inextricably interwoven with the fabric of an international system in which states are incapable of performing some of their intended functions (such as affording security to citizens) but in which those same states seem unable to change the system into a more viable form.

Under pressure from the major powers, the General Assembly adopted in January, 1946, as its first resolution, a proposal to establish an Atomic Energy Commission to be composed of all the members of the Security Council plus Canada. The commission was to formulate and submit to the Security Council plans for eliminating atomic weapons, setting up regulations and safeguards, and assuring the use of atomic energy for peaceful purposes only. The next year the Security Council established the Commission for Coventional Armaments, composed of all Council members, to consider general measures for the reduction of armaments.

Basic differences between the positions of the Soviet Union and the United States on the control of atomic weapons manifested themselves immediately, and elements of these differences have persisted throughout all subsequent negotiations. The United States submitted to the Atomic Energy Commission the Acheson-Lilienthal, or Baruch, Plan, which provided for an international authority to be set up to exercise a monopoly over the ownership, production, and research for peaceful purposes of all atomic material. Atomic weapons would be prohibited, a system of inspection would be instituted, and severe penalties could be imposed by veto-free Security Council actions. When adequate controls were established, the United States would destroy its stockpile of weapons and turn over to the international authority its scientific information on atomic processes. The Soviet representatives insisted on (1) the destruction of existing weapons before discussion of controls, (2) national ownership of atomic facilities, (3) limited and periodic inspection, and (4) the retention of the veto in the Security Council. The Baruch Plan received the endorsement of the majority of the commission but the East-West impasse was irresoluble.

The United States and Soviet positions are explicable in terms of their respective international positions. While the Baruch Plan seemed on its face a generous offer by a state with an atomic monopoly, it preserved that monopoly of basic knowledge by restricting the freedom of any other state to develop and test an atomic weapon. The United States insisted on maintaining its monopoly until a secure system was established, insuring against atomic weapons development by any other state and providing a method of taking effective action against violators of the agreements. The Soviet Union wished to escape from the disadvantaged position of bargaining in which it found itself by developing its own nuclear capability, a process that culminated in its own test of an atomic weapon in 1949. Soviet concepts of protecting national sovereignty were consistent with general long-range Soviet attitudes on sovereignty and were demonstrated by their resistance to inspection, to international authority over nuclear production and development, and to the exemption from the veto of action in the Security Council to apply penalties in cases of violation of agreements.

The post-World War II stalemate over disarmament revives the familiar dichotomy of national positions that persisted throughout the 1920s and 1930s. The Soviet Union frequently states the theme that "the way to disarm is to disarm" or that security results from disarmament and must rest on the good faith of sovereign states expressed through treaty pledges. This theme is similar to the position and approach of the United States and several other states prior to 1940. The current United States insistence on controls and safeguards is reminiscent of the French position during the League of Nations period when France demanded security before disarmament.

In 1952 the consideration of nuclear arms control was merged with that of conventional or nonnuclear arms reduction through the formation of a single Disarmament Commission replacing the two previously separate commissions, but composed, like the Atomic Energy Commission, of the Security Council members plus Canada. The Disarmament Commission was enlarged from twelve to twenty-six members in 1957, and, at the insistence of the Soviet Union, to the full membership of the United Nations in 1958. However, subcommittees and ad hoc bodies have played a more significant role in disarmament negotiations. A subcommittee of Canada, France, the Soviet Union, the United Kingdom, and the United States was established in 1953 to seek reconciliation of opposing views through private sessions. In 1959 the major powers announced that they had agreed to the formation of the Ten Nation Committee, composed of equal numbers of states from the East and West blocs. In 1961 the General Assembly approved an arrangement between the Soviet Union and the United States for a new Eighteen Nation Disarmament Committee (ENDC) to report to the General Assembly and the Disarmament Commission. In 1969 the membership was enlarged to twenty-six, and the title was changed to the Conference of the Committee on Disarmament (CCD). In 1975 five more members were added to the CCD.

Some of the most fruitful disarmament negotiations have been carried on outside the United Nations. The path to agreement is often easiest in private consultations among the major powers. Several of the ad hoc bodies referred to in the previous paragraph have had an ambiguous relationship to the United Nations. This relationship has been described as follows:

> But from 1957 on, the major negotiations on general disarmament have taken place not in the organs of the United Nations but in ad hoc bodies established by agreement of the major powers, in particular the Eighteen Nation Disarmament Committee. These bodies have had only a tenuous connection with the United Nations. They have, at the invitation of the Assembly, utilized the facilities of the United Nations and the services of the Secretariat. At the request of the Assembly, they have submitted reports to the United Nations. The annual discussions on disarmament in the Assembly have taken place largely on the basis of these reports.[4]

Occasional arms control efforts, such as the Strategic Arms Limitations Talks (SALT), have been completely divorced from United Nations sponsorship. Disarmament has been on the agenda of summit conferences among heads of state, as at Geneva in 1955 and at the aborted Paris meeting in 1960.

Although closed meetings of the major powers may be a more appropriate forum than the United Nations organs for certain stages of negotiation on disarmament, the world organization has played a crucial role in the movement for disarmament since 1946. The General Assembly, in particular, has annually prodded its members toward agreement by the spotlight of debate, through recommendations, and by obligingly constituting new bodies in which negotiations may be resumed when any of the major powers find the climate in the previous agency oppressive or disadvantageous. The Secretary-General has also used the moral force of his position and

---

[4] Leland M. Goodrich, Edward Hambro and Anne Simons, *United Nations Charter: Commentary and Documents,* 3rd ed. (New York: Columbia University Press, 1969), p. 120.

influence as well as the facilities of the Secretariat to goad and assist efforts toward disarmament. Thus, the door is kept open for piece-meal agreements that might culminate in larger and larger areas of reconciliation or in general disarmament.

Comprehensive plans for general disarmament have repeatedly been put forward by the major powers since a Soviet proposal in 1948 to reduce immediately all military forces by one-third and to prohibit atomic weapons. Proposals and counterproposals have been so numerous in the ensuing years that a detailed examination of them is of small value. Except as an indication of the pressure for disarmament and the narrowing of the gap between the initial posi-tions of the Soviet Union and the United States, the parade of proposals means little in terms of real progress toward comprehensive disarmament.

How serious have the major powers been in seeking general dis-armament? To what extent have the various plans been a part of a propaganda battle rather than genuine proposals to do away with military arsenals and large military forces? One observer (with whom many analysts agree on this point) expresses his reaction in this way:

> In the years that immediately followed [circa 1952] proposals were pre-sented thick and fast. So much so, in fact, that each side in the discussion presented all the possibilities in the form of their own proposals only to reject them when presented by the other side. It should be recognized that, during this period particularly, members were prone to propose plans which, by their nature and timing, they knew must have been unaccept-able to others. Knowing that they would not be accepted and losing no advantage by proposing them, as much propaganda mileage was obtained from them as possible before they were overtaken by another crop of proposals.[5]

One landmark of the protracted negotiations for comprehensive disarmament was the issuance of a Joint Statement of Principles by the United States and the Soviet Union in September, 1961. These principles, which were to serve as a basis for further discussions, may be summarized as follows:

1. Disarmament should be general and complete with the retention of national forces sufficient only to maintain internal order.
2. Simultaneous with disarmament must be provisions for strengthening the means for peaceful settlement through the United Nations and the estab-lishment of an international peace force.

[5] Ralph Townley, *The United Nations: A View from Within* (New York: Scribner, 1968), p. 95.

3. National facilities that must be eliminated include armed forces, military establishments, training facilities, military expenditures, arms production, stockpiles of nuclear and other weapons, and means of delivery of weapons.
4. Disarmament should proceed by stages with verification of each stage. No state should be disadvantaged at any stage in the disarmament process.
5. An International Disarmament Organization must be created to exercise strict international control over the implementation and verification process. The authorized agents of this organization must have unrestricted access, without veto, to all places as necessary for effective verification.

These principles are high sounding, general, and radical in their provisions for change but have prompted little progress toward implementation.

Proposals for comprehensive disarmament have generally been based on a staged or phased plan for gradually moving to the final goal of complete disarmament. The common pattern in proposals emanating from Moscow, Washington, London, or Paris has been a three-stage process. In 1959 the Soviets presented a plan for the completion of all three stages within four years; later the total time span was extended by six months. Western proposals have allowed more time for each phase and would require at least seven years for completion.

Although differences between eastern and western plans have narrowed, crucial issues remain outside the area of agreement. Matters of timing, degree, and type of disarmament in each phase, the nature of controls and verification in moving from one stage to another, and the provisions for an adequate international security system as a replacement for reliance on armaments are major points of ongoing disagreement between the superpowers. The Soviet Union insists on the elimination of all foreign military bases and the withdrawal of all troops from foreign territory as an initial step, while the United States agrees to partial withdrawal during the second stage (fourth to sixth year) of the process. The Soviet plan calls for the elimination of all nuclear delivery systems except a limited number of intercontinental ballistic missiles in stage one and the destruction of all nuclear stockpiles in stage two; the United States proposes percentage reductions in nuclear weapons and delivery systems in stages one and two with final elimination in the third stage. The United States insists on the establishment of adequate means of control and verification during the first stage, while the Soviet Union would place greater reliance on the good faith of the parties.

No movement toward reconciliation of the approaches to general disarmament has been manifested by the major powers during the past decade. Emphasis has been placed instead on partial measures or a piecemeal approach to lessening the effects of the arms race. The successes of this fractional effort will be examined in the next section of the chapter.

BREAKTHROUGHS IN ARMS CONTROL

Failure to achieve general disarmament has not prevented a series of lesser agreements on specific areas of arms control. Comprehensive and limited approaches to arms control are not incompatible; in fact, some would argue that the piecemeal approach may pave the way and create the climate for the adoption of more comprehensive plans to follow. A series of partial measures may collectively, over time, cover many aspects of a general reduction in preparedness. In the meantime, each step in the series of agreements may remove a specific source of tensions and may, in itself, serve the cause of a more stable and less threatening international situation.

A development only indirectly related to disarmament is the encouragement, under safeguards, of the peaceful uses of atomic energy. In 1953 President Eisenhower suggested to the General Assembly that governments contribute fissionable materials to a new United Nations atomic energy agency. In 1955 the first United Nations Conference on the Peaceful Uses of Atomic Energy met in Geneva and drew up a draft statute for this agency. The revised statute was approved the following year, and, in 1957, the International Atomic Energy Agency (IAEA) began operations with headquarters in Vienna. Although the major aim of the IAEA is to assist countries and disseminate information for the use of atomic energy for peaceful purposes, it has developed a system of controls to prevent the diversion of atomic materials to military uses, and this experience may prove valuable in any control system applied to nuclear military weapons. Nuclear disarmament could also make available reservoirs of talent and materials for peaceful purposes.

Following extensive joint research efforts in Antarctica during the International Geophysical Year (1957-58), twelve nations with territorial and/or scientific interests in the area concluded an Antarctic Treaty in 1959, which, without settling conflicting territorial claims, opened the continent to all countries for research purposes. Military activities of all types are forbidden including nuclear weapons or testing and the dumping of radioactive materials.

By setting up a demilitarized and denuclearized neutral zone, the Antarctic Treaty set a precedent for claiming other areas as the "common heritage of humankind." Limited applications of these principles to outer space and to the sea bed are noted subsequently.

In the mid-1950s India repeatedly urged the cessation of nuclear testing because it endangered human health, well-being, and survival. From 1959 through 1962 the General Assembly passed numerous resolutions calling upon states to refrain from testing in all environments. In 1958 the United States and the Soviet Union convened a conference of scientific experts to determine the feasibility of setting up an effective control system for the detection of violations of a test-ban agreement. The conclusions of the conference were favorable, and the United States, the Soviet Union, and the United Kingdom began negotiations for the discontinuance of nuclear-weapons testing.

The three-power Conference on the Discontinuance of Nuclear Weapons Tests was unable to reach agreement on a satisfactory control system for detecting and verifying underground tests, and the conference was adjourned in January, 1962. However, these same states resumed negotiations in March as a subcommittee of the recently established Eighteen Nation Disarmament Committee (ENDC). After months of prodding by the full committee and by the General Assembly, the three governments announced that they would hold discussions in Moscow in July, 1963.

The Moscow negotiations resulted in agreement on a partial test-ban treaty. Attempts to agree on an inspection or verification system for underground tests were abandoned. The treaty prohibited tests in three environments — the atmosphere, outer space, and under water. Existing detection methods required no additional safeguards or machinery for determining violations in these environments. Parties to the treaty also bound themselves to prevent the escape, beyond their national boundaries, of radioactive debris from underground explosions, and promised not to encourage or participate in any nuclear explosion anywhere that would violate the restrictions assumed under the treaty. More than 120 states have ratified the partial test-ban agreement, but France and the People's Republic of China refuse to adhere to its terms.

Another significant development in 1963 was the opening of the so called hot-line between Washington and Moscow. By establishing a direct communications link between the heads of government of the superpowers the risk of nuclear war through error or miscalculation may be reduced.

In the year following the orbiting of the first earth satellite, the

General Assembly established a Committee on the Peaceful Uses of Outer Space. The Assembly has since that time repeatedly affirmed that outer space and celestial bodies are free to access by all states but are not subject to national appropriation. The United Nations has promoted peaceful cooperation in space, but also a major concern has been to prevent the deployment of nuclear destructive devices in this environment. The test-ban treaty prohibits testing in space but not the orbiting or stationing there of nuclear weapons.

In 1963 the ENDC submitted a draft resolution to the General Assembly on the banning of weapons of mass destruction from outer space. In 1966 these ideas were incorporated into a general Treaty on Principles Governing the Activities of States in the Exploration and Use of Outer Space. Certain provisions of the treaty prohibit the orbiting, installing, or stationing of nuclear or other weapons of mass destruction anywhere in space. The treaty also forbids all military activity on the moon and other celestial bodies. These measures remove a potentially serious threat to the security of nations and to humankind. The treaty came into force in October, 1967.

One approach to controlling nuclear weapons is the prohibition of their introduction into certain geographic areas. The Antarctic Treaty in 1959 incorporates such a provision and is a first step in establishing nuclear-free zones. The African states through the Organization of African Unity (OAU) have exerted pressure for many years to have their continent declared a nuclear-free zone. A greater measure of success has been achieved in Latin America. In 1967 twenty-one Latin American countries signed at Tlatelolco, Mexico, a Treaty for the Prohibition of Nuclear Weapons in Latin America. Recognizing the importance of peaceful uses of nuclear research and energy the treaty forbids only the testing, use, production, acquisition, receipt, storage, and deployment of all nuclear weapons in the Latin American area. A control system and an agency to ensure compliance are also established by the treaty. An attached protocol provides for nuclear powers to signify their cooperation in respecting the terms of the agreement, and the United States and the United Kingdom have done so. The treaty came into force in 1969.

Another partial step toward arms control is the Treaty on the Non-Proliferation of Nuclear Weapons, which was opened for signature in 1968 and which entered into force in 1970. The treaty resulted from nearly ten years of effort in the General Assembly and the ENDC, from extensive negotiations among the nuclear powers, and from the prodding of the Secretary-General bolstered by expert opinion and public pressures from many sources. The terms of the treaty obligate the nuclear powers not to transfer, and the non-nuclear states not to acquire, nuclear weapons. The acquiring of nuclear capability, under safeguards, solely for peaceful purposes is encouraged. To ease the qualms of states not possessing nuclear capabilities, the nuclear powers also promise to negotiate as soon as possible effective measures for stopping the nuclear arms race, for nuclear disarmament, and for general and complete disarmament. Thus, the partial step toward arms control is tied to the need for more sweeping measures that would erase some of the possible disadvantages of nonnuclear states in their relations with the members of the nuclear club.

In the same way that the test-ban treaty of 1963 required supplementation to demilitarize outer space and reserve it for peaceful purposes, the need was also recognized to protect the sea bed and the ocean floor outside national jurisdiction. In 1968 the ENDC began intensive consideration of sea bed demilitarization proposals from the Soviet Union and the United States. In the same year the General Assembly established a permanent Committee on the Peaceful Uses of the Sea Bed and the Ocean Floor beyond the Limits of National Jurisdiction. After nearly three years of effort to expand the scope of a demilitarization treaty, a very limited text was opened for signature in February, 1971. The treaty merely prohibits the placing of weapons of mass destruction, or structures for storing, testing, or launching such weapons, on the sea bed and ocean floor or in their subsoil. It does not interfere with nuclear-armed submarines or detection devices beyond territorial limits or with military installations within territorial waters. Thus, the demilitarization measures adopted for the sea bed fall far short of those adopted for outer space.

Since World War I chemical, bacteriological (biological), and radiological (CBR) weapons have been recognized as potential killers on a massive scale. In 1925 a protocol was signed at Geneva under the terms of which the ratifying states agreed not to use asphyxiating, poisonous, or other gases or biological weapons in war. Recent pressures for the control of these weapons stemmed from (1) the fact that several states, including the United States, had never adhered to the Geneva Protocol; (2) the knowledge that huge stockpiles of varied and sophisticated CBR weapons had been accumulated in a number of countries; (3) the reaction in various parts of the world to the use by the United States in Vietnam of tear gas, herbicides, and defoliants; and (4) the publication of studies and reports, including a 1969 United Nations report by fourteen experts, on the effects of the possible use of these weapons.

The principal conclusions of the 1969 United Nations report may be summarized as follows:

> Were these weapons ever to be used on a large scale in war, no one could predict how enduring the effects would be and how they would affect the structure of society and the environment in which we live. This over-riding danger would apply as much to the country which initiated the use of these weapons as to one which has been attacked. . . .
>
> The prospects for general and complete disarmament under effective international control, and hence for peace throughout the world, would brighten significantly if the development, production and stockpiling of chemical and bacteriological (biological) agents intended for purposes of war were to end and if they were eliminated from all military arsenals.[6]

Beginning in 1966 the General Assembly, the Eighteen Nation Committee on Disarmament (ENDC), and its successor, the Confer-ence of the Committee on Disarmament (CCD) exerted pressure on all states that had not done so to accede to the Geneva protocol of 1925 and urged the major powers to reach agreement on a treaty banning the production and stockpiling of chemical and bacteriologi-cal weapons. The United States and the United Kingdom were willing to agree to a prohibition of bacteriological but not to chemical weapons, while the Soviet bloc and nonaligned states pressed for the inclusion of both. The United States also reserved the right to inter-pret the coverage of the Geneva Protocol as not applying to tear gas, herbicides, and defoliants. However, in 1969 the United States unilaterally renounced the use or production of bacteriological (biological) weapons. President Nixon also announced that the United States would not use lethal and incapacitating chemical weapons except in retaliation for their use by other parties, and he urged the ratification of the Geneva Protocol. In 1971 the major powers agreed to a Convention on the Prohibition of the Develop-ment, Production and Stockpiling of Bacteriological (Biological) and Toxin Weapons and on Their Destruction, which was drafted in the CCD, approved by the General Assembly, and opened for signa-ture in London, Moscow, and Washington, D.C., on April 10, 1972. The Convention entered into force in 1975. The only coverage of chemical weapons remains the prohibition of their use in the 1925 Geneva Protocol.

Outside the United Nations the United States and the Soviet Union have been conducting negotiations at Helsinki and Vienna

---

[6] *Chemical and Bacteriological (Biological) Weapons and the Effects of Their Possible Use,* United Nations Publication, Sales no. E. 69. I. 24 (New York: United Nations, 1969), p. 88. Also issued as UN Document A/7575/Rev. 1 and UN Document S/9292/Rev. 1.

since November, 1969, on strategic arms limitation. These Strategic Arms Limitations Talks (SALT) have considered possibilities for halting or slowing the race to stockpile and develop both defensive and offensive weapons. By 1971 it was clear that the first agreement to come out of the SALT talks would concentrate on the limitation of the deployment of antiballistic missile systems (ABMs) in both countries. Following President Nixon's visit to Moscow in May, 1972, an announcement of accord on ABM limitation was made limiting each country to two sites. A collateral agreement placed a numerical ceiling on certain categories of armament such as ICBM launchers, but excluded from the limitation multiple warheads, bombers, medium-range missiles, the improvement of existing systems, and new technological developments. The net result was an announcement of proposed increased defense budgets in each country. In fact, since the ABM was yet to be deployed, and the numerical ceilings limited only substantial *increases* of certain systems, no *decreases* in defensive or offensive levels were provided by the Moscow or by subsequent agreements.

Negotiations in preparation for a SALT II agreement began in 1972. In 1974 a Vladivostok understanding between President Ford and General Secretary Brezhnev set numerical ceilings for strategic missiles and the number of missiles which could carry multiple warheads. By mid-1978 no further settlement had been made and tensions between the superpowers were somewhat higher than in previous years. The promise of the major powers, incorporated into the Non-Proliferation Treaty, to negotiate nuclear disarmament had not been fulfilled.

A majority of members of the United Nations seek more rapid progress toward security through disarmament. In pursuit of this goal the General Assembly declared the decade of the 1970s as the Disarmament Decade. The members thus hope to dramatize the need for further efforts and to pressure the major powers to convert the meager results of the piecemeal approach into more comprehensive plans for arms reduction.

On the initiative of the non-aligned countries the General Assembly agreed to hold a five-week special session of that body in 1978 to focus world attention on the importance of disarmament. The Special Session on Disarmament was not planned as a negotiating session but as a means of formulating principles and processes for stimulating subsequent negotiations. The session also was an attempt to return the United Nations to a more central role in dealing with a subject which concerned all members, but one on which the organization, to a considerable degree, had been by-passed.

THE NEED FOR CONTROL

In spite of the limited controls discussed above, the arms-race spiral continues upward year by year. After the partial test-ban treaty, the number of tests per year increased, although restricted to a single environment. The 1972 Moscow agreement on limiting ABMs accomplished no reduction of existing armaments levels but only set a limit on future expansion and was followed by plans for increased defense budgets in the United States and the Soviet Union. World armaments expenditures passed the 200-billion-dollar mark in 1969 and 400 billion in 1978. Such an arms burden reduces substantially the capacity of many countries to provide for basic human needs or to take effective measures for rapid economic growth.

Several approaches to arms control and disarmament are possible. One is to continue to rely on deterrence and a balance of terror and to prevent castastrophic war by restraint and the avoidance of error, miscalculation, irrational acts and escalation of small conflicts. Under these conditions, armed conflicts will occur and be restricted to nonnuclear methods. States must be prepared to fight limited wars for limited goals and to hold nuclear capabilities as a guarantee against being the victim of a first strike or as a credible threat against challenge to their basic values and interests. The controls operating in such a milieu are self-help, a balance among states capable of inflicting unacceptable damage upon each other, restraint, credibility, and rationality. No reduction of armaments is probable under these conditions. The failure of any of the controls could bring disaster to all or a major part of the world's population.

A second path to arms control and disarmament is a continuation of the piecemeal approach. Additional steps can be taken to reduce tensions and limit the possibilities for conflict. Among these are the continued negotiation in the SALT talks of restrictions upon the development, testing, and deployment of offensive as well as defensive weapons; the expansion of the partial test-ban agreement to a comprehensive test-ban agreement eliminating all nuclear tests in any environment; disengagement in central Europe with a dismantling of NATO and Warsaw Pact military forces and emplacements of forward based and medium-range weapons systems; unilateral initiatives toward reversing the arms-race spiral with the hope of inducing reciprocal action by other states; and the extension of nuclear free zones to new areas.[7]

[7] Several of these proposals are discussed in detail in Herbert Scoville, Jr., Betty G. Lall, and Robert E. Hunter, "The Arms Race: Steps Toward Restraint," *International Conciliation*, No. 587 (March, 1972). The unilateral initiative approach is advocated by psychologist Charles E. Osgood in *An Alternative to War or Surrender* (Urbana, Illinois: University of Illinois Press, 1962).

The third method of dealing with the arms problem is to negotiate an agreement for general and complete disarmament. Both the United States and the Soviet Union are committed to such a goal in their 1961 Joint Statement of Principles. Both have submitted plans for phased achievement of the total disarmament goal within a 4.5-10-year time span. Numerous General Assembly resolutions have urged general disarmament, and, in 1965, the Assembly proposed the calling of a World Disarmament Conference not later than 1967. The conference was not convened, and the wisdom of calling such a meeting can be questioned when the prospects for success are not bright. Studies by experts have underlined the desirability of eliminating weapons of mass destruction and the economic burden of armament. The nonproliferation treaty contained a commitment to seek total disarmament as soon as possible. Commitments to broad principles are easy to make and may carry with them considerable propaganda value, but the steps toward general disarmament seem, in many ways, as remote as they proved to be in the first half of the twentieth century.

The search for disarmament contains both a dilemma and a paradox. The paradox is that each state searches for security by acquiring a military arsenal, and yet the possession of arms by all states results in greater international threats and the lessening of the sense of security. The existence of modern weapons of mass destruction exacerbates the threat, raises it to a level of total destructive capability previously unimagined, and heightens the feelings of insecurity.

The dilemma for each state is how to promote its national interests in a disarmed world and how to be sure that at each stage of the process of disarming no nation violates its pledges and uses its advantage for the purpose of dominating other nations. It is frequently pointed out that armaments are means and are generally not ends in themselves. States acquire arms in order to achieve certain ends. The elimination of arms can probably never be achieved without the substitution of other means for accomplishing the goals of states. This lesson was apparent in the security demands of states in the disarmament negotiations of the League period and is equally apparent today. Disarmament is primarily a political problem linked to the whole range of problems of the relations of nations in a competitive world. States remain the dominant actors in the international system, and they are reluctant to create other agencies capable of enforcing peace in a disarmed world.

The obstacles to disarmament are the obstacles to international cooperation generally. The forces of nationalism are strong, and the bonds of world community are weak. National competition, fed by suspicion, mistrust, and antagonism, is the order of the day.

Universality of support for any movement seems impossible to achieve. China and France, two nuclear powers, have refused to adhere to the test-ban and nonproliferation treaties. France has boycotted the United Nations disarmament agencies for many years. Nations are reluctant to strengthen the relatively weak United Nations; the creation of international agencies strong enough to enforce peace and to exercise compulsory jurisdiction over disputes seems a remote possibility.

Many scholars have focused their attention upon the problem of the changes necessary to assure a reasonable degree of order in a disarmed world. Most of them forecast the need for at least some surrender of sovereignty in limited areas, but, beyond this minimal change, they disagree on the degree and nature of change required in the international order. Their projections vary from almost no modifications of the existing system to the necessity of a world government with broad areas of authority and means of enforcement.[8]

The arms race goes on. The threat of human annihilation or of a holocaust of unprecedented proportions for present and future generations hangs over the heads of humankind. Thus far the United Nations has been unable and the nations have been unwilling to take effective measures to remove the threat. No problem is more pressing for solution. Research, study, education, and international cooperation and effort on questions of war and peace, disarmament and arms control, and more effective forms of international organization and authority will be required before the problem is solved. Disarmament cannot occur in a vacuum or in the abstract. Security must be sought through substitute means in order for disarmament to occur. Restraint and rationality must be exercised until the new means can be developed.

[8] A partial list of scholars who have published their ideas on the nature of a disarmed world follows: Walter Millis, Richard A. Falk, Richard J. Barnet, Lincoln Bloomfield, Louis B. Sohn, Grenville Clark, Amitai Etzioni, Neil W. Chamberlain, Arthur I. Waskow, Klaus Knorr, Saul H. Mendlovitz, and Roger Fisher.

10

❧

Promoting
Economic Welfare

Over four-fifths of the United Nations' budget is allotted to economic and social activities, and most of its or its affiliated agencies' permanent and temporary personnel are engaged in economic and social work. Since 1960, economic and social development and all of its ramifications have been the main preoccupation of the General Assembly. Activities in these fields are varied and are carried out in almost every country in the world.

It is impossible to separate completely economic from social matters. Problems in these areas usually have both economic and social characteristics and effects. Projects in these areas thus generally serve both sets of needs of individuals.

The United Nations and its agencies also are organized around both economic and social concerns. The Economic and Social Council is a single coordinating and directing agency. The so-called regional economic commissions deal with a combination of economic and social matters. At first the Secretariat was organized into separate economic and social departments but soon these were combined into a less artificial, single department. Although some agencies, such as the World Bank, may suggest a predominately economic character, the country surveys made by the bank cover social as well as economic problems, and the bank's loans are for multiple purposes.

Although economic and social problems are indeed related, for easier classification as topics they will be separated in this and the next chapter according to which area is predominant. This separation also will help to limit the chapters' length and diversity. This chapter examines issues of a more economic nature.

WORLD ECONOMIC INTERDEPENDENCE

Although world trade is not a new phenomenon, its growth rate since 1945 has exhibited exponential characteristics. The value of world exports expressed in constant 1970 dollars (excluding the Communist countries with the exception of Yugoslavia) soared from 63 billion dollars in 1948 to 107 billion dollars in 1958 and to 280 billion dollars in 1970. By 1975 the value had climbed to 370 billion dollars.[1] This nearly sixfold expansion in twenty-seven years is one type of gross indicator of the growing network of exchanges across national boundaries. The amount of goods entering international commercial channels increases at a greater rate than world production, thus contributing to burgeoning interdependence among nations.

International monetary relationships represent another type of economic interdependence. The International Monetary Fund (IMF) was established in 1945 to provide orderly and stable international exchange arrangements looking ideally toward the elimination of all barriers to convertibility of currencies. Although this free exchange may never be attained, consultations and cooperation among states mark postwar efforts to minimize the international effects of national monetary actions. When a government decides to float its currency in the world market, adjustments immediately result in the buying power of that currency and of others. When the United States abandons a long-standing policy linking the dollar to a fixed low price for gold and at the same time imposes a temporary surcharge on imports, the repercussions are felt in all the major money and trading markets throughout the world. When the members of the IMF agree to the creation of special drawing rights (SDRs), the purpose is to create additional reserves in order to stabilize the international monetary system. Together the IMF and its member states seek to substitute cooperation and order for unilateralism and chaos in international monetary affairs.

Another facet of economic interdependence involves the transfer

---

[1] *United Nations Statistical Yearbook,* 1976, Table 14, p. 55.

of technical knowledge and skills from one country to another. This transfer occurs at all levels of scientific, technological, and managerial development. The creation of the Economic and Social Council and more than a dozen specialized agencies under the aegis of the United Nations serves mainly to provide technical assistance to developing countries for the primary goal of raising their standards of living. Technical assistance can be furnished by developed nations to developing ones, but sharing of skills and knowledge among developing societies is also a feature of a multilateral system of agencies and programs. The transfer of technology also involves private as well as public agencies. Grants from the Ford and the Rockefeller foundations supported the development of new strains of cereal grains capable of creating a "green revolution" in the developing areas. The multinational corporations serve as a vehicle for the transfer of often highly sophisticated technology throughout the world, although this channel has operated more among developed economies than from developed to developing systems.

Interdependence has manifested itself in the creation of regional economic communities (or common markets) and of regional development banks. The most fully developed common market is the European Economic Community (EEC), whose membership was expanded in 1973 to include nine central and western European states with a total population of more than a quarter-billion people. (For a more detailed description and assessment of the EEC and other regional agencies, consult chapter 14.) In general, the tendency of regional economic agencies is to break down barriers to the free exchange of goods and persons and to develop common economic policies among the members.

The rapid growth of multinational corporations has contributed to international economic interdependence in respects other than the transfer of technology across national boundaries. A large number of these corporate giants have scattered their production units in a score or more of countries, thus decentralizing this aspect of their operations. Production resulting from foreign investment is nearly double the value of world exports. The flow of investment, goods, technology, profits, and managerial controls are all stimulated by the complex operations of the multinational corporations.

As the world uses its reserves of minerals and fuels, the number of countries that are nearly self-sufficient in resources diminishes and interdependence increases. The use of petroleum as an economic and political weapon in the Middle East crisis of 1973–74 is dramatic proof of the dependence of Europe, Japan, and the United States upon this resource. Lester R. Brown points out that of thirteen basic industrial raw materials, the United States by the end of the century will have to import more than half its supply of twelve of these and will be nearly self-sufficient in phosphate only.[2] Many of the major reserves of minerals and fuels are in developing countries. If these countries tightly control their resources and demand higher prices as the industrialized economies seek increasing supplies from abroad, their financial problems for supporting the process of development could be partially solved. However, resources are so unevenly distributed throughout the world that this brighter outlook for the future would by-pass a substantial number of poor but aspiring states.

Thus, in numerous ways world economic interdependence exists and grows at an accelerating rate. Future effects may be manifested through both conflict and cooperation. If common goals and solutions are sought, greater prosperity may result for an increasing percentage of humanity.

THE UNITED NATIONS NETWORK
OF AGENCIES

The United Nations structure for planning, coordinating, administering, and implementing its economic and social program is very complex, diversified, and decentralized. As stated in the introduction to this chapter, the bulk of the United Nations' resources, both physical and human, is devoted to economic and social activities.

At the apex of the structure are the General Assembly and the Economic and Social Council. The General Assembly, among its manifold responsibilities, provides general direction and supervision for economic and social activities. The Economic and Social Council (ECOSOC) concentrates solely on this work but has difficulty in coordinating the diverse strands of the program. These difficulties are related to the nature of the Economic and Social Council, the scope of the economic and social program, the number and diversity of agencies involved, and ECOSOC's lack of authority over the specialized agencies.

The broad features of the General Assembly and the Economic and Social Council were described in chapter 4. For a review of the structure and functions of these organs, the reader may wish to refer to that portion of the text.

[2] Lester R. Brown, *The Interdependence of Nations*, Headline Series, No. 212 (New York: Foreign Policy Association, October 1972), pp. 43–44.

The complexity of the Economic and Social Council's responsibility for coordination can best be realized by examining, in general outline, the range and types of economic and social agencies in the United Nations system and their relationships to ECOSOC. The general categories include functional commissions, regional commissions, specialized agencies, standing committees, ad hoc committees, and a variety of other bodies and agencies. The relationships of nongovernmental organizations with the United Nations are also carried on primarily through ECOSOC.

In recent years ECOSOC has operated with the assistance of six functional commissions and the present structure of functional commissions has displayed great stability. Three have existed continuously since 1946. These are the Statistical Commission, the Commission on Human Rights, and the Commission on Narcotic Drugs. The Commission on the Status of Women was originally a subcommission of the Commission on Human Rights but was raised to full commission status in 1947. The Population Commission was created at the third session of ECOSOC. The Commission for Social Development was established at the initial meeting of ECOSOC as the Social Commission, but the title was changed in 1966 to reflect the emphasis in its current program. The Commission on Human Rights has a Sub-Commission on Prevention of Discrimination and Protection of Minorities. The Commission on Narcotic Drugs has a Sub-Commission on Illicit Drug Traffic and Related Matters in the Near and Middle East. Several functional commissions and subcommissions have been established, served their purposes, and been discontinued.

The regional commissions represent a moderately effective method of decentralizing some of the planning and programs of ECOSOC. Each regional commission focuses on the problems salient to its geographic area. Five such commissions have been established: the Economic Commission for Europe (ECE), established in 1947; the Economic and Social Commission for Asia and the Pacific (ESCAP) originally established in 1947 as the Economic Commission for Asia and the Far East (ECAFE); the Economic Commission for Latin America (ECLA), established in 1948; the Economic Commission for Africa (ECA), established in 1958; and the Economic Commission for Western Asia (ECWA), established in 1974. In general, membership in each commission is open to all states in the region, except that South Africa has been excluded from participation in the ECA. In the ECA, states such as France, Spain, and the United Kingdom, with special interests in the area, are accorded associate membership, but, in the other regional commissions, outside states with special interests enjoy full membership. The United States is a member of the ECE, the ESCAP, and the ECLA; the United Kingdom, France, and the Netherlands belong to the ECLA and the ESCAP; the USSR has membership in the ESCAP, and Canada is a member of the ECLA. Since 1960 the emphasis on regional decentralization has been increased. Each commission determines its own pattern of organization, and all have established a number of committees to facilitate their efforts in special areas of concern. The commissions hold annual meetings and submit annual reports to ECOSOC.

To provide further assistance for its varied responsibilities, ECOSOC has maintained a flexible and frequently changing group of standing, sessional and ad hoc committees. In 1977 there were standing committees on (1) Non-Governmental Organizations, (2) Negotiations with Intergovernmental Agencies, (3) Housing, Building and Planning, (4) Program and Coordination, (5) Natural Resources, (6) Review and Appraisal, (7) Science and Technology for Development, (8) Crime Prevention and Control, and (9) Development Planning. There was also a standing Commission on Transnational Corporations.

A number of other bodies exist in the economic and social fields which are not as directly subject to ECOSOC direction or control but which are related to ECOSOC interests and for which ECOSOC provides limited coordinating services. These agencies include (1) the United Nations Development Program (UNDP), (2) the United Nations Children's Fund (UNICEF), (3) the United Nations High Commissioner for Refugees (UNHCR), (4) the United Nations Conference on Trade and Development (UNCTAD), (5) the United Nations Industrial Development Organization (UNIDO), (6) the United Nations Institute for Training and Research (UNITAR), (7) the International Narcotics Control Board, (8) the World Food Program, (9) the United Nations Environment Program (UNEP), (10) the United Nations University (UNU), and (11) the World Food Council. Two other coordinating committees, composed of top-level Secretariat personnel from the cooperating agencies, are the Administrative Committee on Coordination and the Inter-Agency Consultative Board of the United Nations Development Program.

One step further removed from ECOSOC control, but subject to limited ECOSOC coordination, are the so-called specialized agencies of the United Nations family of associated organizations. In fact, the specialized agencies are so highly independent of any effective control by United Nations organs that they are generally described as autonomous organizations. Each has its own headquarters, staff, and budget. Each was created in the same manner as the United Nations by an international conference that produced a constitution or charter for the proposed organization in the form of a multilateral treaty. Membership is independent of United Nations membership but is predominantly identical since all agencies aim at near universality, and most agencies have substantially more than 100 members. This overlapping membership probably provides as effective coordination as is provided under the limited controls of ECOSOC, since governments that belong to many agencies will be interested in balancing their interests, controlling relative budgets, and preventing duplication of services or conflict of goals.

After each intergovernmental agency is established by international treaty independently of the United Nations, it becomes a specialized agency of the United Nations by an agreement between the agency and the United Nations. This agreement is negotiated between the agency and the Economic and Social Council subject to approval by the General Assembly. The purpose of the agreement is to spell out the relationships and avenues of coordination between the agency and the United Nations. Although the agreements are not uniform, a pattern of standard provisions exists. The agreements normally include provisions for (1) reciprocal representation at meetings, (2) reciprocal proposal of agenda items, (3) exchange of documents and information, (4) submission of reports by the specialized agencies to the United Nations, (5) prompt consideration by the agencies of recommendations by appropriate United Nations organs, (6) consultation to achieve uniform personnel standards and practices, and (7) submission of agency budgets to the United Nations for review and recommendation. Additional consultation occurs at the administrative level. Coordination also is effected by numerous bodies involved in the planning, financing, and administration of the United Nations Development Program since the United Nations and most of the specialized agencies participate in this cooperative program.

Fifteen specialized agencies operate today in affiliation with the United Nations. One temporary agency, the International Refugee Organization (IRO), existed from 1948 to 1952 and was dissolved. The present agencies follow:

International Labor Organization (ILO)
Food and Agriculture Organization (FAO)
United Nations Educational, Scientific and Cultural Organization (UNESCO)
World Health Organization (WHO)
International Bank for Reconstruction and Development (Bank or IBRD)
International Finance Corporation (IFC)

International Development Association (IDA)
International Monetary Fund (Fund or IMF)
International Civil Aviation Organization (ICAO)
Universal Postal Union (UPU)
International Telecommunication Union (ITU)
World Meteorological Organization (WMO)
Intergovernmental Maritime Consultative Organization (IMCO)
World Intellectual Property Organization (WIPO)
International Fund for Agricultural Development (IFAD)

Two other agencies that resemble specialized agencies in some, but not all, characteristics are the International Atomic Energy Agency (IAEA), discussed in the preceding chapter, and the General Agreement on Tariffs and Trade (GATT), a substitute for an aborted attempt to establish an International Trade Organization.

The Economic and Social Council is also authorized to enter into a consultative relationship with private organizations, generally referred to as nongovernmental organizations (NGOs). These arrangements may be made with international organizations, or, with the consent of the government involved, with national organizations. The United States delegation had established a precedent of extensive consultation with national interest groups at the San Francisco conference. Since both public and private resources are limited and interests overlap, reciprocal benefits often result from this type of coordination and cooperation. The specialized agencies also carry on extensive consultative and cooperative efforts with nongovernmental organizations.

Three categories of NGOs have been established. Category I consists of two dozen organizations having the broadest range of interests in the work of ECOSOC. Category II, with nearly 200 organizations on the approved list, includes agencies interested in a specific aspect of the work. Other NGOs, numbering over 120 and having significant contributions to make to the program of ECOSOC, are placed on what is known as the roster. Approximately 350 other organizations are on the roster because of their consultative status with specialized agencies or other United Nations bodies. Organizations on the roster may send observers to meetings and may submit recommendations only on invitation. Category I and II organizations have the additional privilege of submitting written statements to ECOSOC and making oral statements to the Council's commissions. Category I representatives may also submit agenda items to ECOSOC and may be heard on such items if they are approved for inclusion on the agenda.

Some appreciation of the importance and complexity of ECOSOC's responsibility for coordination should be apparent from the listing in the preceding paragraphs of the scores of agencies and subagencies with which ECOSOC has relationships. Since many of these bodies are immune from its direct control, ECOSOC must depend primarily on consultation, persuasion, and the perceived advantages of cooperation. A fifty-four-member body with limited powers is not an ideal agency of coordination. If coordination is reasonably achieved, the results are due in part to the other avenues of cooperation and control — budgetary allocations, subsidiary agencies performing coordinating functions, administrative cooperation, and coordination through member governments.

PROBLEMS OF ECONOMIC DEVELOPMENT

Countries are generally classified as either developing or developed depending primarily upon their degree of industrialization. Sometimes the categories used are preindustrial, industrial, and postindustrial. In another method of classification, the categories may be underdeveloped, semideveloped, and developed. If only two classes are used to separate developing from developed countries, most experts agree that two-thirds to three-fourths of the world's population live in developing nations.

A profile of the developing states reveals certain common characteristics. These nations, with few exceptions, recently emerged from colonial rule into political independence. Generally a large proportion of the population suffers from severe deprivation in terms of fulfilling human potential and achieving well-being. The broad forms of deprivation are manifested as widespread poverty, illiteracy, hunger, and disease. The more specific characteristics are numerous. Most of the population is engaged in subsistence agriculture using primitive agricultural methods involving hand labor and few tools. Foreign trade is small, and exports are often primarily made up of a single commodity that is either an agricultural product or an unrefined mineral. Dependence on a single source for foreign exchange creates fluctuations in trade revenues as world markets and prices vary from year to year. The absence of manufacturing results in an economy based on primary or unfinished commodities. Manufactured goods are scarce and, for the most part, must be imported.

In the developing countries individual income levels are extremely low. The average per capita income generally falls into the 60–1,000-dollar range. Furthermore, a small wealthy and powerful elite usually controls a large share of the economic resources, while the bulk of the population lives at an even lower level of misery than is indicated by the average income level. A low level of per capita energy consumption is a result of the lack of capital and industrialization. The absence of basic skills and technical knowledge, in combination with other factors, leads to low per capita productivity.

In these countries health and educational facilities are inadequate. Endemic and epidemic diseases are prevalent. Birth and death rates are high. Infant mortality often exceeds 10 percent of all live births, and life expectancy averages twenty years less than in the developed countries. In spite of the high death rates, the population growth rate usually varies between 2 percent and 4 percent, and is almost universally higher than in developed nations. Lack of access to knowledge about and devices for birth control, religious and social barriers to contraception, and economic pressures and desires for large families contribute to population increase at an exponential rate.

In the developing countries malnutrition and hunger contribute to a lack of human vigor. Not only is the daily calorie intake much below the standard of the developed countries, but protein deficiency also threatens to undermine physical and mental health. Basic health care is inadequate with a lack of access to doctors, hospitals, and public or private health facilities.

In most of these countries, in spite of efforts to educate the people, a lack of funds, facilities, and trained personnel results in slow progress toward the elimination of illiteracy. Training above the level of basic literacy is even more scarce so that the development of skills and the provision of secondary and higher education are available to an extremely limited portion of the population. Without skills and knowledge among the general citizenry and without a broad corps of adequately trained political leaders and administrators and industrial managers, progress in economic development is slow and difficult, and is marked by undue reliance upon nonindigenous personnel in managerial positions, especially in the economic structure.

Because both capital and managerial skills are in scarce supply, the developing countries must continue, for a time, to rely on foreign industry to develop their resources. This dependence results in feelings of inferiority, frustration, and resentment. Foreign personnel receive the highest salaries, profits drain out of the country (often to the former colonial power), and the indigenous people exercise little control over the use or exploitation of their own resources.

Low levels of income and the difficulty of saving result in a vicious circle of poverty. In an illiterate, poverty-stricken population incentives for saving and investment are almost totally absent. The struggle for survival and the crises of today dominate the economic life of most individuals.

The needs of the developing states seem infinite. As soon as a determination is made to seek the alleviation of some of the basic problems of development, new sources of frustration arise. Attacks are made upon the causes of endemic and epidemic diseases and the death rate falls, while birth rates continue at a high level. The result is a population explosion, which wipes out a substantial portion of the economic gains in other areas. Population control seems to be almost a necessity in order to generate a rapid rate of economic growth.

Health and educational facilities must be provided for people of all ages. Short courses must be instituted to train midwives and persons with minimal qualifications in a variety of health areas until the cost of more adequate facilities and more highly trained medical personnel can be afforded. Schools must be provided for wiping out illiteracy among the young, but adult education and training are equally important if rapid economic development is to take place. Farmers must learn improved methods of production and the use of simple tools. Enough skills must be taught to facilitate diversification in the economy and a gradual shift toward industrialization and commerce.

The accumulation of capital and its investment in growth-generating economic enterprises is imperative for economic development. Forced savings through taxation may be required even though individual resources are barely enough for subsistence. Foreign loans, grants, and investment may also be necessary, but internal capital must be generated if the economy is ever to reach a takeoff point in energizing the development process. A balance must be attained between incentives for foreign capital to invest and maximization of benefits to the host state. Reinvestment within the country rather than a drain of large profits abroad, adequate compensation to indigenous employees and their progressive access to more highly skilled positions, and the host country's control over the use and conservation of native resources, as well as an adequate return through taxes or joint ownership of business enterprises, are all required if national developmental progress is to be maximized. Bilateral or multilateral grants must be utilized so as to assure their application to growth-generating enterprises or to building the infrastructure essential to an industrializing economy. Loans may be useful unless resources for repayment are accumulated too slowly, in which case loans may become a burden when payment of principal and interest come due. Such a process might lead to a point where more capital resources are being drained from the country than are coming in.

The complexity of the problems faced within a developing economy and the application of efficient methods for maximum progress in escaping from the human deprivations that are involved necessitate a major role for government in the process. Planning and effective administration of programs are essential for rapid growth. National unity and pride must be instilled among the people. Non-economic incentives and promises of future well-being must be substituted for immediate material benefits in order to foster rapid economic growth. In addition to the functions of planning and whipping up support, government must also provide, either directly or indirectly, for the necessary organizational structure to carry out the economic measures within the plan.

There is no guarantee of rapid progress in economic development. The obstacles are self-evident in the previous analysis of needs and conditions. Governments often lack capable personnel for wise planning and able administration of programs. The needs are so vast that choosing priorities is difficult, and marshalling sufficient resources seems impossible. Apathy on the part of the masses and complacency among the elites must be overcome. Drastic social change must occur if development is to succeed. Entrenched interests must be uprooted and prevailing attitudes must undergo radical change. Internal graft, corruption, and inefficiency may frustrate attempts at progress. Those who control private and public foreign resources may balk at involvement except on their own terms. The delicate balancing of forces for development may be beyond the capabilities of the talent available for the task. It is small wonder that much pessimism prevails over the prospects for a substantially more satisfying existence for two thirds of humanity.

DEVELOPMENT PROGRAMS
OF THE UNITED NATIONS

Plans for postwar relief and rehabilitation in Europe and Asia antedate the establishment of the United Nations. In 1943 and 1944, at the height of war activity, the Allied powers established the United Nations Relief and Rehabilitation Administration (UNRRA), held a conference that took the initial steps for the creation of the Food and Agriculture Organization, and, at the Bretton Woods

Conference, drew up the plans for the International Bank for Reconstruction and Development and the International Monetary Fund. The UNRRA was to be a temporary organization, whereas the others were to become specialized agencies affiliated with the emergent United Nations.

The UNRRA served a vital purpose in helping the war-devastated countries of Europe and of Asia to meet their immediate relief needs of food, clothing, and medical supplies at the survival level and to rebuild their economic and social fabric. During 1945–46 the UNRRA furnished more than 3.5 billion dollars worth of supplies for relief and rehabilitation. Recipient governments were required to sell most of the supplies and use the funds for UNRRA-approved rehabilitation projects. UNRRA delivered the goods to the countries, but internal distribution was the responsibility of the receiving state, although the UNRRA maintained surveillance over the process. The entire approach was one of self-help and internal responsibility with external assistance. The United States was the chief donor, supplying more than two-thirds of the goods and money. The program was abruptly terminated in Europe at the end of 1946 and in Asia three months later.

As the organs of the newly created United Nations began operation in 1946, great stress was laid on helping disadvantaged nations and groups. UNICEF was set up to care for the special needs of children. Initially it took over some of the assets of the UNRRA. A temporary specialized agency, the International Refugee Organization (IRO), was created to cope with the residual problems of wartime refugees unresolved by the UNRRA. The Economic and Social Council, from its inception and by intent, focused heavily upon the problems of development and relief. By 1948 it had created regional commissions in Europe, Asia, and Latin America and functional commissions in such fields as population, transport and communications, commodity trade, social questions, and human rights. Also by 1948, in addition to the IRO, nine of the permanent specialized agencies had become affiliated with the United Nations, and administrative coordinating machinery had been established to assure some degree of cooperation with the United Nations. A large share of the activities of these specialized agencies (particularly the bank, the FAO, UNESCO, and the WHO) was directed toward technical or other aid to developing countries. Altogether, the United Nations and its affiliated agencies were much involved in aid to developing nations prior to the launching of the Expanded Program of Technical Assistance in 1950.

The Expanded Program of Technical Assistance (EPTA) represented a United Nations endeavor to supplement the scattered technical assistance efforts previously carried out by ECOSOC and the specialized agencies as parts of their regular programs. It involved cooperation and coordination among the United Nations bodies and most of the specialized agencies to weigh requests from states for technical aid and to allocate the tasks and resources for implementing approved projects to the most appropriate agencies. In order to achieve this coordination and distribution of resources and responsibilities, new coordinating machinery had to be created within the United Nations structure both at the intergovernmental and the administrative levels. The Technical Assistance Administration was established within the United Nations Secretariat, the Technical Assistance Board was charged with administrative coordination among all the agencies involved, and the Technical Assistance Committee of governmental representatives was created to assist ECOSOC in the coordination and supervision of the EPTA.

The initial impetus for the EPTA was President Truman's inaugural address of January, 1949, in which he proposed a sharing of technical knowledge and capital resources with the developing nations. The United States Congress later made available resources for international development on both a multilateral and a bilateral basis with the lion's share of resources being allocated to the bilateral channels. The General Assembly, in November, 1949, approved the plans for the EPTA as the multilateral program to capitalize on the United States initiative. All members of the United Nations were invited to pledge, on a voluntary basis, support to a special and supplementary budget for the support of the EPTA.

The amounts expended for the EPTA projects were always modest. A target of 20 million dollars was set and fully subscribed to for the first eighteen-month period — from July 1, 1950, to December 31, 1951 — with the United States pledging 60 percent of the total. In subsequent years the total pledges increased at a more rapid rate than the number of subscribing states. For example, in 1953, 69 states pledged 22.4 million dollars, while by 1963 the number of states involved was 105 and the subscriptions for the first time passed the 50-million-dollar mark. By 1961 the United States had reduced the proportion of its pledge to 40 percent of the total.

The EPTA concentrated its efforts on the furnishing of individual experts for work in the developing countries and the provision of fellowships for the training abroad of personnel from these nations. By 1965 approximately 9,000 experts had been sent overseas to provide technical advice in developing countries for periods averaging two to three years. More than three times that number of persons had been granted fellowships for relatively short periods of training abroad. At very low cost thousands of persons were exchanged for the purpose of raising the levels of knowledge and skills in the developing states and territories. But the effect of such diverse and fragmented efforts was similar to hunting big game with a shotgun loaded with birdshot. The impact made some impression but never reached the vital centers of the problems on which a concentrated and massive effort must be directed if the hunt is to really succeed. The lack of effective coordination and the scattering of resources among small-scale projects — problems that have plagued most United Nations economic and social programs — have been prime characteristics of the EPTA. Manifold demands from every corner of the globe led to the apportionment of limited resources among as many countries and projects as possible. Something for everyone was the general rule.

In order to provide a new dimension for development aid, a United Nations Special Fund began operations in 1959. The developing states had been pressing for several years for a Special United Nations Fund for Economic Development (SUNFED), the establishment of which was resisted by the affluent states, and the Special Fund represented a substitute more acceptable to the big donors of funds. The Special Fund concentrated on preinvestment projects, each of which averaged considerably larger than EPTA projects and which involved modest expenditures for equipment as well as for the provision of experts to carry out surveys of resources, research, training, and pilot projects. A small number of fellowships were also provided by the fund. The main purpose of the fund was to provide the groundwork and then to stimulate investment from internal and external private and public sources in order to carry out development projects and programs in needy countries.

Over the years, the Special Fund was somewhat more generously supported than the EPTA. After a modest start in 1959, the amounts pledged for the Special Fund gradually outstripped those for the EPTA by ever-widening margins until, in 1965, the total subscribed for the fund was 91.6 million dollars compared with the EPTA's 54 million dollars.

In 1965 the General Assembly decided to merge the Special Fund and the EPTA into a single entity, the United Nations Development Program (UNDP). Better coordination and integration of projects within an overall development plan for each country was thus achieved. The merger was resisted by several of the specialized agencies because of their significant roles in the EPTA. Although the merger resulted in a single administrative structure for coordinating requests for aid, in fact the two components of the program remained identifiable. The level of aid continued to increase yearly under the combined program from 145.6 million dollars in 1965 to nearly 500 million dollars by 1977.

One way to achieve a degree of coordination of development plans and programs at the individual country level is to utilize the United Nations resident representative. While the practice of appointing resident representatives developed gradually, the utility of a single United Nations appointee with a broad perspective over all the multilateral projects within each country is obvious.[3] Because of the breadth of planning and the diversity of international agencies operating in each country, a person who can assist the government in formulating and presenting proposals and who can try to bring some degree of order out of the diverse and scattered field activities of technical advisers from several United Nations agencies can provide a most valuable service.

Ideally, the resident representative should be looked upon by the host government and by the operating agencies as the intermediary channel between the government and the representatives of the agencies. He should also serve as chief United Nations spokesman and diplomat within the country. His office should advise the host government in formulating proposals and presenting them to the United Nations for approval. He should coordinate and evaluate programs to assure the contribution of each project to the broad goals of development. He and his staff can furnish administrative support that can assist both the host government and the agencies and their technicians.

The resident representative never totally achieves these ideals and usually falls far short of achieving perfection. Among the many factors that operate to frustrate the achievement of the ideal are (1) a lack of any grant of broad authority to the resident representative, (2) interagency jealousy and competition, (3) inadequate staff to provide all the services that an overall coordinator and administrator should furnish, (4) lack of adequate planning or cooperation by the host government, and (5) human inadequacies both of spirit and of ability. Without the instruments of authority the resident representative must depend upon persuasion, service, personality, effectiveness, and the building of confidence to enhance his importance in the development process. But for all his skill, he is dealing, in most developing countries, with only the United Nations component of

[3] Gerard J. Mangone, "Field Administration: The United Nations Resident Representative," in Gerard J. Mangone, ed., *UN Administration of Economic and Social Programs* (New York: Columbia University Press, 1966).

development aid, which is far outstripped by more massive bilateral inputs of human and material resources. Until a greater proportion of aid becomes multilateral, and until the resident representative is granted greater authority, the potential of his role in the development process will not be realized. In the meantime, fragmentation leads to inefficiency in planning and in attaining the goals of economic development.

As the number of new, developing nations entering the United Nations multiplied after 1955, demands for increased attention to their economic and social needs were manifested in new United Nations programs. Through their growing majority in the General Assembly, they were able to create new agencies and to focus world attention upon development issues by declaring the 1960s as the United Nations Development Decade and the 1970s as the Second Development Decade. Although the developing nations could not force the affluent states to furnish massive resources for development, they could exert constant pressure for increased attention to their problems and squeeze from the rich reluctant and limited concessions for their benefit.

Planning for the First Development Decade was inadequate and poorly executed. Targets of a 50 percent economic growth rate for the developing nations and an annual resource transfer of 1 percent of national income of the developed states to the developing countries were never achieved. Most of the measures recommended were in the form of exhortations in vague terms lacking any specificity of procedures, priorities, or commitments by which the aims could be achieved.

Planning for the Second Development Decade was done more carefully than in the 1960s, and the measures for implementation of goals were spelled out more specifically, but the means to secure the cooperation of those states possessing a majority of the world's resources were still lacking.[4] The results in the first half of the decade were, therefore, disappointing. A goal of a resource transfer of 1 percent of the GNP of the developed to the developing states was set, with 0.7 percent to come from the public sector. These goals were to be achieved not later than 1975. Throughout the 1960s the government aid component from the sixteen affluent nations that were members of the Development Assistance Commit-

---

[4] "Towards Accelerated Development: Proposals for the Second United Nations Development Decade," Report of the Committee for Development Planning (New York: United Nations, 1970); *International Development Strategy: Action Programme of the General Assembly for the Second United Nations Development Decade* (New York: United Nations, 1970).

tee (DAC) of the Organization for Economic Cooperation and Development (OECD) gradually fell, until in 1969 it reached 0.36 percent of their total GNPs, barely half of the proposed target for 1975. The overall percentage never exceeded this rate in the 1970s in spite of extraordinary efforts by several of the smaller DAC countries to meet the 0.7 percent target. However, the chances for success remain remote as the most affluent member, the United States, continued yearly to decrease its rate of flow of official aid to developing countries. From a rate of approximately 0.32 percent for 1972, the United States' aid as a proportion of GNP declined below that level during the remainder of the 1970s, ranking it among the lowest of the DAC members in percentage terms. The reversal of attitude by the previously most generous of nations dealt a severe blow to the hopes for achieving the goals of the Second Development Decade. Some of the gap was filled by fairly generous OPEC aid, but at least 60 percent of this aid went to Arab states.

Planning for the Second Development Decade was spearheaded by an expert Committee for Development Planning under the aegis of the Economic and Social Council. Their proposals included (1) setting objectives, (2) delineating the means for attaining the objectives, and (3) arrangements for appraisal of progress during the decade. Their recommendations were essentially adopted in a General Assembly resolution of October 24, 1970. In addition to the goal for the transfer of resources discussed above, they proposed a 6 percent average annual rate of economic growth as a minimum target for the developing countries in order to achieve a per capita growth rate of 3.5 percent or more. In the agricultural sector the increase in output was set at a minimum of 4 percent annually and in manufacturing at a minimum of 8 percent. The committee recommended that internal policies be directed toward improvements in income distribution, employment, education, health, and housing, and a slowing of the rate of population growth. The goal for gross domestic savings as a percent of gross product was set at 20 percent in 1980 as compared with about 15 percent in 1970. The average annual increase in imports was targeted at slightly less than 7 percent with a somewhat higher goal for exports. International measures called for included the securing of stable and remunerative prices for primary commodities, the reduction of barriers to imports of primary products, and the establishment of nonreciprocal preferential treatment for exports of developing countries to developed ones.

Review and appraisal of progress toward achieving the goals of the decade were considered essential to the program. It was specified that the Secretary-General, the Committee for Development Planning, the Economic and Social Council, and the General Assembly would engage in a biennial evaluation with the second set of appraisals serving as a mid-decade review and assessment. The results of these appraisals in terms of general progress and goal attainment have been discouraging. Relatively few countries are achieving satisfactory rates of economic development.

The impatience of the developing states with the limited support available through international channels for the attainment of their economic goals led to the formation of the United Nations Conference on Trade and Development (UNCTAD), which was approved by ECOSOC and the General Assembly in 1962 and which met in Geneva for a twelve-week period in 1964. Although 120 countries participated in the Conference, it was dominated by a solid coalition of developing states, "the 77," which, through unity of action, pressed their demands into resolutions adopted by the conference. This group of seventy-seven developing states also signed, at the conclusion of the conference, a joint declaration in which they made clear their intention to treat the conference only as a first step in achieving a greater degree of justice for the impoverished nations. Since 1964 the term "group of 77" continues as a label, although its membership has expanded to well over one hundred states. The guiding spirit of the conference was Raul Prebisch, an economist and former executive secretary of the Economic Commission for Latin America, who was selected to become the Secretary-General of the newly created quasi-autonomous secretariat of the permanent organization of UNCTAD. By creating their own agency, the developing states hoped to establish an effective channel for promoting their interests and for partially by-passing the labyrinth of United Nations agencies surrounding ECOSOC.

The principal demands of the developing states as reflected in the conference resolutions included the following: (1) the stabilization of prices for primary commodities by international arrangements, (2) the lowering of tariffs and other trade barriers on primary commodities, (3) the safeguarding of the developing countries against adverse effects of the disposal of surplus agricultural products, (4) the provision of long-term loans at low rates of interest repayable in local currencies or in goods, (5) loans and grants free of obligations to buy from the granting state or to utilize their shipping and insurance facilities, (6) a net flow of aid from developed states equal to 1 percent of their national income, (7) the encouragement of regional arrangements and integration among developing states as a means of promoting trade and economic growth, and (8) special attention to the needs of the least developed among the developing states.

Altogether twenty-seven principles were approved by the conference. In voting on these principles, a dichotomy became evident between the positions of the developing and the developed states. The solid bloc of developing states produced affirmative votes varying in number between 78 and 116 on each principle. Only five principles were unanimously approved. In general the developed states either opposed or abstained on a majority of issues, with the United States opposing more principles than any other state. This dichotomy is significant in forecasting the difficulties during the following years in eliciting cooperation from the affluent states to speed the development process.

Another set of decisions of the conference led to the creation of permanent machinery for the UNCTAD. Conferences were to be held presumably at three-year intervals, although, in reality, UNCTAD 2 met in New Delhi in 1968, UNCTAD 3 in Santiago in 1972, UNCTAD 4 in Nairobi in 1976, and UNCTAD 5 in Manila in 1979. Between sessions of the conference a Trade and Development Board open to participation by all UNCTAD members meets annually. To assist the board several specialized and expert committees have been set up. Within the United Nations Secretariat a special UNCTAD unit with its own budgetary allocations has been established in Geneva. The UNCTAD is placed directly under the aegis of the General Assembly, thus by-passing much of the jurisdiction of ECOSOC as a coordinating agency. The developing countries sought and obtained their own agency but, in the process, further complicated the already complex United Nations machinery for dealing with development problems in a somewhat orderly and unified manner.

The hopes of the developing states for special concessions through the UNCTAD to meet their perceived needs have been largely frustrated. The fact that the resolutions of each successive conference generally reiterate the same demands as those of UNCTAD 1, and that speeches of third world representatives often concentrate upon blaming the developed states for the lack of substantial progress toward the goals of the development process, dramatizes the disappointment of the developing nations in obtaining outside aid and support. Minor gains have been made in the area of nonreciprocal tariffs, but the general situation remains one of confrontation between rich and poor.

A major thrust of the developing countries' efforts to enlarge their share of global income has been their demand for remunerative and stable prices for primary commodities, the source of most of their foreign exchange. This theme of equitable and reliable prices for their exports has run through every UNCTAD session since 1964.

In 1975, in preparation for the fourth general conference, the UNCTAD secretariat drew up plans for an integrated program for commodities. In 1977 the Paris Conference on International Economic Cooperation endorsed in principle a Common Fund to support the prices of these commodities. Conclusion of a detailed and comprehensive commodity program with the financial support of such a fund, would represent a fundamental gain for the developing states and a significant improvement over the piecemeal approach.

Because the programs of the UNDP and of the specialized agencies for the promotion of the industrialization process in the developing countries were meager and dispersed, these countries pushed through the creation of another organization, similar in structure to the UNCTAD, in the industrialization field. The United Nations Industrial Development Organization (UNIDO) was approved by the General Assembly in 1965 and began operations in 1967. Its purpose is to accelerate the industrialization process in the developing countries with particular emphasis upon the manufacturing sector. Its funds come from the United Nations regular budget, from voluntary contributions, and from allocations from the UNDP. UNIDO has its own "permanent and full time" secretariat in Vienna as a part of the United Nations Secretariat. As with the UNCTAD, a high degree of autonomy, rather than direction from ECOSOC or the UNDP, is guaranteed. A proposal was first made in 1975 to elevate UNIDO to the status of a specialized agency, but difficulties in the planning process delayed the transition for several years.

UNIDO's activities include research, training, pilot projects, surveys, technical aid, seminars, data gathering and analysis, and exchange of information. The critics of UNIDO charge that the establishment of another "autonomous" agency added to the chaos of decentralized and overlapping jurisdiction within the economic and social areas of the United Nations, and that the activities of UNIDO spread too few resources over too many projects resulting in no real impact on the industrialization process. Those that have directly benefited, especially from the field activities of UNIDO, are likely to challenge such an assessment.

Small programs, but significant for development, include Operational Executive and Administrative Personnel Services (OPEX) and United Nations Volunteers. OPEX recruits top-level administrators for government posts in developing countries. While performing their duties, these administrators train indigenous counterparts who will replace them. The United Nations Volunteer program, begun in 1972, recruits young people who use their skills in aiding development programs.

The tendency in recent years in the United Nations is to answer each new problem related to development by creating a new agency or program, and to escape control by the affluent states by giving autonomy to the new agencies and by structuring them so that in their governing bodies the developing states have substantial majorities. Additional funds for development are also sought each year by the United Nations. The result is the constant expenditure of larger sums on a wider variety of projects through dispersed agencies with inadequate means for central planning and coordination.

In the 1970s the UNDP has attempted some reform in its procedures to correct these faults. For most of the developing countries five-year integrated country programs for development have been worked out and priorities have been established within the longer-range plans. This country-oriented approach has been accompanied by administrative restructuring to place more responsibility at the country level. Such attempts to strengthen the leading component of the United Nations development activities are indeed welcome and overdue.

A new dimension was added to the United Nations development efforts in 1974 when the "group of 77" called for a special session of the General Assembly devoted to problems of raw materials and development. From this session came the demand for a New International Economic Order (NIEO) "based on equity, sovereign equality, interdependence, common interest, and cooperation among all states." The less developed nations dominated this and subsequent regular and special General Assembly sessions and pressed hard for a radical reordering of the global economic system to correct what they saw as inequalities and injustices which constantly worked to the disadvantage of the poor countries. The general goals were to accelerate economic and social development and to eliminate the widening gap between rich and poor states.

The aspirations and demands of the developing states for the NIEO incorporated the previously developed programs of the UNCTAD conferences and expanded them. A Charter of Economic Rights and Duties of States adopted by the 1974 General Assembly asserted that every state has the right to exercise exclusive sovereignty over its wealth and natural resources, to regulate foreign investments, and to nationalize, expropriate, or transfer the ownership of foreign property with controversies to be settled under domestic law. This provision was vigorously opposed by the representatives of the developed market economies. Other planks in the NIEO platform stressed the formation of producers' associations and other forms of cooperation among developing countries, the establishment of linkage between the prices of exports of developing countries and the prices of their imports from developed countries, the formulation of commodity agreements, international monetary reforms, and the restructuring of the economic and social sectors of the United Nations system.

The progress toward a new International Economic Order is dependent upon the will and cooperation of individual states, rich and poor. The poor states must remain united in their goals and individually committed and effective in weeding out the internal impediments to development and in vigorously fostering measures that promote economic growth and social progress. Rich states must place the welfare of their less fortunate neighbors in this global village at a higher level of national priority than most have done in the past.

FINANCING ECONOMIC DEVELOPMENT

Some of the programs discussed in the previous section entail substantial financial contributions to the purpose of development. For example, an annual budget of approximately 500 million dollars for UNDP is a considerable sum to be devoted exclusively to aiding the development process. Sums from the regular budgets of the United Nations and many of the specialized agencies, as well as projects carried out by UNIDO, are also earmarked for development supporting activities. Yet these programs provide none of the basic financial resources in the form of loans or grants that the developing countries need in order to stimulate economic growth. The UNDP, the specialized agencies, and similar organizations merely furnish preinvestment needs through information, surveys, demonstrations, expert advice, and training, which are preliminary to investment in agriculture, industry, roads, dams, schools, and the host of other elements for building a more prosperous economy.

Capital is a primary component for development, although, obviously, it can be wasted or misdirected. Infusions of capital, without careful planning and the provision for supplementary conditions for growth, will not necessarily lead to development. Graft, mismanagement, maldistribution of resources, poor planning, or the lack of a balanced social and economic structure of society can lead to failure even though investment capital is available.

The major sources of capital are of three types. In the long run, domestic savings for investment is the most important source if an economy is to be healthy and is to attain an internal dynamic that all developed industrial economies possess. Until this "take-off" point is reached, outside loans or grants are essential. These monies come through either bilateral or multilateral channels. Bilateral sources provide the great bulk of these funds, but multilateral sources are the main focus of this study of international organization.

The initial financial agencies of the United Nations family of specialized agencies were the International Bank for Reconstruction and Development (IBRD or World Bank or Bank) and the International Monetary Fund (IMF or Fund). These are conservative agencies, run by hard-headed bankers and financial experts, and controlled by the affluent states through weighted voting based on contributions of capital. Both organizations came into being in December, 1945, when twenty-eight countries ratified the Bretton Woods Agreements of the previous year.

The World Bank is the largest multilateral source of funds for development. By 1978 the aggregate of all loans made by the Bank passed the 40-billion-dollar mark. In the 1970s the amount of lending per year averaged more than 3 billion dollars, or three to four times the annual volume for the 1960s.

Loans are made by the Bank under rules requiring (1) that all loans must be made to governments or must be guaranteed by governments; (2) that the rate of interest be consistent with the prevalent rate in the world's money markets; (3) that repayment be made within ten to thirty-five years; (4) that loans be made only in circumstances in which other sources are not readily available; (5) that investigations be made of the probability of repayment, considering both the soundness of the project and the financial responsibility of the government; and (6) that sufficient surveillance be maintained by the Bank over the carrying out of the project to assure that it is relatively well executed and managed. The application of some of these rules has carried the Bank into areas not strictly typical of lending institutions. The Bank is heavily involved in technical assistance activities and has made both comprehensive and limited preinvestment surveys, some of which are financed by the Bank and others by the UNDP. The Bank has also provided training for more than 4000 high-level administrative personnel through its Economic Development Institute.

In order to meet a wider variety of financial needs, two affiliates of the Bank have been created since 1956. The first to be established was the International Finance Corporation (IFC), which is intended to stimulate private investment in the developing countries. The IFC acts as a catalyst by furnishing limited investment capital for growth enterprises, in partnership with private investors. In order to increase its impact as a catalyst for private investment, the IFC frequently sells some of its holdings and uses the returns for investment in new enterprises. Although its resources, as compared with the capital and borrowing power of the Bank, are relatively modest, the IFC by 1977 had cumulatively committed more than 1.7 billion dollars in investments. Since it never underwrites more than 25 percent of each enterprise, and since its projects are carefully selected as making a significant contribution to the overall growth of a country's economy, its impact has been of significant proportions.

In 1960 a second affiliate of the Bank, the International Development Association (IDA), was created to provide for the special financial needs of the least-developed countries. Many of the poorest countries cannot bear the debt burden of conventional middle-term loans on the Bank's regular terms. Repayments of principal and interest provide such a drain on their limited resources as to cancel out much of the input of new capital. Countries are eligible for IDA loans if their per capita GNP is less than 375 dollars. Loans are made for fifty years at no interest with only an administrative service charge of three-fourths of 1 percent. No repayment is required during the first ten years, 10 percent of the loan is due during the second ten years, and the remaining 90 percent is payable during the last thirty years. Unlike the Bank and the IFC, whose funds are regenerated through repayments of principal and interest on loans made out of their original capital and borrowing power, the IDA must ask for new voluntary contributions on a continuing basis until such time as substantial repayments of previous loans are due. The response to the IDA requests for increasing amounts of funds to meet the expanding needs of the least-developed states is dependent upon the generosity and sense of obligation of the donor states. Even with a reduction in the previous United States share from 40 percent of the total to 33.3 percent, difficulties were encountered in Congress in 1974 in gaining support for an appropriation of 375 million dollars as the United States' first year's contribution to a four-year projected fund of 4.5 billion dollars for IDA.

Although the Bank and the IDA are legally separate entities, the same administrative structure directs both. After 1968, under McNamara's presidency of the Bank group of agencies, the philosophy common to the two organizations focused upon maximum contributions to the development process, particularly of the poorest states. The IDA's emphasis upon long-range needs became the dominant element in the new philosophy. Attention to the effects of projects on the total economy was intensified. Earlier concentration upon dams, industrial facilities, and transportation was shifted to include substantial support for agriculture, education, and population planning. Another concern in the new philosophy was the impact of projects upon the lowest 40 percent of the people within each national society, those who suffer the most from dire poverty. The benefits of past programs that often accrued only to privileged segments of the society were not considered satisfactory. A trickle-down philosophy of economic benefits was rejected.[5]

Because of the special problems of developing countries that could not qualify for IDA loans, the World Bank in 1975 opened a "Third Window" for loans at intermediate rates of interest of approximately half those of its regular loans. The Third Window loans are subsidized by a special fund raised by voluntary governmental contributions. The money available is relatively small in comparison with IDA or standard Bank lending.

The International Monetary Fund was created in 1945 to provide currency stability and convertibility among the world's nations and to allow countries to borrow from the fund to meet temporary balance-of-payments difficulties. Since the borrowing power of each member is linked to its quota in the IMF, the smaller nations are limited in their power. In 1969, the fund created Special Drawing Rights (SDRs), which are often referred to as paper gold and which were expected to promote trade and development by increasing the supply of international liquidity. SDRs were issued in the amount of approximately 9.5 billion dollars and allowed governments to borrow SDRs as well as other nations' currencies or gold from the IMF in order to correct balance of payments deficits. The value of each unit of SDRs was determined by a "basket" of the world's leading currencies and thus was related to floating exchange rates. By 1976 SDRs were established as the monetary system's principal reserve asset in place of gold or U.S. dollars. However, the use of the SDRs to July 31, 1972, showed that the United States and the United Kingdom together received more benefits from the system than all eighty-nine less-developed members combined.[6] The IMF also offers technical assistance in areas such as tax and budgeting policies, statistics, and central banking. In addition, it operates a training institute for the instruction of fiscal and budgetary officers from developing nations.

One ill-starred venture of the United Nations in the financial area

---

[5] For a more complete discussion of the new philosophy see Paul Dickson, "A Fresh Look at the World Bank," *Vista* (now *Inter Dependent*), (June, 1973), pp. 25, 27, 30, 48–49.

[6] Marjorie M. Milbourn and Mildred Weiss, "Statistical Annexes," *The United States and the Developing World: Agenda for Action 1973* (Washington, D.C.: Overseas Development Council, 1973), Annex B-7, p. 132.

was the establishment in 1966, at the insistence of the developing countries, of the United Nations Capital Development Fund. Because of their opposition to its creation, most wealthy states have refused to contribute to the fund, and the resources made available are extremely limited (only 18 million dollars paid in by 1975) and are mostly in nonconvertible currencies. Because of the disappointing response, the small resources are administered through UNDP rather than by special machinery provided for in the 1966 General Assembly resolution.

Other important sources of multilateral financing for development include the regional and subregional banks, which are discussed more fully in chapter 14. Both the Inter-American Development Bank and the Asian Development Bank have been major sources of development financing for hundreds of projects within their respective regions. The combined loans from these two institutions exceed 25 billion dollars.

In recent years the former figure of only approximately 10 percent of all foreign aid being transferred through multilateral channels has begun to increase slightly. This trend is due, in part, to a decrease in overall United States aid, which has, to date, seen slightly larger cuts in bilateral than in multilateral programs. In spite of the creation of many new agencies for meeting development needs, the demands of the poor countries for capital and other valuable resources seem unlikely to be met through either multilateral or bilateral channels. Continued sacrifice, misery, and reliance on a high degree of self-help seem likely predictions for the poverty-stricken two-thirds of the world in the light of current attitudes in the affluent segments of the globe.

RICH NATIONS AND POOR

Wealth is very unevenly distributed both within national societies and among them. Economic equality may be relatively more closely approximated in a few countries, but inequality is the rule. The Scandinavian countries and China are examples, at different levels of living standards, of countries that may have eliminated the greatest extremes of affluence and deprivation among their citizens.

One general difference, however, between the industrialized and the preindustrial societies is in the size of the segment of the population that lives in conditions of dire poverty. In a preindustrial society a small elite, perhaps 5-10 percent, generally lives either comfortably or extravagantly by twentieth-century standards. The remainder of the population lives far below the standard of minimum essentials that befit human dignity. In the industrial societies, on the other hand, the amenities of social and economic well-being are widely distributed among a large segment of the population.

In the world as a whole the discrepancies between rich and poor are similar to the contrasts of wealth and poverty within a preindustrial nation. If all states are divided into two classes, developed and developing, the developed one-fourth to one-third of the world population enjoys the benefits of possessing more than 80 percent of the gross world product, while in the developing world nearly three times as many people must survive on less than 20 percent of the world's wealth.

Relatively, the gap between rich and poor increases even though small absolute gains are registered by the developing states. A far greater rate of population growth in the poor than in the rich countries exacerbates the problem. Even if a developing country attains a 6 percent economic growth rate, if it also has a rate of population increase of 2.5 percent, which is the average for the developing world, it will require twenty years to double its per capita GNP. In that same period the discrepancy between the rich and poor nations in dollar amounts will have widened even if the rate of economic growth of the rich states is below 3.5 percent per capita.

In relative terms the developing states lose ground in other ways too. Between 1950 and 1970 their share of the value of world trade fell from 30 percent to less than 18 percent. In light of those statistics, their pressures for higher prices and favored treatment for their exports, as expressed through the UNCTAD, seem reasonable. For countries that are already poor their debt and debt service burdens become increasingly oppressive. The debts of the developing states doubled between 1965 and 1973 and doubled again in the next five years. By 1980 their total indebtedness was more than 200 billion dollars. For several countries, repayments of principal and interest threaten to exceed receipts of new loans and grants. Again, it should cause no surprise if these countries request easier terms on their much needed capital in the form of long-term, low-interest loans or outright grants.

In the international arena the frustrations of the developing nations have been expressed through the General Assembly, the Economic and Social Council, the UNCTAD, and conferences of nonaligned states. The poor countries have passed resolutions setting goals for development and creating new machinery, but the problems multiply and intensify, and the impact for dramatic alteration of their plight is slight. Part of the reason for slow progress is that the goals of the developing states are not shared or given high priority by the wealthy nations. Interdependence has not yet produced a common strategy for mutual prosperity. Robert Gregg has referred to a United Nations "performance gap" between less-developed countries' "numerical control of the UN decision-making process and Western state control of the goods and services toward which those UN decisions are directed."[7] This performance gap in the United Nations is indicative of the dissatisfaction of the developing states with their economic status and progress.

A PERSPECTIVE ON THE FUTURE

Several appraisals of development aid were published during 1969–70. One is a report prepared at the instigation of the World Bank by the Commission on International Development under the chairmanship of Lester Pearson. Another is the Capacity Study of the United Nations Development System under the leadership of Sir Robert Jackson. A third is the report of the UN Committee for Development Planning, which helped set the goals for the Second Development Decade. And a fourth is a study made by a Presidential Task Force appointed by President Nixon and chaired by Rudolph Peterson on the subject of international development, with emphasis upon the United States' role.

All of these reports stress the importance of development, point to mutual advantages of rich and poor in promoting it, and set higher goals for the future than the accomplishments of the past in order to accelerate the process. All urge that a larger percentage of aid be distributed through multilateral channels. All agree that the official component of development aid is a more reliable and important stimulus to rapid progress than heavy reliance on private investment for the transfer of resources.

The Jackson report, in particular, stresses the weaknesses of the United Nations system for accomplishing orderly development. Projects have been too small, numerous, and dispersed without sufficient relationship to broad plans either on a global or national basis. Agencies have proliferated and become uncoordinated instead of playing a role in an integrated whole. Clear priorities have not

---

[7] Robert W. Gregg, "UN Economic, Social, and Technical Activities," in James Barros, ed., *The United Nations: Past, Present, and Future* (New York: Free Press, 1972), p. 235.

been set and adhered to. The whole process is chaotic and lacks direction.

Some progress is being made in correcting these deficiencies. Evaluation is an integral part of the process for the Second Development Decade. Countries have been pressured to cooperate with the United Nations in drawing up integrated development plans and in establishing priorities. The World Bank and IDA have stressed education, agriculture, and population planning as basic to healthy development and have begun to measure aid in terms of its impact on the whole society.

Past and present trends, nevertheless, suggest a gloomy prognosis for the 1980s. As happened with the goals of the 1960s, those of the 1970s are also not being met. The transfer of resources to the developing states is far below the targets set by the reports. Cleavages between North and South as expressed through UNCTAD and the General Assembly seem to grow wider. The entrenched privileged segments of the global society seem inadequately concerned with the conditions faced by the disadvantaged two-thirds of humanity.

Immediate and longer-range prospects for the poor nations to improve their lot rapidly seem bleak. World food supply reserves are inadequate for emergencies, and the prospects for mass starvation in many areas are imminent. Population increases are canceling out many of the potential economic gains of the poor countries. The oil shortage of 1973-74 hit the poorest countries particularly hard because of increased prices, which they could not afford, for energy and fertilizer. Projections of the growth of population and GNP for the year 2000 show that more and more people will be living in the underdeveloped world, while the prosperity gap between rich and poor, in relative terms, will widen.

If these dismal prospects for the developing world are not to become reality, the realization of world interdependence must rapidly be converted into a positive philosophy. Facts and foresight prove such a philosophy to be rational. More and more scientists are pointing to the practicality and reality of a spaceship earth concept. In an increasing number of ways the futures of rich and poor are intertwined. The world development process is not a zero-sum game. An expanding pool of benefits is available in which all may share. This is illustrated by the experience within the nations that have already industrialized. The opening of global markets will provide a system of more efficient suppliers and a wider range of customers for an expanding production. Within such a system the developing states may be encouraged to diversify their production and increase their manufacturing output for export.

In a negative sense we are also all fellow travelers on spaceship earth. Without concern for the welfare of the poor nations the rich cannot achieve the stable kind of world relations on which they are dependent for their own future welfare and prosperity. The age of total interdependence is rapidly approaching. Habits and attitudes of national economic rivalry and self-gratification will soon have to give way to a global strategy in order to guarantee survival, progress, and the attainment of well-being for all.

11

❦

Promoting
Social Progress

As explained in the introduction to chapter 10, the economic and social activities of international organizations cannot be distinguished completely, either in theory or in practice. However, those programs generally identified as more social than economic are discussed in this chapter. These topics include human rights, health, food, population, child welfare, labor conditions, education, science, culture, narcotic drugs, and refugee problems.

CHARTER GOALS AND WORLD NEEDS

The social goals of the United Nations are best summarized in the phrase from the preamble of the Charter "to promote social progress and better standards of life in larger freedom." This statement of goals expresses the aspirations of humankind for a fuller, richer, more secure and more satisfying life—a quality of living that promises escape from the meanness of human degradation into the fullness of human dignity. The complete realization of these aspirations would bring about an ideal world from which all pockets of ignorance, poverty, hunger, and disease had been eliminated.

Anyone who views world conditions since 1945 realizes how

short of utopia we are and how little positive progress has been made toward a better life for the majority of humankind. As world population rapidly increases, the percentage of that population living at subhuman levels of education, health, nutrition, and economic well-being remains relatively unchanged despite billions of dollar-equivalents devoted annually to programs for raising social and economic standards of living. In comparative economic terms the rich countries continue to get richer and the poor countries get poorer. A North-South economic and social cleavage lays first claim for world attention over the East-West political cleavage. Pessimistic forecasts for the future of the underdeveloped countries are common. Based on trends of the past twenty-five years the prospects are not bright for the majority of humankind to escape from misery into a "better way of life" during the remainder of this century.

World social and economic needs are of gargantuan proportions. Massive infusions of capital would be required to bring about rapid improvement in the quality of life of hundreds of millions of people who have not shared in the emancipating aspects of economic affluence. But the problems of social change cannot be solved merely by providing huge amounts of capital, even if sufficient quantities were available. The experiments of the postwar years have demonstrated the fallacies of such an approach. The developing countries may be required to generate most of their own capital rather than to depend primarily on outside sources. But beyond capital needs the requirements of planning, social engineering, and social revolution probably outweigh other factors if the kinds of changes are to occur that will "turn the world around" for the developing societies. Only in those countries where enlightened leadership promotes social revolution can societies hope to achieve their aspirations for an escape from human misery. In countries where that quality of leadership fails to emerge, life for the masses will continue to be, in Hobbesian terms, "solitary, poor, nasty, brutish and short."

Although most of the energy and resources for social and economic development must be generated internally, the attitudes of the decision makers of the affluent states toward the "revolution of rising expectations" in the developing world will affect the course and rate of change in those countries. The examples of Soviet and Chinese development may lead one to conclude that a state can carry on massive reforms with a minumum of outside assistance, or even with outside opposition, but these examples may serve as inadequate models for most of the scores of underdeveloped states today. The Soviet Union and China, with their gigantic political, social, and economic base, are in sharp contrast to most of the political units seeking improved social and economic conditions. Dependence upon outside relations is an inescapable reality for a small state lacking in a myriad of necessary elements for rapid development. Whether the developed states will tolerate or encourage revolutionary change, whether they will cooperate and support internal efforts at reform, or whether they will intervene to maintain the status quo can profoundly affect the course of development of those nations trying to throw off the yoke of past conditions. From the developed states the less prosperous will need capital, technical assistance, goods, markets for their products, and, above all, an understanding of their problems and tangible encouragement and aid in their solutions. Without this aid and encouragement progress will be either slow or nonexistent.

Social revolution is an essential ingredient for rapid social development, but social change is interrelated with political and economic change. No state can plan for improved social conditions without concomitant expansion of its economic base and adequate attention to improvement of the quality of government personnel, organization, and programs. Any discussion of social factors is, of necessity, certain to impinge upon the economic and political sectors. No attempt will be made to isolate the social issues discussed in this chapter from the political and economic realities to which they are inextricably related.

In a world of 160 independent states of which two-thirds are classified as underdeveloped or preindustrial, the United Nations can play a minor yet crucial role in the development process. The resources distributed through United Nations agencies are small when compared to the amounts involved in bilateral aid programs or the expenditures for war preparation or the sums that would be required to relieve human deprivation and suffering. An attitude of skepticism and pessimism concerning the United Nations' impact on world economic and social problems seems justified when one compares a total budget measured in hundreds of millions of dollars against the tens of billions that would be necessary annually to satisfy the needs of all persons who live below a decent standard of human dignity. One might also question the amount of change that can be effected by a few thousand civil servants and experts recruited by United Nations agencies, however skilled and devoted to their tasks they may be, when the total needs for social reform are so vast and progress to date seems infinitesimal. National sovereignty and national sensibilities also preclude any global solution to world social problems. National governments must request aid before it can be granted, existing governmental agencies must act as the channels through which aid is administered, and United Nations personnel can carry on their activities within each state only at the sufferance of the governmental authorities of the host state. Global welfare programs must still conform to the theories and patterns of a compartmentalized world of independent, sovereign states in which no significant authority has yet been transferred to the international level.

In spite of all its obstacles and limitations, the United Nations plays an indispensable role in assisting nations to escape from the intolerable conditions that condemn the majority of the world's population to a brutish existence. Although for each country self-help is the main key to the escalation process toward better social and economic standards, small states are dependent on the rest of the world for supportive conditions for their own efforts. Bilateral arrangements are often unattractive because of the degrading psychological effects of dependence that attend such arrangements. Multilateral channels provide an escape from the stigma of dependence since every state can be both donor and recipient in a cooperative effort. Underdeveloped states clamor for the expansion of United Nations development programs as evidenced by the proclamation of the First and Second Development Decades and by the creation of the United Nations Conference on Trade and Development (UNCTAD) and the United Nations Industrial Development Organization (UNIDO). Developed states, among whose primary goals is that of international stability, may gradually see their enlightened self-interest to lie in the direction of channeling increased development effort through multilateral channels. Although United Nations resources may remain small in comparison to both total need and internal national programs, they can provide, if intelligently planned, the necessary catalytic element to turn failure into success in those countries whose own efforts are greatest and best directed.

If any progress is to be made toward a worldwide frontal attack upon ignorance, poverty, hunger, and disease, the United Nations family of agencies is indispensable for coordinating that effort. The United Nations already exists, its goals include the promotion of the better standards of life to which the developing nations aspire, and it has established an elaborate pattern of agencies and programs for working toward the attainment of these goals. No other broad competing or substitute international agencies that can promote world social welfare are in prospect. The present and future role of the

United Nations system has been well summarized by David Owen, who was for nearly twenty-five years a key administrator in the development programs of the United Nations:

> The mobilization and application of the resources needed to carry out a combined attack on the problems of global development will be so immense and pervasive a task as to be beyond the resources of any single institution or grouping of institutions now in existence. . . . It is certainly far beyond the capability of the United Nations system as its exists today. It may be suggested, however, that a modest but nonetheless vital role does await the United Nations system as a focal centre for strategic planning, for co-ordinating programmes of combined action, for harmonizing the actions of governments and international institutions, for directing some key activities, and for assessing the progress made in the implementation of programmes. Financially weak and ill-nourished though it is today, no other systematic grouping of worldwide institutions has the same organizational resources for the purpose.[1]

EMPHASIS ON HUMAN RIGHTS

The question of human rights is concerned with interpersonal relationships and with the relationships of the individual to governmental authority at all levels from local to international. Human rights include those areas of individual or group freedom that are immune from governmental interference or that, because of their basic contribution to human dignity or welfare, are subject to governmental guarantee, protection, or promotion.

Two major ideologies encompassing ideas on human rights, which are in substantial degree antithetical, have emerged in recent centuries. One strand of political thought is represented by the humanistic philosophy of the Enlightenment of the eighteenth century; the other is the ideology of Marxism as developed by Lenin, Mao, and others. Advocates of each ideology are certain of the truth and eventual universal acceptance of their doctrines. Their differences in views on property, class struggle, individualism, equality, and the role of the state leave little ground for agreement upon a universal set of values for the international community. Communist doctrine emphasizes economic and social rights, whereas liberal democratic theory concentrates on civil and political rights. Semantic interpretations can occasionally help to bridge the gaps if each side is allowed to read its own set of meanings into terms such as "democratic" and "freedom," which both use but in different contexts. But as

---

[1] David Owen, "A Combined Strategy," in Richard Symonds, ed., *International Targets for Development* (New York: Harper & Row, 1970), p. 247.

long as major groups of individuals differ sharply on their acceptance of basic values and values systems, the adoption of universally accepted standards of human rights will be difficult to achieve and implement.

Great concern for human rights was not manifest in the League of Nations. The statement of purposes and principles in the Covenant made no reference to human rights. Article 22, which dealt with the mandates system, contained a general and vague commitment, "that the well-being and development of such peoples [governed under mandate] form a sacred trust of civilization." In the section that outlined the conditions to be maintained by the mandatory in the class B mandates, references were included to a "guarantee [of] freedom of conscience and religion" and "the prohibition of abuses such as the slave trade." Article 23, which dealt with economic and social questions, listed among the general obligations of members of the League the securing of "fair and humane conditions of labor for men, women, and children," maintaining "just treatment of the native inhabitants of territories under their control" and entrusting "the League with the general supervision over the execution of agreements with regard to the traffic in women and children and the traffic in opium and other dangerous drugs."

In the peace treaties and in special "minority treaties" at the end of World War I, the Allied powers exacted special obligations from Czechoslovakia, Greece, Poland, Rumania, and Yugoslavia with regard to the rights of minorities within their borders. Although these obligations were not mentioned in the Covenant, the treaties assigned to the League Council the principal responsibility for treaty enforcement and provided that the Permanent Court of International Justice should decide any legal question referred to it under the treaties. In spite of complaints by the eastern European states that they were subject to special obligations not applicable to other states, the League was powerless to universalize these obligations except to the extent of a Council resolution expressing a "hope" that all states would practice as high a standard in the treatment of minorities as was required in the minority treaties.

The mass murders, concentration camps, and other forms of inhuman treatment of individuals and groups of individuals as a part of the official policy of some governments prior to and during World War II provided the impetus for a commitment to the protection and promotion of human rights in the United Nations Charter. The concern for human rights finds expression in the Charter in seven separate references to the subject. "[P]romoting and encouraging respect for human rights and for fundamental freedoms for all without distinction as to race, sex, language, or religion" is declared in Article 1 to be one of the primary goals of the organization. Implementation of this goal is assigned chiefly to the Economic and Social Council, but human rights also come within the scope of responsibilities of the General Assembly and the Trusteeship Council. The Economic and Social Council is given a specific mandate in Article 68 to set up commissions in the area of human rights in addition to such other commissions in economic and social fields as may facilitate its functions. Thus, the prominent role of the subject of human rights in the Charter stands in sharp contrast to the meager attention given it by the League Covenant.

The Economic and Social Council took prompt action to implement its mandate to set up commissions for the promotion of human rights. In 1946 it established the Commission on Human Rights and a Sub-Commission on the Status of Women. The next year this sub-commission was raised to full commission status and the Commission on Human Rights established a new Sub-Commission on Prevention of Discrimination and Protection of Minorities. Except for increases in the membership of these agencies, the general pattern of organization has remained unchanged since 1947.

In 1947 the Commission of Human Rights, under the chairmanship of Eleanor Roosevelt, began work on the Declaration of Human Rights and, in spite of semantic and ideological difficulties, completed the document by the following year. On December 10, 1948, the General Assembly adopted the declaration by a vote of 48–0 with eight abstentions. Members of the Soviet bloc abstained because of the narrowness of coverage of economic and social rights, and South Africa objected to the invasion by the United Nations of an area that, in its judgment, was immune to international jurisdiction. December 10 is commemorated each year as Human Rights Day.

In spite of its nonbinding character, the Declaration of Human Rights has made considerable impact in several directions. It has been cited in court opinions, has influenced national legislation, has been incorporated, in part, into new national constitutions, and has been referred to in the text of international treaties. The declaration has been widely publicized and is frequently alluded to in the organs and agencies of the United Nations. Although unenforceable, it has provided a common standard of conduct against which alleged invasions of rights can be judged in the arena of world opinion.

Seeking to incorporate human rights into the principles of international law, the proponents of human rights in the United Nations next focused their attention upon the task of producing one or more conventions on the subject. If such conventions were widely ratified, the doctrines of the declaration could be converted into binding legal principles voluntarily adhered to by the ratifying states. The speedy adoption of the declaration stands in sharp contrast to the delays and frustrations of working out satisfactory terms for the conventions. For a time a single convention was considered, but, at the insistence of the United States, separate covenants on civil and political rights and on economic, social, and cultural rights were produced. After many years of slow and painstaking effort and compromise, the General Assembly finally approved the two covenants on December 16, 1966, and opened them for ratification. States were slow to ratify, and it was 1976 before the two covenants came into effect with 35 ratifications each. Since treaties bind only those states that ratify them, most of the world is unaffected by the guarantees of the covenants.

In addition to the search for general principles in the field of human rights, United Nations agencies have produced a series of more specialized conventions each directed toward the elimination of interference with specific freedoms or discrimination against a specific group. The ILO and UNESCO as well as the commissions of ECOSOC have been the source of some of these treaties.

The Convention on the Prevention and Punishment of the Crime of Genocide, which was approved by the General Assembly in December, 1948, and which entered into force in January, 1951, is probably the most widely known of these instruments. Genocide is defined as the commitment of acts with intent to destroy or decimate a national, ethnic, racial, or religious group. The impetus for such an international obligation largely stemmed from the Nazi extermination of the Jews, although other allegations of genocide can be traced through earlier history in many countries.

Other subjects dealt with in the more specialized conventions include the abolition of slavery and the slave trade, the abolition of forced labor, discrimination in employment, equal pay for men and women workers, discrimination in education, and political rights of women. The conventions covering these areas are all in force and have been ratified by forty or more states.[2] Of special interest is the Convention on the Elimination of All Forms of Racial Discrimination, which was approved by the General Assembly in 1965 and entered into force in January, 1969. The convention is notable not only for its scope of subject matter, but also because it provides for

[2] For a list of nine key conventions for which the General Assembly has particularly urged additional ratifications, see Vernon Van Dyke, *Human Rights, the United States, and World Community* (New York: Oxford University Press, 1970), pp. 144-45.

an implementing committee to receive complaints and for an optional clause by which adhering states may permit petitions from individuals or groups within their jurisdiction.

Regional organizations have made significant contributions to the safeguarding of human rights. The Council of Europe has adopted a European Convention on Human Rights with optional provision for petitions from individuals or groups and with elaborate machinery and procedures for investigating complaints and for enforcing decisions. Authority is allocated among a European Commission on Human Rights, a European Court of Human Rights, and the Committee of Ministers of the Council. The Organization of American States in 1948 adopted an American Declaration on the Rights and Duties of Man and in 1960 established an Inter-American Commission on Human Rights. This commission has demonstrated remarkable effectiveness, particularly during the Dominican crisis of 1965. Preliminary steps have been taken to set up an Inter-American system similar to the European human rights machinery, and proposals have been made for regional systems in Africa and Southeast Asia, but progress toward these goals is slow.

A paradox confronts humankind in its efforts to promote human rights. On the one hand, the need to protect individual and group rights is apparent from history, and the state is likely to be the perpetrator or silent partner in any infringement of those rights. At the same time, each state is jealous of its sovereign prerogatives, and guarantees of rights have traditionally been a subject almost solely of domestic jurisdiction. Any effective international means for implementation is, therefore, revolutionary in nature and likely to be resisted by conservative nationalist forces.[3] In the United States these forces of resistance were led in the 1950s by Senator Bricker and the American Bar Association and so influenced Secretary of State Dulles that he announced a policy of refusing to submit all human rights conventions to the Senate for approval. A dramatic change of attitude was initiated in 1977 by the Carter administration by making the promotion of human rights a prominent issue in United States foreign policy. However, President Carter was accused of selectively applying pressures to end foreign government persecution of individuals and groups and of meddling in the internal affairs of other states. Moral declaration of rights have much appeal, but the invasion of accepted areas of domestic jurisdiction in order to pro-

[3] Both William Korey, "The Key to Human Rights—Implementation," *International Conciliation*, No. 570 (November, 1968), and Van Dyke, *Human Rights*, stress the problem of implementation as the great obstacle to the achievement of international protection of human rights.

vide international sanctions against state abuse is quite another matter.

Nowhere is the frustration of trying to bring international pressure to bear more vividly illustrated than in regard to the apartheid policies of South Africa. United Nations involvement in this issue was previously detailed in chapter 6. Early resolutions by the General Assembly were based on the provisions of the Charter that obligate all members to promote respect for and observance of human rights, but later resolutions spoke of "crimes against humanity" and "threats to international peace and security." South Africa's response to these measures has been defiance and noncooperation with United Nations agencies. Its main legal pillar has been the domestic jurisdiction clause of Article 2, paragraph 7, of the Charter. South Africa claims that the United Nations is trying to intervene illegally in its domestic affairs and that it has violated no obligation subject to international jurisdiction.

Human rights is an area in which controversy over international authority will continue for some time. The present period represents a transition from purely domestic jurisdiction to increasing international concern. The transition will be complicated by differences in ideology and standards of human rights and by the problems of trying to develop international instruments and models for implementation and enforcement. The emphasis upon human rights in the Charter, the Declaration of Human Rights, and the creation of effective agencies by the Council of Europe are landmarks of new attitudes to come. But, as long as the major powers are unenthusiastic in their endorsement of international action, and, as long as nations such as South Africa can defy international pressures to end race discrimination, the new age of human freedom under effective international guarantees will not have dawned.

PROMOTING IMPROVED HEALTH STANDARDS

Health problems have been a matter of international concern for centuries. Epidemics of cholera, plague, typhus, and influenza have swept across national borders fron ancient times to the present century. Beginning in 1851 a series of international conferences was called to deal with quarantine regulations, and the International Sanitary Convention was adopted in 1903. In 1909 the International Office of Public Hygiene was established in Paris to deal only with quarantine matters. After the establishment of the League of Nations Health Organization, the Paris office continued its functions side by side with the League organization until both were absorbed by the World Health Organization in 1948. In 1902 the Pan American Sanitary Bureau was created and has served, in the scope of its authority, as a model for subsequent organizations. It continues its functions today both independently of and as a regional office of the World Health Organization.[4]

The Health Organization of the League, established in 1923, accomplished much more than its creators or those who limited its financial resources anticipated. It was appraised by most students of League operations as one of the most successful agencies among the League's social and economic divisions. The economic and social work of the League, mainly an afterthought in an organization created primarily to maintain peace, grew throughout the life of the League in importance and prestige, and the Health Organization was a keystone in this development. It carried on activities in epidemic control, research, publication of health information, standardization of vaccines, sponsorship of conferences and lectureships, and direct assistance to governments. It became the principal center for international activities in promoting improved world health standards.

The World Health Organization (WHO) was established as a specialized agency of the United Nations in 1948 and has become the largest of the specialized agencies in terms of budget, and one of the largest in membership. Its headquarters is in Geneva, but its operations are decentralized through six regional committees and regional offices.

In trying to carry out its self-imposed mandate of attaining for all peoples the highest possible level of health, the World Health Organization has engaged in a formidable array of activities. WHO maintains an Epidemiological Intelligence Network for the rapid dissemination of information by telecommunications concerning the outbreak anywhere in the world of cases of cholera, plague, smallpox, and yellow fever. It has initiated massive campaigns for the eradication of malaria, tuberculosis, smallpox, and yaws, and, with the cooperation of governments, tens of millions of people have been treated for each of these communicable diseases. In the case of tuberculosis, WHO research helped produce a new improved vaccine. Costs of effective treatment for mass campaigns against

---

[4] For an excellent summary of both the historical development and the current status and problems of international health agencies, see Freeman H. Quimby, *The Politics of Global Health*, Committee Print in Science, Technology, and American Diplomacy series (Subcommittee on National Security Policy and Scientific Development of U.S.H.R. Committee on Foreign Affairs, May 1971). This document serves as one of the major sources of information for this section.

communicable diseases have been reduced through WHO efforts. WHO supports research and control programs against trachoma, bilharziasis, and leprosy.

In the areas of water supply, sewage disposal, air pollution, and the development and use of insecticides, WHO conducts studies, subsidizes research, and furnishes technical assistance. It provides advice to governments on public-health planning. It has assumed leadership in establishing research programs for heart disease, cancer, drug dependence, and mental health. In trying to overcome the severe shortage of personnel in the health professions, WHO aids in establishing schools and training programs and each year makes about 100 training and exchange grants and provides 3,500 fellowships. Each year it organizes approximately forty short courses and eighty technical conferences. In encouraging research it initiates roughly 200 research contracts annually. WHO is responsible for administering the Code of International Health Regulations adopted in 1969 by the World Health Assembly. It has established quality control for hundreds of drugs in order to establish standards of content and purity.

WHO serves as an information and publication center on health matters by compiling statistics and publishing reports, research studies, monographs, manuals, directories, and several periodicals. It can draw on and disseminate information through several hundred reference centers that have agreed to serve as part of a network that WHO coordinates.

Through collaboration with private and public agencies, WHO expands its influence in every aspect of its program. The reference centers mentioned above are one example of this collaboration; another is the relationship with the Pan American Sanitary Bureau, which serves both as a regional office of WHO and as an arm of the Organization of American States (OAS) with its own program and budget. A substantial portion of the budget of the United Nations Children's Fund (UNICEF) is administered through WHO since the health of children is a prime aspect of their welfare. WHO collaborates with other United Nations specialized agencies in activities that are mutually supportive. The closest relationships are with the Food and Agriculture Organization (FAO), the International Labor Organization (ILO), and the United Nations Educational, Scientific and Cultural Organization (UNESCO). WHO also administers programs and funds as a part of the United Nations Development Program in addition to the programs financed through WHO's regular budget.

Altogether WHO has working agreements and relationships with more than eighty major public and private organizations in the health field in addition to its hundreds of reference centers. For its expertise it depends not only on its own staff, but also on forty-five or more advisory panels and expert committees representing a cross section of health subjects and world talent.

This review of the broad range of WHO activities and collaboration could lead one to assume that great inroads have been made into the problems of world health. When one adds to the picture the fact that, in a country such as the United States, expenditures have been several times as great for bilateral programs as for multilateral activities, and that foundations and private organizations have devoted substantial funds and energy to the alleviation of health problems, the expectations for success might be enhanced even further. Signal advances in some areas have, indeed, been made. The world is well on the way toward the elimination of malaria, smallpox, tuberculosis, and yaws. But the attainment of the goal of the highest level of health for all people is nearly as remote as it was in 1948. Hundreds of millions of humans live without access to medical aid, health services, or sanitary facilities. WHO currently dispenses funds from all sources of more than 250 million dollars annually. The report of the Committee for Development Planning, established by the Economic and Social Council, suggested that in order to meet the needs of the 1970s and to implement the objectives of WHO an annual expenditure of nearly 10 billion dollars from bilateral and multilateral sources would be necessary. In addition to large sums of money, a substantial increase in personnel and adequate planning would be major requirements. As in most international problems, the reallocation of human and monetary resources is not likely to occur in a highly compartmentalized world. The areas of greatest need are those with scarce resources. Without a restructuring of human values, the attainment of a high level of health for the poverty-stricken populations of the world will be a slow and agonizing process.

FOOD AND POPULATION PROBLEMS

For several years following World War II, the Malthusian doctrine gained considerable currency: a world population growth rate of geometric proportions and a food production rate of arithmetical dimensions would bring about the inevitable starvation of a large percentage of the world's future inhabitants. New knowledge about relationships between consumption and production and between production and distribution, and new techniques in agriculture and in birth control and family planning have resulted in more sophisticated approaches to the problem of feeding a growing population. However, the questions of food supply and population are undoubtedly linked and are especially urgent for the future of the developing nations.

Not only are food and population related, but they are, both separately and jointly, intertwined with a broad range of economic and social factors including buying power, land tenure, family structure, underemployment, social and religious beliefs and traditions, health, urban-rural relationships, education, economic and social class structure, industrialization, and international trade and aid, to mention only a partial list of possible linkages. The underdeveloped areas are not only growing in population at a faster rate than the more prosperous industrialized states, but they lack all the other elements necessary to guarantee the achievement of a more satisfying existence for the majority of their people.

World population was in 1976 approximately 4 billion, and at the current rate of increase will double in 35–40 years. More than 70 percent of the world's population now live in underdeveloped countries. In the preindustrial areas the rate of population increase is double the rate in the industrialized areas. By the year 2000 these trends will result in a concentration of 80 percent of the world's population in those countries now classified as underdeveloped. This rapid population growth complicates the planning process for economic development and cancels out a substantial portion of the economic growth in developing countries.

Other demographic factors exacerbate the problems of the underdeveloped states. In a pattern of rapid population increase, the high proportion of nonproductive persons is a significant factor. Children and old persons constitute nearly as high a percentage of the population as those of working age. Finding work for a rapidly growing rural population and for those who migrate to the cities is another formidable problem. The increased demand for health, education, and housing facilities represents a basic drain on the limited available resources for capital investment required for development.

Population control is a sensitive area and limits the possibilities for effective international action. In the first place, several declarations have been adopted since 1966 by the General Assembly and by special conferences that state the principle that the determination of the number and spacing of children is a basic human right of parents. Such declarations have both positive and negative connotations with regard to the relations between individuals and governments. On the one hand, the state may not interfere with the parents' desire to have many or few children. On the other hand, the state may make family planning possible through laws and through informational and educational programs of birth control, abortion, and sterilization. Religious principles may affect individual opinions toward family planning. Other factors include attitudes engendered by high infant mortality and information about, and access to, effective, inexpensive, and convenient birth-control devices and methods. Government and private programs to promote family planning may have contributed to recent substantial reductions in the rate of annual population growth in the Republic of Korea, Taiwan, and Puerto Rico, but the rate of increase in India has dropped only slightly in spite of government efforts favoring population control.

Prior to the 1960s the United Nations limited its population program mainly to fact-finding and statistical analysis. These activities were stimulated by the Economic and Social Council and by its subsidiary Population Commission, which meets at two-year intervals. The work of research and publication was carried on by the Population Division and the Statistical Office of the Secretariat. The program emphasized training in census techniques, the gathering of worldwide census data, and the publication of census data and population trends. The *Demographic Yearbook* published by the Statistical Office is one of the major outputs of these efforts.

Three World Population Conferences have been held. The first met in Rome in 1954, the second in Belgrade in 1965, and the third in Bucharest in 1974. The first two conferences were mainly technical in nature, but the 1974 conference adopted a World Population Plan of Action setting targets for reducing world fertility by 1985, with special emphasis upon developing countries. The Bucharest Conference is treated more fully in the next chapter.

As governments became more concerned with population problems, as the relationship between population growth and economic development was more widely appreciated, and as the role of government in population control became more acceptable, the emphasis in the United Nations population program broadened to include technical assistance and a concern for human welfare. Since 1962 the General Assembly has shown an interest in and concern for the reciprocal aspects of population change and economic development. Regional conferences, seminars, and committees of experts have met frequently to discuss general and specific aspects of population matters. An Asian Population Conference met in 1963 and an

African Population Conference in 1971. Committees of experts were convened in 1964 and 1966 to plan programs of research and action in the population field. In 1969 the United Nations Development Program financed a Seminar on Population Data and Development Planning in Kiev, Ukranian SSR. In 1967 the Secretary-General established a United Nations Fund for Population Activities with a budget target of 5.5 million dollars for five years. From this modest proposal a substantial fund has developed with actual annual pledges of more than 15 million dollars in 1970 and 89 million dollars in 1976. In 1969 an inaugural five-week training course for United Nations Population Program Officers was financed by the fund to prepare specialists for field assignments. The nine specialists in the initial course were given eighteen-month field assignments to aid forty-two governments in identifying population problems and in preparing action projects to be submitted for financing by the United Nations or other sources. The United Nations has gradually become involved in population activities that, twenty years earlier, would have been considered inappropriate for such an organization.

Although nutritional deficiencies exist among the poor living in prosperous countries, the severe problems of world hunger and malnutrition affect mainly the underdeveloped states. The problems include low per capita calorie consumption, protein deficiency, vitamin and mineral deficiencies, high cost of scarce commodities, and inequalities in food consumption among various segments of the population. Hunger and malnutrition lead to health problems and lack of energy. With a rapid growth in population, the poor countries must increase food supplies rapidly and distribute them more equitably if they hope to mobilize the necessary human resources for economic development.

Self-sufficiency in food production is not necessarily the answer for all the underdeveloped states. Per capita gains in income from any combination of sources is their most basic goal. Prior to World War II the underdeveloped areas in general exported a surplus of cereals. During the 1950s the trend was reversed, and the huge surplus of wheat in the United States became one of the chief sources of cereals for the developing countries. The development of new high-yielding varieties of wheat, maize, and rice seemed to promise a "green revolution," which might have restored some of the developing states to a position of self-sufficiency or surplus production of food. Adverse weather conditions, high fertilizer costs, and the slow spread of agricultural technology produced, instead, food shortages and famines in Africa and Asia in the 1970s.

A current emphasis in the fight against hunger is to helping the small farmer in the developing countries to stay on his land and to improve his welfare and buying power. As a part of their "basic needs" philosophy, the World Bank and its affiliates have stressed programs that directly assist poor farmers and their families. Frances Moore Lappé and Joseph Collins in their investigations of the hunger problem have concluded that the answers lie neither in production of more food nor in better distribution, and that such developments as the "green revolution" have contributed simultaneously to more food production and more hunger. They argue that modernization of agriculture in the developing countries has made a business of farming which is profitable only on a larger scale and thus squeezes out the small farmer who becomes landless and unemployed. The displaced farmers are eliminated from both the production and consumption processes. Increased food supplies are diverted from basic human consumption to livestock feed, breweries, or sweeteners for soft drinks. In order to resolve the problem, the small farmers in developing countries need to regain control of the production process in order to feed themselves.[5]

The key international agency concerned with food production and distribution and with nutrition is the Food and Agriculture Organization (FAO) established in 1945 as a specialized agency of the United Nations. The headquarters is in Rome with regional offices throughout the world.

For an organization with an annual regular budget of approximately 85 million dollars to attack the problems of world food supply and nutrition would appear to be an exercise in futility. However, several factors add to the effectiveness of the FAO's efforts. The FAO administers additional funds from several sources including the United Nations Development Program (UNDP), UNICEF, national governments, and nongovernmental organizations. Each of the regional commissions of the Economic and Social Council has an agriculture division jointly staffed by the FAO and the commission. With the International Atomic Energy Commission (IAEA), the FAO has set up a Joint Division of Atomic Energy in Agriculture at IAEA headquarters in Vienna. The FAO collaborates with other specialized agencies, notably the ILO, UNESCO, and WHO. The World Bank has subsidized surveys of national needs, including agricultural requirements, in many underdeveloped countries, and the financial agencies among the United Nations furnished

[5] Frances Moore Lappé and Joseph Collins, "When More Food Means More Hunger," *War on Hunger*, 10, no. 11 (November, 1976), publication of U.S. Agency for International Development, 1–3; 14–15.

loans and grants for agricultural projects promoted through FAO efforts.

Like most of the other specialized agencies of the United Nations, the FAO engages in relatively low-cost activities. It does not undertake large-scale operations or furnish extensive funds for implementing its recommendations. Its major programs involve research, fact-finding, publication, technical assistance, and the promotion of conferences and seminars. The FAO's main role is to furnish information, stimulation, and technical knowledge. If the implementation of proposed programs is costly, the financial resources must come either from within the state where a given program is conducted or from bilateral or multilateral grants or loans.

A brief review of some of the FAO's principal projects will serve to demonstrate the breadth of its activities. In 1960 the FAO inaugurated a Freedom from Hunger Campaign based on private citizen support and programs with FAO advice and stimulation. Projects inspired by the campaign range from land use and irrigation to cooperatives and nutrition education. A perennial activity of the FAO is a survey of the world food and agriculture situation and the publication of regular reports showing the status and trends of food supply and agricultural production. For several years the FAO worked on an Indicative World Plan for Agricultural Development setting forth detailed objectives for food production and supplies for the years 1975 and 1985. Regular surveys are also published covering the state of the world's forests and fisheries. Studies have been made of fishing boats and fishing equipment and methods, and research and technical assistance have been furnished to promote "fish farming" in ponds and flooded rice paddies as a means of increasing the protein intake in underdeveloped countries. As a joint enterprise with WHO, the FAO has developed under the *Codex Alimentarius* a set of international quality standards for food products. The FAO also works closely with UNICEF and WHO in improving child nutrition, especially in the production of powdered milk and inexpensive high-protein foods.

Within the broad area of agriculture, the FAO is concerned with such diverse matters as soils, irrigation, the development of new varieties of seeds, the use of farm machinery and fertilizers, and the elimination and control of livestock diseases. One of the important services of the FAO is the furnishing of fellowships for training personnel in new skills in all the areas of the FAO program. Regional seminars and short courses also contribute to the policy of training for greater self-help in the developing countries, a policy that, it is hoped, will make the maximum contribution to the development process.

In 1961 the General Assembly authorized a three-year World Food Program to begin in January, 1963, with a proposed budget of 100 million dollars in commodities, cash, and services pledged by governments. In 1965 the program was made permanent, and new pledging targets were set. In 1976 the annual budget reached 300 million dollars. The program is run as a joint project of the United Nations and the FAO with an Inter-Governmental Committee for policy direction and a special secretariat for program administration. The purposes of the World Food Program are to relieve emergency food needs and to implement the food portion of economic and social development projects. A unique feature is the use of food as a partial substitute for cash wages for persons engaged in development work. Although its emergency relief is important, the program makes little impact on the total food needs of the developing countries. The United States Agricultural Trade Development and Assistance Act of 1954 (Public Law 480), a bilateral program, far exceeds the World Food Program if its more than 1 billion dollars in average annual resources is compared to the 300 million dollars available to the World Food program. Public Law 480, in turn, represented only 30 percent of the value of United States agricultural exports between 1954 and 1966.[6]

The FAO has been criticized for concentrating too much on statistics and research and too little on leading a grassroots agricultural revolution. The great need, according to Sudhir Sen, is to help develop competent agricultural extension

in as many countries as possible and to bring the benefits of modern science and technology to the door of the farmers coupled with actual field demonstration and the requisite practical guidance.[7]

Sen accuses the FAO of dealing in "grandiose schemes" and massive reports while neglecting means of implementation. He suggests

that the seeds of revolution can be planted in the fields and nourished with fertilizers; that the new forces of dynamism thus introduced in rural environment would be a powerful factor in changing the farmer's attitude; and, working backwards from the field, they would, sooner or later, help burst the institutional rigidities and even compel the authorities to forge new policies and to make necessary institutional and other adjustments.[8]

[6] David R. Wightman, "Food Aid and Economic Development," *International Conciliation*, No. 567 (March, 1968), p. 35.
[7] Sudhir Sen, *United Nations in Economic Development — Need for a New Strategy* (Dobbs Ferry, N.Y.: Oceana Publications, 1969), p. 254.
[8] *Ibid.*, p. 255.

In the Plans that were approved at a World Food Conference in Rome in 1974 for implementing the recommendations of the conference, two basic principles emerged: (1) the FAO was largely bypassed, and (2) national freedom of action and voluntary cooperation were left intact. A World Food Council was created to coordinate the work of diverse international agencies and to carry out conference plans. A pledging target of 10 million tons of annual food aid for developing countries was adopted. Proposals were also accepted for international coordination of *national* grain reserves. The World Food Conference is discussed more fully in the next chapter.

The great practical reality of the United Nations concern for the population and food problems of the underdeveloped nations is that no universal solution could be imposed from outside even if international authority were much greater than it is. Population control is largely a private and domestic matter. In preventing mass starvation, donor nations and international coordinating agencies may be able to act effectively in emergencies, but the prime tools for long-range solutions to food and population problems are information, education, the provision of incentives, and national development plans, programs, and means of implementation.

FOCUS ON CHILD WELFARE

The plight of destitute children has a strong emotional appeal for most persons. Several of the United Nations specialized agencies include in their programs projects that alleviate the needs of the young. WHO is concerned with the health of children, FAO with their nutritional needs, UNESCO with problems of education, and the International Labor Organization (ILO) with child labor. An additional organization, UNICEF, concentrates exclusively on the task of improving the lot of disadvantaged children. Since the 1950s its main concern has been with the condition of children in the developing countries.

At its creation by resolution of the General Assembly in December, 1946, UNICEF was intended to be an emergency organization to care for the European children who were victims of World War II. Hence its full original title, United Nations International Children's Emergency Fund, emphasized the crisis nature of what was planned as a temporary agency. In 1953, when it was made a permanent agency and the word "emergency" was dropped from its official title, its familiar acronym, UNICEF, remained unchanged.

When UNICEF was formed, it had available approximately 30 million dollars in unexpended assets from the United Nations Relief and Rehabilitation Administration (UNRRA). During the period 1946-50, when UNICEF's activities were concentrated in Europe, it provided 112 million dollars in direct assistance to needy European children. At the peak of the European operations, 6 million children received a daily supplementary meal, 5 million were given clothing and shoes, and 8 million received vaccine to inoculate them against tuberculosis.

UNICEF is neither a specialized agency of the United Nations nor an operating agency. Its budget is not raised by assessment but by voluntary contributions from governments and private sources. It was established by resolution of the General Assembly and is not a membership organization, although more than 120 governments make voluntary contributions for its support. It is, as its title suggests, a fund administered under the direction of a thirty-nation executive board with the assistance of a staff incorporated within the United Nations Secretariat and headed by an executive director. Only two persons have served as executive director, the first, Maurice Pate, from 1946 to 1965, and Henry R. Labouisse since 1965. UNICEF grants are made to governments for projects benefitting children, and experts are recruited through WHO, the FAO, UNESCO, or other agencies with UNICEF subsidizing the costs. Governments requesting aid must furnish financial support and personnel so that UNICEF funds have a catalytic or multiplier effect. Government funds for UNICEF-aided projects average two and a half times the UNICEF subsidy.

Financial support for UNICEF has increased substantially since the early 1950s. For the decade 1951-60, UNICEF made direct assistance grants totaling 150 million dollars. For 1961-70 the figure was more than 300 million dollars. In 1965 the budget was 33 million dollars. In December, 1968, the General Assembly expressed deep concern at the magnitude of the unfulfilled needs of children in the developing countries and appealed for an increase in donations to reach an annual goal of 50 million dollars by the end of the First Development Decade. In 1970 the budget exceeded the target by 9 million dollars, and in 1971 a record high of 72 million dollars was reached. At the same time eighteen projects with total costs of more than 10 million dollars had to be put on a deferred list for lack of additional funds, and a new income target of 100 million dollars annually was set for 1975 onward. This target also is annually exceeded.

Private sources of income for UNICEF have gradually risen in both absolute and percentage terms. Today they account for approximately one fourth of UNICEF's resources. In 1970 the volume of UNICEF greeting cards sold was 70 million for a net profit to UNICEF of 4.5 million dollars. Other private donations and such campaigns as the Hallowe'en Trick or Treat for UNICEF account for additional millions from nongovernmental sources.

The range of UNICEF projects may be indicated by the list of categories for which allocations were made by the executive board in May, 1969. In decreasing order of magnitude of expenditure these were (1) permanent health services, (2) education, (3) malaria eradication, (4) nutrition, (5) comprehensive service for children in selected areas of rural development and prevocational training, (6) family and child welfare, and (7) emergency aid. Health services in India alone received an allocation of 10 million dollars. In terms of the types of institutions aided by UNICEF, a summary for 1961-70 shows assistance to 30,000 rural health centers, 55,000 schools, 2,500 teacher-training institutions, and 7,000 family and child welfare centers. During this ten-year period 225 million children were furnished with vaccinations against tuberculosis and almost 15 million were treated for yaws.[9]

In order to encourage countries to emphasize youth in their development plans, a series of international and regional conferences have been sponsored by UNICEF. Conferences of this type have been held in Bellagio, Italy, in 1964, in Santiago, Chile, in 1965 and again in 1969, in Bangkok in 1966, and in Addis Ababa in 1966.

In spite of occasional attacks on UNICEF by right-wing groups in the United States, the organization has been widely acclaimed as one of the most significant developments among the social and humanitarian efforts of the United Nations. In recognition of its great contribution, UNICEF was awarded the Nobel Peace Prize in 1965. Hundreds of millions of children in the developing countries require massive aid if they are, in the future, to make maximum contributions to the economic, social, and political development of their nations. UNICEF is making more than a token impact upon their prospects for a better life.

IMPROVING CONDITIONS OF LABOR

Although other agencies of the United Nations family of organizations engage in limited activities beneficial to workers, it is in the International Labor Organization (ILO) that the bulk of these

---

[9] Much useful information about UNICEF is contained in the General Progress Report of the Executive Director, Henry R. Labouisse, on the twenty-fifth anniversary of the organization, reported in *UN Monthly Chronicle* (April, 1971), pp. 48-60.

efforts are concentrated. Workers are affected by certain aspects of the programs of the Human Rights Commission, UNESCO, and the World Health Organization; the Economic and Social Council discusses and coordinates matters of vital concern to the welfare of the laboring class; the ILO consults with and engages in joint projects with other specialized agencies of the United Nations. But these efforts on behalf of labor are tangential and incidental to the concentration within the ILO of programs for the improvement of conditions for those within each society who are classified as laborers.

The ILO is unique both in its origins and in its system of representation. In response to pressure from several international workers' conferences held during World War I, the Paris peace conference incorporated the Constitution of the ILO into the Treaty of Versailles. Thus, the ILO was established in 1919 in the same manner as the League of Nations as a part of the movement to further world order through international cooperative institutions. In declaring that the ILO should be an autonomous organization associated with the League of Nations, the peace conference established a model that would serve for the relationship of the specialized agencies to the United Nations a quarter of a century later. The ILO's pattern of affiliation with the League based on the twin principles of autonomy and coordination proved more attractive at the San Francisco conference than suggestions for a highly centralized system of agencies. As a continuous organization since 1919 the ILO in 1946 became the first of the specialized agencies to conclude an agreement with the United Nations defining that relationship.

The ILO is typical of most of the other specialized agencies in its tripartite structure. This tripartite organization usually consists of a general conference, or assembly, in which all members are represented, a smaller council, or executive board, which acts as an executive committee between sessions of the larger assembly, and a secretariat, headed by a director-general, which carries out the basic policies established by the conference or assembly. In the ILO these three major organs are given the titles International Labor Conference, Governing Body, and International Labor Office.

Although similar to the other specialized agencies in overall organizational structure, the ILO is unique in its system of representation. The novel feature of ILO representation applies to both the International Labor Conference and the Governing Body, in which there are employers' delegates and workers' delegates as well as government delegates. Each member state is represented in the International Labor Conference by two government delegates, one employers' delegate, and one workers' delegate. In the choice of employers' and workers' delegates, governments are obligated to consult "with the industrial organizations, if such organizations exist, which are most representative of employers or workpeople, as the case may be, in their respective countries."[10] The Governing Body has a similar balance and consists of twenty-eight government representatives, fourteen employers' representatives, and fourteen workers' representatives. Twelve of the government representatives are required to be from the states of "chief industrial importance" and the employers' and workers' representatives are "elected respectively by the Employers' delegates and the Workers' delegates to the Conference."[11] In Communist ideology the identity of interests among government, employers, and workers tends to vitiate the purpose of tripartite representation and has led to charges of a lack of divergent interests and viewpoints among Communist delegates. In general, however, the tripartite formula has received praise and support as a device peculiarly suitable to such an organization as the ILO.

The activities of the ILO may be divided into four major categories. These are (1) standard setting, (2) technical cooperation, (3) research and information, and (4) education and training.

Since the inception of the ILO, standard setting has been a keystone of the organization's program to improve labor conditions, living standards, and workers' rights. The instruments have been international conventions and recommendations adopted by a two-thirds vote of the International Labor Conference. Recommendations are not binding on member states, but the conventions are open to ratification by governments, a process that incorporates them into municipal law. Ideally, the recommendations also affect governmental policies since the substantial support required for passage must reflect an influential segment of concerned opinion in many nations. Beginning with the adoption of six conventions and six recommendations by the first International Labor Conference in 1919, the list of each grew to 151 conventions and 143 recommendations by 1975. More than 4000 ratifications of conventions were certified during this period. While this number seems substantial, it represents an average of less than thirty ratifications for each convention in an organization whose recent membership is approximately 130. States that have recently joined the ILO tend to be low in number of ratifications, but the United States, whose membership dates from 1934, has ratified only seven conventions. In contrast,

---

[10] ILO Constitution, Art, 3, sec. 5.
[11] *Ibid.*, Art. 7.

France, Bulgaria, Spain and Italy have ratified more than 75 of these international instruments, thus incorporating a majority of this labor code into their internal legal systems.

The conventions adopted by the ILO range across a broad spectrum of subjects. Some of the main areas covered include regulations pertaining to hours of work, wages, unemployment, workers' compensation, insurance benefits, and safety. Special groups of workers, including women, young people, seamen, and miners, receive attention in numerous treaties. The two subjects most acceptable to states, as measured by the number of ratifications, are the prohibition of forced labor and the right to organize and bargain collectively. Five of the seven conventions highest in order of number of ratifications deal with these two subjects.

While the standards of the International Labor Code, established by conventions and recommendations, are mainly a reflection of the achievements of the more advanced industrial countries, the ILO's work in technical assistance and economic development is of primary significance to the developing nations, which now make up 70 percent of its membership. Although limited activities involving advisory missions had been sponsored by the ILO since the 1930s, the first expansion of this work into a major program of the ILO was recommended by the director-general, David Morse, in 1949. Supplements to the ILO budget for this purpose became available in 1950 through the United Nations Expanded Program of Technical Assistance. Today more than one half of all ILO activity is in this area.

Although aid sought from the ILO by governments ranges over a broad spectrum of specific projects, a major portion of the technical cooperation activities fall within the general field of manpower or human resources, including vocational training. The means include the recruiting and furnishing of experts, providing fellowships and study grants, and conducting seminars and local and regional training courses. In recent years more than 1,000 experts have been assigned, and a similar number of fellowships and study grants have been awarded annually through the ILO.

Another feature of the technical cooperation program is the development of large-scale cooperative projects involving several United Nations agencies. The ILO acts as the coordinating agency in several of these projects. One of the most spectacular is the Andean Indian Program begun in 1954 and involving the cooperation of the ILO, the FAO, WHO, UNESCO, and the United Nations. The program is also multinational and affects seven million Indians living in Argentina, Bolivia, Chile, Colombia, Ecuador, and Peru.

The purpose is to raise the living standard of these impoverished people living in the high altitudes of the Andes and to integrate them into the social, economic, and political life of their respective countries. The efforts include vocational and handicraft training, agricultural skills, health measures, social welfare, and education, as well as the establishment of ,experimental farms and training centers. By 1966 plans were begun to phase out gradually United Nations activity and to have the involved governments absorb the major responsibilities for the program.

In the area of research and information the ILO performs a function in labor matters similar to that of most other specialized agencies in their respective fields. The ILO is the only comprehensive organization capable of acting as a research and information agency in the field of labor data. Research and information functions are performed by the Central Library and Documentation Branch, the Central Research and Planning Department, the International Occupational Safety and Health Information Center, the Editorial and Translation Branch, and the Public Information Branch of the Geneva office. Publications include, *inter alia*, the quarterly *Official Bulletin*, the monthly *International Labor Review*, the *Year Book of Labor Statistics*, and a variety of studies, handbooks, and manuals. The Public Information Branch also issues press and media releases, films, photographs, posters, and booklets. As a worldwide organization the ILO must furnish publications in several languages, especially in English, French, and Spanish.

In the field of education and training the ILO has established two institutions of special significance. The first is the International Institute for Labor Studies at Geneva, established in 1961. The institute conducts high-level courses on social and labor policy for government and industrial leaders and researchers, concentrating on labor problems in social and economic development. The institute hopes to act as a catalyst for the establishment of similar programs of leadership education in national education centers of developing countries. The second institution of special note is the International Centre for Advanced Technical and Vocational Training at Turin, Italy, which was opened in 1965. The original mandate of the Turin center was to provide technical and vocational training for persons, primarily from developing countries, at more advanced levels than they could obtain in their own countries or regions, and to provide training of instructors in technical cooperation. This mandate has been expanded to include emphasis upon management training for senior and middle-level managers from both industrialized and developing countries. During the first three years of operation the courses at the center enrolled 500 trainees annually, but a target of 1,500 fellowships of four months average duration has been established.

In recent years the work of the ILO has been somewhat decentralized through the creation of a pattern of area offices, regional offices, regional conferences, regional advisory committees, and industrial committees. This decentralization reflects a means of bringing technical cooperation and informational and research activities closer to local sources.

One broad project of the ILO is a World Employment Program launched in 1969. The program is designed as a long-range attack upon problems of unemployment and underemployment. Positive results are hoped for through regional manpower plans developed by ILO's regional agencies.

On November 5, 1975 the United States Secretary of State notified the ILO of the United States' intention to withdraw from the organization. The letter sent by the Secretary of State was in compliance with a two-year notice of intent to withdraw required by the ILO Constitution. The letter also made clear that the United States had no expectation nor desire to withdraw if corrective measures for its complaints were taken. These dissatisfactions centered on recent uneven concern by the ILO for human rights in member states, and increasing politicization of the organization through resolutions of condemnation against particular members which were political targets of the moment, without regard to established procedures and due process. In spite of assertions by Francis Blanchard, the Director-General of the ILO, that the organization had recently adhered to its proper principles and procedures and had performed many useful functions, the United States carried out its threat of withdrawal in November, 1977. The serious loss of 25 percent of the ILO budget was met mainly by the curtailment of services and functions. Several smaller states announced that they would increase their contributions to offset some of the loss.

The ILO can provide no panaceas for assuring the welfare of workers. As with other international agencies, it lacks teeth for enforcing its standards. It lacks sufficient funds for meeting all the demands for technical cooperation in the areas of its competence. But in many areas the ILO has furnished indispensable services to governments and groups of individuals throughout its more than 60 years of existence. The awarding of the Nobel Peace Prize to the ILO in its 50th anniversary year, 1969, was one evidence of esteem and respect. If the United States government can be convinced to rejoin the organization and support its budget, the ILO can continue to play the important role for which it has been noted throughout its history.

COOPERATION IN EDUCATION, SCIENCE AND CULTURE

One of the basic factors in the slow advancement of the development process for two-thirds of the world's people is the wasted human potential associated with high illiteracy and a lack of skills. Overcoming these deficiencies could, in combination with other necessary ingredients for growth, go far toward implementing the "revolution of rising hopes and expectations" sought by the more enlightened leaders of the developing nations.

Since its establishment in 1946, the United Nations Educational, Scientific and Cultural Organization (UNESCO) has concentrated much of its major efforts in the educational portion of its program on the elimination of illiteracy and on training in basic skills. Traditionally literacy has been defined as an ability to read and write. UNESCO has sought a more utilitarian form of literacy through literacy with a social and economic value. The early terminology in UNESCO's program of "fundamental education" has been superseded more recently by a program of "functional literacy," but the goals are essentially identical. The aim of functional literacy is economic and social effectiveness which includes vocational training and skills linked to social and economic development. UNESCO, in cooperation with nongovernmental organizations and the United Nations Development Program, can furnish encouragement, information, research, technical assistance, and demonstration projects for combatting illiteracy, but the major inputs of capital, planning and execution of programs must come from national and local governments determined to solve their own educational problems.

Progress in eliminating adult illiteracy is not encouraging. The extent of illiteracy in the world is estimated by UNESCO to have decreased from 44 percent in 1957 to 34 percent in 1970. Yet, due to population increase, the number of illiterates actually increased during that period by 48 million to a total of 783 million adults. With most of these persons concentrated in the developing countries, the implications for the development process are obvious. Adult illiteracy and the lack of sufficient schools to guarantee even a minimal exposure to formal education of many minors make future prospects for closing the gap between have and have-not nations far from bright.

UNESCO's activities in the field of education, in addition to its literacy program, are far ranging. The linkage between educational problems and the needs of developing nations is at the forefront of several other types of projects in the UNESCO program. For example, UNESCO has supported pilot projects in education for rural development in both Peru and Uganda. Most of the teacher education effort of UNESCO has been focused on the problems of the developing countries. Low-cost and practical school buildings have been planned; curriculum development is emphasized; the production of textbooks and educational materials is fostered; conferences are sponsored between ministers of education and ministers responsible for economic planning; dozens of projects have been financed by the United Nations Development Program and administered and staffed by UNESCO. UNESCO has decentralized some of its educational efforts on behalf of disadvantaged areas by establishing regional offices for education for Africa (in Dakar), for Latin America (in Santiago), and for Asia (in Bangkok).

UNESCO also includes in the educational portion of its program a wide range of activities of general and worldwide significance and value. These activities encompass such processes as the holding of conferences, acting as a clearing-house of information, gathering statistics, conducting research, issuing publications, and cooperating with other organizations interested in educational matters. Important publications that result from UNESCO's role as a clearing-house of information are the *UNESCO Statistical Yearbook*, which includes data on the scientific and cultural as well as the educational aspects of UNESCO's role; the *International Yearbook of Education*, published jointly with the International Bureau of Education; *Study Abroad*, issued biennially in English, French, and Spanish, and listing more than 250,000 scholarships throughout the world; and *Vacation Study Abroad*, listing opportunities for short-term foreign study. UNESCO cooperates with the other United Nations specialized agencies, and dozens of nongovernmental organizations have consultative status with UNESCO, but especially close affinities exist between UNESCO and the International Bureau of Education in Geneva and the International Institute for Educational Planning in Paris.

Two other educational activities implemented by UNESCO resulted from initiatives taken by the United Nations General Assembly. The Assembly declared 1970 as International Education Year, and UNESCO set up special programs to emphasize education during that year. The General Assembly in 1969 agreed to consider a proposal by Secretary-General U Thant for establishing a United

Nations or International University and requested that UNESCO prepare a feasibility study. The results of the study were generally favorable to the proposal, and the university began operations in Japan in 1975.

In the total UNESCO program the emphasis upon the natural sciences ranks close behind education in number and variety of projects and budget allocations. The main source of funds for natural-science projects is not the regular UNESCO budget, but the United Nations Development Program, which supplies more than 70 percent of the resources administered by UNESCO in the natural-science area. Projects include the promotion of fundamental research in science; the establishment of a World Scientific and Technical Information System; studies and assistance to member states in science education, engineering education, and agricultural education; the training of technicians; promotion of research on natural resources and ecological research studies of natural disasters and their causes; hydrology projects and research; oceanography projects and research, including the establishment of an Integrated Global Ocean Station System; nuclear research; and research on the earth's arid zones and their possible uses. In 1957–58 UNESCO assisted in sponsoring the International Geophysical Year.

Over a period of several years, UNESCO developed a program called Man and the Biosphere as a contribution to the total United Nations program on the human environment and pollution problems. Also, in preparation for the United Nations Conference on the Human Environment (Stockholm, 1972), UNESCO produced a plan for a World Heritage Foundation to preserve critical environmental areas and endangered animal and plant species.

Since the bulk of UNESCO's funds for the natural sciences are furnished by the United Nations Development Program, most of UNESCO's activities in this area are in the nature of assisting member states to carry out programs in the natural sciences that will contribute to their economic development—e.g., projects in science education, engineering education, agricultural education, and the training of technicians referred to in the previous list of UNESCO activities. UNESCO also assists and cooperates with nongovernmental organizations such as the International Council of Scientific Unions. Work is further decentralized through the operation of five field science offices for Africa, Latin America, the Arab States, South Asia, and Southeast Asia.

A third broad area of UNESCO's program encompasses the social sciences, humanities, and culture. Although UNESCO devotes a much smaller portion of its budget to these fields than to education or the natural sciences, the variety of activities in these fields is, nevertheless, quite broad. With assistance from the United Nations Development Program, UNESCO assists member governments primarily in three types of projects. These are (1) social-science teaching and research, (2) preservation, presentation, and development of their cultural heritage, and (3) training of museographers and technicians.

One of the methods by which UNESCO widens its area of influence is through subsidies to numerous nongovernmental organizations with which UNESCO maintains close liaison. A sample list of such organizations includes the International Council for Philosophy and Humanistic Studies, the International Social Science Council, the International Political Science Association, the International Sociological Association, the International Economics Association, the International Committee for Social Science Documentation, the International Theater Institute, the International Music Council, the International Association of Plastic Arts, and the International Council of Museums. UNESCO also cooperates with and gives financial support to international and regional institutions such as the African Training and Research Centre in Administration for Development in Tangiers, the Latin American Social Science Faculty in Santiago, and the Center for Coordination of Research and Documentation in the Social Sciences in Vienna.

For many years UNESCO devoted much attention to questions of race in order to refute myths of racial superiority or inferiority. More recently the emphasis in the social sciences has focused on the contributions of the social sciences to development, the study of population and environment problems, the promotion of human rights, and research and teaching on the problems of peace.

One of UNESCO's primary concerns is the preservation of human culture. Studies of Asian, African, Latin American, and European cultures have been encouraged and supported. A massive *History of the Scientific and Cultural Development of Mankind* has been published in several languages. Translations of the masterpieces of literature is a part of UNESCO's program linked with the publication of *Index Translationum*, an annual international bibliography of translations appearing throughout the world. Another major project is the mutual appreciation of eastern and western cultural values. UNESCO has aided states in the preservation and restoration of cultural monuments, including the Nubian monuments of Egypt. Other projects involve the safeguarding of Venice and the restoration of the art treasures of Florence in cooperation with the Italian government.

In the field of art, UNESCO has produced more than thirty sets of color slides with commentary on painting and sculpture and is continuing to produce three or four new sets each year. UNESCO also publishes a *Catalogue of Colour Reproductions of Paintings*, with one edition for the period before 1860 and another for 1860 to the present. These are updated and revised regularly.

Among the important multilateral treaties developed by UNESCO are a Universal Copyright Convention and a Convention on the Free Flow of Educational, Scientific and Cultural Materials. Each has been ratified by more than sixty states.

Finally UNESCO publishes or subsidizes the publication of a number of periodicals in addition to those previously mentioned. These include the *UNESCO Courier*, the *UNESCO Chronicle*, the *UNESCO Bulletin for Libraries*, the *International Social Science Journal*, *Diogenes*, and *Museum*.

One might assume that with such a wide variety of programs UNESCO's impact in the areas of its competence would be substantial. Yet the resources available are extremely limited in relation to the size of the problems, and the obstacles to be overcome are formidable. The scattering of limited resources over such a broad range of activities may in itself act as a limiting factor in effectively coping with educational, scientific, and cultural problems, and UNESCO has frequently been accused of too much diffusion of effort. Another threat, in the mid-1970s, to UNESCO's vitality is the politicizing of the organization and the alienation of governments and scholars by the refusal to allow Israel to participate in certain UNESCO programs. In spite of these criticisms and threats, the fundamental importance of the elements of the UNESCO program for human well-being and enrichment cannot be denied.

CONTROLLING NARCOTIC DRUGS

Narcotic drugs are both a boon to medical science and, at the same time, a threat to individual and societal well-being. The problem is to produce sufficient amounts for medical and scientific needs and to prevent illicit traffic that leads to uncontrolled use or addiction. No one nation can achieve these ends without international cooperation and international instruments of control.

Attempts at narcotics control date back to the period before World War I. In 1912 the first convention on the subject was adopted at The Hague and established essentially the principles and methods of control that have been used in all subsequent agreements. Production, manufacture, and trade in narcotic drugs were to be controlled by law, and permits and records were to be used as regulatory instruments. Opium and its derivatives (morphine and heroin) and cocaine were the chief objects of early regulation, and heroin remains today the chief addictive drug of illicit traffic. The League of Nations established two new agencies, the Permanent Central Opium Board and the Drug Supervisory Body, with limited regulatory powers, and drew up additional more comprehensive conventions to cover the new developments in narcotic-drug production. The system depended for its effectiveness upon government compliance in submitting annual and quarterly reports on production, consumption, stocks, imports and exports of drugs; upon import and export authorizations; and upon state enforcement of the conventions and national supporting legislation.

The United Nations system of control continues the essential features of the League arrangements. The Economic and Social Council early established as one of its functional commissions the Commission on Narcotic Drugs. The supervisory bodies of the League system continued to operate as United Nations agencies. A proliferation of new treaties resulted in pressure for the adoption in 1961 of a so-called Single Convention on Narcotic Drugs. By consolidating the several previous treaties into one, the problem of uniform regulations for all states adhering to the new convention was resolved since some states had previously been selective in their choice of treaties to ratify. At the same time an International Narcotics Control Board replaced the two previous regulatory agencies inherited from the League of Nations.

Before the single convention was in full operation it became apparent that its scope was not sufficiently comprehensive to cover new developments and new problems of drug control. The manufacture of synthetic drugs and the widespread use of amphetamines, barbiturates, hallucinogens, and tranquillizers produced increased pressure for bringing their use under control. In 1971 a Convention on Psychotropic Substances was endorsed by an international conference in Vienna, attended by delegates of seventy-one governments. This convention entered into force in August, 1976 when ratified by the required forty states. Loopholes in the enforcement provisions of the 1961 convention also became apparent, and a conference was called in Geneva in March, 1972, to strengthen these provisions. The protocol which was adopted, amending the single convention, came into force in 1975. Thus the process of consolidation of treaties and control machinery is followed by further proliferation as new problems arise.

As with most social problems, law enforcement alone will not get to the root of the drug-abuse issue. In spite of international conventions and regulatory agencies, national laws and enforcement, and the cooperation of the International Criminal Police Organization (INTERPOL), illicit production, smuggling, drug addiction, and crime committed by sellers and users continue without significant letup. Synthetic drugs are easy to produce and difficult to regulate. The countries of Southeast Asia have been ineffective in controlling the production of opium. Turkey, with United States financial support, cut production by subsidizing poppy farmers to grow substitute crops. At the users' end of the chain, a large number of addicts with no source of cheap or legal supply will make illicit sales so profitable as to invite high risks in supplying the demand. Society continues to grope for the "best" answers to this dilemma. To the control of production, manufacture, trade, and distribution of drugs must be added education, research, and treatment and rehabilitation of addicts if any impact is to be made on drug-abuse problems.

Some new initiatives have been taken by the United Nations in recognition of the growing concern with the illicit drug trade. A United Nations Fund for Drug Abuse Control was established in 1971 with the aim of strengthening existing agencies and enlisting additional support for short- and long-term programs directed against drug abuse. A four-man United Nations Regional Training and Consultative Mission on Narcotics Control to Asia and the Far East was set up under the United Nations Development Program to assist regional governments with establishing effective narcotic-control measures. A United Nations research program staffed by international teams of scientists conducts research at laboratories in Sweden and Switzerland. The battle against drug abuse thus continues on multiple fronts.

REFUGEE PROGRAMS

Wars, revolutions, and natural disasters frequently generate large numbers of refugees. Because of fear of persecution for reasons of race, religion, nationality, or political opinion, or in order to escape from unacceptable living conditions, groups of people move across national boundaries and constitute a problem for the host nation. Small numbers might be readily dispersed or assimilated, but mass movements of thousands or even millions of persons confront the host country with a dilemma of such proportions that international assistance is often welcome or necessary. In addition to the issues involved for the host state, the welfare of the refugees raises questions of individual, local, national, and international concern.

In order to deal with the post-World War I refugee situation, the League of Nations appointed Fridtjof Nansen of Norway as high commissioner for refugees. Most of the original group of refugees resulted from the Russian Revolution of 1917, but additional numbers at irregular intervals from other sources caused the conversion of a temporary program into a permanent activity. The high commissioner developed the Nansen passport, which was accepted by more than fifty states as a permit for displaced persons to cross national boundaries in search of a permanent home. Without authority or monetary resources the Nansen office could only solicit cooperation and aid from governments and private agencies and try to guarantee legal rights to displaced persons.

The trauma of World War II created new millions of refugees. The most satisfactory solutions for refugee problems involve (1) repatriation to the state of origin, (2) assimilation into the host state, or (3) resettlement to a new state willing to absorb a given number of displaced persons. The least desirable situation is to maintain refugee camps for sustained periods, since these camps usually result in unsatisfactory levels of nutrition, housing, and health care and in psychological attitudes of dependence and hopelessness.

By 1947 the large majority of World War II refugees were repatriated to their original states through the efforts of the military occupation authorities with the aid of the United Nations Relief and Rehabilitation Administration (UNRRA). The problem of finding homes for the remaining 1.6 million was transferred in that year to the preparatory commission of a new specialized agency of the United Nations, the International Refugee Organization (IRO). During its short life this organization resettled more than a million persons in countries willing to absorb them and repatriated a few tens of thousands more. By the termination of the IRO's existence in 1951, most of the original group of refugees remaining in the European camps were "hard-core" refugees whom, because of age or other infirmity, no country was willing to accept.

In 1951, on the initiative of the General Assembly, the Office of the United Nations High Commissioner for Refugees (UNHCR) began operations, and through periodic renewals of its authority, continues as the general international agency for refugee protection. The office is nonoperational in its program and is thus dependent on governments and voluntary agencies for staffing the direct-care facilities for refugees. Excluded from the high commissioner's jurisdiction are refugees considered as nationals by the countries granting them asylum and refugees, such as the Palestine group, for whom separate United Nations programs have been established. At first no direct relief assistance was furnished by the UNHCR, but gradually this restriction has been relaxed. However, with an annual budget of slightly over 6 million dollars raised by voluntary contributions, the office must depend primarily on other agencies for the direct aid that refugees require. The mandate for the UNHCR is thus very similar to that of the League of Nations high commissioner. The main functions are (1) furnishing legal protection to refugees, (2) facilitating repatriation, resettlement, and assimilation of refugees, (3) co-ordinating the efforts of governments and private agencies, (4) stimulating international action on behalf of refugees, and (5) providing technical assistance on a very modest scale.

As a basis for the legal protection of refugees, a Convention Relating to the Status of Refugees was adopted in 1951 and came into force in 1954, and in 1967 a protocol was added to enlarge its coverage. The convention specifies the minimum rights of refugees, such as the right to work, to education, to social welfare, to religious freedom, and to access to legal processes. It also provides for the issuance of travel documents and guarantees protection against expulsion under conditions threatening the refugee's life or freedom.

One persistent problem, which has been politically explosive because of emotional overtones, has been that of Palestine refugees displaced as a result of the creation of the Israeli state and the Arab-Israel conflict. In 1950 the United Nations Relief and Works Agency for Palestine Refugees in the Near East (UNRWA) assumed the responsibilities that had been temporarily carried out since 1948 by other agencies. Although, as in the case of the UNHCR, the UNRWA is supported by voluntary contributions, it is an operating agency with much larger financial requirements. On an annual budget of 40–50 million dollars, it has attempted to furnish enough daily food to prevent starvation among more than half of the total of nearly 1.5 million refugees registered with the agency. It has also, because of the large number of children and young people among the refugees, stressed education in its recent programs. Health care is also a necessary element in its services. The intransigence of the major parties to the Middle East dispute leaves these unfortunate people in Syria, Lebanon, the Gaza Strip, the West Bank, and Jordan in the position of pawns in a political struggle marked by invective on both sides, but with no movement toward a solution. The Arabs stress the right of the refugees to return to their original homes, while the Israelis point to the lack of Arab effort to resettle or assimilate these people. In the meantime, hundreds of thousands of persons exist at subhuman levels.

The expectation that refugee problems are transient and will disappear seems ill-founded on the basis of other experience in addition to the Palestine situation. The creation of the IRO for only four years and the original mandate of the high commissioner for only three years demonstrate the illusion that the need for such agencies might be temporary. However, no sooner had the European refugee situation been reduced to manageable proportions (although with fresh inputs, such as Hungarian refugees of 1956), than Africa became the main area of concern. Refugees from Morocco, Tunisia, the Congo, Angola, Rwanda, Mozambique, Portuguese Guinea, and the Sudan swelled the numbers to approximately 1 million with Angola accounting for the largest group. Asian groups included Tibetans and Chinese in Hong Kong. However, all these movements of refugees were dwarfed in 1971 by the sudden influx of at least 7 million persons fleeing to India from the civil war in East Pakistan. Among them disease and starvation became rampant, and the international community was requested to furnish emergency aid at a rate of nearly 1 billion dollars annually. No adequate international machinery exists to channel such massive aid, and the bases of response make the survival (let alone the human dignity) of the refugees highly uncertain. No international commitment to a permanent solution of refugee problems has been made.

FUNCTIONALISM AND WORLD ORDER

Among the theorists who seek a more peaceful and orderly world, one group sees functionalism as the most satisfactory and realistic approach with greater prospects for success than political federation, world empire, or regionalism as alternative paths to the same end. The functionalist believes in the efficacy of a gradualist approach to world order with the attainment of political federation by installments. Since the political rivalry of states is so intense and since state sovereignty is so firmly entrenched, these areas must be bypassed and habits of cooperation must be established and expanded in "nonpolitical" matters in the economic and social spheres. In these spheres problems exist that are relatively free from the conflict of national interests, that appeal to the human sense of social justice, that require international cooperation for solution, and the resolution of which works to the mutual advantage of all. As the world shrinks through science and technology, the amount of economic and social cooperation multiplies while political rivalry and national loyalties seem as intense as ever. The functionalist believes, however, that an ever-increasing amount of economic and social cooperation will eventually build habits of interaction and a broader base of common values that will "spill over" into the political arena. Thus, according to the theory, the obstacles to political integration will gradually be eroded and world unity will be achieved.

Functionalist theory in its basic elements is not new. Émeric Crucé with his emphasis upon travel, trade, the practical arts, and the interdependence of states was, in the seventeenth century, essentially a functionalist. Modern exponents of functionalist theory include David Mitrany and Ernst Haas.

Some support for functionalism is evident in world affairs today. Problems of health, communication, travel, and development, among others, seem both to require international solutions and to be conducive to international cooperation. The United Nations spends three-fourths of its budget on economic and social work, while political questions defy solution. Fifteen specialized agencies epitomize, singly, a fragmented but, collectively, a broad functional approach to world cooperation. Hundreds of nongovernmental organizations associated with the Economic and Social Council and with the specialized agencies are engaged in cooperative activities, and a substantial number of regional organizations work for economic and social ends. With so much activity in these spheres, is it not conceivable that habits of cooperation and the recognition of common interests will eventually carry over into the political arena and make possible the creation of an integrated world political community?

Several possible flaws in functionalist theory need to be examined. The first is the assumption that a clear distinction can be drawn between the political and nonpolitical areas. The solution of the plight of Palestinian refugees is completely intertwined with the political situation in the Middle East. United States temporary withdrawal of financial support from ILO in 1971 was occasioned by charges of undue Communist influence in the organization and similar retaliation against UNESCO in 1975 was prompted by anti-Israeli actions and resolutions. UNCTAD was created by the developing nations in response to North-South cleavages and the failure of GATT to meet the needs of the economically disadvantaged states. The list of examples of impediments to economic and social cooperation because of the clash of political interests could be expanded at great length.

The possibility of transferring habits of cooperation from one field to another may also be questioned. Whereas nations cooperate in economic and social matters, they may at the same time be playing a power game in the Security Council or on political disputes in the General Assembly. Economic cooperation in the European Economic Community, which is often cited as the shining example of the movement toward functional integration, has yet to prove that it will lead to political integration. Global integration will be much more difficult to achieve.

Fundamentally, functionalist theory tends to obscure the divisions in world society symbolized by the sovereignty of states. Just because cooperation in some areas is perceived to be mutually advantageous, there is no assurance that loyalties will be transferred to the international level or that state sovereignty in vital political areas will be surrendered to a higher authority.

Finally, functionalists often claim that ignorance, poverty, hunger, and disease are the "root causes of war" and that the removal of these scourges of humankind will eliminate the basic sources of political conflict. Evidence of this position is found in the constitutions of three of the United Nations' specialized agencies. The UNESCO constitution states "that ignorance of each other's ways and lives has been a common cause [of war] . . . and that peace must therefore be founded, if it is not to fail, upon the intellectual and moral solidarity of mankind." The WHO constitution declares that "the health of all peoples is fundamental to the attainment of peace and security." The ILO constitution claims that "universal peace can be established only if it is based on social justice." These exorbitant claims cannot be historically or empirically substantiated, although there is an increasing amount of internal violence in developing states and growing frustrations could be a breeding ground for future wars.

A rationale exists for international economic and social cooperation without necessarily accepting the claim of the functionalists that world political order is its primary objective or outcome. Alleviating hunger, disease, poverty, and ignorance are worth accomplishing for their own value whether or not they contribute to world peace. The human race is ennobled by its concern for human life and human welfare. Our knowledge of the individual and of societies is insufficient to predict whether selfishness, greed, suspicion, and patriotic fervor will act as stronger forces than those that unite the human race and that overcome the obstacles of divisiveness and rivalry among nations. Limited evidence does exist that habits of cooperation may lead to further cooperative and integrative patterns.

Therefore, without making exaggerated claims that economic and social programs constitute a panacea leading to world harmony, their legitimacy and value can be supported. Since we have never before lived in such an interdependent world, only the future can produce the hard evidence to substantiate the validity of some aspects of functionalist theory.

12

✃

The 1970s:
A Decade
of
World Conferences

Unique to the 1970s is a series of global conferences of which most were initiated through the United Nations General Assembly and which dealt primarily with economic and social problems. The typical pattern for each conference was to select a single topic for attention, set a time period and meeting place for the conference, arrange for preparatory work by existing or specially created agencies, hold a conference of two or more weeks' duration generally open to all states, and adopt a set of principles and an action plan requiring implementation through new or existing United Nations or related agencies.

The most important function of these conferences may have been world consciousness-raising. Harlan Cleveland sums up their significance by stating that

> [I]n the perspective of history [these conferences] may well be seen as historic. These giant sensitivity training sessions, despite the rhetoric of "action programs," are not really called to "do" anything. They are designed to gather a large crowd from all over, and raise the world's attention level for an important part of the interdependent whole.[1]

[1] Harlan Cleveland, *The Third Try at World Order: American Self-Renewal in an Interdependent World* (Princeton, N.J.: Aspen Institute for Humanistic Studies, 1976), p. 78.

Despite this emphasis on the major purpose of the conferences themselves, the follow-up work after each conference was important to sustain international attention and activities on a problem important enough to demand world concern in the first place.

This chapter will deal, in varying detail, with the series of conferences called during the decade of the 1970s. For several of the topics not treated in other chapters some background information is also included.

WORLD CONFERENCE
ON THE HUMAN ENVIRONMENT

Widespread concern that the human race may be potentially as threatened by pollution as it is by nuclear holocaust is a relatively recent phenomenon. The possibility of nuclear contamination of air, water, and soil in a large-scale nuclear war has been realized since Hiroshima and was reemphasized when Japanese fishermen were affected by nuclear fallout in the Bikini test of March 1, 1954. The ultimate peril is dramatized by such a novel as Nevil Shute's *On the Beach*. Localized threats to health from air pollution have existed for many years in such places as Los Angeles and London (before the latter city imposed regulations to reduce the threat), and from water pollution in myriad rivers and lakes, and oil pollution on numerous beaches. But gradually the realization has spread that major environmental problems require international attention, in addition to national and local concern, in order to foresee and forestall the various forms of eco-catastrophe that could overtake humankind.

Attention has recently focused on a wide range of pollutants that threaten the natural balance of the biosphere necessary to sustain healthy human life. A study sponsored by the Massachusetts Institute of Technology identified the following pollutants as worthy of special attention—carbon dioxide; particulate matter; sulfur dioxide; oxides of nitrogen; mercury and other toxic heavy metals; oil; DDT and other hydrocarbons; radionuclides; heat; and nutrients, especially phosphates.[2] Severe problems may exist locally with other pollutants but this list represents the residuals that have global effects on the climate or on ocean or terrestrial ecology, or that create major problems in many countries.

International agencies have given limited attention to problems of the human environment for many years, but the programs have

[2] *Man's Impact on the Global Environment*, Report of the Study of Critical Environmental Problems (Cambridge, Mass.: MIT Press, 1970), p. 227.

been selective, low-scale, and often incidental to the main thrust of
the efforts of these agencies. The pressure for a comprehensive and
better-coordinated effort is of recent origin. A perusal of the activities of the specialized agencies affiliated with the United Nations
reveals that the agencies giving the greatest attention to environmental problems are the World Meteorological Organization (WMO),
which is concerned with air pollution and the climatic effects of pollutants; the World Health Organization (WHO), which is involved in
a wide range of projects in environmental health; UNESCO, which
has sponsored several studies and conferences of experts; the Food
and Agriculture Organization (FAO), whose interests include pesti-
cide accumulation and misuse of the environment; the International
Atomic Energy Agency (IAEA), which is concerned with nuclear
wastes; the Inter-Governmental Maritime Consultative Organization
(IMCO), which has a special interest in oil pollution of the oceans;
and the International Labor Organization (ILO), whose concerns
include atmospheric pollution in the working environment.

The accelerating interest in a global approach to pollution prob-
Obstacles to the solution of environmental problems have also
been evident in the United Nations and its affiliated agencies. In
the FAO the pressure to continue to use DDT to eliminate pests
threatening food production proved greater than the effects of
warnings by scientists of the widespread ecological effects of its
continued use. Another attitude that is slow to respond to the
threats of terracide by pollution is found in the underdeveloped areas
where the problems of pollution are widely conceived as those of the
industrialized nations and any attempt to impose ecological restraints
on development programs may be viewed as unnecessary obstacles
to rapid development. Such negative attitutes toward placing environmental problems high on the list of global priorities may defer
effective measures until the disasters of which many scientists warn
are imminent.

The accelerating interest in a global approach to pollution problems came to a focus in the World Conference on the Human Environment in Stockholm in June, 1972. Swedish leadership in acting
as the host country for this two-week conference was prompted, at
least in part, by problems of mercury poisoning of birds and fish and
other foods consumed by the Swedish people resulting in both national action to combat the threat and in the summoning of an international conference in Sweden in 1966 on the threat of mercury
poisoning. By 1968 enough delegates to ECOSOC and the General
Assembly responded to Swedish prodding for a broad-gauge approach to environmental problems to approve the calling of the 1972
World Conference on the Human Environment.

Preparations for the Stockholm conference were extensive and received special attention by Secretary-General U Thant. Groups outside the United Nations also took supportive action. The month-long study in July, 1970, by fifty United States scientists at Williams College under the sponsorship of the Massachusetts Institute of Technology concentrated on pollution problems of global significance and made recommendations for international action as well as for national and local remedies to combat threats to the environment.[3] In May, 1971, an international assemblage of forty scientists, government officials, and representatives of international agencies met for three days at Rensselaerville, New York, under the joint sponsorship of the Institute on Man and Science and the Aspen Institute of Humanistic Studies to examine the means for combatting global pollution through international action.[4]

Three major instrumentalities were established by the United Nations in preparation for the Stockholm conference. A twenty-seven-nation preparatory committee held four working sessions of approximately two weeks each in 1970-72. The preparatory committee established several intergovernmental working groups charged with producing the text of documents to present to the Stockholm meeting on the subjects of marine pollution, monitoring of the environment, soil preservation, and conservation. One working group was also directed to prepare a draft Declaration on the Human Environment, which, it was hoped, might achieve a place in world esteem equal to that of the Declaration of Human Rights. Under persistent urging by U Thant, Maurice F. Strong, the energetic director of the Canadian International Development Agency, accepted the posts of United Nations under-secretary general in charge of the Secretariat staff in Geneva for conference preparation and of secretary-general of the Stockholm conference. The Secretariat was instructed by the preparatory commission to develop plans for international criteria for pollutant-release limits, for the education and training of specialists in environmental problems, and for the interchange of information on environmental matters. Governments were requested to submit reports on national action programs

[3] *Ibid., passim.*
[4] In addition to the MIT Press publication cited above, a number of other sources are of special value in tracing the private and United Nations preparations for the Stockholm conference. The *Saturday Review* published dozens of articles on the environment. For the global aspects, see especially the issues of January 23, 1971, pp. 42-43; April 3, 1971, pp. 53-57, 61; August 7, 1971, pp. 41-50. See also, Richard N. Gardner, "New Tasks for the '70s," *Vista* (now *Inter Dependent*) May-June, 1970, pp. 39-42, and Stanley Johnson, "Ecocenter-Geneva 1971," *Vista* (now *Inter Dependent*) May–June, 1971, pp. 41-43, 53.

and suggestions for international activity. Specialized agencies of the United Nations were also asked to make reports of past programs and future plans for preserving the environment. UNESCO was invited to assume primary responsibility for developing a constitution for a proposed World Heritage Foundation to preserve environmentally critical areas and endangered animal and plant species of the globe. In order to convince the developing nations of the importance of their full participation in the 1972 conference, regional seminars were organized to bring the impending environmental crisis to their attention. Maurice Strong also initiated a conference of twenty-seven experts who met at Founex, Switzerland, near Geneva, in June, 1971, to study the relationships between development and environment. The report of this conference contributed to an awareness in developing countries that environmental problems were not the exclusive domain of industrialized nations.[5]

In spite of initial misgivings, most of the developing countries agreed to participate in the Stockholm conference, and altogether 113 countries were represented. The USSR and most East European Communist states refused to send delegations as a result of a controversy that led to a decision to exclude the German Democratic Republic. In addition to official delegates from governments, representatives of United Nations specialized agencies and of international nongovernmental organizations were invited as observers, and, in some cases, they were permitted to submit statements to the conference. To provide an outlet for other private groups, the Swedish government arranged an Environment Forum to run simultaneously with the conference in another part of Stockholm. Representatives of almost 200 nongovernmental organizations participated in this Environment Forum.[6]

The United Nations Conference on the Human Environment (UNCHE) approved as its theme "Only One Earth" to emphasize the essential unity and interdependence on the global life-support system. The conference adopted a 26-point Declaration on the Human Environment and a 109-point Action Plan for the guidance of governments and international organizations in implementing a program of environmental protection. The conference also proposed the setting up of permanent international machinery within a United

[5] For the Founex Report and accompanying commentaries by four of the participants see "Environment and Development," *International Conciliation*, No. 586, January 1972.

[6] For a study of the role of nongovernmental organizations in the Stockholm conference, including preparatory and follow-up activities, see Anne Thompson Feraru, "Transnational Political Interests and the Global Environment," *International Organization*, Vol. 28 (Winter 1974), pp. 31–60.

Nations Environment Program (UNEP), and this arrangement was endorsed and implemented by ECOSOC in October and by the General Assembly in December, 1972.

The permanent machinery created by the General Assembly includes a small Environmental Secretariat in which Maurice Strong served as the first executive director; a fifty-eight-member Governing Council to coordinate environmental activities and to promote governmental cooperation; an Environment Fund raised by voluntary contributions with a target of 100 million dollars for the first five years; and an Environment Coordination Board as a subsidiary of the intersecretariat Administrative Committee on Coordination to foster cooperation among the secretariats of the United Nations and its specialized agencies in carrying out environmental projects. It is anticipated that continued activities in support of environmental protection will be carried out by United Nations regional economic commissions, by the specialized agencies, by nongovernmental organizations, and by governments under the leadership of the Environmental Secretariat and the Governing Council. Since no coercive powers exist, the basic principle for successful coordination and effective programs is voluntary cooperation.

The interests of the developing states are protected in two aspects of the UNEP arrangements. Developing countries have a majority of the seats on the Governing Council, and the selection of Nairobi, Kenya, as the site for the Environmental Secretariat is clearly a concession to pressures from the less-developed states. A balance between environmental and development concerns in rich and poor nations may be anticipated.

One major focus of the action program adopted at Stockholm is an "Earthwatch" network to assess current environmental conditions in all parts of the globe and to monitor changes that presage danger. Atmospheric conditions will be monitored for pollutants that threaten health or climatic modification. Marine pollution and the release of toxic substances into the life-support system will be checked, and any threatening changes will be publicized. Earthwatch activities include an International Referral System connecting national information centers to a central data bank in Geneva, an International Register of Potentially Toxic Chemicals, and a Global Environmental Monitoring Service (GEMS) with a projected 110 monitoring stations throughout the world. Another UNEP concern is for endangered species with imperative attention to the extinction of whales. Other topics assigned high priority include human settlements, education, information, transfer of technology, conservation of natural and genetic resources, and energy.

The pace of UNEP activities gradually accelerated after a slow start. In 1976 the Environment Fund dispensed approximately 30 million dollars for a variety of projects. Among those instigated by that date was an early warning system for typhoons in the Bay of Bengal. In May, 1976 an agreement was signed at Barcelona to combat pollution and other environmental problems in the Mediterranean and its coastal states. A regional center was established in Malta to handle oil spills and pollution emergencies. Dumping of certain highly toxic substances into the Mediterranean was prohibited. For another list of substances, dumping was severely restricted. In April, 1978 a similar agreement was drawn up for the Persian Gulf region by eight major oil-producing states. The threat of oil and industrial pollution is especially severe in this area. In October, 1977 a conference sponsored jointly by UNESCO and UNEP in Tbilisi, USSR issued a declaration stressing the importance of environmental education for all ages and through the mass media. These projects represent only a sampling of the varied activities of the UNEP.

The chances for dramatic results in checking the environmental threats are mixed. The impetus toward effective action was provided by the Stockholm conference and by the setting up of special machinery to implement the approved Action Plan. National attitudes toward environmental protection include many negative factors. References have been previously made to the doubts and reservations of the developing countries. In the industrialized countries the energy crisis that developed in 1973 resulted in a possibly temporary but significant deemphasis of environmental concerns. There is danger that, in spite of warnings of impending environmental global catastrophe, higher national priorities will be assigned to rapid economic development and to maintaining the upward spiral of energy consumption than to environmental protection.

It is generally recognized that most effective measures for preventing deterioration of the human environment will depend primarily upon national and local regulations and enforcement. It is unlikely that sovereign states will subject themselves to supranational authority in ecological matters in sharp contrast to the lack of such authority in other areas. The Soviet Union has declared that it favors international, not supranational, machinery for controlling the human environment. Nevertheless, the problems of global pollution, with the threat of eco-catastrophes from many existing sources and trends, present to humankind one more opportunity for cooperative action for the benefit, and possibly the survival, of the whole human race. National action without global planning will probably prove insufficient. A failure to meet potential ecological threats on a global front with foresight and imagination could prove disastrous. Should the scientific evidence suggest the necessity for drastic global measures to preserve a healthy environment, is a world of competing sovereign states capable of developing flexible responses in time to avert catastrophe?

OTHER MAJOR CONFERENCES WITHIN THE ENVIRONMENTAL CONTEXT

During the 1970s, the United Nations Environment Program generated three additional global conferences, each dealing with environmental problems. Those selected for concentrated attention in these conferences were human settlements, water, and desertification.

United Nations Conference on Human Settlements (HABITAT)

Among the recommendations of the Stockholm Conference on the Human Environment was a proposal to convene a global conference on human settlements on certain environmental living conditions relating to patterns of human habitation. This proposal was endorsed by the United Nations General Assembly and culminated in the scheduling of a United Nations Conference on Human Settlements (HABITAT) in Vancouver, Canada, from May 31 to June 11, 1976. HABITAT was the largest world conference to date with representatives from 131 national governments, 6 national liberation movements, 160 nongovernmental organizations, and several intergovernmental organizations.

During the seventeen-month period preceding the sessions, a fifty-six-nation preparatory committee planned the framework and agenda for the conference. Several regional conferences were also convened preliminary to the Vancouver meetings.

The central theme of the conference is summed up in one of the general principles adopted by the delegates, stating that "the improvement of the quality of life of human beings is the first and most important objective of every human settlement policy." Since by the year 2000, nearly 80 percent of the world's population will live in cities, many of the concerns expressed at the conference focused on urban problems in both developed and developing countries. Rural living conditions in less developed states must be improved to relieve the pressures for migration to the cities. The unprecedented growth of miserable slum conditions is already a major problem in the cities of the third-world countries.

The final documents of the conference had three components — a "Vancouver Declaration on Human Settlements, 1976," a set of sixty-four recommendations for national action, and a resolution proposing the establishment of permanent United Nations machinery concerned exclusively with human settlements. Emphasized in these documents was the satisfaction of basic human needs. These include adequate shelter, food, clean water, employment, health, education, training, sanitation, and access to essential services and opportunities for cultural growth, all within a framework of freedom, dignity, and social justice. Priority was to be given to the needs of the most disadvantaged people. Another major theme was land use, stressing the necessity for government planning and land ownership or control.

The potential harmony of the conference was shattered by politicization through the interjection of anti-Israeli and anticolonial issues. Without direct reference to Israel or South Africa, all forms of racism as referred to in General Assembly resolutions were condemned. This allusion includes the contentious characterization of Zionism as a form of racism. The establishment of settlements in territories occupied by force was condemned and declared illegal. A related recommendation requested that the General Assembly instruct the Secretary-General to prepare a report on "the living conditions of the Palestinian people in the occupied territories." Another gratuitous reference to the necessity of implementing the New International Economic Order was included at the insistence of developing states. Most of the states in the affluent, developed, market economy category found the inclusion of these issues, which they interpreted as political and extraneous, to be so objectionable that they either voted against or abstained on the Vancouver Declaration.

A special feature of the conference was the preparation and use by the delegations of more than 200 film and slide presentations. A Canadian offer was endorsed by the Conference and subsequently approved by the General Assembly to establish a United Nations Audio-Visual Center on Human Settlements at the University of British Columbia. The center would reproduce and distribute these and other related materials for worldwide use.

After the conference, until new United Nations machinery was created, the global human settlements activities continued as a part of the United Nations Environment Program. In 1978 the former Economic and Social Council's Committee on Housing, Building and Planning was replaced by a fifty-eight-member Commission on

Human Settlements to assume general supervision of appropriate functions, and a special section of the Secretariat was established under the title, HABITAT, Centre on Human Settlements. The new Commission urged governments to act quickly to meet the proposed target of 50 million dollars for 1978-1981 for human settlement activities. Much of the emphasis at Vancouver had been on the necessity for national action, but the United Nations regional commissions were also urged to enlarge their role in human settlement programs.

United Nations Water Conference

The idea for a global conference on the problems of water supply and utilization originated with the Economic and Social Council's Committee on Natural Resources in 1971 and was endorsed by the parent body in 1973. The HABITAT conference included clean water and sanitation facilities on its list of basic human needs. The United Nations Water Conference met in Mar del Plata, Argentina, March 14-25, 1977.

In preparation for the conference, regional meetings were convened under the auspices of each of the UN regional commissions. Each regional meeting submitted detailed recommendations to the Committee on Natural Resources which then prepared a consolidated report. The Food and Agriculture Organization assumed responsibility for a preliminary action plan on water for agricultural use.

The problems of water supply and utilization are numerous. Water is a scarce resource and much of it is wasted or misused. The best estimates indicate that 40 percent of the world's population lack a supply of safe drinking water. Many areas suffer from floods, drought, soil erosion, and salination. Much more water for irrigation will be needed to increase food supplies for a growing world population. Agriculture today accounts for 80 percent of water use. Water pollution occurs from many sources and water-borne diseases are common.

The recommendations of the conference were wide-ranging, but the results were not especially dramatic. The recommendations were embodied in a "Plan of Action of Mar del Plata." At least 85 percent of the recommendations were to be carried out by national governments. The problem of the water rights of upstream and downstream states sharing river systems remained intractable. A resolution committing states sharing a river basin to inform other states of plans to develop that resource was hotly debated and narrowly adopted. Regional, joint projects were encouraged.

One of the general goals endorsed by the conference was that adequate drinking water and sanitation facilities should be available for all people by 1990. Each country was encouraged to formulate a national water policy and to take action in areas of water resource assessment, supply management, environmental protection, and disaster control. The need for public information and training was stressed. Recommendations for agriculture included measures to improve and extend irrigation, stressing the prevention of flooding, soil waterlogging, and the accumulation of salts or other harmful chemicals. For industrial uses, the emphasis was on recycling, efficient use of water, and waste treatment. With regard to water pollution, states were urged to adopt the principle that direct and indirect costs attributable to pollution should be borne by the polluter.

The spirit of the conference was one of restraint, with the introduction of a minimum of political controversy. Most recommendations were adopted by consensus without a formal vote. One contentious resolution denounced policies or actions by colonizing or dominating powers in occupied territories which denied indigenous control over water resources. Another mildly worded resolution endorsed the rapid settlement of the Panama Canal issue in order to restore Panama's sovereignty over that facility.

In addition to assigning major responsibility for effective measures to national governments, the Plan of Action stressed regional cooperation, including an expanded role for the United Nations regional commissions. Global implementation was to be carried out by the Economic and Social Council, its Committee on Natural Resources, and the United Nations Development Program. No new special funding was recommended, but the Secretary-General was requested to study the mechanisms by which an adequate flow of funds through existing channels could be assured for water-related projects.

UNITED NATIONS CONFERENCE ON DESERTIFICATION

A special environmental problem of geographically widespread impact is that of halting the spread of deserts. The problem overlaps not only that of water supply and utilization, but also has dimensions relating to health, food, population, development, meteorology, culture, science, and technology. According to preliminary studies prepared for the United Nations Conference on Desertification in Nairobi, Kenya, August 29–September 9, 1977, deserts presently cover about 36 percent of the earth's land surface, and desertification threatens another 19 percent affecting 628 million people. The 1972-74 Sahel drought in Africa with its human suffering and long-range implications dramatized this threat. To check the further encroachment of deserts on habitable and productive land requires informed planning in water utilization and in grazing and agricultural practices. The conference emphasized human activities that can turn productive areas into deserts.

The Nairobi conference was convened under the authority of a 1974 General Assembly decision and was attended by representatives of 100 countries as well as by delegates from intergovernmental and nongovernmental organizations. Preparatory work was carried out by individual governments, a scientific symposium, regional conferences, and such United Nations agencies as UNEP, UNESCO, FAO, WMO, and UNDP. UNEP played a key preparatory role by providing six feasibility studies and by acting as the overall planning agency for the conference.

The principal output of the conference was an action plan. Most of the twenty-six recommendations were accepted by consensus. The bulk of them were addressed to national governments, but others required regional or international action for implementation. Governments were urged to establish antidesertification programs as a part of their development plans. Specific recommendations included development and management of water resources; soil conservation and improvement; prevention and control of salinization, waterlogging and alkalinization in irrigated lands; provision of health care services, including family planning for people vulnerable to desertification; preventive and protective strategies against the risks and effects of droughts, including insurance plans; and the substitution of simple, inexpensive sources of energy for those using vegetation.

Implementation at the regional level envisages leadership by the United Nations regional commissions in catalyzing, coordinating and executing joint regional projects and in sponsoring regional technical workshops and seminars. One significant project on which planning is well advanced is for a green belt to check the advance of the north Saharan desert. It is a cooperative enterprise of Egypt, Libya, Algeria, Tunisia, and Morocco. The United Nations role is to elaborate methodologies, coordinate research and provide financial and technical support. Most of the functions will be concentrated in UNEP, unless the General Assembly designates alternative machinery. The General Assembly was also urged to support the work of the World Meteorological Organization and the pertinent activities of the International Council of Scientific Unions.

In a postconference statement, Mostafa Tolba, the Executive

Director of UNEP, estimated the annual cost of corrective measures at 400 million dollars. The conference adopted a recommendation sponsored by the African states for a special international account for plan implementation, but the divided pattern of voting indicated a lack of enthusiasm by affluent potential donor states.

The Conference on Desertification avoided excessive politicization. Nevertheless, two resolutions were adopted against South Africa, another denounced an Israeli document on reclaiming the Negev desert, and one was aimed at the United States' use of chemical weapons in Vietnam.

THIRD UNITED NATIONS CONFERENCE ON THE LAW OF THE SEA

Until fairly recently the problems with regard to the use of the oceans by national states and private actors were relatively simple. The principle of freedom of the seas governed navigation, fish were plentiful, and most states claimed jurisdiction over a three-mile territorial sea adjacent to their shores.

Since 1945 these conditions have changed drastically. Some states now claim jurisdiction over the adjacent waters and seabed to a distance of 200 miles; new methods of fishing threaten the extinction of many species; ocean pollution has become a threat to the marine life system; vast reservoirs of petroleum are being tapped on the continental margins; other valuable minerals may soon be retrieved from the deep ocean floor; submarines and nuclear weapons make possible the use of the oceans as nuclear bases; the widening of territorial claims may close many straits to free navigation; and ocean research has expanded at a rapid pace.

To exacerbate all these problems two opposed sets of interests have emerged. On the one hand, a movement has developed to declare the oceans and seabed as "the common heritage of mankind" and to restrict national jurisdictional claims to a narrow range of territorial waters and seabed. At the other extreme is the desire of some coastal states and private interests to claim sweeping national jurisdiction over nearly one-fourth of the ocean and seabed area wherein lie 90 percent of the mineral and fishing resources. If the most extravagant national claims become universally accepted, any international agency that may be created would be limited in resources to the point that "the common heritage" would be a pittance when distributed for meeting the needs of the remaining disadvantaged countries. Further compounding the problem of finding a solution to these many-faceted issues is the lack of a simple division of coastal versus landlocked or shelf-locked states or of developed versus developing states. Even within states, policy may be dictated by competing orientations among commercial, military, industrial, fishing, research, conservationist, and political interests.

The definition of several terms is necessary to an understanding of the current ocean controversy. The "continental shelf" is the portion of the ocean bottom from low tide to the point at which the slope begins to decline much more sharply. The width of the shelf varies widely but averages just under fifty miles. However, a 1958 international convention, which sets the limits not by the natural contour, but at a water depth of 200 meters, extends this average width to somewhat more than fifty miles. The "continental slope" extends from the edge of the continental shelf sharply downward to the "continental rise" at which point the angle of decline is much less abrupt until it reaches the "abyssal plains" of the "deep ocean floor." The term "continental margin" includes the shelf, slope, and rise, or the entire submerged extension of the continental land mass. These features are illustrated on the accompanying diagram.

The movement toward the extension of national jurisdictional claims over the resources of the continental margins began with a proclamation in 1945 by President Truman that, while not extending the three-mile territorial sea, declared exclusive United States jurisdiction over the resources of the continental shelf, defined as extending to the 200-meter isobath. Other countries, following the lead of the United States, unilaterally enlarged their claims over an extended area, variously covering exclusive jurisdiction over mineral resources, fishing rights, or even full sovereignty over the seas to a distance of as great as 200 miles. By the early 1970s eight states claimed exclusive jurisdiction over a 200-mile territorial sea and four additional states declared title to fishing rights in a 200-mile zone.

In 1958 the United States' assertion of jurisdiction made by President Truman was institutionalized and universalized by the adoption by the Law of the Sea Conference in Geneva of a Convention of the Continental Shelf. Not only did this convention adopt the 200-meter isobath rule for the boundary of the continental shelf, but, in addition, it included an "exploitability clause," which allows the extension of jurisdictional claims beyond the 200-meter depth wherever exploitation of the natural resources of the seabed and subsoil is technically possible. With today's technology such exploitation for petroleum, for example, is possible well beyond the limits of the continental shelf and may soon encompass virtually all of the continental margin.

The 1958 Law of the Sea Conference referred to above was the first in a series of attempts by the international community to reconcile the growing differences among national claims and to create universally recognized standards of international law for the oceans. The United Nations General Assembly instigated this conference, which was preceded by ten years of preparatory work by the International Law Commission. Eighty-six countries (almost every independent state in 1958) were represented in Geneva. The conference approved four conventions and submitted them for ratification by states. In addition to the Convention on the Continental Shelf, these instruments were a Convention on the Territorial Sea and the Contiguous Zone, a Convention on the High Seas, and a Convention on Fishing and the Conservation of the Living Resources of the High Seas. Each of the conventions received sufficient ratifications between 1962 and 1966 to come into force.

The 1958 conference left unanswered certain important questions including the breadth of the territorial sea and conflicting limits on fishing rights. A second United Nations Conference on the Law of the Sea in 1960 failed to resolve these issues.

During the 1960s the urgency of resolving both previously unsettled issues and newly emerging ones mounted. National claims became more diverse at the same time that conflicts over fishing rights, concern over ocean pollution, and the possibility of placing nuclear weapons on the ocean floor caused increasing anxiety. Partial solutions touching only the periphery of the main body of problems were provided by a 1970 Treaty on the Prohibition of the Emplacement of Nuclear Weapons and Other Weapons of Mass Destruction on the Seabed and the Ocean Floor and in the Subsoil Thereof and by a 1972 Ocean Dumping Convention.

A notable proposal for restoring order out of the mounting chaos was made in the United Nations General Assembly in 1967 by Ambassador Arvid Pardo of Malta. With great imagination Ambassador Pardo linked the desirability of restoring order and uniformity in the realm of the oceans to the needs of the developing states for substantial and growing financial resources. He warned against further national appropriation of the seabed. He proposed that the resources of the seabed and ocean floor beyond present national jurisdiction be declared "the common heritage of mankind" to be shared by all states both coastal and landlocked. Ambassador Pardo suggested the setting up of an international seabed authority with jurisdiction to regulate, promote, and protect the common heritage for the benefit of all, but with special attention to the needs of developing states. With increasing exploitation of these resources and with curtailment

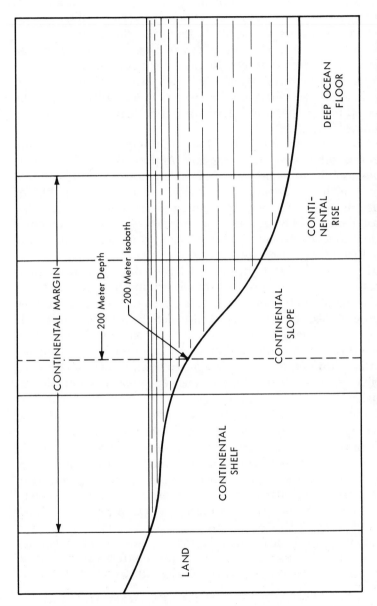

Adapted from Larry L. Fabian, "The Ocean, the United States and the Poor Countries" in *The United States and the Developing World: Agenda for Action* (Washington, D.C., Overseas Development Council, 1973), p. 81, and from John J. Logue, ed., *The Fate of the Oceans* (Villanova, Pa., Villanova University Press, 1972), p. 232.

of extravagant national jurisdictional claims, the prospects for a long-term common heritage of billions of dollars could be foreseen.

The General Assembly in responding to the Pardo initiative set up an ad hoc committee and in the following year a standing committee of forty-two members to study the principles involved in promoting the exploration and exploitation of the resources of the sea and the machinery for an international regime for the seabed. This Seabed Committee, as it is popularly called, was later expanded to eighty-six and then to ninety-one members. In 1970 the committee was converted to a preparatory organ for a third Law of the Sea Conference planned initially for 1973.

As the date for the projected Law of the Sea Conference approached, the difficulties of achieving Ambassador Pardo's goals became increasingly apparent. Some of the most extravagant national jurisdictional claims hardened to the point that the possibility of compromise on universal standards seemed increasingly remote. The diversity of issues to be resolved and of interests to be accommodated added to the difficulty of working out an all-encompassing plan for managing ocean resources. Nations were engaged in enforcement battles over fishing rights in a 12–200-mile zone from their shores. States were issuing licenses for oil drilling beyond the limits of the continental shelf. Several companies were preparing to mine manganese nodules (from which could also be obtained valuable resources of nickel, copper, and cobalt) from the deep ocean floor without waiting for the establishment of an international regime. Several states proposed plans that sought to compromise outstanding national differences, but national intransigence was apparent in the vigorous debates over these proposals.

The debate over differences among the members of the Seabed Committee delayed the proposed opening date for the third Law of the Sea Conference. The first session, purely organizational in character, was held in New York for two weeks in December, 1973. The second session, lasting the entire summer, met in Caracas in 1974. Slowness in resolving basic disagreements among divergent interests required further extended meetings in Geneva or New York each year beginning in 1975.

One reason for the difficulties in formulating a comprehensive treaty is the range of issues with which the conference must deal. Larry Fabian has summed up this problem as follows:

> The conference agenda is awesomely ambitious. Seaward limits of national sovereignty must be drawn. Rights to ocean resources beyond these limits must be spelled out. Ground rules must be set for allocating privileges between coastal states and others wanting access to their adjacent offshore

areas beyond national limits — long-distance fishermen, oil drillers, marine scientists, and civilian and military vessels or aircraft seeking rights of transit or overflight. The conference is to settle the status of international straits, to adopt principles for international revenue sharing from ocean exploitation, and to determine methods for providing technical assistance and resolving international disputes. It must take further steps to control ocean pollution, in conjunction with the recent U.N. Conference on the Human Environment and several international agencies with marine environmental responsibilities. For these and many other issues, the conference is charged with creating a comprehensive regime of ocean law and the political machinery to implement it.[7]

The stakes in the conference are very high. This fact is dramatically presented in the following statement by Earl Anderson:

> This summer [1974], 147 nations will clash in what could be one of the greatest sea battles the world has ever known. They will meet on dry land and they will fight with words. In history books, their encounter will go down as the Third United Nations Law of the Sea Conference.
>
> But it will be a sea battle nonetheless. The stakes are the political and economic future of 70% of the earth's surface — the oceans. And the oceans are becoming a more important and valuable piece of real estate as the world grows more dependent on them and their resources, and as technology opens up new ways to tap them.[8]

Idealists see in the opportunities facing the Law of the Sea Conference the possibility of the greatest breakthrough ever achieved toward universalism. If an international ocean regime is established with shared jurisdiction over the rich resources of the continental margins as well as those of the deep ocean floor, and endowed with real decision-making and enforcement powers, such a step would indeed create a common heritage of great potential. By establishing an international authority with an independent and vast source of revenue, the first substantial penetration would have been made of the wall of national sovereignty. And with these future resources committed to meeting the needs of the development process, the outlook for a stepping up of the rate of development (if combined with other favorable factors of planning, management, and incentives) would be bright.

The possibility of achieving such an ideal is dim. Differences in national interests are too great to be readily reconciled. Positive attitudes toward the surrender of national sovereignty to an international ocean authority are not widely shared. Coastal states that

[7] Larry L. Fabian, "The Ocean, the United States, and the Poor Countries," in *The United States and the Developing World: Agenda for Action* (Washington, D.C.: Overseas Development Council, 1973), p. 80.

[8] Earl V. Anderson, "World's Nations Scramble for Sea's Riches," *Chemical and Engineering News*, March 4, 1974, p. 18.

have been in the process since 1945 of extending their jurisdictional claims are reluctant to surrender any of their unilaterally established "rights." Some progress has been made in the annual sessions of the Law of the Sea Conference in working out compromises on numerous points of controversy, but, at the end of the seventh session in 1978, several hard-core issues still required resolution. These issues included details of control of deep-sea mining by the international authority, rights of access of land-locked states to the resources in the 200-mile economic zones of other states, and the settlement of disputes regarding control of these economic zones.

The costs of failure to reach agreement are very high. The competition for rich ocean resources may convert the "freedom of the seas" into the "freedom of the seize." Coastal developed states and private enterprises may get very rich at the expense of the poor or landlocked countries. Only thirteen states would monopolize more than two-thirds of the areas of the world's oceans if national claims were extended to the middle of the oceans.[9] Altogether the challenge of the oceans presents unprecedented opportunities for achieving cooperation for the benefit of the whole world's population or the equally unprecedented threat of an unbridled race to compete for national control over the oceans' riches. Such a competition would risk the exacerbation of international anarchy, jealousy, and tensions to the point of fomenting uncontrollable forces toward sea battles fought with every conceivable economic, political, and, perhaps even, military weapon.

WORLD POPULATION CONFERENCE

By 1970 the ongoing "population explosion" and its threatened acceleration had become a major concern of government leaders throughout the world. While these officials recognized that national government policies were at the heart of any solutions, they favored a global conference to illuminate the problem and to guide national and international programs to abate the ill effects of uncontrolled population growth.

In 1970 the Economic and Social Council recommended that plans for a population conference be started. The General Assembly approved the proposal, set 1974 as the date, and designated that year as World Population Year. In 1972 the Economic and Social

[9] Bernard H. Oxman, "The Case for the United States Draft Seabed Treaty" in John J. Logue, ed., *The Fate of the Oceans* (Villanova, Pa.: Villanova University Press, 1972) pp. 183–84.

Council named its Population Commission as the preparatory agency for coordinating conference planning activities. Other preliminary studies were contributed by national governments, four symposia of scientific experts, and regional meetings sponsored by the five United Nations regional commissions.

The World Population Conference met in Bucharest, August 19–30, 1974. Participating were representatives of more than 130 national governments, plus observers from several United Nations specialized agencies and other United Nations organizations, from a few national liberation movements, and from more than 100 intergovernmental and nongovernmental organizations.

The primary document from the conference was a World Population Plan of Action. This set a target for the reduction of the average birth rate in developing countries from the present thirty-eight per thousand to thirty per thousand by 1985. Another aim was an average global life expectancy of sixty-two years by 1985 and seventy-four years by 2000. Reduction of infant mortality was accorded high priority. Respect for human life, the quality of human existence, the essentiality of the family, the right of couples to decide the numbers and spacing of their children and to have the information and means to do so, and respect for the sovereignty of states in formulating population policies and programs were declared to be basic principles of the World Population Plan.

Governments were urged to enhance the status of women, to assure them equal responsibility for family planning and to integrate them fully into the educational, social, economic, and political life of their societies, as possible incentives to smaller family size.

The bulk of the responsibilities for implementing the plan were envisaged as resting on national governments. Each government was urged to formulate its own population policy and program consistent with its overall goals and with the principles and aims of the World Plan of Action. Governments were encouraged to utilize the support and facilities of intergovernmental and nongovernmental organizations. United Nations agencies were to undertake the tasks of monitoring, reviewing, and appraising the results of the plan, and were to conduct an intensive review and appraisal every five years for possible modification of goals and recommendations.

In December, 1974 the General Assembly endorsed the World Population Plan of Action and invited governments to take national action to implement it. They designated the Economic and Social Council as the central, policy guidance and review agency, and called upon other United Nations agencies to report to that body on how they could best contribute to the plan's implementation. The General Assembly also recommended increased international aid for population programs, especially through the United Nations Fund for Population Activities (UNFPA). Between 1975 and 1978, annual voluntary contributions to UNFPA grew from 63 million dollars to approximately 100 million dollars.

WORLD FOOD CONFERENCE

Hunger, starvation, and malnutrition are chronic threats or realities to hundreds of millions of people, especially in the least developed countries. Prior to the 1970s, the Food and Agriculture Organization and the World Health Organization had provided technical assistance to alleviate food and nutritional deficiencies, national governments had supplied food through sales, loans, and grants, and the World Food Program had furnished food for emergencies and for development aid. Widespread, severe drought and crop failures in 1972–74 drastically depleted world grain reserves and portended possible catastrophies unless new measures were undertaken, especially by developing countries, to increase food production and facilitate distribution to critical areas.

The United Nations General Assembly in 1973 authorized the convening of the World Food Conference at the suggestion of the Economic and Social Council. Preparatory work was split among ECOSOC, a preparatory committee established by ECOSOC, the Economic Commission of ECOSOC, United Nations Secretariat personnel under the direction of the Secretary-General of the conference, and the Food and Agriculture Organization. The World Food Conference met in Rome, November 5–16, 1974.

The conference produced a Universal Declaration on the Eradication of Hunger and Malnutrition, and a set of twenty other recommendations. Among the principles that made up the Universal Declaration were the following: (1) Freedom from hunger and malnutrition is a basic human right; (2) It is a fundamental responsibility of governments to cooperate for higher food production and more equitable and efficient distribution; (3) Governments should initiate immediately an attack on chronic malnutrition among lower income groups; (4) Each state has a responsibility to remove obstacles and to provide incentives for increasing food production through agrarian, tax, credit, and investment policy reform; (5) Developed states should provide increased and sustained technical, material, and financial assistance on favorable terms to developing states; (6) Barriers to food trade should be reduced or eliminated, and special nonreciprocal trade concessions should be made to developing states.

The list of recommendations of the conference were both routine and innovative. All governments were urged to formulate comprehensive plans for increasing food production and for assuring access to food supplies and adequate nutrition by all segments of the population. The World Bank, regional banks, the United Nations Development Program, the Food and Agriculture Organization, and the United Nations Industrial Development Organization were requested to increase their assistance to agriculture and fisheries in developing countries. It was recommended that the FAO set up a Global Information and Early Warning System on Food and Agriculture. Governments were urged to establish national grain reserves as part of a world food security system. The level of continued food aid was set at 10 million tons of grain annually, and states were urged to channel a greater proportion through the World Food Program. In 1978 the Executive Director of the World Food Program estimated that 85 percent of food aid moved through bilateral channels.

One significant proposal of the conference was a recommendation that the General Assembly establish a World Food Council at the ministerial level, to coordinate all United Nations agencies' food policies and programs, periodically to review problems and policies, and to recommend remedial action. The Assembly promptly established a thirty-six-nation council and directed other United Nations agencies to cooperate with it and report to it.

Another organization created as a result of the Rome conference is the International Fund for Agricultural Development (IFAD) which began in late 1977 as a new member of the family of United Nations specialized agencies. The provisions for this agency are unique in that OPEC countries agreed to furnish at least 40 percent of the 1 billion dollars of initial funds, and the Governing Board has a balanced representation of donor-developed countries, donor-developing countries (OPEC), and recipient-developing countries. The purpose of the Fund is to provide grants and loans on concessional terms to help increase food production in developing countries. The first two loans were made to Sri Lanka and Tanzania and were jointly financed, respectively, by the Asian Development Bank and the International Development Association.

Although such targets as those set for the grain reserves of the world food security system and the proposed pledges for the World Food Program were not being met in the late 1970s, the World Food Conference did lay the foundations for a more adequate attack upon one of the most pressing problems of humankind.

WORLD CONFERENCE OF THE
INTERNATIONAL WOMEN'S YEAR

The principle of equality of the sexes is asserted in the United Nations Charter. One of the functional commissions of ECOSOC, the Commission on the Status of Women, has been active for more than thirty years in trying to bridge the gap between words and deeds in making this principle effective.

The General Assembly proclaimed 1975 as International Women's Year, and a World Conference was convened in Mexico City from June 19 to July 2 as a focal point of the year's activities. The theme of the conference was "Equality, Development, and Peace." The Mexico City meeting was the first global intergovernmental conference on women's issue ever held.

The conference produced the usual types of documents—a declaration of principles, a world plan of action, regional action plans, and miscellaneous resolutions. The declaration of principles affirms the role that women can play in development programs and world peace, and stresses the responsibilities of governments in enabling women to be fully and equally integrated into society. The declaration also states that the achievement of a new international economic order is a precondition for the attainment of women's equality. Furthermore, it condemns imperialism, neocolonialism, racism, apartheid, Zionism, and aggression as obstructing women's rights.

The action plan, subsequently approved by the General Assembly, set minimum targets by 1980 for substantial gains by women in the areas of literacy, vocational training, education, career opportunities, political participation and employment, health education, and parity in civil, political and social rights. Another world conference is planned for 1980 to assess progress toward these goals and to set priorities for the second half of the United Nations Decade for Women (1976–85).

The Mexico City conference was marked by more than usual dissension primarily because of the insistence by representatives of developing countries that the issues of establishing a new international economic order and of racism receive as much attention as the traditional aspects of women's rights. If, as the conference proclaimed, the role of women is a major factor in achieving development, it is noteworthy that the seventh special session of the General Assembly, which was devoted to development and economic cooperation and to which the Mexico City recommendations were submitted, almost totally ignored the possible contributions of women. During this same year, an analysis of the role of women in United Nations Secretariat positions revealed that the percentage of women employees in professional or higher categories was less than one-third that of men employees in those categories. These few indicators signal the manifold difficulties of achieving the degree of equality of status for women targeted at Mexico City.

CONFERENCE ON INTERNATIONAL
ECONOMIC COOPERATION (CIEC)

In December, 1975 the Conference on International Economic Cooperation was convened in Paris on the initiative of the French government. The original intent was for the participants to seek solutions to issues relating to the energy crisis, but the developing states insisted on enlarging the scope to include raw materials and trade, development, and finance. This was not a conference in which all countries participated, but was restricted to eight, western, developed states (with one representing the entire European Economic Community), eight OPEC members, and eleven other developing states. No members of the Communist bloc were included. Nevertheless, the conference dealt with global issues, was regarded as representative of most of the diverse geographic and economic sectors of the world, and was commonly referred to as the "North-South dialogue." As far as the developing countries were concerned, they viewed the broad mission of the conference as furthering the evolution of the new international economic order proclaimed by them in recent special and regular sessions of the UN General Assembly.

The CIEC held its first meeting at the ministerial level (mostly foreign ministers), and then broke into working groups, one for each of the four major divisions of the subject matter covered by the conference. It convened again at the ministerial level for a four-day final session at which the report of the conference was adopted. The conference held sessions intermittently over a period of eighteen months without reaching agreement on most issues. At the invitation of the UN General Assembly, the conference report was submitted for consideration to the Assembly's thirty-first resumed session on September 13–19, 1977. The General Assembly failed to adopt any resolution concerning the receipt of the report. A proposal on behalf of the developed states suggested that the Assembly note with regret that the results of the Conference fell far short of its objectives, and that no real progress had been made toward restructuring the international economic system or solving the most pressing problems of the developing countries. It was further suggested that efforts continue through all appropriate United Nations channels.

A few significant agreements were reached in the Paris talks. One of these was the establishment of a Common Fund to support the prices of commodities produced by developing countries, with details of the plan to be worked out through UNCTAD. Another agreement promised 1 billion dollars in special additional economic aid for low-income countries. Among the major disappointments was the failure to agree on debt-burden relief for poor countries. Other unresolved issues were numerous and wide-ranging. The Paris Conference failed to close the North-South rift.

ADDITIONAL CONFERENCES IN THE LATE 1970s

In the last two years of the 1970s, the pattern of world conferences continued. All were instigated by the economically disadvantaged group of countries, and most of them dealt with issues relating directly to development.

The five-week special session of the General Assembly on disarmament in May–June, 1978, is often referred to as a World Disarmament Conference, the first since the Disarmament Conference of 1932–34. This conference was previously discussed in chapter 9. After prolonged preparation and publicity, the General Assembly constituted itself as a conference devoted to a single subject, although it never anticipated that any break-throughs in the form of disarmament measures would come out of the discussions. The consciousness-raising function and increased pressures for subsequent agreements were the motives for calling the session.

Other global conferences scheduled for 1978 were a World Conference to Combat Racism and Racial Discrimination, in Geneva in August, a Conference on Technical Cooperation among Developing Countries, in Buenos Aires in August–September, and a United Nations Conference on an International Code of Conduct on Transfer of Technology, in Geneva in October–November. In July, 1979, the Food and Agriculture Organization sponsored a World Conference on Agrarian Reform and Rural Development in Rome. The final major conference of the decade, for which elaborate preparations were made over a period of two and a half years, was the

United Nations Conference on Science and Technology for Development, in Vienna in August–September, 1979. The Economic and Social Council's fifty-four-member standing Committee on Science and Technology for Development acted as the general preparatory body for the Conference and enlisted the support of a twenty-four-member advisory committee of scientists and specialists in applied technology. Other groundwork included regional meetings and the preparation of background papers by national governments, regional commissions, intergovernmental and nongovernmental organizations, and the United Nations Secretariat under the direction of the Secretary-General of the conference.

ASSESSMENT OF THE CONFERENCE TECHNIQUE

In the series of forums discussed in this chapter, the clash of diverse national interests has prevented any dramatic break-throughs toward satisfactory solutions to these basic problems. In spite of elaborate preparation, the results of most of the conferences of the 1970s have been meager. The hopes of the economically disadvantaged peoples of the world for a "new deal" in the form of a new international economic order have not been realized. Threats to individual and collective existence for the human race seem intractable.

Yet there are positive aspects to the "talk fests" of the 1970s. Perhaps most important is the fact that rational human beings understand the realities of the human condition and are able to identify those threats demanding attention and action. The alternative is to be a pawn to forces we have neither the will nor the ability to control. To review the subjects covered in the world conferences of the 1970s is to list the most vital issues of present world conditions.

Another revelation that emerges from this phenomenon is that the recognition of a "spaceship earth" concept has made some impact on human consciousness. Interdependence is a fact of life. Otherwise why bother to use global forums in a search for illumination of human problems? The very heart of the demand for a new economic order is the realization of the intricate web of interdependence. Problems of the environment, the oceans, disarmament, or the transfer of technology require international action.

Some partial but positive actions have resulted from the conferences. A worldwide monitoring system for the environment has been set up. Projects to halt the further encroachment of deserts have been initiated. A new fund has been established for aiding agricultural development in poor countries. Economic aid for developing countries has been increased, especially for those with lowest incomes. Numerous other gains can be cited.

Finally, the conferences represent a beginning in a long and evolving process of keeping within manageable proportions the major problems of humanity. Action plans will have to be revised at later dates, and the evolutionary process will be slow, but momentum has been given to an ongoing set of processes for meeting human demands and aspirations.

13

✣

The Struggle
for
Self-Government

Since 1945, the rush to independence has become a stampede, and the old colonialism, based on territorial dominance, has been nearly terminated. The speed of this stampede could not be predicted in 1945. Then, about one-third of the world's population was governed by metropolitan powers in some form of colonialism. Today less than one-half of one percent of the world's population is non-self-governing, and the number of recognized states has doubled. India, Pakistan, and Indonesia account for three-fourths of the liberated population. Much of the rest live in numerous mini-states, many of which have very limited political and economic bases.

From the beginning, the United Nations has declared, in its Charter and in its delegate bodies, its interest in the movement toward self-government. This interest is shown through trusteeship and through decolonialization. The number of trust territories and their populations has represented only a fraction of the colonial domain, with decolonialization making up the bulk of the movement. After India, Pakistan, and Indonesia became independent, and at the peak of the establishment of trusteeship arrangements, only one-tenth as many people lived in trust territories as remained under colonial rule. Today both arrangements have been almost phased out, and only a few remnants of the system remain.

This chapter will examine both trusteeship and political emancipation. The aspirations, achievements, frustrations, and problems
of liberated peoples, and the effect of the emergence of many new
states upon the world community also will be discussed.

THE LEAGUE MANDATES SYSTEM

When the League of Nations was founded, the legitimacy of acquiring colonies was already beginning to be questioned, and, therefore,
a way was sought by which the victorious powers in World War I
could avoid the disapprobation of acquiring the overseas territories
of the defeated powers as outright possessions. General Jan Smuts of
South Africa included a plan for a League-supervised mandate system
in his proposals for an international organization, and this idea was
incorporated into the Covenant as Article 22. Territories taken from
the defeated powers and not yet ready for self-government were to
be placed under the tutelage of "advanced nations" and "this tutelage [was to] be exercised by them as Mandatories on behalf of the
League." Each mandatory was to apply "the principle that the well-
being and development of such peoples form a sacred trust of civilization." The League Council was assigned the responsibility of
supervising the mandates system. The explicit terms of each mandate
were agreed upon between the mandatory and the Council.

To assist the Council in supervising the mandates system, a
Permanent Mandates Commission was constituted. The commission
was composed of experts nominated by the Council and, in order to
ensure their independence and impartiality, no one in a government
role was considered for appointment. Each mandatory was required
to submit an annual report on each territory to the Council. The
Permanent Mandates Commission, rather than the Council, actually
received these reports and supplemented the information through
questioning representatives of the administering authority, often the
governors of the territories. This useful and enlightening procedure
served as a precedent and carried over into the practice of the United
Nations Trusteeship Council.

In spite of severe handicaps, the Permanent Mandates Commission was remarkably successful in its efforts. The commission
possessed no real authority and had to rely upon its reputation for
thoroughness and impartiality to secure a high degree of cooperation
from all parties affected by its work. The annual reports by the
mandatory and the interrogation of responsible administrators were
the main sources of information on which the commission could base

its reports to the Council. No right of inspection by visiting missions existed. The administering states were the channels through which any petitions were screened and forwarded to the Commission. No right of petition was specified in the Covenant, but the right was sanctioned in Council practice. In the definitive historical work on the League of Nations, F. P. Walters points out that at first the administering states resented the commission's inquiries and suggestions.

> But as the time went on its reputation for competence and fairness continued to grow. The mandatories themselves gradually discovered that if on the one hand the reprimands of the Commission were painful, on the other hand its suggestions were helpful and its commendations were a valuable encouragement to the administration in the field. In its last years the Commission was consulted and trusted by mandatory and non-mandatory powers alike.[1]

The territories placed under mandate fell into three categories. Territories formerly belonging to the Turkish empire were considered nearly ready for self-government and came to be known as A mandates. These included Lebanon and Syria under French supervision, and Iraq, Palestine, and Trans-Jordan under British supervision. All of the A mandates achieved full sovereignty between 1932 and 1947. The former German colonies in Central Africa were considered to be further from the attainment of self-rule and were classified as B mandates. Cameroons and Togoland were each split into two territories administered by the British and French; Tanganyika was assigned to British administration; Ruanda-Urundi was made a mandate of Belgium. The C mandates were considered to be incapable of self-rule in the foreseeable future, and, because of their small size or population, or because of contiguity to the territory of the mandatory, the administering powers were permitted to administer them as integral parts of their territory. The C mandates were the former German colonies of South West Africa placed under South African supervision; the Marianas, Caroline, and Marshall Islands assigned to Japan; New Guinea and Nauru under the aegis of Australia; and Western Samoa under the control of New Zealand. All of the B and C mandates except South West Africa became trust territories under the United Nations trusteeship system.

The idea of mandates was frequently criticized as a thinly veiled disguise for expanded colonialism on the part of the victorious powers. Little distinction was drawn between the treatment and administration of mandates and that of other colonies of the metropolitan powers. Progress toward self-rule was slow, and the man-

[1] F. P. Walters, *A History of the League of Nations* (London: Oxford University Press, 1952), Vol. I, p. 173.

datories were under no pressure to advance self-government in the C group of mandates. However, the constant pressure and publicity furnished by the Mandates Commission probably ensured more protection for the rights and well-being of the indigenous peoples than would have been otherwise guaranteed. The mandates system was a first step among several that foreshadowed the eventual doom of the old colonialism.

RUSH TO SELF-GOVERNMENT

Modern colonialism grew out of the age of exploration and discovery during which European explorers and traders gained access to areas of the globe from which Europe had been previously isolated, and European governments laid political and economic claim to those non-European territories. Territorial empires were accumulated by Spain, Great Britain, France, the Netherlands, Portugal, and Belgium, with Germany and Italy later aspirants to imperial rule. Political ambitions and economic gains provided incentives for empire building. Imperialism was accompanied by the establishment of a superior-inferior relationship, by the exploitation of the resources of the non-European territories by the metropolitan powers through both public and private channels, and by a sense of mission to bring the benefits of European civilization and administration to "less-advanced" peoples — an attitude reflected in the phrase "the white man's burden." In the early stages of colonialism the possibilities of self-rule by indigenous populations did not occur to colonial administrators, although paternalistic attitudes concerning the welfare of native inhabitants increasingly developed.

Eventually the European model served as a major force in the dissolution of the overseas empires. Western political and economic revolutions caught the imagination of the dominated groups as possibilities for themselves. Imperial administrators and entrepreneurs, although reserving all top government and management posts for Europeans, were required, by necessity, to train more and more indigenous people for skilled positions and to use education as a means for progressively developing business and government enterprises. Native elites were educated in western universities and embraced western values as goals for their own societies. Members of these elites became leaders in the independence movements, were frequently jailed by colonial administrations, but eventually emerged as national heroes. Gandhi and Nehru in India, Nkrumah in Ghana, and Kenyatta in Kenya are familiar examples.

The impact of the European revolutionary model upon the anti-colonial movement is cogently summarized by Rupert Emerson.

> . . . imperialism has been drawing to a close precisely because it has been fulfilling the historic but inadvertent function of spreading abroad the dynamism inherent in the great Western revolution of modern times. . . . The peoples who were being driven into the modern world by alien masters had learned enough of a lesson to insist that, henceforward, they would themselves take control of their further advance into modernity. To sum the matter up in the briefest fashion: through global conquest the dominant Western powers worked to reshape the world in their own image and thus aroused against themselves the forces of nationalism which are both the bitterest enemies of imperialism and, perversely, its finest fruit.[2]

The first independence movements occurred in the Western Hemisphere and involved transplanted Europeans who inherited the values of the western world. The war for independence in the area that became the United States was followed in the nineteenth century by secession from colonial empires by major segments of Latin America and by Canada. In the early twentieth century Australia and New Zealand, also predominantly inhabited by British emigrants, attained self-rule.

By 1914 the major areas remaining under colonial jurisdiction were in Asia and Africa. The most prevalent pattern was domination by whites of nonwhites. The territories that emerged as independent states between 1910 and World War II were relatively few in number and included South Africa, Saudi Arabia, Yemen, Egypt, and Iraq. Self-rule for hundreds of millions of nonwhites remained as an unachieved goal in 1940.

World War II provided the impetus for accelerating the rush to independence. Japan invaded the British, French, Dutch, United States, and Australian colonies in Southeast Asia and in the Pacific Islands. Only the Philippines, which had been promised early independence, provided formidable resistance to the invaders. Upon the withdrawal of Japanese forces, the Indonesians and Vietnamese seized the opportunity for revolt against the return to Dutch and French rule. India, Pakistan, Burma, Ceylon, and the Philippines rapidly achieved independence after the war. Korea was promised self-rule but became a divided state in the territorial arrangements growing out of the agreements for temporary occupation by Soviet and United States armed forces. In the Middle East the long-awaited

[2] Rupert Emerson, *From Empire to Nation: The Rise to Self-Assertion of Asian and African Peoples* (Cambridge, Mass.: Harvard University Press, 1960), pp. 16–17.

transfer of sovereignty was promptly made to the remaining mandates, which became the states of Syria, Lebanon, Jordan, and Israel.

The war made an impact on other areas that were not immediately granted independence. War-time conditions and the invasion of Belgium, the Netherlands, and France by the Nazi war machine disrupted the pattern of control over colonial possessions. Permanent domination of whites over nonwhites was challenged. Recruitment of colonial forces for fighting outside their borders and increased contacts with military personnel from other countries both within and outside their home base widened the experiences and aspirations of colonial peoples. Allied slogans and aims in the war provided a philosophical basis for the allure of self-determination. The spread of information allowed the attainment of independence by some states to serve as a model and to whet the desire of others for the same goal.

By the early 1950s the major remaining bastion of the old colonialism was in the African continent, and the final assault on this bastion has been clearly heralded. After 1950 the independence movement swept through the continent adding more than forty new states to the four that had previously attained sovereignty. For many years the most stubborn foreign imperial state was Portugal, but, after a change of regime, its policy abruptly shifted and it granted independence to Guinea-Bissau in 1974 and to Mozambique and Angola in 1975. After that date the only large non-self-governing areas were those whose status remained in dispute—South West Africa and Rhodesia.

THE UNITED NATIONS TRUSTEESHIP SYSTEM

No proposals for a system of trusteeship were included in the conversations of the major powers at Dumbarton Oaks; subsequently, at Yalta an agreement emerged providing only (1) that the Charter should include provisions for trusteeship, (2) that the major powers would consult on the matter before the San Francisco conference, and (3) that three categories of territories should be eligible for inclusion as trust territories. The three categories were those eventually incorporated into Article 77 of the Charter and included (1) former mandates under the League of Nations, (2) territories detached from enemy states as a result of World War II, and (3) any other territories voluntarily placed under the system by administering states. The anticipated consultations among the big powers were not held prior to the San Francisco sessions, and, instead, these consultations proceeded simultaneously with the drafting of the trusteeship provisions of the Charter causing inconvenience and delay in committee consideration of the provisions.

At one stage in the postwar planning within the United States State Department, a proposal was made to apply the trusteeship principle to all colonies and dependencies, but this plan was resolutely opposed by the military arm of government. The same proposal was suggested in San Francisco by Australia and the Philippines but was not vigorously pushed and was dropped. As a substitute several states supported the inclusion in the Charter of a declaration on non-self-governing territories, which developed into Chapter XI of the Charter. Details of this declaration, applying to other colonies and possessions not placed under trusteeship, are discussed in a subsequent section of this chapter.

Charter provisions for trusteeship involved several basic changes from those that governed the League mandate system. General supervision of trusteeship matters was shifted from the League Council to the United Nations General Assembly. The Permanent Mandates Commission, composed of experts serving in their private capacity, was replaced by the Trusteeship Council, made up of government representatives. Half of the members of the Trusteeship Council were the states that administered trust territories, thus assuring control over any measures on which the administering states were united. As a gesture toward the desirability of maintaining the services of experts, each member of the Council was requested to "designate one specially qualified person to represent it therein." The territories placed under mandate were specified and classified into A, B, and C categories by the Supreme Allied Council after World War I; all territories placed under trusteeship were to be voluntarily offered by the controlling state under individual agreements, the terms of which could be dictated by the metropolitan power under threat of withdrawing the offer to place the territory under trusteeship. The goal of self-government was indicated in the League Covenant only for category A mandates; trustees were bound by the Charter to promote the political advancement and the "progressive development toward self-government or independence" of all trust territories in accordance with "the freely expressed wishes of the people concerned."

In addition to the obligation to advance trust territories toward self-government or independence, the trustees were committed by Article 76 of the Charter to promote the economic, social, and educational advancement of the inhabitants of the trust territories. Other principles binding the trustees were (1) the promotion of human rights and fundamental freedoms, (2) encouragement of the recognition of the interdependence of peoples, (3) the furthering of international peace and security, and (4) the guarantee of equal treatment in social, economic, and commercial matters for United Nations members and their nationals. On the whole, these obligations served as better protection for the rights and aspirations of the indigenous peoples than had been provided in Article 22 of the League Covenant.

Although three categories of territories were designated as possible subjects of trusteeship agreements, thus opening the door to arrangements that could apply to dozens of non-self-governing territories, only eleven areas administered by seven trustees ever came under the aegis of the Trusteeship Council (as opposed to the fifteen mandated territories under the League). Most of the trust territories were former mandates. The series of trusteeship agreements for the former mandates was approved by the General Assembly (and by the Security Council for the strategic Trust Territory of the Pacific Islands) between December 13, 1946, and November 1, 1947.

A second category of potential candidates for trusteeship status was territories detached from enemy states as a result of World War II. The Pacific Islands group, over which the United States was granted a strategic trusteeship, can be classified in this category as well as in the group of mandates listed above, since Japan held these islands under mandate from the League of Nations. Of the three African colonies detached from Italy, one, Italian Somaliland (joined since 1960 with former British Somaliland into Somalia), was assigned by the General Assembly to Italy as trustee for a ten-year period beginning in 1950. The territory had been under British control in the interval since World War II. The arrangement was unusual (1) because of the assignment of a former enemy state as trustee, (2) because Italy was not yet a United Nations member in 1950, and (3) because Italy was subjected by the terms of the trusteeship agreement to several restrictions and to a degree of United Nations supervision not applicable to the trustees of other territories.

The third category of territories eligible for trusteeship were "territories voluntarily placed under the system by states responsible for their administration." Since no compulsion existed for colonial powers to submit to the inconveniences of international supervision over territories in this category, it is not surprising that no such offers were made.

Another unused feature of the Charter's trusteeship provisions is the possibility of designating the United Nations itself as the trustee over a specified territory. Suggestions were made from time to time for such an arrangement—e.g., with regard to Palestine or Jerusalem—but none ever came to fruition. The United Nations created a Temporary Executive Authority (UNTEA) to administer the area of West Irian for a few months in 1962-63 in the interval between the transfer of jurisdiction from the Netherlands to Indonesia, but this operation most resembled a peacekeeping arrangement, and the Trusteeship Council was not involved. Another provision of the Charter for joint trustees was implemented in the arrangement for Australia, New Zealand, and the United Kingdom to serve as the administering authority over Nauru, but Australia was to act as administrator on behalf of all three.

As plans were being formulated for the trusteeship system, defense spokesmen within the United States government expressed their concern that, on the one hand, outright annexation of territory taken from the Axis powers was contrary to current world opinion, and that, on the other hand, the proposed trusteeship arrangements failed to provide for protection of the security interests of the United States in the Pacific area. In order to accommodate these military pressures, the State Department proposed a unique variation in the trusteeship arrangements by which all or part of a trust territory could be declared a strategic area. Only one territory, the Trust Territory of the Pacific Islands under United States administration, was offered as a strategic area. The Charter provides that all functions performed by the General Assembly in approving regular trusteeship agreements and in exercising supervisory powers shall be exercised by the Security Council for strategic areas. The purpose of this arrangement was apparently to give the United States a potential veto over any action considered adverse to its security interests. In practice the Security Council has never exercised its supervisory powers, although it annually receives reports from the Trusteeship Council as does the General Assembly for all other territories.

In many respects the obligations assumed by the trustee for a strategic area are identical to those applying to other trust territories. The trustee is obligated to promote the political, economic, social, and educational advancement of the inhabitants and the other rights and protections specified in Article 76 of the Charter as applying generally to the inhabitants of trust territories. Annual reports are submitted to the Trusteeship Council on the basis of a uniform questionnaire, visiting missions are sent to the territory at regular intervals, and petitions from the inhabitants are guaranteed a hearing through established procedures of the Trusteeship Council.

The major departures from the normal operation of the trusteeship system as applied to the Trust Territory of the Pacific Islands are in the closing of certain areas for security purposes and in the lack of a review of the Trusteeship Council's annual consideration of matters concerning the territory resulting from the Security Council's default on its exercise of this function. The United States conducted nuclear tests in the area in 1954 and, for a time, declared the Bikini and Eniwetok regions closed to visiting missions. Other members of the Trusteeship Council severely criticized the United States for conducting these tests and charged that the interests and safety of the inhabitants were jeopardized. The uprooting of inhabitants against their will and their removal from their ancestral homes in the area where the tests were conducted was a point of special stress by the critics. The fortification of the islands and the establishment of military, naval, and air bases required no special privileges for the United States since this right applied to all trust territories, a right forbidden in class B and C mandates under the League.

To provide for adequate supervision of the administration of the trust territories, the Charter stipulates the establishment of the Trusteeship Council. The composition of the Council was outlined in chapter 4, and the details need not be repeated here. For the period 1950–55, Italy, as an administering state but a nonmember of the United Nations, sat in the Council without vote but with responsibility for its administration of Somaliland. The prescribed balance between the number of administering and nonadministering members has been tilted in favor of nonadministering states under two circumstances: (1) at various times, as trust territories were granted independence, a temporary imbalance occurred until the expiration of the three-year term of one or more elected members; and (2) after 1968, the two remaining trustees (one after 1975) were overbalanced by the four nonadministering permanent members of the Security Council.

During the most active years of the trusteeship system, the General Assembly exercised tight control over the Trusteeship Council through its Fourth Committee. Although the Charter declares that the Trusteeship Council is a major organ, it also provides ample grounds for the General Assembly to treat the Council as its subordinate body. Of necessity, however, the Trusteeship Council performed the primary functions needed to check on the administration of the trust territories. The Charter provides a broader range of methods for performing these functions than were available to the Mandates Commission of the League.

The special devices available to the Trusteeship Council are (1) annual reports from the administering authority, (2) petitions, and (3) visiting missions. The annual reports are based on a detailed questionnaire, and a special representative, usually a top administrator from the territory under investigation, is subjected to extensive questioning by members of the Council. At the height of Trusteeship Council activities, the volume of petitions from individuals and groups was of such proportions as to require special procedures for handling them. Both oral and written petitions are acceptable, and visiting missions may receive petitions during their visits to a territory. The use of visiting missions is a wholly unprecedented means of checking on the administration of trust territories. These missions are composed of representatives of two administering and two non-administering members of the Trusteeship Council accompanied by the necessary supporting staff. Each territory has been visited at three-year intervals. Each mission attempted to compare by observation the conditions within the territory with the information reported by the trustee and as reflected in previous petitions.

Instead of relying on the Trusteeship Council to provide special investigative missions to determine the wishes of the inhabitants of trust territories regarding the conditions for self-government, the General Assembly assumed direct responsibility for appointing plebiscite administrators or similar agencies in territories nearly ready for independence. The attainment of self-government is one of several areas in which the General Assembly maintained its control over matters that otherwise might have been delegated to the Trusteeship Council.

THE RECORD OF TRUSTEESHIP

Because the composition of the Trusteeship Council was dependent upon the prior adoption of trusteeship agreements, fourteen months were required after the initial session of the General Assembly before the Council could be organized. A proposal to establish a temporary trusteeship organization was rejected, but the General Assembly in February, 1946, urged the mandatory powers to promptly draw up trusteeship proposals and submit them at an early date for General Assembly approval. Accordingly, eight proposed agreements were submitted to the General Assembly for consideration and approval at its reconvened first session in October–December of the same year. In spite of prolonged and sometimes bitter debate over some of the terms of the proposals, all major suggestions for modification were rejected, partially in recognition of the reality that the administering state had a final veto over changes it found unacceptable since all trust arrangements were voluntary, not compulsory.

On December 13, 1946, the Assembly approved all eight agreements and the following day elected two states to provide the necessary balance in the Trusteeship Council between administering and non-administering members.

The Trusteeship Council met for the first time in March, 1947, with ten members. Within the same year trusteeship agreements were approved for the strategic Trust Territory of the Pacific Islands and for Nauru, and two more elective members were added to the Council. The only further territory added to the list was Somaliland, but, since Italy as trustee was not, in 1950, a United Nations member, it sat as a thirteenth nonvoting member of the Council until 1955. In that year Italy's admission to the United Nations required the election by the General Assembly of one additional nonadministering member of the Trusteeship Council. From 1955 to 1960 the composition of the Council was seven administering members (Australia, Belgium, France, Italy, New Zealand, the United Kingdom, and the United States); two nonadministering permanent members of the Security Council (China and the Soviet Union); and five members elected for three-year terms. The attainment of independence by eight trust territories between 1960 and 1968 left temporary majorities of nonadministering states on the Council until the terms of elected members expired. Today only the five permanent members of the Security Council remain as Trusteeship Council members with the nonadministering states outnumbering the administering states four to one.

Twice the Soviet Union has boycotted sessions of the Trusteeship Council. The first occasion was in 1947 ostensibly on the grounds that the trusteeship agreements violated the Charter and were illegal. Soviet objections to the agreements included (1) failure of the trustees to consult all "states directly concerned," as specified in the Charter, in drawing up the agreements, (2) statements in the agreements allowing administration of the territories as integral parts of the administering states, and (3) exemption from Security Council supervision of military and defense measures in the territories. The second Soviet boycott occurred in 1950 over the issue of the representation of China in the Trusteeship Council.

The first trust territory to gain independence was British Togoland in 1957, when it was combined with the Gold Coast, a British colony, to form the new state of Ghana. The future of British Togoland was in doubt for several years preceding 1957 because of conflicting expressions of the wishes of various tribal groups living in the two Togolands and in the Gold Coast. As early as 1947 the General Assembly interjected itself into the controversy by granting oral hearings to representatives of the Ewe people, who lived in an area cutting across all three territories. At various times the General Assembly expressed its support of both (1) a separate Ewe state, and (2) unification of the two Togolands. Unification of the Togolands was given additional support in the report of the 1952 Trusteeship Council's visiting mission to West Africa. By 1954, however, new signals indicated that a majority of the inhabitants of British Togoland probably favored union with the Gold Coast. This desire was verified by a plebiscite in 1956 conducted by the British under the supervision of a United Nations commissioner appointed by the General Assembly. Although the Ewe districts voted two to one in favor of separation from the Gold Coast, the overall margin favoring union with the Gold Coast was 93,365 to 67,422. In accordance with this expression of the will of the people of British Togoland, that territory became an integral part of the new state of Ghana when independence was declared, effective March 6, 1957. In spite of earlier errors based on partial evidence, the wishes of the majority of the inhabitants of the territory were the final determining factor in deciding the future status of British Togoland.

Several trustees set up administrative unions by which a trust territory was administered through a single governmental structure common to the trust territory and an adjoining colony. Ardent advocates of the trusteeship system, in the interests of safeguarding the rights of indigenous inhabitants, were suspicious that such an arrangement would subvert those rights by reducing the trust territory to colonial status. In 1950, at the urging of the General Assembly, the Trusteeship Council established a committee on administrative unions to scrutinize such unions to make sure that the fulfillment of all objectives of the trusteeship system, including the attainment of self-government, were not hampered by these arrangements. Most evidence indicates that administrative unions did not jeopardize the rights of the inhabitants of trust territories nor slow progress toward self-government. The vigilance and supervision of the General Assembly and the Trusteeship Council may have helped to prevent any tendency to use administrative unions as a device for escaping from Charter obligations.

Progress toward independence has been furthered and expedited by the trusteeship system. The accompanying chart shows that eight of the eleven trust territories had attained self-rule by 1962. Although this process was paralleled by the rapid emergence of colonies as new states, the pressures for independence for the trust territories were increased through the supervision of United Nations agencies. Furthermore, the trust territories were, on the average, better pre-

TERRITORIES PLACED UNDER UNITED NATIONS TRUSTEESHIP

Territory	Previous Status	Administering Authority	Duration of Trusteeship	Present Status	UN Membership
Cameroons (British)	Class B Mandate (UK)	United Kingdom	1946–61	Portion incorporated into Nigeria; remainder into Cameroon (1961)	
Cameroons (French)	Class B Mandate (France)	France	1946–60	Independent as Cameroon (1960)	1960
Nauru	Class C Mandate (Australia)	Australia (on behalf of Australia, New Zealand, and UK)	1947–68	Independent (1968)	
New Guinea	Class C Mandate (Australia)	Australia	1946–75	Independent (1975)	1975
Ruanda-Urundi	Class B Mandate (Belgium)	Belgium	1946–62	Independent as separate states of Rwanda and Burundi (1962)	1962
Somaliland (Italian)	Italian Protectorate	Italy	1950–60	Independent and joined with British Somaliland as Somalia (1960)	1960
Tanganyika	Class B Mandate (UK)	United Kingdom	1946–61	Independent (1961); joined with Zanzibar (1964)	1961
Togoland (British)	Class B Mandate (UK)	United Kingdom	1946–57	Joined with Gold Coast as independent state of Ghana (1957)	1957
Togoland (French)	Class B Mandate (France)	France	1946–60	Independent as Togo (1960)	1960
Trust Territory of the Pacific Islands	Class C Mandate (Japan)	United States	1947–	Strategic Trusteeship	
Western Samoa	Class C Mandate (New Zealand)	New Zealand	1946–62	Independent (1962)	1976

pared for self-rule than were many colonies. Pressures on the trustees to expand suffrage, to develop institutions of local government, and increasingly to involve the inhabitants as participants in the government and the administration of the territories paved the way for a smooth transition to self-government.

Economic and social gains were also registered in the trust territories during the period before independence. Evidence of these gains could be found in the annual reports on each territory, in the questioning of the special representatives by the members of the Trusteeship Council, and in the reports of the visiting missions to the various territories. The trustees were under constant pressure to advance the fundamental human rights of free speech, assembly, press, and religion, to improve the status of women, and to abolish racial discrimination and corporal punishment. Other pressures were exerted to show continuous improvement in educational and medical and health facilities, and to develop transportation, communications, and levels of economic well-being of the local population.

The trusteeship system has been less than perfect in its operation. Conflicts between General Assembly and Trusteeship Council jurisdiction and functions have been apparent, although Assembly supervision has tended to prod the Council members and trustees into more diligent efforts to safeguard the interests of indigenous populations. On the whole, the glare of publicity furnished by the varied means of supervision over the administration of the territories has produced salutary results in comparison with the League mandate system or with general colonial administration.

THE CHARTER AND NON-SELF-GOVERNING TERRITORIES

In 1945 when the Charter was written, the anticolonialist movement had not yet attained its momentum of later years. The provisions of Chapter XI entitled "Declaration Regarding Non-Self-Governing Territories" represented, therefore, a set of compromises between colonialism and the emerging pressures for terminating the colonial system. States representing the growing anticolonialist sentiment could effectively demand inclusion of guarantees for subjected peoples but could not establish these guarantees on any except a moral basis and without implementing machinery. Yet Chapter XI subsequently became the instrument for a militant campaign for the immediate granting of self-government and independence to all peoples who had not attained self-rule and political independence.

Chapter XI has been characterized as a bill of rights for all non-self-governing peoples. Since it represented a new precedent in asserting certain rights and since all members of the United Nations accepted obligations toward colonial peoples not clearly recognized previously, its revolutionary nature is evident. Colonial powers agreed, in adhering to Article 73 of the Charter, to "accept as a sacred trust the obligation to promote to the utmost, . . . the well-being of the inhabitants of these territories" and to "recognize the principle that the interests of the inhabitants of these territories are paramount." They further promised to ensure non-self-governing peoples political, economic, social, and educational advancement, just treatment, and the development of self-government and of free political institutions (but not necessarily independence). Colonial powers were additionally obligated to transmit to the Secretary-General statistical and technical information "relating to economic, social, and educational conditions in the territories" that they administered. However, such information was designated as "for information purposes" and no provision was made for the further use of this information. At the insistence of the colonial powers, political data were exempted from inclusion in the reports.

From the earliest years of the United Nations, the anticolonialist forces chipped away at the colonial bastions by seeking to put into operation the principles of Article 73 of the Charter, to expand the coverage of the article to establish the principle of international accountability for the administration of non-self-governing territories, and to mobilize world opinion on behalf of the self-determination of dependent peoples. The assault on colonialism was carried on in the General Assembly, in the Assembly's Fourth Committee, and in a series of ad hoc and semipermanent committees created on the authority of the General Assembly. Frequently recurring themes for debates within these bodies included such questions as (1) what is the scope of the obligation to transmit information under Article 73? (2) how shall such information be dealt with and utilized? (3) what are the criteria for determining non-self-governing status? (4) who has the authority to determine that a territory is non-self-governing? (5) under what conditions may the submission of reports be terminated? (6) by what authority may reports be discontinued?

From the beginning the General Assembly asserted its authority to examine the information submitted by administering states, to debate the issues relating to conditions in non-self-governing territories, and to recommend steps toward the political, economic, social, and educational advancement of indigenous peoples. In 1946 eight states resolved the problem of deciding which territories were subject to the transmission of information by submitting a list of seventy-four territories on which they intended to forward data to the Secretary-General. This list was accepted by the General Assembly as a basis for compliance with Article 73.

In order to utilize the information submitted by metropolitan powers more effectively, the General Assembly in 1946 authorized the establishment of a Committee on Information from Non-Self-Governing Territories. This committee was composed of an equal number of administering and nonadministering states, the latter chosen by the Assembly's Fourth Committee. The pattern of representation was copied from that of the Trusteeship Council. Belgium refused to participate in committee deliberations beginning in 1953, although it continued to transmit information on its colonial possessions. The Committee on Information was not a powerful anticolonialist instrument because of its composition, with the colonial states exerting strong influence; because the committee lacked means, such as the receipt of petitions or the sending of visiting missions, for checking on the accuracy of the reports submitted to it; and because the committee was forbidden by its terms of reference from making specific recommendations on individual territories. The Fourth Committee (in relation to which the Committee on Information was essentially a subcommittee) and the General Assembly, each representing the full membership of the United Nations, were more aggressive in their attitudes on anticolonialism.

As a guide to colonial powers in submitting their annual reports to the Secretary-General the General Assembly approved a type of comprehensive questionnaire entitled "Standard Form for the Guidance of Members in the Preparation of Information to be Transmitted under Article 73(e) of the Charter." Article 73 deliberately omitted political information from the categories on which data was required, but the standard form included optional sections, and several states voluntarily submitted political information. The standard form served as just one of several means for increasing the pressure on colonial powers to rapidly move toward granting independence to non-self-governing peoples.

The lack of a definition for the term "non-self-governing" was partially remedied by the submission in 1946 of the list of seventy-four territories on which the colonial powers intended to submit information. However, within the first few years, states discontinued the forwarding of information on several of these territories claiming, in most cases, a change of status that warranted the cessation. The United Kingdom, for example, asserted that it would be improper to report on any matters on which local autonomy had been granted.

France ceased reports on several overseas departments within the French Union. The United States sent only one report on the Panama Canal Zone because of a protest from Panama, and later discontinued its reports on Puerto Rico when that island was granted the status of a free commonwealth associated with the United States. In 1955, when Portugal and Spain were granted United Nations membership, each asserted that they had no territories on which to report because their overseas territories were integral parts of the homeland. Several colonial powers maintained their exclusive right to determine the status or change of status of territories under their jurisdiction.

The unilateral right of administering states to determine the territories on which they would report and to decide when they would cease to make such reports was disputed by the General Assembly. The Assembly sought to define "non-self-governing territory" through studies conducted with the aid of several special committees, the Secretariat, and the Committee on Information from Non-Self-Governing Territories. The special committees decided that the formulation of a precise definition of such phrases as "a full measure of self-government" in Article 73 of the Charter was impossible, but they developed a list of thirty-four factors to serve as a guide to the General Assembly and the administering states. The Assembly asserted its role in deciding whether to accept the termination of reports on territories whose status was claimed by the colonial powers to have changed, although, in fact, the Assembly lacked any sanctions except moral suasion over reluctant states. The General Assembly also reviewed the change of status of territories such as Indonesia, Puerto Rico, and Greenland and specifically approved the cessation of reports on them. The Assembly asserted that the attainment by a territory of full independence, free association, or integration into a metropolitan state were changes warranting the cessation of reports on that territory.

In general, during the period from 1946 to 1959, the General Assembly and its Fourth Committee exhibited an increasing tendency toward establishing international accountability on the part of colonial powers for their administration of dependent territories. Pressures were exerted to extract more information from metropolitan states and to keep the spotlight of world opinion on their progress in promoting the well-being and political, economic, and social advancement of indigenous populations. The revolution of independence for all non-self-governing peoples was well begun but its more militant aspects remained to be manifested during the 1960s.

INCREASING PRESSURES FOR EMANCIPATION

The year 1960 marks the turning point from mild pressures on metropolitan powers to encourage independence for their colonies to a frontal assault on the legitimacy of the colonial system, accompanied by demands for the immediate termination of all domination of one people over another. This revolution of attitudes was made possible by the influx of new members into the United Nations. The dozen former colonies that were admitted to the United Nations during the period 1955-58 were augmented in 1960 by seventeen new states all of which had experienced the sting of colonial domination and had escaped to self-rule and independence. The previous anticolonialist minority now became a majority in the General Assembly.

The forces of anticolonialism lost no time in launching a frontal assault on the remaining bastions of colonialism. On December 14, 1960, they pushed through the General Assembly a Declaration on the Granting of Independence to Colonial Countries and Peoples by a vote of 90-0 with nine abstentions, with the abstentions cast mainly by colonial powers. The sweeping nature of this document is attested to by Rupert Emerson's characterization of it as "almost an amendment of the Charter."[3]

The 1960 declaration moved from previous assertions that political independence should be progressively forwarded by colonial powers to demands for immediate political freedom as a basic right for all peoples regardless of their stage of political, economic, social, or educational development. The seven main provisions of the declaration may be summarized as follows: (1) the subjugation or domination of any people constitutes a denial of fundamental human rights, is contrary to the United Nations Charter, and serves as an impediment to world peace and cooperation; (2) all peoples have the right to self-determination; (3) the inadequacy of political, economic, social, or educational preparedness should never serve as a pretext for delaying independence; (4) all repressive measures directed against dependent peoples shall cease; (5) all powers necessary for complete independence and freedom should immediately be transferred to the peoples of non-self-governing territories; (6) any attempt to disrupt the national unity and territorial integrity of a country is incompatible with United Nations Charter principles;

[3] Rupert Emerson, "Colonialism, Political Development, and the UN," *International Organization*, Vol. 19, (Summer, 1965), p. 493.

(7) all states shall observe the provisions of the United Nations Charter, the Declaration of Human Rights, and the present declaration in order to secure the sovereign rights and territorial integrity of all peoples.

In order to convert the declaration into a positive instrument for the realization of its principles, the General Assembly in 1961 created the Special Committee on the Situation with Regard to the Implementation of the Declaration on the Granting of Independence to Colonial Countries and Peoples. In this special committee parity of membership between administering and non-administering states (the pattern followed for the composition of the Trusteeship Council and the Committee on Information from Non-Self-Governing Territories) was abandoned in favor of a predominant representation of states with a strong anticolonial bias. In 1962 the original committee membership of seventeen was increased to twenty-four, and since that time the Special Committee of Twenty-Four has served as the common title for the body because of the ponderous official appellation. In 1963, in order to concentrate more anticolonial activities in a single body, the Committee on Information from Non-Self-Governing Territories was abolished and its functions transferred to the Special Committee of Twenty-Four.

In spite of its lack of coercive means, the Committee of Twenty-Four has been aggressive in its demands. Early in its existence it decided to ignore the restriction placed on the Committee on Information to make only recommendations of general application and instead to consider territories on an individual basis. It has attempted to use petitions and investigative commissions to implement its deliberations. It has sought the support of the General Assembly and the Security Council for marshaling world opinion and invoking sanctions against recalcitrant colonial powers. It encouraged the use of the International Court of Justice in the South West Africa controversy and sought ways to offset an unfavorable decision by the Court.

Empirical proof of the effectiveness of the Special Committee of Twenty-Four in hastening the processes of granting independence to non-self-governing peoples may be difficult to produce, but the pressures on the colonial states have been so sharply focused and world opinion has been so preponderant in favor of self-determination that only a few countries are defiant of these influences. Anticolonialism as a major issue preoccupying the majority of United Nations members has been rivaled only by concerns for economic, social, and political development. Regardless of the causes of the process, the addition to United Nations membership since 1960 of fifty former colonies is evidence of the continuing process of decolonization.

PROBLEMS OF RESIDUAL COLONIALISM

In spite of the momentum of the rush to independence, certain remnants of the old colonialism remain. Most of the approximately thirty remaining dependent territories are small islands or groups of islands whose viability as independent political units is doubtful. Some form of political relationship with another state under an arrangement for local self-rule may be the most advantageous solution for these micro-units. Such an arrangement may be acceptable to the majority of United Nations members providing that the option is clearly a free choice by the indigenous inhabitants, although this is not a foregone conclusion since demands for Puerto Rican independence are voiced in the United Nations notwithstanding the islanders overwhelming choice of Commonwealth status rather than independence.

A few colonies are larger and more populous than the microunits referred to above and account for the bulk of the approximately 15 million people who are non-self-governing. The future of Hong Kong, a British Crown Colony of about 4 million people, is enigmatic. The Special Committee of Twenty-Four, for more than a decade, focused most of its attention upon South West Africa, Rhodesia, and Portuguese territories in Africa. The problem of the Portuguese territories was resolved with a dramatic shift of policy by the Portuguese government, which resulted in granting independence to Guinea-Bissau, Mozambique, and Angola in 1974–75. The other two hard-core remnants of colonialism deserve special emphasis.

South West Africa (Namibia)

South West Africa is a large but sparsely populated area lying between South Africa and Angola. After World War I it was taken from Germany and assigned to the administration of South Africa as a class C mandate. By this classification South Africa was permitted to administer South West Africa as an integral part of its own territory.

After the demise of the League and its replacement by the United Nations, South Africa asserted that it was under no obligation to place South West Africa under trusteeship. Instead it claimed the right to annex the territory on the grounds that its former obligations died with the League and that it alone was free to determine the future status of South West Africa.

Criticisms in the United Nations of South Africa's administration of South West Africa focused on the treatment of nonwhites in the area and the intention of South Africa to incorporate South West Africa as an integral part of its own territory. The southern two-thirds of the country, which included the most productive land and the most valuable minerals, was reserved for whites. Africans lived mainly in reserves or homelands and were subjected to contract labor, a pass system, severe penalties for infractions of labor contracts, low wages, and a lack of education and health facilities. White prosperity was maintained at the expense of the Africans.

The role of the International Court of Justice in the South West African question was described in some detail in chapter 8; therefore, only the highlights of this role will be reviewed here. In an advisory opinion in 1950, the Court declared that South Africa's obligations under the mandate continued and that South Africa could not unilaterally modify the status of the territory. In a court case brought by Ethiopia and Liberia, which lasted for six years, a closely divided Court first, in 1962, seemed to accept the right of the plaintiff states to bring the suit, but, in 1966, reversed this ruling. The Court thus left unanswered the substantive questions concerning the further obligations of South Africa and the enforcement of these obligations.

The disappointed United Nations members reacted to the Court's decision with prompt and drastic political measures. Throughout the period 1960–66 the special committees of the General Assembly had repeatedly urged the Assembly to revoke the mandate and assume direct United Nations administration of the territory. On one occasion the Assembly responded to South African plans for separate development for Africans within the territory by declaring that any attempt at partition or annexation would violate the mandate and constitute an act of aggression. Immediately after the Court's decision the General Assembly took up the South West Africa question as a priority item on its 1966 agenda. On October 27 the Assembly declared the mandate to be terminated and South West Africa to be the direct responsibility of the United Nations. In 1968 the General Assembly renamed the territory Namibia.

In order to give substance to its resolution of October 27, 1966, the General Assembly created machinery for carrying out its provisions. First it established a fourteen-member Ad Hoc Committee for South West Africa charged with recommending practical means for administering the territory until independence was granted. Based on the suggestions of the Ad Hoc Committee, the Assembly set up an eleven-member Council for Namibia and authorized the appointment of a   United Nations commissioner for Namibia. Much delay in the appointment of the commissioner resulted from the difficulty of finding a willing, qualified candidate who was acceptable to all United Nations factions including the anticolonialist bloc. In the meantime, the Council for Namibia, which, not unexpectedly, was denied access to the territory by South Africa, proceeded to act as a government in exile.

Beginning in 1969, the Security Council added the weight of its authority to that of the General Assembly in a series of resolutions demanding the withdrawal of South Africa from Namibia. When South Africa ignored an October 4, 1969, deadline for withdrawal set by the Security Council, that body established a subcommittee to study ways and means of implementing its resolutions. France, the United Kingdom, and the United States have opposed full mandatory sanctions against South Africa, and France and the United Kingdom have abstained on the major Security Council resolutions on Namibia. On July 29, 1970, the Council asked member states to declare their nonrecognition of South Africa's jurisdiction over Namibia, to refrain from any acts implying such recognition, and to discourage commercial enterprises, loans, credit, trade, investment and tourism directly or indirectly to Namibia. In February, 1972, the Security Council invited the Secretary-General, in consultation with a three-member group from the Security Council, to consult with "all parties concerned" to enable the people of Namibia to exercise their right to self-determination and independence. In a second resolution the Council requested states to ensure that their corporations adhere to the principles of the Declaration of Human Rights in Namibia.

In 1970 the Security Council asked the International Court of Justice for an advisory opinion on the legal consequences of South Africa's continued presence in Namibia in violation of the Council's resolutions. In June, 1971, the Court issued its opinion in which, by 13-2, it declared that the continued presence of South Africa in Namibia is illegal and that South Africa is under obligation to withdraw its administration immediately. By 11-4 the Court also ruled that United Nations members are under obligation to recognize the illegality of South Africa's presence in Namibia and to refrain from any acts or dealings with the government of South Africa implying recognition of or lending support to such presence and administration.

For several years the puzzle in the Namibia question was how to make the United Nations declarations practical. Military intervention was rejected as too costly and dangerous. World opinion made little impact on the South African government. Economic costs to South Africa of measures imposed from outside as well as of internal resistance eventually softened their attitudes against granting independence to Namibia. In 1978 South Africa agreed to a plan put forward by five major western states that provides for a cease-fire and elections under United Nations supervision. South African acquiescence was obtained under threat of stepped-up economic sanctions. For a time the South West African People's Organization (SWAPO), the leading guerrilla resistance group in Namibia, refused to accept some of the details of the independence plan, but, under increasing pressure from black African states, reluctantly agreed. Assuming that all parties stick to their preliminary commitments, the end of colonial rule over Namibia should be realized.

Rhodesia

Rhodesia (formerly known as Southern Rhodesia) is a landlocked country with common boundaries with South Africa, Botswana, Zambia, and Mozambique. Its population, estimated at approximately 6.5 million, is less than 4 percent white with small numbers of Asiatics and Colored. Apartheid is practiced, and the white minority monopolize political power. The British controlled the territory after 1889 through the British South Africa Company, but in 1923 they granted Rhodesia internal self-government by means of a constitution. White domination became well entrenched under this arrangement, but a new constitution in 1961 further fortified and perpetuated white rule.

Since 1962 the Rhodesian situation has been under almost constant surveillance in the United Nations by the Special Committee on Decolonization (the Committee of Twenty-Four), the General Assembly, and the Security Council. The Committee of Twenty-Four took the position that Rhodesia was a non-self-governing territory within the terms of Article 73 of the Charter and that the United Kingdom was responsible for reporting to the United Nations on conditions in the territory and for advancing the territory toward independence under guarantees of full political rights for all its inhabitants. The British, on the other hand, considered that full internal autonomy had been granted to the Rhodesians under the 1923 constitution and that neither the United Kingdom nor the United Nations could intervene in the domestic affairs of the territory. In 1962 the General Assembly supported the contentions of its Special Committee and called upon the United Kingdom to undertake immediate constitutional changes to secure unqualified political rights for the entire population of Rhodesia.

The Security Council considered the Rhodesian question in 1963, but the United Kingdom exercised its veto to defeat a draft resolution inviting it to prevent the transfer of power to Rhodesia until a representative government had been established. By 1964, under the growing threat of a unilateral declaration of independence by the Rhodesian government headed by Ian Smith, the Security Council requested all states not to accept such a declaration and asked the United Kingdom to take action to prevent the threatened declaration and to implement the measures previously requested by the Assembly so that independence might be achieved under a democratic form of government.

On November 5, 1965, the General Assembly adopted a resolution calling upon the United Kingdom to employ all necessary measures including military force to prevent a unilateral declaration of independence. On November 11 the Smith regime issued the anticipated declaration. Reaction in the United Nations was swift. On the day of the declaration, both the Assembly and the British representative called for an urgent meeting of the Security Council. On the following day the Council condemned the action of the Smith government and called on all states not to recognize the illegal and racist regime and to refrain from rendering assistance to it. On November 20 the Council called upon all states to cut off supplies of arms and military equipment to Rhodesia and to break off voluntarily economic relations including an embargo on petroleum products. It also asked the United Kingdom to eliminate the authority of the minority regime and to establish democratic government in Rhodesia.

The legal position assumed by the British government throughout this period is an interesting phenomenon. As previously mentioned, the British maintained that in 1923 internal autonomy had been granted to the Rhodesians, that the territory did not, therefore, come under the non-self-governing provisions of Article 73 of the Charter, and that Britain could not report on, nor the United Nations inquire into, the internal affairs of the territory. However, the British also maintained that they were opposed to government by minority and that the Smith regime could not, unilaterally, declare its independence. During 1964 and 1965 the British attempted to negotiate terms of settlement with the Smith regime and insisted on the establishment of a majority government as a preliminary step to independence. The unilateral declaration of independence was considered by the British to be an act of rebellion and treason and to establish British authority as the only legitimate government in Rhodesia. Therefore, the British, from this point on, insisted on the legitimacy of United Nations measures to bring down the Smith regime and cooperated with the United Nations in most ways, although they refused to use armed force to put down the insurgency. Immediately after the Rhodesian declaration of independence, the British government cut off arms and economic aid to Rhodesia and invoked monetary, economic, and financial sanctions including the exclusion of Rhodesia from the sterling area.

Sanctions against Rhodesia have been invoked by the Security Council in three stages. The sanctions imposed on November 20, 1965, were voluntary and selective since states were merely requested to comply with a partial embargo of trade with the Rhodesians. In December, 1966, the Council invoked Article 41 of the Charter to require a mandatory boycott of a specified list of the chief exports from Rhodesia and of the supply of petroleum products to Rhodesia. When the Smith regime showed little strain from these limited measures, the Council in May, 1968, adopted comprehensive trade sanctions against Rhodesia, exempting only medical and educational supplies. The sanctions of 1966 and 1968 are the first imposed under Chapter VII of the Charter. In April, 1966, the Security Council set another precedent by authorizing the British to prevent, by the use of force if necessary, the shipment of oil intended for Rhodesia through Portuguese Mozambique ports. Thus the Council authorized a single state to carry out a Council decision under Chapter VII.

On March 1, 1970, the Smith regime proclaimed a republic in Rhodesia under a new constitution and the severing of all ties to the United Kingdom. The British government immediately declared this action to be illegal. On March 18 the Security Council condemned this proclamation by the illegal Smith regime; called on all states to refrain from recognizing or giving assistance to the regime; condemned South Africa and Portugal for continued relations with Rhodesia; demanded immediate withdrawal of South African police and military personnel from Rhodesia; called on states to compel their nationals and companies to conform to previously imposed sanctions; and urged greater assistance to the people of Rhodesia in their struggle for freedom and independence.

The series of United Nations measures failed to bring about the collapse of the Smith government. South Africa continued to trade with Rhodesia and to furnish other forms of assistance, thus thwarting the intended effect of economic sanctions. Gradually South Africa's enthusiasm for this relationship cooled, and the Vorster government applied increasing pressures on the Smith regime for a resolution of the problem. Other states, too, contributed to the ineffectiveness of the trade embargo. Mozambique, before independence from Portugal, served as another outlet for Rhodesian products. Through concealment of sources or destinations of goods in transshipment and through the use of false invoices, several European countries, such as Switzerland, served as surreptitious trading partners of Rhodesia. Portugal in late 1977 and Switzerland in January, 1978, tightened their controls over illegal trade with Rhodesia. The United States, in violation of its United Nations commitment, adopted the Byrd amendment in 1971 authorizing the purchase of Rhodesian chrome; after repeated attempts the amendment was repealed in 1977.

Some of Rhodesia's neighbors were very adversely affected by the sanctions against Rhodesia. Zambia was most seriously hurt by the cutoff of transportation facilities running through Rhodesia and by their previous dependence upon a major source of electricity in Rhodesia. A new pipeline, opened in 1968 through Tanzania, restored Zambia's source of oil. The Chinese built a new railroad to give Zambia a transportation outlet in Tanzania. The United Nations and the British and other governments have provided subsidies to offset part of the losses.

Under pressure from many sources, Smith announced in 1976 his acceptance of the principle of majority rule within two years. Internal troubles contributed to his decision. Each year the Rhodesian economic indicators became increasingly unfavorable, white disaffection built up, black guerrilla resistance spread, and the cost of defense measures strained government resources. In 1977 the United Kingdom and the United States developed a new set of proposals for the transition to majority rule. These proposals, which included the use of a United Nations peacekeeping force, received widespread endorsement but were rejected by the Smith regime and by the guerrilla leaders in Rhodesia.

In March, 1978, Smith made an agreement with three moderate black leaders on a transition to black majority rule by the end of the year. Smith claimed that these leaders, Bishop Abel Muzorewa, Reverend Ndabaningi Sithole, and Chief Jeremiah Chirau, represented 85 percent of the black population of Rhodesia. This arrangement was vigorously denounced by the Patriotic Front guerrilla leaders, by the five neighboring black-controlled "front-line states," by the Organization of African Unity, and by the United Nations Security Council. The Organization of African Unity recognized the Patriotic Front as the only legitimate representatives of the people of Zimbabwe (the African name for Rhodesia). The leaders of the Patriotic Front were Joshua Nkomo, with headquarters in Zambia, and Robert Mugabe, with headquarters in Mozambique. In the Security Council debates, the black leaders with whom Smith had negotiated were repeatedly accused by African representatives of being "black African puppets."

The Security Council resolution of March 14, 1978, "condemns all attempts and manoeuvres by the illegal regime aimed at the retention of power by a racist minority and at preventing the achievement of independence by Zimbabwe." It also calls on the United Kingdom and the Secretary-General to take measures to achieve genuine decolonization in Rhodesia. Because of some of the wording, Canada, France, the Federal Republic of Germany, the United Kingdom and the United States abstained, although they disapproved the unilateral action of the Smith government. Unless all factions in Rhodesia (or Zimbabwe) can reach a reconciliation, guerrilla warfare will be a permanent condition in the area.

PROBLEMS AFTER POLITICAL INDEPENDENCE

Although self-determination and self-rule are attractive goals for politically dominated peoples, independence is no panacea, and the problems following political liberation may seem greater than those previously surmounted. All former colonies are economically under-developed and must face the dilemmas of gradually overcoming poverty, disease, hunger, and illiteracy. Both outside aid and internal savings are required to build a self-generating economy. Without population controls gains in total production may be partially or completely wiped out on a per capita basis. Mini-states lack the economic base to build a viable economic structure independent of heavy reliance on others. Frustrations and impatience with slow progress are almost certain to accompany the struggle for develop-ment. The international community may seem deaf to the appeals of the poor nations for special concessions to help them escape from poverty. The self-interests of the rich are not likely to identify strongly with the welfare of impoverished peoples nor to be out-weighed by humanitarian compassion.

Once the unifying force of the common goal of independence has been removed, the political vitality of the new state must also be strengthened. The development of political consciousness or nation building must be undertaken. Enlistment of all elements of the population is required for rapid development. Heroes of the independence movement may lose their former luster as the hard-ships and frustrations of economic, social, and political development are faced. Fratricidal factional contests must be avoided in order not to dissipate the energies and resources of the new state. Stability in government is difficult to achieve. The struggles for power in Vietnam, Pakistan, Indonesia, Nigeria, and Ghana are but a few reminders of the cleavages that may interfere with the stability required for goal attainment.

The struggle for self-government is a revolution that has nearly run its course. But out of that struggle has emerged the new North-South confrontation of which the world is increasingly conscious. Whether the nations of the globe with the aid of international machinery and cooperative efforts can successfully resolve the new challenges remains to be proven. At this stage it seems certain that the new problems are no less formidable than the old.

14

❦

Varieties
of
Regionalism

One phenomenon of the period since 1945 is the rapid growth in the number of intergovernmental regional organizations. In fact, regional organizations founded since 1945 outnumber those of a universal nature by approximately a two-to-one ratio. Obviously, not all regional agencies perform highly significant functions, but some have assumed important roles in world affairs. The contributions and deficiencies of the major regional organizations is the subject matter of this chapter.

THE PROS AND CONS OF REGIONALISM

Regional organizations are variously defined, often on the basis of geographical proximity of the members. Such definitions are subject to the difficulty of delimiting geographic regions, for there is no general agreement on any natural divisions into which the world may be clearly and conveniently divided. Therefore, while geography may be one factor that aids in determining the regional character of many organizations, the lack of proximity of the members or the failure of an organization to conform to a neat generally recognizable geographic area will not be decisive in excluding certain agencies from consideration in this chapter. The United States, for example, is a member of several organizations that claim regional status and that reach to almost every point of the compass, thus variously identifying the United States with the North Atlantic, American, and Southeast Asian areas. None of the organizations involved conforms to any natural geographic region. The North Atlantic area opens to question whether an ocean represents a unifying factor or a barrier for determining a region; the inclusion of Greece and Turkey in the membership of the North Atlantic Treaty Organization throws further doubt on conformity to regional limits. The now defunct Southeast Asia Treaty Organization was *for* the protection of Southeast Asian countries but it was dominated *by* non-Asian states, which formed a majority of its membership. The membership of the Organization of American States includes all states within North, South, and Central America except Canada, but geographers have never viewed both continents as a single well defined region. The British Commonwealth is also frequently classified as a regional organization, although its members are dispersed around the globe.

As the term is used in this chapter, a "regional organization" is a segment of the world bound together by a common set of objectives based on geographical, social, cultural, economic, or political ties and possessing a formal structure provided for in formal intergovernmental agreements. Although bilateral arrangements can qualify under such a definition, attention will be focused here only on arrangements involving three or more members. At the other end of the scale, limited actual membership in organizations open to all states does not affect their global character since their objectives point toward universality. A regional organization is intended to appeal only to a specified category of states, less than global in scope.

In the twentieth century a cleavage has developed between certain advocates of universalism and some advocates of regionalism. Both sets of antagonists agree that the international system must eventually be modified from the primacy of the nation-state in the direction of a partial surrender of state sovereignty to larger political units. The adversaries concur on the goal of world order and stability and on the inadequacy of the state-centered system for this purpose. Extreme universalists and regionalists each see their own approach to order and stability as the *only* feasible alternative to the deficiencies of the present system. Thus a dichotomy is set up in which the choice is presented as either universalism or regionalism.

The regionalists often include the following claims for the superiority of regionalism over universalism:

1. There is a natural tendency toward regionalism based on the homogeneity of interests, traditions, and values within small groups of neighboring states.

2. Political, economic, and social integration is more easily attained among a lesser number of states within a limited geographic area than on a global basis.

3. Regional economic cooperation provides more efficient economic units than the smaller states, and these larger units can compete successfully in world markets.

4. Local threats to the peace are more willingly and promptly dealt with by the governments of that area than by disinterested states at greater distances from the scene of conflict.

5. By combining states into regional groupings a global balance of power will be maintained and world peace and security will be promoted.

6. The world is not ready to establish global authority sufficient to maintain world peace and promote world welfare. Regionalism is the first step in gaining experience and building areas of consensus toward eventual intergovernmental coordination or integration.

7. Universalists fail to take into account the heterogeneity of political, economic, social, and geographical factors throughout the world that militate against global unity. These differences can be more easily accommodated within a regional framework.

On the other hand, the universalists frequently argue that the following reasons substantiate their preference for universalism over regionalism:

1. World interdependence has created an increasing number of problems that require global solutions. Political, economic, and social problems reach across regional boundaries.

2. Regional resources are often inadequate to resolve the problems of states within the region.

3. Since peace is indivisible only a world organization can deal effectively with threats to the peace that may, if unchecked, spread beyond local or regional limits.

4. Only a universal organization can provide an adequate check on the power of a large state that can often dominate the other members of a regional arrangement.

5. Sanctions against an aggressor are usually ineffective if applied on a regional basis because of sources of aid to the aggressor from outside the region.

6. Regions are imprecise and impermanent. No agreement can be reached on a system of regions into which the globe can be conveniently divided.

7. Regional alliances provide the basis for rivalries and competition for military supremacy among regions leading to greater possibilities for major wars.

8. The existence of numerous, moderately successful universal organizations

demonstrates the desire of governments and peoples to cooperate on a global basis without the necessity of first using regional organizations as laboratories for gradually developing enlarged areas of consensus or community.

Although the claims of the universalists and regionalists, by creating a dichotomy between the two approaches, might seem to preclude an accommodation between them, such an accommodation in fact exists. The choice is not necessarily one of either regionalism or universalism but allows for both regionalism and universalism coexisting in a sometimes competing and sometimes mutually supporting relationship. The relationship of regional with universal organizations may be either antagonistic or harmonious.

In her book *The Majority of One*, Minerva Etzioni discusses the concept of compatibility and incompatibility between regional and universal organizations. Compatibility is defined as the relationship between two organizations by which "the activities of one do not undermine those of the other and vice versa."[1] The antagonism between regionalism and universalism occurs only when the jurisdiction and functions of organizations at the two levels are incompatible. If universal obligations, in case of conflict, prevail over regional obligations, and if regional agencies submit to supervision by global agencies or respond positively to their requests for supportive action, then the basis for a compatible relationship exists. These harmonious or conflicting relationships will be examined with regard to the regional organizations described throughout this chapter. A combination of regionalism and universalism serves to promote the national interests of most states in their advance beyond unilateralism and self-help.

The nature of the problem to be solved determines whether it will best respond to regional or to universal treatment. If the consequences of a problem are regional in nature or scope, then a regional solution is appropriate. On the other hand, a military security system or a form of economic regionalism that tends to foster antagonisms or discriminatory policies toward other states or blocs of states may be considered as subversive of and incompatible with world order and justice through universalism. In determining the balance to be sought between the roles of regional and universal organizations, the effect of each action in promoting order, restraint, and international cooperation should serve as norma-

---

[1] Minerva M. Etzioni, *The Majority of One: Towards a Theory of Regional Compatibility* (Beverly Hills, Cal.: Sage Publications, 1970), p. 18.

tive guides, while actions that increase international tensions and rivalries should be avoided. Both regional and global agencies can contribute to the promotion of the general welfare of humanity, but the myopic view fostered by rival nationalistic movements prevalent in today's world will continue to bolster the misuse or nonuse of both levels of agencies for immediate, narrow, national advantage.

REGIONALISM UNDER THE UNITED NATIONS CHARTER

At the time that the Charter of the United Nations was being formulated, the forces favoring regionalism were sufficiently strong and diverse to require an accommodation for regional organizations within the universal framework. Winston Churchill at first favored the regionalist over the universalist approach to world order, and the Latin American states formed a strong pressure bloc for a recognition of the legitimacy and importance of the role of regional agencies in promoting the aims of international peace, security, and welfare. However, at the San Francisco conference a proposal to provide specific arrangements for regional agencies in the economic and social work of the United Nations was defeated. Consequently, all of the Charter provisions for regional arrangements are limited to the role of regional organizations in the maintenance of international peace and security. However, in practice, regional agencies are extensively utilized in the economic and social spheres, since nothing in the Charter precludes their establishment and since their utility is widely recognized. Those regional economic and social agencies that are part of the United Nations official structure are created under the broad authority of the General Assembly and the Economic and Social Council to establish subsidiary bodies to assist in carrying out their functions.

The primary provisions of the Charter concerning regional arrangements are found in Chapter VIII containing only three articles (Articles 52-54). The most important principles of Chapter VIII are the following: (1) regional agencies may exist for dealing with such issues of international peace and security as are appropriate for regional action as long as their activities are consistent with the purposes and principles of the United Nations; (2) states are encouraged to settle local disputes through regional agencies before referring them to the Security Council; (3) the Security Council may, in turn, utilize such agencies for the settlement of local disputes; (4) with the exception of action against enemy states resulting from World War II, no enforcement action shall be taken by regional agencies without the authorization of the Security Council; (5) the Security Council shall be kept fully informed of activities undertaken or contemplated by regional agencies for the maintenance of peace and security.

These principles clearly were intended to establish that, in case of conflict between the jurisdiction of a regional organization and the United Nations, universalism should take precedence over regionalism. However, through interpretation of such phrases as "local disputes," "enforcement action," and "fully informed," and through intermittent debate concerning the right of the Security Council to assume priority over disputes while they are under consideration by regional organizations, the supremacy of the universalist claim has been substantially undermined.

The most numerous test cases tending to lessen United Nations authority have involved the Organization of American States (OAS). Because of its dominant position within the OAS, the United States has preferred to use regional channels for dealing with conflicts within the Western Hemisphere. In 1954, on the grounds that the situation was under consideration by the OAS, Guatemala was denied access to the Security Council in bringing its charge of aggression against Nicaragua and Honduras. In 1960 Cuba's charges of aggression committed by the United States, and, in 1963, the Haitian complaint against the Dominican Republic were deferred by the Security Council, honoring the priority claimed by the OAS. Although the right of any party to a dispute to appeal to the Security Council at any time is not denied, expediency and political pressures often dictate leaving the dispute to regional consideration.

Article 53 forbids the taking of "enforcement action" by regional agencies without the authorization of the Security Council. Articles 41 and 42 of the Charter specify that the kinds of enforcement available include both military and nonmilitary measures. Yet the meaning of the term "enforcement action" in Article 53 has been, in practice, systematically narrowed to exclude nonmilitary sanctions applied by regional agencies. In 1960 the necessity for the Security Council to approve economic sanctions against the Dominican Republic imposed through OAS action was denied on the grounds that approval only of military action was required by Article 53. The meaning of "enforcement action" was further narrowed during the Dominican crisis of 1965, when the United States was supported in its claim that United States marines and OAS military contingents in the Dominican Republic were there as "peace-keeping forces," not as agents of enforcement within the meaning of Article 53.

Similarly, the requirement of Article 54 that the Security Council at all times be kept fully informed of activities "undertaken or in contemplation" by regional agencies has been eroded through practice. The kinds and scope of information have been limited and "after the fact" instead of keeping the Council fully informed during the planning stages in order that United Nations supervision can be maintained throughout all phases of a dispute or conflict. The Security Council has acquiesced in accepting perfunctory reports from regional organizations outlining in documentary form the results only of actions.

One of the most significant modifications of the Charter through interpretation and state practice applying to regional associations has developed, not under Chapter VIII, but under Article 51, dealing with the right of states to take measures for collective as well as individual self-defense against armed attack. Such a right is limited by requirements that the Security Council be immediately informed of such measures, that the Council's authority and responsibility for maintaining peace and security not be affected thereby, and that the right of self-defense exists only until the Security Council has taken necessary measures to restore and maintain international peace and security. No specific mention of regional arrangements is made in Article 51, but the reference to collective self-defense opens the door to the creation and use of regional organizations for this purpose.

Few regional arrangements capable of mobilization for collective self-defense existed in 1945. The Union of American Republics, as the forerunner of the OAS, and the League of Arab States (Arab League) were the only regional agencies that included collective self-defense among their objectives. The breakdown of East-West cooperation after World War II and the increasing tensions of the Cold War presaged the deadlock of the Security Council on issues involving the maintenance of peace and security in which the major powers had important interests.

The great powers sought security through a series of regional pacts in which the United States took the earliest initiative. The first postwar development of this type did not receive its main impetus from the Cold War. In 1947 the Inter-American Treaty of Reciprocal Assistance (Rio Treaty) established a regional security system for the Western Hemisphere. Other United States-sponsored alliances for military defense quickly followed and were aimed at bolstering the emerging Communist containment policy of the United States government. These included the North Atlantic Treaty Organization (NATO) formed in 1949; the ANZUS Pacific Security Pact in 1951; and the Southeast Asia Treaty Organization (SEATO) in 1954 (disbanded in 1976). Although the United States is not an official member, it has participated in the deliberations and activities of the Central Treaty Organization (CENTO), formerly known as the Council of the Baghdad Pact, dating from 1955. Also in 1955 the Soviet Union responded to the threat of military encirclement by setting up the Warsaw Treaty Organization (WTO) as a capstone to a series of bilateral security treaties among East European states.

Although Article 51 of the Charter emphasizes the supreme authority of the Security Council in matters of self-defense, this article has become an escape hatch from the obligations of universalism toward a revival of an alliance system contributing to a compartmentalization and fragmentation of any potential global unity. The major powers interpret the collective self-defense clause as justifying the creation of military security alliances. These alliances, in turn, exacerbate existing attitudes of divisiveness and hostility. The Security Council's supposedly preeminent role in self-defense situations cannot be exercised when a major power is involved if that power refuses to inform the Council of its defensive measures, as required by Article 51, or when the veto is available to block Council action. The growth of opposing systems of alliances as instruments of collective self-defense attests to the breakdown of cooperation among states with competing ideologies and to the inability of the United Nations to act effectively when the national interests of major powers come into conflict. The Charter attempts to assign to the Security Council ultimate and supreme responsibility for maintaining peace and security, but it provides the Council with inadequate means for enforcement, and it builds into the system the possibilities for deadlock and stalemate. Thus, any hopes for a Council-imposed solution for a situation involving one of the great powers are illusory. Only an era of cooperation and good will among nations or a radically different system of international controls could eliminate the reliance of states upon self-help and collective defense arrangements.

MULTIPURPOSE REGIONAL ORGANIZATIONS

Regional organizations may be classified in several ways based on the nature or scope of their functions or memberships, or possibly on the degree of eventual integration that is sought. One useful and instructive method of classification has been developed by Lynn H. Miller, who divides all regional organizations into three general types, which he labels as (1) cooperative, (2) alliance, or (3) functional.[2] Miller's categories are based on "the single variable of the *security orientation* of component states as expressed through the organizational structure."[3]

For purposes of this chapter, a variation of the above categories will be adopted. Instead of the "cooperative" classification, a more inclusive category of "multipurpose" organizations will be used. The terms "alliance" and "functional" will be retained, and a fourth distinct category of United Nations Regional Commissions will be added.

These latter regional commissions fit neatly into no other group since they form a link between the universal and the regional systems and serve to promote universal goals within specific geographic areas through regional agencies established as a part of the United Nations system. The multipurpose organizations are those whose broad aims and activities reach across the lines that divide political and military matters from those generally classified as economic and social. Alliance-type organizations are those whose military and political orientation is intended to provide security against external actors. Functional organizations are those that promote economic, social, or political collaboration with little or no regard to security factors. The dividing line between all other categories and the multipurpose category is somewhat arbitrary and subjective and is determined by the range and variety of activities pursued by the regional organization. The accompanying chart includes the most important regional organizations within this fourfold classification system.

As defined above, multipurpose organizations are characterized by the range and scope of their functions, aims, and activities. The examination of several multipurpose organizations will serve to demonstrate these characteristics and to illustrate the significance of these agencies in the conduct of world affairs.

Organization of American States (OAS)

The OAS is in several respects the most significant of the multipurpose regional organizations. This significance is established on the basis of the elaborate structure and functions of the OAS and its long, continuous history.

---

[2] Lynn H. Miller, "Regional Organizations and Subordinate Systems," in Louis J. Cantori and Steven L. Spiegel, *The International Politics of Regions: A Comparative Approach* (Englewood Cliffs, N.J.: Prentice-Hall, 1970), pp. 357-78.
[3] *Ibid.,* p. 361.

MAJOR INTERGOVERNMENTAL REGIONAL ORGANIZATIONS

I. Multipurpose Organizations

Title	Acronym	Established	Membership (1976)
Organization of American States (originally, International Union of American Republics)	OAS	1948 (1890)	24
League of Arab States (Arab League)		1945	20
Organization of African Unity	OAU	1963	47
Commonwealth (formerly, British Commonwealth of Nations)		1926	36
French Community		1958	19
Council of Europe		1949	18
Organization of Central American States	ODECA, or OCAS	1952	5
Common Afro-Mauritian Organization	OCAM	1966	10

II. Alliance Systems

Title	Acronym	Established	Membership (1976)
North Atlantic Treaty Organization	NATO	1949	15
Warsaw Treaty Organization	WTO	1955	7
Australia, New Zealand, United States Security Treaty Organization	ANZUS	1952	3
Western European Union	WEU	1954	7
Central Treaty Organization (formerly, Baghdad Pact)	CENTO	1959 (1955)	4

III. Functional Organizations

Title	Acronym	Established	Membership (1976)
Benelux Economic Union	BENELUX	1948	3
European Coal and Steel Community	ECSC	1952	9
European Economic Community	EEC	1958	9 + 6 assoc.
European Free Trade Association	EFTA	1960	6 + 1 assoc.
European Atomic Energy Community	EURATOM	1958	9
Organization for Economic Cooperation and Development	OECD	1961	24
Latin American Free Trade Association	LAFTA	1961	11
Association of Southeast Asian Nations	ASEAN	1967	5
Central American Common Market	CACM	1961	5
Council for Technical Cooperation in South and Southeast Asia (Colombo Plan)		1950	27

Council for Mutual Economic Assistance	COMECON, or CMEA	1949	9
Inter-American Development Bank	IDB	1959	24
African Development Bank	AFDB	1964	41
Asian Development Bank	ASDB	1966	41
Central American Bank of Economic Integration	CABEI	1961	5
European Investment Bank	EIB	1958	9
Nordic Council	NC	1952	5
Conseil de l'Entente	CE	1959	5
Organization of Petroleum Exporting Countries	OPEC	1960	13

IV. United Nations Regional Commissions

Title	Acronym	Established	Membership (1976)
Economic Commission for Europe	ECE	1947	34
Economic and Social Commission for Asia and the Pacific	ESCAP	1947	32 + 4 assoc.
Economic Commission for Latin America	ECLA	1948	32 + 2 assoc.
Economic Commission for Africa	ECA	1958	47 + 4 assoc.
Economic Commission for Western Asia	ECWA	1974	12

The First International Conference of American States in 1890 authorized the establishment of a permanent organization under the title of the International Union of American Republics. As the continuous organ of the union, a central bureau was set up in Washington, D.C., for the primary purpose of disseminating commercial information. Successive Inter-American Conferences in the early twentieth century broadened the functions of the bureau to include a wide range of noncommercial activities. In 1910, in a major reorganization, the title of the organization was changed to the Union of American Republics, and the bureau became the Pan-American Union. A further restructuring in 1948 resulted in the adoption of the present name, the Organization of American States, and the Pan-American Union became the General Secretariat. In 1967 the Third Special Inter-American Conference meeting in Buenos Aires approved a series of Charter amendments that again significantly altered the previous organizational structure. These Buenos Aires amendments took effect in 1970.

The OAS operates through a General Assembly, which meets annually and is designated as the supreme organ. A Permanent Council, consisting of one representative of ambassadorial rank per member state, has its seat in Washington, D.C. The Permanent

Council performs special pacific-settlement functions in addition to serving as the preparatory committee for the General Assembly and carrying out other directives of the Assembly. Two other councils, the Inter-American Economic and Social Council and the Inter-American Council for Education, Science and Culture, supervise extensive programs, draft treaties, and initiate conferences under Assembly guidance. In crisis situations a Meeting of Consultation of ministers of foreign affairs may be summoned at the request of member states. An Inter-American Juridical Committee acts as an advisory body to the OAS and promotes the development and codification of international law within the hemisphere. Other agencies include specialized conferences, specialized organizations in such fields as agriculture, child welfare, women's affairs, health, and Indian affairs, and an Inter-American Commission on Human Rights. The General Secretariat, headed by a secretary-general and employing more than 1,200 staff workers, serves as the administering and coordinating arm of the OAS. The headquarters is in Washington, D.C., and the annual budget is in excess of 40 million dollars.

The aims of the OAS are as comprehensive and diffuse as its structure. These include (1) strengthening the peace and security of the continent, (2) preventing difficulties and ensuring the pacific settlement of disputes among members, (3) providing common action in the event of aggression, (4) seeking the solution of political, juridical, and economic problems among members, and (5) promoting by cooperative action the economic, social, and cultural development of the member states.

The OAS operates in part as an alliance for collective defense. In 1947 a special conference at Rio de Janeiro drew up the Inter-American Treaty of Reciprocal Assistance (Rio Pact). This pact and the OAS charter adopted at Bogotá in 1948 (as amended in 1967) serve as the legal basis for the hemispheric security system. The Rio Pact declares "that an armed attack by any State against an American State shall be considered as an attack against all the American States." This principle is common to the military-alliance arrangements discussed in the next section of this chapter. While the OAS serves a wide range of other functions, this feature establishes an identity of purpose with such organizations as the North Atlantic Treaty Organization and the Warsaw Treaty Organization. The Rio Pact also defined an inter-American security zone extending several hundred miles into the oceans and from pole to pole within which an attack would be treated as if it were made upon the land area of a state. Members of the OAS were obligated to provide individual assistance to the victim of an aggression until a Meeting of Consultation (either of ministers of foreign affairs or of the OAS council) or the United Nations Security Council recommended a course of collective action.

The collective defense features of the OAS have served more as a warning against potential external aggression that might threaten states within the hemisphere than as a defense against military attack. During the 1950s the organs of OAS, in response to United States initiative, adopted a series of resolutions urging safeguards against Communist subversion of individual states. Indirect aggression was thus viewed as the major concern of the defense system. The emergence of Communism in Cuba served as "proof" of indirect aggression and established a base for the further spread of Communist doctrine. Cuba was suspended from participation in the OAS, and Communism was declared to be incompatible with the principles of the OAS. The only direct military threat was the placing of Soviet missiles and missile launchers on Cuban soil in 1962. While the United States carried out all measures for getting the weapons removed, the OAS indicated its willingness to cooperate in collective defensive measures. OAS members served as willing partners, and OAS agencies as convenient tools in supporting United States attitudes in the Cold War.

The OAS has played a much larger role in maintaining peace and promoting the pacific settlement of disputes among states within the hemisphere than it has as a collective defense agency against outside aggression. In these inter-American conflicts the council of the OAS or the ministers of foreign affairs acting as an Organ of Consultation have served as the instruments through which action was taken. In several cases the assistance of the Inter-American Peace Commission as a fact-finding and conciliation agency was vital to a solution. Among the disputes dealt with by the OAS are the following: Costa Rica and Nicaragua (1948-49, 1955-56, 1959); Honduras and Nicaragua (1957); Venezuela and the Dominican Republic (1960-61); Venezuela and Cuba (1963-64, 1967); the Dominican Republic and Haiti (1950, 1963-65); and Panama and the United States (1964). The OAS was particularly effective in bringing about a resolution of the issues in the so-called soccer war between El Salvador and Honduras in 1969-70. The organization also played a supporting role to that of the United States in the interventions into the internal situations in Guatemala in 1954 and in the Dominican Republic in 1965. In the latter case the United States was hard pressed to muster the necessary two-thirds vote for an OAS force to partially replace United States military contingents unilaterally dispatched to Santo Domingo. Many Latin American states resented the pressures from the "colossus of the North" to turn a unilateral violation of domestic jurisdiction into a face-saving collective "peace-keeping" operation under which the United States could claim immunity from United Nations responsibility and jurisdiction.

Throughout their history the OAS and its forerunners have served as instruments of economic and social cooperation. The earliest activities of the International Union of American Republics concentrated on commercial concerns. After World War II economic and social development in Latin America was treated by the United States as secondary to the rebuilding of western Europe. As a result, the Latin American states, prior to 1961, relied more on the United Nations Economic Commission for Latin America (ECLA) than on the OAS for promoting their aspirations for accelerating the development process. In addition to its direct programs, the ECLA encouraged the founding of the Latin American Free Trade Association (LAFTA), the Central American Common Market (CACM), and the Inter-American Development Bank (IDB). After a period of intensified anti-United States feeling, culminating in the physical attacks upon Vice-President Nixon in 1958 in Peru and in Venezuela, a special meeting of foreign ministers in Washington endorsed a number of new economic measures to be carried out through OAS.

The resurgence of OAS economic and social development activities was manifested in the Charter of Punta del Este, which, in 1961, outlined the terms of the Alliance for Progress. The purpose of the alliance was to accelerate the rate of economic and social development by mobilizing the energies and resources of Latin American peoples and governments. Both national and cooperative programs were stressed. A minimum per capita income growth rate of 2.5 percent was set as a target, and additional goals included increased investment and more equitable distribution of income, diversification of national production, more rapid industrialization, increased agricultural productivity and land reform, the elimination of adult illiteracy, the expansion of educational facilities including vocational and technical training, improved health and medical facilities with a target of a five-year increase in life expectancy by 1970, construction of low-cost housing, price stabilization, and the promotion of economic integration. The total investment needs for accomplishing these goals was set at 100 billion dollars for a ten-year period with 80 percent of the total to be generated internally in each developing state and the remaining 20 billion dollars to come from outside sources, not the least of which was to be the United States government.

The results of the Alliance for Progress have been disappointing. The ambitious goals of the program have generally fallen short of realization. The rate of economic growth measured in terms of per capita income has averaged far below the target of 2.5 percent, although a few states have exceeded the goal. As a result of their continued frustrations, Latin American governments have become staunch advocates of the United Nations Conference on Trade and Development (UNCTAD), a combined effort with other under-developed states to establish a claim for special concessions from the developed states for the purpose of closing the economic gap between rich and poor nations.

The OAS Charter is technically compatible with the United Nations Charter and contains more references to the role of OAS as a regional organization under Articles 52–54 of the United Nations Charter than are found in the basic document of any other regional organization. However, as pointed out in the previous section of this chapter, through narrowed interpretation of the obligations of the OAS to submit to United Nations supervision of enforcement actions, the role of the United Nations in the realm of peace and security has been gradually eroded. In practice, according to Minerva Etzioni, the relationship had been transformed from one of compatibility to one of incompatibility.[4] The United States, as the hegemonic power within the OAS, has used the organization for its own purposes and has insulated these actions from effective United Nations control and responsibility. Even the military measures used in Guatemala in 1965 were first converted from unilateral to regional status and then claimed as "peacekeeping" forces immune from the requirement of prior Security Council approval of enforcement measures. Ellen Frey-Wouters sums up the results of the transformation of the security and peaceful settlement provisions of the OAS Charter from compatibility to incompatibility with the United Nations Charter in these terms:

> The primary role of the Latin American members of the OAS in most collective security cases has been to provide a multilateral legitimacy for essentially unilateral U.S. action. The OAS serves to carry out the extra-continental objectives of the U.S., free from any control by the UN. It can be expected that the OAS will continue, at least in the immediate future, to be misused as a means to intervene against regimes of states which do not meet with the approval of the U.S.[5]

More recently, however, the ability of the United States to use the OAS as such a willing tool of United States foreign policy shows

[4] Etzioni, *Majority of One, passim.*
[5] Ellen Frey-Wouters, "The Prospects for Regionalism in World Affairs," in Richard A. Falk and Cyril E. Black, eds., *The Future of the International Legal Order* (Princeton, N.J.: Princeton University Press, 1969), Vol. I, p. 539.

some signs of weakening as Latin American states assert greater independence from United States dominance.

Organization of African Unity (OAU)

The OAU is one of the newest multipurpose regional organizations and is the largest in membership. The OAU emerged in 1963 as an amalgamation of several former subregional groupings of states in Africa. From its original membership of thirty it has grown to include forty-seven states. All members are from Africa, since the Charter does not permit non-African states to join. Only independent and sovereign states are eligible, and admission is by simple majority of the members after notice is given by the applicant state of its intention to accede to the charter.

The purposes of the OAU are the following: (1) to promote the unity and solidarity of the African states; (2) to cooperate and coordinate efforts to achieve a better life for the peoples of Africa; (3) to defend the sovereignty, territorial integrity, and independence of the African states; (4) to eradicate all forms of colonialism from Africa; and (5) to promote international cooperation with due regard to the Charter of the United Nations and the Universal Declaration of Human Rights. The basic principles of the organization, in addition to those implicit in the purposes stated above, include (1) peaceful settlement of disputes by negotiation, mediation, conciliation, or arbitration; (2) unreserved condemnation of political assassination and subversive activities; and (3) affirmation of a policy of nonalignment with regard to all blocs. The condemnation of political assassination and subversive activities was prompted by a series of charges against the government of Ghana by neighboring states, which culminated in the assassination of President Sylvanus Olympio of Togo on the eve of the conference for the adoption of the OAU charter.

At the inception of the OAU, Ghana also led an effort to establish a central political organization with power to formulate a common foreign policy, common planning for economic development, a common currency, and a common defense system. These suggestions for the surrender of national sovereignty were unacceptable to most of the heads of states and governments that approved the charter. The Ghanaian proposal for organic political union was rejected in favor of a loose organization with a limited functional approach to unity.

The supreme organ of the OAU is the annual Assembly of Heads of State and Government. The agenda for the supreme organ is prepared by the Council of Ministers, which meets twice a year to supervise the general work of the organization and which is also called into emergency session when crises so demand. The Council of Ministers is charged with the responsibility of implementing the decisions of the Assembly of Heads of State and Government. A permanent General Secretariat carries on the continuous activities of the organization and provides necessary support for the periodic meetings of the policy-determining organs. The General Secretariat is headed by an administrative secretary-general, a title highly significant in designating the limited initiative conferred upon this officer. Five functional specialized commissions and a Commission of Mediation, Conciliation and Arbitration complete the organizational structure of the OAU.

In bringing about peaceful settlement of disputes among African states, the OAU has a mixed record. In an Algerian-Moroccan border dispute in which fighting broke out in 1963, the efforts of individual African heads of state, an emergency session of the OAU council, and the appointment of an ad hoc commission contributed to a gradual lessening of tensions and hostilities, although no permanent settlement was ever formalized. From 1964 until 1967 guerrilla fighting occurred along the borders of Somalia with Ethiopia and Kenya over the claims of Somalia to the right of incorporation into Somalia of territories occupied by Somali minorities in adjoining states. In spite of attempts at settlement by the OAU, sporadic fighting continued for four years until a reconciliation at the 1967 OAU Assembly of Heads of State. In 1966 and 1967 the political activities of refugees from Rwanda who had fled to Burundi caused tensions between the two countries. The Assembly of Heads of State in 1966 requested President Mobutu of the Congo to mediate the dispute, and his efforts were successful.

In two other disputes disagreement among OAU members led to frustration and stalemate. In the Congo in 1964 and 1965 rebel actions against the Tshombe government split the sympathies of African states. An emergency meeting of the Council of Ministers in 1964 agreed upon the appointment of a ten-nation conciliation commission, but neither this commission nor a subsequent meeting of the council could concur on any course of action. The dispute subsided with the defeat of the rebels and with subsequent changes in the leadership of the Congo government. In the Biafran revolt against the Nigerian government in 1967-70 and the resulting civil war, the OAU proved impotent as a force for conciliation. The majority actions of the OAU were partial to Nigerian sovereignty and violated the requirement of neutrality, which is necessary for conciliation. Some African states supported the Biafran cause, and the OAU made no contribution to the final settlement, which came about by military action.

As might be expected, the failures of the OAU in dispute settlement or amelioration occurred in those situations in which the members were split in their support of the contending parties. Relative success resulted from near unanimity on a course of action or from a desire to provide neutral pressures for a cessation of hostilities.

In numerous areas the OAU has worked closely with the United Nations. In attitudes and sanctions against the white-dominated regime in Rhodesia, the OAU organs have anticipated and pressed for effective United Nations action. Realizing their own lack of military and economic capacity, the African states have agitated through the OAU, the General Assembly, and the Security Council for British measures and United Nations sanctions to bring down the Ian Smith government. Reciprocally the Security Council in 1965, immediately after the unilateral declaration of independence by the Smith regime, specifically called on the OAU to assist in the implementation of its resolution on Rhodesia. Also in 1965, in the area of economic and social cooperation, the OAU and the United Nations Economic Commission for Africa signed an agreement for mutual cooperation on a continuing basis to facilitate economic and social development in Africa.

The OAU in its short life has survived several crises that have threatened its disintegration. Its effectiveness has not lived up to inflated expectations, and its weakness against targets in South Africa, Rhodesia, and Portugal has been painfully apparent. Recently its budget has been cut to more realistic proportions. Although judging its permanent value may be premature, the OAU's modest accomplishments in political, economic, and social matters seem sufficient to justify its past efforts and to predict its continued utility.

League of Arab States (Arab League)

Established in 1945 with seven original members, the Arab League expanded by 1974 to a membership of twenty states. The elements contributing to basic unity among the members include a common religion, language, and culture. Since 1948 a shared hostility toward Israel has provided a powerful motivating force for collective action, but other factors have frustrated this potential for mustering full and united opposition to Israel. The league has been acutely split into factions, and Egypt's aspirations for leadership of a Pan-Arab movement have run into opposition from other Arab rulers. Individual member states have gained little support from the league as a collectivity in their wars and guerrilla activities against Israel.

The scope of activities of the Arab League is extensive, and the work is supported by a Secretariat staff of more than 200. One of the principal instruments (in addition to the pact establishing the league) that outlines the mutual obligations of members is the Treaty of Joint Defense and Economic Cooperation, adopted in 1950. This treaty asserts the principle that armed aggression against any party is an act against all members and obligates each state to assist the attacked state by every appropriate means including armed force. Such sweeping obligations were ignored by the member states in circumstances such as the attacks by Israel, France, and the United Kingdom against the United Arab Republic in 1956. The league has been wholly ineffective against outside threats.

The record of the Arab League in dealing with disputes and military clashes among its own members has been only slightly better than in dealing with external threats. The one notable success was a united effort, including a 3,300-member military force, to prevent Iraq from taking over Kuwait at the time of the latter's independence in 1961. The British first sent troops in response to Kuwait's appeal, and these were replaced by the combined force from five Arab states, with the bulk furnished by Saudi Arabia and the United Arab Republic. These military contingents remained in Kuwait until 1963. The league seemed incapable of resolving other disputes including charges of UAR successive interventions in Tunisia (1958), Lebanon (1958), Jordan (1958 and 1960), and Syria (1962). In the cases of Lebanon and Jordan in 1958, these countries sought the protection of the United States and the United Kingdom respectively in the face of Arab League ineffectiveness. In 1963 Morocco and Algeria turned to the OAU rather than to the Arab League for the conciliation of their border dispute. The league was also paralyzed in the Yemen civil war of 1962-67, in which Saudi Arabia and the UAR were supporting opposing factions.

On certain issues the Arab states have presented a united front. At the United Nations they have spoken with one voice in opposition to Israel and on questions of decolonization. They consistently opposed France on the Algerian, Moroccan, and Tunisian questions and exerted pressure on Britain to free its territories in the Middle East. On these types of issues, the Arab states have spoken and voted as a unit, but they have failed to take cooperative action through the Arab League.

The diversity of interest in the program of the league is demonstrated by the elaborate league machinery. In the political and security realm there is a Council, a Political Committee, a Joint Defense Council, and a Permanent Military Committee. In the area of economic cooperation, the chief organ is an Economic Council, composed of ministers of economic affairs. Other permanent committees are concerned with social and cultural affairs. The Secretariat has departments dealing with political, economic, legal, cultural, press and publicity, administrative and financial, social, and Palestinian matters. There is also an Institute of Arab Studies, an Institute of Arab Manuscripts, a Refugee Boycott Office, and an Anti-Narcotics Office. An Arab Development Bank has been established, and an Arab Economic Union has been formed with the goal of achieving a common market. Other cooperative agencies include a Postal and Telecommunication Union, a Health Organization, and an Arab League Petroleum Bureau. Cooperation among Arab states has been achieved in such areas as educational standardization and teacher exchange. The league maintains an office in New York to facilitate cooperation among Arab states at the United Nations.

From the preceding summary of agencies and activities it is apparent that Arab League deficiencies are not the result of a narrowness of interests or instrumentalities. Economic, social, and cultural cooperation has succeeded to a greater degree than in the political and security realm. In spite of a common basis for political cooperation, intrabloc rivalries and suspicions have prevented closer collaboration and unity of action.

ALLIANCE-TYPE REGIONAL ORGANIZATIONS

As previously defined, alliance-type organizations are those whose military and political orientation is intended to provide security against external actors. All organizations in this category are a response to the Cold War, which developed between the Communist states, led by the Soviet Union, and the so-called free world, led by the United States, in the aftermath of World War II. The attitudes that foster such organizations are based on distrust and hostility rather than on friendly and cooperative relations among nations. The need for security arrangements reflects feelings of insecurity concerning perceived threats from other countries or groups of countries and indicates the conviction that these threats require a collective rather than a unilateral response. The resulting treaty arrangements among allies provide for united military responses to an attack on any member of the alliance so that any use of force will be met with massive counterforce. The intent is supposedly defensive rather than offensive and serves mainly to deter aggression by the prospect of collective retaliation against the aggressor. Potential aggressors are envisioned as being states outside the membership of the alliance, and it is assumed that members of the alliance will not initiate armed attacks against each other.

The members of all current military alliances of this type claim that these pacts are compatible with the United Nations Charter. The provisions of the treaties refer specifically to the right of individual or collective self-defense in Article 51 of the Charter, and the agreements are generally defended as regional organizations within the spirit and purpose of the Charter. The signatories proclaim their support of United Nations purposes and principles and recognize their obligations under the Charter including the pledge to settle all disputes by peaceful means. The parties also recognize the primacy of the Security Council in the maintenance of international peace and security.

In spite of these declarations of support for United Nations principles, the compatibility of these pacts with the spirit of the Charter should be questioned. If all members of the United Nations honored their commitments to renounce the use of force and to settle all disputes by peaceful means, no military alliances would be required. If the collective-security system of the United Nations could be implemented, other military arrangements would be inconsistent with the working of the universal system. By dividing the world into hostile camps, the alliance-type organizations undermine the Charter purposes of developing friendly relations among nations and harmonizing their actions within a universal framework. The attainment of a worldwide spirit of peace, harmony, and cooperation for peaceful change is thus retarded by emphasizing the hostility among blocs of nations suspicious of the intentions of other nations to adhere to Charter principles.

On the other hand, military alliances merely reflect the hostility and lack of harmony among states. The spirit of the Charter was never taken seriously by the world's statesmen. Cleavages and power politics became immediately apparent in the postwar period. Clashes of ideology intensified the rivalries of powerful states. National interests predominated in the interactions among sovereign states. The Cold War became the prime factor of world politics. If military alliances were incompatible with the yearnings for a worldwide system that could assure peace and cooperation among nations, they were a manifestation that such an ideal had not been attained through the creation of the United Nations. Given this kind of world in which national rivalry and suspicion were rampant, a system of rival military alliances seemed necessary for protection of national interests, even if subversive of universal hopes for cooperation and harmony. The response to a potential military threat was an arrangement for military counterforce. Such a response, it may be argued, is not a creator of tensions but only a reflection of existing tensions that must be recognized and acted upon.

Alliance-type organizations have built-in elements of instability. The perceived threat against which each arrangement is directed tends to be greater at the time the organization is formed than on a sustained basis. As changes occur in world relations, the reasons for forming and supporting the alliance become less credible, and the unity of the membership is subject to greater stresses and strains. Doubts arise concerning the legitimacy of maintaining a high degree of hostile relations with the outside power or powers against which the pact is directed. Additional skepticism grows regarding the scope and intensity of the commitment of alliance partners to honor fully their mutual obligations when their own national interests are not vitally affected. Disaffections and disillusionments stem from the practice of the dominant power within the alliance to set a unilateral course in its foreign policy without regard to effects upon lesser alliance partners and frequently with little or no consultation prior to foreign policy actions. France's withdrawal of forces from NATO and Pakistan's renunciation of membership in SEATO are only two of the more dramatic examples of these tendencies toward alliance instability.

The examination of the main features of a sampling of alliance-type organizations will tend to illuminate the nature, importance, and evolution of this type of regional arrangement.

North Atlantic Treaty Organization (NATO)

The largest, most highly organized, and most stable military security alliance is NATO. As the original postwar organization of its type, it served as a model for the other organizations in this category. NATO was formed in response to the possible threat of Soviet military incursions into central and Western Europe. NATO was initiated by the United States as a major element in the containment policy directed against Communist states in general and the Soviet Union in particular. Other closely related elements within the United States containment policy were the Truman Doctrine, the Marshall Plan, the Korean War, SEATO, and the Baghdad Pact.

NATO membership extends geographically from the United States and Canada on the west to Greece and Turkey on the east. Original members included Belgium, Canada, Denmark, France, Iceland, Italy, Luxembourg, the Netherlands, Norway, Portugal, the United Kingdom, and the United States. The treaty was signed in Washington, D.C., in April, 1949, and came into force in August of that year. In 1952 Greece and Turkey joined the alliance, and in 1955 the Federal Republic of Germany completed the roster of fifteen members. In 1966 President De Gaulle announced France's intention to withdraw from participation in the combined NATO military organization in western Europe and requested that military forces and NATO headquarters be removed from French territory. In 1967 the Supreme Headquarters Allied Powers Europe (SHAPE) was moved to Mons, Belgium, and a new Secretariat and Council headquarters was opened in Brussels.

The key provision of the North Atlantic Treaty is the agreement "that an armed attack against one or more of them [the parties to the treaty] in Europe or North America shall be considered an attack against them all." When such an attack occurs, each member state is obligated to assist the member attacked in order to restore and maintain security within the region. However, sovereignty is safeguarded by providing that each member is obligated to take only "such action as it deems necessary." This protection of sovereignty carries over into the command of troops assigned to the European sector. Although an elaborate integrated command structure exists, national officers retain full control over their military contingents, and no orders can be carried out except through national channels. The entire basis for NATO operation consists of consultation, cooperation, and discussion so that each member state retains its full freedom of action. Forces are maintained in the field in Europe with the largest contingents furnished by the United States and Germany. Agreements on levels of forces have been negotiated but not fully implemented. A large and complicated organizational structure has been created. Meetings for consultation are regular and numerous. NATO requires the services of approximately as many administrative personnel as the United Nations (excluding the specialized agencies). But in spite of a large structure and budget, backed potentially by the total military might of the individual members, national decision-making powers remain unimpaired. Attempts to form both an integrated military force and a supranational nuclear capability have failed to materialize. European members are somewhat frustrated by the realization that only the United States policy toward the Soviet Union, including the decision for nuclear retaliation or other flexible response, will really determine their fate in a major confrontation. Freedom of action in reality involves more freedom of decision for some members than for others.

The supreme organ of NATO is the North Atlantic Council, in which all decisions require a unanimous vote. The Council meets at the ministerial level (generally ministers of foreign affairs or defense) at least twice a year and at the level of permanent representatives (ambassadorial rank) on a weekly basis. The secretary-general of NATO is the chairman of the council. The permanent representatives (with the exception of a representative from France since 1966) also meet as a Defense Planning Committee for determining military policy.

An elaborate administrative, committee, and military-command structure operates under the general aegis of the North Atlantic Council. The Secretariat headed by the secretary-general is organized to reflect and support all of the activities and committee structure of NATO. The secretary-general, in addition to presiding over council sessions, prepares the budget, arranges the agenda of meetings and initiates agenda items, supervises the administrative functions with powers to hire and release personnel, and represents NATO in relations with governments and with other organizations. The North Atlantic Council is assisted in its work by a dozen major committees and as many more specialized committees. Examples of primary committees are those concerned with political affairs, defence review, armaments, economic affairs, science, and information and cultural affairs. Specialized committees deal with such matters as European air space, pipelines, and communications. In 1969 a Committee on the Challenges of Modern Society was established to consider environmental problems. This latter activity serves as an example of the nonmilitary interest incorporated within the NATO program. Since an elaborate structure already exists, and as military threats subside, there is a tendency for NATO to seek new activities to justify its continuance on the scale previously developed.

The military command structure is headed by the Military Committee composed of chiefs-of-staff, or their representatives, of all NATO members except France. The defense area is divided into three principal commands, Allied Command Europe, Allied Command Atlantic, and Allied Command Channel, plus a Canada-U.S. Regional Planning Group. Each of the three commands is in turn subdivided into a number of subordinate commands. The Allied Command Europe has always enjoyed the highest prestige because of its assigned strategic area in relation to the Soviet Union and because of its coordinating functions over the various national military contingents that provide defense for western Europe. Persons of the eminence of General Dwight Eisenhower have served as Supreme Allied Commander Europe (SACEUR) at the headquarters in France or Belgium.

Support and enthusiasm for NATO has been subjected to stresses and strains over a quarter century, and priorities for the organization have been shifted within this period. France's disillusionment with United States primacy within the organization and with such problems as the role of German forces in European security culminated in 1966-67 in France's withdrawal from the military arrangements in NATO while retaining membership in the organization for other purposes. NATO's original central purpose of deterrence of the Soviet Union has given way to an equal emphasis on détente between East and West. The so-called Harmel Report, adopted by the council in December, 1967, marked the recognition of détente as a primary function of NATO. In recent years emphasis has been placed upon such policies as disarmament, mutual and balanced force reductions, and a settlement of the future of Germany and Berlin. Accommodation and peaceful relations with the Soviet bloc have replaced implacable hostility and a strong defense posture, although the original military purposes of defense and warnings against relaxing the degree of physical or psychological preparedness are stressed in every report of the council.

Concomitant with the growing emphasis on détente has been the shift of United States policy from that of massive retaliation to one of flexible response. Reluctantly the NATO council was forced to adopt flexible response as its official policy, although such a shift increased the doubt that the United States would risk its own security on behalf of its European allies in many circumstances. Thus, the degree of solidarity of commitment underlying the alliance has been gradually eroded. Yet even as growing détente between East and West tends to bring into question the validity of the purposes of NATO, the organization may be retained for some time as a symbol of unity and as a convenient means of consultation and coordination on matters of common concern to its members.

Warsaw Treaty Organization
(WTO or Warsaw Pact)

Instead of the Soviet Union responding to the formation of NATO by immediately instigating an East European general security arrangement, that country first consolidated its security system by a series of bilateral pacts. However, the entry of West Germany into NATO membership in 1955 is often cited as the trigger that set into motion the formation of the Warsaw Treaty Organization. Other factors that prompted this move were the desire to create a bargaining tool with the West and the provision of justification for keeping Soviet military forces in Hungary and Rumania after the signing of the Austrian State Treaty by the Big Four, which removed the previous grounds for maintaining forces there. Among these reasons subsequent events seem to indicate that the most important was to furnish a bargaining device in dealing with the West.

In its basic elements the Warsaw Pact is almost a carbon copy of the North Atlantic Treaty, although in practice the organizations have not followed identical patterns of organization or behavior. In case of armed attack upon any member, all other members of the WTO are obligated to come to the aid of the victim by all means, including military, that each member deems necessary. Members pledge themselves to peacefully settle disputes among themselves, to promote disarmament, and to consult on matters of mutual concern. One unique feature of the Warsaw Pact is the provision to dissolve the organization upon the conclusion of an all-European security agreement, a recurrent project in Soviet proposals.

The original members of the Warsaw Pact, which was adopted in the Polish capital on May 14, 1955, were Albania, Bulgaria, Czechoslovakia, the German Democratic Republic (GDR), Hungary, Poland, Rumania, and the USSR. Albania ceased its participation in any meetings in 1961, and Rumania has, on many occasions since the mid-1960s demonstrated its discontent with the pact.

Two primary structural devices are provided in the treaty. The first is a Political Consultative Committee, supposedly the supreme policy-determining body. Meetings of this committee have been infrequent but have been attended by high-ranking party and government officials, including first secretaries of the National Communist parties, premiers, and defense and foreign ministers.

The second major body provided for in the treaty is the Unified Command. A Soviet general has always served as commander-in-chief of the joint forces, and ministers of defense from the other pact countries have served as his deputies. A Joint Staff with headquarters in Moscow was established to assist the Unified Command in their direction of WTO forces. Beginning in 1961 frequent joint military maneuvers or exercises were conducted in the various countries allied with the Soviet Union. Soviet troops were initially stationed in the German Democratic Republic, Hungary, Poland, and Rumania, but in 1958 they were withdrawn from Rumania.

The Warsaw Pact has been used to enforce Soviet dominance over its allies. In 1956 it was invoked as the authority for using Soviet troops to suppress the Hungarian revolt. In 1968 joint WTO forces displayed their effectiveness in quashing the attempted Czechoslovakian defection from Soviet influence. Rumanian moves toward greater independence of action were temporarily reversed because of the demonstration in Czechoslovakia of WTO effectiveness against insurgent members of the organization.

Centrifugal forces have been in operation throughout the history of the Warsaw Pact. Albania's defection was accomplished without serious reprisal in 1961. On the other hand, Polish and Hungarian attempts at establishing independent courses of policy in 1956 and Czechoslovakia's changes of basic doctrine in 1968 were dealt with in such a manner as to prevent a break in the alliance relationship. Members have been restive because of the domination of the USSR within the organization. Rumania has, for all practical purposes, ceased to participate actively in the alliance. Czechoslovakia and Hungary have asserted increasingly independent policies.

Externally the rationale for maintaining a strong alliance has diminished. Détente between the USSR and the United States has lessened the sense of threat. The growing Sino-Soviet cleavage has encouraged the movement toward polycentrism within the Communist world. The weakening of NATO through French defection has decreased the pressure for maintaining a strong and united counterforce. The opening up of East-West trade and other relationships, including West German overtures to the eastern European countries, has dissolved the basic hostility that gave impetus to the establishment of rival alliances. The Warsaw Pact remains, therefore, as does NATO, primarily as a symbol of unity and strength and as a bargaining chip in East-West relations.

FUNCTIONAL REGIONAL ORGANIZATIONS

The largest category of regional organizations includes those of the functional type. Functional organizations, as previously noted, are defined as those that promote economic, social, or political collaboration with little or no regard to security factors. A review of the list of functional organizations in the chart on pages 375–76 reveals that the majority of these organizations are formed for the attainment of economic goals of the members. The collaboration of the members achieves mutual economic advantages that cannot be attained through unilateral policies.

According to functional theories of emerging world order,

such as those held by David Mitrany, the habits of collaboration developed in functional areas should eventually spill over into the political sphere and lead to the breakdown of political barriers among states. If these theories have any validity, the proof is not yet strongly evidenced in the behavior of states, which continue to safeguard vigorously their political unity and independence. In fact, steps toward economic union have been partial, gradual, cautious, and reflective of little national enthusiasm for merging national economic institutions except to the degree that national political freedom remains intact. On the other hand, Joseph S. Nye states that

> Before a conflict has reached a stage of open hostilities, micro-regional economic organizations may indeed act to raise the price of conflict and to foster communications and help restructure values in a way that may have a restraining effect on political leaders. . . . After major fighting has broken out, the role of the regional economic organization will be primarily to symbolize the possibility of upgrading a common interest.[6]

Thus, without achieving a broader political community, regional economic organizations may contribute modestly to the maintenance or restoration of peace and the integration of policy.

Functional regional organizations are so numerous that even a brief description of each would require too much space in this chapter. Only a small sampling is presented below. For information on other organizations, the student may consult the *Yearbook of International Organizations*, which will serve as a starting point by outlining such features as the aims, membership, structure, and primary activities of each agency.

European Economic Community
(EEC or Common Market)

The EEC is unique among regional organizations. It represents the greatest advance toward supranationalism of any such organization. Within the economic sphere, broad national decision-making authority has been voluntarily surrendered to collective agencies. Economic integration has been carried further on a wider scope of activities than in any other regional arrangement. Yet, in the basic political functions the integrative process has not followed that of the economic sector, although the two cannot be totally differentiated since much economic decision making is a part of the political

---

[6] J. S. Nye, *Peace in Parts: Integration and Conflict in Regional Organization* (Boston: Little, Brown, 1971), p. 112.

process and the surrender of sovereign powers has, to a remarkable degree, already occurred.

The EEC is also such an unprecedented success story that it has served as a model for other similar experiments and as the most tangible hope of the functionalists to prove that economic integration will lead to eventual political integration. Although this step still seems remote, the EEC has achieved its major economic goals, and this achievement has resulted in rapidly rising prosperity for its component states.

The EEC is an outgrowth of, and is closely associated with, several other organizational developments. The impetus for a European federation predates World War II, and the first step toward an economic union was the formation of a customs union (Benelux), which came into operation January 1, 1948, among Belgium, the Netherlands and Luxembourg. In 1950 French Foreign Minister Robert Schuman proposed a coal and steel community to include six countries, and in 1952 the European Coal and Steel Community (ECSC), composed of the Benelux countries and France, West Germany, and Italy became a reality. In 1954 and 1955 proposals were initiated for expanding the areas of integration of economic policies among the six members of the ECSC into a common market, and in 1957 the Rome treaties were signed creating the European Economic Community and the European Atomic Energy Community (Euratom). Habits of cooperation among European states were also fostered by the establishment in 1948 of the Organization for European Economic Cooperation (OEEC) to implement the Marshall Plan for European recovery; by the creation in 1960–61 of its successor, enlarged in membership, the Organization for Economic Cooperation and Development (OECD); and by the formation in the political arena in 1949 of the Council of Europe.

The creation of the Common Market also gave rise to the establishment of the European Free Trade Association (EFTA) in 1960. EFTA is less integrated and more limited in aims than the EEC but represents a response by European nonmembers of the EEC to the desirability of international cooperation in establishing enlarged trade areas through reducing barriers to trade. The EFTA membership eventually included Austria, Denmark, Finland, Iceland, Norway, Portugal, Sweden, Switzerland, and the United Kingdom. On January 1, 1973, Denmark and the United Kingdom withdrew from the EFTA and became members of the EEC. Ireland also joined the EEC on this date, thus enlarging the EEC membership from six to nine. The remaining EFTA members retained their own organizational relationships, continued their previous trade arrangements with the United Kingdom and Denmark, and negotiated individual trade agreements with the EEC.

Today the EEC, the ECSC, and Euratom share the same common organizational institutions. From the inception of the EEC and Euratom, all three organizations had in common a Parliament and Court of Justice. In 1967 other separate organs were merged into a single Commission and Council of Ministers.

The commission of thirteen members, not more than two of whom may be of the same nationality, is chosen by the Council of Ministers for four-year renewable terms and may be removed only by a two-thirds censure vote of the European Parliament. The commission administers and implements the program of the EEC and is assisted by an administrative staff of more than 5,000. The commission submits an annual report to the European Parliament. It administers a European Development Fund, which has made available to associated countries and territories, mainly in Africa, a total of more than 3 billion dollars. The commission is also advised by an Economic and Social Committee of 101 experts representing a cross section of employers', workers', and consumers' interests.

The real center of power in the Common Market organization is the Council of Ministers. For the most important decisions the foreign ministers participate, but for specialized subjects the appropriate ministers from each of the nine member states sit on the council. Votes are weighted with the ministers of West Germany, France, Italy, and Britain having ten each; Belgium and the Netherlands, five each; Denmark and Ireland, three each; and Luxembourg, one. Decisions are made on less important issues by majority, but on issues of vital national interest, the requirement for adoption is forty-one votes including favorable votes by the ministers of at least six countries. Most important decisions are taken unanimously. The preparatory work for the council is performed by a Committee of Permanent Representatives of ambassadorial rank accredited to the headquarters in Brussels. This group wields great influence in the activities of the council.

Until 1978 the European Parliament represented the legislatures of the constituent countries, but after that year the members were chosen by direct election. It meets at Strasbourg at least six or eight times annually for sessions of approximately a week in duration. The members of the parliament are apportioned as follows: Britain, France, Germany, and Italy — thirty-six each; Belgium and the Netherlands — fourteen each; Denmark and Ireland — ten each; and

Luxembourg — six. The members sit in political, not national, groups. The parliament may question the members of the commission and maintains an elaborate committee structure.

The Court of Justice sits at Luxembourg and hears cases and appeals concerning obligations and disputes under the basic treaties and agreements within the community framework. Cases may involve governments, community agencies, private organizations or firms, or individuals. Penalties may be fixed by the court and there is no appeal from its decisions. Hundreds of cases have been brought before the court.

The success of the Common Market may be measured in terms of its specific accomplishments. The transition period for the full development of a customs union was originally set at twelve to fifteen years but was accomplished in approximately ten years. This customs union abolishes customs duties and quantitative restrictions among the member states and establishes common external tariffs on imports. The community has negotiated much-reduced tariff rates with their outside trading partners. The EEC has also adopted a common agricultural program financed from a central fund involving certain subsidies and incentives for improving agricultural production. Labor mobility from one country to another is virtually achieved and guaranteed, and a common transport policy has been adopted. The states in the community have moved toward a common added-value tax on goods and services and are working to remove restrictions on capital movements. By 1975 the EEC became independent of member assessments, and its budget was financed entirely by community resources, primarily external tariffs and agricultural levies. General policies and targets for economic growth have been adopted and the achieved rates of growth have exceeded those of the United States or the EFTA countries. The EEC has established a European Investment Bank, which has provided loans for such economically disadvantaged areas as southern Italy.

The community is the world's largest trading bloc, and it has served as a magnet to attract new members bringing its total population and GNP into a similar rank with those of the superpowers — the United States and the Soviet Union. In addition to establishing special relationships with African states, the community has accorded Greece, Turkey, Cyprus, Malta, Morocco, and Tunisia associate-membership status. The goal of political union may be remote, but economic integration has been developed to a high degree with mutual benefits for all members.

Council for Mutual Economic Assistance
(CMEA or COMECON)

Under Moscow's leadership COMECON was established in 1949 to promote and coordinate the planned development of the national economies of the East European states, to accelerate their economic and social progress, to encourage industrialization in the less-industrialized areas, to increase labor productivity, and to promote the welfare of the people of the member states. The charter of COMECON was revised in 1959 and again in 1962 with provisions in the latter revision for the admission of non-European members. Active members include Bulgaria, Czechoslovakia, the German Democratic Republic, Hungary, Mongolia, Poland, Rumania, and the USSR. Albania is officially listed as a member but has not participated since 1961. Since 1964 Yugoslavia has taken part in a limited number of activities. COMECON operates through a Council, an Executive Committee, a Committee for Cooperation in Planned Activity, a Committee for Scientific and Technological Cooperation, a Bureau for Integrated Planning Problems, about twenty standing commissions, and several standing conferences. The work is supported by a Secretariat. The headquarters is in Moscow.

One of the central activities of COMECON is the coordination of national economic plans and the exchange of information among members. States are not bound by recommendations to which they have not assented. Cooperative efforts have concentrated on such areas as machine building, radio and electronics, and the chemical and metallurgical industries. A CMEA Institute of Standardization has facilitated the interchangeability of goods and machinery. Specific accomplishments include the setting up of a unified power production system and the creation of a 100,000-unit CMEA Railway-Wagon Pool. In the financial area a system of multilateral accounts in transferable rubles has been adopted, and two banks have been created—an International Bank for Economic Cooperation (IBEC), established in 1964, and an International Investment Bank, which began operations in 1970.

While significant progress toward economic integration, to the mutual advantage of all member states, has been accomplished through COMECON, the degree of integration is evidently much less than in the EEC. With the growing signs of nationalism and independence from Soviet direction and control on the part of such states as Rumania and Hungary, further economic and political integration is likely to be very limited.

Organization for Economic Cooperation and Development (OECD)

The OECD was created in 1961 as the successor to the Organization for European Economic Cooperation (OEEC), whose original purpose was the administration of Marshall Plan aid and European recovery plans. Membership includes the non-Communist European states plus Australia, New Zealand, Japan, the United States, Canada, and Turkey. The aims of the organization include the promotion of optimum economic conditions and financial stability of the members, the development of the world economy, the promotion of economic development of member and nonmember countries, and the expansion of world trade on a nondiscriminatory basis. The headquarters is in Paris.

In addition to a Council, Executive Committee, and Secretariat, the OECD carries on its numerous functions through more than two dozen committees and other subsidiary groups. The broad subject areas include economic policies, the environment, aid to developing countries, trade, financial affairs, science, education, manpower, social affairs, industry, energy, agriculture, and fisheries. The Development Assistance Committee (DAC) includes the seventeen most affluent members, which are the world's principal donors of development aid. The OECD Development Centre aids in research and transfer of knowledge on development problems. A Nuclear Energy Agency is a feature of the OECD operations, and in 1974 an International Energy Agency of eighteen members was created to deal with oil supply and price problems through coordinated policies in stockpiling, conservation, and research into new energy sources.

The OECD maintains working relations with numerous other intergovernmental and nongovernmental organizations. Through consultation, research, exchange of information, and publication the OECD provides a center for coordinating the economic policies of the members among themselves and toward the developing states.

Regional Development Banks

An international phenomenon of the 1960s was the establishment of several regional and subregional development banks. These banks were set up because of discontent with the policies of the

World Bank group of institutions, the inadequacies of the development resources available through existing channels, and the special needs of particular areas that were unlikely to be met by bilateral and global financial programs. The countries in the areas involved sought increased resources, greater flexibility in lending policies, and more local control in the determination of policies and the use of resources. One of the purposes was to provide financing for projects essential to development, such as in education and agriculture for which loans were not readily available from existing sources. Another was to encourage financial support for broad programs rather than for specific projects.

The regional institutions that were created in response to these demands were the Inter-American Development Bank (IDB), the African Development Bank (AFDB), and the Asian Development Bank (ASDB). The IDB became operative in 1960 and the other two in 1966. Subregional financial institutions include the European Investment Bank (EIB), to which reference was previously made in the discussion of the EEC; the International Bank for Economic Cooperation (IBEC) and the International Investment Bank, both of which were previously mentioned in the information on COMECON; the Central American Bank for Economic Integration (CABEI), dating from 1961; and the East African Development Bank, created in 1967 by Kenya, Tanzania, and Uganda. The establishment of so many regional and subregional financial agencies within a decade is part of the movement by the developing countries to join forces to speed the processes of their economic development.

Of the three regional banks, the Inter-American Development Bank, because of its longer period of operation and its generous support from the United States, was able by December, 1975, to commit more than 17.5 billion dollars in loans for 889 projects. The Asian Development Bank grew rapidly and by the end of 1975 had capital stock subscriptions of approximately 7.5 billion dollars and had committed 5.3 billion dollars in loans for 228 projects. The Asian Development Bank was somewhat less successful than the Inter-American Development Bank in raising funds in the world's money markets through the sale of securities. The African Development Bank has suffered from inadequate resources because it has limited its membership to African states, all of which are relatively poor. The Asian Development Bank, in contrast, counts among its members the United States, Canada, Australia, New Zealand, Japan, and twelve European states, as well as its Asian underdeveloped beneficiaries. Japan, Australia, and the nonregional members control a majority of the voting power. In the IDB, because of special and weighted voting requirements, the United States has veto power over major decisions and a virtual veto over other decisions. Regional autonomy over the African bank's policies and decisions is purchased at the cost of inadequate resources.

Thus, the developing states are caught in the dilemma of wishing to control their own destinies but of having to surrender decision-making power to those states who command the bulk of the world's resources in exchange for access to a portion of those resources. Although the major purposes of the regional development banks include the provision for greater flexibility in lending policies and more local control over the allocation of resources, the attainment of these goals in two of the three institutions is dependent upon the sympathy and cooperation with these aims of the affluent contributors of capital. In spite of these difficulties the regional and subregional banks have provided for needs not otherwise met through alternate channels. The financing of cooperative enterprises and attention to the unique problems of each region or subregion are among the contributions of these agencies during the short span of their existence.

UNITED NATIONS REGIONAL COMMISSIONS

As previously noted, no regional decentralization of the economic and social activities of the United Nations was provided for in the Charter; all Charter references to regionalism applied solely to security matters. However, the task of reconstruction and rehabilitation in the war-damaged areas provided the initial impetus for the establishment in 1947 of the Economic Commission for Europe (ECE) and the Economic Commission for Asia and the Far East (ECAFE). The title of ECAFE was changed in 1974 to the Economic and Social Commission for Asia and the Pacific (ESCAP). Pressures from the Latin American states, with support from other under-developed countries in the General Assembly, after a lack of success in the Economic and Social Council, led to the creation in 1948 of the Economic Commission for Latin America (ECLA). Ten years later the beginning of the influx of new African states into United Nations membership brought about the approval of an Economic Commission for Africa (ECA). For many years proposals for a Middle East commission fell prey to the hostility between the Arab states and Israel. As a substitute, a relatively small United Nations Economic and Social Office in Beirut was opened in 1963. Finally, in 1974, it was converted into a full-fledged Economic Commission for Western Asia.

Each of the regional commissions is a subsidiary body of the Economic and Social Council, to which it reports. Although the regional staffs of the commissions in Asia, Latin America, and Africa number 500-600 each, the regional offices must work closely with the Department of Economic and Social Affairs of the United Nations Secretariat, with the United Nations Development Program, with the United Nations Conference on Trade and Development, with such other regional organizations as the OAU, the OAS, or the Colombo Plan, with the specialized agencies of the United Nations, and with the governments of the countries in the area. Their task of trying to provide coordination in economic development is complicated by their lack of authority and by the diversity of channels of operation in each region. The project and individual country orientation of most bilateral and United Nations aid programs makes their work doubly difficult. Rivalries among states or groups of states in the area compound the problem.[7]

The principal structural components of each United Nations regional organization are the secretariat, which is a branch of the United Nations Secretariat, the commission, made up of representatives of governments belonging to the regional organization, and a series of specialized committees. Each commission meets annually or biennially and determines general policy within the limits of United Nations guidelines, programs, and resources. The secretariat prepares for commission and committee meetings, carries on research, implements the programs approved by the commission, and attempts to provide coordination of activities for the region. The executive secretary, as head of the secretariat, occupies a crucial position in providing leadership within the organization and in his relations with member governments.

The major purpose of the regional commissions is to assist in raising the level of economic well-being in their region and to strengthen the economic relations of the countries of the region with each other and with other countries outside the area. Originally the principal activity of each commission was to provide research, surveys, and planning as a basis for coordinated economic development. After 1960 the importance of the commissions was intended to be upgraded by an official United Nations policy to strengthen the commissions and decentralize the United Nations economic activities. This purpose has met with varying degrees of success due to some of the obstacles previously mentioned. The ECLA has enjoyed extensive popularity among Latin American states and has been

---

[7] For example, see James S. Magee, "ECA and the Paradox of African Cooperation," *International Conciliation*, No. 580 (November, 1970), *passim*.

credited with major contributions in the establishment of the Latin American Free Trade Association, the Central American Common Market, the Inter-American Development Bank, and the United Nations Conference on Trade and Development. The ESCAP has promoted such projects as the Mekong River development, the Asian Highway, the Asian Development Bank, and the Asian Institute for Economic Development and Planning. The ECA has some credits also, such as the African Development Bank, but it has failed to gain acceptance among African states to the same degree as the other regional commissions, and its effectiveness has been hampered by internal dissension and by rivalry with the OAU. Forces that tend to emphasize individual projects, individual countries, and diverse agencies impede any attempts at regional coordination.

One of the most effective areas of service and coordination engaged in by the regional commissions is in the dissemination of information and the development of needed skills. The specific methods include workshops, seminars, training institutes, information centers, advisory services, provision of fellowships, research centers, symposia, and conferences. Thousands of persons in the areas have received the direct benefits of these activities. The regional commissions provide only part of the needed services and resources, but they act to stimulate governments and other agencies and to provide coordination of diverse activities.

The regional economic commissions of the United Nations system represent a middle approach between the global goals for which the organization was created and the manifold projects and agencies that carry decentralization to a point bordering on chaos. However, because of their limited resources and influence, and because of their dependence upon the cooperation of governments and numerous agencies, they have never attained a central role in the processes of economic development. Persuasion is a relatively weak tool for uniting and coordinating the disparate elements that tend to protect the sovereignty of states and the autonomy of myriad programs and projects.

GENERAL ASSESSMENT OF REGIONALISM

The proliferation of regional organizations within a period of thirty years could lead to the mistaken conclusion that regionalism is the wave of the future in the redistribution of world political and economic power. The mere establishment of numerous regional agencies as evidence of a new world order would be as misleading as to assume that the establishment of the United Nations and the subsequent increase in the number of universal organizations heralds a new age of world community. Concomitant with these developments has been the emergence of a host of new independent states, seeking separate identities, jealous of their sovereign prerogatives, and determined to seek the promotion of their national interests, not through an onslaught on the state system, but within its framework. The older and more powerful states are equally determined to maintain the established system, to emphasize self-help in their foreign policies, and to exercise extreme caution in movements toward cooperation, coordination, or integration across state boundaries.

No incompatibility need exist between regional and universal organizations. The United Nations has established its own economic commissions to facilitate the achievement of regional goals within a universal framework. Most functional regional organizations are striving for the same kinds of economic and social development as the United Nations family of agencies, and the two levels of effort generally serve to reinforce each other. It is possible for regional economic integration to lead to policies adverse to the interests of other countries, but this problem has not attained major proportions in the broad pattern of functional regional development.

On the other hand, alliance-type organizations, by stressing the hostility between groups of states, tend to retard the attainment of some of the cooperative aims of universal organizations. The OAS, as a multipurpose organization, has also been perverted, through military and political intervention, into an instrument of United States foreign policy within the hemisphere. It has provided a cloak of legitimacy for unilateral United States action. In the process, means were found to isolate the United Nations organs from any effective supervision over disputes within the hemisphere and to rewrite Charter provisions on this subject through restrictive interpretation and practice. This perversion and reinterpretation has occurred in spite of the clear provisions of the UN and OAS charters establishing the priority of United Nations jurisdiction over disputes. However, the economic and social activities of the OAS and other multipurpose organizations are generally supportive of, and compatible with, the goals of universal organizations.

No strong or persistent trend toward regionalism can be discerned on the present world scene. Discontent and dissension are threats to several existing organizations including the OAS, the OAU, the ECA, NATO, the WTO, and COMECON. Resentment of the domination of organizations by single powerful states, the clash of interests among groups of states, and reassertions of sovereign prerogatives are among the factors that act as centrifugal forces destroying the unity of regional agencies. A sufficient community of interests has not been established to outweigh the forces of nationalism and unilateralism. Cooperation for mutual benefit is possible, under these circumstances, but regional integration can occur only at a superficial level.

Regionalism (as well as universalism) possesses limited dynamics of its own. Regionalism exerts little magnetic force that tends to pull states away from the poles of national power and purposes. Regional organizations are formed not for their own sake, but to promote the enhancement of national interests. If functionalism ever results in a surrender of national sovereignty, the current evidence suggests that the period of time in which this will occur is not imminent.

15

International Administration and the Search for Leadership

Because most existing international organizations are based on cooperation among sovereign states, ultimate power remains in these individual member states. Thus, joining an international organization furthers the national interests of each member, and protects and enhances rather than diminishes national sovereignty.

The growth of international agencies also points up the interdependence of nations and the recognition that their destiny and welfare are inextricably linked. No nation can be separate unto itself; its interests need to be accommodated by the cooperation of other states through formal and informal channels. International organizations provide some of these channels.

The establishment of many international organizations creates demands met completely or partly by the formation of secretariats as part of their structure. Among these demands are (1) the efficient administration of programs authorized and supported by the organizations, (2) the provision of leadership and guidance for emerging world community forces, (3) the practice of neutralism among competing national interests, and (4) the provision of an international perspective on international problems and programs.

Secretariats certainly do not provide the only leaders of the world community, but international statespeople are rare among those committed to protect national interests. Although several possibilities for leadership will be examined in this chapter, the unique position of the international civil servant will be emphasized. Other roles performed by a secretary-general and his staff also will be outlined. The development of modern administrative structures through precedent-setting practices provides the justification of combining historical and analytical methods of investigating these matters.

THE DEVELOPMENT OF THE INTERNATIONAL CIVIL SERVICE

Although civil-service traditions at the national level date back many centuries, international secretariats have a history of only approximately 100 years. The first suggestion for a neutral international body of civil servants was incorporated into William Penn's proposal for a general parliament in Europe, published in 1694. Penn suggested a body of clerks modeled after the clerks of the British House of Commons. The first actual use of secretariats attached to permanent international organizations developed in the 1860s and 1870s with the establishment of the International Telegraphic Union, the Universal Postal Union, and the International Bureau of Weights and Measures. However, the secretariat personnel for these organizations did not represent a multinational group of civil servants but were either recruited from the host country or seconded by member governments. The concept of a truly international secretariat with primary responsibility to the organization rather than to national governments was put into practice only with the establishment of the League of Nations.

In planning for the League of Nations, two possible roles were foreseen for the Secretary-General. One of these was the role of international statesman and political leader as contrasted with that of efficient administrator limited to carrying out the will of the delegate bodies of the League. The role of dynamic leader and innovator was tied to the possibility of recruiting a widely recognized national personality respected internationally for his statesmanship and ability. The most frequently mentioned person for this position was Eleutherios Venizelos of Greece, who refused the post. In these early stages the title of chancellor was suggested as appropriate for the leadership type of role. President Wilson briefly considered the possibility of accepting the position but decided against it. Before offering the office to Sir Eric Drummond, the decision was made to drop the title of chancellor in favor of the more indeterminate title of Secretary-General.

The Covenant of the League of Nations provides little insight into the intended nature and role of the Secretariat. The relevant clauses from Article 6 are tersely stated as follows:

1. . . . The Secretariat shall comprise a Secretary-General and such secretaries and staff as may be required.
2. The first Secretary-General shall be the person named in the Annex; thereafter the Secretary-General shall be appointed by the Council with the approval of the majority of the Assembly.
3. The secretaries and staff of the Secretariat shall be appointed by the Secretary-General with the approval of the Council.
4. The Secretary-General shall act in that capacity at all meetings of the Assembly and of the Council.

The first Secretary-General named in the annex to the Covenant was Sir Eric Drummond, and it was his personality and vision of the office that shaped the role of the League's Secretariat. Sir Eric was immersed in the tradition of anonymity and non-partisanship of the British civil service, and he carried these attitudes into the League Secretariat.

Sir Eric Drummond was known to his most intimate associates as an efficient and capable administrator, a man of unimpeachable integrity, and one who effectively practiced quiet diplomacy. Some of the adjectives most frequently used by these associates to describe his qualities are discreet, prudent, modest, quiet, shy, impartial, tactful, cautious, well-informed, and judicious. Because of these personal qualities, combined with the tradition of the British civil service of impartially serving any political party in power, it is no surprise that Sir Eric visualized his role more as an administrator than as a leader. The assumption of this role smoothed his relationships with representatives of governments in the Assembly and Council. They trusted his judgment and appreciated his support and counsel. He never addressed the Council or Assembly, seldom made public speeches, avoided publicity, and limited his reports to a factual accounting of the work of the League.

The description above might lead to the erroneous assumption that Drummond failed to practice any form of leadership in League affairs. He believed that quiet diplomacy behind the scenes was often more effective than public statements. Dag Hammarskjöld later expressed his admiration of this approach by Drummond and partially followed a similar practice. Drummond spent much time in private, behind-the-scenes consultations with government representatives, and his wise counsel combined with his tact and discretion inspired their confidence and trust in him. He traveled extensively to world capitals but again he shunned publicity. He believed in the principles and purposes of the League and furthered them without assuming the role of outspoken advocate.

Drummond is frequently contrasted with Albert Thomas of France whose term as director of the International Labour Office of the International Labour Organization approximately coincided with the tenure of Drummond as League Secretary-General. Thomas was dynamic and outspoken and used his office to assert leadership on behalf of measures he personally advocated. Rather than being reserved, Thomas was an activist who took the initiative in suggesting policy. He was forceful, controversial, and eloquent. He suggested measures and programs to the ILO Conference and Governing Body and vigorously defended his initiatives. He promoted support for his programs by establishing direct contact with constituencies in labor unions, in governments, and among employers. Thomas was a fighter for social justice for labor. He also established a precedent and a model for the later relationship of the specialized agencies to the United Nations by insisting on the autonomy of the ILO and its freedom from undue control by the League Assembly.

To compare and contrast Drummond and Thomas may be both unfair and inappropriate. The foreign ministries, in all probability, would not have tolerated an Albert Thomas as Secretary-General of the League. In a functional organization, dealing with the special problems of labor, he was both accepted and effective. Each man seemed uniquely suited to the demands of his situation and each, then, was able to contribute mightily to the advancement of the cause of international organization.

In one most important respect Sir Eric Drummond was an innovator and pioneer in the development of precedents for secretariats of international organizations. He rejected the concept that personnel of the League Secretariat should be government representatives, that they should be seconded for their positions by their governments, or that they should serve the international agency while being temporarily detached from national civil service. Drummond insisted from the earliest stages that the League Secretariat should be truly international in composition, responsibilities, loyalties, and spirit. Sir Eric was supported in his principles by the Balfour Report to the League in 1920 and by several subsequent reports on administrative policies. The Balfour Report stated that "members of the Secretariat once appointed are no longer the servants of the country of which they are citizens, but become for the time being the servants only of the League of Nations. Their duties are not national but international."

This development of an international civil service was the first experiment of its type. It necessitated appointment of personnel by an international authority. It enabled the assemblage of a competent body of persons from more than thirty states working as an administrative team. Secretariat members were selected on the basis of qualifications for each position and devotion to the principles of the League rather than on the basis of nationality. Reasonable assurances of security of employment and tenure were given, and a corporate spirit was developed under Drummond's leadership.

An exception to the complete internationalization of the Secretariat was made at the Under Secretary-General and Assistant Secretary-General level. Each of the major powers insisted on having one of its nationals in a key position on an assigned basis, so that a Frenchman would always be replaced by a Frenchman, an Italian by an Italian, etc. Germany and Italy, in particular, insisted on home government approval of major appointees and on the duty of their nationals to report important matters to their foreign offices. The degree of national interference at the top level is cogently summarized by Arthur W. Rovine.

> By this time [1926], it was obvious enough that the upper strata of the Secretariat were filled with political appointees responsible in fact not to Secretary-General Drummond, but to their respective foreign offices, with their primary functions being advisory, representative, and liaison with home governments.[1]

Drummond gently but determinedly resisted undue encroachment of these practices upon the international independence of the Secretariat. The experience of the League in this regard is closely paralleled by the later situation in the United Nations both in the matter of the distribution of top administrative posts and in the attacks upon the neutrality of the Secretary-General accompanied by proposals for collective leadership operating under the limitations of a veto power. These United Nations developments will be examined in other sections of this chapter.

The League of Nations Secretariat always operated under conditions of severe limitations of budget and personnel. The number of personnel was a small fraction of the present total for the United Nations Secretariat and was actually less than the administrative staffs of several regional organizations and United Nations specialized

[1] Arthur W. Rovine, *The First Fifty Years: The Secretary-General in World Politics 1920–1970* (Leiden: A. W. Sijthoff, 1970), p. 38.

agencies today. These circumstances, in addition to the philosophy of exercising primarily an administrative role for the Secretariat, set limits on the impact which the Secretariat could exert on world affairs and conditions.

Joseph Avenol, who in 1933 succeeded Eric Drummond, and Sean Lester, who presided over the vestiges of the Secretariat from 1940 to 1946, retained, for the most part, the Drummond philosophy of the role of the Secretariat. Avenol, a French financial expert, was less capable than Drummond of inspiring the confidence of government representatives and the esprit de corps of Secretariat personnel. Because he believed that during most of his term as Secretary-General the League had lost its political impact, he emphasized the technical work of the organization. Sean Lester had the thankless job of holding together a skeleton Secretariat of a practically defunct organization.

THE INTERNATIONAL CIVIL SERVANT IN THE UNITED NATIONS

The Secretariats of the United Nations and of the specialized agencies are the beneficiaries of the principles established by Sir Eric Drummond for the Secretariat of the League of Nations. The substance of the practices initiated by Drummond was incorporated into the United Nations Charter and into the treaties establishing each of the specialized agencies to entrench these principles firmly into the basic concepts of the new organization rather than to leave them open to later negotiation or doubt.

The international character, loyalty, and independence of the Secretariat are fundamental to the effectiveness of an international civil service. The principle of national representation is carried out in the United Nations through the several delegate bodies. The Secretariat's role can only be performed satisfactorily if its members impartially serve the organization as a whole, are loyal to Charter principles, and take their direction from the Secretary-General, not from their home governments.

In Dumbarton Oaks and in San Francisco no fundamental disagreement was expressed with the principles underlying the international loyalty and independence of the Secretariat. The League experience and the desirability of impartiality in carrying out the recommendations of the delegate organs served to foster agreement and minimize dissent concerning the relevant provisions of the Charter.

If a secretariat is international in character, its members must be recruited on a broad geographical basis. Article 101 of the Charter provides that geographical distribution shall be considered but shall be secondary to the more essential requirements of high standards of efficiency, competence, and integrity in recruitment of personnel; no necessary conflict exists between these two sets of principles. Member states of the United Nations have insisted on a distribution of Secretariat posts that allots to each state a resonable "quota" of those posts with regard to both total number of positions and their grade level. This insistence reflects national pride as well as an attitude that national representation should, in a limited sense, carry over into the Secretariat. The Secretaries-General, buttressed by General Assembly support, have contended that efficiency, competence, and integrity must take precedence over geographical distribution, but that a wide variation of national backgrounds, cultures, and experiences among Secretariat personnel enrich the contributions that the Secretariat can make to the work of the organization. The intrinsic value of diversity of staff establishes the compatibility of geographic distribution with the primary standards of efficiency and integrity.

The issue of international loyalty raises some interesting questions. Must national loyalty be sublimated in favor of international loyalty for Secretariat personnel? Are the two loyalties incompatible? What are the demands of international loyalty on the staff member? How do temporary or permanent appointments to the Secretariat affect the attitudes of appointees toward their roles as international and as national actors? Can a member state demand of its nationals a certain standard of national loyalty as a requirement for employment by an international organization?

International loyalty demands that the staff member accept and adhere to the purposes and principles of the organization and faithfully and impartially further these standards in the performance of his or her duties as an international civil servant. The oath required of United Nations Secretariat personnel includes the promise that the employee will discharge assigned functions and regulate his or her personal conduct "with the interests of the United Nations only in view." The international civil servant must abjure the promotion of national interests in favor of impartially serving the interests of the international community. This is a difficult task in a nationalistic world. The staff member must also faithfully serve the Secretary-General or designated head of the secretariat of an international organization and must take instructions only from authorities internal to the organization.

The international civil servant is not required to forswear national allegiance in order to become an effective international agent. In fact, national loyalty, if not carried to the extreme of ethnocentrism and national prejudice, may serve as an effective prerequisite qualification for the international staff member. In general, the narrow or intolerant nationalist will not be inclined to seek employment with an international organization. The United Nations preparatory commission declared that "Loyalty to the Organization is in no way incompatible with an official's attachment to his own country, whose higher interest he is serving in serving the United Nations."

If international loyalty is to be fostered in a secretariat, at least two thirds of the personnel must have permanent status. A career service with adequate pay, promotion, and retirement benefits is essential to the building of an esprit de corps and a devotion to the purposes and principles of the organization that result only from continued experience and interaction among personnel of diverse backgrounds. The career civil servant gradually absorbs the spirit of cooperative enterprise which will ideally dominate the secretariat under skilled and intelligent leadership. The temporary employee, seconded by his government for a one- or two-year term, generally cannot achieve the same degree of loyalty to the organization to which he is briefly assigned, since his permanent career is with his national government or in his home state. His overall hierarchy of loyalties will, therefore, have his national attachments in a priority position. Communist countries have favored short-term international assignments for the majority of their nationals. This attitude is consistent with Communist states' attempts to convert international secretariats from independent to representative agencies. African states, because of internal demands for administrative talent, have been reluctant to release substantial numbers of qualified personnel for long-term careers in international secretariats. Technical experts recruited for field missions in a particular country are often on short-term contracts, but the main burden of the continuous work of international organizations is most effectively borne by career personnel of long experience who have acquired a high degree of impartiality and a sense of international loyalty to the organization and its purposes.

The greatest crisis pertaining to questions of loyalty of United Nations Secretariat personnel involved the dismissal of eighteen United States citizens in 1952–53. Investigations and charges of past or current Communist affiliations of employees in the United States government, particularly in the State Department, spilled over into allegations of Communist leanings among United States nationals in the secretariat. A federal grand jury, without handing down any indictments, charged that "an overwhelmingly large group" of disloyal Americans had infiltrated the United Nations. Several weeks later, Senator Joseph McCarthy, as chairman of the Internal Security Subcommittee of the Senate Judiciary Committee, directed hearings in New York involving eighteen American United Nations civil servants, half of whom were on permanent contract. The number of Americans called to testify amounted to 1 percent of the total number of United States employees of the Secretariat. On the basis of their United States constitutional rights and the independence, under the Charter, of the Secretariat from national jurisdiction, the Americans, on the advice of legal counsel, refused to testify before the grand jury and the subcommittee.

Secretary-General Trygve Lie was caught in the crosscurrents, on the one hand, of American anti-Communist hysteria and official pressure from the host country and, on the other, of the need to protect the independence and integrity of the Secretariat. In spite of the acknowledged right of United States citizens against self-incrimination guaranteed in the Fifth Amendment of the United States Constitution, Lie seemed to feel that refusal to testify represented an overriding threat to the reputation of the Secretariat. He stated that he did not want to employ any United States citizens under suspicion of dedication to the overthrow of their government by force or violence.

Lie first dismissed the temporary employees—those on fixed-term contracts—who had refused to testify. He then sought the advice of a special three-member international panel of eminent legal experts, on which several persons refused to serve. On the advice of the panel, the staff members on permanent contract were also dismissed. The United Nations Administrative Tribunal, in an appeal from those dismissed, found no grounds for misconduct on the part of the accused staff members and awarded substantial compensation to several of them. Early in his term as Secretary-General, Dag Hammarskjöld received approval for changes in the staff regulations clarifying the obligations of staff members and strengthening the Secretary-General's powers of dismissal of employees whose conduct is interpreted as violating the Charter's standards of integrity, independence, and impartiality. At the same time, Hammarskjöld asserted that he would be the final judge of the validity of evidence presented from national sources and that he would refuse to act on unsubstantiated charges against a staff member.

Under an executive order issued by President Truman on January 9, 1953, the United States Civil Service Commission and the

FBI were authorized to carry out loyalty investigations concerning all United States nationals employed by or applying for employment with the United Nations. Trygve Lie succumbed to pressure to allow the investigators to carry on their work on United Nations premises. Dag Hammarskjöld later rescinded this permission since such an invasion by national agents violated the international character of the headquarters. The loyalty investigations delivered a severe blow to the morale of the Secretariat as a whole from which recovery was slow and painful.

Questions of dual loyalties and wide geographical recruitment of staff members are closely related to the international independence of the Secretariat. This interrelatedness is clearly illustrated by the preceding paragraphs. However, the principle of independence merits further consideration.

Articles 100 and 101 of the United Nations Charter are basic to the establishment of the principle of Secretariat international independence. The essential elements in guaranteeing independence are the following: (1) The staff shall not seek or receive instructions from any government or other authority external to the organization. (2) Reciprocally, each member state shall respect the exclusively international character of the responsibilities of the staff and not seek to influence them in the discharge of their responsibilities. (3) Staff members shall refrain from any action reflecting adversely on their position as international officials responsible only to the organization. (4) The Secretary-General shall have the final power of making staff appointments within guidelines approved by the General Assembly.

Perhaps the best analysis of the elements relating to the independent position of the Secretariat was made by Dag Hammarskjöld in a lecture at Oxford University on May 30, 1961.[2] In this lecture Hammarskjöld recognized the dependence of the Secretary-General upon the services of governments to obtain suitable applicants for positions and to provide information concerning their competence and integrity, but he asserted the right of the Secretary-General to make final choices on the basis of the information furnished. He further states that mere suspicion concerning an employee or withholding of evidence from the Secretary-General by a government provided insufficient grounds for dismissal. In summary,

[2] "The International Civil Servant in Law and in Fact," reproduced in Wilder Foote, ed., *Servant of Peace: A Selection of the Speeches and Statements of Dag Hammarskjöld* (New York: Harper & Row, 1963), pp. 329–49.

The interest of the governments in placing certain nationals and in barring the employment of others had to be subordinated, as a matter of principle and law, to the independent determination of the Organization.[3]

Hammarskjöld also pointed out that yielding to pressures from governments to increase substantially the proportion of Secretariat staff on short fixed-term contracts would convert the Secretariat from an "international" to an "intergovernmental" body, would compromise its independence, and would reverse the principles established by the League of Nations and confirmed in Articles 100 and 101 of the Charter. With regard to the integrity of the international civil servant, Hammarskjöld asserted that the staff member must be guided by the common aims and rules of the organization and by recognized legal principles rather than by personal preferences. The staff member must subject himself to self-examination to balance personal judgment against respect for law and truth on behalf of the organization as a whole.

In his Oxford lecture Hammarskjöld also discussed the independence of the Secretary-General in implementing controversial political decisions. This aspect will be discussed in a subsequent section of this chapter dealing more specifically with the office of the Secretary-General.

In order to safeguard the independent position of Secretariat members, they must be free from national jurisdiction in the performance of their official duties. Article 105 of the Charter, and similar provisions in the basic treaties establishing the specialized agencies of the United Nations family, accord to staff officials "such privileges and immunities as are necessary for the independent exercise of their functions in connection with the Organization." Instead of conferring traditional diplomatic privileges and immunities, this clause establishes a functional basis for the privileges and immunities of Secretariat personnel. Such an indefinite standard requires supplemental treaties to identify the extent and limitations of privileges and immunities that are "necessary" for various levels or categories of personnel. In 1946 the General Assembly approved a General Convention on the Privileges and Immunities of the United Nations, which has been ratified by more than 100 countries. This convention enumerates the privileges and immunities that shall be accorded to categories of personnel specified by the Secretary-General but excludes from coverage those locally recruited persons paid on hourly rates. The Secretary-General and Assistant

[3] *Ibid.*, p. 339.

Secretaries-General and their immediate families are accorded full diplomatic privileges and immunities.

Special agreements have been worked out between the United Nations and certain host countries. One such agreement between the United Nations and the Netherlands covers the personnel associated with the International Court of Justice. Switzerland, as a nonmember of the United Nations but as host to the European headquarters of the United Nations, has acceded to a special arrangement with the United Nations. The United States has never ratified the general convention, but in 1947 approved, together with the General Assembly, a Headquarters Agreement. One difficulty is the failure of the Headquarters Agreement to accord exemption from taxation of salaries of United States nationals. Staff assessments have been necessary to reimburse United States nationals employed in the Secretariat in order to maintain equality in salary scales. United States accession to the general convention would alleviate other difficulties arising from discrepancies between that convention and the Headquarters Agreement.

THE ROLE OF THE SECRETARIAT

In much of the literature on the United Nations there is a tendency to treat the role of the Secretariat primarily in terms of the Secretary-General. This tendency is a natural outcome of, among other factors, the publicity accorded to the Secretary-General, the direct confrontations and consultations between him and government representatives, the delegation to him by other organs of broad responsibilities, his constitutional position as head of the Secretariat, and the personal qualities of leadership of successive occupants of the office.

Charles Winchmore has pointed out that, in spite of a close linkage between the Secretariat and its chief officer, the treatment of the Secretariat exclusively in terms of the Secretary-General is to confuse the whole with one of its parts.[4] In evidence of this distinction, one can cite Article 7 of the Charter, in which the Secretariat and not the Secretary-General is designated as a major organ of the United Nations, Article 97, in which the Secretariat is defined as comprised of both the Secretary-General and the staff, and various clauses of Articles 97-101, which deal with both elements of the Secretariat. Drawing this distinction in no way denigrates the impor-

[4] Charles Winchmore, "The Secretariat: Retrospect and Prospect," *International Organization*, Vol. 19 (Summer, 1965), pp. 622-39.

tance of the Secretary-General in the theory or practice of the United Nations, and his activities and leadership deserve special treatment in other sections of this chapter.

One problem of meeting the Charter standard of efficiency reaches beyond the recruitment of competent personnel into the establishment of a rational administrative structure for the assignment of tasks, for the maintenance of lines of communication, for the performance of work requirements, and for the provision of working conditions, equipment, and services that expedite the completion of assignments. The attainment of the goal of efficient organization and management is complicated by the size of the Secretariat, the diversity of cultural backgrounds and language abilities, the range of tasks to be performed, budgetary limitations, the demands for conformity to standards of neutrality, and the dispersal of personnel in many centers around the globe. In other words, the administration of the Secretariat is subject to all of the problems of other complex organizations plus special difficulties relating to worldwide recruitment and dispersal of personnel.

The complexity of the organization of the Secretariat may be appreciated by an examination of the chart on page 418. The organization problem has come under periodic scrutiny by the Secretary-General, the General Assembly, and special committees during the life span of the United Nations. Each Secretary-General has proposed changes in structure to suit his own style and interest in the administrative processes. Trygve Lie, by his own admission, was bored by administrative details, while Dag Hammarskjöld, in contrast, concentrated the supervision of administrative functions in his own office. The preparatory commission worked out detailed prescriptions for administrative organization of the Secretariat, and these were approved by the first session of the General Assembly, thus limiting the freedom of the first Secretary-General to formulate his own structure. The hectic initial recruitment of personnel resulted in geographical imbalances that had to be subsequently corrected. Major reviews of administrative structure and related problems were made in 1954-55, 1960–61, and the mid-1970s. In 1974 the General Assembly created an International Civil Service Commission of fifteen experts to advise the Assembly and the Secretary-General on personnel matters and on the coordination of services within the United Nations family of agencies. Their first set of recommendations in 1977 resulted in a 17 percent reduction in the salary scale for general service personnel in United Nations agencies in Geneva.

Although the United Nations Secretariat is dwarfed by compari-

THE UNITED NATIONS SYSTEM

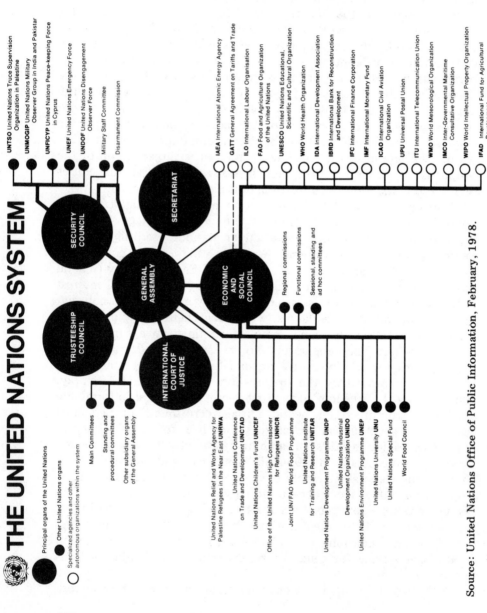

- Principal organs of the United Nations
- Other United Nations organs
- Specialized agencies and other autonomous organizations within the system

TRUSTEESHIP COUNCIL

SECURITY COUNCIL

GENERAL ASSEMBLY

INTERNATIONAL COURT OF JUSTICE

SECRETARIAT

ECONOMIC AND SOCIAL COUNCIL

Main Committees

Standing and procedural committees

Other subsidiary organs of the General Assembly

Regional commissions

Functional commissions

Sessional, standing and ad hoc committees

United Nations Relief and Works Agency for Palestine Refugees in the Near East **UNRWA**

United Nations Conference on Trade and Development **UNCTAD**

United Nations Children's Fund **UNICEF**

Office of the United Nations High Commissioner for Refugees **UNHCR**

Joint UN/FAO World Food Programme

United Nations Institute for Training and Research **UNITAR**

United Nations Development Programme **UNDP**

United Nations Industrial Development Organization **UNIDO**

United Nations Environment Programme **UNEP**

United Nations University **UNU**

United Nations Special Fund

World Food Council

UNTSO United Nations Truce Supervision Organization in Palestine

UNMOGIP United Nations Military Observer Group in India and Pakistan

UNFICYP United Nations Peace-keeping Force in Cyprus

UNEF United Nations Emergency Force

UNDOF United Nations Disengagement Observer Force

Military Staff Committee

Disarmament Commission

IAEA International Atomic Energy Agency

GATT General Agreement on Tariffs and Trade

ILO International Labour Organisation

FAO Food and Agriculture Organization of the United Nations

UNESCO United Nations Educational, Scientific and Cultural Organization

WHO World Health Organization

IDA International Development Association

IBRD International Bank for Reconstruction and Development

IFC International Finance Corporation

IMF International Monetary Fund

ICAO International Civil Aviation Organization

UPU Universal Postal Union

ITU International Telecommunication Union

WMO World Meteorological Organization

IMCO Inter-Governmental Maritime Consultative Organization

WIPO World Intellectual Property Organization

IFAD International Fund for Agricultural Development

Source: United Nations Office of Public Information, February, 1978.

418

son with the 2.8 million employees of the United States government or the work force of giant corporations, it is large and complex when compared with the 700 employees of the League of Nations. The number now approximates 18,000. About one-third of this number work in New York, and the other two-thirds are dispersed in the Geneva office, in the regional commissions, as United Nations country representatives, and in field operations in more than 130 countries. Supervising, controlling, and coordinating such diverse activities and personnel require the application of considerable expertise in administrative skills.

The recruitment of staff on a wide geographical basis, on the one hand, enriches the international character of the Secretariat, but, on the other, complicates the smooth functioning of administrative processes. Communication is hampered when any two people in the Secretariat make oral or written contact in a language in which both are not equally proficient. The necessity to reproduce documents in six official languages is a requirement not demanded of national administrations. Administrative methods and standards of efficiency vary from one country and region to another. Variations in cultural values and ways of life affect the working relationships of personnel both positively and negatively. Achieving an acceptable standard of administrative efficiency among persons of lingual and cultural diversity and with varied administrative training and experience is a difficult task.

Only a minority of the total employees of the Secretariat are subject to international recruitment on a geographical "quota" basis. Language specialists must be employed on the criterion of necessary skills. Positions below the professional level are also exempt and are filled mainly through applications from persons in the local job market. Nevertheless, the most responsible posts are filled by recruitment on a worldwide distribution basis.

Budgetary penury has been a problem of international organizations since the days of the League of Nations. The policy organs assign new tasks to the Secretariat but are less than generous with financial support. Tardiness in paying national assessments and refusal on the part of some members to pay for certain peacekeeping expenses have reduced the organization to pauper status despite annual pleas by the Secretary-General to the members to revitalize the United Nations with a much-needed infusion of funds. Secretariat personnel have faced the constant threat in recent years of pay days without paychecks because of the virtual bankruptcy of the organization. Such uncertainties most assuredly affect the morale of the staff. Financial stringencies also limit the means available to most effectively carry out the multiple tasks assigned to an often overworked staff.

Secretariat personnel must be constantly on guard concerning the national sensibilities and interests of each of the member states of the United Nations. Each staff member must keep in mind that, in reality, he or she has more than 150 bosses to please in addition to his or her superiors in the Secretariat hierarchy. Neutrality demands that each word of a study or report produced within the Secretariat be scrutinized to assure that no offense can be taken by any government delegation. Imagination, creativeness, and literary flair frequently must be stifled in favor of established legal jargon, which has precise and accepted meaning based on past practice and experience. As a result most United Nations documents and reports make for fairly dull reading.

Certain large tasks occupy the energies of most United Nations Secretariat personnel. One of these is the servicing of the 5,000 or more meetings or conferences held annually by United Nations organs or other agencies convening under United Nations auspices. In addition to supplying physical facilities and preparing documentation, studies, and reports, the Secretariat provides highly competent language specialists and translators for both consecutive and simultaneous translation of speeches and debates and for the written reproduction of documents in the six working and official languages — English, French, Russian, Chinese, Spanish, and Arabic.

In the substantive areas of United Nations programs, the bulk of the personnel is engaged in economic and social activities and projects. As the United Nations has instigated more and more operating programs, in addition to the previous tasks of gathering data and issuing studies and reports, the number of employees in the economic and social areas has increased and a larger proportion of this number has been widely dispersed throughout the world. As technical assistance and economic aid through the United Nations have been expanded, United Nations personnel have become closely associated with large numbers of experts engaged by the specialized agencies for field projects. Teamwork between these agents of international organizations and local governmental personnel is also a necessary consequence of the increasing emphasis on economic and social development.

A third major area of activity of Secretariat personnel is the range of internal housekeeping chores necessary in all complex administrative organizations. These activities include financial and accounting services, personnel services, maintenance of physical facilities, supplies, records, library, transportation, security, and other similar services.

Other activities of the United Nations are important or even essential but engage the efforts of smaller numbers of staff members. Some of these other areas include political and security council affairs, non-self-governing territories and trusteeship affairs, legal matters and public information. The Secretary-General also maintains a staff of personal advisers and assistants whose role will be discussed in the following section.

TASKS AND INFLUENCE OF THE SECRETARY-GENERAL

Although the staff of the United Nations Secretariat and the Secretary-General are interdependent in their functions, the Secretary-General's position and responsibilities are, in many respects, unique, and he is assigned a central role as an administrator and leader in the organization. The Charter specifies several powers and functions that the Secretary-General is expected to exercise. Article 97 designates him as the "chief administrative officer of the Organization." Article 98 requires that he submit "an annual report to the General Assembly on the work of the Organization," and Article 101 empowers him to appoint the staff "under regulations established by the General Assembly." These functions were all previously exercised in the practice, if not in the mandate, of the Secretary-General of the League of Nations. The expansion of the United Nations Secretary-General's role into the political realm is based primarily on a broad interpretation of the provision of Article 98 that the Secretary-General "shall perform such other functions as are entrusted to him" by the General Assembly, Security Council, the Economic and Social Council, and the Trusteeship Council, and on the succinct statement comprising Article 99 that "the Secretary-General may bring to the attention of the Security Council any matter which in his opinion may threaten the maintenance of international peace and security." Although Article 99 has rarely been specifically invoked to call meetings of the Security Council, its implications, when added to the delegation of authority under Article 98 and the other general powers of the Secretary-General, have served as a basis for political activism by the Secretary-General.

The evolution of the role of the Secretary-General in the area of executive leadership has resulted more from other factors than from deliberate grants of power in the Charter. Any constitutional document becomes a living instrument only through practice and application to a series of actual events and circumstances. The role of the Secretary-General has expanded beyond the intentions of the architects of the Charter in response to demands that could not have been foreseen in 1945. This expansion has come about through broad interpretation of the general and specific terms of the Charter, through delegation of responsibilities to the Secretary-General by the Security Council and General Assembly (usually with either the approval or the acquiescence of the major powers), and through the initiative of successive Secretaries-General in seeking freedom of maneuver and in enhancing possibilities for leadership by all available means within the limits of each political situation. The personality, philosophy, and diplomatic skills of each incumbent of the office have affected the parameters of his action and influence in expanding executive leadership.

One factor affecting the Secretary-General's ability to exercise leadership is his relationship with other top-level administrators and executive personnel in the Secretariat. In San Francisco a proposal to elect a number of deputy directors in the same manner as the Secretary-General was rejected on the grounds that such a procedure would limit the freedom of the Secretary-General and subject him to political restraints. However, the Big Five proceeded to reach agreement on a distribution of top posts among their countries and to put forward the names of particular candidates whom they expected the Secretary-General to appoint. The Soviet Union was allotted the position of Assistant Secretary-General (later Under-Secretary) for Political and Security Council Affairs; the United States took the post in Administrative and Financial Services; the United Kingdom was assigned to Economic Affairs; Social Affairs went to France, and Trusteeship to China. Such an arrangement would have gone far toward negating the Secretary-General's independence from political control if each Secretary-General had not taken steps to by-pass these chief assistants and to centralize decision making in his executive office. Andrew Cordier of the United States served as executive assistant to both Lie and Hammarskjöld. When Hammarskjöld reorganized the Secretariat, he added two Under-Secretaries for Special Political Affairs to serve as special assistants without portfolio. U Thant, in another reorganization, stated that he should consult his eight principal advisers or other officials individually or collectively according to circumstances. Thus, the successive Secretaries-General maintained some flexibility of control in spite of the pressures from major powers to dilute the principle of international independence of the Secretariat.

The Secretary-General is chief administrator or manager of the organization. His strategic position at the intersection of the political and administrative sectors of the organization provides him with opportunities for offering initiative and leadership in both sectors.

He maintains contacts with governments and their representatives in the United Nations delegations. He has available an independent, substantial, and usually adequate communications system including telephone, telegraph, television, radio, press, library, and documentation facilities. He personally performs those administrative tasks in which he is most interested and which most enhance his position of leadership, and delegates to others the remainder. He appoints Secretariat personnel, within the constraints previously outlined, and is the primary source of plans for restructuring the administrative framework, a process fundamental to improvement of administrative effectiveness and efficiency. In carrying out his administrative functions, the Secretary-General must represent the epitome of discretion and neutrality among member states. At the same time he must uphold the principles and purposes of the organization.

In attempting to unify the staff as an efficient administrative unit, the Secretary-General confronts a paradoxical set of factors. Centrifugal forces (in addition to the representational basis for appointment of heads of major departments and offices, and short-term contracts for a minority of employees) include the compartmentalization of the Secretariat into its specific functions and activities. Each employee tends to identify with his or her own unit and to develop a loyalty to his or her administrative chief. In stimulating changes of policy, the Secretary-General is frustrated by attitudes of immobility and resistance to innovation by staff members who cling to established procedures and whose security is protected by staff regulations enforced with the aid of a Staff Association and a Staff Council.

Opposed to these centrifugal forces are the unifying factors available to the Secretary-General. Insofar as the Staff Council has been utilized to develop policy concerning staff welfare, an esprit de corps has been established for the entire Secretariat. The staff members are inclined to rally behind the maximalist philosophy of the Secretary-General because an expansion of executive power is shared by all members of the Secretariat. The career international civil servants also develop, in common with the Secretary-General, a devotion to the broad principles and purposes of the organization, which binds them together in a sense of mission. Finally, the Secretary-General must inspire his staff by his leadership and by seeking their support in their common efforts.

In preparing the budget the Secretary-General is dealing with both political and administrative implications of the document. Allocation proposals determine changes in program emphasis and affect the tasks to be performed by Secretariat personnel. The

Secretary-General by no means has a free hand in budgetary matters. His proposals are subject to review by the General Assembly through the Advisory Committee on Administrative and Budgetary Questions and the Fifth Committee, where attitudes of conservatism and economy prevail. The near-bankrupt condition of the United Nations since 1962 has had a serious impact on staff morale and on budget planning.

Article 63 of the Charter assigns to the Economic and Social Council the task of coordinating the activities of the specialized agencies and the United Nations in economic and social projects, but, of necessity, the Secretary-General is the chief coordinator. In its first year of operation, the Economic and Social Council authorized the Secretary-General to establish an Administrative Committee on Coordination composed of the administrative heads of the specialized agencies and to serve as its chairman. This committee attempts to prevent duplication of effort and any working at cross-purposes and to allocate tasks among the diverse agencies and subagencies. Other efforts at coordination by the Secretary-General are carried out through the preparation of reports for the Economic and Social Council and through multiagency cooperative activities in such areas as technical assistance and economic development.

The most significant and controversial extensions of the Secretary-General's power have been in the political realm. The history of this development has been marked by periods of euphoria concerning the Secretary-General's accomplishments followed by bitter attacks upon his person and office by one or another of the member states, including the big powers.

Trygve Lie was, at times, a severe critic of the major powers' failure to live up to Charter principles. In 1950 he interjected his Twenty-Year Program for Peace into the situation of the East-West Cold War in an attempt to restore the United Nations as an effective instrument for peace and collective security. His attempt at negotiation with the major powers to support his proposals received an especially cold reception in Moscow, inspired no efforts at implementation by any major power, and fell victim to the Korean War. In his annual reports to the General Assembly, Lie called upon the great powers to seek agreement on world problems. He also spoke out in press conferences and made public statements against regional security pacts, such as NATO, as inconsistent with Charter intentions concerning regional arrangements and collective self-defense and as inimical to global solutions of global problems.

In the first dispute to come before the Security Council, the Secretary-General was criticized, at various stages, by the Soviet

Union and the United States but managed to establish an important principle concerning his political prerogatives. When, in 1946, Iran and the United States insisted, with Lie's reluctant acquiescence, that the dispute over failure of the Soviet Union to withdraw troops from Iranian territory by an agreed deadline be placed on the Security Council agenda, the Soviet representative walked out in protest. When both Iran and the Soviet Union wished to drop the item from the agenda before the troop withdrawal was complete, Lie supported this position in a document based on legal opinion, but the United States mustered sufficient votes to retain the question on the agenda. At the same time, Lie's assertion of authority under Article 99 to intervene in Security Council affairs with oral or written statements at any time during debate was opposed by the United States but subsequently upheld and established as a general rule of procedure. In ensuing months his right to make similar statements to the General Assembly on his own initiative was established along with his right to conduct investigations to determine whether matters should be brought before these bodies. These tools gave the Secretary-General political powers unprecedented in the experience of the League of Nations.

In the early stages of the Palestine dispute, Trygve Lie strongly supported the partition plan approved by the General Assembly and urged the major powers to enforce it through Security Council action including, if necessary, the furnishing of military forces. As in other situations, Lie felt a duty to speak for the collective interest of the United Nations as a whole. He procured several hundred personnel for observation and truce supervision in Palestine and worked closely with the mediator and other United Nations agents in arranging a truce.

Lie alienated first the United States and later the Soviet Union by his stand on other major United Nations issues. In 1950 he strongly endorsed the seating of Communist Chinese delegates in the United Nations and thus incurred the wrath of the United States. With the outbreak of the Korean War, his support for military measures under the aegis of the United Nations evoked hostility by the Soviet Union to the point of their opposing the extension of his term and of totally boycotting him throughout the remainder of his tenure in office. In the loyalty investigations during the last months of Lie's tenure, he was severely criticized by the delegates of many states for his failure to oppose strongly the overzealous activities of agents of the United States government, which critics saw as a threat to the independence and integrity of the Secretariat.

Dag Hammarskjöld as Secretary-General contributed more to

the position of executive leadership of that office than any other incumbent. His contributions came as a result of circumstances to which he responded by building a body of theory and practice that expanded the role of the Secretary-General in unprecedented directions and dimensions. In the end, his actions and ideas brought him and his office under bitter attack from the representatives of the Soviet Union, who perceived his claims as inimical to great-power sovereignty and dominance in world politics.

One of Hammarskjöld's earliest assignments that allowed him some leeway in exercising his diplomatic talents was a request from the General Assembly that the Secretary-General seek the release of fifteen American flyers downed on United Nations missions and imprisoned in China. The Assembly resolution provided no specific guidelines and permitted Hammarskjöld to use "the means most appropriate in his judgment." Since the resolution also condemned the Chinese action, Hammarskjöld wisely decided to use, instead, as his basis of authority for a mission to Peking, his general authority as Secretary-General. Although no dramatic announcement followed his four-day visit, all the flyers were released within the next seven months.

The Suez Canal crisis of 1956 provided much broader mandates and opportunities for the exercise of discretion and initiative by the Secretary-General. The Security Council was deadlocked by British and French vetoes requiring an emergency session of the General Assembly under the Uniting for Peace Resolution. The General Assembly called for a cease-fire, and a withdrawal of forces behind the previously established armistice lines, and directed the Secretary-General to submit within forty-eight hours plans for the recruitment and dispatch of a United Nations Emergency Force to the Middle East to secure compliance with these provisions.

All of the guidelines, details for raising a peacekeeping force, and the actual direction of the operations were delegated to Hammarskjöld by the General Assembly. Negotiations with the governments that were to furnish personnel as well as with the belligerents for the withdrawal of their forces were necessary. Egypt finally agreed to the deployment of United Nations forces upon parts of its territory after Israel's refusal to accept such an occupying group, and the first UNEF troops reached Egyptian territory eleven days after the adoption of the General Assembly's resolution.

A new principle and concept evolved with the formation of the UNEF. Peacekeeping by a police-type force was substituted for collective-security action dependent upon the might of the major powers. "Preventive diplomacy" and "peacekeeping" entered the lexicon of the United Nations. The Secretary-General directed the forces through his appointee, General Burns of Canada, in contrast to the earlier arrangement in Korea that the United States furnish the direction of the combined forces there.

Hammarskjöld also assumed responsibility for the clearing of the Suez Canal, which had been blocked by ships sunk by the Egyptians. The task was completed within four months (which was ahead of all predictions) by a salvage operation involving personnel or equipment from at least eight countries.

The Hungarian crisis, which occurred almost simultaneously with the Suez dispute, provided no opportunity for the Secretary-General to widen his powers or display his ability to carry out successfully a mission assigned by the political organs of the United Nations. The General Assembly requested Hammarskjöld to take such initiatives as were available to investigate the invasion of Hungary by Soviet troops and to ascertain the facts concerning the intervention. In the face of Soviet intransigence, no entry to Hungarian territory was possible, and United Nations influence was negligible.

As additional crises faced the United Nations, Hammarskjöld's added to his philosophy of an enlarged leadership role for the Secretary-General. Not only were specific mandates from the political organs to be flexibly and generously interpreted, but an independent role for the Secretary-General was asserted for situations in which the resolutions lacked specificity or in which authorization was totally lacking. Hammarskjöld proclaimed his right and duty to fill vacuums when no basis of authority existed except the general principles and aims of the Charter and a broad interpretation of the Secretary-General's grants of power in that document.

The Lebanese crisis of 1958 demonstrates Hammarskjöld interpretation of his independent position. In response to a Security Council's directive, he formed an observer group to investigate Lebanese charges of infiltration across its border with Syria by United Arab Republic partisans. After the dispatch of United States Marines to Lebanon at President Chamoun's invitation, all subsequent proposals in the Security Council to provide additional guidance and authority for further action by the Secretary-General failed because of Soviet vetoes. Hammarskjöld declared that under these circumstances he would fill the vacuum by taking such additional measures as he judged appropriate. He increased the observer group sufficiently for effective border surveillance. After he instigated a pledge of mutual nonintervention by the Arab states, and after the observers made a further report on minimal infiltration across Lebanese borders, all foreign forces and the observer group were withdrawn from Lebanon.

Independent action by Hammarskjöld without first requesting

guidance from the political organs of the United Nations was demonstrated by the situations in the dispute between Cambodia and Thailand in 1958–60 and in the internal conditions in Laos in 1959–61. In the Cambodian-Thailand dispute Hammarskjöld advised against taking the matter to the Security Council in order to avoid any possible hardening of conflicting East-West positions. With informal consent from the major powers, he appointed a personal special representative who brought about a reconciliation between the two countries. When a further dispute flared up in 1960, another special representative of the Secretary-General conducted negotiations with Cambodian and Thai diplomats at United Nations headquarters in New York, which led to the signing of terms of settlement.

In the Laotian situation Hammarskjöld twice made personal visits to Laos to urge a position of neutrality in accordance with the Geneva agreements of 1954. Hammarskjöld resisted requests from the Laotian government for the establishment of a peacekeeping force in Laos, but, following his second visit, he appointed a series of personal representatives who were only temporarily successful in delaying the effects of outside intervention.

Hammarskjöld's assumptions of independent authority reached their highest peak and met their greatest challenge in the Congo crisis of 1960–61. In 1960, to meet the Congo emergency, he invoked, for the first time, his authority to call a meeting of the Security Council. In the early stages of the crisis the Security Council provided broad guidelines under which Hammarskjöld raised a peacekeeping force to aid the central government in restoring order and to supervise the withdrawal of Belgian and mercenary forces from the Congo. When the internal political situation became confused and when the secession of Katanga and other provinces was threatened, Hammarskjöld repeatedly returned to the Council for clarification of his instructions. In the face of inadequate guidelines and the necessity for quick decisions in emergencies, he did not hesitate to use his own judgment or to support the decisions of his deputies in the Congo. When the Security Council became deadlocked and when outside forces were intervening to influence the internal political situation, Hammarskjöld turned to the General Assembly for support and direction.

Because of the confused political situation in the Congo and the clash of external interests, the guidelines furnished by both the Security Council and the General Assembly became increasingly inadequate, and Hammarskjöld was faced with making personal decisions or refusing to act at all. In assessing his responsibilities Hammarskjöld rejected the course of inaction. He declared that, instead, his decisions, regardless of offense to any member states, should be based on (1) Charter principles and purposes, (2) widely accepted legal rules and precedents, especially those found in United Nations resolutions, (3) consultations with the personnel of the permanent missions to the United Nations or with advisory committees of the type established for the UNEF and Congo operations, and, finally, (4) his own personal judgment based on his integrity and exercise of conscience with self-examination concerning his objectivity and neutrality.[5]

When the Soviet Union's representatives decided that Hammarskjöld's policies in the Congo were inimical to Soviet interests, they mounted an attack upon him personally and upon the office of Secretary-General. Asserting that no man is neutral, Khrushchev demanded in the General Assembly that Hammarskjöld resign and that the single office be modified to a "troika," or three-member collective executive body, representing the socialist, western, and neutralist groups of states. Under this arrangement the interest of each bloc would be safeguarded by vesting each member of the "troika" with veto power. Thus, the arena for political struggle would be broadened to include the Secretariat, and the independent international role of the Secretariat, established forty years earlier by Drummond, would be abandoned.

Hammarskjöld refused to resign and defended the integrity of his office. He declared that "this is a question not of a man but of an institution."[6] He reminded the members of the organization that the Congo was their operation, not his, but if they failed to furnish positive direction, he had no choice but to follow his own conviction.[7] He asserted that the Soviet proposal for a triple executive would destroy the effectiveness of the United Nations. Hammarskjöld appealed to the small nations on the basis that they, not the big powers, needed the protection of the organization, and that he would remain in his post if the large majority wished him to do so.[8] He repeatedly received what amounted to overwhelming votes of confidence in the General Assembly, and the neutralist states rejected the Soviet proposal for giving them representation in the leadership of the Secretariat by substituting a "troika" for a single Secretary-General. However, Hammarskjöld's effectiveness, from September, 1960, until his death a year later, was diminished by the active hostility of the Soviet Union.

[5] Foote, *Servant of Peace*, pp. 346–48.
[6] *Ibid.*, p. 316.
[7] *Ibid.*, p. 317.
[8] *Ibid.*, pp. 318–19.

U Thant, during his ten years as Secretary-General, did not further develop the philosophy of the office or establish startling precedents, but he acted discreetly in a series of crises, consolidated the gains of his predecessors, kept the support of the big powers, and acted as spokesman on the issues of greatest concern to the developing nations. Throughout his tenure of office he was plagued by the financial crises that the members were unable or unwilling to resolve. He played a constructive role in political disputes such as those involving the Congo, Cyprus, West Irian, and the Cuban missile crisis. He was criticized in some quarters for the rapid withdrawal of the UNEF force from the Middle East in 1967. He was outspoken but ineffective in trying to bring an end to the Vietnam War. In general he maintained the principles established by Lie and Hammarskjöld and judiciously exercised the previously established prerogatives. His successor, Kurt Waldheim, continued along a similar line. Both Thant and Waldheim were restricted in their opportunities for initiative and independence by the development of a community of interest among the big powers to control political situations and to prevent the Secretary-General and the General Assembly from expanding their powers through default and deadlock in the Security Council. The combination of fewer vacuums to be filled, a less aggressive personal style, and the lessons to be learned from the painful clashes of Lie and Hammarskjöld with the major powers contributed to a lower profile in leadership for Thant and Waldheim.

BASES OF INFLUENCE AND LEADERSHIP

In an international organization such as the United Nations, leadership is shared by the personnel in the Secretariat and the governments of the member states. The unique position of the Secretary-General has been detailed and illustrated in the previous section. As the major spokesman for an international, objective approach to problems, based on Charter principles and goals, he epitomizes the advocacy of the utilization of the United Nations for the maintenance of peace and for the improvement of the human condition through economic and social cooperation.

Other members of the Secretariat sometimes share in this leadership role. Ralph Bunche, who served as Director of the Division of Trusteeship Affairs of the Secretariat prior to his appointment as Acting United Nations Mediator in Palestine, received the Nobel Peace Prize in 1950 for his mediation efforts in the Middle East.

Andrew Cordier, who served as executive assistant to the Secretary-General from 1946 to 1961, and C. V. Narashimhan, who succeeded to the post and served for twelve years, were key figures in decision making in the Secretary-General's office. Paul Hoffman, as director of both the United Nations Special Fund and its enlarged successor, the United Nations Development Program, left his mark on the economic and social development efforts of the United Nations. In the same area of concern, Gunnar Myrdal, as executive secretary of the Economic Commission for Europe, and Raul Prebisch, as executive secretary of the Economic Commission for Latin America, established reputations as vigorous leaders and innovators. Much leadership credit for economic and social activities of the United Nations must also be given to Philippe de Seynes, undersecretary-general for Economic and Social Affairs in the administrations of Hammarskjöld, Thant, and Waldheim. In this position he directed the largest and most active segment of the Secretariat.

In many cases the Secretary-General requires the services of a personal representative to go to a crisis area to investigate, mediate, and report on conditions and events. In these instances he often selects a trusted, capable, and judicious member of the Secretariat. Among those who have ably served in this capacity is Pier Spinelli, who during his ten-year tenure as director of the European Office of the United Nations in Geneva was given assignments to the Middle East, Yemen, and Cyprus as special representative of Hammarskjöld and of Thant. Secretary Thant also relied on José Rolz-Bennett to act as his personal representative in West New Guinea in 1962, in Cyprus in 1964, in the dispute between Guinea and the Ivory Coast in 1967, and in Algeria in 1968.

Several able and distinguished leaders have headed the secretariats of the specialized agencies affiliated with the United Nations. Among the many who might be cited for their leadership qualities, Eugene R. Black, who served as president of the International Bank for Reconstruction and Development for fourteen years, and Robert S. McNamara, who became its president in 1968, are noteworthy. McNamara has engaged in a vigorous campaign to funnel a much larger share of the bank's loans into the International Development Association with the goal of speeding up the development process in the countries that most need financial aid.

If the United Nations is to make progress toward achieving its goals, leadership must come from the member governments as well as from the Secretariat. Heads of delegations, if they have a firm basis of support within their governments, may make major contributions to the success of the organization. Lester Pearson of Canada has distinguished himself as an innovator in United Nations affairs. He served as president of the General Assembly in 1952. He is credited with being the father of the idea for the United Nations Emergency Force. In recognition of his contributions he received the Nobel Peace Prize in 1957.

Charles Malik of Lebanon and Eleanor Roosevelt of the United States worked persistently in the Commission on Human Rights to produce the Universal Declaration on Human Rights. Carlos P. Romulo of the Philippines is another head of a national delegation who distinguished himself as a spokesman for a strengthened United Nations. Adlai Stevenson combined outstanding talent with an enthusiasm for the role of the United Nations, but he was frequently frustrated by a lack of support from Washington for his personal preferences on the United States stance in the organization.

Heads of governments have occasionally utilized the United Nations to carry out proposals for the achievement of universal goals. Two such proposals are noteworthy. In 1949 the General Assembly developed the Expanded Program for Technical Assistance in response to the multilateral aspects of President Truman's Point Four Proposals in his inaugural address of that year. In 1953 President Eisenhower used the General Assembly as a forum for his Atoms for Peace proposal, and this culminated in the formation of the International Atomic Energy Agency.

Secretaries-General sometimes reach into national government services to recruit talent for special assignments. An example is Robert K. A. Gardiner of Ghana, who was appointed as chief of the United Nations Congo Operation in 1962–63 and in the latter year was chosen executive secretary of the Economic Commission for Africa. Major-General Indar Jit Rikhye of India served as chief of staff of the UNEF in 1958-60 and became military advisor to the Secretary-General in 1960. During his eight years in the latter post, he also was assigned to United Nations forces in the Congo, West Irian, Yemen, and Cyprus. Of special note is the service of Gunnar Jarring, who, while serving as Swedish ambassador to the USSR, took on, in 1967, a prolonged and difficult assignment as special representative of the Secretary-General to attempt to mediate the dispute in the Middle East.

Many other individuals could be cited for meritorious service on behalf of United Nations goals. Restraints imposed within the larger arena of world politics have limited the leadership roles exercised by the individuals who have participated in this work.

THE NEED FOR INTERNATIONAL LEADERSHIP

Since 1970 both the United Nations and its Secretariat have been subject to increased criticism. A series of appraisals of United Nations personnel policies generally agree that the quality of Secretariat personnel has fallen below optimum standards. One critical study concentrates a large share of the blame on member states' advocacy of unqualified candidates for appointment to positions and the Secretariat's lack of resistance to such pressure.[9] Some corrective measures in recruitment policies have been initiated, but important tasks will be assigned to the United Nations only if there is confidence in its competency to perform those tasks. This requirement also applies to other international organizations.

In a chaotic and increasingly interdependent world more orderly processes for settling disputes and for achieving economic and social cooperation are needed. States that insist on a myopic national view of the international scene can contribute little to the resolution of international problems. International organizations provide one set of existing channels through which such problems can be cooperatively attacked. Since the opportunities for leadership within international agencies are so restricted by the attitudes and policies of governments, it is from within these governments that an impetus toward utilizing the full potential of international organization must originate. The need is for national leaders with enough vision to recognize both the threats and the means toward removing those threats that exist in an interdependent world. The exercise of leadership in and through the United Nations and other international organizations could help to diminish the sources of tensions and restore confidence in human capabilities for peacefully resolving conflicts and problems.

[9] Seymour M. Finger and John Mugno, *The Politics of Staffing the United Nations Secretariat* (New York: The Ralph Bunche Institute on the United Nations, The Graduate School and University Center of the City University of New York, 1974).

16

Transnational Relations and International Organization

The constant change in world relations affects individuals, states, businesses, and organizations—domestic or international, public or private. Better transportation and communication link people, ideas, and commodities across national borders to a degree never before possible.

These changes force states and international organizations to adjust their policies and operations in order to maintain their relevance in international relations. Nongovernmental organizations in business, labor, and many other fields encroach upon states' prerogatives and escape government control. Often the network of contacts and transactions among nongovernmental actors threatens to undermine state sovereignty in important areas and questions the adequacy of the state-centric model of international relations.

Although transnational activities have been carried on for centuries, they have only recently become of major significance. And even more recently have scholars focused attention on these activities as important factors in current and future political relationships deserving increased analysis. There still is much to be learned about these activities, but it is known that transnational relations are now important and will be more so in the future. Because there is sure to be more concentration on the study of transnational relations, the fields of international relations and international organization may even need to be redefined so as to accommodate dimensions previously largely ignored.

DEFINITIONS AND PERSPECTIVES

Because the study of transnational relations is relatively new, some of the terminology applied to this area is little understood and sometimes lacks precision. To guide the student in distinguishing between interstate and transnational relations, a few definitions are in order. Not all scholars would subscribe to the same use of terms, but the definitions adopted below are based on those used in the summer, 1971, issue of *International Organization*. These are selected because twenty scholars writing on various aspects of the theme "Transnational Relations and World Politics" agreed to accept the general definitions supplied by the editors of the issue.[1]

The basic term used by the editors, Keohane and Nye, is "transnational interaction." A transnational interaction is "the movement of tangible or intangible items across state boundaries when at least one actor is not an agent of a government or an international organization."[2] This definition focuses on the activities of nongovernmental organizations and individuals involved in the transfer of goods, money, credit, information, or persons from one country to another. States or intergovernmental organizations may be involved in transnational interactions, but they need not be, since the interaction may be between nongovernmental organizations or individuals only.

In the lexicon of Keohane and Nye, the term "transnational interaction" is not as broad as "transnational relations," since the latter also includes interactions involving governmental subunits and subunits of international organizations as well as nongovernmental actors. Complex organizations, whether governmental or nongovernmental, are scarcely monolithic and may be properly treated as multidimensional. The Secretary-General of the United Nations or the Central Intelligence Agency of the United States government

---

[1] Robert O. Keohane and Joseph S. Nye, Jr., eds., "Transnational Relations and World Politics," *International Organization*, Vol. 25 (Summer, 1971). This publication, which makes no claim to comprehensive coverage of the subject, is at this time the best broadgauge treatment of the many facets of transnational relations and is a basis and guide for further investigation of the area.

[2] *Ibid.*, p. 332.

may play independent roles, on occasion, from those taken through "normal" or traditional policy channels.

Transnational or nongovernmental international organizations may be divided into two broad categories. One is the nonprofit organization of which there are approximately 3000 with the number increasing by nearly 5 percent per year. The other category is the multinational business enterprise organized for profit, the number of which varies from 250 to 1,000 depending on the definition of how widespread the activities of such an enterprise must be in order to qualify as multinational.

Definitions of multinational business enterprises are generally imprecise in setting standards for inclusion or exclusion of particular firms. Some definitions are based primarily on the number of countries in which a corporation or conglomerate has assets, earnings, manufacturing facilities, or sales. Other definitions stress such factors as the percentage of overseas assets or sales, centralized control, or tendency toward a global perspective.

Economic and social historians cite evidence of the prior existence of transnational interactions and relations. One example is the influence of various religious movements over several centuries. In the Middle Ages the Roman Catholic Church was a major political force commanding human allegiance outrivaling that of any secular ruler. The Church straddled the line between temporal and secular power through ownership and political rule over vast territories. In the struggle for supremacy between church and state in the late Middle Ages, the Roman Church only gradually lost ground in the political realm to kings and emperors.

Another historical example of the significance of transnational activities is the close affinity of private and public agencies that assured the dominance of British world power in the nineteenth century. British manufacturers, traders, and financiers played a key role in the preponderance of British political influence in an empire encompassing one fourth of the land area of the globe and in the preeminence in commercial and financial as well as political relations with other states. Robert Gilpin emphasizes strongly the importance of this precedent for modern transnationalism.

> One may reasonably argue, I believe, that in certain respects the regime of the Pax Britannica was the Golden Age of transnationalism. The activities of private financiers and capitalists enmeshed the nations in a web of interdependencies which certainly influenced the course of international relations. In contrast to our own era, in which the role of the multinational corporation in international economic relations is unprecedented, the private institutions of the City of London under the gold standard

and the regime of free trade had a strategic and central place in world affairs unmatched by any transnational organization today.[3]

In spite of a plethora of historical examples of transnational interactions, the period since 1945 is particularly noteworthy as the era in which transnationalism has come into its own both as a phenomenon and as a subject for increased scholarly investigation and analysis. Multinational corporations are becoming larger, more numerous and more influential with each passing year. They cannot yet be described as ubiquitous, but their spread will be watched with interest by governments and by students of international relations, business, and economics. International nonprofit organizations are also proliferating at an unprecedented rate since 1945, and the possibilities for political influence multiply as improved transportation and communications increase the facilities for linking members and groups across national boundaries. Complex interactions are encouraged by close working relationships between intergovernmental organizations, such as the United Nations or its specialized agencies, and nongovernmental organizations. Nongovernmental organizations not only enjoy consultative status with intergovernmental organizations but frequently enter into working relationships with them for the attainment of commonly shared goals. The distinction between public and private functions becomes blurred in this as well as in numerous other areas.

The impossibility of separating public from private, domestic from foreign, and political from economic and social matters calls into question previously narrow concepts of the political process. If the political process is defined in terms of the authoritative allocation of values, then private actions in the economic and social realms, which affect the values available to other actors, are political actions. If these actions have an impact across state boundaries, they are transnational.

A broad definition of the political process points to the inadequacy of the state-centric model of world politics. The state-centric model tends to view the actions of nongovernmental actors as outside the political process. It assigns to them the status of environmental factors affecting the political process but not part of it. The justification for this approach rests on the monopolization of certain forms of coercive power by states. By excluding transnational actions from the main elements of the world political system, the model is

[3] Robert Gilpin, "The Politics of Transnational Economic Relations," *International Organization*, Vol. 25 (Summer, 1971), p. 406.

simplified and becomes more manageable. At the same time the state-centric model may lose much potential explanatory power by assigning to transnational factors a secondary status only incidental to world politics. Recent analysis of transnational factors reveals their direct relevance for and participation in the political process. A model that includes them as primary, not secondary, inputs into the political system will undoubtedly prove more satisfactory as a basis for research than the state-centric pattern that may be more manageable but lacking in inclusiveness of significant and perhaps powerful actions that are political in nature.

No specific model for study and research will be endorsed here. What is important is a recognition that any matrix of interactions in world politics is lacking in recognition of important transnational factors if only states and international organizations are included as active units. For the reader the salient fact to consider is the necessity to emphasize the role of nongovernmental actors in political affairs. No picture of world politics is complete if the complex pattern of interactions between transnational actors and governmental actors is ignored or treated as peripheral to the interactions of states and international organizations. The significance of transnational interactions will be clarified further in successive sections of this chapter.

NONPROFIT TRANSNATIONAL ACTORS AND ACTIVITIES

One category of transnational interaction results from the movement of persons across national boundaries. The dimensions of this movement have not been computed with great accuracy, but, according to the best estimates, the number of persons involved annually is several millions and the rate of increase per year is more than 10 percent. The rapid growth of personal movement is due not only to improved transportation facilities, but also to the creation of new governmental and private programs supporting the exchange of persons and to complex economic, sociological, and psychological motives related to increased knowledge about other countries and peoples. The interactions that take place involve both the persons who move across national boundaries and the persons residing in the host countries. If we are interested in the impact of these transnational interactions, we must consider the effects on the host population as well as the influence on the person who goes abroad. The question of impact or influence can also involve contacts with persons or policy makers in the home state during or after the foreign experience.

In relation to world politics, some movements of persons are much more significant than others. One scholar who has attempted to analyze those aspects of personal interchange that have a positive influence toward breaking down barriers among states and promoting accommodative policies is Robert C. Angell. He believes that national barriers may be more easily removed by the pressure exerted by "influentials" on their own policy makers than by the strengthening of international organizations or by any other means. An increasing number of this influential elite is engaging in transnational interactions each year. The thesis stated by Angell is that

> policy-makers are being subjected increasingly to a stream of influence from elites toward accommodation among nations, a stream that derives in part from the growing amount of transnational participation with positive effects on these elites. . . . The present hypothesis emphasizes the influence that the transnational experiences of members of national elites has on their home governments and thus ultimately on the relations among nations. Participation in the world social system is seen as affecting the nature of the world political system via national foreign policies.[4]

In sorting out those transnational interactions that have a positive influence toward accommodation among nations, Professor Angell rejects from his analysis all tourist travel and other transient contacts that make little impact upon the attitudes and values of the participants or the population of the host country. Among the types of contacts which are of sufficient duration and intensity to affect national elites, he includes

Study abroad
Teaching and research abroad
Migration for long-term or permanent settlement abroad
Visiting relatives and friends abroad
Participation in foreign work camps and the Peace Corps
Technical assistance missions
Work in foreign religious missions
Residence abroad for business reasons
Residence abroad in military service
Participation in international nongovernmental organizations
Membership in secretariats of United Nations agencies[5]

The individuals in these categories are often acting on behalf of or are supported by a private organization or governmental

---

[4] Robert C. Angell, *Peace on the March: Transnational Participation* (New York: Van Nostrand Reinhold, 1969), p. 26.
[5] *Ibid.*

agency, but they engage in *personal* interactions that may change their attitudes and cause them to exert accommodative influence upon governmental policy makers. The identity of purposes between these individuals and public policies or the programs of nongovernmental organizations is demonstrated by other recent studies.[6] The role of individuals may often be difficult to distinguish from the role of organizations or agencies in which those individuals participate, but their personal impact should be noted as a separate aspect of transnational interactions. Changes in personal attitudes are an additional factor in world politics beyond the actions of governments and organizations.

Personal transnational interaction can have both positive and negative effects upon the development of accommodation among nations. Some contacts may reinforce attitudes of national chauvinism, hostility, and the protection of sovereignty. Interactions that may be negative in their effects include (1) interactions between those in military service abroad and segments of the host population; (2) the impact of foreign religious missionaries upon members of the host population who are not direct beneficiaries of their religious and social activities; and (3) the interaction between businessmen residing abroad and competitors or others who resent the drain of profits to foreign investors.

In balancing the positive and negative effects of personal interaction, Professor Angell calculates an overwhelming influence on the side of accommodation among nations. Not only is this the case, but annually the increment of positive influence is increasing. With present trends he foresees these forces assuming extensive proportions before the close of the century and predicts that national accommodative policies will reflect the multiple influences of personal transnational participation. To predict an end to international conflict is unrealistic and naive, but the atmosphere in which interstate interactions occur may be ameliorated by the impact of the web of personal relationships.[7]

[6] Examples include Philip H. Coombs, *The Fourth Dimension of Foreign Policy: Educational and Cultural Affairs* (New York: Harper & Row, 1964); Andrew M. Scott, *The Revolution in Statecraft: Informal Penetration* (New York: Random House, 1965); Robert Blum, ed., *Cultural Affairs and Foreign Relations*. For the American Assembly. (Englewood Cliffs, N.J.: Prentice-Hall, 1963); Herbert C. Kelman and Raphael S. Ezekiel, *Cross-National Encounters: The Personal Impact of an Exchange Program for Broadcasters* (San Francisco: Jossey-Bass, 1970); James N. Rosenau, *National Leadership and Foreign Policy: A Case Study in the Mobilization of Public Support* (Princeton, N.J.: Princeton University Press, 1963).

[7] For more details concerning these conclusions, see Angell, *Peace on the March*, Chap. 11.

Several United Nations special programs represent joint efforts between the United Nations and private groups and individuals, and embody goals fostering international understanding and amity. One of these is the United Nations International School which was begun by Secretariat personnel in 1947 to provide basic education in an international atmosphere. In the area of development, a United Nations Volunteers program was initiated in the 1970s to appeal mainly to an international corps of young people anxious to participate in development projects. In 1965 the United Nations Institute for Training and Research (UNITAR) began operations. Its regular staff is supplemented by scholars on temporary assignment to UNITAR. The Institute has published dozens of research studies and also conducts training seminars for new members of government delegations and their staffs and for United Nations related civil service positions. Another research enterprise linking the private world of scholarship with the United Nations is the United Nations University which first began operations in 1975 at its headquarters in Tokyo. The purpose is to energize research on global problems through a network of public and private research institutes and universities.

Another dimension of transnational relations is the development of a web of international nongovernmental organizations (NGOs) with the most rapid expansion occurring since 1945. The *Yearbook of International Organizations* for 1974 gives data on 2,470 such organizations as compared with only 280 intergovernmental units including 34 in the United Nations family of associated agencies. The *Yearbook* uses certain criteria for inclusion in their NGO list. These criteria exclude all groups operating in only two countries; those that are not truly international in their aims, membership, structure, and financial support; those that are an integral subdivision of another organization; and educational institutions, secret societies, and social clubs. In the 1977 edition of the *Yearbook* many national organizations were added to the listing because of the increasing interaction between them and United Nations and regional agencies. Although the annual rate of increase since 1945 in the number of NGOs is probably less than half the increment rate of growth in interpersonal transnational interactions, it is nevertheless substantial, with an annual increase of 4.7 percent for the period 1954-68.[8] Even with allowance for the increase in world population, the move-

[8] Kjell Skjelsbaek, "The Growth of International Nongovernmental Organization in the Twentieth Century," *International Organization*, Vol. 25 (Summer, 1971), p. 425.

ment is a dynamic one and promises to continue to be an increasing
factor in world politics for the next several decades.

International nongovernmental organizations have been created
in almost every conceivable field of human concern from religion to
transport and from art to science. According to broad categories
adopted for classification purposes by the Union of International
Associations in the *Yearbook of International Organizations*, the
most numerous types of organizations in rank order are those in (1)
commerce and industry, (2) health and medicine, (3) science, and (4)
international relations. Between 1957 and 1971 the categories
showing the greatest percentage increase were (1) technology, (2)
agriculture, (3) science, and (4) economics and finance.

Nongovernmental organizations do not operate in a vacuum
hermetically sealed off from each other or from governments and
intergovernmental organizations. One of the major purposes of
focusing greater attention on the study of nongovernmental actors
is to assess the interactions between them and governments so that
the political process may be examined in its fullest dimensions.
Knowledge of the importance of these interactions is at an elemen-
tary stage, but preliminary investigations indicate a complex pattern
of relationships warranting further study.

One indication of the interaction between NGOs and intergovernmental organizations is the provision for consultative status of NGOs
within United Nations agencies. The most sought-after consultative
status is granted by the Economic and Social Council. The breadth
of ECOSOC's mandate explains the large number of NGOs that have
been granted consultative status, including nearly 700 organizations
divided into three categories according to the extent of their involvement in ECOSOC's program. All of the specialized agencies except
the Universal Postal Union and the financial group also enter into
consultative agreements with NGOs. The number of NGOs that have
such a relationship varies from 15 organizations for the World
Meteorological Organization to more than 400 for UNESCO. The
United Nations Children's Fund, the United Nations Conference on
Trade and Development, the International Atomic Energy Agency,
and the United Nations Industrial Development Organization also
grant consultative status to substantial numbers of NGOs.

The relationships between United Nations agencies and hundreds
of NGOs demonstrate the impossibility of effectively separating
public from private organizations. The working arrangements involve
bonds of mutual support and interdependence. Lines of information, research, and administration flow back and forth between
United Nations and private agencies. The pattern is one of coopera-

tion and division of labor for common ends rather than a sharp cleavage between public and private sectors.\Transnational interactions operate extensively through these channels.

Many cases can be cited of the political impact of transnational actors. A few examples will illustrate the interrelationships of governmental and private groups.

Plane hijackings have been a cause of much concern to governments, airlines, and the public. It has been estimated that nearly two thirds of all hijackings have been committed for political reasons. Revolutionary organizations such as the Popular Front for the Liberation of Palestine have engaged in spectacular hijackings for the purpose of securing the release of political prisoners. Passengers and crew have been held hostage, and threats have been made to destroy the aircraft. A series of hijackings culminated in 1970 in the diversion of three aircraft belonging to TWA, Swissair, and BOAC to an isolated airstrip in Jordan and a Pan American 747 to Cairo. After lengthy negotiations the passengers were freed in exchange for the release of Popular Front members from prisons in West Germany, Switzerland, and the United Kingdom. Similar incidents involving other revolutionary organizations have occurred frequently in various parts of the world.[9]

Nongovernmental organizations play a key role in aerial hijacking and in other aspects of transnational air transport. One of these is the International Federations of Airline Pilots' Associations (IFALPA). Pilots assume primary responsibility for the safety of passengers, crew, and aircraft during a hijacking attempt. IFALPA is composed of national associations of pilots in fifty countries and has among its goals assisting and advising in the development of a safe and orderly system of air transportation and the promotion of safe working conditions. IFALPA has agreed to boycott all air traffic to states unwilling to take effective antihijacking measures. In August, 1968, it called for a boycott of routes to Algeria in retaliation for the detention in Algeria of plane, crew, and passengers of an El Al aircraft. The boycott was canceled when the Algerian government gave assurances that the release would be made promptly.

Another example of IFALPA's effectiveness was its threat of a strike in protest of a revision in 1966 by the International Civil Aviation Organization (ICAO) of the safety rules in the North Atlantic air corridor. The proposed rule reduced the distance between

[9] For a discussion of many facets of the hijacking problem see articles by Narinder Aggarwala, Michael J. Fenello, and Gerald F. FitzGerald in "Air Hijacking: An International Perspective," *International Conciliation*, No. 585 (November, 1971).

planes from 120 to 90 miles. The rule was rescinded as a result of IFALPA's protest.

Governments, intergovernmental organizations, and transnational organizations engage in an intricate pattern of interactions in the air transport arena. Public and private ownership of airlines complicate the pattern. The International Air Transport Association (IATA), whose members are more than 100 scheduled airlines from 84 countries, sets fares for scheduled airline service. In addition to the organization of pilots, other airline employees are affiliated with the International Transport Workers Federation. Governments and the ICAO adopt regulations affecting interstate carriers, but private groups — including those mentioned above, manufacturers of aircraft and equipment, and labor organizations — engage in interactions that affect the pattern of airline control, service, and operation.[10]

In the 1970s terrorism has moved from the national to the transnational level and from plane-hijacking to a wider range of terrorist techniques. The transnational dimensions of terrorism are established when there is collusion among the Popular Front for the Liberation of Palestine, the Japanese Red Army, and the German Baader-Meinhof Gang. Transnational dimensions are demonstrated by Lebanon, Iraq, and South Yemen serving as training centers for terrorists of various nationalities and by Libya, South Yemen, and Lebanon serving as sanctuaries for various terrorist groups. Access of terrorist groups to weapons from international sources is another transnational aspect of terrorism. Red Brigades in Italy kidnap or cripple industrialists and kidnap, try, and kill Aldo Moro, the leading Italian political figure, but see their ultimate mission as the ideological triumph of a European brand of communism. Even the media, as transnational agencies, become partners of the terrorists by giving to them the publicity which they seek. This publicity, plus the reactions of governments and publics, offer to a few hundred terrorists an influence far beyond their numbers. Some lessons have been learned in combatting terrorism, but its transnational aspects will remain a persistent problem for the foreseeable future.

Science is inherently and traditionally transnational. An example of a transnational scientific organization of transcendent significance is the International Council of Scientific Unions (ICSU). The ICSU is the coordinating agency for sixteen constituent international scientific unions in the exact and natural sciences. Membership also

---

[10] For additional details see Robert L. Thornton, "Governments and Airlines," *International Organization*, Vol. 25 (Summer, 1971), pp. 541–53.

includes the principal scientific academies, national research councils, and associations of scientific institutions in sixty countries. The ICSU has consultative status with ECOSOC, UNESCO, and the International Atomic Energy Agency, and working relations with the World Meteorological Organization, the Food and Agricultural Organization, the International Telecommunication Union, and the World Health Organization. Inter-Council coordinating committees have been established with the International Council for Philosophy and Humanistic Studies and with the Council for International Organizations of Medical Sciences. The ICSU was primarily responsible for the organization of the International Geophysical Year, the International Year of the Quiet Sun, and the International Biological Programme. Its committees on oceanic research, antarctic research, space research, water research, and science and technology in developing countries all deal with politically significant and sensitive subject areas. The ICSU is obviously involved in a complex pattern of interactions with governments, intergovernmental organizations, and other nongovernmental organizations.

Several activities of the ICSU demonstrate the meshing of public and private interests. The idea for the International Geophysical Year (IGY) originated with individual scientists. The ICSU soon became interested in the project and, in 1952, established the Special Committee for the IGY, which became the planning and coordinating agency for the program. The IGY lasted officially for eighteen months from July 1, 1957, to December 31, 1958, and enlisted the cooperation of scientists from sixty-six nations. Special areas of concern were space, the weather, the oceans, and the frigid zones. All of these are of major interest to governments, and such activities as space probes and satellite programs required governmental cooperation. Governmental financial support was obtained for many IGY projects. UNESCO also makes annual grants for scientific research through the ICSU, and, in 1957, made a special grant to the Special Committee for the IGY. During and following the period of the IGY, another of the United Nations specialized agencies, the World Meteorological Organization (WMO) acted as the collecting and publishing agency for meteorological data by establishing an IGY Meteorological Data Centre. In this work the WMO maintained close liaison with the Special Committee for the IGY.

The ICSU is also cooperatively involved with intergovernmental organizations in the promotion of space research programs. The role of two subagencies of the ICSU — the Committee on Space Research (COSPAR) and the Inter-Union Commission on Frequency Allocations for Radio Astronomy and Space Science (IUCAF) — will serve to illustrate the web of interactions among nongovernmental, governmental, and intergovernmental units.[11]

COSPAR was first established by the ICSU in 1957, a few days before *Sputnik I* was launched into orbit. Membership consisted of both national members — representing scientific academies, research councils, or governments in states most active in space research — and representatives of scientific unions that belong to the ICSU. Almost immediately, political pressure was interjected into the formulation of the terms of the COSPAR charter by proposals from the Soviet Union to expand the list of national members to include the Ukraine, Byelorussia, and several states of eastern Europe. A limited veto power was given to the United States and the Soviet Union over financial assessments and certain relationships with the United Nations. National committees have been formed to cooperate with COSPAR, and some of these are controlled by governments. Thus, COSPAR is linked with governments in its composition and control.

COSPAR also interacts with intergovernmental organizations interested in space research. These working relationships are most involved with the World Meteorological Organization (WMO) and the International Telecommunication Union (ITU). Weather data from satellites and space communication are areas of joint interest with COSPAR. Edward Miles also states that

> Among NGOs, COSPAR has played the leading role both by providing advice to the UN General Assembly and by acting as an international referee in disputes involving claims of probably harmful effects of experiments.[12]

COSPAR is at the center of international cooperation in space research because it comprises the greatest reservoir of international expertise in the field. Planning in COSPAR represents the frontiers of space knowledge and research. COSPAR can serve other purposes, such as the provision of a center for the collection and dissemination of scientific space data, but its greatest asset is its pooling of the best talent in space research. Because of this central role, the interactions that exist between it and governments, intergovernmental organiza-

---

[11] For additional details to those outlined below, see Edward Miles, "Transnationalism in Space: Inner and Outer," *International Organization*, Vol. 25 (Summer, 1971), pp. 602–25; and Hugh Odishaw, "International Cooperation in Space Science" in Lincoln P. Bloomfield, ed., *Outer Space: Prospects for Man and Society*. For the American Assembly. (Englewood Cliffs, N.J.: Prentice-Hall, 1962), pp. 105–22.

[12] Miles, "Transnationalism in Space," p. 614.

tions, and other NGOs are a natural development in an interdependent world.

An area of both competition and cooperation between governments and private agencies is in the allocation of radio frequencies for specific uses. The international agency that registers all frequency requests is the International Frequency Registration Board (IFRB), a subdivision of the ITU. The power of the IFRB does not extend to the allocation of frequencies, which must be determined by bargaining in international conferences. Frequency allocations have great economic value, affecting private business interests, but governments are the agents that engage in the process of compromise to determine the allocation of frequencies within the spectrum.

Radio astronomers and space scientists were dissatisfied with the first allocation of frequencies for space purposes in 1959. In 1960 the ICSU set up the Inter-Union Commission on Frequency Allocations for Radio Astronomy and Space Science (IUCAF) to promote the interests of scientists in lobbying with their governments and with the ITU. The IUCAF is composed of representatives of the International Astronomical Union, the International Scientific Radio Union, and COSPAR, all of which are constituent units or committees of the ICSU. Prior to the 1963 Extraordinary Administrative Radio Conference on Space Radiocommunications, the IUCAF communicated its needs to the IFRB. As a result of IUCAF efforts approximately 15 percent of the radio frequency spectrum was allocated for space purposes. Multiple pressures of a transnational nature were required to achieve this end.

Not all foundations perform as transnational actors, but a number of United States and European foundations carry on overseas programs that have a substantial impact on world politics. According to the *Directory of European Foundations* issued in 1969, about 12 percent of the resources of European-based foundations was allocated for international programs. In the United States the percentage of expenditure on international activities has declined sharply since 1966. The 1971 edition of *The Foundation Directory* indicates that 21 percent of foundation expenditure was allotted to international projects in 1966 and only 7 percent in 1970.

Two United States foundations stand out in international programming. These are the Ford Foundation and the Rockefeller Foundation, which rank first and third in total assets among American as well as world foundations. In 1971 the Ford Foundation allotted more than 29 percent of its total grants to its international programs. From available data the Rockefeller percentage is more difficult to compute, since several of their projects have international components. But the percentage for international projects appears to be somewhat higher than the Ford percentage.[13]

The Ford Foundation officially states that its fundamental objective is the advancement of human welfare. More specifically, its aims include contributions toward eliminating the causes of war and the strengthening of democratic institutions and processes. Its international program is organized around three fields of activity: (1) development assistance, (2) population, and (3) European and international affairs. The international division of the foundation is larger than any of its other program divisions in both expenditure and personnel. Within the international division's program approximately 60 percent of expenditures are allocated to development assistance. Both the Ford and the Rockefeller foundations maintain large field staffs in the developing countries to stimulate, plan, coordinate, influence, and oversee local projects.

The official seal of the Rockefeller Foundation proclaims a goal as comprehensive and global as that of the Ford Foundation. This goal is declared to be "the well-being of mankind throughout the world." Any realistic approach to achieving this aim would necessarily involve the foundation in transnational activity.

Since its inception in 1913, the Rockefeller Foundation has been notable for its support of health and biomedical programs particularly in Latin America. In recent years this emphasis continues, but other major preoccupations of the field staff are with programs in Latin America, Asia, and Africa for the conquest of hunger and the development of universities. The largest program expenditure is for research on problems of population.

Both the Ford and the Rockefeller foundations deserve special credit for the "green revolution," which promises to expand cereal production in many agriculturally primitive societies. The green revolution involves the development of high-yielding seeds together with the use of fertilizers, water, and planting and cultivation techniques to produce remarkably increased yields per unit of land. Other experiments have produced grain varieties with substantially increased protein content. Protein-deficient diets are endemic to many societies living at poverty levels. Ford and Rockefeller foundation

---

[13] Data is based on "The Ford Foundation Annual Report 1971" and "The Rockefeller Foundation President's Review and Annual Report 1970." For additional information on the Ford Foundation see Peter D. Bell, "The Ford Foundation as a Transnational Actor," *International Organization*, Vol. 25 (Summer, 1971), pp. 465-78, and *The Ford Foundation in the 1960's* (New York: Ford Foundation, July, 1962).

funds have jointly supported four institutes largely responsible for the green revolution. These are the International Rice Research Institute in the Philippines, the International Maize and Wheat Improvement Center in Mexico, the International Center of Tropical Agriculture in Colombia, and the International Institute of Tropical Agriculture in Nigeria. In 1970 Dr. Norman E. Borlaug, a member of the Rockefeller field staff attached to the International Maize and Wheat Improvement Center, received the Nobel Peace Prize for his contributions to the development of the new varieties of wheat.

The international programs of the Ford and the Rockefeller foundations bring the foundation personnel into constant and intricate interaction with personnel representing governments, universities, intergovernmental organizations, and other private agencies. The annual reports of the foundations are replete with evidence of these interactions. Governments have given land and financial support to institutes created by the foundations, and repeated references are made in the reports to the necessity for governments to take over projects initiated through Ford and Rockefeller grants. Agencies of host governments with which interactions frequently occur are ministries of health, agriculture, education, home affairs, labor, external affairs, and finance; commissions or offices of national planning; presidential commissions; local planning organizations; population commissions; and publicly supported universities. One purpose of foundation grants is to provide training for government officials. Many of the foundation programs are closely coordinated with the activities of the United States Agency for International Development and, in fewer cases, with the Canadian Development Agency. The United States National Institutes of Health has supported programs in which the foundations played a role. In Latin America cooperation with such regional organizations as the Organization of American States, the Inter-American Development Bank, and the Latin American Demographic Center is cited in the foundations' reports. Among international intergovernmental agencies the program with which the foundations interact to the greatest extent is the United Nations Development Program, but frequent interactions also occur with the World Health Organization, the Food and Agriculture Organization, the United Nations Educational, Scientific and Cultural Organization, and the International Bank for Reconstruction and Development.

The pattern of cooperative interactions in which the foundations are involved is, indeed, most intricate and extensive. The impact, in some cases, can already be assessed; other evaluations must be based on future developments. The foundations may be able to generate only modest changes in comparison with the vast needs of under-developed nations, but their efforts are made at critical points in terms of the generally recognized reforms that are required and desired.

Many more examples of nonprofit transnational actors and their activities could be described, but those presented above may serve as a representative cross section of this phenomenon. By realizing that this presentation is only a portion of the whole, the student may appreciate the complexities of the web of interdependencies that characterize world political affairs and recognize the need to assess the role of individuals and nongovernmental organizations in the political process.

THE MULTINATIONAL CORPORATION

Multinational business enterprises deserve special treatment because they are different from nonprofit organizations in nature, size, and degree of impact on world politics. Furthermore, they have recently come under increased scrutiny by governments, businessmen, and scholars because of the realization of their growing importance in economic and political affairs and because of the complex patterns of interactions between them and other actors, especially states and international organizations. Projections of current growth trends indicate an increasing influence of the multinational corporation (or transnational corporation in United Nations' parlance) in world politics during the remainder of the century. Reactions to this future influence vary from welcoming the process as the key to an emerging world community to pointing with alarm to the prospect of irresponsible concentrations of economic power in the hands of an elite. The future role of the multinational business enterprise in perpetuating or closing the prosperity gap between rich and poor nations is also an area of interest and concern.

One simple measure of the impact of multinational corporations is the enormity of the resources controlled by these conglomerates. The annual *Fortune* lists of the largest United States and foreign industrial corporations ranks corporations according to their annual sales. In 1976 the sales of five United States and one European-based conglomerate exceeded 25 billion dollars each. Exxon and General Motors sales throughout the world amounted to nearly 50 billion dollars each, which is roughly equal to the entire gross domestic product of Argentina, almost double that of Finland, and more than three times that of the Philippines or New Zealand. The largest foreign-based corporation, Royal Dutch Shell, has sales of more than 36 billion dollars, which is approximately equal to the gross domestic product of Austria, Denmark, or South Africa.

The United States dominates the field of multinational giants. The two largest conglomerates — Exxon and General Motors — are based in the United States. Only four of the World's top fifteen enterprises have their parent companies outside the United States — Royal Dutch Shell ranking third, National Iranian Oil ranking seventh, British Petroleum ranking ninth, and Unilever ranking twelfth. The United States and Europe together are preponderant as bases for the industrial giants. Of the ten largest which are based outside the United States, only one, National Iranian Oil, is non-European.

The simultaneous development of (1) a world market, (2) the rapid expansion of multinational corporations, and (3) the necessity for modern governments to exercise controls in order to maintain stability and economic growth presents dilemmas for both business and government. Economic factors occupy a larger share of the political spectrum than ever before. The doctrine of laissez faire has been long abandoned even in the least controlled national economic systems. The multinational business enterprise seeks to gain greater freedom by establishing subsidiaries in many countries, but is subjected to controls by both the home and the host nations. Multinational corporations have great flexibility in moving goods, money, personnel, and technology across national boundaries, and this flexibility increases their bargaining power with governments. In dealing with such giants, governments must be sure that they maintain control over tax revenues, inflation, trade balances, balance of payments, trade restrictions, monetary values, credit policies, employment, and economic planning. The complex interplay of economic and political factors is greatly affected by the activities of multinational business enterprises. The business conglomerates, by controlling such enormous resources and so great a share of the market, play a leading role in the areas of control sought by governments.

Most multinational firms are highly centralized and are dominated by the parent company. The managers are from the home state, research is centralized, autonomy for foreign subsidiaries is limited, technology is exported from the parent company, profits are often repatriated, and the policies of the firm conform closely to the economic and foreign policies of the home government. As multinational corporations grow larger, as they recognize that not all managerial and research talent is monopolized by one country, and as they accommodate more to local conditions, they may move from an ethnocentric to a geocentric orientation.

Professor Howard Perlmutter uses the term "geocentric" to describe a type of business attitude that is world oriented. Some of the characteristics of a geocentric-type organization include complex and interdependent organization, collaboration between headquarters and subsidiaries in decision making, worldwide perspective, worldwide recruiting and interchange of personnel, and multidirectional communication among units of the corporation.[14] If a number of large and powerful business enterprises eventually shift their orientation from a national to a geocentric emphasis, the implications for state policy could be extensive.

The acquisition of subsidiaries by foreign parent corporations is both welcomed and resisted by the governments of the host countries. Professor Jack Behrman has cogently summarized the dilemma of the host government in facing the incursion of foreign-dominated business enterprises.

> The host government is caught in a "love-hate" syndrome. It wants the contributions to wealth and economic growth that the multinational enterprise can provide because they add to its power within the country, as well as internationally. At the same time it dislikes and fears the results: the incursions on national sovereignty and technological independence. The host government finds multinational enterprises difficult to live with, but, so long as it seeks to increase national power, equally unpleasant to live without. . . . It appears to the host government that a trade-off may be required between sovereignty and greater wealth.[15]

The advantages and the disadvantages to the host government may be analyzed in more specific terms. Behrman suggests, "The contributions lie mainly in the areas of capital formation, technology and management skills, regional development, competition, and balance of payments."[16] The concerns of the hosts include the fear of industrial dominance, the fear of technological dependence, and the disturbance to economic plans."

An aspect of the flexibility of the multinational corporation is its freedom to establish subsidiaries in countries that provide the

[14] Howard V. Perlmutter, "The Tortuous Evolution of the Multinational Corporation," *Columbia Journal of World Business*, Vol. 4 (January-February, 1969), pp. 9-18.

[15] Jack N. Behrman, *National Interests and the Multinational Enterprise: Tensions Among the North Atlantic Countries* (Englewood Cliffs, N.J.: Prentice-Hall, 1970), pp. 7-8.

[16] *Ibid.*, p. 13.

[17] *Ibid., passim.*

most favorable conditions. Furthermore, when a parent company decides to close a subsidiary, it may evoke strong repercussions from the host government because of the loss of local employment. Compromise and accommodation mark the bargaining positions of host governments and business enterprises in determining the location and the status of subsidiary business units.

The establishment of foreign subsidiaries also entails both benefits and costs for the home government of the parent corporation. Incentives for businesses to become multinational include not only economy of operation and access to markets but also possible tax advantages through flexible accounting procedures. The outflow of investment is a factor in the international balance of payments. The United States, as the base for the largest multinational business enterprises, has imposed governmental controls over foreign investment, the export of goods or technology to designated areas, and antitrust violations by multinational corporations. Under authority derived from the Trading with the Enemy Act and the Export Control Act, the United States has been able to prohibit sales to such areas as Cuba or Mainland China from both United States-based businesses and from their foreign subsidiaries. When such sales are not contrary to the law of the state in which the subsidiary is located, this amounts to an extension of United States law and foreign policy across national boundaries. A similar situation arises from the extension of United States antitrust jurisdiction to cases affecting the international business holdings of American-based corporations.

The existence of multinational corporations results in many conflicts of law. Host states resent and fear the intrusion of the jurisdiction of the home state in regulating business practices as an invasion of their sovereignty. Even without the application of domestic law across national boundaries, the erosion of sovereignty and independence occurs to some degree because of the identity of interests between corporations and their home governments.

Host governments are not helpless in protecting their interests against the invasion of foreign capital and the threat of diminution of national sovereignty. They may refuse to grant corporate charters to subsidiaries of foreign businesses. They may place conditions upon the ownership and behavior of subsidiaries. They may restrict the freedom of businesses whose products are closely related to national security. They may encourage and subsidize local businesses to increase their competitiveness. Governments may seek protection against undesirable practices through regional and international agreements and associations and through diplomatic channels when conflicts occur. Businesses are subject to the threat of nationalization with or without adequate compensation.

The threat of nationalization carries with it complex economic and political ramifications. The foreign business subsidiary is hostage to the host state. The home state also becomes hostage to the attitudes and the practices of the multinational enterprise in its foreign operations. The corporation seeks guarantees from the home government against loss from confiscation of its foreign properties. The negative attitude of the United States government toward public ownership is reflected in its foreign economic and political policies. Public ownership, in turn, may work to the advantage of a state only if it possesses sufficient resources and technology to compete in the international arena. Again, internal psychological factors may dictate policies not economically advantageous.

The complex interplay of political and economic factors is illustrated by the nationalization of the Anglo-Iranian Oil Company in 1951.[18] The British government owned 51 percent of the stock of Anglo-Iranian. The terms of the agreement regarding oil revenues gave three times as much income to the British treasury as to the Iranian treasury. Several oil-producing countries had won more favorable terms from international oil companies. Premier Mohammed Mossadegh announced the nationalization of the Anglo-Iranian Company, which had a monopoly of Iranian oil production. The British took their case to the International Court of Justice and to the Security Council without attaining satisfaction, and, with the cooperation of other states, imposed an oil boycott on Iran. The boycott virtually paralyzed Iranian operations for three years as the British drew on oil reserves in Kuwait and elsewhere. Tensions grew between Premier Mossadegh and the Shah as the premier sought new revenues from wealthy Iranians, instituted new land policies, tried to gain control of the military, and moved to cut the Shah's personal income and allowances. The United States Central Intelligence Agency (CIA) played a decisive role in engineering a coup that overthrew the Mossadegh regime. In the new oil agreements that followed, 40 percent of the shares were assigned to British Petroleum and 40 percent to United States firms. The CIA agent who directed the coup later became a vice-president of Gulf Oil Corporation.

While industrially developed nations generally welcome multinational subsidiaries as more beneficial than harmful, the same case

---

[18] These details are reviewed in Michael Tanzer, *The Political Economy of International Oil and the Underdeveloped Countries* (Boston: Beacon Press, 1969), pp. 321-26.

does not clearly apply to developing areas. In the less developed countries the industries affected have frequently been extractive in nature with a major drain of resources to the host country. In general, multinational corporations establish manufacturing subsidiaries in other developed countries, not in underdeveloped ones. Only one-fourth of the business activities of transnational industries are conducted in the developing countries. Two-thirds of United States direct manufacturing investment has gone to Canada and to Europe, with only one-third for the rest of the world. Canadian and European subsidiaries account for three-fourths of the value of sales by United States foreign manufacturing affiliates. The repatriation of handsome profits from extractive industries plus the problem of servicing public and private debts leaves little investment income within developing countries for economic growth. Furthermore, the technology that is cheaply exported from one developed country to another may be inappropriate for transfer to an underdeveloped economy. Employment of local labor may represent a higher good in a labor-rich economy than mechanized efficiency suitable to Europe or North America. United States or European industries geared to mass consumption buttressed by advertising may, if introduced in areas of low industrialization, create demands inappropriate to national needs and divert resources from enterprises more basic to development. Fundamental problems of economic growth are often ignored by local elites who link their interests with foreign business enterprises backed by a powerful government. Local governments are no match for the bargaining power of large developed states whose means for rewards and punishment are formidable. The identity of government and business interests compounds the problem for the weak state.

The growth of multinational corporations presents ethical and philosophical problems. Democratic values are affected by the emergence of powerful transnational businesses capable of affecting the distribution of goods and of influencing or by-passing governmental policy. Trends toward a deterioration of democratic control resulting from the size, complexity, and bureaucratization of government are exacerbated by the development of powerful transnational actors only partially responsible and responsive to public pressures exercised through governmental channels. The possible threat to democratic values represented by the multinational corporation deserves further attention by philosophers, political scientists, and others concerned with maintaining responsibility in political and social affairs.

Inevitably, the United Nations has become involved with the

question of the rapid growth and expanding influence of the multi-national corporations. In 1972 ECOSOC created a group of twenty eminent persons to study the role and the impact of these corporate giants and to recommend steps or methods leading toward international accountability or regulation. In 1974, as a first step, ECOSOC created two permanent bodies to keep the problems of the multinationals under scrutiny — a forty-eight-member intergovernmental Commission on Transnational Corporations and a United Nations Center on Transnational Corporations. By 1977 the Center had a staff of fifty-five persons. The Commission established as its first priority the development of a code of conduct for the activities of transnational corporations and this task, due to its complexities and to the competing interests involved, required continuous study and negotiations over a period of several years. In the meantime, the Organization for Economic Cooperation and Development, in 1976, adopted a voluntary code of conduct for transnationals, which, because it represented the position only of affluent states, was considered inadequate by third-world standards.

Several other major tasks were undertaken by the Commission and the Center. The Commission, besides working on the code of conduct, gave special attention to means for halting corrupt practices involving transnational corporations. The Center was requested to work in four primary areas in addition to its support activities on a code of conduct. These were (1) the establishment of a comprehensive information system; (2) research into the political, legal, economic, and social effects of the operations of transnationals; (3) technical cooperation programs to strengthen the negotiating capacities of developing countries in their dealings with transnational corporations; and (4) attempts to more precisely define the term "transnational corporations." In 1977 the Commission adopted, in a vote divided along North-South lines, a resolution requesting transnational corporations to cease further investment in South Africa and to disengage progressively from that country. The Commission also enlisted the services of a panel of experts to advise on the development of uniform national standards of accounting and reporting by transnational corporations.

The role of multinational corporations will continue as a persistent issue in many forums inside and outside the United Nations. One danger to the welfare of developing countries is that a code of conduct and related measures might contain provisions considered so inimical to the interests of transnational enterprises that they would withdraw from those countries. Such a trend would be a major blow to development aspirations and to the realization of a new international economic order.

POSSIBLE IMPACT OF TRANSNATIONAL ACTORS

There is little doubt that the accelerated rate of growth of transnational actors of diverse types since 1945 has complicated the political picture and brought into serious question the adequacy of the state-centric model of world politics. This growth is a natural outcome of scientific and technological developments that shrink global distances and increase access from one part of the world to another. The process was well under way before social scientists became aware of its far-reaching implications and realized that current trends indicate a rapidly enlarged future role of transnational actors.

Will the effects of the future expansion of transnationalism be benign or malignant, utopian or diastrous? Informed opinions vary so widely as to be inconclusive. The principal point of agreement is that political relationships will become increasingly complex. Whether methods of dealing with information and ideas can be harnessed to control the complex relationships to the benefit of most of humanity is not clear.

Some students of transnational trends forecast the decline or eventual demise of the national state. Professor Charles Kindleberger welcomes the replacement of the nation-state as an economic unit by multinational corporations as a natural and beneficial development.[19] J. J. Servan-Schreiber points to the lack of adequate political response to the American challenge by European governments or by the European community and predicts that, unless new policies are rapidly adopted, the third greatest industrial power will soon be not Europe, but American industry in Europe. As multinational corporations move toward a geocentric perspective, they may become independent centers of economic power rivaling the power of large states.

Other forecasters predict the breaking down of national barriers and the adoption of more accommodative policies among states. The state would continue to operate as the primary political unit, but its freedom to use the most hostile means of persuasion would be circumscribed. Robert Angell attributes a movement toward peace to the increased exchange of elites who will bring growing pressure on their home governments for international accommodation and cooperation.

Those who adopt Marxist theory see the multinational corporation as an extension of the imperialism of powerful capitalist states.

[19] Charles P. Kindleberger, *American Business Abroad: Six Lectures on Direct Investment* (New Haven, Conn.: Yale University Press, 1969).

In their view the partnership between business and the state is a manifestation of the control of the state by capitalists who use economic and political power to exploit foreign societies. Underdeveloped countries will continue to become poorer unless they revolt against their oppressors.

Regardless of the philosophical or theoretical orientation of the observer, the fact is that the developing states have been by-passed by the mainstream of the transnational movement. Developed countries have been the principal actors in the programs of international nongovernmental organizations and in the exchange of persons. Multinational corporations are based in developed nations and prefer investing most of their resources in other developed areas rather than risk their capital in less stable political and economic units. Unless prosperous states or multinational actors adopt more accommodative policies toward the poor countries, the escape of those countries from poverty may be indefinitely postponed. Hopeful beginnings have been made through the programs of the Ford and the Rockefeller foundations, the United Nations Development Program, national economic aid programs, the Organization of Petroleum Exporting Countries (OPEC), the United Nations Conference on Trade and Development (UNCTAD), and the United Nations Industrial Development Organization (UNIDO), but the impact has been disappointing in relation to relative needs.

Most observers forecast the continued importance of both the nation-state and transnational actors. States still command a monopoly of certain forms of coercive force and elicit the loyalty of millions of citizens. The increase of transnational activity will not radically alter the role of states in the near future. The political process will become increasingly complex, and the web of interactions will affect the behavior of governments. The realization of advantages in the utilization of international organizations may well enhance the further development of such organizations as a means of channeling cooperative actions for mutual gain. The study of political phenomena must encompass a wide range of actors and activities and a pattern of interactions of such complexity as to challenge the ingenuity of scholars. States will continue to serve as instruments of control but will undergo change as pressures from other sources exert influence on world political affairs.

17

❧

International
Organization
in
Retrospect and Prospect

It is appropriate at this point in our study of international organization to assess the progress of and the prospects for international
organization, by examining its problems and accomplishments and
by estimating its probable and potential role in world affairs. Several
questions establish the outlines of this assessment. How far has
international organization progressed since the first international
unions or since the League of Nations? Have the principles of international organization been valuable or have they been unrealistic
ideals? Has the proliferation, since 1945, of international agencies,
both regional and global, caused significant changes in international
affairs, or have these agencies operated on only the fringes of the
international system without great effect on the principal forces
shaping international human relationships? Have international organizations provided services and channels for interaction indispensable
to, or at least valuable for maintaining an orderly international
system? If these services and channels have been indispensable or
valuable, have nations and national leaders been willing to, and capable of using them wisely? Is international organization of only
marginal use, is it the answer to the future, or is it a transitional
step in developing a new international order? Of course, not all
these questions can be answered definitively, but trying to answer

them will be useful in placing the role of international organization into current and future perspective.

SOURCES OF PESSIMISM

If the major contribution that international organization can make to world affairs is to aid in breaking down barriers that divide the peoples of the world, the progress to date in eliminating those barriers often seems discouraging. Cleavages among nations appear to be nearly as wide and deep as ever in modern history. Deeply ingrained in human consciousness is a sense of loyalty and identity built around the nation-state. This sense of identity compartmentalizes the world into 160 sovereign, competing political units. Little evidence exists that substantial numbers of people living in these 160 political units feel any strong mutual ties with the whole of humanity or share with them a common sense of values. In spite of lip service accorded to codes of religious, ethical, or moral principles that profess the unity of the human race, the hierarchy of individual and national values assigns priority to the elements of divisiveness, not unity. Humanitarianism is still smothered by particularism. The order of the day is rivalry rather than cooperation. Rivalry among nations is fostered by suspicion, fear, and perceived self-interests. National and individual goals concentrate on immediate economic gain or protection of economic advantage, and any promises of long-range mutual benefits from international cooperation are greeted with impatience and doubt.

In spite of the rhetoric of détente, the competition of ideologies is far from a dead issue. Divergent networks of political and economic ideas as support for antagonistic political and economic systems have not lost their currency and vitality. Human welfare and freedom are not universally accepted standards as basic concepts for political organization and action. In spite of professions of a willingness to coexist, the basis for cooperation between competing political units remains limited because of fundamental differences in perspectives. Conviction concerning the correctness of the underlying principles and values of one's own system lends impetus to a missionary zeal to bring enlightenment concerning the validity of these "truths" to the entire human race. A sense of historical destiny bolsters up this crusading spirit and hinders the process of accommodation. National barriers are thus reinforced rather than broken down by the influence of ideology.

Perceived economic interests are among the most powerful forces for cleavage among nations. Movement toward economic unity has been limited and tension-ridden. Even in the European Economic Community, usually cited as the model for economic unions, the path to cooperation and solidarity has not been smooth. Segmentation and rivalry remain the order of the day. Each country's economic and monetary system elicits the support of individuals to a degree unrivaled at the transnational or international level. Personal economic well-being is identified with the national economic system to the point that foreign economic activities are often perceived as threats to both personal and national economic prosperity in terms of jobs, prices, markets, and profits.

Economic rivalry persists as the dominant attitude over economic cooperation. Among developed states adversary relationships mark the bargaining process by which compromises can be reached that lead to limited cooperation. In trade and tariff arrangements the interests of internal segments of the working, management, and entrepreneurial population must be protected as a first priority. Individual interest thus becomes linked to and identified with national interest. The state remains as the main instrumentality for safeguarding and promoting individual and group economic welfare.

Economic interests also serve as a basis for the hardening of antagonism between rich, industrial, developed nations and poor, preindustrial, developing nations. The United Nations Conference on Trade and Development has emerged as the symbol of the demands of the have-not countries and as the forum for the espousal of their cause. Their frustrations and impatience with economic progress are expressed through resolutions stating recurrent themes— recurrent because so little headway is made toward the achievement of the goals of the development process. Rightly or wrongly the developing states blame the affluent nations for much of their plight because the rich states dominate the international economic system and because massive transfers of economic resources are not made from the haves to the have-nots on terms most favorable to the perceived interests of the latter. In 1974–75 the developing countries used special and regular sessions of the General Assembly for the promotion of a "New International Economic Order." After initial resistance, most notably by the United States, a spirit of cautious accommodation of North-South interests emerged.

Although science and technology continue to shrink global dimensions, and problems multiply that demand worldwide solutions, national leaders persist, in their rhetoric and behavior, in emphasizing parochial rather than universal viewpoints and interests.

The components of interdependence expand at exponential rates, but traditions and habits linked to the past prevent the application of dynamic and imaginative ideas and techniques appropriate for a new future of which many of the elements have already emerged today. The problems of spaceship earth will not be solved by Neanderthal approaches. A revolution in social and political thinking is required to avoid a series of potential catastrophes whose signs are already evident, but a sense of urgency has not yet permeated the centers of power and decision.

Conflicts and wars flare up in all corners of the globe with alarming frequency. In spite of the ever-increasing destructiveness of weapons and in spite of apprehensions concerning the escalation of the level of conflict from conventional to nuclear warfare, people wage wars that the United Nations is unable to prevent or rapidly bring under control. On some occasions, such as in the series of Middle East conflicts, the effects are lessened by action taken through United Nations agencies, while in other cases involving the great powers, such as in Czechoslovakia and Vietnam, the United Nations and the principles of the Charter are ignored. The desirability of arms limitations and controls is overwhelmed by an arms race in which the nations of the world spend more than 400 billion dollars each year on weapons and means of destruction. Security is sought through a balance of terror and threat, rather than through cooperation for the peaceful settlement of disputes and the elimination of war. World priorities place military preparedness above the values of human life and welfare.

In this highly competitive world climate international organizations tend to languish rather than flourish. New agencies are created in substantial number but are unable to realize much of their potential. Organizations are based on the principle that the sovereignty of the members will remain intact and undiminished. States retain all their prerogatives of ultimate decision making and cooperate through international organizations when their perceived national interests are enhanced rather than diminished or threatened by such cooperation. International organizations become the convenient tools of foreign policy of the individual states. Most of the energies and resources of each state are reserved for bilateral not multilateral activities. As soon as a regional or global organization is perceived as taking an action or series of actions inimical to the internal interests of one or more members, the spirit of cooperation disappears and the vitality of the organization to act as an agent of regional or global interests is sapped to feed the demands of special national concerns.

SUMMARY OF ACHIEVEMENTS

In spite of the rather gloomy picture of a sharply divided world painted above, there is a more optimistic view of the contributions of international organization to world peace and human welfare that should be presented. In such a presentation one's expectations should not anticipate a high degree of perfection in the performance of international organizations since humans are fallible and all human institutions are imperfect. In seeking greater harmony and improved standards of justice in an increasingly interdependent, yet always competitive, international system, the degrees of harmony and justice will always be relative and subject to perfectability. Furthermore, international organizations have never been assigned a major role in an age dominated by national sovereign states. Therefore, in this assessment of achievements, we should look for those elements in the performance of international organizations that have positively, although modestly, moved toward the amelioration of human relations across national boundaries and toward securing a higher standard of justice, especially for that segment of humanity who live under the constant threat of hunger, poverty, illiteracy, and disease or who are denied an effective voice in determining their own political, social, and economic destiny.

The first evidence of the positive role of international organizations is the growth of the movement in establishing hundreds of public, and even larger numbers of private, international organizations, a movement which began in the nineteenth century and has accelerated steadily in almost every successive decade. The value placed upon the existence of a general organization was demonstrated by the pressure to establish the United Nations in 1945 to replace the dormant League of Nations. Supplementing the general organization are dozens of specialized agencies, regional commissions, and service agencies in the economic and social areas. Outside the United Nations orbit rapid expansion has occurred in the creation of regional organizations of a variety of types, including several with a broad range of purposes. Surely, the momentum of the movement for establishing so many diverse agencies must reflect a conviction on the part of national leaders that such organizations perform useful functions within the international system.

Another evidence of the conviction that international organizations have considerable utility is the clamor for membership. Almost every eligible state seeks membership in a variety of organizations, and withdrawals are rare. Even for mini-states the benefits of participation are judged to outweigh the costs, although these costs are a real economic burden.

In the political area international organizations have a mixed record but some notable successes. Regional organizations such as the OAS and the OAU have served as channels for containing conflicts among their members and restoring peace. When the right combination of conditions and attitudes prevails, the members of the United Nations have used the Security Council and the General Assembly for dispute settlement. The Middle East is a notable example of repeated recourse to the United Nations as an agency for ending hostilities and restoring relative peace. The United Nations has demonstrated its flexibility and adaptability in controlling conflicts by the selection of appropriate means mentioned in the Charter for the peaceful settlement of all manner of disputes, and by the development of new techniques including cease-fires, preventive diplomacy, and a variety of forms of United Nations presences including peacekeeping forces. One of the most significant contributions to peace has involved the insulation of power vacuums from great-power direct involvement or confrontation.

Although international law, because of its nature and sources, develops slowly in a world of sovereign states, the United Nations has fostered modest but significant advances toward building a more satisfactory body of world law. Through interpretations and applications of Charter principles, through the efforts of the International Law Commission, and through decisions and advisory opinions of the International Court of Justice, the right of the international community to concern itself with denials of human rights and justice has been repeatedly affirmed. Special emphasis has been placed on the rights of all peoples to self-government. Treaties exempting areas of potential conflict from national competition contribute much to a vital area of law. Agreements concerning outer space, and a number of nuclear free zones are prime examples. If a comprehensive law of the seas can be developed, including an international authority with jurisdiction beyond national limits, a major breakthrough in the development of international law will have been achieved. The United Nations has invested several years of intensive preparatory effort to try to bring about such an achievement, but the intransigence of competitive national interests may temporarily block the realization of the ideal of a common-heritage concept for the oceans.

One of the least tangible, but potentially most significant, contributions of international organizations to a more orderly and cooperative world is the provision of multiple contacts among national

Although the study of international organizations generally emphasizes intergovernmental or public activities, these cannot be separated from the role of private actors. With world interdependence increasing at exponential rates, both old and new private actors take on increased importance. New business giants in the form of multinational corporations defy control and analysis in conventional terms. Their impact on future international relations will undoubtedly be massive, but whether, on balance, they will become agents of change for good or evil is still in debate. They may contribute to a global perspective, but their own status as centers of power or as contributors to economic development could have either benign or malignant effects on the welfare of the mass of humanity. Multinational corporations both reflect and contribute to global interdependence. As a subject of continued analysis they deserve much attention for both their positive and negative inputs into the emerging global system. Other transnational interactions, such as the increased interchange of persons and ideas, probably contribute more positively than negatively to the breakdown of provincial attitudes that compartmentalize the world. Recent acceleration of such transnational forces provides hope for future global security and welfare by helping to build the economic and social foundations for global community without which political cooperation cannot flourish.

Among the most important contributions of international organizations to the security and well-being of humanity is the provision of channels and programs for dealing with short-range and long-range crises. If a series of disasters for humankind is to be prevented or contained within manageable limits, and if these incipient crises affect multiple states, it is imperative that means be provided for cooperative action to avoid the engulfment of large segments of the world community in a major cataclysm.

The possibilities for disaster range over a broad spectrum of political, social and economic problems. In the political realm the persistent threat is that of nuclear destruction. Even in the area of peaceful uses of atomic energy, the IAEA's safety standards for preventing accidents affecting the lives and health of millions of persons living in the vicinity of nuclear power plants do not eliminate all concerns and fears of the possibility of such accidents. For the preindustrial societies of the world the major long-range crisis is a crisis of development and the elimination of gross inequalities between rich and poor countries. Priorities for speeding the processes of development are expressed through such programs as the two Development Decades, the UNCTAD, UNIDO, the UNDP, the IDA, and the New International Economic Order. Other transcendent crises of such proportions as to threaten all or substantial segments of humanity include a deteriorating environment, uncontrolled population growth, an inadequate food supply, a broad range of problems relating to the use of the oceans, shortages due to accelerating use and depletion of finite energy and other resources, and illicit traffic in drugs.

A variety of international organizations are concerned with these crises and can and do serve as agencies for cooperative action in avoiding the threats that these crucial problems present to the fragile life-support system of our biosphere. A mental scanning of the range of agencies discussed throughout the previous chapters would remind one of an exhaustive list of regional and global organizations and suborganizations whose major activities include various aspects of present and future crisis management. There is no assurance that the efforts of nations working through this broad range of international agencies will or can prevent catastrophes from engulfing major segments of humankind, but without recourse to international action the endeavors of individual states will surely fail to stem the tide of impending disaster. In these crisis areas the interdependence of the globe is clearly dramatized.

Finally, in assessing the positive values of international organizations, their role as agents of integration and aggregation of interests across national boundaries should be noted. Constant interaction among government representatives and international civil servants in the meeting rooms, offices, corridors, and lounges of these diverse organizations gradually build habits and attitudes that facilitate and foster cooperation. As common problems are attacked that obviously will not respond to parochial, national solutions, the advantages of integrated approaches through regional and global agencies become increasingly apparent. International organizations thus serve as instruments for raising the level of consciousness concerning the realities of world interdependence, and they provide the means for an integrated approach to an attack on problems that, through other channels, defy resolution. Unless the objective scientific facts concerning the spaceship-earth concept are matched by a heightened awareness of the political and social implications of those facts, humanity could be faced with conditions that have slipped beyond the point of control. Through a process of integration and aggregation of interests, international organizations provide a most important means of supplying the balance to make humankind the beneficiary rather than the victim of rapid change.

FUTURE NEEDS AND PROSPECTS

The preceding assessment of positive and negative contributions of international organizations to human welfare is not wholly reassuring for future prospects concerning the role of such agencies. International organizations must be viewed within the larger context of the international system. That system is still dominated by national states that arrogate to themselves the claim of sovereignty or ultimate authority in their international relationships and that assign to international organizations a role subservient to their own convenience and interests. Of course, these interstate relationships are responses to the basic parochialism, selfishness, and fears that are engrained in the minds, emotions, and attitudes of the peoples of the world and their leaders.

But, ever since the beginning of the Industrial Revolution, economic, social, and political change in those countries in which this revolution occurred has accelerated with each successive decade, and, in the past twenty-five years, those tides of change have revolutionized the demands of the three quarters of the human race previously untouched by these dynamic forces. At the same time, the further developments of science and technology and the expansion of the industrialization processes have brought about both a shrinking of the globe and a condition of worldwide interdependence. Our growing body of knowledge has furnished the means, if wisely applied, to enhance the well-being of most of the world's people. It also has produced, in its applications, unprecedented problems that threaten the lives and security of all humanity. A catalog of these threats include nuclear incineration and poisoning, the exhaustion of finite resources, overpopulation, mass starvation, deterioration or destruction of the earth's life-support system, and the denial of justice and dignity to an ever-enlarging mass of humanity who populate the underdeveloped portion of the world. Our knowledge has not only expanded our potential for either disaster or enhanced well-being, but it has also furnished the means for foreseeing, however imperfectly, future trends and problems and for guiding human affairs toward those policies that increase human welfare and avoid disaster.

Throughout this study the increasing role of international organizations in the years since 1945 has been repeatedly noted and documented. The complex system of agencies created by the member states of the United Nations represents as much development over the League of Nations system as the League represented over the sporadic and meager organizational efforts of the nineteenth century. Concomitant with the proliferation of United Nations agencies, regional and nongovernmental organizations have been established in ever-increasing numbers. As global time and distance continue to shrink and as world interdependence bcomes more and more apparent, the existing trends toward the creation of international and transnational organizations will continue. The needs of a small, fragile, and interdependent planet cannot be met by the independent activities of 160 political units. Cooperation among these units is the minimum essential for promoting the common interests in which each has a share. Collective approaches to problems become increasingly necessary if the world situation is not to deteriorate. International organizations, based as they are on the principle of voluntary cooperation, provide acceptable means of collective consultation and action.

At the present stage of history, the United Nations system of agencies, as well as regional and transnational organizations, provide a bridge between the old and the new world order. On the one hand, they act as a conservative force against radical change by conforming to the status quo and by further institutionalizing the present international framework. On the other hand, they reflect the necessity for orderly, cooperative action in attacking the common problems of humanity. As the range of common problems broadens, organizations spring up in response to the need for united effort toward the possible solution of these mutual problems. Since cooperation is dependent upon the will of the involved parties, and since will is partially shaped by perceived needs, the future utility and increased role of international organizations seem assured. Past trends in the development of international organizations project themselves into the future as forecasts of the formation of more organizations performing a wider range of activities at a constantly accelerating pace.

It may well be that change will occur in the next twenty years at such a rate that revolutionary modifications in the international system will be required to adapt to the new developments. It is also possible that some of the potential sources of global disaster will threaten all or major segments of humanity with extinction. In either case the nation-state system and a system of international organizations based on voluntary cooperation among sovereign states may, of necessity, give way to a radically new international order. The clash between sovereignty and interdependence may require the relinquishment of substantial areas of sovereign prerogatives. Short of such radical threats or changes, both the nation-state and international organizations as instruments of cooperative action will survive and thrive. Both interdependence and the shrinking of global dimensions will require adjustments and will enhance the role of international organizations.

A great deal of attention has recently been focused on the many areas of potential threat to human survival in the next quarter or half century. Such predictions of doom certainly require our closest scrutiny and our most intelligent and diligent efforts to forestall disaster. This type of prediction reflects pessimism concerning human capability to solve problems, to cooperate in their solution, and to evolve institutions and social frameworks adequate to support the processes of problem solving.

The other side of the coin is the capability of the human race to survive. Humanity has a resilience that has been demonstrated throughout thousands of years of adaptability to change. As thinking creatures humans have developed an ingenuity of incredible proportions. There is no assurance that humanity will not be overcome by conditions partially of its own making, but ingenuity and adaptability give hope for continued survival.

The short history of international organizations is one demonstration of human ingenuity and adaptability. Their rapid development is a prime example of how humanity responds to changing needs. This development has not yet reached its zenith. If, at some future date, other instruments, which are better suited to that time, are required, we should, with some confidence, assume that present forms of organization will then be modified or replaced by more appropriate tools for promoting human welfare. Until that relatively remote period is reached, human reliance on the general type of international organizations familiar today will continue and will increase.

Bibliography

GENERAL SOURCES

A primary source is the *United Nations Documents*, which include records of meetings, reports, research studies, and communications from governments. The documents of the specialized agencies are also included in the listings in the *United Nations Documents Index*. Regional and other organizations generally publish voluminous records, which are also primary sources of information.

Other basic publications of the United Nations include:

"Annual Report of the Secretary-General on the Work of the United Nations"
Everyman's United Nations, 8th ed., 1968.
Everyman's United Nations — Supplement, 1971.
United Nations Demographic Yearbook
United Nations Statistical Yearbook
United Nations Treaty Series
Yearbook of the United Nations

The documents of the San Francisco conference, which produced the United Nations Charter, appear in *Documents of the United Nations Conference on International Organization*, 22 vols. Vols. 1–16 were published in 1945–46 in London and New York by the United Nations Information Organizations in cooperation with the Library of Congress. Vols. 17–22 were published in 1954–55 in New York by the United Nations.

472

Privately published sources of fundamental importance include:

Deadline Data on World Affairs. Includes an updated chronology of events in the United Nations.

Goodrich, Leland M., Edvard Hambro, and Anne P. Simons. *United Nations Charter: Commentary and Documents* (3rd ed.). New York: Columbia University Press, 1969.

Issues Before the General Assembly of the United Nations. Annual volumes. New York: United Nations Association of the United States of America.

"Reports of the Commission to Study the Organization of Peace."

Worldmark Encyclopedia of the Nations, 1, *The United Nations,* (5th ed.). New York: John Wiley & Sons, Inc., 1976.

Yearbook of International Organizations, (16th ed.). Brussels: Union of International Associations, 1977.

Periodicals published by the United Nations Office of Public Information are indispensable in supplying current information. The following series have been published:

United Nations Bulletin (August, 1946–June, 1954). Weekly through December, 1947, then twice monthly.

United Nations Monthly Chronicle (since May, 1964).

United Nations Review (July, 1954–April, 1964). Monthly.

The two most valuable privately published periodicals are *International Organization* and *International Conciliation* (discontinued in 1972).

SELECTED BIBLIOGRAPHY BY CHAPTERS

Chapter 1 By Way of Introduction

CLAUDE, INIS L., JR. *The Changing United Nations.* New York: Random House, 1967.

KAPLAN, MORTON A., ed. *The Revolution in World Politics.* New York: John Wiley, 1962.

MANGONE, GERARD J. *A Short History of International Organization.* New York: McGraw-Hill, 1954.

NICHOLAS, H. G. *The United Nations as a Political Institution,* (4th ed.). New York: Oxford University Press, 1971.

Chapter 2 A Great Experiment —
The League of Nations

CECIL, LORD ROBERT. *A Great Experiment.* New York: Oxford University Press, 1939.

League of Nations. *The Development of International Cooperation in Economic and Social Affairs.* Geneva: League Secretariat, August, 1939.

MILLER, DAVID HUNTER. *The Drafting of the Covenant*. New York: Putnam, 1928, 2 vols.
WALTERS, F. P. *A History of the League of Nations*. London: Oxford University Press, 1952, 2 vols.

Chapter 3 The Genesis of the United Nations

EAGLETON, CLYDE. "The Charter Adopted at San Francisco." *American Political Science Review*, 39 (October, 1945), 934-42.
GOODRICH, LELAND M. "From League of Nations to United Nations." *International Organization*, 1 (February, 1947), 3-21.
——, EDVARD HAMBRO, and ANNE P. SIMONS. *United Nations Charter: Commentary and Documents*, (3rd ed.). New York: Columbia University Press, 1969.
"Report to the President on the Results of the San Francisco Conference...." Department of State Publication 2349, Conference Series 71. Washington, D.C.: Government Printing Office, 1945.
RUSSELL, RUTH B., and JEANETTE E. MUTHER. *A History of the United Nations: The Role of the United States, 1940-45*. Washington, D.C.: The Brookings Institution, 1958.

Chapter 4 Basic Principles and Organization of the United Nations

BAILEY, SYDNEY D. *The Procedure of the UN Security Council*. Oxford: Clarendon Press, 1975.
Basic Facts About the United Nations. New York: United Nations, 1977.
Everyman's United Nations, (8th ed.). New York: United Nations, 1968.
GOODRICH, LELAND M., EDVARD HAMBRO, and ANNE P. SIMONS. *United Nations Charter: Commentary and Documents*, (3rd ed.). New York: Columbia University Press, 1969.

Chapter 5 Some Basic Issues of the United Nations

ALKER, HAYWARD R., JR., and BRUCE M. RUSSETT. *World Politics in the General Assembly*. New Haven, Conn.: Yale University Press, 1965.
BAILEY, SYDNEY D. "Veto in the Security Council." *International Conciliation*, no. 566 (January, 1968).
KAY, DAVID A. "The Impact of the African States on the United Nations." *International Organization*, 23 (Winter, 1969), 20-47.
KEOHANE, ROBERT O. "Political Influence in the General Assembly." *International Conciliation*, no. 557 (March, 1966).
NEWCOMBE, HANNA, MICHAEL ROSS, and ALAN G. NEWCOMBE. "United Nations Voting Patterns." *International Organization*, 24 (Winter, 1970), 100-21.
"The Problem of Membership in the United Nations." Staff Study No. 3, Subcommittee on the United Nations Charter, Committee on Foreign Relations, United States Senate, 83rd Congress, 2nd Session. Washington, D.C.: Government Printing Office, 1954.

"The Problem of the Veto in the United Nations Security Council." Staff Study No. 1, Subcommittee on the United Nations Charter, Committee on Foreign Relations, United States Senate, 83rd Congress, 2nd Session. Washington, D.C.: Government Printing Office, 1954.

"Representation and Voting in the United Nations General Assembly." Staff Study No. 4, Subcommittee on the United Nations Charter, Committee on Foreign Relations, United States Senate, 83rd Congress, 2nd Session. Washington, D.C.: Government Printing Office, 1954.

RUSSELL, RUTH B. *The General Assembly: Patterns/Problems/Prospects.* New York: Carnegie Endowment for International Peace, 1970.

STOESSINGER, JOHN G. *The United Nations and the Superpowers*, (4th ed.). New York: Random House, 1977.

——, and ASSOCIATES. *Financing the United Nations System.* Washington, D.C.: The Brookings Institution, 1964.

Chapter 6 Peaceful Settlement of Disputes

CLAUDE, INIS L., JR. "The OAS, the UN, and the United States." *International Conciliation*, no. 547 (March, 1964).

FALK, RICHARD A., and CYRIL E. BLACK, eds. *The Future of the International Legal Order*, Vol. III, *Conflict Management*. Princeton, N.J.: Princeton University Press, 1971.

GOODRICH, LELAND M. and ANNE P. SIMONS. *The United Nations and the Maintenance of International Peace and Security.* Washington, D.C.: The Brookings Institution, 1955.

"Pacific Settlement of Disputes in the United Nations." Staff Study no. 5, Subcommittee on the United Nations Charter, Committee on Foreign Relations, United States Senate, 83rd Congress, 2nd Session. Washington, D.C.: Government Printing Office, 1954.

STEVENSON, ADLAI E. *Looking Outward: Years of Crisis at the United Nations.* New York: Harper & Row, 1963.

Chapter 7 Collective Security and its Alternatives — Theory and Practice

BOYD, ANDREW. *Fifteen Men on a Powder Keg: A History of the United Nations Security Council.* New York: Stein and Day, 1971.

BOYD, JAMES M. *United Nations Peace-Keeping Operations: A Military and Political Appraisal.* New York: Praeger, 1971.

COX, ARTHUR M. *Prospects for Peacekeeping.* Washington, D.C.: The Brookings Institution, 1967.

FABIAN, LARRY L. *Soldiers Without Enemies: Preparing the United Nations for Peacekeeping.* Washington. D.C.: The Brookings Institution, 1971.

FINGER, SEYMOUR M. "The Maintenance of Peace," *Proceedings of the Academy of Political Science*, 32, no. 4, 1977, 195–205.

FINKELSTEIN, MARINA S., and LAWRENCE S. FINKELSTEIN, eds. *Collective Security.* San Francisco: Chandler Publishing, 1966.

GOODRICH, LELAND M. *Korea: A Study of the U.S. Policy in the United Nations.* New York: Council on Foreign Relations, 1956.

JAMES, ALAN. *The Politics of Peace-Keeping.* Published for The Institute for Strategic Studies. New York: Praeger, 1969.

LEFEVER, ERNEST W. *Crisis in the Congo: A United Nations Force in Action.* Washington, D.C.: The Brookings Institution, 1965.

MOSKOS, CHARLES C., JR. *Peace Soldiers: The Sociology of a United Nations Military Force.* Chicago: University of Chicago Press, 1976.

STEGENGA, JAMES A. *The United Nations Force in Cyprus.* Columbus, Ohio: Ohio University Press, 1968.

Chapter 8 The Search for
Justice Under Law

CORBETT, PERCY E. *The Growth of World Law.* Princeton, N.J.: Princeton University Press, 1971.

FALK, RICHARD A., and CYRIL E. BLACK, eds. *The Future of the International Legal Order,* Vol. I, *Trends and Patterns.* Princeton, N.J.: Princeton University Press, 1969.

HENKIN, LOUIS. *How Nations Behave: Law and Foreign Policy.* Published for The Council on Foreign Relations. New York: Praeger, 1970.

HIGGINS, ROSALYN. *The Development of International Law Through the Political Organs of the United Nations.* London: Oxford University Press, 1963.

International Court of Justice Yearbook. The Hague: International Court of Justice.

JENKS, C. WILFRED. *A New World of Law?* London: Longmans, Green, 1969.

JESSUP, PHILIP C. *The Price of International Justice.* New York: Columbia University Press, 1971.

SYATAUW, J. J. G. *Decisions of the International Court of Justice: A Digest,* 2nd ed. Leiden: A. W. Sijthoff, 1969.

Chapter 9 Controlling the
Instruments of War

Arms Control: Issues for the Public. Published for The American Assembly. Englewood Cliffs, N.J.: Prentice-Hall, 1961.

ART, ROBERT J., and KENNETH N. WALTZ, eds. *The Use of Force: International Politics and Foreign Policy.* Boston: Little, Brown, 1971.

BARGMAN, ABRAHAM. "Nuclear Diplomacy," *Proceedings of the Academy of Political Science,* 32, no. 4, 1977, 159-169.

BLOOMFIELD, BETH. "Strategic Arms Limitation," *Proceedings of the Academy of Political Science,* 32, no. 4, 1977, 184-194.

"Chemical and Bacteriological (Biological) Weapons and the Effects of Their Possible Use." Report of the Secretary-General, United Nations. New York, United Nations, 1969.

"Economic and Social Consequences of the Arms Race and of Military Expenditures." Report of the Secretary-General, UN Document A/8469/Rev. 1. New York, United Nations, 1972.

EDWARDS, DAVID V. *Arms Control in International Politics.* New York: Holt, Rinehart and Winston, 1969.

FALK, RICHARD A., and SAUL H. MENDLOVITZ, eds., *The Strategy of World Order,* Vol. IV, *Disarmament and Economic Development.* New York: World Law Fund, 1966.

SCOVILLE, HERBERT, JR., BETTY G. LALL, and ROBERT E. HUNTER. "The Arms Race: Steps Toward Restraint." *International Conciliation*, no. 587 (March, 1972).

SIVARD, RUTH LEGER. *World Military and Social Expenditures 1977*. Leesburg, Virginia: WMSE Publications, 1977.

SLOCOMBE, WALTER. "Controlling Strategic Nuclear Weapons," Headline Series, no. 226. New York: Foreign Policy Association, June, 1975.

World Military Expenditures and Arms Trade, 1963-1973. U.S. Arms Control and Disarmament Agency. Washington, D.C.: Government Printing Office, 1975.

Chapter 10 Promoting Economic Welfare

BROWN, LESTER R. "The Interdependence of Nations," Headline Series, no. 212. New York: Foreign Policy Association, October, 1972.

FERGUSON, C. CLYDE, JR. "The Politics of the New International Economic Order," *Proceedings of the Academy of Political Science*, 32, no. 4, 1977, 142-58.

GREGG, ROBERT W. "UN Economic, Social, and Technical Activities," in *The United Nations, Past, Present, and Future*, ed. James Barros. New York: Free Press, 1972.

"International Development Strategy: Action Programme of the General Assembly for the Second United Nations Development Decade." New York: United Nations, 1970.

"The International Development Strategy: First Over-all Review and Appraisal of Issues and Policies." Report of the Secretary-General, New York: United Nations, 1973.

MANGONE, GERARD J., ed. *UN Administration of Economic and Social Programs*. New York: Columbia University Press, 1966.

SCHACHTER, OSCAR. *Sharing the World's Resources*. New York: Columbia University Press, 1977.

SEN, SUDHIR. *United Nations in Economic Development—Need for a New Strategy*. Dobbs Ferry, N.Y.: Oceana Publications, 1969.

SHARP, WALTER R. *The United Nations Economic and Social Council*. New York: Columbia University Press, 1969.

SYMONDS, RICHARD, ed. *International Targets for Development*. New York: Harper & Row, 1970.

"Towards Accelerated Development: Proposals for the Second United Nations Development Decade." Report of the Committee for Development Planning. New York: United Nations, 1970.

Chapter 11 Promoting Social Progress

BROWN, LESTER R. "The Social Impact of the Green Revolution." *International Conciliation*, no. 581 (January, 1971).

JENKS, C. WILFRED. *Social Justice in the Law of Nations: The ILO Impact After Fifty Years*. London: Oxford University Press, 1970.

JOHNSTON, G. A. *The International Labour Organization, Its Work For Social and Economic Progress*. London: Europa Publications, 1970.

JOYNER, CHRISTOPHER C. "The United States' Withdrawal from the ILO International Politics in the Labor Arena." *International Lawyer*, 12 (Fall, 1978), 721-39.

KOREY, WILLIAM. "The Key to Human Rights — Implementation." *International Conciliation*, no. 570 (November, 1968).

LABOUISSE, HENRY R. "For the World's Children — UNICEF at 25." *UN Chronicle*, 8 (April, 1971), 48-60.

MORSE, DAVID A. *The Origin and Evolution of the I.L.O. and Its Role in the World Community.* Ithaca, New York: New York State School of Industrial and Labor Relations, Cornell University, 1969.

NANES, ALLAN S. *Beyond Malthus: The Food/People Equation.* Committee Print, Subcommittee on National Security Policy and Scientific Developments, Committee on Foreign Affairs, U.S. House of Representatives, 92nd Congress, 1st Session. Washington, D.C.: Government Printing Office, 1971.

PREGEL, BORIS, HAROLD D. LASSWELL and JOHN McHALE, eds. *World Priorities.* New Brunswick, N.J.: Transaction Books, 1977.

QUIMBY, FREEMAN H. *The Politics of Global Health.* Committee Print, Subcommittee on National Security Policy and Scientific Developments, Committee on Foreign Affairs, U.S. House of Representatives, 92nd Congress, 1st Session. Washington, D.C.: Government Printing Office, 1971.

"Symposium on the Role of the United States in Specialized International Organizations." Hearing before the Committee on Governmental Affairs, United States Senate, 95th Congress, 1st session, June 15, 1977. Washington, D.C.: Government Printing Office, 1977.

VAN DYKE, VERNON. *Human Rights, The United States, and World Community.* New York: Oxford University Press, 1970.

WADDEL, IAN G. "International Narcotics Control." *American Journal of International Law*, 64 (April, 1970), 310-23.

"World Population: A Challenge to the United Nations and Its System of Agencies." Report of a National Policy Panel established by the United Nations Association of the United States of America. New York: United Nations Association of the United States of America, May, 1969.

Chapter 12 The 1970s: A Decade of World Conferences

FERARU, ANNE THOMPSON. "Transnational Political Interests and the Global Environment." *International Organization.* 28 (Winter, 1974), 31-60.

HOLLICK, ANN L., and ROBERT E. OSGOOD. *New Era of Ocean Politics.* Baltimore: Johns Hopkins University Press, 1974.

LOGUE, JOHN J., ed. *The Fate of the Oceans.* Villanova, Pa: Villanova University Press, 1972.

"Man's Impact on the Global Environment." Report of the Study of Critical Environmental Problems. Cambridge, Mass.: MIT Press, 1970.

"Report of the Committee on Conferences." United Nations General Assembly, Official Records, 32nd Session, Supplement no. 32. New York: United Nations, 1977.

SCHACHTER, OSCAR. *Sharing the World's Resources.* New York: Columbia University Press, 1977.

SWING, JOHN TEMPLE. "The Law of the Sea," *Proceedings of the Academy of Political Science*, 32, no. 4, 1977, 128-141.

WEISS, MILDRED. "The Lawless Depths: The Need for an International Oceans Regime" in *The U.S. and the Developing World: Agenda for Action 1974.* Published for the Overseas Development Council. New York: Praeger, 1974.

Chapter 13 The Struggle for
Self-Government

ALLEN, PHILIP M. "Self-Determination in the Western Indian Ocean." *International Conciliation*, no. 560 (November, 1966).

CHOWDHURI, R. N. *International Mandates and Trusteeship Systems: A Comparative Study*. The Hague: Martinus Nijhoff, 1955.

EMERSON, RUPERT, "Colonialism, Political Development, and the UN." *International Organization*, 19 (Summer, 1965), 484–503.

———. *From Empire to Nation: The Rise to Self-Assertion of Asian and African Peoples*. Cambridge, Mass.: Harvard University Press, 1960.

KAY, DAVID A. "The United Nations and Decolonization" in *The United Nations: Past, Present, and Future*, ed. James Barros. New York: The Free Press, 1972.

MURRAY, JAMES N., JR. *The United Nations Trusteeship System*. Illinois Studies in the Social Sciences, 40. Urbana: University of Illinois Press, 1957.

Chapter 14 Varieties of Regionalism

BALL, M. MARGARET. *The OAS in Transition*. Durham, N.C.: Duke University Press, 1969.

BEER, FRANCIS A., ed. *Alliances: Latent War Communities in the Contemporary World*. New York: Holt, Rinehart and Winston, 1970.

CANTORI, LOUIS J., and STEVEN L. SPIEGEL, *The International Politics of Regions*. Englewood Cliffs, N.J.: Prentice-Hall, 1970.

ETZIONI, MINERVA M. *The Majority of One: Towards a Theory of Regional Compatibility*. Beverly Hills, Cal.: Sage Publications, 1970.

FEDDER, EDWIN H. *NATO: The Dynamics of Alliance in the Postwar World*. New York: Dodd Mead, 1973.

FELD, WERNER J. *The European Community in World Affairs: Economic Power and Political Influence*. Port Washington, N.Y.: Alfred Pub. Co., 1976.

GREGG, ROBERT W. "Program Decentralization Through the Regional Economic Commissions" in *UN Administration of Economic and Social Programs*, ed. Gerard J. Mangone, New York: Columbia University Press, 1966.

KORBONSKI, ANDRZEJ "The Warsaw Pact." *International Conciliation*, no. 573 (May, 1969).

MAGEE, JAMES S. "ECA and the Paradox of African Cooperation." *International Conciliation*, no. 580 (November, 1970).

NYE, JOSEPH S. *Peace in Parts: Integration and Conflict in Regional Organization*. Boston: Little, Brown, 1971.

SINGH, MANMOHAN. "Regional Development Banks." *International Conciliation*, no. 576 (January, 1970).

WORONOFF, JON. *Organizing African Unity*. Metuchen, N.J.: Scarecrow Press, 1970.

Chapter 15 International Administration
and the Search for Leadership

BAILEY, SYDNEY D. *The Secretariat of the United Nations*. New York: Carnegie Endowment for International Peace, 1962.

FINGER, SEYMOUR M., and JOHN MUGNO. *The Politics of Staffing the United Nations Secretariat.* New York: The Ralph Bunche Institute on the United Nations, The Graduate School and University Center of the City University of New York, 1974.

FOOTE, WILDER, ed. *Servant of Peace: A Selection of the Speeches and Statements of Dag Hammarskjöld.* New York: Harper & Row, 1963.

FOSDICK, RAYMOND B. *The League and the United Nations After Fifty Years: The Six Secretaries-General.* Newtown, Conn.: Raymond B. Fosdick, 1972.

ROVINE, ARTHUR W. *The First Fifty Years: The Secretary-General in World Politics, 1920–1970.* Leiden: A. W. Sijthoff, 1970.

SCHWEBEL, STEPHEN M. *The Secretary-General of the United Nations: His Political Powers and Practice.* Cambridge, Mass.: Harvard University Press, 1952.

"The UN Secretary-General: His Role in World Politics." 14th Report, Commission to Study the Organization of Peace. New York: Commission to Study the Organization of Peace, 1962.

WINCHMORE, CHARLES. "The Secretariat: Retrospect and Prospect." *International Organization,* 19 (Summer, 1965), 622–39.

ZACHER, MARK W. *Dag Hammarskjöld's United Nations.* New York: Columbia University Press, 1970.

Chapter 16 Transnational Relations and International Organization

AGGARWALA, NARINDER, MICHAEL J. FENELLO, and GERALD F. FITZ-GERALD. "Air Hijacking: An International Perspective." *International Conciliation,* no. 585 (November, 1971).

ANGELL, ROBERT C. *Peace on the March: Transnational Participation.* New York: Van Nostrand Reinhold, 1969.

BEHRMAN, JACK N. *National Interests and the Multinational Enterprise: Tensions Among the North Atlantic Countries.* Englewood Cliffs, N.J.: Prentice-Hall, 1970.

BERGSTEN, C. FRED, THOMAS HORST, and THEODORE H. MORAN. *American Multinationals and American Interests.* Washington, D.C.: Brookings Institution, 1978.

KEOHANE, ROBERT O., and JOSEPH S. NYE, JR., eds.. "Transnational Relations and World Politics." *International Organization,* 25 (Summer, 1971).

KINDLEBERGER, CHARLES P., ed. *The International Corporation.* Cambridge, Mass.: MIT Press, 1970.

ODISHAW, HUGH. "International Cooperation in Space Science" in *Outer Space: Prospects for Man and Society,* ed. Lincoln P. Bloomfield. For the American Assembly. Englewood Cliffs, N.J.: Prentice-Hall, 1962, 105–22.

PERLMUTTER, HOWARD V. "The Tortuous Evolution of the Multinational Corporation." *Columbia Journal of World Business,* 4 (January–February, 1969), 9–18.

RUBIN, SEYMOUR J. "The Transnational Corporations," *Proceedings of the Academy of Political Science,* 32, no. 4, 1977, 120–27.

SCOTT, ANDREW M. *The Revolution in Statecraft: Informal Penetration.* New York: Random House, 1965.

SERVAN-SCHREIBER, J. J. *The American Challenge,* trans. Ronald Steel. New York: Atheneum, 1968.

TANZER, MICHAEL. *The Political Economy of International Oil and the Underdeveloped Countries.* Boston: Beacon Press, 1969.

"Terrorism: The World at Bay." Transcript of special events production broadcast by WHYY, Philadelphia. Kent, Ohio: PTV Publications, 1978.

TURNER, LOUIS. *Invisible Empires: Multinational Companies and the Modern World.* London: Hamish Hamilton, 1970.

Chapter 17 International Organization in Retrospect and Prospect

GOODRICH, LELAND M. *The United Nations in a Changing World.* New York: Columbia University Press, 1974.

KAY, DAVID A., ed. *The Changing United Nations: Options for the United States.* Proceedings of the Academy of Political Science, 32, no. 4, 1977.

"Reform and Restructuring of the U.N. System." Department of State Pub. 8940, International Organization and Conference Series 135, June, 1978.

"Report of the President's Commission for the Observance of the Twenty-Fifth Anniversary of the United Nations." Washington, D.C.: Government Printing Office, 1972.

"The United Nations in the 1970s: A Strategy for a Unique Era in the Affairs of Nations." Report of a National Policy Panel Established by the United Nations Association of the United States of America. New York: United Nations Association of the United States of America, 1971.

"The United Nations: The Next Twenty-Five Years." 20th Report, Commission to Study the Organization of Peace. Dobbs Ferry, N.Y.: Oceana Publications, Inc., 1970.

I

❧

Charter
of
the United Nations

WE THE PEOPLES OF THE UNITED NATIONS determined

to save succeeding generations from the scourge of war, which twice in our lifetime has brought untold sorrow to mankind, and

to reaffirm faith in fundamental human rights, in the dignity and worth of the human person, in the equal rights of men and women and of nations large and small, and

to establish conditions under which justice and respect for the obligations arising from treaties and other sources of international law can be maintained, and

to promote social progress and better standards of life in larger freedom,

    and for these ends

to practice tolerance and live together in peace with one another as good neighbours, and

to unite our strength to maintain international peace and security, and

to ensure, by the acceptance of principles and the institution of methods, that armed force shall not be used, save in the common interest, and

to employ international machinery for the promotion of the economic and social advancement of all peoples,

    have resolved to combine our efforts

    to accomplish these aims

Accordingly, our respective Governments, through representatives assembled in the city of San Francisco, who have exhibited their full powers found to be in good and due form, have agreed to the present Charter of the United Nations and do hereby establish an international organization to be known as the United Nations.

CHAPTER 1
PURPOSES AND PRINCIPLES

Article 1

The Purposes of the United Nations are:

1. To maintain international peace and security, and to that end: to take effective collective measures for the prevention and removal of threats to the peace, and for the suppression of acts of aggression or other breaches of the peace, and to bring about by peaceful means, and in conformity with the principles of justice and international law, adjustment or settlement of international disputes or situations which might lead to a breach of the peace;

2. To develop friendly relations among nations based on respect for the principle of equal rights and self-determination of peoples, and to take other appropriate measures to strengthen universal peace;

3. To achieve international co-operation in solving international problems of an economic, social, cultural, or humanitarian character, and in promoting and encouraging respect for human rights and for fundamental freedoms for all without distinction as to race, sex, language, or religion; and

4. To be a centre for harmonizing the actions of nations in the attainment of these common ends.

Article 2

The Organization and its Members, in pursuit of the Purposes stated in Article 1, shall act in accordance with the following Principles.

1. The Organization is based on the principle of the sovereign equality of all its Members.

2. All Members, in order to ensure to all of them the rights and benefits resulting from membership, shall fulfil in good faith the obligations assumed by them in accordance with the present Charter.

3. All Members shall settle their international disputes by peaceful means in such a manner that international peace and security, and justice, are not endangered.

4. All Members shall refrain in their international relations from the threat or use of force against the territorial integrity or political independence of any state, or in any other manner inconsistent with the Purposes of the United Nations.

5. All Members shall give the United Nations every assistance in any action it takes in accordance with the present Charter, and shall refrain from giving assistance to any state against which the United Nations is taking preventive or enforcement action.

6. The Organization shall ensure that states which are not Members of the United Nations act in accordance with these Principles so far as may be necessary for the maintenance of international peace and security.

7. Nothing contained in the present Charter shall authorize the United Nations to intervene in matters which are essentially within the domestic jurisdiction of any state or shall require the Members to submit such matters to settlement under the present Charter; but this principle shall not prejudice the application of enforcement measures under Chapter VII.

CHAPTER II
MEMBERSHIP

Article 3

The original Members of the United Nations shall be the states which, having participated in the United Nations Conference on International Organization at San Francisco, or having previously signed the Declaration by United Nations of 1 January 1942, sign the present Charter and ratify it in accordance with Article 110.

Article 4

1. Membership in the United Nations is open to all other peace-loving states which accept the obligations contained in the present Charter and, in the judgment of the Organization, are able and willing to carry out these obligations.

2. The admission of any such state to membership in the United Nations will be effected by a decision of the General Assembly upon the recommendation of the Security Council.

Article 5

A Member of the United Nations against which preventive or enforcement action has been taken by the Security Council may be suspended from the exercise of the rights and privileges of membership by the General Assembly upon the recommendation of the Security Council. The exercise of these rights and privileges may be restored by the Security Council.

Article 6

A Member of the United Nations which has persistently violated the Principles contained in the present Charter may be expelled from the Organization by the General Assembly upon the recommendation of the Security Council.

CHAPTER III
ORGANS

Article 7

1. There are established as the principal organs of the United Nations: a General Assembly, a Security Council, an Economic and Social Council, a Trusteeship Council, an International Court of Justice and a Secretariat.

2. Such subsidiary organs as may be found necessary may be established in accordance with the present Charter.

Article 8

The United Nations shall place no restrictions on the eligibility of men and women to participate in any capacity and under conditions of equality in its principal and subsidiary organs.

CHAPTER IV
THE GENERAL ASSEMBLY

Composition

Article 9

1. The General Assembly shall consist of all the Members of the United Nations.
2. Each Member shall have not more than five representatives in the General Assembly.

Functions and Powers

Article 10

The General Assembly may discuss any questions or any matters within the scope of the present Charter or relating to the powers and functions of any organs provided for in the present Charter, and, except as provided in Article 12, may make recommendations to the Members of the United Nations or to the Security Council or to both on any such questions or matters.

Article 11

1. The General Assembly may consider the general principles of co-operation in the maintenance of international peace and security, including the principles governing disarmament and the regulation of armaments, and may make recommendations with regard to such principles to the Members or to the Security Council or to both.
2. The General Assembly may discuss any questions relating to the maintenance of international peace and security brought before it by any Member of the United Nations, or by the Security Council, or by a state which is not a Member of the United Nations in accordance with Article 35, paragraph 2, and, except as provided in Article 12, may make recommendations with regard to any such questions to the state or states concerned or to the Security Council or to both. Any such question on which action is necessary shall be referred to the Security Council by the General Assembly either before or after discussion.
3. The General Assembly may call the attention of the Security Council to situations which are likely to endanger international peace and security.
4. The powers of the General Assembly set forth in this Article shall not limit the general scope of Article 10.

Article 12

1. While the Security Council is exercising in respect of any dispute or situation the functions assigned to it in the present Charter, the General Assembly shall not make any recommendations with regard to that dispute or situation unless the Security Council so requests.

2. The Secretary-General, with the consent of the Security Council, shall notify the General Assembly at each session of any matters relative to the maintenance of international peace and security which are being dealt with by the Security Council and shall similarly notify the General Assembly, or the Members of the United Nations if the General Assembly is not in session, immediately the Security Council ceases to deal with such matters.

Article 13

1. The General Assembly shall initiate studies and make recommendations for the purpose of:

a. promoting international co-operation in the political field and encouraging the progressive development of international law and its codification;

b. promoting international co-operation in the economic, social, cultural, educational, and health fields, and assisting in the realization of human rights and fundamental freedoms for all without distinction as to race, sex, language, or religion.

2. The further responsibilities, functions and powers of the General Assembly with respect to matters mentioned in paragraph 1(b) above are set forth in Chapters IX and X.

Article 14

Subject to the provisions of Article 12, the General Assembly may recommend measures for the peaceful adjustment of any situation, regardless of origin, which it deems likely to impair the general welfare or friendly relations among nations, including situations resulting from a violation of the provisions of the present Charter setting forth the Purposes and Principles of the United Nations.

Article 15

1. The General Assembly shall receive and consider annual and special reports from the Security Council; these reports shall include an account of the measures that the Security Council has decided upon or taken to maintain international peace and security.

2. The General Assembly shall receive and consider reports from the other organs of the United Nations.

Article 16

The General Assembly shall perform such functions with respect to the international trusteeship system as are assigned to it under Chapters XII and XIII, including the approval of the trusteeship agreements for areas not designated as strategic.

Article 17

1. The General Assembly shall consider and approve the budget of the Organization.
2. The expenses of the Organization shall be borne by the Members as apportioned by the General Assembly.
3. The General Assembly shall consider and approve any financial and budgetary arrangements with specialized agencies referred to in Article 57 and shall examine the administrative budgets of such specialized agencies with a view to making recommendations to the agencies concerned.

Voting

Article 18

1. Each member of the General Assembly shall have one vote.
2. Decisions of the General Assembly on important questions shall be made by a two-thirds majority of the members present and voting. These questions shall include: recommendations with respect to the maintenance of international peace and security, the election of the non-permanent members of the Security Council, the election of the members of the Economic and Social Council, the election of members of the Trusteeship Council in accordance with paragraph 1(c) of Article 86, the admission of new Members to the United Nations, the suspension of the rights and privileges of membership, the expulsion of Members, questions relating to the operation of the trusteeship system, and budgetary questions.
3. Decisions on other questions, including the determination of additional categories of questions to be decided by a two-thirds majority, shall be made by a majority of the members present and voting.

Article 19

A Member of the United Nations which is in arrears in the payment of its financial contributions to the Organization shall have no vote in the General Assembly if the amount of its arrears equals or exceeds the amount of the contributions due from it for the preceding two full years. The General Assembly may, nevertheless, permit such a Member to vote if it is satisfied that the failure to pay is due to conditions beyond the control of the Member.

Procedure

Article 20

The General Assembly shall meet in regular annual sessions and in such special sessions as occasion may require. Special sessions shall be convoked by the Secretary-General at the request of the Security Council or of a majority of the Members of the United Nations.

Article 21

The General Assembly shall adopt its own rules of procedure. It shall elect its President for each session.

Article 22

The General Assembly may establish such subsidiary organs as it deems necessary for the performance of its functions.

CHAPTER V
THE SECURITY COUNCIL

Composition

Article 23

1. The Security Council shall consist of fifteen Members of the United Nations. The Republic of China, France, the Union of Soviet Socialist Republics, the United Kingdom of Great Britain and Northern Ireland, and the United States of America shall be permanent members of the Security Council. The General Assembly shall elect ten other Members of the United Nations to be non-permanent members of the Security Council, due regard being specially paid, in the first instance to the contribution of Members of the United Nations to the maintenance of international peace and security and to the other purposes of the Organization, and also to equitable geographical distribution.

2. The non-permanent members of the Security Council shall be elected for a term of two years. In the first election of the non-permanent members after the increase of the membership of the Security Council from eleven to fifteen, two of the four additional members shall be chosen for a term of one year. A retiring member shall not be eligible for immediate reelection.

3. Each member of the Security Council shall have one representative.

Functions and Powers

Article 24

1. In order to ensure prompt and effective action by the United Nations, its Members confer on the Security Council primary responsibility for the maintenance of international peace and security, and agree that in carrying out its duties under this responsibility the Security Council acts on their behalf.

2. In discharging these duties the Security Council shall act in accordance with the Purposes and Principles of the United Nations. The specific powers granted to the Security Council for the discharge of these duties are laid down in Chapters VI, VII, VIII, and XII.

3. The Security Council shall submit annual and, when necessary, special reports to the General Assembly for its consideration.

Article 25

The Members of the United Nations agree to accept and carry out the decisions of the Security Council in accordance with the present Charter.

Article 26

In order to promote the establishment and maintenance of international peace and security with the least diversion for armaments of the world's human and economic resources, the Security Council shall be responsible for formulating, with the assistance of the Military Staff Committee referred to in Article 47, plans to be submitted to the Members of the United Nations for the establishment of a system for the regulation of armaments.

Voting

Article 27

1. Each member of the Security Council shall have one vote.

2. Decisions of the Security Council on procedural matters shall be made by an affirmative vote of nine members.

3. Decisions of the Security Council on all other matters shall be made by an affirmative vote of nine members including the concurring votes of the permanent members; provided that, in decisions under Chapter VI, and under paragraph 3 of Article 52, a party to a dispute shall abstain from voting.

Procedure

Article 28

1. The Security Council shall be so organized as to be able to function continuously. Each member of the Security Council shall for this purpose be represented at all times at the seat of the Organization.

2. The Security Council shall hold periodic meetings at which each of its members may, if it so desires, be represented by a member of the government or by some other specially designated representative.

3. The Security Council may hold meetings at such places other than the seat of the Organization as in its judgment will best facilitate its work.

Article 29

The Security Council may establish such subsidiary organs as it deems necessary for the performance of its functions.

Article 30

The Security Council shall adopt its own rules of procedure, including the method of selecting its President.

Article 31

Any Member of the United Nations which is not a member of the Security Council may participate, without vote, in the discussion of any question brought before the Security Council whenever the latter considers that the interests of that Member are specially affected.

Article 32

Any Member of the United Nations which is not a member of the Security Council or any state which is not a Member of the United Nations, if it is a party to a dispute under consideration by the Security Council, shall be invited to participate, without vote, in the discussion relating to the dispute. The Security Council shall lay down such conditions as it deems just for the participation of a state which is not a Member of the United Nations.

CHAPTER VI
PACIFIC SETTLEMENT OF DISPUTES

Article 33

1. The parties to any dispute, the continuance of which is likely to endanger the maintenance of international peace and security, shall, first of all, seek a solution by negotiation, enquiry, mediation, conciliation, arbitration, judicial settlement, resort to regional agencies or arrangements, or other peaceful means of their own choice.
2. The Security Council shall, when it deems necessary, call upon the parties to settle their dispute by such means.

Article 34

The Security Council may investigate any dispute, or any situation which might lead to international friction or give rise to a dispute, in order to determine whether the continuance of the dispute or situation is likely to endanger the maintenance of international peace and security.

Article 35

1. Any Member of the United Nations may bring any dispute, or any situation of the nature referred to in Article 34, to the attention of the Security Council or of the General Assembly.

2. A state which is not a Member of the United Nations may bring to the attention of the Security Council or of the General Assembly any dispute to which it is a party if it accepts in advance, for the purposes of the dispute, the obligations of pacific settlement provided in the present Charter.

3. The proceedings of the General Assembly in respect of matters brought to its attention under this Article will be subject to the provisions of Articles 11 and 12.

Article 36

1. The Security Council may, at any stage of a dispute of the nature referred to in Article 33 or of a situation of like nature, recommend appropriate procedures or methods of adjustment.

2. The Security Council should take into consideration any procedures for the settlement of the dispute which have already been adopted by the parties.

3. In making recommendations under this Article the Security Council should also take into consideration that legal disputes should as a general rule be referred by the parties to the International Court of Justice in accordance with the provisions of the Statute of the Court.

Article 37

1. Should the parties to a dispute of the nature referred to in Article 33 fail to settle it by the means indicated in that Article, they shall refer it to the Security Council.

2. If the Security Council deems that the continuance of the dispute is in fact likely to endanger the maintenance of international peace and security, it shall decide whether to take action under Article 36 or to recommend such terms of settlement as it may consider appropriate.

Article 38

Without prejudice to the provisions of Articles 33 to 37, the Security Council may, if all the parties to any dispute so request, make recommendations to the parties with a view to a pacific settlement of the dispute.

CHAPTER VII
ACTION WITH RESPECT TO THREATS TO THE PEACE, BREACHES OF THE PEACE, AND ACTS OF AGGRESSION

Article 39

The Security Council shall determine the existence of any threat to the peace, breach of the peace, or act of aggression and shall make recommendations, or decide what measures shall be taken in accordance with Articles 41 and 42, to maintain or restore international peace and security.

Article 40

In order to prevent an aggravation of the situation, the Security Council may, before making the recommendations or deciding upon the measures provided for in Article 39, call upon the parties concerned to comply with such provisional measures as it deems necessary or desirable. Such provisional measures shall be without prejudice to the rights, claims, or position of the parties concerned. The Security Council shall duly take account of failure to comply with such provisional measures.

Article 41

The Security Council may decide what measures not involving the use of armed force are to be employed to give effect to its decisions, and it may call upon the Members of the United Nations to apply such measures. These may include complete or partial interruption of economic relations and of rail, sea, air, postal, telegraphic, radio, and other means of communication, and the severance of diplomatic relations.

Article 42

Should the Security Council consider that measures provided for in Article 41 would be inadequate or have proved to be inadequate, it may take such action by air, sea, or land forces as may be necessary to maintain or restore international peace and security. Such action may include demonstrations, blockade, and other operations by air, sea, or land forces of Members of the United Nations.

Article 43

1. All Members of the United Nations, in order to contribute to the maintenance of international peace and security, undertake to make available to the Security Council, on its call and in accordance with a special agreement or agreements, armed forces, assistance, and facilities, including rights of passage, necessary for the purpose of maintaining international peace and security.

2. Such agreement or agreements shall govern the numbers and types of forces, their degree of readiness and general location, and the nature of the facilities and assistance to be provided.

3. The agreement or agreements shall be negotiated as soon as possible on the initiative of the Security Council. They shall be concluded between the Security Council and Members or between the Security Council and groups of Members and shall be subject to ratification by the signatory states in accordance with their respective constitutional processes.

Article 44

When the Security Council has decided to use force it shall, before calling upon a Member not represented on it to provide armed forces in fulfilment of the obligations assumed under Article 43, invite that Member, if the Member so desires, to participate in the decisions of the Security Council concerning the employment of contingents of that Member's armed forces.

Article 45

In order to enable the United Nations to take urgent military measures, Members shall hold immediately available national air-force contingents for combined international enforcement action. The strength and degree of readiness of these contingents and plans for their combined action shall be determined, within the limits laid down in the special agreement or agreements referred to in Article 43, by the Security Council with the assistance of the Military Staff Committee.

Article 46

Plans for the application of armed force shall be made by the Security Council with the assistance of the Military Staff Committee.

Article 47

1. There shall be established a Military Staff Committee to advise and assist the Security Council on all questions relating to the Security Council's military requirements for the maintenance of international peace and security, the employment and command of forces placed at its disposal, the regulation of armaments, and possible disarmament.

2. The Military Staff Committee shall consist of the Chiefs of Staff of the permanent members of the Security Council or their representatives. Any Member of the United Nations not permanently represented on the Committee shall be invited by the Committee to be associated with it when the efficient discharge of the Committee's responsibilities requires the participation of that Member in its work.

3. The Military Staff Committee shall be responsible under the Security Council for the strategic direction of any armed forces placed at the disposal of the Security Council. Questions relating to the command of such forces shall be worked out subsequently.

4. The Military Staff Committee, with the authorization of the Security Council and after consultation with appropriate regional agencies, may establish regional sub-committees.

Article 48

1. The action required to carry out the decisions of the Security Council for the maintenance of international peace and security shall be taken by all the Members of the United Nations or by some of them, as the Security Council may determine.

2. Such decisions shall be carried out by the Members of the United Nations directly and through their action in the appropriate international agencies of which they are members.

Article 49

The Members of the United Nations shall join in affording mutual assistance in carrying out the measures decided upon by the Security Council.

Article 50

If preventive or enforcement measures against any state are taken by the Security Council, any other state, whether a Member of the United Nations or not, which finds itself confronted with special economic problems arising from the carrying out of those measures shall have the right to consult the Security Council with regard to a solution of those problems.

Article 51

Nothing in the present Charter shall impair the inherent right of individual or collective self-defence if an armed attack occurs against a Member of the United Nations, until the Security Council has taken measures necessary to maintain international peace and security. Measures taken by members in the exercise of this right of self-defence shall be immediately reported to the Security Council and shall not in any way affect the authority and responsibility of the Security Council under the present Charter to take at any time such action as it deems necessary in order to maintain or restore international peace and security.

CHAPTER VIII
REGIONAL ARRANGEMENTS

Article 52

1. Nothing in the present Charter precludes the existence of regional arrangements or agencies for dealing with such matters relating to the maintenance of

international peace and security as are appropriate for regional action, provided that such arrangements or agencies and their activities are consistent with the Purposes and Principles of the United Nations.

2. The Members of the United Nations entering into such arrangements or constituting such agencies shall make every effort to achieve pacific settlement of local disputes through such regional arrangements or by such regional agencies before referring them to the Security Council.

3. The Security Council shall encourage the development of pacific settlement of local disputes through such regional arrangements or by such regional agencies either on the initiative of the states concerned or by reference from the Security Council.

4. This Article in no way impairs the application of Articles 34 and 35.

Article 53

1. The Security Council shall, where appropriate, utilize such regional arrangements or agencies for enforcement action under its authority. But no enforcement action shall be taken under regional arrangments or by regional agencies without the authorization of the Security Council, with the exception of measures against any enemy state, as defined in paragraph 2 of this Article, provided for pursuant to Article 107 or in regional arrangements directed against renewal of aggressive policy on the part of any such state, until such time as the Organization may, on request of the Governments concerned, be charged with the responsibility for preventing further aggression by such a state.

2. The term enemy state as used in paragraph 1 of this Article applies to any state which during the Second World War has been an enemy of any signatory of the present Charter.

Article 54

The Security Council shall at all times be kept fully informed of activities undertaken or in contemplation under regional arrangements or by regional agencies for the maintenance of international peace and security.

CHAPTER IX
INTERNATIONAL ECONOMIC AND SOCIAL
CO-OPERATION

Article 55

With a view to the creation of conditions of stability and well-being which are necessary for peaceful and friendly relations among nations based on respect for the principle of equal rights and self-determination of peoples, the United nations shall promote:

 a. higher standards of living, full employment, and conditions of economic and social progress and development;

 b. solutions of international economic, social, health, and related problems; and international cultural and educational co-operation; and

c. universal respect for, and observance of, human rights and fundamental freedoms for all without distinction as to race, sex, language, or religion.

Article 56

All Members pledge themselves to take joint and separate action in cooperation with the Organization for the achievement of the purposes set forth in Article 55.

Article 57

1. The various specialized agencies, established by intergovernmental agreement and having wide international responsibilities, as defined in their basic instruments, in economic, social, cultural, educational, health, and related fields, shall be brought into relationship with the United Nations in accordance with the provisions of Article 63.
2. Such agencies thus brought into relationship with the United Nations are hereinafter referred to as specialized agencies.

Article 58

The Organization shall make recommendations for the coordination of the policies and activities of the specialized agencies.

Article 59

The Organization shall, where appropriate, initiate negotiations among the states concerned for the creation of any new specialized agencies required for the accomplishment of the purposes set forth in Article 55.

Article 60

Responsibility for the discharge of the functions of the Organization set forth in this Chapter shall be vested in the General Assembly and, under the authority of the General Assembly, in the Economic and Social Council, which shall have for this purpose the powers set forth in Chapter X.

CHAPTER X
THE ECONOMIC AND SOCIAL COUNCIL

Composition

Article 61

1. The Economic and Social Council shall consist of fifty-four Members of the United Nations elected by the General Assembly.

2. Subject to the provisions of paragraph 3, eighteen members of the Economic and Social Council shall be elected each year for a term of three years. A retiring member shall be eligible for immediate re-election.

3. At the first election after the increase in the membership of the Economic and Social Council from twenty-seven to fifty-four members, in addition to the members elected in place of the nine members whose term of office expires at the end of that year, twenty-seven additional members shall be elected. Of these twenty-seven additional members, the term of office of nine members so elected shall expire at the end of one year, and of nine other members at the end of two years, in accordance with arrangements made by the General Assembly.

4. Each member of the Economic and Social Council shall have one representative.

Functions and Powers

Article 62

1. The Economic and Social Council may make or initiate studies and reports with respect to international economic, social, cultural, educational, health, and related matters and may make recommendations with respect to any such matters to the General Assembly, to the Members of the United Nations, and to the specialized agencies concerned.

2. It may make recommendations for the purpose of promoting respect for, and observance of, human rights and fundamental freedoms for all.

3. It may prepare draft conventions for submission to the General Assembly, with respect to matters falling within its competence.

4. It may call, in accordance with the rules prescribed by the United Nations, international conferences on matters falling within its competence.

Article 63

1. The Economic and Social Council may enter into agreements with any of the agencies referred to in Article 57, defining the terms on which the agency concerned shall be brought into relationship with the United Nations. Such agreements shall be subject to approval by the General Assembly.

2. It may co-ordinate the activities of the specialized agencies through consultation with and recommendations to such agencies and through recommendations to the General Assembly and to the Members of the United Nations.

Article 64

1. The Economic and Social Council may take appropriate steps to obtain regular reports from the specialized agencies. It may make arrangements with the Members of the United Nations and with the specialized agencies to obtain reports on the steps taken to give effect to its own recommendations and to recommendations on matters falling within its competence made by the General Assembly.

2. It may communicate its observations on these reports to the General Assembly.

Article 65

The Economic and Social Council may furnish information to the Security Council and shall assist the Security Council upon its request.

Article 66

1. The Economic and Social Council shall perform such functions as fall within its competence in connexion with the carrying out of the recommendations of the General Assembly.
2. It may, with the approval of the General Assembly, perform services at the request of Members of the United Nations and at the request of specialized agencies.
3. It shall perform such other functions as are specified elsewhere in the present Charter or as may be assigned to it by the General Assembly.

Voting

Article 67

1. Each Member of the Economic and Social Council shall have one vote.
2. Decisions of the Economic and Social Council shall be made by a majority of the members present and voting.

Procedure

Article 68

The Economic and Social Council shall set up commissions in economic and social fields and for the promotion of human rights, and such other commissions as may be required for the performance of its functions.

Article 69

The Economic and Social Council shall invite any Member of the United Nations to participate, without vote, in its deliberations on any matter of particular concern to that Member.

Article 70

The Economic and Social Council may make arrangements for representatives of the specialized agencies to participate, without vote, in its deliberations and in those of the commissions established by it, and for its representatives to participate in the deliberations of the specialized agencies.

Article 71

The Economic and Social Council may make suitable arrangements for consultation with non-governmental organizations which are concerned with matters within its competence. Such arrangements may be made with international organizations and, where appropriate, with national organizations after consultation with the Member of the United Nations concerned.

Article 72

1. The Economic and Social Council shall adopt its own rules of procedure, including the method of selecting its President.
2. The Economic and Social Council shall meet as required in accordance with its rules, which shall include provision for the convening of meetings on the request of a majority of its members.

CHAPTER XI
DECLARATION REGARDING
NON-SELF-GOVERNING TERRITORIES

Article 73

Members of the United Nations which have or assume responsibilities for the administration of territories whose peoples have not yet attained a full measure of self-government recognize the principle that the interests of the inhabitants of these territories are paramount, and accept as a sacred trust the obligation to promote to the utmost, within the system of international peace and security established by the present Charter, the well-being of the inhabitants of these territories, and, to this end:

a. to ensure, with due respect for the culture of the peoples concerned, their political, economic, social, and educational advancement, their just treatment, and their protection against abuses;

b. to develop self-government, to take due account of the political aspirations of the peoples, and to assist them in the progressive development of their free political institutions, according to the particular circumstances of each territory and its peoples and their varying stages of advancement;

c. to further international peace and security;

d. to promote constructive measures of development, to encourage research, and to co-operate with one another and, when and where appropriate, with specialized international bodies with a view to the practical achievement of the social, economic, and scientific purposes set forth in this Article; and

e. to transmit regularly to the Secretary-General for information purposes, subject to such limitation as security and constitutional considerations may require, statistical and other information of a technical nature relating to economic, social, and educational conditions in the territories for which they are respectively responsible other than those territories to which Chapters XII and XIII apply.

Article 74

Members of the United Nations also agree that their policy in respect of the territories to which this Chapter applies, no less than in respect of their metropolitan areas, must be based on the general principle of good-neighbourliness, due account being taken of the interests and well-being of the rest of the world, in social, economic, and commercial matters.

CHAPTER XII
INTERNATIONAL TRUSTEESHIP SYSTEM

Article 75

The United Nations shall establish under its authority an international trusteeship system for the administration and supervision of such territories as may be placed thereunder by subsequent individual agreements. These territories are hereinafter referred to as trust territories.

Article 76

The basic objectives of the trusteeship system, in accordance with the Purposes of the United Nations laid down in Article 1 of the present Charter, shall be:

a. to further international peace and security;

b. to promote the political, economic, social, and educational advancement of the inhabitants of the trust territories, and their progressive development towards self-government or independence as may be appropriate to the particular circumstances of each territory and its peoples and the freely expressed wishes of the peoples concerned, and as may be provided by the terms of each trusteeship agreement;

c. to encourage respect for human rights and for fundamental freedoms for all without distinction as to race, sex, language, or religion, and to encourage recognition of the interdependence of the peoples of the world; and

d. to ensure equal treatment in social, economic, and commercial matters for all Members of the United Nations and their nationals, and also equal treatment for the latter in the administration of justice, without prejudice to the attainment of the forgoing objectives and subject to the provisions of Article 80.

Article 77

1. The trusteeship system shall apply to such territories in the following categories as may be placed thereunder by means of trusteeship agreements:
  a. territories now held under mandate;
  b. territories which may be detached from enemy states as a result of the Second World War; and
  c. territories voluntarily placed under the system by states responsible for their administration.
2. It will be a matter for subsequent agreement as to which territories in the foregoing categories will be brought under the trusteeship system and upon what terms.

Article 78

The trusteeship system shall not apply to territories which have become Members of the United Nations, relationship among which shall be based on respect for the principle of sovereign equality.

Article 79

The terms of trusteeship for each territory to be placed under the trusteeship system, including any alteration or amendment, shall be agreed upon by the states directly concerned, including the mandatory power in the case of territories held under mandate by a Member of the United Nations, and shall be approved as provided for in Articles 83 and 85.

Article 80

1. Except as may be agreed upon in individual trusteeship agreements, made under Articles 77, 79, and 81, placing each territory under the trusteeship system, and until such agreements have been concluded, nothing in the Chapter shall be construed in or of itself to alter in any manner the rights whatsoever of any states or any peoples or the terms of existing international instruments to which Members of the United Nations may respectively be parties.
2. Paragraph 1 of this Article shall not be interpreted as giving grounds for delay or postponement of the negotiation and conclusion of agreements for placing mandated and other territories under the trusteeship system as provided for in Article 77.

Article 81

The trusteeship agreement shall in each case include the terms under which the trust territory will be administered and designate the authority which will exercise the administration of the trust territory. Such authority, hereinafter called the administering authority, may be one or more states or the Organization itself.

Article 82

There may be designated, in any trusteeship agreement, a strategic area or areas which may include part or all of the trust territory to which the agreement applies, without prejudice to any special agreement or agreements made under Article 43.

Article 83

1. All functions of the United Nations relating to strategic areas, including the approval of the terms of the trusteeship agreements and of their alteration or amendment, shall be exercised by the Security Council.
2. The basic objectives set forth in Article 76 shall be applicable to the people of each strategic area.
3. The Security Council shall, subject to the provisions of the trusteeship agreements and without prejudice to security considerations, avail itself of the assistance of the Trusteeship Council to perform those functions of the United Nations under the trusteeship system relating to political, economic, social, and educational matters in the strategic areas.

Article 84

It shall be the duty of the administering authority to ensure that the trust territory shall play its part in the maintenance of international peace and security. To this end the administering authority may make use of volunteer forces, facilities, and assistance from the trust territory in carrying out the obligations towards the Security Council undertaken in this regard by the administering authority, as well as for local defence and the maintenance of law and order within the trust territory.

Article 85

1. The functions of the United Nations with regard to trusteeship agreements for all areas not designated as strategic, including the approval of the terms of the trusteeship agreements and of their alteration or amendment, shall be exercised by the General Assembly.
2. The Trusteeship Council, operating under the authority of the General Assembly, shall assist the General Assembly in carrying out these functions.

CHAPTER XIII
THE TRUSTEESHIP COUNCIL

Composition

Article 86

1. The Trusteeship Council shall consist of the following Members of the United Nations:

a. those Members administering trust territories;

b. such of those Members mentioned by name in Article 23 as are not administering trust territories; and

c. as many other Members elected for three-year terms by the General Assembly as may be necessary to ensure that the total number of members of the Trusteeship Council is equally divided between those Members of the United Nations which administer trust territories and those which do not.

2. Each member of the Trusteeship Council shall designate one specially qualified person to represent it therein.

Functions and Powers

Article 87

The General Assembly and, under its authority, the Trusteeship Council, in carrying out their functions, may:

a. consider reports submitted by the administering authority;

b. accept petitions and examine them in consultation with the administering authority;

c. provide for periodic visits to the respective trust territories at times agreed upon with the administering authority; and

d. take these and other actions in conformity with the terms of the trusteeship agreements.

Article 88

The Trusteeship Council shall formulate a questionnaire on the political, economic, social, and educational advancement of the inhabitants of each trust territory, and the administering authority for each trust territory within the competence of the General Assembly shall make an annual report to the General Assembly upon the basis of such questionnaire.

Voting

Article 89

1. Each member of the Trusteeship Council shall have one vote.

2. Decisions of the Trusteeship Council shall be made by a majority of the members present and voting.

Procedure

Article 90

1. The Trusteeship Council shall adopt its own rules of procedure, including the method of selecting its President.

2. The Trusteeship Council shall meet as required in accordance with its rules, which shall include provisions for the convening of meetings on the request of a majority of its members.

Article 91

The Trusteeship Council shall, when appropriate, avail itself of the assistance of the Economic and Social Council and of the specialized agencies in regard to matters with which they are respectively concerned.

CHAPTER XIV
THE INTERNATIONAL COURT OF JUSTICE

Article 92

The International Court of Justice shall be the principal judicial organ of the United Nations. It shall function in accordance with the annexed Statute, which is based upon the Statute of the Permanent Court of International Justice and forms an integral part of the present Charter.

Article 93

1. All Members of the United Nations are *ipso facto* parties to the Statute of the International Court of Justice.
2. A state which is not a Member of the United Nations may become a party to the Statute of the International Court of Justice on conditions to be determined in each case by the General Assembly upon the recommendation of the Security Council.

Article 94

1. Each Member of the United Nations undertakes to comply with the decision of the International Court of Justice in any case to which it is a party.
2. If any party to a case fails to perform the obligations incumbent upon it under a judgment rendered by the Court, the other party may have recourse to the Security Council, which may, if it deems necessary, make recommendations or decide upon measures to be taken to give effect to the judgment.

Article 95

Nothing in the present Charter shall prevent Members of the United Nations from entrusting the solution of their differences to other tribunals by virtue of agreements already in existence or which may be concluded in the future.

Article 96

1. The General Assembly of the Security Council may request the International Court of Justice to give an advisory opinion on any legal question.

2. Other organs of the United Nations and specialized agencies, which may at any time be so authorized by the General Assembly, may also request advisory opinions of the Court on legal questions arising within the scope of their activities.

CHAPTER XV
THE SECRETARIAT

Article 97

The Secretariat shall comprise a Secretary-General and such staff as the organization may require. The Secretary-General shall be appointed by the General Assembly upon the recommendation of the Security Council. He shall be the chief administrative officer of the Organization.

Article 98

The Secretary-General shall act in that capacity in all meetings of the General Assembly, of the Security Council, of the Economic and Social Council, and of the Trusteeship Council, and shall perform such other functions as are entrusted to him by these organs. The Secretary-General shall make an annual report to the General Assembly on the work of the Organization.

Article 99

The Secretary-General may bring to the attention of the Security Council any matter which in his opinion may threaten the maintenance of international peace and security.

Article 100

1. In the performance of their duties the Secretary-General and the staff shall not seek or receive instructions from any government or from any other authority external to the Organization. They shall refrain from any action which might reflect on their position as international officials responsible only to the Organization.

2. Each Member of the United Nations undertakes to respect the exclusively international character of the responsibilities of the Secretary-General and the staff and not to seek to influence them in the discharge of their responsibilities.

Article 101

1. The staff shall be appointed by the Secretary-General under regulations established by the General Assembly.

2. Appropriate staffs shall be permanently assigned to the Economic and Social Council, the Trusteeship Council, and, as required, to other organs of the United Nations. These staffs shall form a part of the Secretariat.

3. The paramount consideration in the employment of the staff and in the determination of the conditions of service shall be the necessity of securing the highest standards of efficiency, competence, and integrity. Due regard shall be paid to the importance of recruiting the staff on as wide a geographical basis as possible.

CHAPTER XVI
MISCELLANEOUS PROVISIONS

Article 102

1. Every treaty and every international agreement entered into by any Member of the United Nations after the present Charter comes into force shall as soon as possible be registered with the Secretariat and published by it.

2. No party to any such treaty or international agreement which, has not been registered in accordance with the provisions of paragraph 1 of this Article may invoke that treaty or agreement before any organ of the United Nations.

Article 103

In the event of a conflict between the obligations of the Members of the United Nations under the present Charter and their obligations under any other international agreement, their obligations under the present Charter shall prevail.

Article 104

The Organization shall enjoy in the territory of each of its Members such legal capacity as may be necessary for the exercise of its functions and the fulfilment of its purposes.

Article 105

1. The Organization shall enjoy in the territory of each of its Members such privileges and immunities as are necessary for the fulfilment of its purposes.

2. Representatives of the Members of the United Nations and officials of the Organization shall similarly enjoy such privileges and immunities as are necessary for the independent exercise of their functions in connexion with the Organization.

3. The General Assembly may make recommendations with a view to determining the details of the application of paragraphs 1 and 2 of this Article or may propose conventions to the Members of the United Nations for this purpose.

CHAPTER XVII
TRANSITIONAL SECURITY ARRANGEMENTS

Article 106

Pending the coming into force of such special agreements referred to in Article 43 as in the opinion of the Security Council enable it to begin the exercise of its responsibilities under Article 42, the parties to the Four-Nations Declaration, signed at Moscow, 30 October 1943, and France, shall, in accordance with the provisions of paragraph 5 of that Declaration, consult with one another and as occasion requires with other Members of the United Nations with a view to such joint action on behalf of the Organization as may be necessary for the purpose of maintaining international peace and security.

Article 107

Nothing in the present Charter shall invalidate or preclude action, in relation to any state which during the second World War has been an enemy of any signatory to the present Charter, taken or authorized as a result of that war by the Governments having responsibility for such action.

CHAPTER XVIII
AMENDMENTS

Article 108

Amendments to the present Charter shall come into force for all Members of the United Nations when they have been adopted by a vote of two thirds of the members of the General Assembly and ratified in accordance with their respective constitutional processes by two thirds of the Members of the United Nations, including all the permanent members of the Security Council.

Article 109

1. A General Conference of the Members of the United Nations for the purpose of reviewing the present Charter may be held at a date and place to be fixed by a two-thirds vote of the members of the General Assembly and by a vote of any nine members of the Security Council. Each Member of the United Nations shall have one vote in the conference.

2. Any alteration of the present Charter recommended by a two-thirds vote of the conference shall take effect when ratified in accordance with their respective constitutional processes by two thirds of the Members of the United Nations including all the permanent members of the Security Council.

3. If such a conference has not been held before the tenth annual session of the General Assembly following the coming into force of the present Charter,

the proposal to call such a conference shall be placed on the agenda of that session of the General Assembly, and the conference shall be held if so decided by a majority vote of the members of the General Assembly and by a vote of any seven members of the Security Council.

CHAPTER XIX
RATIFICATION AND SIGNATURE

Article 110

1. The present Charter shall be ratified by the signatory states in accordance with their respective constitutional processes.

2. The ratifications shall be deposited with the Government of the United States of America, which shall notify all the signatory states of each deposit as well as the Secretary-General of the Organization when he has been appointed.

3. The present Charter shall come into force upon the deposit of ratifications by the Republic of China, France, the Union of Soviet Socialist Republics, the United Kingdom of Great Britain and Northern Ireland, and the United States of America, and by a majority of the other signatory states. A protocol of the ratifications deposited shall thereupon be drawn up by the Government of the United States of America which shall communicate copies thereof to all the signatory states.

4. The states signatory to the present Charter which ratify it after it has come into force will become original Members of the United Nations on the date of the deposit of their respective ratifications.

Article 111

The present Charter of which the Chinese, French, Russian, English, and Spanish texts are equally authentic, shall remain deposited in the archives of the Government of the United States of America. Duly certified copies thereof shall be transmitted by that Government to the Governments of the other signatory states.

IN FAITH WHEREOF the representatives of the Governments of the United Nations have signed the present Charter.

DONE at the city of San Francisco the twenty-sixth day of June, one thousand nine hundred and forty-five.

II

Members
of
the United Nations

MEMBERS OF THE UNITED NATIONS — DATE OF MEMBERSHIP, AREA, POPULATION, AND ASSESSMENT

Member	Date of UN Membership	Total Area (square kilometers)	Population (latest UN estimate)	Percentage of UN Budget Assessment
Afghanistan	19 Nov. 1946	647 497	19 803 000	0.01
Albania	14 Dec. 1955	28 748	2 548 000	0.01
Algeria	8 Oct. 1962	2 381 741	17 304 300	0.10
Angola	1 Dec. 1976	1 246 700	6 511 000	0.02
Argentina	24 Oct. 1945	2 766 889	25 719 000	0.84
Australia	1 Nov. 1945	7 686 848	13 642 800	1.54
Austria	14 Dec. 1955	83 849	7 514 000	0.64
Bahamas	18 Sep. 1973	13 935	170 849	0.01
Bahrain	21 Sep. 1971	622	259 000	0.01
Bangladesh	17 Sep. 1974	143 998	76 815 000	0.04
Barbados	9 Dec. 1966	431	247 400	0.01
Belgium	27 Dec. 1945	30 513	9 889 000	1.08
Benin	20 Sep. 1960	112 622	3 197 000	0.01
Bhutan	21 Sep. 1971	47 000	1 202 000	0.01
Bolivia	14 Nov. 1945	1 098 581	5 789 300	0.01
Botswana	17 Oct. 1966	600 372	693 000	0.01
Brazil	24 Oct. 1945	8 511 965	109 180 600	1.04
Bulgaria	14 Dec. 1955	110 912	8 760 971	0.14
Burma	19 Apr. 1948	676 552	31 002 000	0.01
Burundi	18 Sep. 1962	27 834	3 864 000	0.01
Byelorussian SSR	24 Oct. 1945	207 600	9 350 900	0.41
Canada	9 Nov. 1945	9 976 139	23 140 000	3.04
Cape Verde	16 Sep. 1975	4 033	303 066	0.01
Central African Empire	20 Sep. 1960	622 984	2 610 000	0.01
Chad	20 Sep. 1960	1 284 000	4 115 839	0.01
Chile	24 Oct. 1945	756 945	10 454 387	0.09
China	24 Oct. 1945	9 596 961	852 133 000	5.50

Country	Date			
Colombia	5 Nov. 1945	1 138 914	24 372 100	0.11
Comoros	12 Nov. 1975	2 171	314 000	0.01
Congo	20 Sep. 1960	342 000	1 390 000	0.01
Costa Rica	2 Nov. 1945	50 700	2 012 481	0.02
Cuba	24 Oct. 1945	114 524	9 331 977	0.11
Cyprus	20 Sep. 1960	9 251	639 000	0.01
Czechoslovakia	24 Oct. 1945	127 869	14 918 186	0.84
Democratic Kampuchea	14 Dec. 1955	181 035	8 354 000	0.01
Democratic Yemen	14 Dec. 1967	332 968	1 749 387	0.01
Denmark	24 Oct. 1945	43 069	5 072 516	0.64
Djibouti	20 Sep. 1977	22 800	300 000	0.01
Dominica	6 Dec. 1978	750	75 000	0.01
Dominican Republic	24 Oct. 1945	48 734	4 835 207	0.02
Ecuador	21 Dec. 1945	283 561	7 305 000	0.02
Egypt	24 Oct. 1945	1 001 449	38 067 000	0.08
El Salvador	24 Oct. 1945	21 393	4 123 323	0.01
Equatorial Guinea	12 Nov. 1968	28 051	316 000	0.01
Ethiopia	13 Nov. 1945	1 221 900	28 667 800	0.01
Fiji	13 Oct. 1970	18 272	580 000	0.01
Finland	14 Dec. 1955	337 009	4 726 616	0.44
France	24 Oct. 1945	547 026	52 915 000	5.82
Gabon	20 Sep. 1960	267 667	530 000	0.01
Gambia	21 Sep. 1965	11 295	538 200	0.01
German Democratic Republic	18 Sep. 1973	108 178	16 786 057	1.33
Germany, Federal Republic of	18 Sep. 1973	248 577	61 498 000	7.70
Ghana	8 Mar. 1957	238 537	10 309 007	0.02
Greece	25 Oct. 1945	131 944	9 165 000	0.35
Grenada	17 Sep. 1974	344	96 000	0.01
Guatemala	21 Nov. 1945	108 889	6 256 199	0.02
Guinea	12 Dec. 1958	245 957	4 529 000	0.01
Guinea-Bissau	17 Sep. 1974	36 125	534 000	0.01
Guyana	20 Sep. 1966	214 969	782 805	0.01
Haiti	24 Oct. 1945	27 750	4 668 162	0.01
Honduras	17 Dec. 1945	112 088	3 141 000	0.01
Hungary	14 Dec. 1955	93 030	10 596 000	0.33
Iceland	19 Nov. 1946	103 000	220 100	0.02

(continued)

Member	Date of UN Membership	Total Area (square kilometers)	Population (latest UN estimate)	Percentage of UN Budget Assessment
India	30 Oct. 1945	3 129 316[a]	610 077 000[a]	0.68
Indonesia	28 Sep. 1950	2 027 087	139 616 000	0.14
Iran	24 Oct. 1945	1 648 000	33 900 000	0.40
Iraq	21 Dec. 1945	434 924	11 505 234	0.08
Ireland	14 Dec. 1955	70 283	3 162 000	0.15
Israel	11 May 1949	20 700	3 464 900	0.23
Italy	14 Dec. 1955	301 225	56 189 000	3.38
Ivory Coast	20 Sep. 1960	322 463	5 017 000	0.02
Jamaica	18 Sep. 1962	10 962	2 057 000	0.02
Japan	18 Dec. 1956	372 313	112 767 795	8.64
Jordan	14 Dec. 1955	97 740	2 779 000	0.01
Kenya	16 Dec. 1963	582 644	13 847 000	0.01
Kuwait	14 May 1963	17 818	1 030 500	0.15
Lao People's Democratic Republic	14 Dec. 1955	236 800	3 383 000	0.01
Lebanon	24 Oct. 1945	10 400	2 961 000	0.03
Lesotho	17 Oct. 1966	30 355	1 038 500	0.01
Liberia	2 Nov. 1945	111 369	1 751 000	0.01
Libyan Arab Jamahiriya	14 Dec. 1955	1 759 540	2 444 000	0.16
Luxembourg	24 Oct. 1945	2 586	358 000	0.04
Madagascar	20 Sep. 1960	587 041	8 266 000	0.01
Malawi	1 Dec. 1964	118 484	5 175 000	0.01
Malaysia	17 Sep. 1957	329 749	12 300 000	0.09
Maldives	21 Sep. 1965	298	122 000	0.01
Mali	28 Sep. 1960	1 240 000	5 844 000	0.01
Malta	1 Dec. 1964	316	303 685	0.01
Mauritania	27 Oct. 1961	1 030 700	1 318 000	0.01
Mauritius	24 Apr. 1968	2 045	894 774	0.01

Mexico	7 Nov. 1945	1 972 546	62 329 189	0.79
Mongolia	27 Oct. 1961	1 565 000	1 488 000	0.01
Morocco	12 Nov. 1956	446 550	17 828 000	0.05
Mozambique	12 Sep. 1975	783 030	9 444 000	0.02
Nepal	14 Dec. 1955	140 797	12 857 243	0.01
Netherlands	10 Dec. 1945	40 844	13 769 913	1.42
New Zealand	24 Oct. 1945	268 676	3 138 400	0.26
Nicaragua	24 Oct. 1945	130 000	2 233 000	0.01
Niger	20 Sep. 1960	1 267 000	4 727 292	0.01
Nigeria	7 Oct. 1960	923 768	64 750 000	0.13
Norway	27 Nov. 1945	324 219	4 026 000	0.45
Oman	7 Oct. 1971	212 457	791 000	0.01
Pakistan	30 Sep. 1947	803 943[a]	72 368 000[a]	0.07
Panama	13 Nov. 1945	75 650	1 718 700	0.02
Papua New Guinea	10 Oct. 1975	461 691	2 829 000	0.01
Paraguay	24 Oct. 1945	406 752	2 724 391	0.01
Peru	31 Oct. 1945	1 285 216	16 090 496	0.06
Philippines	24 Oct. 1945	300 000	43 751 320	0.10
Poland	24 Oct. 1945	312 677	34 362 133	1.39
Portugal	14 Dec. 1955	92 082	9 448 800	0.19
Qatar	21 Sep. 1971	11 000	95 000	0.02
Romania	14 Dec. 1955	237 500	21 445 698	0.24
Rwanda	18 Sep. 1962	26 338	4 289 000	0.01
Samoa	15 Dec. 1976	2 842	151 200	0.01
Sao Tome and Principe	16 Sep. 1975	964	81 000	0.01
Saudi Arabia	24 Oct. 1945	2 149 690	9 240 000	0.23
Senegal	28 Sep. 1960	196 192	5 114 600	0.01
Seychelles	21 Sep. 1976	280	59 226	0.01
Sierra Leone	27 Sep. 1961	71 740	3 111 000	0.01
Singapore	21 Sep. 1965	581	2 278 200	0.08
Solomon Islands	19 Sep. 1978	28 446	200 000	0.01
Somalia	20 Sep. 1960	637 657	3 261 000	0.01
South Africa	7 Nov. 1945	1 221 037	26 129 000	0.42
Spain	14 Dec. 1955	504 782	35 971 000	1.53
Sri Lanka	14 Dec. 1955	65 610	14 270 000	0.02
Sudan	12 Nov. 1956	2 505 813	16 126 000	0.01

(continued)

Member	Date of UN Membership	Total Area (square kilometers)	Population (latest UN estimate)	Percentage of UN Budget Assessment
Surinam	4 Dec. 1975	163 265	435 000	0.01
Swaziland	24 Sep. 1968	17 363	496 835	0.01
Sweden	19 Nov. 1946	449 964	8 222 310	1.24
Syrian Arab Republic	24 Oct. 1945	185 180	7 595 895	0.02
Thailand	16 Dec. 1946	514 000	42 960 000	0.10
Togo	20 Sep. 1960	56 000	2 283 350	0.01
Trinidad and Tobago	18 Sep. 1962	5 128	1 081 550	0.03
Tunisia	12 Nov. 1956	163 610	5 737 000	0.02
Turkey	24 Oct. 1945	780 576	40 163 400	0.30
Uganda	25 Oct. 1962	236 036	11 942 690	0.01
Ukrainian SSR	24 Oct. 1945	603 700	49 100 000	1.53
Union of Soviet Socialist Republics	24 Oct. 1945	22 402 200[b]	256 670 000[b]	11.60
United Arab Emirates	9 Dec. 1971	83 600	229 000	0.07
United Kingdom	24 Oct. 1945	244 046	55 927 600	4.52
United Republic of Cameroon	20 Sep. 1960	475 442	6 531 000	0.01
United Republic of Tanzania	14 Dec. 1961	945 087	15 606 923	0.01
United States of America	24 Oct. 1945	9 363 123	215 118 000	25.00
Upper Volta	20 Sep. 1960	274 200	6 174 000	0.01
Uruguay	18 Dec. 1945	176 215	3 101 000	0.04
Venezuela	15 Nov. 1945	912 050	12 361 090	0.39
Vietnam	20 Sep. 1977	330 980	46 520 000	0.03
Yemen	30 Sep. 1947	195 000	6 870 000	0.01
Yugoslavia	24 Oct. 1945	255 804	21 560 000	0.39
Zaire	20 Sep. 1960	2 345 409	25 629 237	0.02
Zambia	1 Dec. 1964	752 614	5 182 000	0.02

[a]Excluding data for Jammu and Kashmir.
[b]Including the figures of Byelorussian SSR and Ukrainian SSR.

Index

15.00